The Web of Data

Aidan Hogan

The Web of Data

 Springer

Aidan Hogan
Department of Computer Science
Universidad de Chile
Santiago de Chile, Chile

ISBN 978-3-030-51582-9   ISBN 978-3-030-51580-5   (eBook)
https://doi.org/10.1007/978-3-030-51580-5

This Springer imprint is published by the registered company Springer Nature Switzerland AG
The registered company address is: Gewerbestrasse 11, 6330 Cham, Switzerland

For all those without whom this book would not have been possible.

To all those without whom it would have been finished sooner.

Preface

The idea of a "Web of Data", as discussed in this book, has been around since at least 1998, when Berners-Lee referenced his plan *"for achieving a set of connected applications for data on the Web in such a way as to form a consistent logical web of data"*. Myriad developments have taken place since then towards realising a Web of Data, including standards, languages, protocols, tools, optimisations, theorems, and more besides. These developments have more recently been deployed on millions of websites, where most users interact with the Web of Data on a daily basis, perhaps without realising it.

The core objective of the Web of Data is to publish content on the Web in formats that machines can process more easily and accurately than the human-friendly HTML documents forming the current "Web of Documents". As the Web becomes increasingly machine readable, increasingly complex tasks can be automated on the Web, yielding more and more powerful Web applications that are capable of discovering, cross-referencing, filtering, and organising data from numerous websites in a matter of seconds.

Assume, for example, that we are running a recipe website. Rather than only describing the recipe in the text of a paragraph – like "This easy dessert recipe for Pecan Pie takes around 20–25 minutes ..." – the first step of the Web of Data is to publish structured DATA about the recipe that is easier for machines to process than natural language. The data can be populated from the underlying database we use for the website, and can be embedded within the webpages we already have, or can be published as separate documents. Ideally we can use a data format that is also used by other recipe sites, such that external applications – e.g., search engines – can compile together these data from different sources, allowing users to quickly QUERY for recipes by type, difficulty, duration, etc. Such applications will then point users back to our website for more details about the recipes of interest to them.

Next we would like to add allergy information to allow users to filter recipes that are not safe for them to eat; for example, if a user is allergic to tree nuts, they would like to quickly rule out recipes using almonds, cashews, chestnuts, pecans, pistachios, or ingredients made using such nuts, including marzipan, certain liqueurs, etc. However, allergies are potentially complex to model in our data, and we need to avoid offering false or misleading information. Rather than manage this sort of information ourselves, we can LINK the ingredients of our recipes to an official, central repository of nutritional data, which defines the SEMANTICS of different types of foods, such as to state that cashews, chestnuts, etc., are types of tree nuts; that all tree nuts are culinary nuts; that legumes (like peanuts) are culinary nuts, but not tree nuts; etc.

What started out as some simple data about recipes slowly expands over time and becomes more and more diverse, allowing our users to find which of our recipes are of more relevance to them through increasingly detailed queries. But as new recipes are added, we start to find recipes with incomplete data (e.g., durations are missing in some cases), or inconsistent information (e.g., recipes requiring a pasta machine are marked "easy"). Hence we start to implement mechanisms for VALIDATION, checking that every recipe has a title, a description, a duration, etc., that recipes marked as easy require equipment from a common list of utensils, etc. These validation mechanisms help us to identify, prioritise and address potential quality issues that might affect our users as the recipe data expand and grow more diverse.

Finally, we will consider a user who has a (hypothetical, as of yet) personal software agent with local access to sensitive data, such as the user's location, medical issues, culinary preferences, available utensils, etc. Based on a query from the user, such an agent may then venture out on this expanding Web of Data, discover recipe sites like ours, discover product lists of local supermarkets, discover nutritional recommendations associated with the users' medical issues (if any), and pull all of these data together in order to recommend a list of safe recipes they can make at home with ingredients available for delivery from a nearby supermarket. The user can then browse this list of recipes, ordering or filtering by price, duration, calories, etc., perhaps even visiting our website for the details of a recipe that catches their eye.

The scenario we describe here, of course, is not nearly as straightforward to put into practice as we seem to suggest. Considering each part in detail raises various technical questions and challenges regarding how we structure data, how queries should be formulated, how links to remote data can be specified, the types of semantics we need, how constraints are formulated for validation, and so forth. However, there have also been over two decades of work on proposals to address these questions, particularly within the *Semantic Web* community, which has brought forward the most concrete and complete instantiation of a Web of Data seen to date, with detailed standards and recommendations relating to DATA, QUERIES, LINKS, SEMANTICS, VALIDATION and more besides. These proposals have been adopted on the Web, with the standards proposed for data being promoted by popular search engines and used on millions of websites. Standards for queries, links, semantics and validation are also being increasingly adopted for specific use-cases.

The primary undertaking of this book is then to draw together these proposals, to motive and describe them in detail, to provide examples of their use, and to discuss how they contribute to – and how they have been used thus far on – the Web of Data. The book is aimed at students, researchers and practitioners interested in learning more about the Web of Data, and about closely related topics such as the Semantic Web, Knowledge Graphs, Linked Data, Graph Databases, Ontologies, etc. The book can serve as a textbook for students and other newcomers, where it motivates the topics discussed, offers accessible examples and exercises, etc.; it can also serve as a reference handbook for researchers and developers, where it offers up-to-date details of key standards (RDF, RDFS, OWL, SPARQL, SHACL, ShEx, RDB2RDF, LDP), along with formal definitions and references to further literature.

The book is structured around nine chapters, as follows:

INTRODUCTION: Chapter 1 introduces the book, discussing the shortcomings of the current Web that illustrate the need for a Web of Data.

WEB OF DATA: Chapter 2 provides an overview of the fundamental concepts underlying the Web of Data, and discusses some current use-cases on the Web where such concepts are already deployed.

RESOURCE DESCRIPTION FRAMEWORK (RDF): In Chapter 3, we describe RDF: the graph-structured data model proposed by the Semantic Web community as a common data model for the Web.

RDF SCHEMA (RDFS) AND SEMANTICS: In Chapter 4, we describe RDFS: a lightweight ontology language used to define an initial semantics for terms used in RDF graphs.

WEB ONTOLOGY LANGUAGE (OWL): In Chapter 5, we describe OWL: a more expressive ontology language built upon RDFS that offers much more powerful ontological features.

SPARQL QUERY LANGUAGE: In Chapter 6, we describe a language for querying and updating RDF graphs, with examples of the features it supports, and a detailed definition of its semantics.

SHAPE CONSTRAINTS AND EXPRESSIONS (SHACL/SHEX): Chapter 7 introduces two languages for describing the expected structure of – and expressing constraints on – RDF graphs for the purposes of validation.

LINKED DATA: In Chapter 8, we discuss the principles and best practices proposed by the Linked Data community for publishing interlinked (RDF) data on the Web, and how those techniques have been adopted.

CONCLUSIONS In Chapter 9, we wrap-up with open problems and more general discussion on the future of the Web of Data.

A website associated with the book – http://webofdatabook.org/ – contains complementary material, including solutions for exercises, slides for classes, raw data for examples, a comments section, and more besides.

Santiago, Chile; April 2020   *Aidan Hogan*

Acknowledgements

First, I would like to thank colleagues and students past and present, who have introduced me to this topic, worked with me on this topic, or whom I have introduced to this topic. I have learnt a lot from all of you.

I would like to thank Thanh Tran and Gong Cheng who were instrumental in making this book happen.

I would like to thank Ralf Gerstner of Springer for his guidance, support, and immense patience during the lengthy preparation of this book.

I would like to thank the observant and patient reviewer whose detailed feedback helped to improve this manuscript.

I would like to thank family and friends for reminding me on occasion that there was perhaps more to life than this book and its topic.

Finally, thanks to Analí for supporting me throughout this journey, and doing all of those important things, both big and small, that needed to be done so that I could keep my head buried in this endeavour.

Contents

Chapter 1
Introduction

While we may be aware of the myriad ways in which the modern Web helps us in our everyday lives, we are probably far less aware of its fundamental limitations. Though its successes need no introduction, the Web is far from perfect and it is only by trying to consider its limitations that we could hope to improve upon it. Immediately we may think that the Web could be faster or cheaper or more reliable or more widely available, but this relates more to the underlying Internet than to the Web.[1] Rather we are interested in fundamental limitations of the Web itself that can potentially be addressed by the technology available to us now or (at least) in the near future.

A key limitation of the Web arises when the information we seek is not available on one webpage or website but rather spread over many. Finding the director of a popular theatrical movie is easy with a search engine since there are many webpages about such movies that will include the name of the director and are accessible through a single click from the results. Finding the start times of movies by Japanese directors showing tonight in nearby cinemas, however, is more difficult since we are not going to find one existing webpage with the specific answer; instead, the answer will need to be cross-referenced from the websites of various cinemas, online maps, movie databases, etc. Likewise finding the nearest supermarket that sells all the ingredients of an online recipe, or finding music events next weekend in cities with cheap return flights, or any number of other such tasks, require manually pulling together information from sources spread across the Web.

Drawing together information from multiple sources on the modern Web is mostly performed manually by human users. Since humans are relatively slow and inaccurate at processing lots of information, often only a small subset of the potentially relevant information that the Web has to offer can be considered when trying to solve more complex tasks. Often users will thus

---

[1] Though often conflated, the Internet refers to the communication network of computers (also used for email, video calls, etc.), while the Web refers to the standards and protocols used to publish and interlink documents on the Internet (as viewable in a browser).

A. Hogan, *The Web of Data*, https://doi.org/10.1007/978-3-030-51580-5_1

be forced to compromise and accept incomplete or approximate answers that are "good enough", depending on their patience and the nature of the task. Such users may even tacitly accept such compromises as somehow *necessary*.

On the other hand, while machines are much *much* more efficient at processing large amounts of information, the idea of a general-purpose algorithm that can navigate the Web for us and automatically connect the dots needed to solve myriad complex tasks still seems far beyond the reach of current technology. Even with recent advancements in Machine Learning, an algorithm operating on the current Web that could automatically isolate the online shopping websites of nearby stores, automatically navigate their pages and extract the details of products for sale, automatically recognise that the *zucchini* mentioned on the U.S. recipe site is the same as the *courgette* in the New Zealand supermarket, automatically determine that *tomato ketchup* does not match the *four tomatoes* of the recipe, and so forth, and then later solve similar complex tasks relating to movies or concerts or whatever we need in that moment – such an algorithm would require an almost human-level understanding of the content of the webpages in question, implying a general form of Artificial Intelligence that remains without precedent.

The fundamental problem is that the Web was originally conceived of as a platform for humans to share documents to be read by other humans. Most of the content of the Web is surfaced as webpages containing formatting instructions to make them pleasant for humans to read and understand, with links to other webpages offering related information. Machines, on the other hand, are mostly used to generate, send, retrieve and display such webpages for users, playing the role of a passive messenger: the information content of such webpages is mostly opaque to the machines that pass them around.

In order to automate increasingly complex tasks on the Web, rather than waiting around for a strong, general Artificial Intelligence that can emulate a human-like understanding of the current *human-readable* Web, what if we rather rethink the Web itself? In particular, what if we could begin to transform the Web to make its vast content more (and more) *machine-readable*?

If machines from different websites could directly exchange *data* amongst themselves – data that they could process and act upon in a more meaningful way than what is currently possible over human-readable webpages – these machines could collaborate to cross-reference such data amongst themselves before packaging the relevant content into a single, concise webpage of results for the user. In this scenario, it would not be merely one website generating a webpage for the user, but potentially the Web itself collaborating to get the answers sought. This would not be limited to one specific type of task, nor even to one specific domain of data, but would span the Web and the full range of complex tasks that could benefit from the Web's *collective* content.

This is the ambitious vision of the *Web of Data*: an evolution of the Web with standards and practices whereby machines can exchange data amongst themselves and can process and act upon that data in more meaningful ways. If machines on the Web were empowered to exchange data in a format they can process with more accuracy and depth than typical webpages, they could potentially do *much* more on the Web, leading to higher levels of automation in complex tasks that humans currently perform manually (if at all).

The goal of this book will then be in exploring this ambitious idea of a *Web of Data* and to discuss in detail some of the current standards and techniques by which it is currently being realised. The core technical question underlying this book is then: *how can we best organise and structure the content of the Web to enable higher levels of machine readability, and ultimately, higher levels of automation for (complex) everyday tasks?*

But first, we must start by trying to better characterise the problem with the contemporary Web that this Web of Data aims to address.

1.1 The Latent Web

If you were unsure what the capital city of Chile was, you could find out on the Web by typing words like "chile capital" into your favourite search engine and it would return you some list of webpages that may state something like "The capital of Chile is Santiago". In fact, your search engine may even tell you in a box directly on the results page, saving you a mouse-click.

On the current Web, with the help of search engines, it is easy to find out the capital of Chile – or its population, or the movies showing tonight in a given cinema, or whether or not lemons contain citrus, or the current temperature in Paris – because such information has been made *explicit* on the Web: there are webpages available that explicitly state that information.

However, a lot of information is left *implicit* on the Web. This sort of information can often require much more work to acquire.

Example 1.1

Julie is a literature student. For her thesis work, she needs to find a list of Nobel Laureates in Literature who fought in a war, the year they were awarded the Nobel prize, and the name of the war(s) they fought in. From the list of such laureates on Wikipedia, she ends up manually checking the article for each laureate, looking for mentions of wars or conflicts, hoping she doesn't miss something.

The raw information Julie needs is available on the Web: she can find a list of Nobel Laureates in Literature, and she can check on the Web if they were involved in a war or not. Hence the answer is available on the Web, just not explicitly on a single webpage that she can quickly find through a search engine. Instead Julie will have to cross-reference different webpages.

The reason why the information Julie seeks has not made explicit on the Web is that it is quite specific: there is not a lot of demand for that precise information, and hence, unfortunately for Julie, there is less motivation for someone to make that particular information explicit on a single webpage.

There may be other reasons why a user is interested in finding something specific on the Web other than writing a report for university; for example, they may be searching for something in a specific context, such as something personalised, or something in a particular place, or at a particular time.

> **Example 1.2**
>
> Frank has a friend calling over tonight for dinner. He's looking for new recipe ideas for a dessert on the Web. His friend is intolerant to citrus. Looking through various recipe websites, many of the desserts he finds would take too long to make, or would require equipment he does not have, or involve citrus fruits, or require weird ingredients that he is not sure where to buy, or don't look delicious, and so on.

Frank can find lots of dessert recipes on the Web, and can probably find lots of citrus-free recipes. Many recipe sites will support faceted search where he can filter the presented list of recipes by the total preparation time or rating. He can search individual ingredients to ensure that they are citrus-free. He can find a map of local supermarkets and their opening hours. Many of these local supermarkets will have an online shopping site where he can find the availability, quantity, price, allergy warnings, etc., of products.

But while there are undoubtedly plenty of recipes on the Web that perfectly suit Frank's needs, in having to manually filter through lots of irrelevant results and cross-check ingredients manually, he will only be able to consider a handful of suitable recipes: he may have to settle on finding one or two options that are good enough and only use widely-available ingredients. And inevitably the supermarket that Frank goes to won't have strawberries.

The next example involves information a user did not even seek.

> **Example 1.3**
>
> Anna is bored so she checks out what's on in a couple of local cinemas. She looks at the movie listings and searches for details about a few movies whose titles look interesting, eventually picking a movie in her favourite cinema. Unfortunately, on her way there, she finds out that the metro line serving the cinema has been closed all day, so instead of paying for a taxi, she returns home. Later that week she finds out that one of the movies showing in a nearby cinema whose title did not look interesting at first glance was by one of her favourite directors.

If Anna had been "recommended" timely information from the Web about the problems with the metro and about the directors of the movies in the cinema listings, she would not have chosen that cinema nor that movie. In this case, Anna was not aware of what she needed from the Web.

Could we build a Web where Julie doesn't need to cross-reference 114 webpages to get a complete list of veteran laureates for her thesis, or where Frank can quickly see only those recipes that match his objective criteria with suggestions on local supermarkets where he can pick up the ingredients needed, or where Anna is shown personalised information about the movies in the local cinema and warned that the metro line is out of service? The challenge inherent in all these examples is that they require information that can only be gained by considering the content of several webpages.

Thus far we have focused on examples of users or "consumers" of the Web. But the lack of automated methods to combine and process information from various webpages also implies costs for the publishers of content, since it encourages high levels of redundancy in order to make information available to users on a single webpage in the language of their preference.

> **Example 1.4**
>
> In Wikipedia, the goals scored by a football player are given in the "info-boxes" – the data about an **entity** appearing in the top right-hand side of an article – of the respective article about the player. Every time a football player scores a goal, to keep the online encyclopaedia up-to-date and consistent, current editors must manually update the values of the goals-scored field in the articles of several languages. Likewise, as a convenience for readers, Wikipedia will often keep an explicit list of the top scorers for a given team, or a given season, or a given tournament, or some combination of such criteria, where these lists may also need to be updated, potentially for different languages. Thus a single goal scored by a player may require updates to tens or hundreds of articles, manually replicating that information in a multitude of locations for the convenience of Wikipedia's readers.

Given that machines are unable to automatically find, process and adapt information to a particular user's needs – for example, automatically collating a list of top goal scorers for a particular tournament from the individual webpages of relevant matches – publishers will rather often replicate redundant information across different webpages for the convenience of users.

In summary, given that the content of the Web is primarily human-readable, machines cannot piece together information from multiple sources; this in turn puts the burden on users to manually integrate the information they need from various webpages, and, conversely, on publishers to redundantly package the same information into different individual webpages to meet the most common demands of (potential) users of the website.

We then coin the phrase "*Latent Web*" as a way to refer to the sum of the factual information that cannot be gained from a single webpage accessible to users, but that can only be concluded from multiple webpages; for example, the directors of movies, the movie times in cinemas, etc., are not part of the Latent Web, as they can all be found on individual pages accessible to users through a search engine request; however, the list of movies by Japanese directors showing tonight in nearby cinemas forms part of the Latent Web, assuming that the list is not accessible to the user on a single webpage.

The vision of the Web of Data is then to harness the Latent Web by making more and more content on the Web available in increasingly machine-readable formats, paving the way for automated methods that can draw together factual information from multiple sources according to a specific user's needs. It is important to note that the Web of Data should not be seen as an alternative to replace the current Web, but rather as a way to enhance the current Web, whereby the types of ideas discussed in this book increasingly form part of the foundations of the Web itself. More practically, we will show that by improving the machine-readability of the explicit content of the Web, this in turn will pave the way for automated methods that make the implicit content of this immense Latent Web increasingly accessible to users, and that all of this is possible *today*, with currently available technology.

1.2 The Current Web

In order to motivate making the content of the Web more machine readable, let us first look at the actual structure of the current Web, the concrete challenges it poses to automated **interpretation** by machine, and some methods by which limited forms of such interpretation are currently attempted.

The Web – like any form of communication – is predicated on agreement.

The first form of agreement on the Web relates to the protocol – specifically the **Hypertext Transfer Protocol (HTTP)** – used to request and send documents. The second form of agreement relates to how documents can be identified and located, which is enabled through the **Uniform Resource Locator (URL)** specification and other related concepts. The third form of agreement relates to how the content of webpages should be specified, which is codified by the **Hypertext Markup Language (HTML)** specification; we will focus on this latter aspect of the Web for now.

1.2.1 Hypertext Markup Language (HTML)

HTML documents use a lightweight and broadly agreed-upon SYNTAX, MODEL and SEMANTICS to communicate rendering instructions to machines, conveying how the author of the document intends the page to be displayed in a browser on the client side. Assuming the author of the document and the client that displays it agree on how the HTML document should be rendered, then the reader will see the document as the author intended.

The SYNTAX of HTML involves use of, for example, angle brackets and slashes to indicate tags, such as <title>, that are not part of the primary content. A machine can then identify these tags in the body of the document and use them to break down the document into its individual parts.

The MODEL of HTML is tree-based, allowing elements to be nested inside other elements. For example, the <title> tag can appear as a *child* (directly nested within) the <head> part of the document, indicating that the title is part of the **metadata** about the document. Conversely, the <img> tag – used to identify an image – would typically appear as an *ancestor* (recursively nested within) the <body> part of the document, indicating that the image is part of the main content of the document. Such elements form abstract trees.

The SEMANTICS of HTML is hard-coded into a specification for developers to follow, where it states, for example, that the <title> tag is used to indicate the title of the document that should be displayed in the window or tab-bar of the browser, the <img> tag is used in the body of the document to indicate the location of an image that the application should retrieve and display at that part of the document's body, and so forth. Developers of browsers can then read the documentation and hard-code interpretation of these semantics into their engines. The meaning of HTML tags is sufficiently detailed – the semantics sufficiently unambiguous – that different compliant browsers coded by different developers should yield analogous results.

Finally, since the content of the Web is **decentralised**, LINKS are of fundamental importance for recommending, connecting, locating and traversing webpages in an ad hoc manner, weaving HTML documents into a Web [52].

HTML documents are thus machine readable, but in a limited sense: a machine can automatically interpret and act upon the content of these documents, but only for displaying the document and supporting its links.

Example 1.5

We give examples of three HTML webpages with links denoted by dashed lines (underlined phrases refer to hyperlinks to other documents not appearing in the example):

Nobel Laureates

We list Nobel laureates ordered by category then year.

Literature

Year	Awardee
1901	Sully Prudhomme
...	...
1953	Winston Churchill
1954	Ernest Hemingway
...	...
1964	Jean-Paul Sartre[†]
...	...
1983	William Golding
...	...
1985	Claude Simon
...	...

[†]Sartre declined.

Peace

Year	Awardee
1901	Henry Dunant
1901	Frédéric Passy
...	...

...

William G. Golding

Sir William Gerald Golding CBE (1911–1993) was a British novelist, playwright and poet. His most celebrated works include the novels "Lord of the Flies", and "Rites of Passage" for which he was awarded the Booker Prize.

...

He joined the Royal Navy in 1940, commanding a landing ship at the Normandy Invasion on D-Day.

...

Invasion of Normandy

On June 6th 1944 (D-Day), the Western Allies of World War II assaulted Nazi occupation forces from the sea at Normandy, as part of Operation Overlord.

...

A snippet of the HTML of the left-hand webpage follows, where "⬚⋯⬚" indicates that part of the HTML is omitted for brevity:

```
<html>
<head>
 <title>Nobel Laureates</title>
</head>
<body>
 <h1>Nobel Laureates</h1>
 <p>We list Nobel laureates ordered by category then year.</p>
 <h2>Literature</h2>
 <table border="1">
  <tr>
   <th>Year</th>
   <th>Awardee</th>
  </tr>
  <tr>
   <td>1901</td>
   <td><a href="http://ex.org/SP">Sully Prudhomme</a></td>
  </tr>
  ⬚⋯⬚
 </table>
 <h2>Peace</h2>
 ⬚⋯⬚
</body>
</html>
```

The SYNTAX is based on angle brackets and slashes to delimit tags that the machine can interpret; for example, `<tr>` tags indicate the start of a table row and `</tr>` tags indicate the end of the row.

The MODEL is tree-based, with nested tags forming a hierarchy:

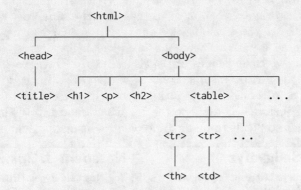

The SEMANTICS are (primarily) hard-coded instructions in browsers for interpreting these tags, for example, to use the content of the `<title>` field to display in the task-bar or tab-bar, and so forth.

Each LINK in the webpage is specified by means of a URL, such as `http://ex.org/SP`, which encodes a location that can be resolved to a webpage using HTTP. The context of the link is given by special tags, where above we see examples of `<a href="...">` tags that contain link text (aka. anchor text) and the URL. Other types of links can be given in HTML; for example, `<img>` tags can be used to give the URL of a remote image that should be embedded into the webpage.

1.2.2 Interpreting HTML Content

HTML documents are only machine readable in a most shallow sense: since HTML outlines a limited, "need-to-know" semantics, the machine only has just enough understanding of the document to be able to display it. Though various new terms have been added to HTML over the years, and other standards have contributed further syntaxes and semantics specifying how pages can be formatted and interacted with, the primary content of a typical Web document is still trapped in a format intended for human consumption: the bulk of information content on the Web is still opaque to machines.

Example 1.6

The information in the webpages of Example 1.5 are easy for a human who reads English and understands the context of war, literature, Nobel prizes, etc., to consume. However, a machine cannot interpret the primary content of the pages in the same way we can.

To try to see these webpages from a more machine perspective, let us jumble the letters between the tags, keeping the tags – like `<tr>` and `</tr>`, which machines are specifically instructed to interpret – intact. Let us further assume that the webpages still encode the same information. Although the resulting webpages are equally as machine readable as before according to the HTML standard, to us humans, it is much more difficult to understand what is being spoken about:

Lucys Sedgyefyz

Ny sozf Lucys sedgyefyz ugwygyw ci befyjugi fhyl iyeg.

Sofygefdgy

Iyeg	Enegwyy
1901	Zdssi Rgdwhummy
...	...
1953	Nolzful Bhdgbhoss
1954	Yglyzf Hymoljnei
...	...
1964	Vyel-Reds Zegfgy[†]
...	...
1983	Nossoem Juswolj
...	...
1985	Bsedwy Zomul
...	...

[†]Zegfgy wybsolyw.

Ryeby

Iyeg	Enegwyy
1901	Hylgi Wdlelf
1901	Pgýwýgob Rezzi
...	...

...

Nossoem J. Juswolj

Zog Nossoem Jygesw Juswolj BCY (1911–1993) nez e Cgofozh lutysozf, rseigojhf elw ruyf. Hoz muzf bysycgefyw nugqz olbsdwy fhy lutysz "Sugw up fhy Psoyz", elw "Gofyz up Rezzejy" pug nhobh hy nez enegwyw fhy "Cuuqyg Rgoay".

...

Hy vuolyw fhy Guies Leti ol 1940, bummelwolj e selwolj zhor ef fhy Lugmelwi Oltezoul ul W-Wei.

...

Oltezoul up Lugmelwi

Ul Vdly 6th 1944 (W-Wei), fhy Nyzfygl Essoyz up Nugsw Neg OO ezzedsfyw Leao ubbdrefoul pugbyz pgum fhy zye ef Lugmelwi, ez regf up Urygefoul Utygsugw.

...

By jumbling the letters, we have broken the semantic connection from this information to the real world – the connection by which the reader can meaningfully interpret the information. Breaking this connection, we can then more clearly see the information from the perspective of a machine that can never make such a connection: we can see titles and words and tables and links (as explicitly indicated in the HTML syntax), but we cannot make sense of them. Our challenge then is to format such content in a way that the machine can *emulate* a meaningful, human-like interpretation of the information it encodes.

In order to organise the *content* of such HTML webpages – if we wanted to build, say, a search engine – we could instruct a machine to parse out individual words between spaces, and index which words appear in which documents. We could also instruct it to identify which words appear in the title, which appear in links to documents, and so forth, and to determine how well-linked the document is. These are the principles upon which modern search engines are based: inverted indexes that map words to the documents, relevance measures based on the density of query terms in each such document compared to the average density, and importance measures such as how well-linked a document is [29]. Such principles – and the nature of the Web itself – underlie the immoderate success of such engines, where with some select keywords, and a simple search in mind, a user rarely even needs to venture beyond the first page of results.

But for more complex searches and tasks, more advanced methods are needed. Deeper analyses of text (in webpages) is an active topic of research, particularly in the area of Information Extraction [92], where concepts from Natural Language Processing [257], Machine Learning [58], Information Retrieval [29] and so forth, are applied to the problem of extracting structured information from unstructured sources of text; this area has grown increasingly important to apply automated processing techniques to the vast quantities of text-based information available on the Web, for example as produced on social networking sites, micro-blogging platforms, wikis, and so forth.

Example 1.7

In order to more deeply analyse the content of the three webpages from Example 1.6, we could instruct a machine to apply a variety of Information Extraction techniques, some of which we will now exemplify. We give the name of specific techniques in italics for reference. We initially use obfuscated text in the examples to give a better idea of how these techniques look from a machine perspective and why they are non-trivial (which may not be otherwise as obvious); thereafter we explain the obfuscated terms. Along these lines, using Information Extraction techniques, machines could be instructed (or trained) to:

- detect related words like "lutysz" and "lutysozf" that have a common root form ("lutys"), suggesting, for example, that a keyword search for the former should perhaps return documents containing the latter, and vice versa (*stemming*);

  - lutysz/novels, lutysozf/novelist, lutys/novel;

- learn from frequency distributions that words like "elw" and "e" occur very frequently (*stop-words*), while terms such as "sedgyefyz" are much more rare (*inverse-document frequency*);

```
      - elw/and, e/a, sedgyefyz/laureates;
```

- learn that some pairs of words like "ubbdrefoul" and "pugbyz" occur sequentially more frequently in text than one might expect in a random distribution (*n-gram analysis*) while words like "lutysozf", "rseigojhf", "ruyf" and "Cuuqyg" tend to appear in the same regions of text (not necessarily sequentially) more often than would be expected of unrelated words (*topic extraction*);

```
      - ubbdrefoul/occupation, pugbyz/forces, lutysozf/novelist,
        rseigojhf/playwright, ruyf/poet, Cuuqyg/Booker;
```

- apply a list of reference words to ascertain whether a text is positive or negative in sentiment, for example, to assign a positive score to a text for appearances of words such as "bysycgefyw", or "enegwyw", while assigning a negative score to appearances of words such as "Neg" or "ezzedsfyw" (*sentiment analysis*).

```
      - bysycgefyw/celebrated, enegwyw/awarded, Neg/War,
        ezzedsfyw/assaulted;
```

- guess from capitalisation that "Zdssi Rgdwhummy" is a name of something, and perhaps use a reference list to guess that it's the name of something called a "rygzul" (*named-entity recognition*);

```
      - Zdssi Rgdwhummy/Sully Prudhomme, rygzul/person;
```

- guess that the "Nossoem Juswolj" of the left-hand webpage probably refers to the same thing as the "Nossoem J. Juswolj" of the right-hand page it links to (*entity resolution*);

```
      - Nossoem Juswolj/William Golding,
        Nossoem J. Juswolj/William G. Golding;
```

- recognise that "lutys' is something called a noun, that "nez" is a past conjugation of a verb, etc. (*part-of-speech tagging*);

```
      - lutys/novel, nez/was;
```

- extract some relationships from the text with a simple sentence structure, for example:

$$\underbrace{\texttt{Nossoem J. Juswolj}}_{subject} \underbrace{\texttt{ngufy}}_{verb} \underbrace{\texttt{Sugw up fhy Psoyz}}_{object}$$

which may allow for asking queries such as for all objects related to by the subject "Nossoem J. Juswolj" with the verb "ngufy" across all documents analysed (*relation extraction*);

> – Nossoem J. Juswolj/William G. Golding, ngufy/wrote,
>   Sugw up fhy Psoyz/Lord of the Flies;
>
> • guess that all things mentioned in the second column of the first
>   table of the left-hand webpage are of the same type ("Enegwyy"), and
>   maybe extract other relations from the tables (*table understanding*);
>
> – Enegwyy/Awardee;
>
> • attempt to answer a question like "nhobh Lucys sedgyefyz ol So-
>   fygefdgy pudjhf ol e neg?" (*question answering*);
>
> – nhobh Lucys sedgyefyz ol Sofygefdgy pudjhf ol e neg?/
>   which Nobel laureates in Literature fought in a war?.

Thanks to decades of intensive research efforts – as well as the growing availability of better corpora and an exponentially increasing computational power – we have enjoyed the benefits of a long and steady stream of advancements in machine understanding of natural language in specific areas, such as machine translation, speech recognition, or answering questions. Anyone who has used services such as Google Translate, Siri, etc., would have experienced these advancements first-hand, but also probably the limitations of current technology. Despite decades of intensive research efforts, we still appear to be (at least) a long way away from a *general purpose* machine that can emulate a human-like understanding of natural language. Referring back to Example 1.7, in particular with respect to the latter tasks such as relation extraction and question answering, we are still far from developing general techniques that are reliable in the sense of returning only correct results (*precision*) and all correct results (*recall*) when evaluated on, for example, small datasets manually labelled with the answers by human experts.

So why are these tasks challenging? Focusing on *Natural Language Understanding* [9], we can mention the following problems that machines face:

• There are many ways to express equivalent information. Taking a very simple example: "*Mary is John's child*", "*Mary is a child of John*", "*John is the parent of Mary*", etc. Taking a more complex example: "*This blueberry cake recipe, which takes 90 minutes to prepare, is suitable for coeliacs*", "*This gluten-free blueberry cake recipe takes 1 h 30 m to make*".
• The same referent can have multiple possible references; for example, "*the United States*", "*the U.S.*", "*the US*", "*USA*", "*EE.UU.*" etc.
• Conversely, different referents may share the same name; for example, "*Boston*" may be the name of a U.S. city, a rock band, the self-titled album of that rock band, a breed of terrier, etc.
• Likewise, many words and phrases that are written the same may have multiple meanings. For example, "*lead*" is a homograph that may refer, amongst other meanings, to a metal or to first place, which renders sentences such as "*John took the lead.*" ambiguous without further context.

- Other words may have subtly different (polysemous) meanings in everyday language. For example, in the sentence "*the local mayor married Jane and John*", our immediate assumption is (probably) that the mayor presided over the marriage ceremony, not that they were married with Jane and John. Other cases may be even more subtle: in the sentences "*the movie costs $4 to rent per night*" and "*the director was paid $4 million to make the movie*", we would naturally distinguish between a physical copy of the movie and the more abstract notion of the movie.
- Information may be split over multiple clauses that use references such as pronouns that may be difficult to resolve; for example, compare the "*she*" in both: "*Jane tried to follow her late grandmother's recipe, but she had not included details of the cooking times.*" and "*Jane tried to follow her late grandmother's recipe, but she had forgotten to buy lemons*".
- Some terms are more specific forms of others; for example, "*John is the father of Mary*" implies that "*John is the parent of Mary*"; more formally, "*father*" in this context is a hyponym of "*parent*", its hypernym.
- Oftentimes in language, the literal meaning is not intended (where even the word "*literally*" cannot always be taken literally).

These examples give an idea of some of the challenges faced by machines in the area of Natural Language Understanding, and as a consequence, the challenges faced by machines in processing the implicit content of the current Web. Indeed, one of the overarching reasons why machines are so far from a human-level understanding of text is that machines cannot experience the world in the same way us humans do. While we can instruct machines on various forms of (what is termed in the Artificial Intelligence community as) "*common-sense knowledge*", they will never experience the *qualia* of what we describe to them, in terms of the bitterness of lemons, the thrill (or boredom) of watching a movie, etc. Without this context, machines are at a major disadvantage when trying to understand subtlety in prose, such as recognising that deceased grandmothers do not typically buy lemons.

Problems like (deep) Information Extraction and Natural Language Understanding are hard, especially when considering something as large and diverse as the Web. So towards our goal of making the Latent Web accessible to automated methods, *wherever possible*, it makes sense to try to avoid these difficult problems – of making machines understand human language – altogether. Avoiding such problems is at the heart of the Web of Data, whose main goal is to make the Web's content more (and more) machine-readable to allow machines to do more (and more) sophisticated tasks automatically. We will elaborate more on the Web of Data in the next chapter.

Chapter 2
Web of Data

Previously we discussed how the current Web is intended to be human-readable, where the bulk of content is made available as text documents formatted in HTML. But machines have as difficult a time in making sense out of our human language as we would have decoding their raw binary content and turning it into textual or visual output. What comes easily to humans is often difficult for machines, and what is easy for machines is often difficult for humans. For humans and machines to work together most effectively, we often must meet somewhere in the middle. The goal of the Web of Data, then, is not to try to make machines understand our natural language, but instead to meet machines in the middle: to allow machines to exchange content between themselves in a structured format that they can do more with algorithmically, without requiring human intervention or guidance.

A key question underlying the Web of Data is thus: how should the content of the Web be organised to make it more machine-readable? In order to meet machines in the middle, we can start by considering the following steps:

- Use a canonical form of expressing factual claims with as simple a sentence structure as possible, avoiding pronouns, irony, etc.
- Use one name to refer to one thing, e.g., *the United States*.
- Use unambiguous names that refer to one thing, e.g., *Boston (Rock Band)*.
- Write queries using a structure analogous to the data.
- Make the semantics of terms explicit, for example, that *father* and *mother* are hyponyms of *parent*.
- Provide links to discover relevant information in remote locations.

Each step increases machine readability. However, these steps imply a raft of technical and social challenges: some factual claims may be contextual or contentious; if we assume one name to refer to one thing, who should decide which names to use; how can we ensure that the same identifiers are used consistently in different locations across the Web; and so forth. For the Web of Data to work, these challenges will need to be addressed. First however, we will illustrate how these (idealised) steps increase machine-readability.

© Springer Nature Switzerland AG 2020

A. Hogan, *The Web of Data*, https://doi.org/10.1007/978-3-030-51580-5_2

2.1 Overview

This chapter discusses the main concepts underlying the vision of the Web of Data with the goal of making the content of the Web increasingly machine-readable. The remainder of the chapter is structured as follows:

Section 2.2 describes some of the concepts by which the Web can be made increasingly machine-readable.

Section 2.3 discusses some examples on the current Web where the aforementioned concepts of the Web of Data are already in use.

2.2 Web of Data: Concepts

The prospect of making the content of the Web more machine readable raises a number of key questions. To begin with, how should DATA be structured on the Web? Should we structure factual data as tables, or trees, or graphs? Next we must consider how QUERIES over that data should be expressed. What sorts of features should a query language support? Thereafter, we need to think about how the meaning of the data (and queries) should be made explicit for machines in terms of how SEMANTICS can be represented. Is there a set of generic *terms* (such as "is-a" or "specialises") whose semantics we can hard-code into machines, such that we can then use those generic terms to define new domain-specific terms on the fly ("lemon is-a citrus-fruit", "father specialises parent")? Subsequently we may think about how we should define CONSTRAINTS against which data can be validated. How can we ensure, for example, that data published on a website meet some minimal guarantees of completeness needed for an application? Finally, since it should not be assumed that the world's knowledge will be packaged up neatly on one Web server, how can we provide LINKS to connect everything together into a *Web*?

In this section, we discuss these five fundamental concepts underlying the Web of Data: DATA, QUERIES, SEMANTICS, CONSTRAINTS, and LINKS.

2.2.1 Data

How data are represented affects the manner in which they can be subsequently used. Representations of data have thus been constantly evolving to try to meet increasingly complex – and sometimes orthogonal – demands.

One of the milestones of this evolution was the emergence of **relational databases** for representing, managing, and querying tables of data, whose foundations were formalised by Codd in the late 60's/early 70's [98], and which have been the subject of continuous study and incremental improvement ever since, including the development of the **Structured Query Language (SQL)** and a variety of optimised relational database engines. Relational databases are broadly adopted for representing and managing data.

However, in some scenarios, relational databases can be awkward to use. Relational databases work best when one can define, *a priori*, a **schema** for the data based on the sets of tables in which to store data and the columns they contain; furthermore, the schema should not need to change often, and the data contained in tables should be relatively complete. Such assumptions work well in the context of banks or libraries, for example, where the types of data that need to be represented do not change often, and where relatively complete information is available for clients, users, etc. In other scenarios, however, designing and maintaining a domain-specific schema to which the data must conform may not be feasible. When integrating data from multiple sources on the Web, for example, a more flexible data representation that relaxes the requirement for a schema would be more fitting.

Hence the concept of **semi-structured data** emerged to characterise scenarios where the data in question do not conform to a typical relational database schema: where attributes may have multiple values, or no values, where the attributes themselves might change, and so forth. For such scenarios, the **eXtensible Markup Language (XML)** was proposed as a similar format to HTML, allowing not only tags for formatting webpages, but also arbitrary tags that could be used to describe data following a tree-based structure. Much later, **JavaScript Object Notation (JSON)** arrived as a popular, lightweight alternative to XML; like XML, JSON is also tree-based. Alternatively, **Comma Separated Values (CSV)** is a lightweight format for representing semi-structured tabular data (with a schema being optional).

However, in many semi-structured domains, the connections between the things being described may contain cycles that are not so natural to represent in a tree-based data structure (e.g., to describe a social network, we may wish to say that Alice is connected to Bob who is connected to Claire who is connected to Alice). Furthermore, in some domains there may not be a clear hierarchy with which to describe the data, requiring one to be artificially imposed on the data (e.g., should we organise users in a dating site by city first, and then by gender; or by gender, then city; or simply represent a flat list of users where specific gender and city values are repeated for each user?).

Other semi-structured data models are based on graphs. Like tree-based data models, graphs are semi-structured, and do not rely on a fixed domain-specific schema. Unlike tree-based data models, graphs allow for conceptually representing cycles, and do not require a hierarchy to be imposed.

There are then a variety of models (e.g., tables, trees, graphs) and formats (e.g., SQL, CSV, JSON, XML), etc., by which data can be represented. While a Web of Data should ideally offer support for all, in order to define standards and begin to build applications, agreeing on one core data model is of key importance, where we will argue in this book that graphs offer the most natural option, following the high-level intuition that data embedded on the Web are inherently incomplete and semi-structured (not following a fixed schema) and do not naturally conform to a (hierarchical) tree-structure. Selecting a graph-based data model does not preclude support for other models and formats: data modelled as tables or trees or otherwise can be mapped to graphs using techniques that shall be described later (in Chapter 8).

Example 2.1

We will now illustrate one way in which a subset of the content of the webpages in Example 1.5 can be better structured in order to make that content more accessible to processing by automated methods:

(SullyPrudhomme,awarded,NLP1901)
(NLP1901,year,1901)
(NLP1901,type,NobelLiteraturePrize)
(NLP1901,accepted,true)
...
(JeanPaulSartre,awarded,NLP1964)
(NLP1964,year,1964)
(NLP1964,type,NobelLiteraturePrize)
(NLP1964,accepted,false)
...
(WilliamGolding,awarded,NLP1983)
(NLP1983,year,1983)
(NLP1983,type,NobelLiteraturePrize)
(NLP1983,accepted,true)
...
(HenryDunant,awarded,NPP1901I)
(NPP1901I,year,1901)
(NPP1901I,type,NobelPeacePrize)
(NPP1901I,accepted,true)
(FrédéricPassy,awarded,NPP1901II)
(NPP1901II,year,1901)
(NPP1901II,type,NobelPeacePrize)
(NPP1901II,accepted,true)
...

(WilliamGolding,nationality,British)
(WilliamGolding,type,Novelist)
(WilliamGolding,type,Playwright)
(WilliamGolding,type,Poet)
(WilliamGolding,wrote,LoTFlies)
(LoTFlies,type,Novel)
(WilliamGolding,wrote,RofPassage)
(RofPassage,type,Novel)
(RofPassage,awarded,BookerPrize)
...
(WilliamGolding,fought,NormandyInv)

(NormandyInv,start,1944-06-06)
(NormandyInv,type,SeaInvasion)
(NormandyInv,location,Normandy)
(NormandyInv,attacking,WestAllies)
(NormandyInv,defending,Nazis)
(NormandyInv,partOf,OpOverload)
(OpOverload,type,MilitaryOperation)
(OpOverload,partOf,WorldWarII)
(WorldWarII,type,War)

This can be considered the verbatim "source" content of each document: there is no HTML or other markup code used; instead each document is now a set of sentences, where each sentence is a claim following a simple *3-tuple* (or *triple*) structure. We will later show how these triples conceptually form a graph of data. Furthermore, certain terms in the data – such as WilliamGolding or NormandyInv – can link to remote sources with relevant data, as denoted by dashed arrows.

Remark 2.1

We will often refer to *semi-structured data* as simply *structured data* since semi-structured data is still structured even if it does not necessarily conform to a relational-style schema.

Discussion 2.1

FRANK: But could you not simply represent these triples in a relational table with three attributes?

AIDAN: Yes you can, and in practice some people do.

FRANK: So why don't we use the relational model?

AIDAN: Well this graph model is much simpler than the relational model, where instead of having a set of tables, we have one, and instead of each table having an arbitrary number of columns, our table has three columns. This simplified model makes it easier to combine two sources of triple data: just take the union of both triple tables. We no longer need to combine relational schemata since each source has only one table. On the other hand, with this simplified model, we can still capture all of the data that one can capture in a relational database. So we end up something more simple and more flexible than the relational model. This will be explained in more detail later when we discuss the RDF data model based on graphs.

Example 2.2

Let's take the following subset of sentences, combined from the three documents in Example 2.1, representing information that William Golding won the Nobel Prize for Literature in 1983 and participated in the Normandy Invasion, along with details of the prize and the invasion:

(WilliamGolding,awarded,NLP1983)	(WilliamGolding,fought,NormandyInv)
(NLP1983,year,1983)	(NormandyInv,partOf,OpOverload)
(NLP1983,type,NobelLiteraturePrize)	(OpOverload,partOf,WorldWarII)
(NLP1983,accepted,true)	(WorldWarII,type,War)

It is straightforward to automatically combine such sentences from multiple locations: simply take the union. Where consistent naming is provided across sources, such sources can complement the information that each provides about an entity, such as, in this case, William Golding.

We can say that the model is *triple-based*, or that it is *graph-based*: each triple in the data of the form (x, y, z) can be viewed as a directed, labelled edge in a graph of the form $x \xrightarrow{y} z$. Viewing the above data from this graph-based perspective, we arrive at the following graph, which spans the information present in the original three documents:

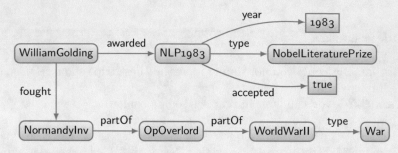

To extend this graph, we can easily add new nodes and/or new labelled edges between nodes (including cycles) by adding more triples, for example, by importing further documents with this format.

Although we no longer have HTML markup indicating how the content should be presented, and we no longer have any more prose text to read, as humans, we can still understand what is being said – more or less – in these data because we can still recognise terms such as War. However, while a machine could be taught to recognise certain **datatype values** like 1983 as a number it can add to another number, or true as a boolean that it can negate to create another boolean, terms like War are effectively an opaque symbol to a machine: they have no real significance other than their own identity.

Example 2.3

From the perspective of a machine, the data from Example 2.2 would appear something like (assuming *un*familiarity with astrology):

$$(\Omega, \mathbb{m}, \delta) \quad (\Omega, \Upsilon, \aleph)$$
$$(\delta, \bar{\epsilon}, 1983) \quad (\aleph, \mathrm{P}, \mathrm{D})$$
$$(\delta, \text{4}, \mathbb{C}) \quad (\mathrm{D}, \mathrm{P}, \hbar)$$
$$(\delta, \sigma, \text{true}) \quad (\hbar, \text{4}, \mathbb{M})$$

Here we replace terms like WilliamGolding, awarded and NLP1983 in the sentences with opaque symbols like Ω, $\mathbb{m}$ and δ. We do not replace datatype values since intuitively machines can recognise their form.

Since we replace each mention of each non-datatype term (e.g., WilliamGolding) consistently with the same symbol (e.g., Ω) in a one-to-one manner, the data have not really changed from the perspective of a machine: it is us humans that assign some sort of meaning to terms like WilliamGolding or symbols like Ω; in other words, by removing familiar terms, we see that from the machine's perspective, the above data could be talking about pretty much anything for all the machine knows.

Without access to the real-world meaning of terms used in the data, the machine can still be instructed to do useful processing using **symbolic methods** applied with respect to the structure of the graph formed by the data.

A good way to understand what we mean by symbolic methods is through the "Chinese Room" analogy put forward by Searle [356], whereby a person who understands no Chinese – neither verbal nor written – is placed in a sealed room. On one side of the room, the occupant is passed questions in Chinese as "input". On the other side of the room, the occupant must return answers to these questions in Chinese as "output". To help with this, the room contains a large book of rules that state how to match patterns in the input questions and how to respond to them with the output answers. Importantly, the book never translates nor explains the Chinese symbols, it just states how to shuffle, combine and exchange these symbols in order to construct answers to questions. At no point does the occupant understand what the Chinese symbols actually mean and yet, it *may* be possible, with a sufficiently efficient occupant and a sufficiently detailed rule book, for the occupant to give the appearance to the outside world of being a Chinese speaker who (to some extent) *understands* the question and can respond in Chinese with a meaningful answer. Searle then draws a philosophical distinction between the Chinese speakers outside the room and the person inside the room in terms of how they are processing and understanding the information.

Leaving aside philosophical questions of the requisites of intelligence, the analogy illustrates the goal underlying symbolic methods: we can consider the occupant in the room as a machine that – without understanding the meaning underlying these symbols in the same way we as humans do – can manipulate symbols taken from the input, using something like a rule-book, to produce an output that is *meaningful* for us in response to a *query*.

In Chapter 3, we describe the **Resource Description Framework (RDF)**: a graph-based data model we can use to structure Web content as a graph.

2.2.2 Queries

Even if we structure data on the Web in this graph-based manner (per Example 2.2), it is still unclear how the machine should answer a question like the one that Julie originally had (in Example 1.1): *which Nobel laureates in Literature have fought in wars?* From the perspective of the machine, it would be much more straightforward if we could also structure the question in a similar way to the data. This gives rise to the notion of (structured) *queries*.

Example 2.4

In the following, we will use terms like WilliamGolding to give a human perspective and symbols like Ω to give a better idea of the perspective of a machine that assigns no significance to such terms.

Let us take the data from Example 2.2 (and the symbolic version from Example 2.3) and let's assume to start with, we wish to get a list of wars from these data, and in the interest of meeting the machine half-way, assume we structure the query in a similar way to the data:

$$(?w, type, War)$$

Here ?w is a variable that can match any term in the data. We see that if we map this variable to WorldWarII, we get a sentence in the original data. Hence we can return WorldWarII as an answer. On the other hand, if we mapped ?w to WilliamGolding, we would get a sentence that is not supported by the data; hence WilliamGolding is not an answer.

Let's look at the same query from the machine's perspective:

$$(?w, ⅄, \text{ẘ})$$

In this case, ?w will map to $\hbar$ since $(\hbar, ⅄, \text{ẘ})$ is in the data. Without understanding the terms, so long as the data and the query are structured in the same way, answers can be retrieved algorithmically using symbolic methods that match the query pattern against the data.

This is an example of a simple question that can be represented as a query with a single sentence. However, we can consider more complex queries that combine multiple query sentences together as a **conjunction**, intuitively meaning that each answer must satisfy all sentences combined.

Example 2.5

Again over the same data from Examples 2.2 and 2.3, let us this time consider a more complex query from the perspective of the machine without concern for its intuitive meaning:

$$(?a, ጤ, ?p), (?p, ⅄, ℂ)$$

This is an example of what is called a **conjunctive query**, which means that implicitly, we wish to find ways to match the variables such that the entire query is a subset of the known data.

It may help if we formulate both the query and the data in terms of a graph. To start with, here are the symbolic data drawn as a graph:

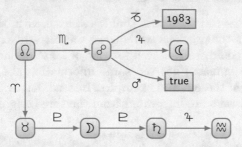

And here is the query drawn as a graph, with variable nodes dashed:

Now we wish to find ways to map the variables in the query graph to fixed symbols in the data graph such that the query graph becomes a sub-graph of the data graph. If we map ?a to ♌ and ?p to ♐ in this query graph, we get the following sub-graph of the data:

In other words, the query is mapped to the following triples:

$$(♌,♏,♐), \quad (♐,♃,☾)$$

This matching of the query to the data can be performed algorithmically by the machine and the match found serves as an answer.

Hence without understanding that we were asking about people who won Nobel Prizes for Literature, assuming that the given query is structured in a similar manner to the data:

$$(\text{?a,awarded,?p}), \quad (\text{?p,type,NobelLiteraturePrize})$$

the machine can return WilliamGolding (♌) and NLP1983 (♐) as results using conceptually straightforward symbolic methods.

If we consider the original dataset from Example 2.1, we could find further answers for the same query using the same symbolic methods:

?a	?p
SullyPrudhomme	NLP1901
JeanPaulSartre	NLP1964
WilliamGolding	NLP1983
. . .	. . .

Of course, in the raw webpages that we started with, the information we have derived from the previous two queries was already explicit on the Web. For example, we could easily search for "list of wars" or "nobel literature prize winners" and (as humans) get the same information the machine has just computed for us in these initial examples. Instead, let us now consider some queries whose answers are integrated from the three original documents.

Example 2.6

To start with, consider the following query asking for British poets who have been awarded the Nobel Prize for Literature:

$$(?a, awarded, ?p), \ (?p, type, NobelLiteraturePrize),$$
$$(?a, type, Poet), \ (?a, nationality, British)$$

If we consider applying this query using the same symbolic methods as discussed before but this time over the merge of all data from the three documents, we would find (at least) the following answer:

?a	?p
WilliamGolding	NLP1983
. . .	. . .

Deriving this first answer requires cross-referencing two explicit sources. Assuming we had similar information for other matching poets, such as Rudyard Kipling, T. S. Eliot, Doris Lessing, etc., we could apply the same process over more sources to derive these answers as well.

Answers to this query can be drawn from multiple sources because:

- both the query and the data follow an analogous simple structure;
- since all sources used the same simple sentence structure, we can merge sources by simply taking the union of all sentences;
- naming is consistent across sources: WilliamGolding is used to refer to the same person across all three documents and the query (and we assume it is only used to refer to that person).

Of course, we may not always be so lucky; indeed, assuming everyone on the Web agrees on the name of everything seems particularly naive. We will revisit ways to relax these assumptions at a later stage in the book.

We can further consider various extensions to conjunctive queries for:

- checking multiple options;
  - e.g., find Nobel laureates in Peace OR Literature that fought in wars;
- or matching optional information;
  - e.g., find Nobel laureates in Peace or Literature that fought in wars and give their nationality IF AVAILABLE;
- or aggregating data;
  - e.g., find the AVERAGE AGE of Nobel laureates in Economics;
- or matching paths in the data;
  - e.g., find all conflicts that were RECURSIVELY part of World War II;
- and so forth.

Hence conjunctive queries are the *basis* of expressing more complex queries over graphs of data. Along these lines, in Chapter 6, we will talk about the **SPARQL Protocol And RDF Query Language (SPARQL)** [169], which offers the ability to express conjunctive queries, all of the aforementioned extensions, and more, over the graph-based RDF data model. We will also talk about the expense of answering such queries: though conceptually straightforward, evaluating such queries can be computationally demanding.

2.2.3 Semantics

Thus far, we have seen examples where we can process queries that reflect the data directly, meaning that we can simply match the query with the data to find results. This can effectively be achieved on the level of data and queries alone. However, in other cases, the machine may not be so lucky: in other more complex cases, the machine may need some encoding of the *semantics* of the data to generate **inferences** for relevant (implicit) answers.

Example 2.7

Let us consider the following query over the running example:

(?a,awarded,?p), (?p,type,NobelPrize), (?p,year,1983)

Intuitively, we would consider WilliamGolding (with NLP1983) as an answer to this query, amongst other winners of Nobel prizes in that year. However, in our original data, we have no mention of a term NobelPrize – only of terms such as NobelLiteraturePrize and NobelPeacePrize. While we as humans – knowing a little something of the Nobel awards – can see an obvious connection between NobelPrize and NobelLiteraturePrize or NobelPeacePrize, the machine cannot see such a connection. One could argue that the machine could compute some similarity between these names and try derive meaning from that, but while this may work in some cases, it would fail in many others and is precisely the type of unreliable heuristic we are trying to avoid in general. Rather it would be better to instruct the machine explicitly about the semantics of these terms in a manner it could process using symbolic methods.

From the perspective of the machine, the query looks like:

$$(?a, ℳ, ?p), (?p, ♃, Ⅱ), (?p, ♅, 1983)$$

On the other hand, the data relevant to William Golding are:

$$(Ω, ℳ, ♂), (♂, ♃, ℂ), (♂, ♅, 1983)$$

The machine cannot generate an answer because the symbol Ⅱ in the query does not match the symbol ℂ in the data.

However, we could provide the machine with a **rule**, as follows:

$$(?x, ♃, ℂ) → (?x, ♃, Ⅱ)$$

Intuitively this states that every time we find something that matches the premise of the left, we can conclude that which is on the right for that match. For example, since we have the sentence $(♂, ♃, ℂ)$, we can apply this rule to infer that the sentence $(♂, ♃, Ⅱ)$ must hold based on the rule and the input sentence. We would now have:

$$(Ω, ℳ, ♂), (♂, ♃, ℂ), (♂, ♃, Ⅱ), (♂, ♅, 1983)$$

With this extra sentence, we can now answer the original query with ?a matched to Ω (WilliamGolding) and with ?p matched to ♂ (NLP1983). Hence, given the query, rule(s), and data, the machine can use symbolic methods to infer that William Golding should feature in an answer.

From a human perspective, we created a rule stating that anything that is of type Nobel Prize in Literature is also of type Nobel Prize:

$$(?x, type, NobelLiteraturePrize) → (?x, type, NobelPrize)$$

We then used this rule to infer that since William Golding's prize is of type Nobel Prize in Literature, it must also be more generally of type Nobel Prize, and thus it must match this criterion of the query.

Of course, we could likewise create rules for other types of Nobel Prizes, and most importantly, we can apply these rules to help answer other queries relating to Nobel Prizes. We can create these generic rules once and use them to help answer arbitrary queries in future.

In this previous example, we use a rule that makes explicit some semantics for the terms/symbols in the data, thus allowing to materialise some implicit data that generates answers to our query.

Again however, it would not be difficult to find an explicit list of Nobel Prize winners in 1983 on the Web of Documents. Thus, let's instead finally turn to the information that Julie sought in Example 1.1: Nobel laureates in Literature that fought in a war, returning the year they were awarded the Nobel prize, and the war(s) they fought in.

Example 2.8

To generalise the case of William Golding for Julie's question, we may be tempted to write the following conjunctive query:

(?a,awarded,?p), (?p,type,NobelLiteraturePrize), (?p,year,?y),
(?a,fought,?b), (?b,partOf,?c), (?c,partOf,?d), (?d,type,War)

This will indeed match the data for William Golding. However, implicit in this query is a path of partOf relations of length 2, representing that the Normandy Invasion was part of Operation Overlord, which was part of World War II. However, other Nobel laureates in Literature may be denoted as fighting directly in a war (a path of 0 partOf relations), or in an operation that is denoted as directly being part of a war (a path of 1 partOf relation), or in a conflict of a battle of an operation of a war (a path of 3 partOf relations), etc., where these laureates would not be returned although intuitively they would be valid answers.

There are a number of ways to solve this. We could run multiple queries with different lengths, but this would not be a general solution since we do not know a priori how many queries we would need to run. We could instead extend the query language to support querying of arbitrary-length paths, which would be a quite general solution; however, this would require increasingly more complex queries to be able to capture even basic semantics for terms, and would preclude the possibility of the machine pre-processing some semantics before queries arrive.

Rather than look at the query, let us first start with the following rule, which tells the machine that the partOf relation is **transitive**:

(?x,partOf,?y), (?y,partOf,?z) → (?x,partOf,?z)

Unlike the previous rule we saw, which states that all prizes of type Nobel Prizes in Literature are also Nobel Prizes, this rule has a conjunctive premise on the left-hand side. Thus for example given the data:

(NormandyInv,partOf,OpOverlord), (OpOverlord,partOf,WorldWarII)

From the above rule and these two sentences, we could then infer:

(NormandyInv,partOf,WorldWarII)

As a side note, for a longer path of partOf relations, we could apply the rule recursively over the input data and the inferred data to compute the transitive closure of the partOf relation; for example, assume we had started with an additional sentence:

(OmahaLanding,partOf,NormandyInv),
(NormandyInv,partOf,OpOverlord),
(OpOverlord,partOf,WorldWarII)

Applying the above rule once, we arrive at:

(NormandyInv,partOf,WorldWarII),
(OmahaLanding,partOf,OpOverlord)

Applying the above rule again (recursively) over the union of the input and inferred statements thus far, we get:

(OmahaLanding,partOf,WorldWarII)

Having encoded the transitives semantics of the partOf relation, let us now add a second recursive rule:

(?x,partOf,?y), (?y,partOf,?z) → (?x,partOf,?z)
(?u,fought,?v), (?v,partOf,?w) → (?u,fought,?w)

Let us again consider the following input sentences:

(WilliamGolding,fought,NormandyInv),
(NormandyInv,partOf,OpOverlord),
(OpOverlord,partOf,WorldWarII)

By applying the first rule and then the second, the machine can infer:

(NormandyInv,partOf,WorldWarII),
(WilliamGolding,fought,OpOverlord),
(WilliamGolding,fought,WorldWarII)

In other words, these two rules enable the machine – using symbolic methods – to automatically infer from the data that William Golding fought in World War II by virtue of the fact that he fought in a battle that was part of an operation that was part of this war. In other words, by these two rules, we add the following dotted edges to the graph:

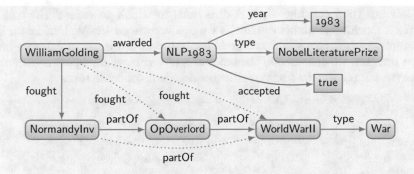

We can now ask a simpler, more general query:

(?a,awarded,?p), (?p,type,NobelLiteraturePrize), (?p,year,?y),
(?a,fought,?b), (?b,type,War)

Representing this query graphically:

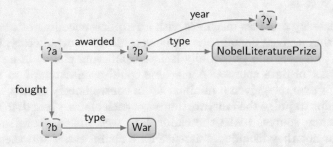

With this query and the two previous rules, we can compute the answer:

?a	?p	?y	?b
WilliamGolding	NLP1983	1983	WorldWarII
...	...	...	...

Likewise, with analogous data for other authors, with the same rules and similar symbolic methods, we would get answers representing the other Nobel laureates in Literature who fought in wars.

Hence, with some added semantics, the machine can now answer Julie's query in an automated fashion by integrating data from multiple sources and deriving some implicit data using rules – implicit data that will match the query and generate additional answers. This saves Julie the need to manually cross-check the content coming from multiple sources on the Web. On the other hand, from the perspective of the machine, the use of semantics greatly simplifies the queries that need to be answered: rather than users having to capture the semantics of terms in custom queries, these semantics can be expressed a priori in the form of generic rules that support all queries.

We can then consider various directions in which to extend the sort of explicit machine-readable semantics we can encode on the Web of Data. For example, with a very slight syntactic extension of the types of rules we have seen thus far, we can encode the semantics of terms with respect to **inconsistency**: with respect to what constitutes a logical contradiction.

Example 2.9

We could use the following rule to state that a given Nobel prize cannot be both a Nobel Prize in Literature and a Nobel Peace Prize:

(?x,type,NobelLiteraturePrize), (?x,type,NobelPeacePrize) → false

The term false in the conclusion of the rule indicates that an inconsistency has been found, meaning that any data matching the premise constitutes a logical contradiction with respect to the defined semantics of the terms NobelLiteraturePrize and NobelPeacePrize.

Inconsistency provides machines with an explicit encoding of what sorts of claims within a given domain should be considered contradictory, which can be useful to detect and potentially isolate conflicting claims in a given data source or set of data sources. A machine could even attempt to repair the conflict; for example, given a minimal set of contradictory claims, a machine may attempt to judge the trustworthiness of each claim – based, for example, on how many sources make the claim, how well linked those sources are, whether or not they include a reference for a claim, etc. – and then suppress the claim(s) deemed by the algorithm to be the least "trustworthy" [69].

Whatever the semantics that the rules define, we can imagine them being published alongside the data, giving an explicit encoding of the semantics of the terms used in that data, allowing the machine to deductively derive implicit conclusions. In fact, when we define rules for terms such as partOf, we are defining the semantics of a term that can be reused across not only several documents, but several domains (such as wars, geography, biology, astrology, etc.). Inherent in this reuse – at least ideally – is an agreement as to the semantics of the terms codified by the rules, allowing for implicit conclusions to be drawn across documents and even various domains. For example, if a publisher wishes to use partOf, then they should agree with the transitives semantics; otherwise, they *should* use another term, for if they do not, they may not enjoy the inferences a machine will generate.

Rather than codifying the semantics of terms in rules, another option is to codify such semantics using the same model (and forms of links) as we use for the data. To enable this, we could define the semantics of special terms in a global standard allowing those terms to be used in the data. As a consequence, this would allow us to avoid having to exchange rules separately from data; we could now simply exchange data using terms with special semantics, succinctly embedding semantics directly into the data.

Example 2.10

Rather than exchanging the following rule from Example 2.7:

$$(?x,type,NobelLiteraturePrize) \rightarrow (?x,type,NobelPrize)$$

instead we could exchange a special sentence as follows:

$$(NobelLiteraturePrize,subClassOf,NobelPrize)$$

We can now define a special semantics for this type of sentence. For example, we can define a generic rule that can form part of a standard:

$$(?x,type,?c), (?c,subClassOf,?d) \rightarrow (?x,type,?d)$$

Now if we take the following data together with this rule:

$$(NLP1983,type,NobelLiteraturePrize)$$
$$(NobelLiteraturePrize,subClassOf,NobelPrize)$$

we can infer:

$$(NLP1983,type,NobelPrize)$$

We can then reuse this special sentence for other similar cases:

$$(NobelPeacePrize,subClassOf,NobelPrize),$$
$$(NobelEconomicsPrize,subClassOf,NobelPrize),$$
$$(War,subClassOf,Conflict),$$
$$...$$

If we define the prior rule as part of a global standard, then we can avoid the need to exchange rules for domain-level terms like NobelPeacePrize, NobelEconomicsPrize, War, and so forth; instead we can exchange sentences of the above form embedded with or linked from the data.

In this case, we define the semantics of a **class** term: a class can be intuitively considered to be a collection of entities that share some commonalities, such as Person, with **instances** like WilliamGolding, WinstonChurchill, etc.; or War, with instances like WorldWarII, ColdWar, VietnamWar, etc.

Aside from classes, we could likewise consider using similar means to define the semantics of **properties**: the terms denoting the type of relationship encoded by the sentence, such as partOf, year, wrote, etc.

Example 2.11

To replace the following rule from Example 2.8:

$$(?x,partOf,?y),\ (?y,partOf,?z) \rightarrow (?x,partOf,?z)$$

we can exchange the following special sentence:

$$(partOf,type,TransitiveProperty)$$

We can now define a special semantics for this type of sentence. For example, we can define a generic rule that can form part of a standard:

$$(?x,?p,?y),\ (?y,?p,?z),\ (?p,type,TransitiveProperty) \rightarrow (?x,?p,?z)$$

Now if we take the following data together with this rule:

$$(partOf,type,TransitiveProperty),$$
$$(NormandyInv,partOf,OpOverlord),$$
$$(OpOverlord,partOf,WorldWarII)$$

we can likewise infer:

$$(NormandyInv,partOf,WorldWarII)$$

We can then reuse this special sentence for other similiar cases:

$$(ancestor,type,TransitiveProperty),$$
$$(descendent,type,TransitiveProperty),$$
$$(olderThan,type,TransitiveProperty),$$
$$...$$

If we define the previous rule as part of a global standard, we can then obviate the need to exchange rules for domain-level terms like partOf, ancestor, descendent, olderThan, and so forth; instead we can exchange sentences of the above form embedded with or linked from the data.

Finally we could likewise capture inconsistency.

Example 2.12

Instead of the following rule from Example 2.9:

$$(?x,type,NobelLiteraturePrize),\ (?x,type,NobelPeacePrize) \rightarrow false$$

we could state:

$$(NobelPeacePrize,disjointWith,NobelLiteraturePrize)$$

or equivalently:

$$(NobelLiteraturePrize, disjointWith, NobelPeacePrize)$$

We could then consider the following meta-rule:

$$(?x, type, ?c), (?x, type, ?d), (?c, disjointWith, ?d) \rightarrow false$$

This would capture the same semantics as the original rule.

However, in this hypothetical global standard, there is nothing limiting us to defining the semantics of special terms like subClassOf or TransitiveProperty using rules: we can use whatever sort of formalism we wish to define special terms in the global standard so long as we can develop techniques for machines to over the data in a manner compliant with those semantics. Importantly, we may wish in some cases to define semantics for special terms in a way that is impossible with rules of the form we have seen.

Example 2.13

As a simple case where rules of the form we have seen are insufficient to define the intuitive semantics of the data, we can consider datatype values. For example, take these two triples:

$$(WinstonChurchill, dateOfBirth, 1874\text{-}30\text{-}12),$$
$$(JeanPaulSartre, dateOfBirth, 1905\text{-}06\text{-}21)$$

In this case, the terms 1874-30-12 and 1905-06-21 can be considered datatype values – in this case dates – that have a regular syntactic form with which the machine can perform useful operations. Now let's imagine we wished to create a generic rule that infers that Winston Churchill is older than Jean-Paul Sartre and likewise for other pairs of persons. One option would be to make an ordering of all dates explicit in the data, perhaps with a transitives property. This would be less practical than defining a special semantics for datatype values that specifies how the machine should extract the year, month and date, and then compare dates based on year, then month, then date [313].

Instead of using symbolic methods to define the semantics of datatype values, it instead would seem better to have a global standard that defines such semantics, allowing, for example, in the case of dates, to define a syntactic form that allows machines to unambiguously extract the year, the month, the day, as well as to compare different datatype values.

This could be used to define a more complex rule formalism that allows **built-in functions** for performing common operations on supported datatype values, e.g., to compare dates, or extract the year of a date, or add two numbers, and so forth. In fact, there is an existing Web standard that defines precisely such a semantics for **datatypes**, called **XML Schema Definition (XSD)** [313], as will be described in more depth in Chapter 3.

Aside from datatype values, however, we can find other purely symbolic cases where rules are not enough to express the intuitive semantics of terms.

> **Example 2.14**
>
> Let us consider the following sentence:
>
> (NobelPrize,unionOf,<NobelPeacePrize,. . . ,NobelLiteraturePrize>)
>
> Here, for brevity, we use <A,B,C> as syntactic sugar for a list of terms; in Chapter 3, we will discuss how such a list can be encoded using plain triples. In the above example, we can assume that the list above contains all types of Nobel prize. Intuitively, we are stating here that NobelPrize is a class of instances where each instance must also be an instance of at least one of NobelPeacePrize, NobelLiteraturePrize, etc. Put another way, the instances of the class NobelPrize are a union of the instances of the classes NobelPeacePrize, NobelLiteraturePrize, etc.
>
> How would we go about defining these semantics using rules?
>
> To start with, we could see that the above statement intuitively implies that if something is an instance of, say, NobelPeacePrize, then it must be an instance of NobelPrize. Hence we can start with the rules:
>
> (?x,type,NobelPeacePrize) → (?x,type,NobelPrize)
> (?x,type,NobelLiteraturePrize) → (?x,type,NobelPrize)
>
> . . .
>
> In fact, as we saw in Example 2.10, we could instead represent the above rules using sentences with a special subClassOf term (which in fact would be implied by the above unionOf sentence).
>
> However, thus far we have only captured part of the semantics. Consider if we have the following statement:
>
> (NP1981,type,NobelPrize)
>
> What does the above unionOf sentence tell us in this case?
>
> Intuitively, we should conclude that NP1981 must also be of type at least one of the classes NobelPeacePrize, or NobelLiteraturePrize, etc., yet we have not covered this semantics of unionOf with the above rules. The problem is that the rules we are using are suited to deal with conjunction ("*and*"), but in this case we have a **disjunction** ("*or*"): NP1981 is of type NobelPeacePrize *or* NobelLiteraturePrize *or* . . .
>
> Now imagine, for example, that the machine were able to conclude that NP1981 could not be an instance of any of the classes in the union

other than NobelPeacePrize without causing an inconsistency.[a] Combined with the above semantics, we should be able to conclude that NP1981 is of type NobelPeacePrize. But without support for disjunction, the machine will not be able to draw this conclusion.

For this reason, (a finite set of) rules of the form that we have seen (i.e., that do not support disjunction in this case) would be sufficient to only partially define the semantics of a special term such as unionOf.

---

[a] Perhaps, for example, the machine finds out that NP1981 was won by an organisation, and the other types of Nobel prize cannot be won by organisations.

In the case of unionOf, the types of rules we have been using are not enough to completely define its semantics; however, since the exchange of semantics and the definition of semantics are decoupled, in the global standard that defines the semantics of special terms like unionOf, we can use, for example, **set theory** to formally define what these terms mean – after all *union* is a set theoretical notion. Or we could use something like **first-order logic** to encode the semantics. Most importantly, we are free to define these terms the best way possible, or even to define these terms in multiple interoperable ways, and offer a choice of implementation options for supporting such semantics.

This leads us to the concept of an **ontology**, which can be thought of as data embedded with special terms – like subClassOf, TransitiveProperty, disjointWith, unionOf – that are defined with an explicit, machine-processable semantics. To define ontologies, we need an **ontology language** that provides a standard set of special terms of this form, as well as a formal definition of the agreed-upon semantics of these terms capturing, in an unambiguous manner, the conclusions that can be drawn from data that use such terms.

On the Web, we currently have two such standards, namely **RDF Schema (RDFS)**, which defines some basic terms like subClassOf, and the **Web Ontology Language (OWL)**, which defines a much broader range of special terms, including TransitiveProperty, disjointWith, unionOf, and much much more. We will speak about these standards in Chapters 4 and 5 respectively.

2.2.4 Constraints

We previously argued why relational tables would not be a good choice when considering a core data model for the Web: in particular, how could a detailed, relational-style schema be defined for the Web? We further argued that graphs would seem a more apt choice due to their flexibility for modelling diverse, incomplete data, where nodes and edges can be added as needed, without restriction. On the other hand, by foregoing the need for a graph to *conform* to a particular high-level structure, while we gain flexibility when modelling data, the resulting data may be more difficult to subsequently work with in applications. For these reasons, it would be useful to be able to *optionally* define high-level structures (called **shapes**) to which graphs should conform, and to which constraints can be added against which graphs can be validated.

Example 2.15

Consider the following description of a Nobel prize:

(NP1981,type,NobelPrize)
(NP1981,year,1981)
(NP1981,year,1982)

Though the data would form a perfectly valid graph, clearly the data would not be particularly useful for a variety of reasons, including:

- the specific type of prize is not given;
- two years are specified, where a prize should have one.
- no winner is specified; etc.

Using the forms of semantics previously described (specifically using OWL), we can provide some definitions that would be able to generate an inconsistency for prizes with more than one year. However, such semantics consider the data that are *given* in a graph, and cannot require an RDF graph to provide data, such as the specific type of prize, or the winner of a prize. If we wished to rather impose some minimal requirements on the descriptions of Nobel prizes – in terms of completeness, multiplicities, etc. – we would thus often need something else.

One proposal would be to define a shape for Nobel prizes. Represented graphically, a shape may would look something like:

SHAPE: NobelPrize(x)

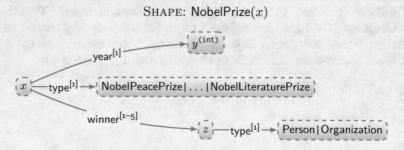

Intuitively, this shape describes a Nobel prize (x) with a single year y of type int; a single type that is one of NobelPeacePrize, ..., Nobel-LiteraturePrize (listing all six possible types); and one-to-five winners that must be of type Person or Organization (but not both). This shape thus encodes a variety of constraints against which selected nodes in a graph can be validated: in this case, nodes (possibly implicitly) of type NobelPrize can be validated against this shape and its constraints.

If validated against this shape, the aforementioned data would fail for a variety of reasons, including the definition of two years, the absence of a specific type of Nobel prize, and the absence of a winner and its type. While such a shape cannot directly verify that the data about each Nobel prize are true, or that all Nobel prizes are described, validating a graph with respect to such a shape at least offers some basic guarantees about the graph that may be important for applications.

Two related languages have been proposed for defining shapes over (RDF) graphs, namely **Shapes Constraint Language (SHACL)** and **Shape Expressions Language (ShEx)**. We will describe these languages in Chapter 7.

2.2.5 Links

In the same way that *links* are fundamental to the Web of Documents, they are likewise fundamental to the Web of Data: they enable machines to traverse and discover structured content spanning the Web.

In Example 1.5, we briefly discussed how links work in HTML webpages. In many ways, links on the Web of Data work using very similar principles.

To start with, we observe that terms such as WilliamGolding, start, Normandy, etc., that we have used thus far in examples are problematic: when considering the Web, we want to avoid conflicts on names, where for example another completely unrelated William Golding was a member of the Canadian House of Commons from 1932–1949; or where a start could refer to the starting location of a race rather than the starting date of an invasion; or where there are several places in the world called Normandy. To avoid such naming conflicts on the Web, we must thus use more specific identifiers for the entities that we describe on the Web of Data – not just plain strings.

A natural option is to reuse the naming scheme of the Web itself to name entities – such as the author William Golding, the class War, the start relation, the French region Normandy, etc. – that we wish to describe in the data. A problem with this, however, is that the identifier scheme traditionally used on the Web – the URL scheme – is used to identify webpages and other documents on the Web, not the entities in the real world we may wish to describe in our data, such as people, places, classes, properties, etc.

Example 2.16

Given a webpage about the author Sully Prudhomme with the
URL http://ex.org/SP, we may be tempted to simply reuse that URL
as an identifier for the real-life author:

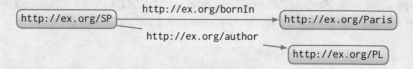

But we may also wish to provide some data about the original webpage itself – perhaps now or perhaps at a later date – such as the fact
that it was authored by Petri Liukkonen.

```
                        http://ex.org/bornIn
http://ex.org/SP ──────────────────────────► http://ex.org/Paris
                  http://ex.org/author
                                         ──► http://ex.org/PL
```

Now we have a naming conflict: the webpage was not born in Paris and
the person was not authored by Petri Liukkonen.

It seems natural that we should reserve URLs for identifying the documents at the given location. Even if we don't wish to describe them with
data right now, we may wish to in future. The question then is: how can we
identify real-world things in a manner compatible with the current Web?

Aside from URLs, the Web also defines the notion of a **Uniform Resource
Identifier (URI)**, which generalises URLs in the sense that URLs refer to both
the identity and location of a **resource**, whereas a URI only needs to establish
the identity of a resource. This means that while a webpage can have a URL
since it has a location on the Web (which also serves as its identifier: its URL
is also its URI), the author William Golding cannot have a URL since he
himself cannot have a location on the Web; instead he can have a URI.

By using Web identifiers (URIs) like http://ex.org/place/Normandy to
name things in our graph-based model – in the data, the queries, the rules,
the ontologies, etc. – we can address a number of key issues. First of all,
URIs help to solve the problem of naming conflicts: a publisher can create
a namespace (e.g., http://ex.org/place/) within a domain (ex.org) that
they control and create identifiers under the namespace that are much more
likely to be unique than generic terms like Normandy.

Perhaps more importantly, using such identifiers enables links to be embedded into the data. While a URI for a person, a place, a war, etc., should
not directly be the location of a document, it can point *indirectly* to a related
document, either by using a special type of HTTP redirect, or by using a
fragment identifier. We will now provide brief examples of both.

Example 2.17

In Example 2.1, we saw two examples of links – from the terms WilliamGolding and NormandyInv to documents about them – but we did not discuss how these links could be implemented in practice.

Taking the former link, assume that the document has the URL http://ex.org/WG. To enable this link, instead of using the term WilliamGolding to identify the author, we can use a URI such as http://ex.org/person/WG that has a special type of redirect to the URL of the document describing the author.

```
                                                    ┌─────────────────────────┐
                                                    │ URL: http://ex.org/NP   │
┌───────────────────────────────────────────────────────────────────────────┐
│ (http://ex.org/person/SP , http://ex.org/prop/awarded , http://ex.org/NP#Lit1901) │
│ ...                                                                         │
│ (http://ex.org/person/WG , http://ex.org/prop/awarded , http://ex.org/NP#Lit1983) │
│ ...                                                                         │
└───────────────────────────────────────────────────────────────────────────┘

              REDIRECT                               ┌─────────────────────────┐
             (SEE OTHER)                             │ URL: http://ex.org/WG   │
                ↓
┌───────────────────────────────────────────────────────────────────────────┐
│ (http://ex.org/person/WG , http://ex.org/prop/wrote , http://ex.org/book/LoTFlies) │
│ (http://ex.org/person/WG , http://ex.org/prop/name , "William Golding")     │
│ (http://ex.org/person/WG , http://ex.org/prop/type , http://ex.org/class/Novelist) │
│ ...                                                                         │
└───────────────────────────────────────────────────────────────────────────┘
```

As an aside, note that per the second triple in the second document, it is important when using URIs to identify entities to additionally provide a human-readable *label* for that entity, where the value – in this case "William Golding" – will have a string datatype.

Returning to the matter of linking, the URI used to identify William Golding in both documents (http://ex.org/person/WG) is different from the URL for the document that describes him in more detail (http://ex.org/WG), but upon looking up the former URI, one can still retrieve the latter document through a redirect. Hence the former URI still serves as a link to related content, even though it does not directly denote a location (i.e., it is not itself a URL).

This is just one example of a link. One could expect other URIs in the example to likewise link to related content about them. For example, http://ex.org/person/SP may link to a similar document describing the author Sully Prudhomme, while http://ex.org/prop/awarded may redirect to a document defining some semantics for that term.

Using such redirects is just one type of recipe to enable links through URIs. Another recipe is exemplified with http://ex.org/NP#Lit1983, where #Lit1983 is a fragment identifier that can be removed to find the location of the document; in other words, fragment identifiers can be used to generate multiple URIs within a given document where no such URI will be the exact location of the document (which will be given by the respective URI without the fragment identifier).

To support links on the Web of Data, all we need is to use Web identifiers – in the form of URIs – to identify the things we describe, and forward URIs to some relevant data when they are looked up. With this method, we don't need any special markup or property to denote a link: any URI used as a name can implicitly offer a link to elsewhere on the Web where more data about that named thing can be found. Thus a given website need not describe every resource it mentions in its data; rather it can use an external name that will forward to an external description of that resource. For example, to identify the books written by an author, a website could simply use an identifier that forwards to a document on a website specialising in books.

When this concept is used to link data expressed with the graph-structured data model previously spoken about – more specifically the RDF data model, which inherently supports the use of URIs for naming things[1] – across the Web, the concept is known as **Linked Data** [46, 181]. In the past decade, hundreds of datasets have been published following Linked Data best practices in a wide variety of different domains [346], forming what is arguable the first tangible instantiation of a Web of Data. However, while Linked Data provides a set of principles by which structured data can be interlinked on the Web, publishers who consider adopting these principles will inevitably face a broad range of non-trivial questions, including:

- How can legacy data (XML, CSV, etc.) be supported?
- When should links to external datasets be provided?
- How should ontologies be defined and reused?

Addressing these and other challenges is the subject of Chapter 8.

2.3 The Current Web of Data

The idea of a "Web of Data" is not original to this book; in fact, it has been around for (at least) over two decades. For example, we can find references to a "web of data" attributable to Berners-Lee (the inventor of the Web) dating back to 1998 [45]. Likewise, we have seen over two decades of work in the areas of the **Semantic Web** [45, 53] and over a decade of work in the area of Linked Data [181] trying to realise this vision of a Web of Data.

Given that the idea of a Web of Data has been around for a while, it seems pertinent to ask: *have these Web of Data techniques seen adoption?*

Taking a step back, the discussion thus far has painted a rather ambitious vision of what a Web of Data might look like, but has not addressed the important question of what path we can take to get there from where we

---

[1] In its most recent version [103], RDF supports **Internationalised Resource Identifiers (IRIs)**, which generalise URIs by allowing non-ASCII characters – such as accented characters, Chinese symbols, etc. – from the Unicode standard to be used.

are now: how can we motivate publishers to start producing increasingly structured data, how can we begin exploiting this additional structure to improve the experience of common users – *where should we start?*

Though we are still arguably far from a mature Web of Data as envisaged, for example, by Berners-Lee in 1998 [45, 195], to help to start to answer the above questions, we will now give four prominent examples of how such techniques have been adopted on the current Web. These examples will give four different perspectives on the types of concrete problems that a Web of Data can not only solve in theory in future, but has already begun to emerge to solve in practice. Such examples may then serve as the starting points from which the Web of Data can continue to evolve in future.

2.3.1 *Wikidata*

In Example 1.4, we already discussed how every time a football player scores a goal, in order to keep Wikipedia consistent and up-to-date, a small army of editors must get to work updating that goal in various locations, including the multiple language versions of the respective article(s) for that player, as well as articles that list the top-scoring players in a tournament or team or country, or the top-scoring teams in a tournament or country, and so on, and so forth. Needless to say, the problem is not specific to football goals.

The *Wikimedia Foundation* – the non-profit organisation dedicated to managing free, collaboratively edited educational content, including the Wikipedia encyclopaedia and a variety of other prominent projects – thus initiated work on *Wikidata* [397]: a collaboratively-edited **knowledge graph** composed of structured data that can support a variety of Wikimedia projects, most notably Wikipedia itself. The vision of Wikidata is to curate the structured data needed by Wikipedia in a single location and in a language agnostic manner. Thus, for example, the vision of Wikidata is that when a goal is scored by a football player, it can be updated in a single location on Wikidata and later propagated to various language versions and various list articles – wherever it is needed. This will ultimately lead to a more consistent view of data across Wikipedia while reducing the manual burden on editors.

Much like Wikipedia, Wikidata centres around the description of entities, where each entity has its own article to which editors can add claims about that entity; the principal difference with Wikipedia is that on Wikidata, all claims must follow a fixed structure. In Example 2.18, we illustrate the structure of Wikidata with sample data available about William Golding.[2]

---

[2] See https://www.wikidata.org/wiki/Q44183

Example 2.18

The following is a subset of real data available from the Wiki-data article on William Golding (available at the time of writing):

> **William Golding [Q44183]**
>
> | | |
> |---|---|
> | date of birth [P569] | "19 September 1911" |
> | date of death [P570] | "19 June 1993" |
> | notable work [P800] | Lord of the Flies [Q271764] |
> | occupation [P106] | writer [Q36180] |
> | | poet [Q49757] |
> | | novelist [Q6625963] |
> | | screenwriter [Q28389] |
> | | science fiction writer [Q18844224] |
> | award received [P166] | Nobel Prize in Literature [Q37922] |
> | | point in time [P585]   "1983" |
> | conflict [P607] | World War II [Q362] |
> | military branch [P241] | Royal Navy [Q172771] |
> | IMDb ID [P345] | [http://www.imdb.com/name/nm0325717/] |
> | ... | ... |

We can then summarise the internal structure of Wikidata as follows:

- Every entity in Wikidata is associated with a unique Q-code, where, for example, the Q-code for William Golding is Q44183, and the Q-code for World War II is Q362. These Q-codes are used to avoid language-specific identifiers and potential issues with ambiguity. Each such Q-code is associated with a Wikidata URI that serves as an Web identifier for the entity, where the URI resolves to a document containing the structured data about that entity.
- Every property in Wikidata is associated with a unique P-code; for example, the property date of birth has the P-code P569. P-codes are the equivalent of Q-codes for properties and are also associated with URIs. In fact, similar descriptions can be edited for properties.
- Different properties can take different types of values. Exemplified in the figure are datatype values (e.g., 19 September 1911), entities (e.g., Q362), and external links (e.g., the IMDb link). There are other possible values, such as **existential variables** to state that an entity has some unknown value for a given property, for example, to state that someone who was murdered has an unknown killer.
- A single property can have multiple values, as per occupation.
- A given value on a given property can be *qualified* with additional information in the form of a set of property-value pairs called *qualifiers*. We see such an example with the claim that William Golding received the Nobel Prize in Literature, which is qualified with the

year in which he won. Qualifier properties act similarly as the properties found directly on an entity and can take the same sorts of values; however, qualifiers cannot themselves be qualified.

- Though not shown in the example, each entity can be associated with labels in multiple languages, where one can change the language and request a view with labels from another language.
- There are also some other features not included in the example, most important of which is support for external references for a given claim, where all claims should (ideally) be associated with an external reference, since – like Wikipedia – Wikidata is not considered a primary source. Another feature is the ability of editors to assign a rank to the values on a property; for example, an editor may assign a higher rank to poet than screenwriter as values for occupation if the entity wrote more poetry than screenplays.

As of February 2020, Wikidata contained close to one billion claims about 78 million entities and had over 21 thousand active users.

Wikidata contains triples at its core, and thus follows a graph-like structure, where from Example 2.18, one could consider $Q44183 \xrightarrow{P607} Q362$ as an edge in a graph. Though this graph-based view is complicated somewhat by the presence of qualifiers, references, ranks, etc., it is possible to capture such information in a graph (see [121, 186] for details; we will discuss the issue of modelling more complex types of information as graphs later in Chapter 3).

The structured data available through Wikidata is not only of use within the Wikimedia family of projects, but is also useful in the broader context of the Web. The developers of Wikidata thus decided to publish versions of the data using RDF as a standard exchange format, providing a public query service where users can issue SPARQL queries over the knowledge graph (available at https://query.wikidata.org/). Results are generated from the claims spanning all Wikidata articles, allowing users and other clients to find answers for complex questions in the language of their choice. The query interface further supports a variety of visualisations using maps, timelines, graphs, etc., in order to present results in a more engaging way.

Example 2.19

The reader may have noticed that the sample data given in Example 2.18 for William Golding on Wikidata corresponds to the type of data Julie needed in Example 1.2. In fact, assuming Julie could formulate her search – for all Nobel Laureates who fought in a war, the year they were awarded the Nobel prize and the name(s) of the war(s) they fought in – as the following SPARQL query:

```
PREFIX wd: <http://www.wikidata.org/entity/>
PREFIX wdt: <http://www.wikidata.org/prop/direct/>
PREFIX p: <http://www.wikidata.org/prop/>
PREFIX ps: <http://www.wikidata.org/prop/statement/>
PREFIX pq: <http://www.wikidata.org/prop/qualifier/>
PREFIX rdfs: <http://www.w3.org/2000/01/rdf-schema#>

SELECT DISTINCT ?laureateName ?awardYear ?warName ?warStart ?warEnd
WHERE {
  ?laureate p:P166 ?award .               # Winner of some prize
  ?award ps:P166 wd:Q37922 .              # Prize is Nobel Pr. in Lit.
  ?award pq:P585 ?awardDate .             # Get the date of the award
  BIND(YEAR(?awardDate) AS ?awardYear)    # Get the year of the award
  ?laureate wdt:P607 ?war .               # Find war(s) laureate was in
  ?war rdfs:label ?warName .              # Get name(s) of war(s)
  ?war wdt:P580 ?warStDate .              # Get date the war started
  BIND(YEAR(?warStDate) AS ?warStart)     # Get year the war started
  ?war wdt:P582 ?warEndDate .             # Get date the war ended
  BIND(YEAR(?warEndDate) AS ?warEnd)      # Get year the war ended
  ?laureate rdfs:label ?laureateName .    # Get name of laureate
  FILTER(LANG(?warName)="en"              # Only English labels
  && LANG(?laureateName)="en")            #  ... names only
} ORDER BY ?awardYear ?warStart           # Oldest award (then war) first
```

She could issue the above query to the aforementioned Wikidata query service to get the following results (generated in February 2020):

laureateName	awardYear	warName	warStart	warEnd
Sully Prudhomme	1901	Franco–Prussian war	1870	1871
Henryk Sienkiewicz	1905	World War I	1914	1918
Carl Spitteler	1919	World War I	1914	1918
Winston Churchill	1953	Mahdist War	1881	1899
Winston Churchill	1953	Second Boer War	1899	1902
Winston Churchill	1953	World War I	1914	1918
Ernest Hemingway	1954	World War I	1914	1918
Ernest Hemingway	1954	Spanish Civil War	1936	1939
Ernest Hemingway	1954	World War II	1939	1945
Albert Camus	1957	World War II	1939	1945
Jean-Paul Sartre	1964	World War II	1939	1945
Jean-Paul Sartre	1964	Algerian War	1954	1962
Michail Sholokhov	1965	World War II	1941	1945
Samuel Beckett	1969	World War II	1939	1945
Heinrich Böll	1972	World War II	1939	1945
Eugenio Montale	1975	World War I	1914	1918
William Golding	1983	World War II	1939	1945
Claude Simon	1985	Spanish Civil War	1936	1939
Camilo José Cela	1989	Spanish Civil War	1936	1939
Günter Grass	1999	World War II	1939	1945

Answers are automatically drawn from 22 different Wikidata articles. These results would require a lot of manual effort to achieve if using, for example, the traditional Wikipedia encyclopaedia, where Julie would most probably have to manually check the article for every Nobel laureate in Literature: more than one hundred articles.

We will discuss more about SPARQL and the particular query that generated these results later in Chapter 6.

Of course as a typical Web user, Julie is unlikely to know enough SPARQL to create such a query, but internal tools are under development to make querying graph-structured datasets like Wikidata more user friendly [255]. More broadly, Wikidata is improving the experience of many users on the current Web in ways that they may not even realise. Aside from internal use-cases within the Wikimedia Foundation, other organisations are using Wikidata to power end/user applications, including Apple's Siri [255].

However, in the same sense that Wikipedia is only one website on the Web of Documents, Wikidata is likewise only one dataset on the Web of Data. Wikidata is a **centralised** dataset under the administration of the Wikimedia Foundation, and has fixed notability requirements, where for an entity to have an article on Wikidata, it must have gained attention in traditional media or other notable sources. Thus while Wikidata serves to answer Julie's query about Nobel laureates, it would not serve Frank's needs to find recipes since most recipes are not notable for Wikimedia's purposes.

2.3.2 Knowledge Graphs

All of the challenges we have described thus far for the Web also apply, at a more local level, to individual organisations and communities, who often struggle to fully exploit the vast amounts of relevant data accessible to them from diverse sources. Such groups have been turning to knowledge graphs as a way to address these challenges. A knowledge graph is based on a large graph of data, where nodes represent entities of interest and edges represent relationships between them. This graph is often enriched with various forms of schemata, rules, ontologies, and more besides, to help validate, structure and define the semantics of the underlying graph. In practice, a knowledge graph then provides a common substrate of knowledge for an organisation or community that can be assembled, curated and refined over time [297].

The announcement of the Google Knowledge Graph was a pivotal moment for knowledge graphs in general, motivated by an effort from Google to shift closer towards **semantic search** while still keeping its traditional document search functionality [297]. This shift can be seen in the variety of ways that the modern Google search engine tries to integrate direct answers (in the form of structured data) into its results page, rather than just a list of relevant documents with the given keywords. Current efforts centre around trying to match a user's keyword query with structured data about a particular entity, where that structured data is potentially integrated from multiple sources. The Google Knowledge Graph then collects and curates knowledge about entities and their relations taken from a wide variety of sources.

One of the main applications of the Google Knowledge Graph is to generate "knowledge panels" on entities that are mentioned in a keyword query.

Example 2.20

The following image shows the knowledge panel displayed on the right-hand side of the Google results page of the keyword search for "william golding" alongside the documents that match the query.[a]

The knowledge panel contains a selection of images, a brief abstract taken from Wikipedia (when available), and a set of structured claims about the author. The panel may contain further details, such as quotes, a map, etc., depending on the type of entity in question.

---

[a] Google and the Google logo are registered trademarks of Google Inc., used with permission.

Another application is to give direct answers to user's queries.

Example 2.21

If a user types in a keyword search such as "spouse william golding", above the ranked list of documents matching the query, the user will also receive the following structured answer:[a]

William Golding / **Spouse**

Ann Brookfield

m. 1939–1993

---

[a] Google and the Google logo are registered trademarks of Google Inc., used with permission.

Computing the direct answer shown in Example 2.21 relates to the problem of question answering that we mentioned previously in Section 1.2. Using its knowledge graph, Google can now answer a subset of commonly asked questions and/or questions that follow a simple common pattern.

Knowledge graphs would later be adopted by a variety of organisations and communities. Broadly these knowledge graphs fall into one of two categories: enterprise knowledge graphs, and open knowledge graphs.

Enterprise knowledge graphs are used internally within companies to manage knowledge (typically) for commercial use-cases. Prominent examples of industries that have announced knowledge graphs include not only Web search (Google, Microsoft, etc.) as previously discussed, but also commerce (Airbnb, Amazon, eBay, etc.), finance (Accenture, Bloomberg, Wells Fargo), social networks (Facebook, LinkedIn, etc.), amongst others. Typical use-cases involve enhancing advertising, business analytics, conversational agents, recommendations, search, transport automation, and more besides.

Open knowledge graphs, on the other hand, are published on the Web in the interest of the public good. A prominent open knowledge graph is Wikidata, as previously discussed [255]. Other knowledge graphs have been published on the Web as "Linked Open Data", which we discuss in Section 2.3.4.

In terms of their relation to the Web of Data, knowledge graphs often use many of the standards and techniques discussed in this book to represent and leverage knowledge. As such, open knowledge graphs – like Wikidata and others discussed later – form part of the Web of Data. Although enterprise knowledge graphs are not published on the Web, they can potentially use the Web of Data as a rich external source. More broadly speaking, the Web of Data itself can be seen as a decentralised global knowledge graph forming a substrate of knowledge for the Web that grows and evolves over time.

2.3.3 Schema.org and the Open Graph Protocol

While the previous discussion on Wikidata and open knowledge graphs in general have dealt with large graphs being published by organisations in a centralised manner, we can also find more decentralised examples of how the Web of Data is being used today across a broad range of websites. Two salient examples relate to Schema.org and the Open Graph Protocol.

Schema.org [160] is an initiative sponsored by a collaboration of Google, Microsoft (who operate the Bing search engine), Yahoo! and Yandex (the largest Russian search engine) with the conceptual goal, again, of moving closer to the goal of semantic search in their respective search engines. One of the initial motivating applications of Schema.org was for the search engines to provide users with more information for each result than simply a title, a URL, and a short snippet from the corresponding document.

Example 2.22

In the following, we see a list of the top-three search results for the keyword query "lemon meringue" taken from the Google search engine.[a] Each result points to a recipe webpage on a different website.

Grandma's Lemon Meringue Pie Recipe - Allrecipes.com
allrecipes.com/recipe/15093/grandmas-**lemon-meringue**-pie/ ▾
★★★★⯪ Rating: 4.6 - 1,622 reviews - 40 min - 298 cal
This pie is thickened with cornstarch and flour in addition to egg yolks, and contains no milk." ... To Make **Lemon** Filling: In a medium saucepan, whisk together 1 cup sugar, flour, cornstarch, and salt. Stir in water, **lemon** juice and **lemon** zest.

Ultimate lemon meringue pie | BBC Good Food
www.bbcgoodfood.com/.../ultimate-**lemon-meringue**-pie ▾
★★★★⯪ Rating: 4.6 - 182 votes - 3 hr 15 min - 480 cal
For the pastry, put the flour, butter, icing sugar, egg yolk (save the white for the **meringue**) and 1 tbsp cold water into a food processor. ... While the pastry bakes, prepare the filling: mix the cornflour, sugar and **lemon** zest in a medium saucepan. ... Try some of our other lemony treats ...
Lemon meringue pie · Little lemon meringue pies · Ultimate meringue

Classic Lemon Meringue Pie recipe from Betty Crocker
www.bettycrocker.com/...**lemon-meringue**.../8f991b88-55b... ▾
★★★★⯪ Rating: 4.5 - 144 votes - 3 hr 45 min - 430 cal
Taste a classic recipe! This pie is bursting with fresh **lemon** taste and a sweet, creamy real **meringue** topping. ... Use Betty Crocker® pie crust mix for the scratch pie crust in this recipe and save time.

We see that aside from a title, URL, text snippet and image, the results contain some embedded structured data, such as the rating, the number of reviews/votes, the preparation time, and the number of calories. These data allow the user to make a quick comparison of recipes, where we can see, for example, that the first recipe will be much faster to prepare than the latter two. Such at-a-glance comparison may not have been possible for users with just plain text snippets.

---

[a] Google and the Google logo are registered trademarks of Google Inc., used with permission.

The technical question then is: how does Google generate these results? Or more specifically, how does Google know the image, rating, preparation time, number of calories, etc., to display in these search results?

One option would be for Google to extract such information automatically from the HTML webpages themselves. However, as seen in Example 2.22, different recipes will come from different sites, where each site will have a different way not only of structuring the HTML pages, but also of representing analogous information: some websites may rate recipes out of 10, or 100; some may offer calorie information per ingredient, and so forth. While Google could try to implement automatic methods to extract data from websites, doing so broadly and accurately is beyond current technology. On the other hand, Google could implement methods to extract such data from specific, popular websites – for example, by manually specifying patterns that match specific HTML trees found on specific websites – but in this case, firstly, only certain popular websites would be covered, and secondly, Google would be breaking neutrality by giving algorithmic preference to certain websites.

The situation is of course similar for other search engines. Rather than trying to extract such data from the raw HTML content, the more practical solution was instead to simply ask the publishers of websites to explicitly embed machine-processable structured data themselves into the HTML webpages indicating precisely the details that could be used to enrich the descriptions of search results. Rather than each search engine giving different incompatible instructions on how to embed such data into their webpages, they decided to collaborate to design a common specification: Schema.org.

Example 2.23

The following is an example of Schema.org markup embedded in the webpage of the second search result from Example 2.22:

```
<ul class="nutrition" itemprop="nutrition" itemscope
  itemtype="http://schema.org/NutritionInformation">
  <li>
    <span class="nutrition__label">kcal</span>
    <span class="nutrition__value" itemprop="calories">480</span>
    ...
  </li>
</ul>
```

This is HTML code for displaying a list. However, one can also see some additional non-HTML markup with attributes such as `itemprop`, `itemscope`, and `itemtype`. One can also see that the `itemtype` attribute takes a value that is a URI on the `schema.org` domain. This markup will not affect what the user sees on the webpage, but is rather denoting structured data that Google and other search engines can extract from the presentational markup and use to enrich search results.

Similar markup is present in the above webpage to encode ratings, preparation time, etc., and likewise in the other two webpages, and in the other recipe webpages published by those three websites.

Discussion 2.2

JULIE: What's to stop websites from publishing falsified data, for example, to increase the ratings on their recipes?

AIDAN: This is just a new form of spam. Search engines have been fighting spam since day one (and have gotten quite good at it). Likewise reputable sites should understand that there are consequences for being caught spamming. In terms of concrete anti-spam techniques, different search engines probably have different measures to counteract falsified data. As a general example, Schema.org recommends to avoid "hidden data", meaning that any embedded values should be visible to visitors of the webpage. Looking back at Example 2.23, though the `itemprop` attribute and its value are hidden, the value for calories will be visible on the webpage. Thus if the websites want to lie to Google about the calories (or rating) data of the recipe, they also have to lie to their visitors. In the medium-to-long term, the website will thus lose reputation and visitors.

Publishers can choose to use **Microdata**, **RDF in Attributes (RDFa)** or **JavaScript Object Notation for Linked Data (JSON-LD)** to embed data. Microdata is the format seen in in Example 2.23. RDFa and JSON-LD are both directly compatible with the aforementioned graph-structured RDF model that will be discussed in more detail in Chapter 3. All three of these formats can be embedded into the HTML of an existing webpage, obviating the need for publishers to maintain two versions – the human-readable HTML version and the machine-readable structured data version – of each recipe.

Of course, Schema.org is not only limited to embedding data about recipes into websites, but covers a wide range of domains. In terms of semantics, Schema.org offers a broad **vocabulary** of class and property terms on its webpage that can be used to describe recipes, stores, products, events, movies, and many other types of entities. Associated with each class is a hierarchy of more general super-classes and a list of properties (possibly inherited from super-classes) that can be used to describe that class. Associated with each property is the class or datatype that a value for that property should take.

Embedding structured data into webpages has a clear **Search Engine Optimisation (SEO)** benefit for publishers: having enriched search-result snippets attracts more users to click on those links in search engines, and thus drives more traffic and more revenue to those webpages. On the other hand, embedding such structured data has a relatively low cost for publishers in cases where webpages are populated from underlying databases, in which case the new markup should be injectable into the webpage without much effort; otherwise, if the data for a given property is not available in a database, it can simply be omitted until, for example, its SEO value outweighs the cost of adding it. Given these incentives for publishers, Schema.org has been widely adopted [61], with 2016 estimates stating that it was used on at least 12 million websites and on around 31% of webpages [160].

The second initiative we can point to is the Open Graph Protocol, which has been led by Facebook. Though the application and details are slightly different, the Open Graph Protocol shares many similarities to Schema.org and arose from a similar technical problem. First, when a Facebook user posts a link to a given webpage, Facebook tries to provide not just the raw URL, but also a summary of what that page is about: Facebook not only wants to have an image and title to display, but also wants to know the type of entity the webpage is talking about: is it a movie, a song, a book, etc. Second, Facebook often offers an embedded pane on external webpages where users can click to specify that they like the page, see which of their friends liked the page, or even comment on the page; in this scenario, Facebook also wants more details on what's being liked or commented on.

The Open Graph Protocol has also become widely adopted [61], in particular due to the direct benefits for publishers of drawing increased traffic from comments on Facebook itself, as well as embedding low-cost social features directly into their own webpages. For instance, in Example 2.18, we mentioned that Wikidata offers external IMDb links for its entities. IMDb embeds lightweight structured data about movies and TV series though the Open Graph Protocol. Data published through the Open Graph Protocol is consumed not only by Facebook, but also search engines and other parties on the Web. In terms of syntaxes, publishers can choose to use RDFa or HTML5; again, the former syntax will be discussed in Chapter 3.

Through the examples of Schema.org and the Open Graph Protocol, we see that publishers can be incentivised to provide structured data, and furthermore, that the experience of common users can benefit in quite direct – perhaps even mundane ways – from increasingly structured content on the broader Web (not just specialised websites like Wikidata). Both examples are significant because they arose from the technical needs of major organisations on the current Web and have received wide adoption; they thus they help us establish precedent that having content in increasingly structured formats on the Web can have a practical value proposition not only for search engines, social networks and their users, but also for the publishers of such data.

On the other hand, Schema.org and Open Graph Protocol are (perhaps) only a partial precedent for the sort of Web of Data we could hope to have in future. In the original applications for Schema.org and the Open Graph Protocol, there was little or no need to consider integration with external vocabularies, nor to consider integration of data about the same entities from different webpages. Hence to keep things as simple as possible for publishers while accomplishing the original motivating applications, both specifications chose to largely downplay the roles of both semantics and links.

Example 2.24

Referring back to Frank's search needs in Example 1.1, Schema.org does offer relevant vocabulary to describe recipes[a], including preparation time, cooking time, etc. Thus we could, in principle, use these values to restrict results in the search engine to only show webpages for recipes that take less than an hour. Such filtering can be applied over recipes from different websites using Schema.org.

Likewise, one can describe products in Schema.org[b], where one can describe brands, offers with prices, production date, product codes, similar products, etc.; one can also describe local businesses[c], with location, opening times, catalogues of products or other offers, contact details, and so forth. A supermarket can use this vocabulary to describe itself and the products it contains, which in turn may be of help to Frank in finding supermarkets with the ingredients he needs.

However, the vocabulary of Schema.org is limited; for example, it does not currently include any terms to specify that a recipe is a dessert recipe, nor to specify what sort of equipment a recipe requires, and so forth. While one can extend the Schema.org vocabulary to add such details[d], the specification does not offer any guidelines on how to define the semantics for the new vocabulary [306] – for example, to state that a dessert recipe is a sub-class of recipe – nor does it offer ideas on how multiple sites may hope to agree on custom vocabulary.

Likewise, the values for many of the aforementioned properties – including ingredients – are all strings, not URIs, meaning that there are no links to further structured data about an entity, nor the possibility, for example, for a supermarket and a recipe site to link to some common identification system for ingredients and products relating to them.

---

[a] See http://schema.org/Recipe

[b] See http://schema.org/Product

[c] See http://schema.org/LocalBusiness

[d] See http://schema.org/docs/extension.html

In summary, Schema.org and Open Graph Protocol are two precedents where the principles of the Web of Data have been adopted by tens of millions of websites and benefit millions of users of search engines by providing more detailed results. Though promising, in these two cases, publishers are restricted to following rather narrow, centralised specifications on how to describe structured data, and typically offer few links to related data. However, from these broad roots may grow richer specifications and data in future [160].

2.3.4 Linking Open Data

Traditionally the Web has been used not only to share webpages, but also to share documents containing structured data, be it contained in spreadsheets, raw database dumps, XML files, JSON files, custom text formats, proprietary formats requiring special software, and so forth. These developments led to an increasing awareness of the common value of sharing data in an open manner, be it in terms of educational, scientific, political or economic benefits – an awareness that became consolidated under the idea of "Open Data". The founding principle of the Open Data movement is to recognise the value of having data that anyone is free to use and share as they wish, to offer specific access and licensing mechanisms by which such sharing can take place, and to encourage organisations to make data openly available in this manner,

While many organisations may wish or need to close or restrict access to datasets due to commercial, legal or ethical reasons, there are many situations in which offering open access to datasets is clear: scientists may wish to share experimental data to support their community; governments may wish to share datasets in the interests of transparency and the hope that the data can be used to build applications for the public good; online communities may wish to openly share user-contributed and user-curated data collections rather than have them be exploited commercially by a third party; etc.

However, while data have long been shared on the Web, this practice of publishing *Data on the Web* has never directly led to a *Web of Data*, in particular because such data were rarely linked, nor were any of the practices on how data could be linked made clear. Likewise, different models and formats were used in different situations, semantics and agreement on vocabulary were never a priority, and so forth. Most often, data were published in custom formats and thus required custom tools to parse, interpret and take value from. Without the provision of links or explicit semantics, each dataset is effectively isolated, preventing the automated integration of data from multiple sources, limiting the potential usage of the data.

Assuming we wish to support – on a technical level – individuals or groups who want to make a dataset openly available on the Web, the first key question we must try to answer is: *how best should one represent and publish structured data on the Web in an open manner such that it can have as broad an impact as possible?* Answering this question is key to unlocking the potential of the Open Data initiative and – indeed – the potential of the Web.

Possible technical answers to this question have already been discussed in depth in this chapter. Relatedly, in March 2007, a **World Wide Web Consortium (W3C)** Community Project called "Interlinking Open Data" – subsequently shortened to "Linking Open Data" (LOD) – was originally launched. The goal of the Linking Open Data project has been twofold: (i) introduce the benefits of RDF, Linked Data, etc., to the broader Open Data community [63, 181] and in so doing (ii) to bootstrap the *Web of Data* by creating, publishing and interlinking RDF exports from these open datasets.

However, adopting technologies such as RDF and Linked Data is associated with a significant cost for publishers: it is much cheaper to simply upload data in whatever "raw format" is most convenient. Thus it was important to find a core message by which to convey to publishers the reasons why they might benefit from such technologies (without getting into the abstract sorts of discussion in this chapter). The core message was distilled by Berners-Lee [46] into the Linked Data "5 Star Scheme" summarised as follows:

> ⋆   PUBLISH DATA ON THE WEB UNDER AN OPEN LICENSE
> ⋆ ⋆   PUBLISH STRUCTURED DATA
> ⋆ ⋆ ⋆   USE NON-PROPRIETARY FORMATS
> ⋆ ⋆ ⋆ ⋆ USE IRIs TO IDENTIFY THINGS
> ⋆ ⋆ ⋆ ⋆ ⋆ LINK YOUR DATA TO OTHER DATA

—**paraphrased from Berners-Lee [46]**

Each additional star is promoted as increasing the potential reusability and interoperability – and thus the potential impact – of the publishers' data. For example, in moving from "⋆ ⋆" to "⋆ ⋆ ⋆", a publisher may switch from publishing a table in a Microsoft Excel spreadsheet – which is a proprietary format that requires special software to access programatically – to using a simpler text format such as CSV – which can be interpreted more conveniently by a wider range of much simpler software. We will discuss this "5 Star Scheme" in more detail in Chapter 8.

In summary, while the Open Data community had data to publish but didn't have best practices on how to publish it, the Linked Data community had best practices to publish data but oftentimes didn't have data to publish. The Linking Open Data initiative was thus successful in encouraging a wide variety of Open Data publishers to follow these Linked Data best practices. There are now hundreds of datasets available on the Web publishing in this manner [346], including contributions from governments (e.g., the UK and US governments), media outlets (e.g., the BBC, New York Times, Thompson Reuters), various scientific communities (e.g., biomedical datasets, bibliographical collections), Web companies (e.g., Wikimedia, Google) etc.

Each such dataset is published using RDF as a core data model. Each such dataset uses URIs to identify entities and link to remote datasets. Many datasets offer a SPARQL query service where users can issue structured queries. The Linking Open Data community has also encouraged agreement – where possible – on the use of vocabularies, where the semantics of such vocabularies is often specified using the RDFS and OWL languages.

Thus the Linking Open Data community have been responsible for fostering the closest instantiation of a true Web of Data we have seen to date, with diverse parties publishing diverse interlinked datasets using diverse interdependent vocabularies. However, although there are surely many interesting applications possible over the datasets that have been published, such applications have been slow to emerge, particularly applications that can discover and incorporate new datasets on-the-fly. In trying to characterise why that might be the case, a number of high-level challenges have been revealed:

- Linking Open Data intended to bootstrap a Web of Data by getting publishers to make data available using the aforementioned best practices, but without any specific application in mind. In the case of Schema.org, the specification originated from the motivating application of generating rich snippets in search results and, in some sense, did just enough to realise that goal. In the case of Linking Open Data, the goal was to publish data in a generic manner to facilitate the broadest range of applications possible. The hope was that by first getting data out there, applications would naturally emerge. In some sense, publishing became an ends rather than a means: the focus of the community was on publishing data, where dealing with how that data would be used was postponed. The downside of this strategy is that how data are published affects how it can be used.
- Following on from the previous point, a major emerging challenge has been the *quality* of data, where quality is defined as being "fit for purpose". However, in the context of Linking Open Data, the "purpose" is often not well-defined. Quality is – in certain important aspects – application-dependent, but without a fixed application in mind, the quality of a dataset is difficult to properly assess (though work is ongoing, it remains a subject of open research [407]). Without a target application in mind, there is no feedback loop to know if data are modelled appropriately, or what is missing for a dataset to have more impact in practice.
- Publishing data that follow Linked Data best practices is costly. First, converting data to RDF can be an expensive process, especially for data that are most naturally represented in other models, e.g., tabular data; modelling data adequately in RDF requires expertise, which a lot of publishers lack. Second, generating high-quality, well-defined links is an expensive process, often requiring a lot of manual intervention. Third, relevant vocabularies are decentralised, meaning that it can be difficult for publishers to know what terms are available to use in their domain. Fourth, semantics have been a contentious issue, where the RDFS and OWL standards are highly technical specifications that publishers have struggled with and that – in any case – do not always meet the needs

of publishers. Coupled with a lack of tangible direct applications, it is difficult to convince publishers to take on these costs, or even for them to be able to assess the quality of their data, links, ontologies, etc.

- The sorts of techniques we need to build applications over such data for non-expert users – like Julie, Frank and Anna – have still not been adequately explored. First, while it is certainly the case that the available datasets can answer interesting questions that users may have, it is not clear precisely how accurately or what types of questions the datasets are sufficient to answer. Second, though techniques for querying and **reasoning** over structured data have been well-explored in local settings, applying these techniques in a Web setting has received insufficient attention. Third, usability is still a major issue, where we lack interfaces that will aid non-expert users to represent their search needs in sufficient detail for the retrieval engine to respond with good answers [195].

The Linking Open Data initiative has thus uncovered a broad range of practical, social and technical challenges that must be first acknowledged and then addressed before a true Web of Data can become a reality. These challenges are far from trivial, but on the other hand, the potential impact that the result – a fully-fledged Web of Data – could have should motivate more work towards addressing these challenges. As we discuss in this book, a lot of the groundwork needed to address these challenges has already been laid by the Semantic Web and Linked Data research communities.

2.4 Summary

In this chapter, we have discussed and motivated some of the main concepts underlying the Web of Data. More specifically, we discussed how data can be modelled, how queries should be expressed, how semantics can be made explicit, how constraints can be specified, and how links can be provided between data published on the Web. The chapters that follow in the book then describe concrete standards that have been proposed to instantiate these five concepts. We also discussed some of the most prominent examples of applications on the Web that currently rely on these concepts – namely: Wikidata, Google's Knowledge Graph, Schema.org, the Open Graph Protocol, and Linking Open Data – discussing how they relate to and depend on the Web of Data. These examples offer precedent for the practical benefits of being able to exchange increasingly machine-readable content on the Web. Conversely they have also revealed a number of open challenges to be addressed towards advancing the vision of the Web of Data even further.

2.5 Discussion

Discussion 2.3

FRANK: How does the Web of Data relate, specifically, to concepts such as the Semantic Web and Linked Data?

AIDAN: The Web of Data, for me, is a more general notion than the Semantic Web, referring to the idea of publishing and interlinking data on the Web, rather than just documents. As Berners-Lee put it, for example: *"The Semantic Web is a web of data"* [45]. Here we have started with the more general notion of the Web of Data in terms of making the content of the Web increasingly machine-readable. However, the most concrete and detailed proposal on how to achieve this Web of Data vision currently lies within the Semantic Web standards: RDF, RDFS, OWL, SPARQL, SHACL, ShEx, etc. The Linked Data principles then specify how these standards can be deployed on the Web to form a Web of Data. So while these terms are sometimes used interchangeably, in this book, we take the view of the Web of Data as the goal, and the Semantic Web and Linked Data as the (furthest-advanced) means to achieve that goal.

JULIE: A Web of Data sounds like a good idea in theory. But it seems like there are a lot of practical challenges to overcome in terms of the quality and trustworthiness of data, getting people to agree on vocabularies, building applications, and so forth.

AIDAN: Yes, it is certainly an ambitious vision, but one that could revolutionise the Web, and one that is thus undoubtedly worth pursuing as far as we can, for even a partial realisation of this vision could have major impact on the Web, and in turn, on our society. While later chapters will address these challenges you mention, they remain far from solved, and this book certainly does not contain all the answers. However, much like the original Web, it is not necessary that all challenges be addressed *a priori*: rather, once the foundations are in place, the Web of Data may evolve from relatively simple applications towards increasingly complex use-cases in an organic way. This book then describes these foundations while this chapter has already introduced some of the initial applications that may represent the seeds of what is yet to come.

Chapter 3
Resource Description Framework

On the Web, we may already find data published in a variety of diverse formats, including CSV, JSON, XML, to name but a few of the most popular. Each such format conforms to a particular abstract model, where for example CSV represents tables, while JSON and XML both represent trees. Each particular format brings with it its own inherent pros and cons, and the question of which format is best to use may depend on the particular dataset at hand and the particular applications envisaged for it. Likewise we may use different tools and languages to work with different formats. For example, for querying CSV data, we may consider loading them into a relational database and using SQL to interrogate them; on the other hand, for querying XML, we would rather use something like **XML Path (XPath)** or **XML Query (XQuery)**.

However, when different datasets on the Web use different formats with different models, we face the problem of how to work with – and in particular integrate – data coming from different sources. To start with, we may end up having to convert CSV to XML or XML to CSV or JSON to XML, and so forth; such conversions are often non-trivial and may thus require the intervention of a human data-expert to achieve a good result. On the other hand, we may try to use tools that support multiple formats, such as relational databases that support embedding and querying XML or JSON as values in tables; this then delays the burden of integration until query time, where complex queries that span formats and models must be designed.

Ideally we could rather *avoid* the problem of having to integrate heterogeneous data formats by selecting *one standard format* for publishing and exchanging data on the Web. Where legacy data reside in other formats, we could map that data to the standard format. Where applications require data in a legacy format, we could map from the standard format to legacy formats. Hence we could potentially avoid the problem of having to define pairwise mappings between all such potentially relevant formats. A standard data format would also serve as a foundation to begin to build further tools and languages that support that format – a foundation for the Web of Data.

© Springer Nature Switzerland AG 2020
A. Hogan, *The Web of Data*, https://doi.org/10.1007/978-3-030-51580-5_3

However, the idea of having one standard data format for the Web raises a number of practical questions. First and foremost, what should such a format look like and what abstract model should it follow? How can we ensure that such a format can naturally represent diverse datasets from a variety of domains? What format would allow us to integrate data more easily and effectively? And finally: how can we be confident that we are not just making the problem of heterogeneous formats *worse* by adding yet another format?

While these questions may not have definitive answers, the potential benefit of having a standard data model for the Web has prompted the W3C standards body to propose the Resource Description Framework (RDF) to fill such a role. As we will discuss, RDF prescribes a graph-structured data model that is inherently more flexible and easier to integrate than trees or tables. Furthermore, RDF is designed with the Web in mind, featuring a global naming scheme that uses native Web identifiers. As such, RDF offers the ingredients necessary to build a *"Giant Global Graph"* of data, where individual documents describe part of a data graph that (assuming agreement on Web identifiers) can be interlinked to form a cohesive global graph of data.

To better justify this vision, and to look critically at whether or not RDF provides answers to the previously outlined questions for a common data model (and if so, how), we must first discuss the standard in more detail.

3.1 Overview

As its name may suggest, the Resource Description Framework (RDF) is a standard framework for describing resources [258]. Resources are anything with identity that one could consider describing in data, including *virtual entities* like webpages, websites, desktop files; *concrete entities*, such as books, people, places, stores; *abstract entities*, such as categories, animal species, points in time, ancestry relationships; and so forth.

Historical Note 3.1

RDF first became a W3C Recommendation in early 1999 [245], with a revised version of the standard re-released later in 2004 [258]. More recently, in 2014, the RDF 1.1 standard was officially released [351], adding some minor revisions to the earlier 2004 version, standardising some new syntaxes and introducing some new abstract concepts. In this chapter, we will describe the updated RDF 1.1 version; we will often simply discuss RDF and leave the version implicit.

The remainder of this chapter is structured as follows:

Section 3.2 describes the **RDF terms** used to refer to resources; these form
the basis of the data model.

Section 3.3 discusses how RDF terms (**IRIs, literals, blank nodes**) can be
combined to form statements in the form of **RDF triples**.

Section 3.4 discusses how sets of triples form **RDF graphs**, giving rise to
graph-structured data.

Section 3.5 outlines how the **RDF vocabulary** can be used to model certain
oft-needed patterns in a standard matter.

Section 3.6 describes how multiple RDF graphs can be identified and grouped
into an **RDF dataset**.

Section 3.7 discusses in more detail the issues arising from the presence of
blank nodes in RDF graphs and datasets.

Section 3.8 outlines some concrete RDF syntaxes used to serialise RDF
graphs and datasets.

Sections 3.9 and 3.10 conclude the chapter with a summary and discussion.

3.2 Terms

RDF terms are used to refer to the resources that RDF intends to describe.
There are three distinct types of RDF terms with different purposes: IRIs,
literals and blank nodes. We now discuss each in turn.

3.2.1 Internationalised Resource Identifiers (IRIs)

In natural language, we may consider identifying resources using simple
strings like Boston. However, as argued previously in Chapter 2, simple strings
are prone to ambiguity: for example, Boston could be interpreted as referring
to a U.S. city, the greater metropolitan area in which the U.S. city of the same
name is based, a rock band, a breed of terrier, and so forth. In the broader
context of the Web, such identifiers would inevitably lead to naming clashes:
for example, if one publisher stated that the resource Boston has a population of 646,000, and another publisher elsewhere on the Web stated that
the resource Boston has the lead-singer Brad Delp, combining both sources
of information on the resource Boston would lead to strange consequences.
Considering that other publishers may likewise use Boston to mean different
things, combining data from such sources would lead to a surrealistic mess.

To avoid such confusion and ambiguity when identifying resources, RDF
reuses the native global naming scheme of the Web. A tempting choice might
then be to use URLs; however, URLs are used exclusively to identify and denote the location of *documents*, and as such, are not suitable for identifying
general resources such as cities (e.g., Boston), singers (e.g., Brad Delp), and so

forth. Hence a generalisation of URLs – called Uniform Resource Identifiers (URIs) [51] – was proposed, with the idea that URIs can serve as identifiers for generic resources; while all URLs are URIs, only those URIs that directly indicate the location of a document are URLs. However, URIs themselves have a significant drawback: they are limited to a subset of ASCII characters, meaning no diacritics, no support for alphabets such as kanji or cyrillic, etc.; such characters need to be encoded with *percent encoding*, such that a substring "Québec" becomes the significantly less readable "Qu%C3%A9bec". Hence the IRI was proposed as a generalisation of URIs to allow such characters, permitting substrings such as "Québec" [118]. While RDF was originally based on URIs, the use of IRIs was introduced in RDF 1.1.

Thus in RDF, a resource such as Boston would be identified by a global IRI as exemplified in Figure 3.1. A typical IRI is composed of various parts, primarily the SCHEME, which denotes the protocol by which information about the resource could be located (if available); the HOST, which provides the location of a server as either a physical IP address or – more commonly, per the example – a hierarchical domain name; the PATH, which typically refers to the file location where information about the resource is kept on the server; and a FRAGMENT, which refers to something contained with a file. Parts such as the FRAGMENT may not always be given; likewise the HOST and PATH may contain more or fewer sub-parts. Indeed, this is merely an example of a common form of IRI; other valid IRIs may come with different schemes (e.g., mailto:ahogan@dcc.uchile.cl or urn:isbn:978-1-61499-382-7), or with a non-default port (e.g., http://example.org:8080/), or with a dynamic query string (e.g., http://example.org/search?q=boston), and so forth.

Fig. 3.1 Anatomy of a typical IRI

In the core RDF standard, IRIs are considered analogous to string identifiers: their composition in terms of schemes, hosts, paths, etc., are not of core importance until higher levels are considered (in particular the real benefit of using IRIs as identifiers will become much more concrete when we discuss Linked Data later in Chapter 8). At the level of RDF, the most important aspect of IRIs is that they constitute a global naming scheme that is compatible with the Web. When the same IRI is used by multiple RDF datasets, it is clear that multiple datasets are talking about the same resource. This also avoids the problems of ambiguity associated with simple strings such as Boston: as long as the two publishers use different IRIs to identify Boston the city and Boston the band, no naming clash will occur.

Conversely, one may ask: *what happens if two different publishers use two different IRIs to identify the same resource?* In this book, we will refer to such IRIs as **coreferent**: as referring to the same thing. In fact, since the Web is only loosely-coordinated – where it seems both unfeasible and undesirable to expect all publishers to agree on one IRI naming scheme for all possible resources of interest – coreferent IRIs commonly appear in practice. To cater for such inevitable situations on the Web, RDF does not take a **Unique Name Assumption (UNA)**: in other words, RDF allows multiple IRIs to refer to the same resource. However, additional processing must be conducted to identify cases of coreference, which is important when integrating data about a given set of resources from multiple locations; otherwise information about a given resource cannot be combined from multiple locations. We will discuss how coreferent IRIs can be handled later in Chapter 8.

Finally, since IRIs are cumbersome, many RDF syntaxes (discussed in more detail in Section 3.8) use prefixes as shorthand. For example, we may define the prefix `ex:` as `http://data.example.org/city/`, where `ex:Boston` would then refer to `http://data.example.org/city/Boston` (per prefix replacement), `ex:Galway` to `http://data.example.org/city/Galway`, and so forth. In this book, we will often use such prefixed names as shorthand for IRIs. In Table 3.1, we list some core prefixes relating to RDF standards that will be mentioned in this section, using `ex:` as an example prefix.[1]

Table 3.1 Core prefixes for the Semantic Web standards

Prefix	Value
rdf:	http://www.w3.org/1999/02/22-rdf-syntax-ns#
xsd:	http://www.w3.org/2001/XMLSchema#
rdfs:	http://www.w3.org/2000/01/rdf-schema#
owl:	http://www.w3.org/2002/07/owl#

3.2.2 Literals

If only IRIs were allowed in RDF, then there would be no way to provide human-readable information like titles, descriptions, dates, numeric values, etc., to RDF descriptions: though one can use an IRI to identify, say, the number 2, the relation between that IRI and that number could never be formally defined; rather it could only understood as referring to the number 2 by convention. To get around this problem, RDF also includes *literals* as terms: lexical strings that can represent numbers or booleans or dates, etc.

---

[1] We also follow *de facto* consensus on common prefixes, as listed on `http://prefix.cc/`.

In RDF 1.1, a literal may consist of (two of) three parts [103]:

a lexical form: a Unicode string;
a datatype IRI: identifies the "type" of literal;
a language tag: indicating the human language of the text.

The most basic form of literal in RDF consists only of a *lexical form*: a simple string like "Strawberry Cheesecake". These are sometimes known as plain or simple literals. Simple literals can optionally be associated with a *language tag* (following BCP47 [316]) where, for example, "Aluminum sulfate"@en specifies that the string is in English, and "Aluminium sulphate"@en-UK more specifically states that it is in the UK dialect of English.

The third ingredient of RDF literals is the datatype IRI, which denotes a datatype indicating how the lexical form should be interpreted; for example, the lexical form "2" could be interpreted as the number 2 or the character 2, where the datatype IRI indicates the appropriate value. Datatype IRIs are written using a double-caret symbol, where "2"^^xsd:integer is an example literal indicating the number 2; conversely, "2"^^xsd:string is a literal indicating the string "2". The datatypes themselves specify a *lexical space*, a *value space*, and a *lexical-to-value mapping*. The lexical space is the set of lexical forms that the datatype permits. The value space is the set of all values to which lexical forms can be mapped. The lexical-to-value mapping states how lexical forms can be interpreted as referring to the value space.

> **Example 3.1**
>
> Take the datatype (identified by the IRI) xsd:integer. This datatype contains "2" in its lexical space but not "2.0" or "broccoli"; its value space consists of $\mathbb{Z}$, the countably infinite set of all integers; its lexical-to-value mapping would map the lexical forms "2", "02", "+2", etc., onto the same value: the number 2 itself.

> **Remark 3.1**
>
> Strictly speaking we should distinguish between the datatype IRI and the datatype itself. We will generally not draw such a distinction, however, since it quickly becomes tedious and unnecessarily indirect; hence, when we say, e.g., "the datatype xsd:integer", strictly we mean "the datatype *identified by* xsd:integer".

The full set of built-in datatypes that RDF 1.1 supports is listed in Table 3.2. Most datatypes come from the XSD standard [313, 103], with two additional RDF-specific datatypes for HTML and XML data. Some datatypes

Table 3.2 List of datatypes supported in RDF 1.1 [313, 103]

Datatype IRI	Example Lexical Forms	Note
	BOOLEAN	
xsd:boolean	"true", "false", "1", "0"	Case sensitive
	NUMERIC	
xsd:decimal	"-2.320"	Any precision
└ xsd:integer	"-3"	Any precision, $x \in \mathbb{Z}$
└ xsd:long	"-9223372036854775808"	$-2^{63} \leq x < 2^{63}$
└ xsd:int	"+2147483647"	$-2^{31} \leq x < 2^{31}$
└ xsd:short	"-32768"	$-2^{15} \leq x < 2^{15}$
└ xsd:byte	"127"	$-2^7 \leq x < 2^7$
└ xsd:nonNegativeInteger	"0", "4"	$0 \leq x < \infty$
└ xsd:positiveInteger	"+1", "3152"	$1 \leq x < \infty$
└ xsd:unsignedLong	"18446744073709551615"	$0 \leq x < 2^{64}$
└ xsd:unsignedInt	"+4294967295"	$0 \leq x < 2^{32}$
└ xsd:unsignedShort	"65535"	$0 \leq x < 2^{16}$
└ xsd:unsignedByte	"+255"	$0 \leq x < 2^8$
└ xsd:nonPositiveInteger	"0", "-4"	$x \leq 0$
└ xsd:negativeInteger	"-3152"	$x < 0$
xsd:double	"1.7e308" "-4.9E-324", "NaN", "INF", "-INF"	IEEE 64-bit floating point
xsd:float	"3.4E38", "-1.4e-45", "NaN", "INF", "-INF"	IEEE 32-bit floating point
	TEMPORAL	
xsd:time	"05:04:12", "05:04:12Z", "05:04:12.00-10:00"	Z indicates +00:00 time-zone
xsd:date	"2012-02-29", "2012-12-31+04:00"	Time-zone optional
xsd:dateTime	"2012-12-31T00:01:02.034"	Time-zone optional
└ xsd:dateTimeStamp	"2012-12-31T00:01:02+04:00"	Time-zone required
xsd:duration	"P6Y9M15DT25H61M4.2S", "P6Y4.2S"	6 Years (...) 4.2 Seconds
└ xsd:dayTimeDuration	"P2DT8H14S"	No month or year
└ xsd:yearMonthDuration	"-P89Y13M"	No days or time
xsd:gDay	"---15", "---01-13:59"	Day recurring every month
xsd:gMonth	"--12", "--01+14:00"	Month recurring every year
xsd:gMonthDay	"--02-29", "--03-01Z"	Date recurring every year
xsd:gYear	"1985", "-0005"	A year ($-y$ indicates B.C.)
xsd:gYearMonth	"1985-05", "-0005-02"	A specific month
	TEXT	
xsd:string	" tab-> <-tab "	Most Unicode characters
└ xsd:normalizedString	" multiple-> <-spaces "	No \r, \n, \t
└ xsd:token	"one-> <-space"	No leading or double spaces
└ xsd:language	"en", "en-UK", "en-uk", "zh-yue-Hant"	Generalises BCP47 [316]
└ xsd:name	"ns:some_name"	XML names
└ xsd:NCName	"some_name"	XML names: no colons
└ xsd:NMTOKEN	"1some_name"	XML names: 1st char relaxed
xsd:base64Binary	"QS5ILiBuZWVkcyBhIHNtb2tlLg=="	Base-64 encoded strings
xsd:hexBinary	"2e2e2e20616e6420616c636f686f6c2e"	Hexadecimal strings
xsd:anyURI	"http://example.com/",	Full IRI strings
rdf:HTML	"<div class="display">some data</div>"	Well-formed HTML content
rdf:XMLLiteral	"<flavour><fruit>apple</fruit></flavour>"	Well-formed XML content

from XSD are not included as they assume an enclosing XML document (e.g., xsd:QName) or represent sequences rather than atomic values (e.g., xsd:IDREFS). The hierarchy shown in the leftmost column of Table 3.2 denotes which datatypes are derived from which. The central column provides some examples of valid lexical forms while the rightmost column provides high-level notes for each datatype. We further categorise the presented datatypes under the following four informal categories:

BOOLEAN: A single true/false datatype.

NUMERIC: A set of datatypes referring to numerical values. There are two distinct categories: one refers to precise numerical values (falling under `xsd:decimal`) and the other refers to IEEE floating point approximations of numeric values (either `xsd:double` or `xsd:float`).

TEMPORAL: A set of datatypes for defining dates, times, durations and recurring/partial dates according to a Gregorian calendar.

TEXT: A set of datatypes generally referring to strings of characters, possibly encoded or following a pre-established syntax.

The hierarchies shown in the left-hand column of Table 3.2 indicate which datatypes are derived from (loosely speaking "are more specific than") which other datatypes. Datatypes that are not derived from other datatypes are known as primitive datatypes. Derived datatypes aim to restrict the lexicon/values of their parents. The lexical and value space of derived datatypes are a subset of those ancestors from which they are recursively derived. Likewise, the lexical-to-value mapping for the lexical space of a derived datatype corresponds with its ancestor datatypes. Hence, any derived datatype can be interpreted using any of its ancestor datatypes.

Example 3.2

Per Table 3.2, the datatype `xsd:byte` is recursively derived from `xsd:integer`, which is derived from `xsd:decimal`. As such, the lexical and value space of `xsd:byte` is a subset of the lexical and value space for `xsd:integer`, which in turn is a subset of the lexical and value space for `xsd:decimal`: any string like `"2"` that is in the lexical space for `xsd:byte` is in the lexical space for `xsd:integer` and `xsd:decimal`. Likewise, even though `"2.0"` is not in the lexical space of `xsd:byte` or `xsd:integer`, the literals `"2"^^xsd:byte`, `"2"^^xsd:integer`, `"2"^^xsd:decimal`, and `"2.0"^^xsd:decimal` all refer to the same value: the number 2.

Remark 3.2

From Table 3.2, one may note that the datatypes `xsd:double` and `xsd:float` are considered as primitive datatypes distinct from `xsd:decimal`. Intuitively, the latter datatype refers to exact values while the former two datatypes refer to floating point (approximate) values. Hence, strictly speaking, for example, `"2"^^xsd:double` and `"2"^^xsd:decimal` should be considered as different values: the former refers to a set of real numbers that round to 2 under double-precision floats (specified by IEEE 754), rather than the exact value 2. In practice, however, these values can be compared (possibly using casting).

Discussion 3.1

ANNA: Why do we need so many datatypes? In particular, why do we
   need derived datatypes like xsd:byte or xsd:nonNegativeInteger
   when we could just use the primitive datatype xsd:decimal for all
   numbers? After all, the values in the former datatypes are contained
   in the latter primitive datatype.
AIDAN: The datatypes come from XML Schema, whose main focus is
   validation. The idea is that if you have an age value, for example,
   you might want to say it takes a value from xsd:nonNegativeInteger
   to allow for validating values. In the next chapter we will see that
   we can do something similar for RDF. So in general, if we think
   that such types of validation may be an important feature to have
   further down the road, we may want to keep such derived datatypes.
ANNA: So are they often used in practice?
AIDAN: Some are and some are not. An analysis conducted by Glimm
   et al. [144] in 2011 of a corpus of millions of RDF documents crawled
   from the Web found frequent usage of some datatype IRIs like
   xsd:dateTime, xsd:boolean, xsd:integer, etc.; but the same study
   found little usage of xsd:time, xsd:token, xsd:gDay, etc.; and no
   usage of xsd:name, xsd:hexBinary, xsd:base64Binary, etc.

Exercise 3.1

What datatype literals would best indicate the following:

1. *December 18th, 2014, 18:47 at UTC−4*
2. *18:47 at UTC−4*
3. *The year 1984*
4. *The human age 22*
5. *The journey duration 1 hour 22 minutes*
6. *The birthday December 18th*
7. *The apartment number 204*

An important aspect of datatypes is their cardinality (number of values).
Most of the datatypes have a value space that is countably infinite.[2] Others
– such as those identified by the IRIs xsd:long, xsd:unsignedlong, and their
derived datatypes – have a bounded cardinality: a finite number of values.

An even more important aspect of datatypes is the ordering possible over
their value space. Although the lexical forms of the datatypes can always

---

[2] A countably infinite set is one where every value in the set can be mapped one-to-one
to a natural number. Since lexical values are assumed to be of finite length over a finite
alphabet (a subset of Unicode), there are no uncountably infinite concrete datatypes.

be compared using string comparison, applications often require datatype literals to be ordered by their value, not their string. For numeric datatypes, this is straightforward since their value spaces have a total ordering, meaning that every pair of values is comparable. However, ordering in the case of other datatypes is more complex: sometimes only a partial order is possible.

Example 3.3

Consider two literals `"2"^^xsd:byte` and `"14"^^xsd:byte`. Ordering the *lexical strings* would lead to the latter literal being considered lower than the former since "14" < "2" lexicographically speaking. Many applications – e.g., one sorting cities by population – would instead require a natural numeric ordering over such literals such that $2 < 14$; this is given by the ordering of the *value space* of the datatype.

However, although a lexical ordering is always possible, a value ordering is not. Consider two literals `"16-05-1985T04:00:00"^^xsd:dateTime` and `"15-05-1985T23:00:00+02:00"^^xsd:dateTime`. Now the question is: which *value* – or in other words, which point in time – came first? The answer is unclear since the time-zone is omitted from the first literal: if that time-zone were `-03:00`, both would refer to the same point in time, but without the time-zone, the literals cannot be ordered by value. An application that wanted to sort a list of global earthquakes by the date-time they were detected may thus not be able to order the results consistently. For this reason, the datatype referred to by `xsd:dateTimeStamp` was introduced, making time-zones mandatory and thus enforcing a total order within that derived datatype.

In RDF 1.1, all literals are interpreted as having a datatype IRI. If a literal is presented without an explicit datatype – e.g., `"Aluminium sulphate"` – then it is assumed to have the datatype IRI `xsd:string`.[3] An exception to this rule is if the literal has a language tag – e.g., `"Aluminium sulphate"@en-UK` – in which case the special datatype `rdf:langString` is implied.

User-defined datatypes are allowed by the RDF 1.1 standard; however, the standard provides no mechanisms for defining new datatypes as being derived from existing datatypes, or having a specific lexical or value space.[4] In other words, it is fine to use custom datatype IRIs that the RDF standard does not directly recognise, but they must be defined elsewhere – e.g., in custom code or another standard – if they are to be interpreted correctly.

---

[3] Though `"Aluminium sulphate"` and `"Aluminium sulphate"^^xsd:string` refer to the same value (i.e., they are coreferent), the two terms are considered different in RDF.

[4] We will discuss the definition of custom datatypes in OWL in Chapter 5.

Example 3.4

RDF allows us to use literals with custom datatypes such as
"8848"^^ex:metres or "48"^^ex:inches. However, RDF implementations are not required to understand custom datatypes of this form,
in terms of being able to order them, convert between them, etc.

Remark 3.3

We wish to emphasise that the values denoted by literals should
also be considered as resources in the context of RDF. In fact, IRIs
can also be used to refer to the same resources as literals. Thus, IRIs
and literals are both sets of RDF terms that refer to resources. Taking
"2.0"^^xsd:decimal and "2"^^xsd:integer, these are two distinct RDF
terms that by definition refer to the same value: they are coreferent.
We could also invent an IRI ex:2 to refer to the number 2 (as done by
Vrandečić et al. in their Linked Open Numbers dataset [398]): this IRI
would then be coreferent with the two literals noted previously (though
such a coreference cannot yet be made explicit with RDF alone).

3.2.3 Blank Nodes

In some cases, having to identify a resource with a globally unique IRI or a
literal may be restrictive, impractical and/or unnecessary.

In the first such case, we may wish to represent the existence of unknown
values, to say, for example, that the Old English poem *Beowulf* has an author,
but that the author is not known. We could completely omit authorship information from the data, but then we lose information: that the poem has *some*
author. Alternatively, we could just use a fixed IRI to represent unknown
values. But how would we encode that semantics? In other words, how would
we avoid external consumers misinterpreting all such works of literature with
unknown authorship as having the same author called "Unknown"@en? Would
we require them to implement custom code or queries to handle this specific
case? Perhaps we could create a different IRI for each unknown author, but
in that case, external consumers of the data would still require custom code
or queries to, for example, find all works of unknown authorship.

In another case, we may wish to refer to a resource that is difficult to
identify in a globally unique sense, such as a goal scored in a sporting event:
to create a globally unique IRI for such a goal, we would need to combine the
exact time of the goal and an identifier for the match, which in turn may need
to include, perhaps, the two teams playing, the sport, the date and time, etc.;

another option would be to create a random string that is unique with high probability, but to get sufficient entropy, we may need to create long IRIs.

RDF offers an alternative option for such cases: blank nodes, which are interpreted as representing the existence of *some* resource, rather than as identifying a specific resource. Blank nodes are typically (and herein) represented with an underscore prefix, such as _:bnode34. Hence in the first case, we can use a blank node as a general solution to represent the unknown author of *Beowulf* and a fresh blank node in each such case for other works. In the second case, we can simply use a blank node to refer to the goal, which we can assume to be implicitly "identified" by the data that describes it.

To capture such cases, blank nodes in RDF are interpreted as existential variables, meaning that they denote the existence of something rather than being interpreted as global identifiers. A subsequent question that then arises is: how do we ensure that blank nodes are globally unique? For example, if we use _:b to denote the author of Beowulf and the goal previously described in two different locations, we do not want these to be interpreted as the same variable. For this reason, rather than requiring blank nodes with high-entropy globally-unique labels, RDF simply defines blank nodes as variables having a local scope. Hence _:b the author of Beowulf and _:b the goal are not considered the same if the data are found in two different locations.

These features of blank nodes give rise to some notable characteristics that will be discussed later in Section 3.7, but for now, it suffices to consider blank nodes as placeholders for resources not identified by an IRI or a literal.

Discussion 3.2

FRANK: Are these blank nodes related to NULLs in databases?

AIDAN: Partially, yes. NULLs are used to fill values that – for whatever reason – are not given in a relational table. But in most relational database engines, NULLs are not named, meaning they can only appear in one place in one table. On the other hand, in RDF, within a given local scope, blank nodes can be used multiple times, for example to describe the time of a goal, the player who scored it, and so forth. Also, relational NULLs do not have a fixed semantics and can mean that the value exists but is not known, or does not exist, or is not applicable, or is withheld for other reasons. Conversely blank nodes have a fixed semantics in RDF: that some value exists.

3.2.4 Defining RDF Terms

Finally, we come to a formal definition of the set of RDF terms, setting up notation we will use throughout the book.

> **Definition 1 (RDF Terms).** Let **I** denote the set of IRIs, **L** the set of RDF literals and **B** the set of RDF blank nodes. These three sets are pairwise **disjoint**: they share no elements. The set of *RDF terms* is defined as the union of these three sets: **I** ∪ **L** ∪ **B**.

3.3 Triples

While RDF terms are used to identify resources, RDF triples are used to describe resources: to make statements about them. Triples are inspired by one of the simplest forms of sentence structure in natural language: subject–verb–object sentences, as demonstrated in Figure 3.2.[5] However, oftentimes sentences wish to express a more complex relationship between a subject and object than a simple verb. In this case, per Figure 3.2, the resulting relationship can be generalised (loosely speaking[6]) as a "predicate".

Lemon contains Citrus

SUBJECT   VERB   OBJECT

Fig. 3.2 A subject–verb–object (SVO) sentence

Boston has population 646,000

SUBJECT   PREDICATE   OBJECT

Fig. 3.3 A subject–predicate–object (SPO) sentence

In a similar fashion, an RDF triple is a simple statement composed of three ordered elements: subject, predicate and object. However, as discussed in the previous section, simple strings like "Boston" are not suitable identifiers for use in RDF. Instead, as shown in Figure 3.4, each of the three positions of the triple – subject, predicate and object – are filled by a single RDF term. The first two triples correspond to the simple sentences we saw previously. The third triple briefly exemplifies use of a blank node to state that the Voynich

---

[5] ... at least for a language like English that typically places terms in this order.

[6] The sentence "*Boston has population 646,000*" takes considerable liberties with English grammar and how it defines a predicate – and in a grammatically correct sentence such as "*The population of Boston is 646,000*" or "*Boston's population is 646,000*", the subject, predicate and object would not correspond with Figure 3.2. But the analogy serves to indicate why the positions of a triple were called "subject", "predicate" and "object".

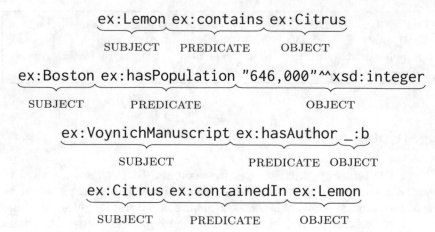

Fig. 3.4 Four example RDF triples

Manuscript has an author, but that author is unidentified/unknown. The fourth triple has the exact same intended meaning as the first triple, but where subject and object roles are reversed; although the subject of a triple is often considered to denote the "primary resource" being described by the triple, this is often an arbitrary distinction since "inverse predicates" can be defined that swap subject and object roles while describing the same thing.

Triples have some restrictions on the positions in which different types of RDF terms can be placed:

1. IRIs can appear in any position: subject, predicate or object;
2. literals can only appear in the object position;
3. blank nodes can only appear in the subject or object position.

Stated equivalently:

1. subjects can only contain IRIs or blank nodes;
2. predicates can only contain IRIs;
3. objects can contain IRIs, blank nodes or literals.

These restrictions are due to design decisions made at the outset of RDF: namely that relations must always be named, that it doesn't make sense to use a literal as a relation[7], and, more controversially, that literals are "secondary resources" that should not be the main *subject* of RDF descriptions.[8]

---

[7] Recall that a literal like "has population" refers to the actual string and thus cannot refer to a relation of the same name.

[8] The possibility of relaxing these restrictions, and in particular allowing literals in the subject position, was discussed by the RDF 1.1 Working Group, but no action was taken. However, the standard provides a non-normative definition of "**generalised triple**", which is an extension of RDF that removes such restrictions.

Following what we have discussed – and building upon Definition 1 for RDF terms – we can now provide a brief formal definition for an RDF triple:

Definition 2 (RDF triple). An *RDF triple* $t := (s, p, o)$ is any element of the set $\mathbf{IB} \times \mathbf{I} \times \mathbf{IBL}$,[a] where $s \in \mathbf{IB}$ is called the *subject*, $p \in \mathbf{I}$ is called the *predicate* and $o \in \mathbf{IBL}$ is called the *object*.

---

[a] In this book, we may use concatenation of set names as a shortcut for set union; e.g., **IBL** denotes $\mathbf{I} \cup \mathbf{B} \cup \mathbf{L}$.

Equivalently, this definition states that any triple (s, p, o) such that s is an IRI or blank node; p is an IRI; and o is an IRI, blank node, or literal; is an RDF triple. This conceptual definition is useful for talking about RDF in general mathematical terms without having to worry, for example, about what syntax a particular RDF document is written down in.

Being based on triples, the RDF data model has a fixed arity (a fixed width or number of terms in each tuple) of 3. As we will see, this plays an important role in how RDF data from different sources can be combined. One may, however, reasonably ask why RDF was not originally based on pairs (2-tuples) or quads (4-tuples), for example. The concise answer is that 3 is the lowest arity needed to conveniently represent arbitrary information using unordered sets.[9] The following example gives an idea of the problem faced when representing arbitrary information with sets of pairs.

Example 3.5

Consider trying to state that lemon contains citrus and cookies contain gluten using a set of pairs. We could try:

$$(\mathsf{ex{:}Lemon}, \mathsf{ex{:}contains}), (\mathsf{ex{:}contains}, \mathsf{ex{:}Citrus})$$
$$(\mathsf{ex{:}Cookies}, \mathsf{ex{:}contains}), (\mathsf{ex{:}contains}, \mathsf{ex{:}Gluten})$$

In this case, however we do not know if lemon contains citrus, or gluten, or both, and likewise for cookies. So we can try assign an ID to each statement and say:

$$(\mathsf{ex{:}1}, \mathsf{ex{:}Lemon}), (\mathsf{ex{:}1}, \mathsf{ex{:}contains}), (\mathsf{ex{:}1}, \mathsf{ex{:}Citrus})$$
$$(\mathsf{ex{:}2}, \mathsf{ex{:}Cookies}), (\mathsf{ex{:}2}, \mathsf{ex{:}contains}), (\mathsf{ex{:}2}, \mathsf{ex{:}Gluten})$$

But now we don't know if citrus contains lemon, or citrus lemon contains, or contains lemon citrus: we do not know the position (and hence roles) of the terms in the statement. So it might be tempting to try:

---

[9] Here assuming that the terms in the tuples are atomic symbols: i.e., that one cannot somehow parse the first term in a pair into two terms to make a triple.

```
(ex:Lemon,ex:containsCitrus)
(ex:Cookies,ex:containsGluten)
```

But now we are limited in how we can *query* the data: we cannot easily query, for example, for all the things that lemon contains: if we used triples, we could find all triples with subject ex:Lemon and predicate ex:contains, but using pairs as above, we have to do something like write a regular-expression against the string of the term.

Another attempt might be:

```
(ex:Lemon,ex:contains1),(ex:contains1,ex:Citrus)
(ex:Cookies,ex:contains2),(ex:contains2,ex:Gluten)
```

But now we cannot query for what things are contained in what other things, and indeed, we would need to know that ex:contains1 is used for lemon if we wanted to query for what lemon contains.

A final attempt might be something along the lines of:

```
(ex:contains1,ex:contains1S),(ex:contains1S,ex:Lemon)
(ex:contains1S,ex:contains1P),(ex:contains1P,ex:contains)
(ex:contains1P,ex:contains1O),(ex:contains1O,ex:Citrus)

(ex:contains2,ex:contains2S),(ex:contains2S,ex:Cookies)
(ex:contains2S,ex:contains2P),(ex:contains2P,ex:contains)
(ex:contains2P,ex:contains2O),(ex:contains2O,ex:Gluten)
```

This would potentially work if we could distinguish structural terms such as ex:contains1P from the domain terms such as ex:Lemon. In general, however, this is clearly verbose and not particularly practical. It would be much easier to simply use triples.

We will see examples of representing more complex forms of data as triples later in this chapter, and we will also discuss how quads are sometimes used to succinctly capture higher-level information about triples.

3.4 Graphs

The core unit of data in RDF is the triple, where a set of triples is then called an *RDF graph*.

Definition 3 (RDF graph). An *RDF graph* G is a subset of $\mathbf{IB} \times \mathbf{I} \times \mathbf{IBL}$; i.e., an RDF graph is a set of triples.

Since RDF graphs are set-based, the ordering of triples does not matter. RDF graphs are called as such because a triple (s,p,o) fits closely with the notion of a directed labelled edge in a graph, where the predicate can be considered a label for the directed edge from the subject node to the object node: $s \xrightarrow{p} o$. An RDF graph is then a set of such edges forming a graph.

Example 3.6

Consider the following set of triples:

ex:LemonCheesecake	rdfs:label	"Lemon Cheesecake"@en
ex:LemonCheesecake	ex:contains	ex:Lemon
ex:LemonCheesecake	ex:contains	ex:Cookies
ex:LemonCheesecake	ex:contains	ex:Sugar
ex:LemonCheesecake	ex:contains	ex:CreamCheese
ex:Lemon	rdfs:label	"Lemon"@en
ex:Lemon	rdfs:label	"Limón"@es
ex:Lemon	ex:contains	ex:Citrus
ex:Cookies	ex:contains	ex:Sugar
ex:Cookies	ex:contains	ex:Gluten

This set of triples is, by definition an RDF graph. Considering a predicate as a directed labelled edge from subject to object, we can represent these RDF data graphically as follows.

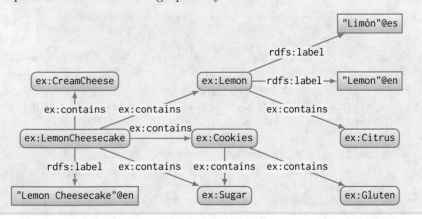

Remark 3.4

In RDF, we may sometimes wish to describe terms appearing in predicate positions. As a result, in an RDF graph, edge labels (i.e., predicates) can sometimes also appear as nodes.

ex:contains	rdfs:label	"Contains"@en
ex:Lemon	ex:contains	ex:Citrus

This would be drawn as follows:

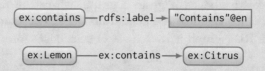

The node ex:contains in the first triple is still considered as referring to the same resource as the edge-label on the second triple.

At its core, RDF is then a graph-structured data model based on triples. Being graph-structured means that RDF is quite a generic and flexible data model. One can arbitrarily add new edges to the graph from any node to any other node with any edge. One can likewise introduce new nodes and edge labels arbitrarily, so long as they abide by the restrictions on which RDF terms can be placed in which positions: an IRI can serve as a labelled edge (predicate) or source node (subject) or target node (object); a literal can serve as a target node (object); though not yet shown, a blank node can serve as a source node (subject) or target node (object). Likewise, one can combine multiple RDF graphs that do not contain blank nodes quite straightforwardly into one RDF graph by taking the union of all triples in the input graphs.

Discussion 3.3

FRANK: How does this all relate with graph databases like Neo4J? Don't they also use a graph-based data model?

AIDAN: Yes, Neo4J and other graph databases often use a data model called *property graphs* [10]. The core idea of property graphs is that nodes and edges can be associated with a set of attribute–value pairs, and hence they can be seen as forming a more complex data model than RDF. However, whatever one can express as a property graph, one can also express as RDF. Also, property graphs are typically considered for applications with closed centralised datasets, whereas the aim of RDF – by using IRIs as identifiers – is to enable publishing data in an open and decentralised manner on the Web.

FRANK: Why then do both such data models exist?

AIDAN: Well RDF pre-dates such graph databases by a significant margin. Both came from different use-cases. RDF originates from the goal of publishing data on the Web. Graph databases like Neo4J came from use-cases where one wishes to have a data model more flexible than, for example, relational tables, and where one wishes to do graph-like queries, such as to find nodes connected by arbitrary-length paths. However, features of graph databases have been included and extended in the standard query language for RDF, called SPARQL (as we discuss later in Chapter 6).

FRANK: So when should we use one or other other?

> AIDAN: That is a difficult question and probably it would be a good idea to check out the survey by Angles et al. [10] and the paper by Hernández et al. [187] for more details. But in summary, RDF and SPARQL are standards implemented by multiple engines and are much more "webby" than the typical graph databases (aside from being standardised, they use Web identifiers, for example). Hence for publishing or consuming data on the Web, RDF and SPARQL are designed for that. On the other hand, in some local applications, using the property graph model might be advantageous.

3.5 Vocabulary and Modelling

The RDF data model centres around sets of triples, which provides a conceptually straightforward graph-based data model. This foundational data model is, as we will show, sufficient to represent complex claims about the world (though admittedly sometimes in an indirect manner). In this section, we discuss how to model more complex data as triples and describe some of the core built-in IRIs that the RDF standard provides for modelling certain patterns. We also give some insights into the strengths and weaknesses of RDF for modelling different types of data.

3.5.1 Classes and Properties

RDF descriptions are composed of two high-level types of conceptual elements: **properties** and **classes**. Properties are the relationships that hold between pairs of resources: they are terms that are primarily used in the predicate position.[10] Classes are groups of resources with some conceptual similarities: classes group resources of the same type. A resource can be a member of multiple classes. A member of a class is often called an **instance** of that class; the class of a resource is often called its type.

RDF provides a built-in property to denote instances of classes, as well as a built-in class to capture all properties.

---

rdf:type: a property for relating an instance to its class.
rdf:Property: the class of all properties.

---

[10] Though the terms "property" and "predicate" are sometimes considered synonymous in RDF, there is a subtle distinction. While we can think of a predicate as the middle position of an RDF triple or the term that fills it, a property refers to the relationship itself or the term that represents it. A property term may appear in multiple triples and in locations other than the predicate position, as will be shown in Example 3.7.

Example 3.7

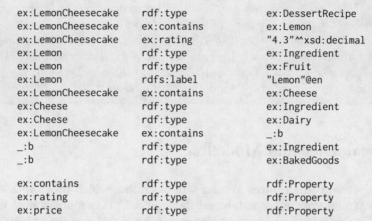

Consider the following triples:

```
ex:LemonCheesecake    rdf:type       ex:DessertRecipe
ex:LemonCheesecake    ex:contains    ex:Lemon
ex:LemonCheesecake    ex:rating      "4.3"^^xsd:decimal
ex:Lemon              rdf:type       ex:Ingredient
ex:Lemon              rdf:type       ex:Fruit
ex:Lemon              rdfs:label     "Lemon"@en
ex:LemonCheesecake    ex:contains    ex:Cheese
ex:Cheese             rdf:type       ex:Ingredient
ex:Cheese             rdf:type       ex:Dairy
ex:LemonCheesecake    ex:contains    _:b
_:b                   rdf:type       ex:Ingredient
_:b                   rdf:type       ex:BakedGoods

ex:contains           rdf:type       rdf:Property
ex:rating             rdf:type       rdf:Property
ex:price              rdf:type       rdf:Property
```

Here we encounter six class IRIs: ex:DessertRecipe, ex:Ingredient,
ex:Fruit, ex:Dairy, ex:BakedGoods and rdf:Property; instances for
these classes are defined using the rdf:type property. We likewise
see five property IRIs: ex:contains, ex:rating, rdf:type, rdfs:label
and ex:price; the first two are used to relate two resources (i.e., appear in the predicate position) *and* are declared as being in the class
rdf:Property, the next two are used to relate two resources without being declared, and the final term is declared but not used in the predicate
position. In RDF, note that properties need not be explicitly declared
as type rdf:Property and declared properties need not be used.

Remark 3.5

It is conventional in RDF that classes are given uppercase singular names and properties and datatypes are given lowercase singular
names. This applies not only for core built-in vocabulary but is also
common usage for user-defined terms. (Though its name may be misleading, rdf:Property is in fact a class: the class of all properties.)

Classes and properties thus provide a high-level **vocabulary** – a set of RDF
terms – for general use in RDF descriptions. A single property or class may
be used to describe an arbitrary amount of instances. Vocabularies can be
trivially reused across different independent RDF sources. Datasets that agree
on vocabularies are better integrable since they "speak the same language".

The semantics of classes and properties can thereafter be made explicit using standards layered on top of RDF, where one can define, for example, that the property ex:contains is the inverse of ex:containedIn (per Figure 3.4), or that any instance of ex:DessertRecipe is also an instance of the more general class ex:Dessert. We will discuss standards for defining the semantics of classes and properties in more detail in Chapters 4 and 5.

3.5.2 *n-ary Relations*

RDF is well-suited for representing **binary relations**: directed, named relationships between two resources. However, it is not as well suited for relationships with a higher *arity* between more than two resources.

Example 3.8

Although it is trivial to represent claims involving binary relations such as "Boston has population 646,000" in triples (per Figure 3.4), more complex claims such as "Boston had population 646,000 as of the year 2014" require more careful consideration. In the latter claim, there are three resources involved in the population relation: the city Boston, the value 646,000, and the year 2014.

The first option to encode complex relations as triples is to use more specific properties that denote more specific types of relationships.

Example 3.9

One could represent the statement "Boston had a population of 646,000 as of the year 2014" in RDF with a single triple:

```
ex:Boston          ex:population2014     "646000"^^xsd:integer
```

Different properties can be defined likewise for different years. However, this approach encodes two dimensions into the predicate where, for example, finding out the year of a population reading would require parsing the IRI term. This may also lead to a large number of properties.

A more general approach is to model a complex relation as a first-class resource. This approach is known as *n*-**ary relation** modelling. For this, the RDF vocabulary defines a special property, called "rdf:value", which indicates the main value of the *n*-ary relation resource.

> `rdf:value`: relates an n-ary relation to its main value.

However, other properties can be (and often are) used.

Example 3.10

One could represent the statement "Boston had a population of 646,000 as of the year 2014" in RDF as follows:

```
ex:Boston        ex:population    ex:BostonP2014
ex:BostonP2014   rdf:value        "646000"^^xsd:integer
ex:BostonP2014   ex:year          "2014"^^xsd:gYear
```

This pattern preserves the full structure of the original statement, with the population value and the year given separate terms. The IRI `ex:BostonP2014` identifies an abstract resource representing the value of the population of Boston in 2014; such a resource is effectively an n-ary relation. The `rdf:value` property can be used to represent the "main" value of the n-ary relation. Likewise, more attributes can be added to the n-ary relation; for example, one could provide a source dimension to `ex:BostonP2014` or any number of other dimensions.

The use of the `rdf:value` property is not mandatory to model such relations in RDF. We could also write, for example:

```
ex:Boston        ex:statistic     _:bpb2014
_:bpb2014        ex:population    "646000"^^xsd:integer
_:bpb2014        ex:year          "2014"^^xsd:gYear
_:bpb2014        rdf:type         ex:PopulationStat
_:bpb2014        rdfs:label       "Pop. 646000 (2014)"
```

This time the "n-ary relation" is denoted by the blank node `_:bpb2014`. The modelling has also been generalised: the `rdf:type` triple may indicate different types of statistics, such as population, record temperature, monthly rainfall, crime rates, etc. The final triple gives a human-readable summary of the statistical relation.

There are many possible variations on the theme of n-ary predicates, but the general idea is that an RDF resource need not refer to something concrete like the city Boston, or the year 2014, or the binary relation has-population, or the value 646,000; a resource can also refer to something intangible, such as a complex relation involving an arbitrary number of resources, each with a different role in the relation (e.g., a population reading for a given city in a given year). This observation allows for modelling complex statements in RDF.

3.5.3 Reification

In a similar vein to n-ary relations is the notion of **reification** in RDF, which likewise allows for making complex claims in RDF, but rather involves talking about statements themselves. In this case, an RDF resource is created that refers to an RDF triple itself. The RDF standard provides the following built-in vocabulary for expressing reification:

---

rdf:Statement a class denoting RDF triples.
rdf:subject relates an RDF triple to its subject.
rdf:predicate relates an RDF triple to its predicate.
rdf:object relates an RDF triple to its object.

Example 3.11

Take the following triple:

```
ex:Boston              ex:population         "646000"^^xsd:integer
```

This triple is missing the year information. We can reify the statement and associate it with a year as follows:

```
_:bpt2014              rdf:subject           ex:Boston
_:bpt2014              rdf:predicate         ex:population
_:bpt2014              rdf:object            "646000"^^xsd:integer
_:bpt2014              ex:year               "2014"^^xsd:gYear
_:bpt2014              rdf:type              rdf:Statement
```

The first three triples identify the triple being reified. The fourth triple associates the year with the reified triple. The fifth triple indicates that the blank node _:bpt2014 denotes a reified triple. One could likewise annotate further information about the triple, such as a source, etc.

It is important to note that declaring a reified triple is distinct from stating the triple directly: the second reified graph above does not state or otherwise imply the triple contained in the first direct graph. To understand why, one should consider that a reified triple may be annotated as being "false": thus care must be taken when "dereifying" triples.

Reification is solely intended to make statements about triples themselves within the RDF model. However, the RDF reification model is quite cumbersome, introducing at least a $3\times$ overhead in the number of triples involved and requiring additional processing to resolve information. Still, for use-cases that require talking about triples *using only triples*, RDF reification (or something similar) is the only solution – the other option being to extend the model.

Example 3.11 provides a "well-formed" instance of reification: the reification resource is expected to have one subject, one predicate and one object defined per the illustrated pattern. However, RDF does not validate such patterns: any RDF graph that follows Definition 3 – in other words, any set of valid triples – can be considered a valid RDF graph.

Discussion 3.4

ANNA: I'm not sure I understand the difference between n-ary relations and reification. When should I use one versus the other?

AIDAN: The distinction is not quite black and white, and certainly there is a significant conceptual overlap between the two, but intuitively speaking, one would use n-ary relations to represent relations with more than two "arguments", such as the population example. On the other hand, reification refers to the idea of describing individual triples within the triple-based model itself; for example, to annotate each triple in an input RDF graph with a particular type of value – perhaps a probabilistic truth value, a temporal interval of truth, a reference to its source, etc. – and represent the output as an RDF graph. In the former case, we are describing the population of a city at a given time, whereas in the latter case, we are describing a triple itself. However, both are applicable for many of the same use-cases. In general, however, n-ary relations should be preferred as a more direct option: considering complex relations as resources themselves. For example, a population reading, a marriage, an employment, a presidency: though we may consider these to be relations, there is nothing stopping us from considering these as resources just like cities, people, businesses, countries, etc. (And when we consider *triples* as resources, that is precisely reification.)

Further Reading 3.1

Further reading about n-ary relations can be found in the W3C Working Group Note by Noy and Rector [296]. Further options for n-ary relations and reification – and their advantages and disadvantages – can be read about in the paper by Hernández et al. [186]. We highlight that features such as reification are quite controversial and sometimes seen as unnecessarily complicating the RDF specification; for example, Berners-Lee [48] (amongst others) has called for such features to be deprecated. Furthermore, an alternative to reification is to consider *RDF datasets*, where triples can be grouped into **named graphs**; we will discuss this novel feature of the RDF 1.1 standard later in Section 3.6.

3.5.4 Containers and Collections

The core of the RDF model is the notion of an RDF graph: an unordered set of triples. As such, RDF does not support an inherent ordering between triples. Instead, where ordering is important, RDF introduces two alternative conventions: **containers** and **collections**.

Containers are intended to be concise representations of groups of resources that may have an ordering. There are three types of containers represented by three different built-in classes:

`rdf:Bag` the class of containers whose ordering is insignificant;
`rdf:Seq` the class of containers whose ordering is significant;
`rdf:Alt` the class of containers containing a list of alternatives;
`rdf:_1` ... `rdf:_n` relates a container to one of its elements.

The containers associated with each of these three classes are identical: each class is used only to give an informal indication of the intention of the container. The members of each container are specified using properties of the form `rdf:_n` where n is any positive (non-zero) integer.

Example 3.12

One may wish to state ingredients for a recipe in the order they are added. To do so in RDF, one option is to use containers:

```
ex:Lemonade            ex:ingredients          _:1singreds
_:1singreds            rdf:_1                  ex:Water
_:1singreds            rdf:_2                  ex:Sugar
_:1singreds            rdf:_3                  ex:Lemon
_:1singreds            rdf:type                rdf:Seq
```

Such a container could be used to encode an ordering of the ingredients for lemonade: water is added first, then sugar, then lemon.

However, containers are cumbersome to process: checking for members of containers requires special support for the syntax of the countably infinite set of properties of the form `rdf:_n`.[11]

Addressing the shortcomings of containers, RDF introduces collections, which are akin to linked lists. They are more specific than containers: their structure encodes a fixed sequential ordering and they are explicitly terminated. RDF provides four built-in vocabulary terms to represent containers:

---

[11] Like reification, Berners-Lee [48] has also called for deprecation of containers from the core RDF standard.

rdf:List the class of all containers; note that list and container are
    essentially synonyms in the context of RDF;

rdf:first relates a list to its element;

rdf:rest relates a parent list to a sub-list;

rdf:nil refers to the empty list, also used to terminate a list.

Example 3.13

The following collection encodes an ordered list of ingredients:

ex:Lemonade	ex:ingredients	_:l1
_:l1	rdf:first	ex:Sugar
_:l1	rdf:rest	_:l2
_:l2	rdf:first	ex:Water
_:l2	rdf:rest	_:l3
_:l3	rdf:first	ex:Lemon
_:l3	rdf:rest	rdf:nil

The blank nodes _:l1, _:l2 and _:l3 refer to (sub-)lists. These could
be typed as rdf:List. The linked-list structure of such collections can
be more easily seen when we render these triples graphically:

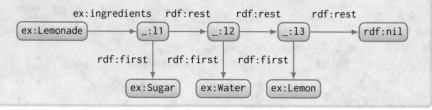

Both containers and collections have a "standard form". For instance, the
list in Example 3.13 follows the standard form of what is often called a "well-
formed list": one element associated with each sub-list, one successor sub-list,
a terminating empty list. However, as per reification, the core RDF model
does not validate such patterns: an RDF graph with an ill-formed list is still
a valid RDF graph. Likewise, for example, an RDF graph with a collection
typed with both rdf:Seq and rdf:Bag is still a valid RDF graph.

3.6 Datasets

Oftentimes applications will want to operate over multiple distinct RDF
graphs without simply merging them. For example, an application collecting RDF data from multiple sources on the Web may need to track which
triples came from which source since not all sources may be equally trust-

worthy. Another application may need to store multiple versions of the same RDF graph at different points in time. For applications that need to segregate and identify different RDF graphs, RDF 1.1 defines the notion of an **RDF dataset**, which is a dictionary of RDF graphs, consisting of:

- one **default graph**: an RDF graph (that may be empty),
- zero or more **named graphs**: pairs consisting of (i) a *name* that can be an IRI or a blank node, and (ii) an *RDF graph* (that may be empty).

We provide a brief formal definition:

Definition 4 (RDF dataset). An RDF dataset D is defined as a default graph and a set of named graphs; more formally speaking, $D := \{G, (x_1, G_1), \ldots, (x_n, G_n)\}$ where G and $G_1, \ldots, G_n$ are RDF graphs and each term in $x_1, \ldots, x_n$ is a *name* that is either an IRI or a blank node (i.e., $\{x_1, \ldots, x_n\} \subseteq \mathbf{IB}$). Each pair of the form (x_i, G_i) $(1 \le i \le n)$ is called a *named graph* and G is called the *default graph*. Each name is unique for the RDF dataset (i.e., it holds that $x_i \ne x_j$ for all $1 \le i < j \le n$) although names may appear freely *within* any graph.

In the context of an RDF dataset, names can be thought of as mapping to individual RDF graphs. For example, names may refer to a Web location from which the RDF graph was sourced, or to a specific version of a graph, etc. The default graph may refer to the union or merge of data in the other graphs, or to the most recent version of the different named versions of the graph, or even to an empty graph, and so forth. The purpose of a default graph and the relation between a name and its graph are not specified by RDF 1.1 [103], but are rather left open for different interpretations in different applications. Likewise, though tempting, a name should not even be considered as *identifying* a graph since, for example, the same name might be used in different RDF datasets to refer to completely different graphs.

Example 3.14

The following depicts an example RDF dataset with four named graphs coming from Frank's profile information, a local supermarket and a recipe site. In this scenario, the four named graphs may represent, for example, four Web documents containing RDF data.

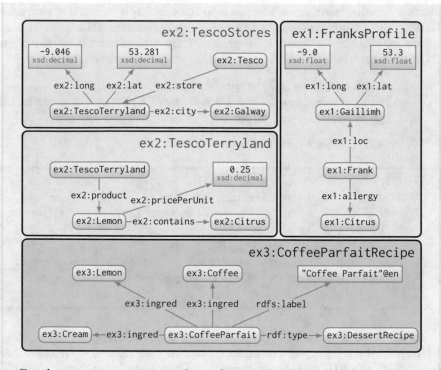

Graph names are written in large font inside the pane for that graph. Graph names are unique although they can be mentioned *within* different graphs (as per ex2:TescoTerryland). In this example, a default graph is not shown; the default graph could, for example, be empty, or could contain the merge of data from all named graphs.

Remark 3.6

In practical scenarios, **quadruples** or **quads** $(s,p,o,g) \in \mathbf{IB} \times \mathbf{I} \times \mathbf{IBL} \times \mathbf{IB}$ are often used to serialise or represent such datasets, where given a dataset D, a quad (s,p,o,g) intuitively represents that the triple (s,p,o) is contained in the graph with name g. In other words, each named graph $(x,G) \in D$ is instead represented as $G \times \{x\}$ taking the product of all triples in G and the graph name x. For instance, from Example 3.14, we could represent that the triple

   ex2:Lemon   ex2:contains   ex2:Citrus

is in the graph named ex2:TescoTerryland with the following quad:

        ex2:Lemon   ex2:contains   ex2:Citrus   ex2:TescoTerryland

One complication in a quad-based representation of a dataset arises with the default graph: this can be represented as a separate set of triples, or by simply assuming a fixed graph name for the default graph. We will discuss serialisations of RDF datasets in more detail in Section 3.8.7.

3.7 Blank Nodes

As previously discussed, blank nodes avoid having to identify every node with an IRI/literal, which can be convenient to represent unknown values, or to avoid having to create a globally unique identifier for all resources (which in turn enables – as we will discuss later – various convenient shortcuts in RDF syntaxes [196], particularly for representing collections in RDF). But this convenience comes at a cost: the presence of blank nodes in RDF graphs introduces a number of complications that we will now discuss.

3.7.1 Isomorphism of RDF Graphs

Recall that blank nodes are locally-scoped RDF terms that indicate the existence of a resource without identifying it: in other words, blank nodes are existential variables. Furthermore, the labels of these blank nodes do not have a particular significance outside of their local scope; in other words, the blank nodes of an RDF graph can be relabelled in a one-to-one manner without changing how it should be interpreted. This gives rise to the notion of **RDF isomorphism** whereby two RDF graphs that are identical up to blank node labels – where the blank nodes of one graph can be relabelled in a one-to-one manner to make the two graphs identical – are considered isomorphic. Intuitively, one can consider isomorphic RDF graphs as having the same structure independently of how blank nodes are labelled.

A loose analogy would be to consider the variables in a query written in a language like SQL or perhaps even the local variables in a method for an imperative language like Java:[12] one could relabel such local variables in a one-to-one (i.e., bijective) manner without changing the "meaning" of that query or method. Likewise, the blank nodes in an RDF graph can be relabelled (one-to-one) without changing the meaning of the RDF graph. Additionally, local variables with the same name used in different queries or methods are not considered as referring to the same thing. Likewise, blank nodes can be considered to have a local "scope" within an RDF graph.

---

[12] It is important to note that these are not existential variables like blank nodes, but they suffice for the analogy.

Example 3.15

Consider the following two RDF graphs with G on the left and G' on the right:

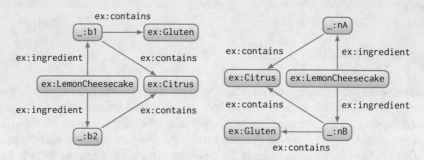

The first graph can be read as stating that Lemon Cheesecake has an ingredient that contains gluten and an ingredient that contains both gluten and citrus. The second graph can be read identically. Although drawn differently, if we map _:b1 $\leftrightarrow$ _:nB and _:b2 $\leftrightarrow$ _:nA, we can see that we get the same graph(s) differing only in blank node labels. Hence both RDF graphs are considered isomorphic.

We capture this idea more formally, starting with a preliminary definition for a blank node mapping where a blank node can map to any RDF term, whereas IRIs and literals are mapped to themselves.

Definition 5 (Blank node mapping and relabelling). We define a *blank node mapping* μ as one that maps blank nodes to RDF terms, and literals and IRIs to themselves. More formally:

- $\mu(c) = c$ for all $c \in \mathbf{IL}$, and
- $\mu(b) \in \mathbf{ILB}$ for all $b \in \mathbf{B}$

Now let G be an RDF graph. We overload notation and let $\mu(G) :=$ $\{(\mu(s), p, \mu(o)) \mid (s, p, o) \in G\}$ denote the application of a blank node mapping μ to an RDF graph G (i.e., the image of G under μ). We call μ a *blank node relabelling* if and only if $\mu(b) \in \mathbf{B}$ for all $b \in \mathbf{B}$.

Definition 6 (Isomorphic RDF graphs). Let G and G' be two RDF graphs. These RDF graphs are *isomorphic*, written $G \cong G'$, if and only if there exists a one-to-one blank node relabelling μ such that $\mu(G) = G'$.

Example 3.16

Returning to Example 3.15, if we consider a one-to-one blank node relabelling μ such that $\mu(\_:b1) = \_:nB$ and $\mu(\_:b2) = \_:nA$, we see that $\mu(G) = G'$, and hence G and G' are isomorphic: $G \cong G'$.

RDF isomorphism indicates when two RDF graphs carry the same meaning. For example, two different systems may parse an RDF document from the same location, and if that document contains implicit blank nodes without labels (which is allowed by most RDF syntaxes, as discussed later), the systems may create different labels for these blank nodes. An RDF isomorphism check would then be required to see if these RDF graphs potentially came from the same document. However, such checks can be expensive.

Remark 3.7

Given two RDF graphs, deciding whether or not they are isomorphic can be computationally costly in certain cases. To gain an intuition of why that might be the case, take the following two RDF graphs (where we omit a fixed edge label :p for brevity):

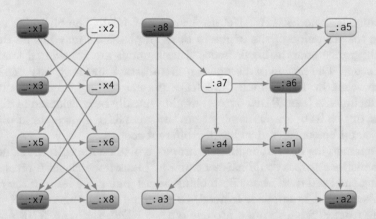

Though it may not be immediately obvious, these two RDF graphs are also isomorphic. One can, for example, map the blank nodes of the same colour in both graphs to achieve the same graph ($\_:xn \leftrightarrow \_:a(9-n)$).

The problem of deciding if two RDF graphs are isomorphic is GI-complete [194], meaning that it is in the same complexity class as the standard **graph isomorphism** problem. The problems in this class are not known to be in P nor to be NP-complete. In practice however, worst-cases are quite exotic and rare [194] (where, e.g., the above example could be handled efficiently with known well-known algorithms).

Discussion 3.5

ANNA: How important is this notion of isomorphism? Could we build
a Web of Data without such a notion?

AIDAN: Perhaps. The notion arises because we have blank nodes in
RDF graphs, which as we discussed can be useful for specifying
that something has a value, but that the value is not known or has
not been explicitly identified. So if we consider a data model where
we can define nodes without a fixed identity, then we will end up
with this question of RDF isomorphism. If we remove blank nodes,
then the problem disappears: we can check if two graphs are the
same by simply checking that the two sets of triples are the same.
But if we rather keep blank nodes, we need to check for a one-to-
one mapping to determine RDF isomorphism. On the other hand,
blank nodes are pretty useful for modelling more complex patterns
in graphs, and for enabling intuitive shortcuts in RDF syntaxes.

3.7.2 Merging RDF Graphs

Without blank nodes, two RDF graphs can be trivially combined into one by
taking the set union of the triples in both graphs. This may not be the case
if both graphs contain blank nodes. Blank nodes are considered local to a
given *scope*. The notion of a scope is quite abstract and may vary depending
on the scenario; for example, two RDF graphs coming from two different
Web documents (aka. RDF sources) would typically be considered in different
scopes, or two RDF graphs coming from the same RDF source but at different
times could be considered as having different scopes.

When merging data from different scopes, a blank node with the same label
in two distinct scopes could naively cause a "blank node clash" – erroneously
merging the local data about both blank nodes under one term in the output
– if a set union is applied. Instead, to combine two or more RDF graphs
coming from different scopes into one output RDF graph, an **RDF merge** is
used. The idea is to first relabel the blank nodes in one or both graphs such
that they no longer share blank nodes, and then take the union.

Definition 7 (RDF merge). Let G_1 and G_2 be two RDF graphs. An
RDF merge of G_1 and G_2, denoted herein as $G_1 + G_2$, is given as $G_1' \cup G_2'$,
where G_1' and G_2' are relabelled versions of G_1 and G_2 respectively such
that $G_1' \cong G_1$, $G_2' \cong G_2$ and G_1' and G_2' share no blank nodes.

The RDF merge of two RDF graphs is unique up to blank nodes labels: all possible RDF merges are pairwise isomorphic. Hence the structure of the graph produced by an RDF merge is fixed even if the blank node labels may vary depending on how the input graphs are relabelled.

Example 3.17

Consider the following RDF graphs, G_1 (left) and G_2 (right):

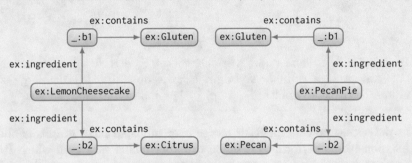

If we were to naively combine these two graphs using a plain set union $G_1 \cup G_2$, we would get the following graph:

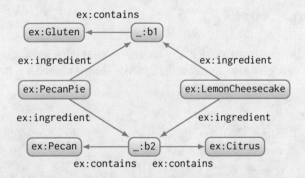

This graph does not follow from the original input graphs G_1 and G_2: ex:LemonCheesecake was not previously stated to share ingredients with ex:PecanPie. Likewise, ex:LemonCheesecake now has an ingredient containing ex:Pecan, which it did not have before.

Instead, using an RDF merge, $G_1 + G_2$, we would get the following:

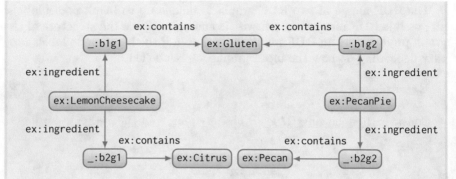

By keeping the blank nodes distinct, the merged RDF graph contains the same information as the original two graphs. This RDF merge is unique up to isomorphism (i.e., up to the blank node labels chosen).

In practice, applying an RDF merge over multiple RDF graphs is about as inexpensive as performing a union of triples. This ease with which RDF graphs can be combined is a non-trivial property of the data model.

3.7.3 Lean Graphs

Finally, we briefly mention for the moment that the existential nature of blank nodes can give rise to redundancy. We show this with a brief example.

Example 3.18

Looking at graph G (or equivalently G') of Example 3.15, it states the following two things:

1. Lemon Cheesecake has some ingredient (_:b1) that contains gluten and citrus;
2. Lemon Cheesecake has some ingredient (_:b2) that contains citrus.

The second statement follows from the first: the second statement is redundant. Hence one could remove the two triples involving _:b2 from G and it would still contain precisely the same information.

> **Remark 3.8** (i)
>
> Looking at G, it may be tempting to consider that the graph shows two different ingredients: one with gluten and another with gluten *and* citrus. However this is not the case. Recall that blank nodes refer to the *existence* of an ingredient rather than a specific ingredient.

An RDF graph without such redundancy is called a **lean RDF graph**, and with such redundancy is called a **non-lean RDF graph**. We will precisely formalise this notion of redundancy in RDF – this notion of (non-)lean graphs – when we speak in more detail about the semantics of RDF in Chapter 4.

3.7.4 Blank Nodes in RDF Datasets

Considering blank nodes in RDF datasets, the (default/named) RDF graphs in an RDF dataset *may* be considered as being in the same scope: in other words, graphs in the same RDF dataset *may* share blank nodes that refer to the existence of the same thing. Likewise, two datasets can be considered *dataset-isomorphic* if they are the same up to blank node labelling.

> **Definition 8 (Isomorphic RDF datasets).** Taking two RDF datasets $D := \{G, (x_1, G_1), \ldots, (x_n, G_n)\}$ and $D' := \{G', (x'_1, G'_1), \ldots, (x'_n, G'_n)\}$, they are considered *dataset-isomorphic*, written $D \cong D'$, if and only if there exists a one-to-one blank node mapping μ such that:
>
> - $\mu(G) = G'$, and
> - (x_i, G_i) is in D if and only if $(\mu(x_i), \mu(G_i))$ is in D'.

In other words, if we can use a single one-to-one blank node mapping to make all of the names *and* all of the graphs of one dataset identical to the other, then those two datasets are isomorphic.

> **Remark 3.9** (i)
>
> Other related notions such as the merge of two RDF datasets, lean RDF datasets, etc., have not been defined as part of the RDF 1.1 standard. In fact, it is not clear what would be a suitable semantics for such RDF datasets, where a variety of options exist and were extensively debated by the W3C – the standardisation body behind RDF and related standards – without reaching agreement. A summary of the alternatives discussed has been provided by Zimmermann [408].

3.8 Syntaxes

Having looked at examples of how to formulate more complex types of structured data in triples, we now come to the topic of how to *serialise* RDF: how to write RDF down in files for storage, parsing and processing. For the purposes of serialising RDF, machine-parsable *syntaxes* are required. A number of standard syntaxes have been proposed for RDF down through the years, each with its own advantages and disadvantages which make them suitable for different settings [245, 42, 152, 40, 39, 185, 366]. However, despite their superficial differences, all such syntaxes can be parsed (with minor exceptions) into an RDF graph. As such, an RDF-aware tool does not need to be customised for different syntaxes: tools can be built over the core data model of triples such that supporting a new syntax merely requires a reader and a writer for that syntax. We now give an overview of these syntaxes.

3.8.1 RDF/XML

The oldest standard RDF syntax (originally recommended in 1999 [245]) is **RDF/XML** [42], which is based on the widely deployed XML standard. The original rationale behind the syntax was that existing tools and languages for XML could be used as the basis for building RDF tools and languages, thus helping to bootstrap the new RDF standard in practice. Unfortunately, as we will later discuss, representing RDF graphs as XML was perhaps not as straightforward nor as fruitful as was originally anticipated. We will give a flavour of the syntax with an example; however, we first assure the reader that understanding all of the details is not critical for our purposes.

Example 3.19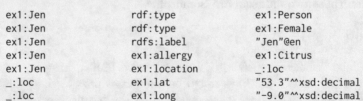

Take the following set of triples (slightly adapting the RDF graph named ex1:JensProfile in Example 3.14):

ex1:Jen	rdf:type	ex1:Person
ex1:Jen	rdf:type	ex1:Female
ex1:Jen	rdfs:label	"Jen"@en
ex1:Jen	ex1:allergy	ex1:Citrus
ex1:Jen	ex1:location	_:loc
_:loc	ex1:lat	"53.3"^^xsd:decimal
_:loc	ex1:long	"-9.0"^^xsd:decimal

These triples can be serialised in RDF/XML as follows:

```
<?xml version="1.0"?>
<!DOCTYPE img [
  <!ENTITY xsd "http://www.w3.org/2001/XMLSchema#">
]>
<rdf:RDF
  xmlns:rdf="http://www.w3.org/1999/02/22-rdf-syntax-ns#"
  xmlns:rdfs="http://www.w3.org/2000/01/rdf-schema#"
  xmlns:ex1="http://ex1.org/#">
  <ex1:Person rdf:about="http://ex1.org/#Jen">
    <rdf:type rdf:resource="http://ex1.org/#Female" />
    <rdfs:label xml:lang="en">Jen</rdfs:label>
    <ex1:allergy rdf:resource="http://ex1.org/#Citrus" />
    <ex1:location>
      <rdf:Description>
        <ex1:lat rdf:datatype="&xsd;decimal">53.3</ex1:lat>
        <ex1:long rdf:datatype="&xsd;decimal">-9.0</ex1:long>
      </rdf:Description>
    </ex1:location>
  </ex1:Person>
</rdf:RDF>
```

The document is valid XML, with balanced start and end tags, etc. The snippet starts by declaring XML entities and IRI prefixes used in the body. The root XML node in the body is always `rdf:RDF`. The names of XML nodes thereafter – like `ex1:Person`, `rdfs:label`, etc. – either refer to classes or to properties; one exception is `rdf:Description`, which denotes a resource that may not have a type. Subject and object resources can be identified by IRIs using built-in attributes like `rdf:about` (typically for subjects) or `rdf:resource` (typically for objects). Literals are specified either using attributes or text within tags. Language tags can be specified with the built-in attribute `xml:lang`. Datatype IRIs are given with the built-in attribute `rdf:datatype`.

Nesting generally follows "stripes" where an initial subject layer (like `ex1:Person` referring to the type of `ex1:Jen`) contains a list of predicate nodes as direct children (like `rdfs:label`, `ex1:allergy`, `ex1:location`), which may themselves contain a nested subject/object node (`rdf:Description` referring to a type-less blank node), which again may recursively nest predicate nodes (`ex1:lat`, `ex1:long`), and so on recursively. These striped layers – SUBJECT → PREDICATE → (SUBJECT|OBJECT) → PREDICATE → ... – encode triples.

RDF/XML also provides various convenient shortcuts for representing containers, collections, reification, etc.

However, this syntax has been the subject of some criticism. As Beckett [37] – an editor on the (revised) RDF/XML standard – put it:

"The problems of writing down a graph in a sequential document representing a tree such as the XML DOM has proved too hard to make it easy to do and clear."

In this quote, DOM refers to the Document Object Model: a tree-based abstract representation of an XML or HTML document. As per Example 3.19, the core message is that RDF/XML is not an intuitive syntax to read, to write or even to process. The original rationale behind RDF/XML (ca. 1999 [245]) – that RDF data written in an XML-based syntax would allow RDF to be processed by existing XML tools – was, in hindsight, perhaps naive. The main problem with processing RDF/XML data using XML tools and standards is the myriad ways in which the same triple and thus the same (isomorphic) RDF graph can be represented in the syntax, as we now illustrate.

Example 3.20

The same set of triples from Example 3.19 can be represented equivalently in RDF/XML (with new syntax conventions) as follows:

```xml
<?xml version="1.0"?>
<!DOCTYPE img [
  <!ENTITY xsd "http://www.w3.org/2001/XMLSchema#">
]>
<rdf:RDF
  xmlns:rdf="http://www.w3.org/1999/02/22-rdf-syntax-ns#"
  xmlns:rdfs="http://www.w3.org/2000/01/rdf-schema#"
  xmlns:ex1="http://ex1.org/#">
  <rdf:Description
      xml:lang="en"
      rdf:about="http://ex1.org/#Jen"
      rdfs:label="Jen">
    <rdf:type rdf:resource="http://ex1.org/#Person" />
    <rdf:type>
      <rdf:Description rdf:about="http://ex1.org/#Female" />
    </rdf:type>
    <ex1:allergy>
      <rdf:Description rdf:about="http://ex1.org/#Citrus" />
    </ex1:allergy>
    <ex1:location rdf:nodeID="loc" />
  </rdf:Description>
  <rdf:Description rdf:nodeID="loc">
    <ex1:long rdf:datatype="&xsd;decimal">-9.0</ex1:long>
    <ex1:lat rdf:datatype="&xsd;decimal">53.3</ex1:lat>
  </rdf:Description>
</rdf:RDF>
```

Some of the new conventions used include the use of multiple initial subject nodes, using attributes to specify literals (per `rdfs:label`) and the use of explicit blank node labels (using `rdf:nodeID`).

Although the XML DOMs of the two documents are completely different (i.e., how the nodes are nested), the RDF graph parsed from this RDF/XML would be equivalent (i.e., isomorphic) with the one parsed from the previous RDF/XML snippet. Thus, for example, if one were to try specify an XML path through the RDF data to locate the type(s) of the current node (e.g., ex1:Jen), it may be given as the name of the current node (per Example 3.19), or it may be the value of the rdf:resource attribute on a child node called rdf:type (per ex1:Person above), or it may be the rdf:about attribute on a rdf:type/rdf:Description path (per ex1:Female above), and so on.

The end result was that RDF/XML was a difficult format to work with and aside from using XML parsers to load the DOM, existing XML tools were not useful to more deeply process or query RDF. In practice, systems often convert RDF/XML to a more "direct" triple-centric graph-based representation, where RDF/XML is rarely directly processed or modelled internally as XML. In summary, the triple/graph-based nature of RDF is obscured by its representation in the RDF/XML syntax, which perhaps made RDF more difficult to understand in the early days than was necessary.

Despite its limitations, for many years, RDF/XML was still promoted as *the* RDF syntax [258]. As a result, RDF/XML is widely used in legacy data and is sometimes still considered *the* compliance format [190]. It is thus useful to have some passing familiarity with the syntax (and its limitations); having given an overview and some discussion, we point the reader to the official W3C RDF/XML specification for more details [41].

3.8.2 N-Triples

The most basic RDF syntax is **N-Triples**: a line-based syntax for RDF first (indirectly[13]) standardised in 2004 [152] and later updated in 2014 [40].

Example 3.21

The same triples from Example 3.19 can be serialised in the N-Triples syntax as follows:

```
<http://ex1.org/#Jen> <http://www.w3.org/1999/02/22-rdf-syntax-ns#type> <http://ex1.org/#Person> .
<http://ex1.org/#Jen> <http://www.w3.org/1999/02/22-rdf-syntax-ns#type> <http://ex1.org/#Female> .
<http://ex1.org/#Jen> <http://www.w3.org/2000/01/rdf-schema#label> "Jen"@en .
<http://ex1.org/#Jen> <http://ex1.org/#allergy> <http://ex1.org/#Citrus> .
<http://ex1.org/#Jen> <http://ex1.org/#location> _:loc .
_:loc <http://ex1.org/#lat> "53.3"^^<http://www.w3.org/2001/XMLSchema#decimal> .
_:loc <http://ex1.org/#long> "-9.0"^^<http://www.w3.org/2001/XMLSchema#decimal> .
```

---

[13] N-Triples was initially standardised as a syntax for representing test-cases, rather than a fully-fledged recommended RDF syntax in its own right [152].

> The syntax has a triple per line: a subject term, a predicate term and an object term. Terms are separated by a space or a tab. Each triple is terminated by a period (aka. full-stop). IRIs must be written in full and delimited by angle brackets. Literals and blank nodes are written using the same conventions we have used previously. Each line of the data stands completely independently as an RDF triple.
>
> Aside from reordering the lines or renaming the blank nodes (which again do not matter in RDF), the snippet above is *almost* the only way to write down the data from Example 3.19 as N-Triples.

In addition to the example syntax provided, comment lines can be embedded in a file using '#' as a prefix. Line feeds, carriage returns, quotes and backslashes used in literals must be escaped with \n,\r, \" and \\, resp.

We noted in the example that the snippet is *almost* the only way in which the given RDF can be written down: the only variances possible are minor syntactic details such as the use of tab instead of space to delimit terms, etc. Thus N-Triples also provides a slightly stricter canonical syntax for RDF called Canonical N-Triples [40, §4], which adds further minor syntactic restrictions to standard N-Triples where, for example, only spaces must be used to delimit terms (not tab), comments are disallowed, etc.

The line-based format of N-Triples make it a popular choice for serialising large dumps of RDF data and for streaming applications: since each line can be directly and independently consumed as a triple, and assuming a canonical representation for each triple, one can count triples, sort/unique triples, extract triples matching a certain regex, split/concatenate files, etc., using standard line-based tools such as those provided by UNIX (e.g., cat, grep, sort, sed, etc.). Likewise if an application encounters a syntax error in the middle of a large file of, say, tens of billions of triples, it can opt to recover by skipping that triple and moving on to the next line; such recovery would not be as straightforward or clean in a syntax like RDF/XML.

The main drawbacks of N-Triples are that it is not very human-readable and it is far from concise: the data contain a lot of repetitions of long IRIs with common prefixes. No shortcuts are available for common RDF patterns. Thus data sizes are larger than necessary (though standard compression techniques like GZip can achieve high performance over such repetitions).

3.8.3 Turtle

Perhaps the most human-friendly syntax – both in terms of reading and writing – is the **Terse RDF Triple Language (Turtle)**, which aims to allow "RDF graphs to be completely written in a compact and natural text form, with abbreviations for common usage patterns and datatypes" [39]. Though

Turtle was standardised for the first time in 2014 as part of the RDF 1.1 effort [39], it had been documented and used in implementations for many years previously [38]. Turtle is thus supported by many legacy tools that long pre-date 2014. Turtle is in a similar family of syntaxes as N-Triples, where both are inspired by **Notation3 (N3)** [49].[14]. In fact, every valid N-Triples file is also a valid Turtle file. However, Turtle further allows a variety of useful abbreviations and shortcuts in order to make serialising RDF more concise.

Example 3.22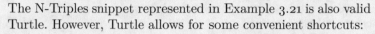

The N-Triples snippet represented in Example 3.21 is also valid Turtle. However, Turtle allows for some convenient shortcuts:

```
@base <http://ex1.org/> .
@prefix rdfs: <http://www.w3.org/2000/01/rdf-schema#> .
@prefix ex1: <http://ex1.org/#> .
  <#Jen> a <http://ex1.org/#Person> , ex1:Female ;
    rdfs:label "Jen"@en ;
    <#allergy> <#Citrus> ;
    ex1:location [ ex1:lat 53.3 ; ex1:long -9.0 ] .
```

This serialises an RDF graph isomorphic to the previous examples.

There are three options to specify IRIs; the following three options are equivalent assuming the base and prefix IRIs are defined as above:

1. written in full: `<http://ex1.org/#Person>`;
2. using a base IRI: `<#Person>`;
3. using a prefixed name: `ex1:Person`.

Instead of repeating the subject, a semi-colon denotes that the subject is being reused. Likewise, a comma can be used to indicate that the subject and predicate are being reused. The term 'a' can be used as a shortcut for the commonly-used term `rdf:type`. Blank nodes can be nested by using square brackets '`[]`'. Finally, certain unquoted literals can be interpreted as datatype literals, including:

- unquoted numbers without decimal points, parsed as `xsd:integer`;
- unquoted numbers with decimal points, parsed as `xsd:decimal`;
- scientific notation (e.g., `-1.9E03`), parsed as `xsd:double`;
- booleans (either `true` or `false`), parsed as `xsd:boolean`.

Turtle also provides a convenient shortcut for RDF collections, which greatly simplifies their inclusion in Turtle documents.

---

[14] It is a common misconception that N3 is an RDF syntax (the title of the most authoritative documentation "Notation3 (N3): A readable RDF syntax" [49] probably does not help). However, N3 represents a strict superset of RDF. Turtle can be thought of roughly as the intersection of RDF and N3.

Example 3.23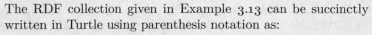

The RDF collection given in Example 3.13 can be succinctly written in Turtle using parenthesis notation as:

```
@base <http://ex.org/#> .
  <Lemonade> <ingredients> ( <Sugar> <Water> <Lemon> ) .
```

This collection would otherwise have to be written as (here using the next most concise form with nested implicit blank nodes):

```
@base <http://ex.org/#> .
@prefix rdf: <http://www.w3.org/1999/02/22-rdf-syntax-ns#> .
  <Lemonade> <ingredients> [
   rdf:first <Sugar> ; rdf:rest [
     rdf:first <Water> ; rdf:rest [
       rdf:first <Lemon> ; rdf:rest rdf:nil
     ]
   ] .
```

Due to its relative conciseness and readability, Turtle is often used in scenarios where data need to be revised or edited manually. Furthermore, the standard query language for RDF follows a similar syntax. In this book, we will often use Turtle in examples for precisely these reasons. For full details on the syntax, we refer the reader to the latest W3C specification [39].

Remark 3.10

Referring back to the usefulness of blank nodes in RDF, we note that the sorts of syntactic shortcuts we have seen thus far are made possible by blank nodes, which obviate the need to name every node in the RDF graph explicitly. For instance, looking at Example 3.23, the Turtle shortcut for RDF Collections assumes that the implicit subject nodes of the list can be labelled automatically and that those labels should not affect the RDF graph. If IRIs were used to "fill in the gaps", (i) we could potentially have naming clashes with parsers generating existing IRIs referring to something different elsewhere, and (ii) unless every parser agreed on which IRIs to use for that particular collection in that particular graph, different parsers would produce different RDF graphs. Using blank nodes to fill the gaps, different parsers produce isomorphic RDF graphs and do not need to worry about naming clashes.

Exercise 3.2

*Model the following (incomplete) data as an RDF graph in Tur-
tle syntax. Be sure to specify datatypes and language tags as appropriate
and to use classes where appropriate. You do not need to model information not explicitly given, even if obvious from background knowledge
(e.g., that New York is a city). You also do not need to explicitly declare
properties to be members of the class* rdf:Property.

*The apartment block with address "146, 5th Avenue, New York, US", has 24
floors and 120 apartments. It was constructed in the year 1976. The second
floor of the apartment block has 5 apartments: 201, 202, 203, 204 and 205.
Apartment 201 is a one-bedroom apartment with two people living there:
John Smith and his wife Mary Smith. Both John and Mary have been living
in the apartment since October 12th, 2013. Before that, Simon Murphy lived
in apartment 201 from December 1st, 2011 to October 12th, 2013. Next door
to apartment 201, in apartment 202, lives Jim O'Brien and his son Harry
O'Brien; Jim has been living there since May 12th, 2001 and Harry since
June 5th, 2009. Apartment 202 has two bedrooms.*

You should use an online Turtle validator (see the book's homepage
http://webofdatabook.org *for links) to check the syntax of your Turtle
file. Note that there is no unique solution but that the exercise raises
some relevant challenges for modelling information as an RDF graph.*

3.8.4 RDFa

The **RDF in Attributes (RDFa)** [3] syntax allows for embedding RDF data directly into XML-based documents. RDFa was first recommended by the W3C
in 2008 [3] for embedding RDF into **eXtensible HyperText Markup Language
(XHTML)** documents (which are similar to HTML documents but with the
additional requirement that they further be valid XML documents). RDFa 1.1
was subsequently designed to relax some of the reliance on XML/XHTML-
specific namespaces, which crucially meant that RDFa could be embedded
into a broader range of HTML documents, such as HTML 4.0 or HTML 5.0;
RDFa 1.1 reached recommendation status in June 2012, with a minor revision
subsequently released a little over a year later in August 2013 [185].

The core motivation for RDFa is to allow Web publishers to embed structured information directly into legacy (X)HTML Web documents, rather than
hosting separate documents offering "pure" RDF. In other words, instead of
hosting a human-readable version of a document and a machine-readable
version of a document, publishers can simply embed machine-readable data
in the human-readable document markup. By reducing infrastructural overhead, RDFa hopes to lower the barrier-to-entry for publishing RDF data,
allowing to "*augment visual data with machine-readable hints*" [3].

In total there are three profiles to consider:

RDFa 1.0 [3]: limited to use with XML-based documents supporting built-in namespace features, such as XHTML.

RDFa 1.1 Core [185]: allows use of custom namespace features that are compatible with, e.g., HTML5.

RDFa 1.1 Lite [185]: a lightweight subset of RDFa 1.1 Core that simplifies the syntax but is still sufficient for many use-cases.

We now give a brief example of how RDFa 1.1 can be used to embed triples into HTML documents.

Example 3.24

The following exemplifies how triples can be embedded into a simple HTML5 webpage about a recipe using RDFa 1.1.

```
<!DOCTYPE html>
<html>
<head>
  <meta charset="utf-8" />
  <title>Recipe for Coffee Parfait</title>
  <base href="http://ex.org/" />
</head>
<body vocab="http://ex.org/#" lang="en"
  prefix="rdfs: http://www.w3.org/2000/01/rdf-schema#">
  <div typeof="Recipe" resource="#CoffeeParfait">
    <h1 property="rdfs:label">Coffee Parfait</h1>

    <p>Time: <span property="minutes" datatype="xsd:integer"
                    content="25">25 mins</span></p>

    <h2>Ingredients:</h2>
    <ul rel="ingredient">
      <li about="#Yolk" property="rdfs:label">Egg Yolk</li>
      <li about="#Sugar" property="rdfs:label">Sugar</li>
      <li about="#Cream" property="rdfs:label">Cream</li>
      <li about="#Coffee" property="rdfs:label">Coffee</li>
    </ul>
  </div>
</body>
</html>
```

The document is a valid HTML5 document that can be rendered in a browser. The syntax specifying the serialisation of triples is embedded into the HTML5 document itself, shown in bold above.

There are three main HTML/RDF 1.1 Lite features that can be used to define shortcuts for IRIs: base is used to define a base IRI against which relative resource IRIs will be resolved; prefix can be used to define a map of namespace shortcuts for IRIs; and vocab defines the prefix used for classes and properties in the absence of a namespace. RDFa also supports common prefixes, like `rdf:`, `rdfs:`, `xsd:`, that will be mapped to their usual values (see Table 3.1) even if not defined.

A resource can be initialised with a class (`typeof`) and an IRI identifier (`resource` or `about`). Nested properties can then be defined for those resources (`property`). Text nodes are interpreted as literal values; `datatype` can be used to specify a datatype IRI; otherwise if there is an in-scope `lang` definition, it will be applied to the literal. A text node can be overwritten using `content` so as to provide a different human-readable value and machine-readable value. The `rel` attribute can be used to specify a group of properties. Note that from these features, the `about`, `datatype`, `content` and `rel` attributes are part of an extended RDFa 1.1 Core syntax and are not part of RDFa 1.1 Lite.

In the above example, the order of the elements of the HTML list will not be preserved in the RDF output. From the above snippet, the following RDF data can be extracted (represented in Turtle format):

```
@prefix rdfa: <http://www.w3.org/ns/rdfa#> .
@prefix ex: <http://ex.org/#> .
@prefix rdfs: <http://www.w3.org/2000/01/rdf-schema#> .
@prefix xsd: <http://www.w3.org/2001/XMLSchema#> .

<http://ex.org/> rdfa:usesVocabulary ex: .

ex:CoffeeParfait a ex:Recipe ;
    rdfs:label "Coffee Parfait"@en ; ex:minutes 25 ;
    ex:ingredient ex:Coffee , ex:Cream , ex:Yolk , ex:Sugar .

ex:Coffee rdfs:label "Coffee"@en .
ex:Cream rdfs:label "Cream"@en .
ex:Yolk rdfs:label "Egg Yolk"@en .
ex:Sugar rdfs:label "Sugar"@en .
```

The first triple is an implicit feature of RDFa: such triples are exported for values of `vocab` attributes. The rest of the triples represent the remaining structure of the RDFa document.

RDFa (1.1) has been adopted for use in a variety of applications, including Facebook's Open Graph Protocol and the Schema.org initiative by Google, Yahoo!, Microsoft and Yandex; these initiatives were discussed in Section 2.3.

These examples give an idea of the main features of RDFa. For more detail on the RDFa (1.1) syntax, we refer the reader to the RDF 1.1 Primer [184].

3.8.5 JSON-LD

JavaScript Object Notation for Linked Data (JSON-LD) [366] is a syntax
for encoding triples in JSON data. In fact, the JSON data model already has
some inherent similarities with RDF, where one could consider a JSON object
as an RDF resource, and JSON attribute–value pairs as RDF predicate–
object pairs, etc. Thus the key contribution of JSON-LD is to provide a
syntactic scheme by which global IRI identifiers can be associated with JSON
objects, attributes and values. Once this IRI specification is in place, the
mapping from JSON to RDF becomes relatively straightforward.

Example 3.25

The following snippet illustrates how the RDF data from Example 3.24 could be likewise represented in JSON-LD.

```
{
  "@context": {
    "xsd": "http://www.w3.org/2001/XMLSchema#",
    "@base": "http://example.com/",
    "@vocab": "http://example.com/#",
    "label": "http://www.w3.org/2000/01/rdf-schema#label",
    "minutes": {
      "@id": "minutes",
      "@type": "xsd:integer"
    },
    "@language": "en"
  },
  "@id": "#CoffeeParfait",
  "@type": "Recipe",
  "label": "Coffee Parfait",
  "minutes": "25",
  "ingredient": [
    { "@id": "#Yolk", "label": "Egg Yolk"},
    { "@id": "#Sugar", "label": "Sugar"},
    { "@id": "#Cream", "label": "Cream"},
    { "@id": "#Coffee", "label": "Coffee"}
  ]
}
```

The RDF that can be extracted from the above snippet corresponds with the Turtle data given in Example 3.24 after dropping the first (RDFa-specific) rdfa:usesVocabulary triple.

The context indicates how attribute strings and values should be mapped to RDF terms. In this case, the context specifies the standard xsd: prefix, a base IRI as a default for resolving generic value strings (e.g., #CoffeeParfait, #EggYolk, etc.), a vocab IRI as a default for resolving attribute strings and type-values (Recipe, minutes, ingredient), an IRI specifically for the label attribute name (which overrides the default vocab declaration and indicates that the value should be considered a literal not an IRI), as well as an IRI and value-type for the minutes attribute. A default language is also provided. Contexts can be imported from other JSON-LD documents on the Web or can be applied to vanilla JSON documents to extract triples.

In the body of the JSON data, @id can be used to provide the identifier for the subject and @type as a shortcut for the standard rdf:type property. The data will be mapped to RDF following the guidelines laid out in the context. Any attribute–value without a known mapping to an RDF term will be silently skipped in the export.

By default, JSON arrays are mapped in a lossy manner: the order of their elements is lost. However, often this order information is important; hence, JSON-LD allows for specifying the keyword @list on arrays

Example 3.26

The RDF list extracted from the following JSON-LD snippet will be equivalent to the one shown previously in Example 3.13:

```
{
  "@context": {
    "@base": "http://example.com/",
    "@vocab": "http://example.com/#"
  },
  "@id": "Lemonade",
  "ingredient": {
    "@list" : [
        { "@id": "Sugar" } ,
        { "@id": "Water" } ,
        { "@id": "Lemon" }
    ]
  }
}
```

Here the @list keyword specifies that the order of the array should be represented in the output using an RDF list.

JSON-LD also has a wide range of other features not exemplified above, such as identifiers for blank nodes, RDF dataset representations, inverse properties, and so forth. For more information on these features, we refer the interested reader to the official W3C specification [366].

Remark 3.12   (i)

JSON-LD can represent triples that are not valid RDF triples: principally, JSON-LD allows blank nodes to be used in the predicate position. In such cases, the specification recommends that the blank node terms in the predicate position are mapped – either by the producer or consumer – to IRIs, or that generalised RDF (RDF that places no restrictions on the usage of RDF terms) is output [366].

At the time of writing, however, a new version of JSON-LD is under development, called JSON-LD 1.1 [229]. This new version states that allowing blank nodes as predicates is considered obsolete, and may be removed in future. We refer to the JSON-LD 1.1 candidate recommendation for details of this and other (proposed) changes [229].

3.8.6 Summary of RDF Graph Syntaxes

We now provide a brief summary of the different RDF syntaxes:

RDF/XML [41]: an XML-based syntax; the first standard RDF syntax.
- *Pros*: XML-compatible; widely supported.
- *Cons*: unintuitive; diverse XML can represent the same RDF data.

N-Triples [40]: simple line-based syntax for RDF.
- *Pros*: simple to serialise, parse, and process.
- *Cons*: verbose; full IRIs are less human-friendly.

Turtle [39]: human-friendly syntax for RDF.
- *Pros*: most human-friendly to read and write; concise.
- *Cons*: more complex to parse and process.

RDFa [185]: syntax embeddable in HTML webpages.
- *Pros*: allows for managing one webpage for humans and machines.
- *Cons*: requires extraction from a webpage; can be unintuitive.

JSON-LD [366]: a JSON-based RDF syntax.
- *Pros*: JSON-compatible; widely used; intuitive; supports datasets.
- *Cons*: incompatibilities with RDF (resolved in JSON-LD 1.1 [229]).

3.8.7 RDF Dataset Syntaxes

Thus far, all of the syntaxes are only used to encode RDF graphs. However, with the advent of RDF 1.1, the W3C have recommended a number of syntaxes for serialising RDF datasets. Though not mentioned before, JSON-LD offers support for serialising RDF datasets. Other dedicated syntaxes have been proposed for RDF datasets, including **N-Quads** [87] and **TriG** [88].

JSON-LD [366] provides syntax for naming and scoping RDF graphs.
N-Quads [87] extends N-Triples syntax with an optional fourth element that
    indicates the name of the RDF graph to which the given triple belongs.
TriG [88] extends Turtle syntax to allow for scoping parts of the Turtle data
    into different graphs.

Example 3.27

In order to give a flavour of how JSON-LD, N-Quads and TriG are used to serialise RDF datasets, we provide a succinct example of one named graph with two triples and a default graph with one triple.
    We first give the data in JSON-LD, where the `@graph` keyword can be used to group triples into named graphs:

```
[
  {
    "@context": {
      "@base": "http://ex.org/",
      "@vocab": "http://ex.org/#"
    },
    "@id": "G-A",
    "@graph": [
      {
        "@id": "Anne",
        "knows": [
          { "@id": "Frank" },
          { "@id": "Julie" }
        ]
      }
    ]
  },
  {
    "@context": {
      "@base": "http://ex.org/",
      "@vocab": "http://ex.org/#"
    } ,
    "@id": "Anne" ,
    "name" : "Anne"
  }
]
```

Next we show the same data in N-Quads, which extends N-Triples to allow a fourth (optional) element indicating a named graph:

```
<http://ex.org/Anne> <http://ex.org/#knows> <http://ex.org/Frank> <http://ex.org/G-A> .
<http://ex.org/Anne> <http://ex.org/#knows> <http://ex.org/Julie> <http://ex.org/G-A> .
<http://ex.org/Anne> <http://ex.org/#name> "Anne" .
```

Like N-Triples, N-Quads does not support any shortcuts, and is particularly well suited to line-based processing. Any valid N-Triples document is also a valid N-Quads document (with a single default graph only).

Finally we show the data in TriG, which extends upon Turtle and allows named graphs to be specified as follows:

```
@base <http://ex.org/> .
@prefix ex: <http://ex.org/#> .
<G-A> {
  <Anne> ex:knows <Frank> , <Julie> .
}
<Anne> ex:name "Anne" .
```

Like Turtle, TriG is perhaps the most "human-friendly" and concise of the three syntaxes. The same types of shortcuts as supported by Turtle are supposed likewise by TriG, where every valid Turtle document is also a valid TriG document (with a single default graph only).

We refer to the respective W3C specifications for further details [366, 87, 88].

3.9 Summary

In this chapter, we provided a primer on RDF 1.1, where we detailed the types of terms that RDF permits, how they are combined to form triples, and how sets of triples form graphs. Thereafter we discussed the notion of classes and properties, and outlined the core vocabulary that RDF provides to describe bags, lists, n-ary relations and reification. We then discussed how multiple graphs can be named and combined to form an RDF dataset. We subsequently discussed some complications that arise from allowing blank nodes in RDF graphs and datasets. Finally we illustrated various syntaxes for RDF with examples, and discussed their relative strengths and weaknesses.

The RDF standard(s) provides a flexible, graph-structured data model. Thus RDF provides a concrete MODEL and set of SYNTAXES from which we can (potentially) begin to build a Web of Data. Likewise, the use of Web identifiers (IRIs) to name entities will allow us to embed LINKS in RDF.

3.10 Discussion

Discussion 3.6

JULIE: So to create the Web of Data we need RDF?

AIDAN: Well we need *something like* RDF: a core data model that is standardised, agreed upon, and flexible for many use-cases, with the ability to use globally-unique Web identifiers. RDF has all the fundamental ingredients we need.

FRANK: So then data in formats like JSON, XML, CSV or Microdata would not form part of the Web of Data?

AIDAN: The problem with such formats is that they are difficult to integrate. For example, imagine trying to integrate a CSV file with a JSON file: how would you do it? Even integrating CSV with CSV or JSON with JSON or XML with XML is difficult. On the other hand, with RDF, to initially integrate two graphs, you can simply take the union (keeping blank nodes distinct). So it is not that JSON, XML or CSV would not form part of the Web of Data, but we would need a way to integrate data in such formats with data represented in other formats. One way to do that would be by mapping them – for example, using JSON-LD, or methods discussed later – to a common data format, like RDF. This would save having to map all such formats in a pairwise manner, for example. Furthermore, RDF then serves as the cornerstone for further standards, as will be described in the chapters that follow.

Chapter 4
RDF Schema and Semantics

Every day, we as humans make simple logical deductions to communicate and understand the world around us. Some deductions are fundamental to interpreting language, such as to conclude that any *"ape"* is also an *"animal"*, or that the term *"niece"* refers to the *"daughter"* of a *"sibling"*. Yet other deductions may relate less explicitly to language and more to our understanding of how the world works; for example, we may understand that the *"niece"* of a *"human"* must also be a *"human"*, not by definition in the language (this would not be found, for example, in the dictionary definition of *"niece"*), but as a consequence of how we understand the real world.

Though crucial to emulate some form of *"understanding"* of its content, machines on the current Web are not typically empowered to make such deductions in any general, systematic way. The burden of deduction is thus rather left to the humans – be they the developers of a website or its users. Such processes of deduction are often repetitive and the burden may need to be repeated on many websites. What, then, of the idea of empowering machines on the Web to draw such deductions automatically on our behalf? If we could begin to empower machines in this fashion, they could start to draw together and make sense of Web data at an unprecedented scale. We can start by instructing machines on how to make relatively simple deductions that will later form the basis for more complex deductions.

> **Example 4.1**
>
> The Wikidata knowledge graph (as was discussed in Section 2.3.1) publishes user-curated data on the Web using the RDF standard. In this knowledge graph, we can find data about a wide variety of entities of a wide variety of *types* (aka. *classes*). One such type is an *astronomical body*, which includes increasingly more specific types, forming a class hierarchy as depicted in the following:

© Springer Nature Switzerland AG 2020
A. Hogan, *The Web of Data*, https://doi.org/10.1007/978-3-030-51580-5_4

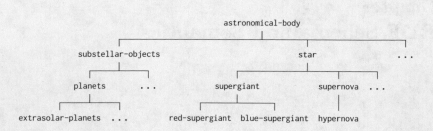

Now let's say we wished to find *a list of the names of all astronomical bodies discovered this century* from the (entire) knowledge-base. To facilitate these types of query, we could consider three options:

1. Editors of the knowledge-base would explicitly type each entity (e.g., *Betelguese*) with all of its (super-)types, (e.g., not only *red supergiant*, but also *supergiant / star / astronomical body*).
2. Each user who wishes to pose such a query would write it in such a way as to capture all of the relevant sub-types, such as *red supergiant, supergiant, galaxy, extrasolar planets*, and so forth.
3. The sub-type relations are provided by the editors and later can be used to automatically deduce the types of a specific entity.

Clearly the third option should greatly reduce the manual load on the (human) editors and users of the knowledge-base, especially since the number of types (*supergiant, galaxy*, etc.) is far less than the number of specific instances of those types (*Betelguese, Andromeda*, etc.). Generalising this idea, we may want to apply much more diverse forms of deductions over such a knowledge-base: not only over astronomical bodies, or even types/classes, but also perhaps over relations/properties (e.g., to define that a *planet* has the same *constellation* as its *parent star*), or more complex patterns (e.g., the *child astronomical body* of a *star* must be of type *substellar object*), and so forth. Hence ideally we would have some declarative means to specify the semantics of such terms, combined with a general process of deduction to be able to automatically conclude, for example, that if the entity *Betelguese* is a *red supergiant*, then it must also be a *supergiant*, a *star*, an *astronomical body*, that its children (if any) must be *substellar objects*, and so forth.

While the previous example involves deductions applied to one knowledge graph on one website (Wikidata), we would also like to be able to apply such deductions over multiple sources of data on the Web.

Example 4.2

Imagine a user wishing to find *dessert recipes* that are *citrus-free*. Every recipe website will have a different way of finding *citrus-free* recipes, all of which will be based on human deduction: be it through an explicit query hard-coded by the developers to avoid ingredients like *lemon* or *lime*, or a tagging system where users can annotate recipes with allergy information, or use of explicit keywords in the description, or simply assuming that the user will filter the search results manually by themselves. But in all such cases, the process of deduction is the same: *recipes* with *ingredients* that *contain citrus* themselves *contain citrus*. Rather if these recipes were described in a (more-or-less) standard way across websites, and if we had an external source of data about which foods contain citrus, a machine could – assuming a suitable process of deduction – apply automatic filtering of recipes containing citrus without requiring any specific interfaces.

As previously discussed in Section 2.2.3, for machines to be able to make such deductions, we need mechanisms to make the logical SEMANTICS of the vocabulary used in the machine-readable data explicit, be it to define the relations between terms in the vocabulary (e.g., "*brother*" is a "*sibling*" who is "*male*"), or to define patterns that capture common-sense knowledge (e.g., that the "*child*" of a "*human*" is "*human*"). While us humans must still provide the machines with such semantics, the idea is to do so in a general manner to allow reuse of such semantic definitions and automated deductive systems across the Web. Machines can then apply deductions automatically on our behalf, emulating a more human-like understanding of the Web's content.

Along these lines, two main standards have been proposed for defining semantics over RDF data: **RDF Schema (RDFS)** and the **Web Ontology Language (OWL)**. The RDFS standard suffices to express the semantic definitions needed to automate the deductions given in the following example.

Example 4.3

Take for example the following RDF triple:

```
ex:WilliamGolding      ex:wroteNovel          ex:LordOfTheFlies
```

Let us assume that in the same `ex:` vocabulary we also have the properties `ex:authored` and `ex:contributedTo`, and we also have the classes `ex:Novelist`, `ex:Author`, `ex:Person`, `ex:Novel`, `ex:LiteraryWork`. A person who speaks English could thus assume that if the above triple were true, then the following triples would also intuitively hold true as a consequence within that given vocabulary:

ex:WilliamGolding	rdf:type	ex:Novelist
ex:WilliamGolding	rdf:type	ex:Author
ex:WilliamGolding	rdf:type	ex:Person
ex:LordOfTheFlies	rdf:type	ex:Novel
ex:LordOfTheFlies	rdf:type	ex:LiteraryWork
ex:WilliamGolding	ex:authored	ex:LordOfTheFlies
ex:WilliamGolding	ex:contributedTo	ex:LordOfTheFlies

That person would assume these latter seven triples hold true because of some background knowledge about the world and the semantics of English: all novels are written by novelists, all novels are literary works, anyone who wrote a novel must have contributed to that novel, and so forth. Thus if a person were to ask for all novelists in the data, they would (ideally) expect that ex:WilliamGolding be returned as an answer on the basis of the original triple stating that he wrote a novel, even if he were not explicitly typed as a novelist in the data.

If a machine is to give the expected behaviour in this case, it will need to have some semantics made explicit about the vocabulary.

While RDFS suffices for the kinds of deductions shown in Example 4.3, more complex definitions are supported by the OWL standard. This chapter will first deal with RDFS while the following chapter will deal with OWL.

4.1 Overview

In this chapter, we will first introduce RDFS: a lightweight extension of the RDF vocabulary that allows for explicitly defining the types of semantics that were needed in Example 4.3. We will then discuss how the semantics of RDF and RDFS can be defined formally and, indeed, why such a formal definition is important. Finally, we discuss a set of rules that can be used to draw deductive conclusions over data using the RDF and RDFS vocabulary.

Historical Note 4.1

The first draft of the RDF Schema (RDFS) specification was published in April 1998 as a W3C Working Note [80]. The original 1998 proposal was heavily modified in later versions. The modern RDFS specification became a W3C Recommendation in early 2004 [79] along with the first version of a formal RDF semantics [179]. An updated RDFS 1.1 version of the specification [81], along with an updated formal semantics [180], were released in February 2014 alongside RDF 1.1. This chapter reflects the updated versions of the RDFS 1.1 and RDF Semantics 1.1 standards (unless the version is otherwise specified).

The remainder of this chapter is structured as follows:

Section 4.2 introduces the RDFS vocabulary with examples of the types of
   semantics it can express.
Section 4.3 discusses the formal definition of the semantics of the RDF and
   RDFS vocabularies.
Section 4.4 describes inference rules that can be used to make deductions
   over data using the RDF(S) vocabulary.
Sections 4.5 and 4.6 conclude the chapter with a summary and discussion.

4.2 RDFS Vocabulary

RDFS extends the RDF vocabulary with a set of novel terms that form the
RDFS vocabulary. Most of these terms are assigned a fixed semantics. We
now describe these terms grouped by their purpose.

4.2.1 Sub-class, Sub-property, Domain and Range

Within the RDFS vocabulary are four key terms that allow for specifying
well-defined relationships between classes and properties and that form the
heart of RDFS [286], as follows:

---

rdfs:subClassOf relates a class C with a class D such that all instances
   of C are instances of D.
rdfs:subPropertyOf relates a property P with a property Q such that
   any pair of resources related by P must also be related by Q.
rdfs:domain relates a property P to a class C such that if P relates
   resource x to resource y, then x is an instance of C.
rdfs:range relates a property P to a class C such that if P relates
   resource x to resource y, then y is an instance of C.

We now describe these four RDFS terms in more detail.

An RDF(S) class C is considered a *sub-class* of an RDF(S) class D if any
instance of C is also an instance of D. In this case, rdfs:subClassOf makes
explicit this semantic relation between C and D.

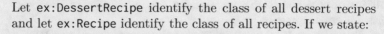

Example 4.4

Let `ex:DessertRecipe` identify the class of all dessert recipes and let `ex:Recipe` identify the class of all recipes. If we state:

```
ex:DessertRecipe        rdfs:subClassOf         ex:Recipe
```

we represent the claim that any instance of the dessert recipe class must also be an instance of the recipe class. So if we further state:

```
ex:DessertRecipe        rdfs:subClassOf         ex:Recipe
ex:LemonPie             rdf:type                ex:DessertRecipe
```

from these claims would follow the conclusion:

```
ex:LemonPie             rdf:type                ex:Recipe
```

Observe that it must hold that every class is a sub-class of itself, and that the sub-class relation is transitive, meaning that if C is a sub-class of D and D is a sub-class of E, then C must be a sub-class of E.

Example 4.5

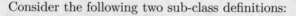

Consider the following two sub-class definitions:

```
ex:VeganRecipe          rdfs:subClassOf         ex:VegetarianRecipe
ex:VegetarianRecipe     rdfs:subClassOf         ex:Recipe
```

Trivially we can say that each class is also a sub-class of itself since the rule "*C is considered a* sub-class *of an RDF(S) class D if any instance of C is also an instance of D*" trivially holds when $C = D$.

```
ex:VeganRecipe          rdfs:subClassOf         ex:VeganRecipe
ex:VegetarianRecipe     rdfs:subClassOf         ex:VegetarianRecipe
ex:Recipe               rdfs:subClassOf         ex:Recipe
```

Next consider the following additional triple:

```
ex:LemonPie             rdf:type                ex:VeganRecipe
```

We can first conclude:

```
ex:LemonPie             rdf:type                ex:VegetarianRecipe
```

and thereafter:

```
ex:LemonPie             rdf:type                ex:Recipe
```

From this we can see that any time x is an instance of class C, where class C is a sub-class of D and class D is a sub-class of E, then x must be an instance of class E. Hence intuitively we can consider `rdfs:subClassOf` to be transitives, and in this case we could conclude:

ex:VeganRecipe	rdfs:subClassOf	ex:Recipe

Next, an RDF property P is considered a *sub-property* of an RDF property Q if any pair of resources related by P is also related by Q. In this case, `rdfs:subPropertyOf` makes explicit the relation between P and Q.

Example 4.6

Let `ex:hasIngredient` identify the relation from a recipe to its individual ingredients and let `ex:contains` identify the relation from some resource to some other resource it contains. If we state:

ex:hasIngredient	rdfs:subPropertyOf	ex:contains

we represent the claim that any two resources related by the former property must also be related by the latter. So if we further state:

ex:LemonPie	ex:hasIngredient	ex:Lemon

from these two claims would follow the conclusion:

ex:LemonPie	ex:contains	ex:Lemon

As was the case for sub-class, every property is a sub-property of itself, and the sub-property relation is again transitives.

Example 4.7

Let's consider:

ex:hasTopping	rdfs:subPropertyOf	ex:hasIngredient
ex:hasIngredient	rdfs:subPropertyOf	ex:contains

From these two triples, we can conclude:

ex:hasTopping	rdfs:subPropertyOf	ex:hasTopping
ex:hasIngredient	rdfs:subPropertyOf	ex:hasIngredient
ex:contains	rdfs:subPropertyOf	ex:contains

and:

ex:hasTopping	rdfs:subPropertyOf	ex:contains

The intuition is similar as before for sub-class in Example 4.5.

Next, an RDF property P is considered to have the *domain C* if any resource in the subject position of the relation P is also an instance of C. In this case, `rdfs:domain` defines the relation between P and C.

Example 4.8

If we state:

ex:hasIngredient	rdfs:domain	ex:Recipe
ex:LemonPie	ex:hasIngredient	ex:Lemon

from these two claims would follow the conclusion:

ex:LemonPie	rdf:type	ex:Recipe

Finally, an RDF property P is considered to have the *range C* if any resource in the *object* position of the relation P is also an instance of C. In this case, `rdfs:range` defines the relation between P and C.

Example 4.9

If we state:

ex:hasIngredient	rdfs:range	ex:Ingredient
ex:LemonPie	ex:hasIngredient	ex:Lemon

from these two claims would follow the conclusion:

ex:Lemon	rdf:type	ex:Ingredient

Remark 4.1

A common misconception is that `rdfs:domain` and `rdfs:range` act as a form of constraint, ensuring respectively that the subject or object resource of a given relation is typed with a given class. This is not directly the case in RDF(S), where data are assumed to be incomplete and such definitions are used to "complete" the data by inferring the appropriate type rather than to flag the data as missing a type. Another related misconception is that `rdfs:domain` and `rdfs:range` are used to check that the type of a subject or object resource is "correct": this is not always the case since a resource can be typed under multiple classes.

For example, if we had the following triples:

ex:hasIngredient	rdfs:range	ex:Ingredient
ex:LemonPie	ex:hasIngredient	ex:Lemon
ex:Lemon	rdf:type	ex:Colour

These triples do not necessarily indicate a problem from the perspective of RDFS. Rather we can conclude the additional triple:

```
ex:Lemon                 rdf:type                 ex:Ingredient
```

Now ex:Lemon simply has two types. Nowhere have we explicitly defined that something cannot be an instance of both ex:Colour and ex:Ingredient (this can be defined in OWL, discussed in Chapter 5).

Another related and common mistake is to assign multiple domains (or multiple ranges) to a property with the intention of saying that the subject (or object) is of one of those types; for example:

```
ex:hasBakingTime      rdfs:domain          ex:CakeRecipe
ex:hasBakingTime      rdfs:domain          ex:CasseroleRecipe
ex:hasBakingTime      rdfs:domain          ex:PieRecipe
. . .                 . . .                . . .
```

If the intent in this example is to state that having a baking time indicates that the recipe is *either* a cake, or a pie, or a casserole, then this usage of rdfs:domain is mistaken since any recipe with a defined baking time will be concluded to have *all* of these types. Instead, to satisfy that intent, it would be more appropriate to define the domain of this property as a class that generalises these possible types:

```
ex:hasBakingTime      rdfs:domain          ex:OvenRecipe
```

where we could further define:

```
ex:CakeRecipe         rdfs:subClassOf      ex:OvenRecipe
ex:CasseroleRecipe    rdfs:subClassOf      ex:OvenRecipe
ex:PieRecipe          rdfs:subClassOf      ex:OvenRecipe
. . .                 . . .                . . .
```

(On a side note, it will be possible to define this disjunctive "or" style semantics using class unions in OWL, described in Chapter 5.)

It is then possible to draw conclusions – or **entailments** – from data using RDFS terms. More specifically, given a particular semantics, we can define a notion of entailment between two RDF graphs such that if we hold the first graph to be true, then we must also hold the second graph to be true under that semantics. In this case, the second graph "says nothing new" that was not already covered – possibly implicitly – by the first graph. Equivalently – and slightly more formally – we say that if A entails B under a given semantics, then there is no "possible world" where A is true and B is false (a similar intuition will be used to more rigorously define entailment in Section 4.3).

Example 4.10

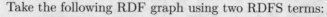

Take the following RDF graph using two RDFS terms:

ex:hasIngredient	rdfs:range	ex:Ingredient
ex:Ingredient	rdfs:subClassOf	ex:Comestible
ex:LemonPie	ex:hasIngredient	ex:Lemon

If we consider a semantics that defines the meaning of these two RDFS terms, then the following RDF graph is entailed by the above graph:

ex:LemonPie	ex:hasIngredient	ex:Lemon
ex:Lemon	rdf:type	ex:Ingredient
ex:Lemon	rdf:type	ex:Comestible

The second graph directly follows as a consequence of the semantics from the first graph: it says nothing new that could not already be concluded from the first graph per the semantics of the RDFS terms.

Exercise 4.1

Provide the RDF Schema triples needed to entail the latter seven triples from the original triple given in Example 4.3.

4.2.2 Annotations

Aside from these four key terms for sub-property, sub-class, domain and range, RDFS also defines various other auxiliary terms. The first four terms are used to annotate resources with useful (human-readable) information.

---

rdfs:label is a property that relates a resource with a human-readable label giving its name.

rdfs:comment is a property that relates a resource with a human-readable comment describing it in more detail.

rdfs:seeAlso is a property that relates a resource with a location on the Web that contains information about it.

rdfs:isDefinedBy is a property that relates a resource with a location on the Web that provides a definition of it.

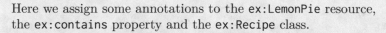

Example 4.11

Here we assign some annotations to the ex:LemonPie resource,
the ex:contains property and the ex:Recipe class.

ex:LemonPie	ex:contains	ex:Lemon
ex:LemonPie	rdf:type	ex:Recipe
ex:LemonPie	rdfs:label	"Lemon Pie"@en
ex:LemonPie	rdfs:label	"Tarta de Limon"@es
ex:LemonPie	rdfs:comment	"A quick recipe for Lemon Pie"@en
ex:LemonPie	rdfs:isDefinedBy	<http://ex.org/lemonpie.ttl>
ex:LemonPie	rdfs:seeAlso	<http://ex.org/lemondesserts.ttl>
ex:contains	rdf:type	rdf:Property
ex:contains	rdfs:label	"contains"@en
ex:contains	rdfs:comment	"Denotes the contains relation"@en
ex:contains	rdfs:isDefinedBy	<http://ex.org/recipes.ttl>
ex:Recipe	rdfs:label	"Recipe"@en
ex:Recipe	rdfs:comment	"Class of gastronomic recipes"@en
ex:Recipe	rdfs:isDefinedBy	<http://ex.org/recipes.ttl>

Multiple of any such property can be defined for any resource, where
we see, for example, multilingual labels (one in English, another in
Spanish) being assigned to the ex:LemonPie resource. Human-readable
comments and labels are crucial additions to the description of terms,
allowing humans to understand what is being intuitively defined.

On the other hand, the rdfs:isDefinedBy and rdfs:seeAlso properties provide links to a document that "define" the resource, or that
contain related information about the resource, respectively.

These four terms do not have specific semantics: they provide a minimal-
istic set of agreed-upon terms for basic annotations. For example, by putting
rdfs:label in the standard, we have a fixed property to query for the human-
readable name of a given resource, rather than (in theory at least) having to
deal with custom properties like ex1:label, ex2:name, ex3:title, etc.

4.2.3 Meta-Classes

RDF defines the "meta class" rdf:Property as the class of all properties.
Along similar lines, RDFS defines four new "meta classes":

rdfs:Resource is the class of all resources.
rdfs:Literal is the class of all literal values.
rdfs:Datatype is the class of all datatypes.
rdfs:Class is the class of all classes (including itself).

These five classes – a form of "semantic bookkeeping" – are associated with a lightweight semantics that we will now illustrate with an example.

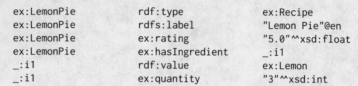

Example 4.12

Let's take the following RDF graph:

```
ex:LemonPie          rdf:type              ex:Recipe
ex:LemonPie          rdfs:label            "Lemon Pie"@en
ex:LemonPie          ex:rating             "5.0"^^xsd:float
ex:LemonPie          ex:hasIngredient      _:i1
_:i1                 rdf:value             ex:Lemon
_:i1                 ex:quantity           "3"^^xsd:int
```

Let's start with the semantics of rdf:Property. Every property is an instance of this class, where every relation appearing in the predicate position of a triple must be a property. Hence we can conclude:

```
rdf:type             rdf:type              rdf:Property
rdfs:label           rdf:type              rdf:Property
ex:rating            rdf:type              rdf:Property
. . .                . . .                 . . .
```

Again we emphasise that despite its name, rdf:Property is a *class* whose instances are properties (it itself is not a property).

Next let's consider the semantics of rdfs:Resource. We stated that everything is an RDFS resource, and so we can conclude:

```
ex:LemonPie          rdf:type              rdfs:Resource
rdf:type             rdf:type              rdfs:Resource
ex:Recipe            rdf:type              rdfs:Resource
rdfs:label           rdf:type              rdfs:Resource
ex:rating            rdf:type              rdfs:Resource
ex:hasIngredient     rdf:type              rdfs:Resource
_:i1                 rdf:type              rdfs:Resource
. . .                . . .                 . . .
```

In RDFS, *everything* is a resource, even classes, even properties – even properties in the RDFS vocabulary. On a side note, if everything is a resource, then that leads us to conclude the following:

```
rdfs:Resource        rdf:type              rdfs:Resource
```

As discussed in more detail later, classes *can* contain themselves!

But if everything is a resource, what about the literals in that case? The problem is that we cannot directly state something like:

```
"5.0"^^xsd:float     rdf:type              rdfs:Resource
```

Though this can be concluded from the semantics of rdfs:Resource, syntactically RDF does not allow literals in the subject position. A trick sometimes used in RDFS is thus to use a fresh blank node to represent literals in the subject position:

```
_:b1                    rdf:type                    rdfs:Resource
```

This blank node is created specifically to represent "5.0"^^xsd:float in the subject of a triple. Such blank nodes are sometimes called **surrogate blank nodes**, used to encode literals in subject positions.

Though surrogate blank nodes are not so important when dealing just with rdfs:Resource, we can also use them support the semantics of rdfs:Literal and to "convert" datatypes into regular classes.

```
_:b1                    rdf:type                    rdfs:Literal
_:b1                    rdf:type                    xsd:float
```

This has some minor significance in that it allows us to reason about a datatype as a regular class: a class of specific datatype values. Observe that from the above example intuitively follows:

```
xsd:float               rdfs:subClassOf             rdfs:Literal
```

Every datatype is a sub-class of rdfs:Literal.

As a minor aside, what would be the datatype of "Lemonade"@en? Perhaps xsd:string? In fact, in RDF 1.1, a new datatype was introduced for strings with language tags; for this literal we would have:

```
_:b2                    rdf:type                    rdf:langString
```

In RDF 1.1, literals without an explicit datatype or language tag are implicitly assigned the datatype xsd:string.

Relatedly, RDFS gives us the class rdfs:Datatype:

```
xsd:float               rdf:type                    rdfs:Datatype
rdf:langString          rdf:type                    rdfs:Datatype
```

Typically an RDFS reasoner will support a specific set of datatypes, which will be typed as above.

Next we have the class of all classes: rdfs:Class. Anything that has an instance (specified by rdf:type) must be a class.

```
ex:Recipe               rdf:type                    rdfs:Class
rdf:Seq                 rdf:type                    rdfs:Class
rdf:Resource            rdf:type                    rdfs:Class
xsd:float               rdf:type                    rdfs:Class
rdf:langString          rdf:type                    rdfs:Class
. . .                   . . .                       . . .
```

In fact, following this logic, we will find:

```
    rdf:Class               rdf:type                rdfs:Class
```

In this case, `rdfs:Class` is the class of all classes; hence it contains itself. Class membership can also be **symmetric**:

```
    rdf:Class               rdf:type                rdfs:Resource
    rdf:Resource            rdf:type                rdfs:Class
```

Everything is a resource, including the class of classes. On the other hand, the class of all resources is a class. Likewise note that since everything is a resource, we can also conclude:

```
    ex:Recipe               rdfs:subClassOf         rdfs:Resource
    rdf:Seq                 rdfs:subClassOf         rdfs:Resource
    rdfs:Class              rdfs:subClassOf         rdfs:Resource
    . . .                   . . .                   . . .
```

Since everything is a resource, every class C is trivially a sub-class of `rdfs:Resource` since it holds that any instance of C must also be a resource. As a final remark, note that in the case of a latter triple, something can be both an instance of and a sub-class of a class.

In this previous example, we saw certain triples that only use terms from the RDF vocabulary – for example, that `rdf:type` is a type of `rdf:Property` – or that only used terms from the RDF and RDFS vocabulary – for example, that `rdfs:Class` is a sub-class of `rdfs:Resource`. These triples do not rely on the input data but hold universally according to the semantics of these RDF(S) terms: such triples are called RDF(S)-valid triples. RDF(S)-valid triples are entailed by even an empty graph!

Exercise 4.2

Consider (individually) the following triples:

```
    rdf:Property            rdf:type                rdfs:Class
    rdf:Property            rdfs:subClassOf         rdfs:Class
    rdf:Property            rdf:type                rdfs:Resource
    rdf:Property            rdfs:subClassOf         rdfs:Resource
    rdfs:subClassOf         rdfs:subPropertyOf      rdfs:subClassOf
    rdfs:subClassOf         rdfs:subPropertyOf      rdf:type
    rdf:type                rdfs:range              rdfs:Class
    rdf:type                rdfs:range              rdfs:Resource
    rdfs:Datatype           rdfs:subClassOf         rdfs:Literal
```

Can you figure out which triples are RDF(S)-valid and which not based on the previous discussion? Can you justify your decisions?

An important observation from the previous example is that, in RDF(S), classes can also be instances. In Example 4.12, we saw some strange examples of this, where, for example, `rdfs:Class` is both a sub-class and an instance of `rdfs:Resource`. However, in some use-cases, it may be quite natural to wish to describe something that is both an instance and a class.

Exercise 4.3

Consider the following triples:

ex:Kanzi	rdf:type	ex:Bonobo
ex:Bonobo	rdfs:subClassOf	ex:Chimpanzee

Which of the following options would intuitively be more appropriate:

ex:Bonobo	rdfs:subClassOf	ex:Species
ex:Chimpanzee	rdfs:subClassOf	ex:Genus

or

ex:Bonobo	rdf:type	ex:Species
ex:Chimpanzee	rdf:type	ex:Genus

Why would your choice be the more appropriate one?

A final observation from the previous examples is that we can use the RDF(S) vocabulary to describe the RDF(S) vocabulary itself. In fact, we can reuse this vocabulary however we wish; this flexibility can be useful.

Exercise 4.4

Consider the following triples:

ex:Kanzi	rdf:type	ex:Bonobo
ex:Bonobo	ex:inGenus	ex:Chimpanzee
ex:Chimpanzee	ex:inOrder	ex:Primate

Assume we would like to add some RDF(S) triples to be able to infer that instances of ex:Bonobo *are instances of both* ex:Chimpanzee *and* ex:Primate, *and that instances of* ex:Chimpanzee *are instances of* ex:Primate. *For example, we wish to be able to conclude:*

ex:Kanzi	rdf:type	ex:Chimpanzee
ex:Kanzi	rdf:type	ex:Primate

One way to enable these entailments would be to state:

ex:Bonobo	rdfs:subClassOf	ex:Chimpanzee
ex:Chimpanzee	rdfs:subClassOf	ex:Primate

However, another way would be to state something in RDFS about the two properties ex:inGenus *and* ex:inOrder *of the following form:*

```
    ex:inGenus              ???                 ???
    ex:inOrder              ???                 ???
```

Complete these two triples.
  Finally, would the following triple make sense for this example?

```
    ex:inGenus         rdfs:subPropertyOf    ex:inOrder
```

In fact, we can easily start to (re)define some very strange things.

Exercise 4.5

Assume you are a Web of Data vandal and you inject this triple into a naive system that applies RDFS inferencing:

```
    rdf:type           rdfs:subPropertyOf    rdfs:subPropertyOf
```

What kinds of effects would this triple have?

Such issues raise questions about how applications can trust RDFS definitions they find on the Web. We will discuss such issues in Chapter 8.

4.2.4 Containers

Remark 4.2

RDF containers are not often used, and as discussed in Section 3.5.4, there have been calls to deprecate them. Hence some authors have chosen to simply ignore these terms from the RDFS vocabulary [286]. With this proviso, we include discussion for completeness.

Finally, wrapping up the RDFS vocabulary, the standard defines terms to help deal with RDF containers, as were described in Section 3.5.4.

> `rdfs:Container` is the class of all RDF containers (a super-class of
>   `rdf:Bag`, `rdf:Seq` and `rdf:Alt`)
> `rdfs:ContainerMembershipProperty` is the class of all container membership properties (i.e., properties of the form `rdf:_n`).
> `rdfs:member` is a super-property of all container membership properties.

We now give an example of the semantics of these terms.

Example 4.13

Let us again take the data from Example 3.12 where we describe a recipe for lemonade giving an ordered list of ingredients using an RDF container (as described in Section 3.5.4).

ex:Lemonade	ex:ingredients	_:1singreds
_:1singreds	rdf:_1	ex:Water
_:1singreds	rdf:_2	ex:Sugar
_:1singreds	rdf:_3	ex:Lemon
_:1singreds	rdf:type	rdf:Seq

Imagine a user now wished to query for all the ingredients of such a recipe (where they do not care about the order). This would be a pain unless they knew beforehand how many ingredients there were. However, with the help of the `rdfs:member` property, we can now conclude:

_:1singreds	rdfs:member	ex:Water
_:1singreds	rdfs:member	ex:Sugar
_:1singreds	rdfs:member	ex:Lemon

Now if the query engine supports the semantics of RDFS, the user would not need to specify `rdf:_1`, `rdf:_2`, `rdf:_3`, etc., in the query, but could instead use the generic `rdfs:member` property in their query.

Likewise, per the `rdfs:Container` term, we could conclude:

_:1singreds	rdf:type	rdfs:Container

Per `rdfs:ContainerMembershipProperty`, we could conclude:

rdf:_1	rdf:type	rdfs:ContainerMembershipProperty
rdf:_2	rdf:type	rdfs:ContainerMembershipProperty
...	rdf:type	rdfs:ContainerMembershipProperty

In fact, an infinite number of such triples can be concluded.

Remark 4.3

The latter group of (infinite) triples in the previous example are in fact RDFS-valid: they only involve terms in the RDF(S) vocabulary and always hold true, even for an empty graph. Given that there are an infinite number of such triples, this would rule out the idea of naively trying to write down *everything* that can be concluded from the RDFS semantics: even an empty graph entails infinite triples! One option is to only write down those triples for terms of the form `rdf:_n` that actually appear in the given data. Another option is to build systems that do not need to immediately make every entailment explicit, but rather do so as needed. We will discuss this more in the following section(s).

4.3 RDF(S) Model-Theoretic Semantics

We previously enumerated the terms in the RDFS vocabulary and provided some intuitive definitions based on examples. However, if we wish to build automated entailment procedures over data using such vocabulary, we will have to be much more precise in defining precisely what each such term means, and which graphs should entail which as a result. The key question then is: how should we define precise notions of entailment over RDF(S) data?

AIDAN: Actually such translations are often used in papers to prove certain results. However, the question then is: how is first-order logic defined? In fact, we will define RDF(S) semantics in a similar way to how first-order logic is (often) defined, thus arriving at a more general mathematical definition rooted in set theory. (Another problem with defining the semantics in first-order logic is that it cannot express the transitive closure of a binary relation [123].)

The RDF(S) standard outlines an abstract semantics based on **model theory**, which comprises a rigorous mathematical definition of how RDF graphs should be interpreted and which RDF graphs entail which others [180].

Example 4.14

Let us first return to Example 4.4 where we intuitively illustrated the semantics of sub-class with the following triple t_1:

```
ex:DessertRecipe        rdfs:subClassOf        ex:Recipe
```

Rather than using a list of rules, how could we more directly define the semantics of sub-class in mathematical language?

To start with, we could say that `ex:DessertRecipe` refers to a *set* of things in the real-world: the set of dessert recipes. Let us denote that set by D. We could likewise say that `ex:Recipe` refers to a *sct* of things in the real-world: the set of recipes R. Now when we have a sub-class triple of the above form, we could say, mathematically, that this means that the set denoted by the term on the left (D) is a *subset* of the set denoted by the term on the right (R): in this case, $D \subseteq R$.

Let us now consider the semantics of `rdf:type` with triple t_2:

```
ex:LemonPie             rdf:type              ex:DessertRecipe
```

We will consider that `ex:LemonPie` refers to a particular thing in the world: the recipe for lemon pie (denoted l). How can we mathematically define the semantics of this `rdf:type` triple? We can say that given the triple t_2, then mathematically it means that the thing denoted on the left (l) is an element of the set denoted on the right (D), giving $l \in D$.

Now, when we have that $l \in D$ and $D \subseteq R$, it follows mathematically that $l \in R$ (for if it were not, then we would have a clear contradiction).

Hence it might be tempting to say that the above two triples must entail – based on our mathematical arguments – the triple t_3:

```
ex:LemonPie             rdf:type              ex:Recipe
```

But we are not yet there. Before continuing, can you see the problem?

The problem is that thus far we have used the following style of condition to define the semantics of the RDF terms:

if a triple holds, **then** a mathematical condition holds

In other words, we have gone from RDF(S) to mathematics, but have not yet gone from mathematics to RDF. Although we have concluded that $l \in D$, to entail t_3, we need a condition of the form:

if a mathematical condition holds, **then** a triple holds.

or combining both directions into one statement:

a triple holds **if and only if** a mathematical condition holds

So to entail t_3 from $l \in D$, we need to say that an RDF triple with the predicate `rdf:type` holds *if and only if* the thing denoted by the subject is an element of the set of things denoted by the object. With this stronger statement, we have outlined a (minimal) way to mathematically define the entailment of t_3 from t_1 and t_2.

Exercise 4.6

*What about the **reflexive** and transitive sub-class entailments in Example 4.5? What would we need to add to Example 4.14 to justify these entailments in our mathematical definitions?*

Exercise 4.7

How might we model sub-property relations in a similar mathematical manner as discussed for sub-class relations?

Model theory – as applied to RDF – then abstractly involves:

1. a mapping from the RDF world onto a mathematical structure (e.g., to map classes to sets and resources to elements of those sets);
2. reasoning over that pre-defined mathematical structure (e.g., to state that if $a \in C$ and $C \subseteq D$, then $a \in D$);
3. a mapping back from the mathematical structure to the RDF world.

Thus instead of defining a special notion of entailment specifically for RDF, entailments arise on the more general mathematical level – in this case on the level of set theory – and are mapped back to the RDF level.

In defining a model theory semantics, we will also be forced to precisely define what individual terms mean – for example, what it means to say "rdfs:Resource *denotes the class of all resources*". We will thus remove any ambiguity on the question of which graphs entail which. With this more general **mathematical semantics**, we can thus define new tasks with respect to the language, irrespective of a given procedure. For such tasks, we can define new procedures and prove formal properties of those procedures (such as **soundness** and **completeness**) with respect to the mathematical definitions.

The RDF Semantics standard then defines four different model theoretic semantics, which build upon each other:

SIMPLE SEMANTICS considers no special vocabulary nor datatypes.
D SEMANTICS adds support for a fixed set of datatypes.
RDF SEMANTICS adds support for RDF vocabulary.
RDFS SEMANTICS adds support for RDFS vocabulary.

We will now talk about each of these semantics in turn.

4.3.1 Simple Semantics

The most "bare bones" model theoretic semantics defined by the RDF 1.1 Semantics standard is the (so-called) **simple semantics**. This semantics considers no datatypes nor RDF nor RDFS vocabulary, but rather deals with defining a mathematical structure onto which RDF graphs can be mapped.

4.3.1.1 Simple Interpretations

At the core of the RDF model theory is the notion of an interpretation: one can think of this, in our context, as an abstract mathematical description of a possible world that may (or may not) be described by an RDF graph, and mappings from RDF terms and triples to that possible world. The most simple type of RDF interpretation is called a **simple interpretation**, which provides no special interpretation for datatypes nor any specific vocabulary.

Before we define an interpretation, let us look at an example that gives the intuition of what we are trying to achieve.

Example 4.15

We wish to define the semantics of an RDF graph mathematically in terms of what it describes in the real world: people, places, interests, food, etc. Here is an example real world with some things:

This world exists independently of any RDF graph. Each symbol here can be seen as possibly representing something in the real world, where for example, we can consider 👨 as a specific flesh-and-blood man in the real world (unfortunately we cannot embed one on the page) and where we can consider 5 as the real world value for five. Also the position of things on the page is not important: there is no ordering.

How can we describe this world mathematically?

To start with, we can describe this world as a set of things, where we will call that set I_R (I for *interpretation*, which is what we are defining; R for *resources*, which is what we call elements of the world in RDF):

$$I_R := \{\text{🐝},\text{📈},\text{♫},\text{🦇},\text{👨},\text{📱},2,\text{♉},\text{☻},\text{☺},\text{✈},\heartsuit,\text{🚹},5,\text{🚲},\text{🚺},\text{☺},\text{♌}\}$$

Since sets do not permit duplicates, thus far we have stated mathematically that we cannot have duplicate things in the world described.

Our world is pretty boring thus far. We might like to know, for example, what is the relation between 👨 and ☻. For this, we will introduce (binary) relations into our world that may connect one resource to another (or even itself). For example, ☆ might be the relation that connects people in our world to their particular star-sign.

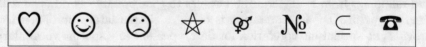

We again define these relations mathematically using a set that we can call I_P (I again for *interpretation*; P for *properties*, which denote different types of binary relations present in our world):

$$I_P := \{\text{☺},\text{⚤},\heartsuit,\text{№},\text{☎},\text{☺},\subseteq,\text{☆}\}$$

Again we see that these relations are unique, but as we will see in a moment, we can still use a particular relation to connect multiple pairs of resources. (We should also note that we have some things in I_R appearing again in I_P; these sets are not disjoint, but can share elements: we have properties that we may wish to describe as resources and how they relate to other resources. On the other hand, not all elements of I_P need to be contained in I_R in this definition.)

Still, even though we now have *two* boxes – I_R and I_P – our constructed world is pretty boring since we still don't know, for example, which relation in I_P connects 🧑 and ☕ in I_R (if any). Hence let's reveal how the binary relations from I_P connect pairs of resources in I_R:

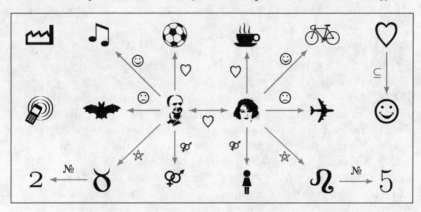

How can we define this mathematically? Actually, there's a few more-or-less equivalent ways. The first option would be to define a set of all the triples of the form $\{(🧑,\heartsuit,☕),\ldots,(\heartsuit,\subseteq,☺)\}$. However, for reasons that will become clear, it will be a little more convenient to define a function from elements of I_P to sets of pairs of resources in I_R, which we shall call I_{EXT} (where EXT refers to the *extension* of a property, which is the set of pairs of resources it relates); for example:

$$I_{EXT}(\heartsuit) := \{(☕,🧑),(🧑,☕),(☕,🦇),(🧑,⚽)\}$$

The function I_{EXT} will be defined likewise for all properties in I_P. In the case of the property ☎, note above that $I_{EXT}(☎) = \emptyset$; in other words, not all properties in I_P have to relate some resources in I_R. Also note that not all resources in I_R need to be involved in a relation.

In fact, we are done describing our example world. This mathematical structure – I_R, I_P and I_{EXT} – is sufficient to model a (possible) world that an RDF graph is talking about. However, to define an interpretation, we somehow need to bridge from the RDF world to this mathematical model of a world. For this, we will need to map elements from the RDF level – from RDF terms – to the world.

To start with, we wish to formalise the idea that IRIs name resources. For this, we will define a mapping I_S (the S has no obvious meaning, but we can think of *signifies* as a mnemonic) from IRIs onto resources and properties in the union of I_R and I_P. In fact, I_S is defined as an infinite map that must map all IRIs; here we define just a few examples: $I_S(\text{ex:Eve}) := \text{❂}$, $I_S(\text{ex:Adam}) := \text{👨}$, $I_S(\text{ex:Cycling}) := \text{🚲}$, $I_S(\text{ex:loves}) := \heartsuit$ and $I_S(\text{ex:likes}) := \text{☺}$. Since I_S is a function, each IRI can only refer to one resource or property. However, multiple IRIs can be used to refer to the same resource or property (i.e., I_S does not necessarily map unique inputs to unique outputs: it is not necessarily *injective*). For example, we could have a second IRI $I_S(\text{ex:Biking}) := \text{🚲}$ or $I_S(\text{ex:enjoys}) := \text{☺}$. This formalises the idea that RDF does not have a UNA: a resource (or property) can have multiple names.

Now that we have mapped IRIs, we need to map literals. A simple interpretation has a *partial* mapping I_L from literals onto resources in I_R. For example, $I_L(\text{"2"\^{}\^{}xsd:integer}) = 2$ or $I_L(\text{"5"\^{}\^{}xsd:integer}) = 5$ or $I_L(\text{"5.0"\^{}\^{}xsd:decimal}) = 5$. On the level of simple interpretations, we can even map $I_L(\text{"2"\^{}\^{}xsd:integer}) = \text{🚲}$; of course this makes no sense, where intuitive restrictions on the interpretations of datatypes will be defined in an extension of simple semantics discussed later. (Note that as a result of such restrictions, I_L will not be defined for certain invalid values – such as $I_L(\text{"blue"\^{}\^{}xsd:boolean})$ – which is why it is defined here as a *partial* mapping.)

The previous example (hopefully) gives the intuition behind a simple interpretation, which we can then define more formally as: follows.

Definition 9 (Simple interpretation). A *simple interpretation* I consists of two sets and three mappings [180]. The two sets are:

1. a non-empty set of resources I_R called the **universe** (aka. *domain*[a]) of the interpretation;
2. a set I_P called the *properties* of the interpretation.

The three mappings are:

1. a mapping I_{EXT} from I_P to $2^{I_R \times I_R}$;[b]
2. a mapping I_S from IRIs to $I_R \cup I_P$;
3. a partial mapping I_L from literals to I_R.

---

[a] The term "domain" here should not be confused with rdfs:domain. To avoid confusion, we will prefer "universe" or simply I_R.

[b] Here 2^S denotes the powerset of S; in other words, I_{EXT} maps a property to a set of pairs of resources in I_R.

A simple interpretation thus sets up a possible world (I_R, I_P and I_{EXT}) and then defines a mapping from RDF terms (IRIs and literals) to elements of that world (I_S, I_L). In fact, the elements of that possible world do not really matter: having "real-world" resources and properties just helps the intuition. What matters is the mathematical structure we use. In fact just with the definition of a simple interpretation, we have already started to formally narrow down how RDF describes a possible world: multiple IRIs can refer to the same resource or property, a property can be a resource but does not (yet) necessarily have to be, a literal cannot refer to a property, etc.

> **Remark 4.4**
>
> In this book, we will often have said something like
>
> - "the resource ex:Eve"; or
> - "the property ex:hates"
>
> More accurately, we should say
>
> - "the resource identified by the IRI ex:Eve"; or
> - "the property identified by the IRI ex:hates"
>
> But that would be as tedious as saying in everyday speech "the person whose name is 'Eve'" rather than simply just "Eve". Hence we will continue just using the first simpler form of speaking.
>
> At the same time, we do wish to highlight the difference between the names of resources and properties (IRIs), and the actual resources and properties (☞, ☺, and so on). Names are in the RDF graph, whereas resources and properties are in the world being described.

> **Remark 4.5**
>
> Simple interpretations are infinite since they map all IRIs to some value in the universe. More advanced interpretations that consider datatypes (discussed later) are also infinite since they consider all possible datatype values. However, finite versions of RDF-related interpretations have been studied as domain-restricted RDF [317] and have been discussed in a non-normative section of the W3C standard under "finite interpretations" [180]. We do not discuss this topic here.

4.3.1.2 Simple Satisfiability

An interpretation can be defined independently of an RDF graph: interpretations and RDF graphs are independent objects. The most important aspect of (simple) interpretations is that they can be used to assign a truth value to an RDF graph following a list of formal semantic conditions, which indicate whether or not the RDF graph "fits within" the possible world defined by the interpretation under the mapping also defined by the interpretation. We first provide an example to give the intuition; note that for now, we focus on using simple interpretations to apply truth values to **ground RDF graphs**: i.e., RDF graphs that do not mention blank nodes anywhere.

Example 4.16

Take the following RDF graph G:

ex:Eve	ex:loves	ex:Adam
ex:Adam	ex:loves	ex:Eve
ex:Eve	ex:likes	ex:Cycling

The interpretation I given in Example 4.15 can be used to assign a truth value to G with the following intuition ...

First we need to map all the terms in the RDF graph G to resources and properties. For now, we see that the RDF graph contains no literals; we will deal with literals later. Hence we are only interested in the I_S mapping, where we had $I_S(\text{ex:Eve}) := \text{🙂}$, $I_S(\text{ex:Adam}) := \text{😀}$, $I_S(\text{ex:Cycling}) := \text{🚲}$, $I_S(\text{ex:loves}) := \heartsuit$ and $I_S(\text{ex:likes}) := \odot$.

Next, we can draw these triples in the image of the I_S mapping:

We see that the result is intuitively a sub-graph of the original interpretation in Example 4.15, and hence the interpretation I assigns G to the value true. We can denote this as $I(G) = \text{true}$.

Otherwise, if it were not a sub-graph, we would have $I(G) = \text{false}$.

Remark 4.6

Just because there exists an interpretation that assigns an RDF graph the value true does not mean it's true in reality: rather it should be read as stating that, from the perspective of the machine, the RDF graph could be describing a consistent world. Where this will become useful is to compare the (mathematical) worlds that two RDF graphs could be describing: the sets of interpretations that assign each RDF graph the value true. Such a comparison will form the basis of our definition of entailment, discussed in Section 4.3.1.3.

We now give a more formal definition of an interpretation assigning truth values to RDF graphs, as illustrated intuitively in Example 4.16.

Definition 10 (Simple truth assignment for ground graphs). Let I be a simple interpretation. Let $I_{LS}(l) := I_L(l)$ if l is a literal and let $I_{LS}(i) := I_S(i)$ if i is an IRI. Then I can be used to assign a truth value to ground triples and graphs per the following *semantic conditions*:

- If (s, p, o) is a **ground RDF triple**, then $I(s, p, o) :=$ true if $I_S(p) \in I_P$ and $(I_S(s), I_{LS}(o)) \in I_{EXT}(I_S(p))$. Otherwise $I(s, p, o) :=$ false.[a]
- If G is a ground RDF graph and there exists $t \in G$ such that $I(t) =$ false, then $I(G) :=$ false . Otherwise $I(G) :=$ true.

---

[a] Recall from Definition 9 that I_L is a partial mapping that may not be defined for all literals. If o is a literal and $I_L(o)$ is undefined, then $I(s, p, o) :=$ false. Consequently, if I_L is undefined for a literal appearing in G, then $I(G) =$ false.

The RDF graph does not need to be a complete description of the possible world: the RDF graph just needs to "partially fit" a subset of the world being mapped to. This indicates that the semantics of RDF follow the **Open World Assumption (OWA)**: intuitively speaking, this means that data are assumed to be potentially incomplete such that if data are not known to be true, they are not assumed to be *false* but are rather simply considered *unknown* (conversely, under the **Closed World Assumption (CWA)**, positive facts/statements not known to be true are assumed to be false).

Remark 4.7   (i)

If one considers publishing RDF on the Web, assuming that unknown data were false would seem unwise since the Web is open and unbounded, where new data and datasets are constantly being added, revised and removed. As we will see, the OWA has significant consequences for RDF and the standards layered on top.

Example 4.17

We work through Example 4.16 using Definition 10.

1. No literals appear in the graph.
2. All three triples are ground. For the first triple, $I_S(\text{ex:loves}) = \heartsuit$ where $\heartsuit \in I_P$, and $(I_S(\text{ex:Eve}), I_{LS}(\text{ex:Adam})) = (\text{⬮}, \text{⬯})$ where $(\text{⬮}, \text{⬯}) \in I_{EXT}(\heartsuit)$. Hence the first triple is assigned true by the interpretation I, and likewise for the other two triples.

3. The graph contains no false triple, hence it is assigned true by I.

Under the image of I_{LS}, the RDF graph does not completely describe the possible world of the interpretation, yet it is assigned the value true. However, this does not mean that additional triples such as:

ex:Eve   ex:loves   ex:Coffee

are considered false even if not known to be true.

Exercise 4.8

Take the interpretation I from Example 4.15 (from which we have that $I_P(\text{ex:loves}) := \heartsuit$). Now take the following RDF graph G:

    ex:A   ex:loves   ex:B
    ex:A   ex:loves   ex:C
    ex:A   ex:loves   ex:D

Note that we did not explicitly give values for $I_S(\text{ex:A})$, $I_S(\text{ex:B})$, $I_S(\text{ex:C})$, $I_S(\text{ex:D})$, but recall that these must have values since I_S must map every IRI to an element of $I_R \cup I_P$. Is there a set of values that I_S can assign to ex:A, ex:B, ex:C and ex:D such that $I(G) = \text{true}$? If so, can you give an example? If not, can you argue why?

Exercise 4.9

Take again the interpretation I from Example 4.15, recalling that $I_P(\text{ex:likes}) := \smiley$. Now consider the following RDF graph G:

    ex:X   ex:likes   ex:Y
    ex:Y   ex:likes   ex:X

Is there a way to define I_S for ex:X and ex:Y such that $I(G) = \text{true}$?

We conveniently ignored literals in examples until now. On the level of simple interpretations, literals have no special meaning, and hence I_L can map any literal to any resource in I_R (a bit like I_S). However there are two subtle differences with I_S. First, I_L is only relevant for mapping the *objects* of RDF triples since literals cannot appear elsewhere. Second, I_L was defined in Definition 9 to be a *partial* mapping, meaning that it may not be defined for some literals; if an RDF graph G contains a literal l that I_L does not map, then $I(G) := \text{false}$. We will now look at some examples.

Example 4.18

Take the following RDF graph G:

| ex:Taurus | ex:ordinal | "2"^^xsd:integer |
| ex:Leo | ex:ordinal | "5"^^xsd:integer |

Take again the interpretation I from Example 4.15, and assume that $I_S(\text{ex:Taurus}) := ♉$, $I_S(\text{ex:Leo}) := ♌$ and $I_P(\text{ex:ordinal}) := №$. Now, if we define I_L for the two literals such that $I_L(\text{"2"^^xsd:integer}) = 2$ and such that $I_L(\text{"5"^^xsd:integer}) = 5$, then $I(G) = \text{true}$.

In the previous case, the literals "happened" to be mapped to their intuitive values, but this need not be the case in general. Take the graph:

| ex:Eve | ex:loves | "2.0"^^xsd:decimal |

On the level of simple interpretations, there's nothing to stop us defining $I_L(\text{"2.0"^^xsd:decimal}) = ♘$ or $I_L(\text{"2.0"^^xsd:decimal}) = ♣$ such that $I(G) = \text{true}$. Since literals don't have any special meaning yet, there's nothing to force us to map them to what they should intuitively correspond to (though we can if we wish).

Finally, in both of the above cases, I_L was defined for all literals in the RDF graph. However, I_L is a partial mapping, meaning it does not need to be defined for all literals. Assume the following RDF graph:

| ex:Eve | ex:loves | "Coffee"^^xsd:string |

If $I_L(\text{"Coffee"^^xsd:string})$ is undefined, then $I(G) := \text{false}$.

With respect to the last case, we highlight that having one interpretation assign an RDF graph false does not mean that the graph is false: it just means that it does not fit with that particular interpretation.

Exercise 4.10

Does there exist a simple interpretation that assigns false to the empty RDF graph?

Exercise 4.11

Does there exist a simple interpretation that will assign false to any (ground) non-empty RDF graph?

Thus far we have only spoken of applying simple interpretations for ground RDF graphs: i.e., for RDF data without blank nodes. Recall that blank nodes act like existential variables in RDF: they don't point to a specific resource in the universe like an IRI or a literal; rather they refer to the existence of some resource. We now define how simple interpretations can be used to assign truth values to RDF graphs with blank nodes. We start with an example.

Example 4.19

The case with blank nodes is similar to the ground case, but as we will see, it has a subtle twist. Take the following RDF graph G:

   ex:Eve   ex:loves   _:b1

Referring again to the interpretation given in Example 4.15, recall that $I_S(\text{ex:Eve}) = $ ☻, $I_S(\text{ex:loves}) = \heartsuit$. Now let us consider a new mapping A from blank nodes to elements in I_R; this is similar in principle to I_S for IRIs except that A is not part of the interpretation, and A only needs to map the blank nodes in the graph (not all blank nodes). Using the interpretation given in Example 4.15, there are two possible mappings of this form such that if we extend I with either, we can intuitively get G to fit inside I: either $A_1 = \{(\_\texttt{:b1}, ☙)\}$ or $A_2 = \{(\_\texttt{:b1}, \text{🙂})\}$.[a] If there exists any such mapping for blank nodes, we say that $I(G) := \mathsf{true}$.

Next take the following extended RDF graph G':

   ex:Eve   ex:loves   _:b1
   _:b1   ex:loves   _:b2

Now there are two possible mappings that will yield $I(G')$: this time either $A_1' = \{(\_\texttt{:b1}, \text{🙂}), (\_\texttt{:b2}, ☻)\}$ or $A_2' = \{(\_\texttt{:b1}, \text{🙂}), (\_\texttt{:b2}, ☻)\}$. Hence once again we have that $I(G') = \mathsf{true}$.

Last consider the following RDF graph G'':

   _:b1   ex:loves   _:b1

This time we cannot map _:b1 to anything that fits the interpretation: no resource in I is narcissistic enough to $\heartsuit$ itself. Hence $I(G'') := \mathsf{false}$.

---
[a] Here we use the notation for a mapping $M = \{(a,b),(b,c),(c,d)\}$ such that $M(a) = b$, $M(b) = c$, $M(c) = d$, and M is undefined for any other input.

Most importantly, the mapping from blank nodes to resources is not set in the simple interpretation I. The existence of any such mapping A will suffice to generate a truth value. As a result, while interpretations may vary based on which IRIs or literals map to which resources, by definition they cannot vary based on which blank nodes map to which resources.

To formalise truth assignment with blank nodes, we need to add a short modification to the semantic conditions in Definition 10.

Definition 11 (Simple truth assignment). Let I be a *simple interpretation* and let A be a mapping from blank nodes to the universe I_R. Define AI_{LS} to be a mapping such that:

- $AI_{LS}(x) = I_{LS}(x)$ if x is a literal or IRI;
- $AI_{LS}(x) = A(x)$ otherwise (if x is a blank node).

Let G be an RDF graph (that may contain blank nodes). $I(G) :=$ true if there exists a mapping A such that for every triple (s,p,o) in G, $I_S(p) \in I_P$ and $(AI_{LS}(s), AI_{LS}(o)) \in I_{EXT}(I_S(p))$. Otherwise $I(G) :=$ false.

Example 4.20

Let's take an isomorphic version (see Section 3.7.1) of the RDF graph G' from Example 4.19 where blank nodes have been relabelled.

ex:Eve	ex:loves	_:c1
_:c1	ex:loves	_:c2

Let's call this graph H'. Any interpretation I that gives $I(G') =$ true must also give $I(H') =$ true since given whatever A existed to satisfy $I(G') =$ true, we can just relabel the blank nodes the same way in A to create a new mapping A^* that witnesses $I(H') =$ true: whatever A mapped _:b1 to in I_R, now A^* will map _:c1 to, and whatever A mapped _:b2 to in I_R, now A^* will map _:c2 to.

However, if we renamed an IRI:

ex:Cycling	ex:loves	_:c1
_:c1	ex:loves	_:c2

The interpretation presented in Example 4.15 will assign the value false to this graph since $I_S(\text{ex:Cycling}) := $ 🚲 and no satisfactory mapping of A exists to map the graph to I_{EXT}. (Of course other interpretations exist that would assign this graph as true.)

The core point here is that we can change the mapping of blank nodes without changing the interpretation, but we cannot change the mapping of IRIs without changing the interpretation.

If interpretations represent possible worlds that an RDF graph could be describing, a natural question to ask is: can there exist an RDF graph that does not describe any possible world (i.e., is not assigned true by any interpretation)? This question leads us to the notions of **models** and **satisfiability**:

Definition 12 (Simple model). Given a simple interpretation I and an RDF graph G, we say that I *simple-satisfies* G if and only if $I(G) =$ true; in this case, I is called a *simple model* of G.

Definition 13 (Simple satisfiability). An RDF graph G is *simply satisfiable* if it has any simple model; otherwise it is *simply unsatisfiable*.

Unsatisfiable RDF graphs are indicative of an error: there are no possible consistent worlds that this RDF graph describes, so it has no possible models. On the other hand, although satisfiable RDF graphs are internally consistent, the interpretations that satisfy them may not reflect reality: they may still contain nonsense so long as that nonsense is mathematically consistent. In fact, every RDF graph is simply satisfiable since every RDF graph is satisfied by at least a **Herbrand interpretation**: an interpretation where RDF terms are considered as mapping to themselves. This is a valid interpretation since there is no restriction on what the resources in the universe denote.

Example 4.21

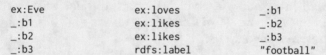

Take the RDF graph:

ex:Eve	ex:loves	_:b1
_:b1	ex:likes	_:b2
_:b2	ex:likes	_:b3
_:b3	rdfs:label	"football"

This has a variety of simple interpretations that satisfy it. One such model is the Herbrand interpretation where the universe consists of the RDF terms themselves, the RDF terms map to themselves, and the triples also map to their corresponding relations in the universe:

- $I_R := \{\text{ex:Eve}, \_\text{:b1}, \_\text{:b2}, \_\text{:b3}, \text{"football"}\}$;
- $I_P := \{\text{ex:loves}, \text{ex:likes}, \text{rdfs:label}\}$;
- $I_{EXT}(\text{ex:likes}) := \{(\_\text{:b1}, \_\text{:b2}), (\_\text{:b2}, \_\text{:b3})\}$,
  $I_{EXT}(\text{ex:loves}) := \{(\text{ex:Eve}, \_\text{:b1})\}$, and
  $I_{EXT}(\text{rdfs:label}) := \{(\_\text{:b3}, \text{"football"})\}$;
- $I_S(\text{ex:Eve}) := \text{ex:Eve}$, $I_S(\text{ex:loves}) := \text{ex:loves}$ and
  $I_S(\text{ex:likes}) := \text{ex:likes}$ (I_S is the identity on all IRIs);
- $I_L(\text{"football"}) := \text{"football"}$ (I_L is undefined for other literals).

This is a valid simple interpretation and one that trivially satisfies the RDF graph, where $A := \{(\_\text{:b1}, \_\text{:b1}), (\_\text{:b2}, \_\text{:b2}), (\_\text{:b3}, \_\text{:b3})\}$ is sufficient to satisfy the blank nodes. Simple Herbrand interpretations like this one trivially exist for any RDF graph.

> **Exercise 4.12**
>
> Given an RDF graph G, a simple Herbrand interpretation can
> be constructed specifically to satisfy G. But can you design a fixed simple
> interpretation that can satisfy any RDF graph G? Can you design such
> a simple interpretation that is minimal in the size of $I_R \cup I_P$?

Since all RDF graphs are simply satisfiable, the notion of unsatisfiability
will only play an important role when more complex semantics are considered.

4.3.1.3 Simple Entailment

The real value of interpretations lies in how they can be used to formally
compare different RDF graphs: one can compare the "semantic content" of
different RDF graphs by comparing their models. Thus given two RDF graphs
G and H and a given semantic notion of interpretation, we can ask:

- *Does H say the same as G?* Formally we can check that G and H have
  the same set of models.
- *Does H say a subset of what G says?* Formally we can check that the
  models of H are a superset of those for G.
- *Does H say something new that G does not?* Formally we can check that
  H has a model that G does not.

Framed another way, initially a machine knows nothing of the world. As
more and more facts are added about the (open) world, the picture of the
world that the machine sees becomes more and more specific and the interpretations must become more detailed to assign true to all claims. Likewise
an empty RDF graph is assigned true by any simple interpretation: the machine knows nothing specific so any world is possible. As one then starts to
add more and more content to an RDF graph, one starts to rule out possible interpretations that would assign true to that RDF graph: the more
meaningful content an RDF graph has, the fewer the interpretations assign
it true. Additional content removes possible worlds that could be described
by requiring interpretations to be more specific to fit the data.

These intuitions lead us to the important notion of **simple entailment**.

Definition 14 (Simple entailment). Given two RDF graphs G and
G', the graph G *simple-entails* the graph G' (denoted $G \models G'$) if and
only if every simple model of G is also a model of G' (or in other words,
the set of simple models for G is a subset of the simple models for G').

Definition 15 (Simple equivalence). Given two graphs G and G', if G simple-entails G' ($G \models G'$) and G' simple-entails G ($G \models G'$), then we say that G and G' are *simply equivalent* (denoted $G \equiv G'$; in other words, the set of simple models for G and G' is the same).

Example 4.22

The notion of entailment between two RDF graphs – $G \models G'$ – is very important, as is the idea of how it relates to the sets of models that G and G' permit. Hence we will try to illustrate and reinforce this **concept** with a concrete and detailed example.

Let us consider a set of interpretations such that $I_R := \{\text{🧔}, \text{👩}\}$ and $I_P := \{\heartsuit\}$. This gives rise to four *possible* relations in the universe:

Hence given I_R and I_P, we can consider 16 configurations for I_{EXT} corresponding to the powerset of these 4 relations:

1 $I_{EXT}(\heartsuit) = \{\}$
2 $I_{EXT}(\heartsuit) = \{(\text{🧔}, \text{🧔})\}$
3 $I_{EXT}(\heartsuit) = \{(\text{🧔}, \text{👩})\}$
4 $I_{EXT}(\heartsuit) = \{(\text{👩}, \text{🧔})\}$
5 $I_{EXT}(\heartsuit) = \{(\text{👩}, \text{👩})\}$
6 $I_{EXT}(\heartsuit) = \{(\text{🧔}, \text{🧔}), (\text{🧔}, \text{👩})\}$
7 $I_{EXT}(\heartsuit) = \{(\text{🧔}, \text{🧔}), (\text{👩}, \text{🧔})\}$
8 $I_{EXT}(\heartsuit) = \{(\text{🧔}, \text{🧔}), (\text{👩}, \text{👩})\}$
9 $I_{EXT}(\heartsuit) = \{(\text{🧔}, \text{👩}), (\text{👩}, \text{🧔})\}$
10 $I_{EXT}(\heartsuit) = \{(\text{🧔}, \text{👩}), (\text{👩}, \text{👩})\}$
11 $I_{EXT}(\heartsuit) = \{(\text{👩}, \text{🧔}), (\text{👩}, \text{👩})\}$
12 $I_{EXT}(\heartsuit) = \{(\text{🧔}, \text{🧔}), (\text{🧔}, \text{👩}), (\text{👩}, \text{🧔})\}$
13 $I_{EXT}(\heartsuit) = \{(\text{🧔}, \text{🧔}), (\text{🧔}, \text{👩}), (\text{👩}, \text{👩})\}$
14 $I_{EXT}(\heartsuit) = \{(\text{🧔}, \text{🧔}), (\text{👩}, \text{🧔}), (\text{👩}, \text{👩})\}$
15 $I_{EXT}(\heartsuit) = \{(\text{🧔}, \text{👩}), (\text{👩}, \text{🧔}), (\text{👩}, \text{👩})\}$
16 $I_{EXT}(\heartsuit) = \{(\text{🧔}, \text{🧔}), (\text{🧔}, \text{👩}), (\text{👩}, \text{🧔}), (\text{👩}, \text{👩})\}$

Note that for each of these sixteen configurations of I_{EXT}, we still have an infinite number of interpretations since we have not restricted

I_S (nor I_L), which may vary in an infinite number of ways in how they map the infinite set of IRIs (and literals) to $\{🧑,☻,♡\}$. (Observe that I_S, in particular, is required to map *all* IRIs by definition.)

Now let's take two RDF graphs; G_1:

ex:A   ex:loves   ex:B

and G_2:

ex:A   ex:loves   ex:A

The question (which is worthwhile for the reader to attempt to answer before continuing) is: *which graph entails which?*

Rather than give the answer directly, we will work it out. Per Definition 14, $G \models G'$ if and only if every model of G is also a model of G'. Let us thus now consider the models of G_1 and G_2 from the example.

An interpretation I is a model of G if and only if it assigns true to G, meaning that the structure of G can be mapped to the structure of I according to the rules of Definition 11. Let us consider the sets of interpretations we previously outlined with 16 configurations for I_{EXT}. We can find models for G_1 within configurations 2–16 of I_{EXT}, but not configuration 1 since it contains no relation that G_1 could be interpreted as describing. We take examples for other configurations:

- Considering the set of interpretations with I_{EXT} configuration 2, any such interpretation where $I_S(\text{ex:A}) := 🧑$, $I_S(\text{ex:loves}) := ♡$ and $I_S(\text{ex:B}) := 🧑$ is a model of G (otherwise it is not a model of G).
- Considering the set of interpretations with I_{EXT} configuration 3, any such interpretation where $I_S(\text{ex:A}) := 🧑$, $I_S(\text{ex:loves}) := ♡$ and $I_S(\text{ex:B}) := ☻$ is a model of G (otherwise it is not a model of G).
- ...
- Considering the set of interpretations with I_{EXT} configuration 6, any such interpretation where $I_S(\text{ex:A}) := 🧑$, $I_S(\text{ex:loves}) := ♡$ and either $I_S(\text{ex:B}) := 🧑$ or $I_S(\text{ex:B}) := ☻$ is a model of G (otherwise it is not a model of G).
- etc.

Let us now consider models of G_2. We can only find such models in configurations 2, 5–8, 10–16 of I_{EXT} that have a reflexive $♡$ relation (where some resource loves itself); in more detail:

- Considering the set of interpretations with I_{EXT} configuration 2, 6, 7 or 12, any such interpretation where $I_S(\text{ex:A}) = 🧑$ and $I_S(\text{ex:loves}) = ♡$ is a model of G_2 (otherwise it is not a model).

- Considering the set of interpretations with I_{EXT} configuration 5, 10, 11 or 15, any such interpretation where $I_S(\text{ex:A}) = $ ☻ and $I_S(\text{ex:loves}) = \heartsuit$ is a model of G_2 (otherwise it is not a model).
- Considering the set of interpretations with I_{EXT} configuration 8, 13, 14 or 16, any such interpretation where either $I_S(\text{ex:A}) = $ 😟 or $I_S(\text{ex:A}) = $ ☻ and $I_S(\text{ex:loves}) = \heartsuit$ is a model of G_2 (otherwise it is not a model).

To answer the original question, we will now ask: are all models of G_1 also models of G_2 (to check if $G_1 \models G_2$)? Conversely we will later ask: are all models of G_2 also models of G_1 (to check if $G_2 \models G_1$)?

We will start with the former question. Observe that we already discussed how there are models of G_1 with configurations 2–16, whereas there are only models of G_2 with configurations 2, 5–8, 10–16. Hence we immediately see that there are models of G_1 that are not models of G_2; for example, models that do not have a reflexive $\heartsuit$ relation can be models of G_1 but not G_2. As a result, we have that $G_1 \not\models G_2$; in other words, the semantics considers that G_2 says something new over G_1.

Next we consider the latter question: are all models of G_2 also models of G_1? Let's choose to analyse configuration 2 of I_{EXT}. An interpretation with configuration 2 is a model of G_1 if and only if $I_S(\text{ex:A}) := $ 😟, $I_S(\text{ex:loves}) := \heartsuit$ and $I_S(\text{ex:B}) := $ 😟. On the other hand, an interpretation with configuration 2 is a model of G_2 if and only if $I_S(\text{ex:A}) := $ 😟 and $I_S(\text{ex:loves}) = \heartsuit$. Thus, if we took an interpretation with configuration 2 where $I_S(\text{ex:A}) := $ 😟, $I_S(\text{ex:loves}) = \heartsuit$ and $I_S(\text{ex:B}) := $ ☻, it would be a model of G_2 but not G_1. Hence we see that not all models of G_2 will be models of G_1 and hence we have that $G_2 \not\models G_1$; in other words, the semantics considers that G_1 says something new over G_2.

This latter non-entailment is a rather subtle point: G_1 states that "*resource A loves resource B*" (possibly, under the UNA, where $A = B$), and G_2 states that "*resource A loves itself*", so a reasonable question then is why G_1 does not follow from G_2? The answer is that G_1 uses a specific *constant* ex:B whose mapping can vary in different interpretations, which in turn affects the sets of models for G_1 (but not G_2); to further illustrate this, consider G_3:

ex:A   ex:loves   ex:C

This will not be entailed by or from G_1 or G_2: the constants used are different, which will change the models of the graph (specifically the function I_S will differ for models of G_1, G_2 and G_3). More generally, the choice of IRIs matters to the semantics and to entailment!

Let us now consider two final examples with blank nodes; G_1':

_:a	ex:loves	_:b

and G_2':

_:a	ex:loves	_:a

Which entailments now hold between G_1, G_2, G_1' and G_2' (if any)?

The models of G_1' are (like G_1) given by configurations 2–16, but where the only condition for interpretations with these configurations is that $I_S(\texttt{ex:loves} = \heartsuit)$. For example, taking an interpretation I with configuration 2, then so long as $I_S(\texttt{ex:loves}) = \heartsuit$, there exists a mapping A that will map _:a to 🧍 and _:b to 🧍. Given that the conditions for being a model of G_1' (that the interpretation has some relation for $I_S(\texttt{ex:loves})$; e.g., $\heartsuit$ in the example interpretations we consider) are strictly weaker than those for G_1, we have that any model of G_1 will be a model of G_1', from which we conclude that $G_1 \models G_1'$, whereas $G_1' \not\models G_1$.

Along similar lines, the conditions for being a model of G_1' are strictly weaker than those for G_2 as well, meaning that $G_2 \models G_1'$ (but not $G_1' \models G_2$). (We will formally prove such entailments to hold in Lemma 1.)

The models of G_2' are (like before for G_2) only given by configurations 2, 5–8, 10–16 with reflexive $\heartsuit$ relations, but where the only condition within these configurations is that $I_S(\texttt{ex:loves}) = \heartsuit$. We can then abstract that the general conditions for being a model of G_2' (have some *reflexive* relation for $I_S(\texttt{ex:loves})$) are again strictly weaker than those for G_2, and hence that $G_2 \models G_2'$ (but $G_2 \not\models G_2'$).

Regarding entailment between G_1' and G_2', we can see that the conditions for being a model of G_1' (that the interpretation has some relation for $I_S(\texttt{ex:loves})$) are also strictly weaker than those for G_2' (that the interpretation has some *reflexive* relation for $I_S(\texttt{ex:loves})$), and hence that any model of G_2' must be a model for G_1' (but not vice versa), allowing us to conclude that $G_2' \models G_1'$ (but $G_2' \not\models G_1'$).

Finally we are left to consider entailment between G_1 and G_2'. We can observe that $G_2' \not\models G_1$ since the conditions for being a model of G_2' are weaker than those for G_1, but are they *strictly* weaker? In other words, can we have models of G_1 that are not models of G_2'? ...

Exercise 4.13

Does $G_1 \models G_2'$ hold in Example 4.22? Justify why (not).

Given two RDF graphs G and G', this definition now gives us a mathematically unambiguous condition for whether or not G entails G' under simple semantics. However, it does not *directly* lead to an algorithm to decide entailment: we cannot enumerate all possible interpretations and make sure that each one satisfying G also satisfies G' since there are infinite interpretations.

However, perhaps we can find other conditions between G and G' that we can prove to be equivalent to the condition in Definition 14 but that are more practical to verify with an algorithm for checking if $G \models G'$.

To start with, let's consider a simple condition to verify simple entailment in some cases: if G' is a sub-graph of G, then G must simple-entail G'.

Lemma 1. *Given two RDF graphs G and G', if $G' \subseteq G$, then $G \models G'$.*

Exercise 4.14

Can you sketch a proof argument for Lemma 1?

This lemma is a start: it would not be difficult to come up with a practical algorithm to check if G' is a sub-graph of G (i.e., it G contains all the triples of G'). Hence when $G' \subseteq G$, we have a procedure to confirm that $G \models G'$. But what if we are asked to check if $G \models G'$ when $G' \nsubseteq G$?

First let's take the simpler case where G' is ground. In this case, the following result can be proven:

Lemma 2. *Given RDF graphs G and G' where G' is ground, then $G \models G'$ if and only if $G' \subseteq G$.*

Exercise 4.15

Can you sketch a proof argument for Lemma 2?

This result states that in cases where G' is ground, the condition in Definition 14 for $G \models G'$ is equivalent to the condition that G' is a sub-graph of G. With this result, we can again check the entailment between these two RDF graphs – $G \models G'$? – by checking the equivalent condition of whether or not G contains all of the triples of G'. Likewise, with the proof that these two conditions are equivalent, we can know that such an algorithm is sound (only returns false when $G \models G'$ is false) and complete (only returns true when $G \models G'$ is true) with respect to the semantics of simple entailment – but of course these guarantees only apply when the graph G' is ground.

Unfortunately, if G' contains blank nodes, the situation is a bit more complex since to establish that $G \models G'$, we need to find a mapping from the blank nodes in G' to terms in G. In the following we use the notion of a blank node mapping μ from Definition 5, which maps blank nodes to RDF terms.

> **Definition 16 (Graph instances).** Let G be an RDF graph and μ be a blank node mapping. Then we call $\mu(G)$ an *instance* of G.

Example 4.23

Let's take the following RDF graph G:

_:b1	ex:hates	_:b2
_:b2	ex:hates	_:b3

Given $\mu := \{(\_:b1, \_:b1), (\_:b2, \_:b2), (\_:b3, \_:b3)\}$, we can see that $\mu(G) = G$, and so G is an instance of itself. In fact, every graph is always an instance of itself. A ground graph only has itself as an instance.

Given $\mu := \{(\_:b1, ex:Adam), (\_:b2, ex:Eve), (\_:b3, "Apples")\}$, the following RDF graph is also an instance of G:

ex:Adam	ex:hates	ex:Eve
ex:Eve	ex:hates	"Apples"

Given $\mu := \{(\_:b1, ex:Adam), (\_:b2, ex:Eve), (\_:b3, ex:Adam)\}$, the following RDF graph is also an instance of G:

ex:Adam	ex:hates	ex:Eve
ex:Eve	ex:hates	ex:Adam

Given $\mu := \{(\_:b1, \_:b1), (\_:b2, \_:b1), (\_:b3, \_:b1)\}$, the following RDF graph is also an instance of G:

_:b1	ex:hates	_:b1

Note, however, that G is not an instance of the latter graph.

Given any two RDF graphs G and G', it is then possible to prove that $G \models G'$ if and only if an instance of G' is a sub-graph of G; in other words:

Theorem 1. $G \models G'$ *if and only if there exists a blank node mapping μ such that $\mu(G') \subseteq G$* [180].

Example 4.24

Let's take the following RDF graph G:

ex:Adam	ex:hates	_:b1
_:b1	ex:hates	ex:Adam
ex:Adam	ex:loves	ex:Cycling

and the graph G':

| _:b1 | ex:hates | _:b2 |
| _:b2 | ex:hates | _:b3 |

Taking $\mu := \{(\_:b1, ex:Adam), (\_:b2, \_:b1), (\_:b3, ex:Adam)\}$ is sufficient to show that there exists a μ such that $\mu(G') \subseteq G$ (the first two triples of G are an instance of G'). Theorem 1 then implies that $G \models G'$.

Exercise 4.16

If you succeeded with Exercise 4.15, can you now sketch a brief proof argument for Theorem 1?

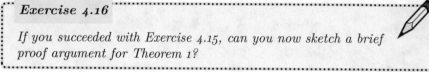

This result directly leads to an algorithm for checking simple entailment – $G \models G'$? – this time between RDF graphs that may contain blank nodes: check if G' has any instance that's a sub-graph of G. We can, for example, use a brute-force algorithm that tries every possible mapping from the blank nodes in G' to the RDF terms in G until we find one that gives $\mu(G') \subseteq G$ (we just need to find one to satisfy the condition). Since both sides of the mapping are finite, we know we will have to search finitely many mappings, so the process will eventually terminate with an answer. However, though finite, there are exponentially many mappings, so such a process will often be inefficient. In fact, though we can have more sophisticated algorithms that perform better in practice that this brute-force search, given two RDF graphs G and G', determining if there exists a μ such that $\mu(G') \subseteq G$ is a hard problem: it is not known whether or not an algorithm that performs better than exponential in the worst case for this problem even exists.

Remark 4.8

Checking the simple-entailment "$G \models G'$?" is known to be NP-complete [317]. Based on Theorem 1, checking entailment is equivalent to finding a blank node mapping from G' to a sub-graph of G. Given a mapping μ, we can verify that $\mu(G') \subseteq G$ in polynomial-time: hence the problem is in NP. Furthermore, given that finding a blank node mapping is equivalent to finding a *homomorphism*, we can trivially reduce **graph homomorphism** to simple entailment; since the former problem is a well-known NP-complete problem, so too is simple entailment.

> **Remark 4.9**
>
> The RDF 1.1 Semantics specification also mentions a brute-force
> procedure that enumerates and checks a finite subset of interpretations
> sufficient to decide entailment [180]. We do not discuss this in detail.

In summary, simple semantics defines the notions of properties and resources, the lack of UNA for RDF terms, the use of the OWA (which is in
fact a "default" assumption), and the existential semantics of blank nodes.

4.3.1.4 (Non-)Lean Graphs

In Section 3.7 and in Example 3.18, we previously discussed the notion of
lean and non-lean RDF graphs, where blank nodes can lead to triples that
are (semantically-speaking) redundant. In light of the previous definitions,
we can now be a little more formal and say that given an RDF graph G, if
we can remove triples from G while keeping the graph semantically (simply)
equivalent to G, then the triples we remove are semantically redundant; if it
is possible to remove triples this way, then G is non-lean; otherwise it is lean.

We now give a formal definition and example of this notion of lean.

Definition 17 ((Non-)Lean RDF graphs). If an RDF graph G has
a proper sub-graph G' (i.e., $G' \subsetneq G$) such that $G' \models G$, then G is called
a *non-lean RDF graph*. Otherwise G is *lean*.

> **Example 4.25**
>
> Take the following RDF graph G:
>
> | | | |
> |---|---|---|
> | ex:Eve | ex:loves | ex:Adam |
> | ex:Adam | ex:loves | ex:Football |
>
> G is a lean RDF graph: if you remove a triple you remove "useful" infor-
> mation that changes the models of the graph. By this same argument,
> it is not difficult to prove that all ground RDF graphs are lean.
>
> Now rather take the following RDF graph G':
>
> | | | |
> |---|---|---|
> | ex:Eve | ex:loves | ex:Adam |
> | _:b1 | ex:loves | _:b2 |
> | ex:Eve | ex:loves | _:b2 |
> | ex:Adam | ex:loves | _:b3 |

This time, G' is non-lean. Intuitively speaking, the graph states that (1) Eve loves Adam, that (2) something loves something that is loved by Eve, and that (3) Adam loves something. But note that, intuitively speaking, (2) is redundant in the presence of (1).

More formally, let G'' be the following RDF graph:

ex:Eve	ex:loves	ex:Adam
ex:Adam	ex:loves	_:b3

Now $G'' \subsetneq G'$ and $G'' \models G'$;[a] thus G' is non-lean: G' contains redundancy such that G' and G'' contain the same information and have the same models. On the other hand, G'' is lean: removing any triple from G'' will change its models, or, intuitively speaking, will remove the information that either Eve loves Adam, or that Adam loves something.

---

[a] The simple entailment $G'' \models G'$ can be shown by the existence of a blank node mapping μ such that $\mu(_:b1) = $ ex:Eve and $\mu(_:b2) = $ ex:Adam where $\mu(G') \subseteq G''$. Furthermore, $G' \models G''$ since $G'' \subseteq G'$. Hence G' and G'' are simple-equivalent.

Remark 4.10

Since one can continue arbitrarily introducing fresh blank nodes to create triples that map back to the original graph, although an RDF graph G may simple-entail only a finite number of lean RDF graphs, it may simple-entail an infinite number of non-lean RDF graphs.

Again, Definition 17 does not directly suggest any algorithm to check if G is lean, nor to compute a lean graph to which it is equivalent (often called "*the core*" of G [162], which is unique up to isomorphism). However, using Theorem 1, we can rephrase the condition of Definition 17 to state that if G has a blank node mapping to a proper sub-graph of itself, then it is non-lean: i.e., we can check to see if there exists a mapping μ such that $\mu(G) \subsetneq G$. Again, we can use this idea to implement algorithms for checking if G is lean, or checking if G' is a core of G, though it is not known if there exists an algorithm for either problem that is better than exponential in the worst-case.

Remark 4.11

For the reader familiar with computational complexity, we remark that the problem of deciding if G is lean is coNP-complete [162]. The problem of deciding if G' is a core of G is DP-complete [162].

4.3.2 Datatype (D) Semantics

Taken on its own, simple semantics is quite *inexpressive*: the semantic conditions are quite shallow and do not allow for expressing interesting claims about the world in a formal way. Instead, simple semantics serves as a mathematical foundation for defining other richer types of semantics, where the RDF Semantics specification [180] further defines the meaning of datatypes and the RDF and RDFS vocabularies, which we will discuss in turn.

Here we will first discuss the semantics of datatypes, which is layered on top of simple semantics. We will assume a set D of supported datatypes, which may include, for example, those datatypes listed previously in Table 3.2. With some extensions to the concepts defined already for simple semantics, our goal is to to define notions of D-interpretations, D-satisfiability and D-entailment that formalise the (intuitive) semantics of such datatypes. Hence the framework we follow will be the same – defining interpretations, satisfiability and entailment analogously as for simple semantics – but adding some new semantic conditions along the way to support datatype literals.

4.3.2.1 D Interpretations

In simple interpretations, I_L is a partial mapping responsible for interpreting some subset of literals. However, the nature of I_L is not specified at the level of simple interpretations: simple interpretations can map (or not map) literals to any resource in the universe they wish. We already saw in Example 4.18 that this could get weird, where we talked about how an interpretation could define I_L such that $I_L(\text{"2.0"}^{\wedge\wedge}\text{xsd:decimal}) = $ ☺ or $I_L(\text{"42"}^{\wedge\wedge}\text{xsd:decimal}) = $ ☂. The goal of D interpretations then – assuming that xsd:decimal is included in the set of supported datatypes D – is to restrict I_L to map, e.g., $I_L(\text{"2.0"}^{\wedge\wedge}\text{xsd:decimal}) = 2$. The most important aspect of the semantics is to know when multiple datatype literals map to the same value; e.g., $I_L(\text{"2.0"}^{\wedge\wedge}\text{xsd:decimal}) = I_L(\text{"2"}^{\wedge\wedge}\text{xsd:byte}) = 2$.

Towards this goal, each supported datatype in D is assumed to be a specific global datatype with an externally defined *lexical-to-value mapping*; in other words, D entailment does not define how each datatype is mapped, but rather assumes that the implementation knows how to map literals in the recognised datatypes to values based on some external specification, and that the same datatype will be treated likewise by other implementations. For example, D interpretations assume that the mapping $I_L(\text{"2.0"}^{\wedge\wedge}\text{xsd:decimal}) = 2$ is defined in the respective XSD specification [313], and likewise for other XSD datatypes. By not defining details of specific datatypes, D-semantics remains general and extendible for supporting new datatypes.

> **Remark 4.12** (i)
>
> The datatype rdf:langString is not defined by XSD and requires special attention: it will be handled explicitly in D entailment since it is defined within RDF itself.

The set of recognised datatypes may vary depending on the application. For minimal compliance with the RDF standard, an engine must recognise two datatypes: rdf:langString and xsd:string. However, the standard implicitly recommends support for all datatypes listed in Table 3.2. Other custom datatypes can be supported in D interpretations where it is assumed that these datatypes are defined and documented in a global manner such that independent implementations will treat them the same.

Towards defining D interpretations, take a simple interpretation I and assume as given a lexical-to-value mapping $L2V$ that takes a datatype IRI from D and a lexical string and maps it to the appropriate value in the value space of that datatype; for example, $L2V(I_S(\texttt{xsd:decimal}),\texttt{"2.0"}) = 2$. This $L2V$ mapping is externally defined for each recognised datatype IRI in D except for rdf:langString. A D interpretation is then defined as follows.

Definition 18 (D interpretation). Let D be a set of IRIs identifying datatypes. Let I be a simple interpretation. I is also a D *interpretation* if the following two additional semantic conditions hold:

- If rdf:langString is in D, then for every language-tagged literal $l := (s,t)$ where s is the lexical string and t the language tag, $I_L(l) = (s,t')$ where t' is the lower-case version of t.
- For every other IRI d in D, $I_S(d)$ gives the datatype identified by d and for every literal $l := (s,d)$ where s is the lexical string and d the datatype IRI, $I_L(l) = L2V(I_S(d),s)$.

This definition states that a D interpretation must map a literal with a given datatype (e.g., xsd:decimal) and lexical string (e.g., "5.0") to the value given by datatype's lexical-to-value mapping (e.g., the number 5).

If the datatype of a literal is unrecognised – i.e., it does not appear in D – then the D interpretation can map it to any value as per a simple interpretation. If a literal with a recognised datatype is ill-typed – meaning that its lexical form doesn't match the given datatype; e.g., "true"^^xsd:decimal – the $L2V$ mapping has no value and the literal cannot denote anything; I_L is undefined for such values and the D interpretation assigns that triple false.

The notions of D models, D satisfiability. D unsatisfiability, etc., follow naturally from their simple counterparts. That is to say: the D models of an RDF graph are the D interpretations that assign it true; an RDF graph is

D-satisfiable if it has a D model; otherwise it is D-unsatisfiable. However, unlike under the simple semantics, RDF graphs can be D-unsatisfiable: RDF graphs containing recognised but ill-typed literals are D-unsatisfiable – they cannot possibly be describing a world consistent with respect to D semantics.

Example 4.26

A literal like `"true"^^xsd:dateTime` is ill-typed: the lexical form cannot be mapped to a value for that datatype. A triple or graph mentioning such a literal is D unsatisfiable if and only if D contains the datatype IRI `xsd:dateTime`: there is no D interpretation supporting that datatype that is a model of such a graph. On the other hand, if the datatype is not recognised – i.e., if `xsd:dateTime` is not supported by D – the mapping of the literal by I_L is not restricted by such a D interpretation, which can map that term to any resource, and in the process, potentially assign true to a graph containing it.

4.3.2.2 D Entailment

The notion of D entailment extends naturally from simple entailment by replacing simple interpretations with D interpretations: a graph G D-entails a graph G' if and only if every D interpretation that satisfies G also satisfies G'. Fundamentally D entailment extends simple entailment to consider the equivalence of datatype literals (i.e., different lexical strings mapping to the same datatype value). The notion of D equivalence extends likewise.[1]

Example 4.27

Assume that D includes the datatypes `xsd:integer`, `xsd:decimal`, `xsd:string` and `rdf:langString`. The XSD datatypes are interpreted according to the hierarchy outlined in Table 3.2, where `xsd:integer` is derived from `xsd:decimal` and hence will have a subset of the values of `xsd:decimal`. Then consider the following RDF graph G:

ex:LemonPie	ex:rating	"4"^^xsd:decimal
ex:LemonPie	rdfs:label	"Lemon Pie"@en-us
ex:LemonPie	ex:code	"X54Y"^^xsd:string

This RDF graph D-entails the following graph G':

---

[1] The notions of lean and cores are usually kept specific to simple semantics ... though, we suppose, there's nothing fundamental to stop us from also talking about D-lean graphs and D-cores that do not contain any redundancy under D semantics.

ex:LemonPie	ex:rating	"04"^^xsd:integer
ex:LemonPie	rdfs:label	"Lemon Pie"@en-US
ex:LemonPie	ex:code	"X54Y"
_:recipe	ex:rating	"+4.00"^^xsd:decimal

The latter triple combines D entailment and simple entailment (which D entailment is based on). In fact, both graphs are D equivalent: they D-entail each other and thus permit the same D interpretations.

Exercise 4.17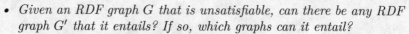

Given that D semantics now permits (D-)unsatisfiable graphs, what effect does this have on entailment? More specifically:

- *Given an RDF graph G that is unsatisfiable, can there be any RDF graph G' that it entails? If so, which graphs can it entail?*
- *On the other hand, if G' is unsatisfiable, can it be entailed by any RDF graph G? If so, which graphs can entail it?*

(Note that the question is not specific to D semantics, but relates to the more general notions of models, unsatisfiability and entailment.)

Since there can be an infinite number of lexical forms that map to the same datatype value – for example, "2"^^xsd:decimal, "2.0"^^xsd:decimal, "2.00"^^xsd:decimal, etc. – an RDF graph may D-entail an infinite number of (lean) triples and thus RDF graphs. A practical method to implement methods for D entailment is thus – where possible – to canonicalise literals with supported datatypes such that a single canonical lexical form is chosen for each value. This canonicalisation process may include, for example:

- adding the xsd:string to every plain literal without a language tag;
- converting literals with more specific derived datatypes to literals with the more general dataypes from which they are derived (see Table 3.2);
- removing leading zeros and trailing zeros in numerics, etc.; lowercasing language tags; and so forth for each supported datatype.

Let $C_D(\cdot)$ denote such a canonicalisation procedure for RDF graphs with respect to the recognised datatypes D. Given two RDF graphs G and G', assuming both graphs are D-satisfiable, to test if G D-entails G', we can check if $C_D(G)$ simple-entails $C_D(G')$. (If G is D-unsatisfiable, we can return true; otherwise if only G' is D-unsatisfiable, we can return false.) Thus with an appropriate canonicalisation procedure for D in hand, we can reduce checking D-entailment to checking simple-entailment of the canonicalised graphs.

Example 4.28

Taking the graphs in Example 4.27, assume we wish to check if G D-entails G'. We can first apply the aforementioned canonicalisation process; G is already canonical ($C_D(G) = G$), whereas $C_D(G')$ is:

ex:LemonPie	ex:rating	"4"^^xsd:decimal
ex:LemonPie	rdfs:label	"Lemon Pie"@en-us
ex:LemonPie	ex:code	"X54Y"^^xsd:string
_:recipe	ex:rating	"4"^^xsd:decimal

Then we can check if $C_D(G)$ simple-entails $C_D(G')$.

4.3.3 RDF Semantics

We discussed in Section 3.5 how the RDF vocabulary can be used for various modelling patterns, such as the use of classes and properties, the specification of containers and collections, as well as the representation of n-ary predicates and the reification of claims. We now formally define the RDF semantics, which includes the semantics of such terms. More specifically, RDF semantics extends upon D semantics with additional semantic conditions relating to the core RDF vocabulary as follows [180] (for n any non-zero natural number):

> rdf:type, rdf:subject, rdf:predicate, rdf:object, rdf:first, rdf:rest, rdf:value, rdf:nil, rdf:List, rdf:langString, rdf:Property, rdf:_n

Remark 4.13

Other RDF terms – like rdf:Bag or rdf:Statement – do not have any special meaning in RDF semantics, primarily because we cannot conclude anything about them using just the RDF vocabulary. For example, RDF properties are defined so we can conclude, e.g.:

rdf:type	rdf:type	rdf:Property
rdf:subject	rdf:type	rdf:Property
. . .	. . .	. . .

On the other hand, for rdf:List and rdf:nil, we can say:

rdf:nil	rdf:type	rdf:List

However, we cannot say anything interesting yet about, e.g., rdf:Bag.

We continue in a similar manner as before: we start by defining an RDF interpretation and then discuss RDF entailment.

4.3.3.1 RDF Interpretations

RDF interpretations add some additional semantics with respect to class instances using the `rdf:type` property: in particular, memberships of the built-in class `rdf:Property` and the supported datatypes. To define these class memberships, we must first think about how we are going to define classes in an interpretation. There are two options we could consider:

- One would be to define a semantic notion of classes, where classes are an inherent part of the possible world being described.
  - To give an idea, we could define a set of classes I_C (similar to I_P), extend I_S to be able to map to I_C, and define a function I_{CEXT} that maps elements of I_C to subsets of I_R.
- The second option is to define a syntactic notion of classes, where, intuitively, `rdf:type` is seen semantically as a relation like any other.

Example 4.29

Let us assume $\mathfrak{Z}$ refers to the class of zodiac signs with (at least) the IRI `ex:Zodiac`, and let us assume we wish to define an interpretation where the class will have two instances: $\mathfrak{R}$ (`ex:Leo`) and $\eth$ (`ex:Taurus`).

We could define classes semantically with I_C, I_{CEXT} and I_S such that, for example, $\mathfrak{Z} \in I_C$, $I_{CEXT}(\mathfrak{Z}) := \{\eth, \mathfrak{R}\}$, and $I_S(\texttt{ex:Zodiac}) := \mathfrak{Z}$.

Or we could define classes purely syntactically (without needing I_C or I_{CEXT}). Assume that $\triangleright$ denotes the type relation: $I_S(\texttt{rdf:type}) := \triangleright$. Now we can define I such that $(\mathfrak{R}, \mathfrak{Z}) \in I_{EXT}(\triangleright)$ and $(\eth, \mathfrak{Z}) \in I_{EXT}(\triangleright)$.

For now, we will define the RDF semantics using a syntactic definition of classes. (When we introduce RDFS later, we will switch to a semantic definition of classes for convenience.) With this in mind, an RDF interpretation extends a D interpretation with semantic conditions to state that all properties are instances of the `rdf:Property` class, and that all datatype values are instances of their (supported) datatype.

Definition 19 (RDF interpretation). Let I be a D interpretation that recognises the datatype IRIs `rdf:langString` and `xsd:string`. I is also an RDF interpretation if it satisfies the following three conditions:

- x is in I_P if and only if $(x, I_S(\texttt{rdf:Property})) \in I_{EXT}(I_S(\texttt{rdf:type}))$.
- For every datatype IRI d in D, $(x, I_S(d))$ is in $I_{EXT}(I_S(\texttt{rdf:type}))$ if and only if x is in the value space of $I_S(d)$.
- The set of RDF **axiomatic triples** is satisfied (see Figure 4.1).

```
rdf:type      rdf:type  rdf:Property .
rdf:subject   rdf:type  rdf:Property .
rdf:object    rdf:type  rdf:Property .
rdf:first     rdf:type  rdf:Property .
rdf:rest      rdf:type  rdf:Property .
rdf:value     rdf:type  rdf:Property .
rdf:nil       rdf:type  rdf:Property .
rdf:_n        rdf:type  rdf:Property .
```

Fig. 4.1 RDF axiomatic triples

RDF interpretations have an underlying D entailment for a given set of recognised datatypes D. As such, we may more accurately write RDF_D interpretations to denote an RDF interpretation recognising a given set of datatypes D. However, for general discussion we do not care about the nature of D (except that it contains at least rdf:langString and xsd:string) in which case we will simply speak about RDF interpretations.

The first semantic condition ensures that [*if:*] every instance of the class rdf:Property is a property in I_P and [*only if:*] every property in I_P is an instance of rdf:Property. Note that this gives a formal definition for what we said early: that "rdf:Property *is the class of all properties*".

The second condition ensures that [*if:*] all values in a datatype (according to $L2V$) are typed accordingly with rdf:type for that datatype and [*only if:*] all values typed with rdf:type to a given datatype are values in $L2V$.

The third condition specifies a set of triples that must always hold true in every RDF interpretation, essentially hard-coding the set of built-in RDF properties into the semantics. In other words, under RDF semantics, these "axiomatic triples" should be implicitly considered part of any RDF graph.

As before for the extension of simple semantics to D semantics, notions of RDF models and RDF (un)satisfiability extend analogously. Recognised datatypes may now cause new types of unsatisfiability under RDF semantics.

Example 4.30

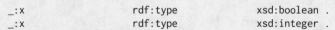

We borrow this example from the RDF 1.1 Semantics document [180]. Take the following RDF graph:

```
_:x                 rdf:type            xsd:boolean .
_:x                 rdf:type            xsd:integer .
```

Assuming both datatypes are recognised by D, the graph is RDF_D-unsatisfiable since the value spaces of the two datatypes in question are known to be *disjoint*: something cannot be an instance of both.

Aside from these new examples of unsatisfiability, the new semantic conditions for RDF semantics do not "restrict" anything about RDF graphs; for example, while the first semantic condition ensures that all properties in an interpretation must be instances of the class rdf:Property, this does not mean that all properties in an RDF graph need to be explicitly typed with rdf:Property. These definitions rather have the opposite effect: an RDF interpretation will fill in these details on behalf of an RDF graph it satisfies.

Example 4.31

Consider the RDF graph:

ex:Adam   ex:loves   ex:Eve

The simple interpretation I discussed in Example 4.15 is not a valid RDF interpretation unless we have that $I_S(\text{rdf:type}) \in I_P$ and that $(\heartsuit, I_S(\text{rdf:Property})) \in I_{EXT}(I_S(\text{rdf:type}))$, and likewise for the other conditions defined on RDF interpretations. In other words, we are not forcing the RDF graph to explicitly type properties, we are forcing the RDF interpretations that satisfy the RDF graph to explicitly type the properties, and thus "fill in" the missing details.

Whether or not an RDF graph has, for example, explicitly typed all properties it uses will thus not affect the RDF models it has. This then leads us to a notion of RDF entailment that is agnostic to such details.

4.3.3.2 RDF Entailment

Given two RDF graphs G and G', as before, we say that G RDF-entails G' if and only if every RDF model of G is also an RDF model of G'.

Perhaps the most useful new RDF entailment is that properties can be automatically typed. Thus we have formalised the first semantic conditions on the vocabulary of RDF(S) itself, useful for (slightly) richer entailment.

Example 4.32

Consider again the RDF graph G from Example 4.31:

ex:Adam   ex:loves   ex:Eve

Let us also consider G':

ex:Adam   ex:loves   ex:Eve
ex:loves   rdf:type   rdf:Property

As discussed in Example 4.31, both G and G' have the same RDF models. Hence G RDF-entails G' and vice versa: they are semantically equivalent under RDF semantics.

> **Exercise 4.18**
>
> *Let's be more explicit with Example 4.32. Although G' simple-entails G (since $G' \subset G$), G does not simple-entail G'; hence there exists a simple model of G that is not a simple model of G'. Can you describe a simple model that shows G does not simple-entail G'? Why is this simple model not enough to show that G does not RDF-entail G'?*

Under RDF semantics, the empty graph entails triples that are satisfied by any RDF interpretation: these are called the *RDF-valid triples*, which include the RDF axiomatic triples added to the interpretation (see Figure 4.1).

Remark 4.14

The set of axiomatic triples is infinite since membership of the class identified by `rdf:Property` will be inferred for all container membership property terms of the form `rdf:_n`. Hence even an empty RDF graph RDF-entails an infinite number of (lean) RDF triples and thus RDF graphs.[a] Thus again, a practical system will not be able to materialise all entailments possible under RDF semantics, but may rather have to (e.g.) only consider container membership properties appearing in the data, or perhaps even just ignore those entailments since they are of questionable practical value [286].

Likewise, in theory, an infinite number of type triples would be entailed for all literals that can be interpreted by a recognised datatype with a countably infinite number of valid lexical strings (e.g., `xsd:string`). However, since literals cannot appear in the subject position of an RDF triple, they must be represented instead with surrogate blank nodes, limiting the amount of lean triples that can be entailed.

---

[a] Unlike unsatisfiable graphs however, not *all* possible graphs are entailed.

Remark 4.15

RDF interpretations can be extended to allow for supporting arbitrary datatypes. However, recalling that an RDF interpretation requires that at least the datatype IRIs `rdf:langString` and `xsd:string` are recognised by D (see Definition 19), a reasonable question is to ask: why are only these datatypes *required* to ensure compatibility? Surely if the standard required that systems supported a wider range of datatypes, this would improve interoperability of such systems.

The answer is that the combination of RDF and D semantics for arbitrary datatypes can already lead to exotic entailments that one might not expect. The following example is taken from the RDF 1.1 Semantics document [180]; consider the following RDF graph G:

ex:a	ex:p	"true"^^xsd:boolean
ex:a	ex:p	"false"^^xsd:boolean
ex:v	rdf:type	xsd:boolean

Assuming xsd:boolean is in D, this graph RDF$_D$-entails G':

ex:a	ex:p	ex:v

Intuitively, if a system adds support for the xsd:boolean datatype to RDF entailment, that system must understand that any boolean can refer to only one of two values. Hence no matter what value ex:v takes above in a particular RDF$_D$-model of G (be it true or false), it must also model G': if ex:v takes true, G' follows from the first triple of G; otherwise it follows from the second; in either case G' follows from G.

Note that G does not D-entail G', nor would G RDF$_D$-entail G' if xsd:boolean were not recognised by D. Rather, G' is entailed from a combination of the RDF semantics and the semantics for datatypes.

Such entailments arise from the fact that certain datatypes may have a fixed number of values (unlike xsd:string or rdf:langString). Indeed xsd:boolean is far from special in this regard and we could consider similar examples with xsd:byte or xsd:long (though such examples would take up considerably more space). In general, we can see that supporting these sorts of datatype entailments in a practical system could cause significant problems, especially when combined with further semantic conditions as defined later for richer vocabularies.

Hence if we wished to build systems for deciding entailments that support a broader variety of datatypes, we would need to be careful in how they interact with other semantic conditions to ensure that all entailments are supported (or rather instead accept *incompleteness*: the possibility that the system may miss certain standard entailments).

In summary, with RDF semantics, we are starting to see some non-trivial entailments taking place. But yet, RDF semantics only serves as a foundation for more *expressive* semantics that allow for making (and entailing) more "interesting" machine-processable claims relating to the world(s) described.

4.3.4 *RDFS Semantics*

We have extensively discussed formal aspects of the RDF semantics such that we should be able to determine which RDF graphs entail or are equivalent to which RDF graphs under which semantics, or even which RDF graphs are unsatisfiable nonsense under which semantics. But mostly we have discussed rather dry – but necessary – foundational ideas rooted in model theory. Though we can interpret blank nodes and datatypes and so forth using the semantics encountered thus far, we still cannot express even the simple types of reasoning captured in Example 4.3, which aimed to motivate the chapter.

However, we now come to define the semantics of the following RDFS vocabulary, which covers the types of entailments we need in such applications.

```
rdfs:domain, rdfs:range, rdfs:Resource, rdfs:Literal, rdfs:Datatype,
    rdfs:Class, rdfs:subClassOf, rdfs:subPropertyOf, rdfs:member,
  rdfs:Container, rdfs:ContainerMembershipProperty, rdfs:comment,
            rdfs:seeAlso, rdfs:isDefinedBy, rdfs:label
```

We once again start with the notion of an RDFS interpretation before moving on to discuss RDFS entailment.

4.3.4.1 RDFS Interpretations

In order to formalise the meaning of the RDFS vocabulary discussed in Section 4.1 – and to formally define the entailments possible through that vocabulary – the $\text{RDFS}_{(D)}$ semantics extends $\text{RDF}_{(D)}$ semantics with additional semantic conditions, which we will define presently.

In the discussion of RDF interpretations, we mentioned that there are two options to define classes: a semantic notion and a syntactic notion (see Example 4.29). While RDF interpretations chose the syntactic option, RDFS chooses the semantic option, adding I_C, I_{CEXT}, etc., to the RDFS interpretations. This will be useful when defining sub-classes, for example. However, it is important to note that I_C and I_{CEXT} are defined in terms of I_R and $I_{EXT}(\text{rdf:type})$, meaning that we do not change the structure of the interpretation when extending it for RDFS: we are just adding some new notation.

Since the definition involves a long list of semantic conditions, we provide some explanation within the definition as to the purpose of each condition. These semantic conditions will pave the way for more powerful – and thus practical – forms of entailment, and will also give a general abstract idea of how more complex semantic languages can be formalised through model theory. As we will see, more than one semantic condition can be associated with a particular term of the RDFS vocabulary.

Definition 20 (RDFS interpretation). Let I be an RDF$_D$ interpretation. Let $I_{CEXT}(y)$ denote the *extension of a class y*:

$$I_{CEXT}(y) := \{x \mid (x, y) \in I_{EXT}(I_S(\text{rdf:type}))\},$$

and let I_C denote the set of classes such that:

$$I_C := I_{CEXT}(I_S(\text{rdfs:Class})).$$

Let I_{LV} denote the set of literal values in I_R, which includes all values v where there exists a literal l such that $I_L(l) = v$; other literal values that are not mapped by a specific literal may also be included in I_{LV}.

I is an *RDFS$_D$ interpretation* if it abides by the following additional semantic conditions:

- $I_{CEXT}(I_S(\text{rdfs:Literal})) = I_{LV}$.
  - States that rdfs:Literal denotes the class of all literal *values*

- $I_{CEXT}(I_S(\text{rdfs:Resource})) = I_R$.
  - States that rdfs:Resource denotes the class of all resources

- $I_{CEXT}(I_S(\text{rdf:langString})) = \{I_L(x) \mid x \text{ is a lang-tagged literal}\}$.
  - States that the rdf:langString datatype is the datatype of all language-tagged strings

- If $d \in D$ and d is not rdf:langString, then $I_{CEXT}(I_S(d))$ is the value space of the datatype $I_S(d)$.
  - States that the class extension of a recognised datatype is the value space of that datatype

- If $d \in D$, then $I_S(d)$ is in $I_{CEXT}(I_S(\text{rdfs:Datatype}))$.
  - States that rdfs:Datatype contains all known datatypes, including but not limited to recognised datatypes in D

- If $(x, y) \in I_{EXT}(I_S(\text{rdfs:domain}))$ and $(u, v) \in I_{EXT}(x)$, then $u \in I_{CEXT}(y)$.
  - Formalises the core semantics of the rdfs:domain property as previously described

- If $(x, y) \in I_{EXT}(I_S(\text{rdfs:range}))$ and $(u, v) \in I_{EXT}(x)$, then $v \in I_{CEXT}(y)$.
  - Formalises the core semantics of the rdfs:range property as previously described

- If $(x, y) \in I_{EXT}(I_S(\text{rdfs:subPropertyOf}))$, then $I_{EXT}(x) \subseteq I_{EXT}(y)$ and $x \in I_P$, $y \in I_P$.
  - Formalises the core semantics of the rdfs:subPropertyOf property as previously described

> - States that both resources in a sub-property relation are properties
>
> - If $p \in I_P$, then $(p,p) \in I_{EXT}(I_S(\texttt{rdfs:subPropertyOf}))$.
>   - States that the $\texttt{rdfs:subPropertyOf}$ property is reflexive on I_P: the set of all properties
>
> - If $(x,y) \in I_{EXT}(I_S(\texttt{rdfs:subPropertyOf}))$
>   and $(y,z) \in I_{EXT}(I_S(\texttt{rdfs:subPropertyOf}))$,
>   then $(x,z) \in I_{EXT}(I_S(\texttt{rdfs:subPropertyOf}))$.
>   - States that the $\texttt{rdfs:subPropertyOf}$ property is transitive
>
> - If $(x,y) \in I_{EXT}(I_S(\texttt{rdfs:subClassOf}))$, then $I_{CEXT}(x) \subseteq I_{CEXT}(y)$ and $x \in I_C$, $y \in I_C$.
>   - Formalises the core semantics of the $\texttt{rdfs:subClassOf}$ property as previously described
>   - States that both resources in a sub-class relation are classes
>
> - If $x \in I_C$, then $(x, I_S(\texttt{rdfs:Resource})) \in I_{EXT}(I_S(\texttt{rdfs:subClassOf}))$.
>   - States that if x is a class, then x is a sub-class of $\texttt{rdfs:Resource}$
>
> - If $c \in I_C$, then $(c,c) \in I_{EXT}(I_S(\texttt{rdfs:subClassOf}))$.
>   - States that the $\texttt{rdfs:subClassOf}$ property is reflexive on I_C: the set of all classes
>
> - If $(x,y) \in I_{EXT}(I_S(\texttt{rdfs:subClassOf}))$
>   and $(y,z) \in I_{EXT}(I_S(\texttt{rdfs:subClassOf}))$,
>   then $(x,z) \in I_{EXT}(I_S(\texttt{rdfs:subClassOf}))$.
>   - States that the $\texttt{rdfs:subClassOf}$ property is transitive
>
> - If $x \in I_{CEXT}(I_S(\texttt{rdfs:ContainerMembershipProperty}))$, then $(x, I_S(\texttt{rdfs:member})) \in I_{EXT}(I_S(\texttt{rdfs:subPropertyOf}))$.
>   - States that all container membership properties are a sub-property of the $\texttt{rdfs:member}$ property
>
> - If $x \in I_{CEXT}(I_S(\texttt{rdfs:Datatype}))$, then $(x, I_S(\texttt{rdfs:Literal})) \in I_{EXT}(I_S(\texttt{rdfs:subClassOf}))$.
>   - States that all datatypes are a sub-class of the class of literals
>
> - The set of RDFS axiomatic triples is satisfied (see Figure 4.2).

Thus, an RDFS_D interpretation extends an RDF_D interpretation with a long list of semantic conditions used to formalise the meaning of the RDFS vocabulary (as discussed in Section 4.2). Among these semantic conditions, arguably the most important are those that relate to the four core RDFS terms: $\texttt{rdfs:subClassOf}$, $\texttt{rdfs:subPropertyOf}$, $\texttt{rdfs:domain}$, and $\texttt{rdfs:range}$ [286]. Other features are used for instantiating meta-classes and datatypes, as well as for handling the semantics of container membership properties.

Example 4.33

In Example 4.14, we sketched some initial ideas for mathematically formalising the semantics of sub-class. Since then we have more concretely formalised these ideas. However, the ideas remain the same; in fact, it may be useful to see how our model theory has better formalised some of the ideas sketched there. First, in simple interpretations, we already generalised and formalised the idea that terms can denote things (which includes sets of things or relations between things):

- $I_R(\texttt{ex:LemonPie}) = l$,
- $I_{CEXT}(I_R(\texttt{ex:DessertRecipe})) = D$,
- $I_{CEXT}(I_R(\texttt{ex:Recipe})) = R$.

More recently, in the definition of RDFS interpretations, we have also formalised the idea that "*an RDF triple with the predicate* `rdf:type` *holds if and only if the thing denoted by the subject is an element of the set of things denoted by the object*" as follows:

$$I_{CEXT}(y) := \{x \mid (x,y) \in I_{EXT}(I_S(\texttt{rdf:type}))\}.$$

Here we have formalised that if we have the triple:

ex:LemonPie   rdf:type   ex:DessertRecipe

then an RDFS model must have $l \in D$; on the other hand, if we knew that $l \in D$, then to equate both sets above, the model would have to have the above triple. Thus the definition above maps in both directions: from the mathematical level to the RDF level and vice versa.

Finally, to capture the semantics of sub-class mathematically, in the definition of RDFS interpretations, we had the following condition:

If $(x,y) \in I_{EXT}(I_S(\texttt{rdfs:subClassOf}))$, then $I_{CEXT}(x) \subseteq I_{CEXT}(y)$

Thereafter, this condition, combined with the triple:

ex:DessertRecipe   rdfs:subClassOf   ex:Recipe

means that an RDFS model must satisfy $D \subseteq R$. If we also know that $l \in D$, we can reason that $l \in R$, which can be mapped back to the corresponding `rdf:type` triple as previously discussed:

ex:LemonPie   rdf:type   ex:Recipe

Remark 4.16 (i)

One may observe that some semantic conditions in Definition 20 are defined in an *if–then* manner rather than an *if and only if* manner. For example, for sub-class, we have the following condition:

- If $(x,y) \in I_{EXT}(I_S(\text{rdfs:subClassOf}))$, then $I_{CEXT}(x) \subseteq I_{CEXT}(y)$.

but we do not have that:

- If $I_{CEXT}(x) \subseteq I_{CEXT}(y)$ then $(x,y) \in I_{EXT}(I_S(\text{rdfs:subClassOf}))$.

In other words, given a sub-class triple, we enforce that the corresponding sets in the model must be subsets, but if we know that the corresponding sets must be subsets in all models, the interpretation does require us to state in RDFS that they are sub-classes.

To better illustrate this, consider the following RDF graph G:

rdf:type   rdfs:domain   ex:Instance

This states that anything that has a type is an instance. Now, everything (in $I_R \cup I_P$) is an instance of rdfs:Resource so everything must also be of type ex:Instance: mathematically, per the definition of RDFS interpretations, we could prove that any RDFS model of G must have that $I_{CEXT}(I_S(\text{rdfs:Resource})) \subseteq I_{CEXT}(I_S(\text{ex:Instance}))$ (and also that $I_{CEXT}(I_S(\text{ex:Instance})) \subseteq I_{CEXT}(I_S(\text{rdfs:Resource}))$, though this is trivial since any class is directly defined to be a sub-class of resource). Perhaps one might then expect that G should RDFS-entail:

rdfs:Resource   rdfs:subClassOf   ex:Instance

Under the *if–then* semantics of RDFS sub-class, this is not the case since nowhere do the definitions state that if $I_{CEXT}(x) \subseteq I_{CEXT}(y)$ then $(x,y) \in I_{EXT}(I_S(\text{rdfs:subClassOf}))$. However, if we had an *if and only if* semantics for RDFS sub-class covering the previous condition, this entailment would hold as part of standard RDFS entailment.

Why then does RDFS use *if–then* semantics for certain definitions? The short answer is that *if and only if* semantics is harder for practical systems to support in a complete manner since we would need to consider the possibility of various types of "exotic" entailments of the above form. Instead, RDFS tries to find a trade-off between expressive semantics and ease of support in practical systems.

We will return to this issue again in Section 4.4.5.

```
rdf:type                            rdfs:domain  rdfs:Resource ; rdfs:range  rdfs:Class    .
rdfs:domain                         rdfs:domain  rdf:Property  ; rdfs:range  rdfs:Class    .
rdfs:range                          rdfs:domain  rdf:Property  ; rdfs:range  rdfs:Class    .
rdfs:subPropertyOf                  rdfs:domain  rdf:Property  ; rdfs:range  rdf:Property  .
rdfs:subClassOf                     rdfs:domain  rdfs:Class    ; rdfs:range  rdfs:Class    .
rdf:subject                         rdfs:domain  rdf:Statement ; rdfs:range  rdfs:Resource .
rdf:predicate                       rdfs:domain  rdf:Statement ; rdfs:range  rdfs:Resource .
rdf:object                          rdfs:domain  rdf:Statement ; rdfs:range  rdfs:Resource .
rdfs:member                         rdfs:domain  rdfs:Resource ; rdfs:range  rdfs:Resource .
rdf:first                           rdfs:domain  rdf:List      ; rdfs:range  rdfs:Resource .
rdf:rest                            rdfs:domain  rdf:List      ; rdfs:range  rdf:List      .
rdfs:seeAlso                        rdfs:domain  rdfs:Resource ; rdfs:range  rdfs:Resource .
rdfs:isDefinedBy                    rdfs:domain  rdfs:Resource ; rdfs:range  rdfs:Resource .
rdfs:comment                        rdfs:domain  rdfs:Resource ; rdfs:range  rdfs:Literal  .
rdfs:label                          rdfs:domain  rdfs:Resource ; rdfs:range  rdfs:Literal  .
rdf:value                           rdfs:domain  rdfs:Resource ; rdfs:range  rdfs:Resource .
rdf:_n                              rdfs:domain  rdfs:Resource ; rdfs:range  rdfs:Resource .
rdf:Alt                                          rdfs:subClassOf  rdfs:Container .
rdf:Bag                                          rdfs:subClassOf  rdfs:Container .
rdf:Seq                                          rdfs:subClassOf  rdfs:Container .
rdfs:ContainerMembershipProperty    rdfs:subClassOf  rdf:Property   .
rdfs:Datatype                                    rdfs:subClassOf  rdfs:Class      .
rdfs:isDefinedBy  rdfs:subPropertyOf  rdfs:seeAlso .
rdf:_n  rdf:type  rdfs:ContainerMembershipProperty .
```

Fig. 4.2 RDFS axiomatic triples ($n > 0$ is any natural number)

Exercise 4.19

All classes, properties and literal values are also resources under RDFS semantics. Argue why this must be the case.

In the definition of an RDFS interpretation, the four core RDFS properties – rdfs:domain, rdfs:range, rdfs:subPropertyOf and rdfs:subClassOf – are used to define the semantics of the RDF and RDFS vocabulary itself, in the form of the RDFS axiomatic triples (see Figure 4.2).

Example 4.34

Assuming that the semantic conditions and axiomatic triples for rdfs:domain and rdfs:range are in place, stating that an RDFS interpretation must also satisfy the following two axiomatic triples:

```
rdf:rest                rdfs:domain             rdf:List
rdf:rest                rdfs:range              rdf:List
```

obviates the need for the following extra semantic conditions:

- If $(x, y) \in I_{EXT}(I_S(\text{rdf:rest}))$, then $x \in I_{CEXT}(I_S(\text{rdf:List}))$ and $y \in I_{CEXT}(I_S(\text{rdf:List}))$.
- $I_S(\text{rdf:rest}) \in I_P$ and $I_S(\text{rdf:List}) \in I_C$.

> **Remark 4.17**
>
> One may notice the following triple in Figure 4.2:
>
> | rdfs:member | rdfs:domain | rdfs:Resource |
> |---|---|---|
>
> While this axiomatic triple is by no means incorrect, it is reasonable to ask: why is the domain of this property not rdfs:Container? The standard is not clear on this point, but aside from being an oversight, it may be that this was to allow rdfs:member to be used on resources that are not containers, such as (perhaps in the future) lists.

By definition, all RDFS axiomatic triples are RDFS-entailed by even an empty RDF graph: under RDFS semantics, they always hold. However, they are not the only triples to always hold under RDFS semantics: as before, this set of triples that always hold is called the RDFS-valid triples, which includes (but is not limited to) the RDFS axiomatic triples.

> **Example 4.35**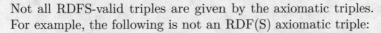
>
> Not all RDFS-valid triples are given by the axiomatic triples. For example, the following is not an RDF(S) axiomatic triple:
>
> | rdfs:member | rdf:type | rdf:Property |
> |---|---|---|
>
> However, the triple always holds under RDFS semantics due to the following semantic conditions (the first defined for RDF interpretations with the latter two defined for RDFS interpretations):
>
> - x is in I_P if and only if $(x, I_S(\texttt{rdf:Property})) \in I_{EXT}(I_S(\texttt{rdf:type}))$.
> - If $(x, y) \in I_{EXT}(I_S(\texttt{rdfs:subPropertyOf}))$, then $I_{EXT}(x) \subseteq I_{EXT}(y)$ and $x \in I_P$, $y \in I_P$.
> - If $x \in I_{CEXT}(I_S(\texttt{rdfs:ContainerMembershipProperty}))$, then $(x, I_S(\texttt{rdfs:member})) \in I_{EXT}(I_S(\texttt{rdfs:subPropertyOf}))$.
>
> combined with at least one RDFS axiomatic triple of the form:
>
> | rdf:_n | rdf:type | rdfs:ContainerMembershipProperty |
> |---|---|---|
>
> Hence the original triple is RDFS-valid: it is satisfied by every RDFS interpretation and thus RDFS-entailed by even the empty graph.

The notions of RDFS satisfaction, models and (un)satisfiability then follow as before: an RDFS interpretation I satisfies an RDF graph G if and only if I satisfies all of its triples, in which case I is an RDFS model of G; an RDF graph is RDFS-satisfiable if and only if it has an RDFS model.

Exercise 4.20

Construct an RDF graph that is RDF_D satisfiable but $RDFS_D$ unsatisfiable.

Exercise 4.21

Is the following graph $RDFS_D$-satisfiable?

ex:A	rdf:type	rdfs:Literal

4.3.4.2 RDFS Entailment

Finally, we are left with the natural notion of RDFS entailment: G RDFS-entails G' if and only if every RDFS model of G is an RDFS model of G'.

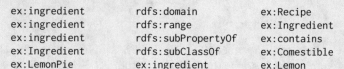

Example 4.36

Take the following RDF graph:

ex:ingredient	rdfs:domain	ex:Recipe
ex:ingredient	rdfs:range	ex:Ingredient
ex:ingredient	rdfs:subPropertyOf	ex:contains
ex:Ingredient	rdfs:subClassOf	ex:Comestible
ex:LemonPie	ex:ingredient	ex:Lemon

This graph RDFS-entails:

ex:LemonPie	rdf:type	ex:Recipe
ex:Lemon	rdf:type	ex:Ingredient
ex:LemonPie	ex:contains	ex:Lemon
ex:Lemon	rdf:type	ex:Comestible
ex:ingredient	rdf:type	rdf:Property
ex:ingredient	rdfs:subPropertyOf	ex:ingredient
ex:Ingredient	rdf:type	rdfs:Class
ex:Ingredient	rdfs:subClassOf	ex:Ingredient
ex:contains	rdf:type	rdf:Property
ex:contains	rdfs:subPropertyOf	ex:contains
ex:Comestible	rdf:type	rdfs:Class
ex:Comestible	rdfs:subClassOf	ex:Comestible
ex:LemonPie	rdf:type	rdfs:Resource

...

Also entailed would be other RDFS-valid triples, triples from simple entailment, D entailment, and RDF entailment.

We are finished formalising the semantics of RDFS with model theory!

4.4 RDF(S) Inference

Thus far we have introduced the terms in the RDF and RDFS vocabularies, given examples of what conclusions can be drawn from data using those terms, and given formal definitions of the semantics of RDF(S) and entailments possible through such terms. However, we have not spoken in detail about how a machine could leverage such a semantics to perform useful tasks: we have not discussed how practical systems can perform *inference* with respect to the RDFS semantics and these formal notions of entailment.

> **Remark 4.18**
>
> The terms *infer/inference* are often used almost interchangeably with *entail/entailment*. The terms based on "*entail*" refer conceptually to what follows as a consequence from what, whereas the term "*infer*" refers to a process of *computing* entailments. Thus in our context, a graph entails another graph, but a machine infers a new graph.
>
> Another term one may encounter is *reasoning*. Again reasoning refers to a process of determining what follows as a consequence from what and thus relates to inference. However, reasoning is (subtly) a more general term, where there are various forms of reasoning:
>
> **deductive reasoning** involves applying rules over premises to derive conclusions and is the main subject of Logic. For example, given the rule "*any recipe containing lemons contains citrus*" and the premise "*this recipe for lemon meringue contains lemons*", then the conclusion that *this recipe for lemon meringue contains citrus* must follow.
> **inductive reasoning** involves learning patterns from lots of examples – such that can be applied to future examples – and is the main subject of Machine Learning. For example, given a set of recipes and their ingredients where some are tagged as "*dessert*" and others not, inductive reasoning could extract the pattern that recipes with ingredients like "*sugar*", "*strawberries*", etc., are important to predict the presence of the "*dessert*" tag on a particular recipe, while ingredients like "*chicken*", "*pasta*", etc., help predict its absence.
> **abductive reasoning** is somewhat more subtle but involves deriving a likely explanation for an observation based on a rule. For example, if we observe that *lemon meringue is bitter*, and we know as a rule that *a dish containing a lot of citrus will be bitter*, a possible explanation for the observation is that *lemon meringue contains a lot of citrus* (though there may be other reasons why it is bitter).
>
> Various specific types of inference may be defined for these varied types of reasoning. Here we deal with deductive reasoning since we are generally concerned with "crisp" data and entailments.

Table 4.1 RDF and RDFS inference rules (in Turtle-like syntax)

ID	*if* G matches	*then* G **RDFS**$_D$**-entails**
rdfD1	?x ?p ?l . (?l a literal with datatype IRI dt(?l) $\in D$)	?x ?p _:b . _:b a dt(?l) .
rdfD2	?x ?p ?y .	?p a rdf:Property .
rdfs1	?u $\in D$	?u a rdfs:Datatype .
rdfs2	?p rdfs:domain ?c . ?x ?p ?y .	?x a ?c .
rdfs3	?p rdfs:range ?c . ?x ?p ?y .	?y a ?c .
rdfs4a	?x ?p ?y .	?x a rdfs:Resource .
rdfs4b	?x ?p ?y .	?y a rdfs:Resource .
rdfs5	?p rdfs:subPropertyOf ?q . ?x ?p ?y .	?x ?q ?y .
rdfs6	?p a rdf:Property .	?p rdfs:subPropertyOf ?p .
rdfs7	?p rdfs:subPropertyOf ?q . ?q rdfs:subPropertyOf ?r .	?p rdfs:subPropertyOf ?r .
rdfs8	?c a rdfs:Class .	?c rdfs:subClassOf rdfs:Resource .
rdfs9	?c rdfs:subClassOf ?d . ?x a ?c .	?x a ?d .
rdfs10	?c a rdfs:Class .	?c rdfs:subClassOf ?c .
rdfs11	?c rdfs:subClassOf ?d . ?d rdfs:subClassOf ?e .	?c rdfs:subClassOf ?e .
rdfs12	?p a rdfs:ContainerMembershipProperty .	?p rdfs:subPropertyOf rdfs:member .
rdfs13	?d a rdfs:Datatype .	?d rdfs:subClassOf rdf:Literal .

One method of inference we could consider is *materialisation*, where a machine computes valid entailments from a graph and makes them explicit. Then we can take the merge of input and materialised data and perform queries over that merge. Another option might be to perform *query rewriting* where an input query is expanded to retrieve more answers over the raw input data; for example, a query for all instances of the class *astronomical bodies* may be expanded to cover all sub-classes of *astronomical bodies*, such as *galaxy*, *star*, etc. (assuming that the appropriate RDFS definitions are in place).

In fact there are many general tasks we could consider that can leverage the types of entailment we have illustrated for various practical purposes, and various ways in which those tasks could be implemented algorithmically. But to start with, we need some way to represent or encode those semantics in an explicit manner that machines can read, process, and act upon.

4.4.1 RDF(S) Rules

Perhaps the most obvious encoding of the RDF(S) semantics for inference is to use *rules* that encode *if–then* conditions over the data, such that *if* some premise is matched by the data, *then* a given entailment holds. The RDF Semantics document [180] provides a non-normative list of rule-like patterns that a machine can execute over a given graph to generate valid inferences. We list these rules in Table 4.1 (recall that "a" denotes a shortcut for rdf:type); the rules follow a straightforward *if–then* pattern, where for every *if* pattern matching a sub-graph G, the associated *then* pattern is entailed by G – according to the RDF(S) semantics – using the same variable substitution. We can then use these rules, for example, to materialise entailments.

Remark 4.19 ⓘ

The *if/then*-clauses of a rule are often called the *antecedent/consequent* or *body/head* of a rule. Rules can be found in various communities with different names, such as Datalog in databases, Horn clauses in Logic Programming, etc.

Example 4.37

To materialise RDFS entailments, we can apply the rules in Table 4.1 recursively until a fixpoint is reached (this process is sometimes known as a "chase" and the fixpoint is sometimes known as the "closure"). To illustrate, let's take the following RDF graph G:

```
ex:hasIngredient    rdfs:domain          ex:Recipe
ex:hasIngredient    rdfs:range           ex:Ingredient
ex:hasIngredient    rdfs:subPropertyOf   ex:contains
ex:hasIngredient    rdfs:subPropertyOf   ex:requires
ex:Ingredient       rdfs:subClassOf      ex:Comestible
ex:LemonPie         ex:hasIngredient     ex:Lemon
```

Let's start by applying the rule rdfs5 on the data. If we look at matches for the body of rdfs5 on the data in G, we will find:

?p	?q	?x	?y
ex:hasIngredient	ex:contains	ex:LemonPie	ex:Lemon
ex:hasIngredient	ex:requires	ex:LemonPie	ex:Lemon

Binding the head of the same rule using these solutions produces two new triples we can add to G:

```
ex:LemonPie         ex:contains          ex:Lemon
ex:LemonPie         ex:requires          ex:Lemon
```

Next we could try rule rdfs9, but we would not yet find solutions in G to match its body. If we then try applying rdfs3 to G, we would add:

```
ex:Lemon            rdf:type             ex:Ingredient
```

Now if we try rdfs9 again, this time we would find the following entailment to add to G:

```
ex:Lemon            rdf:type             ex:Comestible
```

... and so on. The order in which we apply rules does not matter so long as we continue until we are sure that no rule can produce a new conclusion and a fixpoint for G is reached.

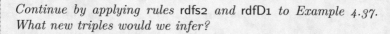

Exercise 4.22

Continue by applying rules rdfs2 and rdfD1 to Example 4.37. What new triples would we infer?

Example 4.37 does not use all rules in Table 4.1. Rules such as rdfD2, rdfs4a, rdfs4b, rdfs6, etc., encode trivial internal properties of the RDFS vocabulary, like that everything is a resource, or any property is a sub-property of itself, and so on, and so forth (as seen previously in Example 4.12).

The reader may also have noticed mention of D in Table 4.1: this refers to the set of supported datatypes (formally defined in Section 4.3.2). The reader may further have noticed that two of the rules look strange: rdfD1 and rdfs1. These rules help to support inferencing over datatypes as was discussed in Example 4.12, where rdfD1 is used to create and type surrogate blank nodes (implicitly, the blank node _:b in the head will be a fresh blank node generated each time, typed with the datatype of that literal), and where rdfs1 explicitly types each supported datatype in D as rdfs:Datatype.

Example 4.38

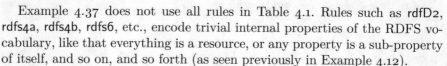

In Example 4.12, we briefly alluded to the need for surrogate blank nodes; for instance, if we had a triple of the form:

```
ex:LemonPie            ex:rating            "5.0"^^xsd:float
```

we might like to infer that:

```
"5.0"^^xsd:float    rdf:type    rdf:Literal
"5.0"^^xsd:float    rdf:type    xsd:float
```

but since we cannot have literals in the subject position, we rather create a fresh surrogate blank node just for the literal:

```
ex:LemonPie            ex:rating            _:z
_:z                    rdf:type             xsd:float
_:z                    rdf:type             rdf:Literal
```

Per the formal definitions of RDF entailment (see Section 4.3), the original triple RDF$_D$-entails these latter three triples assuming that xsd:float is recognised by D. In the interest of completeness, covering this inference is then the purpose of the rule rdfD1 in Table 4.1.

4.4.2 RDF(S) Axiomatic Triples

We previously defined a set of RDF axiomatic triples (Figure 4.1) and RDFS axiomatic triples (Figure 4.2) that always hold true, even for an empty graph. In fact, the rules in Table 4.1 are not sufficient to infer these triples; this omission, in turn, may lead to the omission of further inferences.

Example 4.39

Consider the triple:

    ex:hasTopping   rdfs:subPropertyOf   ex:hasIngredient

Intuitively, under RDFS, this triple should entail:

    ex:hasTopping   rdf:type   rdf:Property
    ex:hasIngredient   rdf:type   rdf:Property

However, there is no way to infer these triples from Table 4.1.

To cover such inferences, we can simply add the aforementioned RDF and RDFS axiomatic triples to the graph prior to applying the rules in Table 4.1.

Exercise 4.23

Find a minimal set of RDFS axiomatic triples (Figure 4.2) that need to be added prior to applying the RDFS inference rules (Table 4.1) in order to achieve the missing inferences in Example 4.39.

One complication is the presence of an infinite number of axiomatic triples mentioning rdf:_n. The recommended solution is to only add these triples for the terms of the form rdf:_n that are mentioned in the input graph, or in the case of an entailment check, the graph proposed to be entailed [180].

Remark 4.20

Figure 4.1 and Figure 4.2 do not include all RDF-valid and RDFS-valid triples, respectively. For example:

    rdfs:member   rdf:type   rdf:Property

is RDFS-valid, but is not included in the set of RDFS axiomatic triples (since it follows from other axiomatic triples and the inference rules).
    On the other hand, some of the axiomatic triples in Figure 4.1 and Figure 4.2 are redundant. For example, stating:

rdf:type	rdfs:domain	rdfs:Resource

is unnecessary when we have rule rdfs4a.

In summary, the set of RDF(S) axiomatic triples is neither maximal nor minimal: some RDF(S) valid triples are not included, while some RDF(S) axiomatic triples can be inferred by other means.

4.4.3 Generalised Triples

This far, we have defined the RDFS inference procedure as first adding axiomatic triples, and next applying rules until a fixpoint. However, before finalising the procedure, we must tackle one final complication – this time due to restrictions on what terms can appear where in an RDF triple. We already discussed how we sometimes need surrogate blank nodes to represent literals in the subject position of a triple. However, there are additional positional restrictions on RDF triples; namely, literals and blank nodes cannot appear as predicates. Do these latter restrictions cause problems?

Example 4.40

Inspired by an example from the RDF Semantics document [180], take the following (perhaps not so natural) RDF graph:

ex:hasMother	rdfs:subPropertyOf	_:b
_:b	rdfs:domain	ex:Child
ex:John	ex:hasMother	ex:Mary

Now consider the following (valid RDF) triple:

ex:John	rdf:type	ex:Child

Should this triple be entailed by the original three triples? According to the RDFS semantics defined in Section 4.3, the answer is yes. In summary, if we were to forget about the restrictions on where terms can be placed in RDF triples, we could infer the following:

ex:John	_:b	ex:Mary
ex:John	rdf:type	ex:Child

However, the first intermediary triple has a blank node in the predicate position and hence it cannot be written down in the materialisation procedure. The second triple is valid RDF and is RDFS-entailed from the original graph but may not have been inferred (due to being inferred from a "valid" but non-RDF triple).

> 1. Add the RDF [and RDFS] axiomatic triples to G (adding at least all of those corresponding to the rdf:_n terms explicitly mentioned in G, or if G contains no such terms, adding the corresponding triples for rdf:_1).
> 2. Apply the RDF [and RDFS] inference rules over G, recursively adding the conclusions back to the graph and reapplying rules until no new conclusions are formed: i.e., until a *fixpoint* is reached. Generalised triples should be allowed in this process.

Fig. 4.3 RDF[S] inference procedure

Thus, aiming towards inferring all expected entailments, the RDF Semantics specification endorses inferring generalised triples, where term–position restrictions on RDF triples are relaxed to allow blank nodes, IRIs and literals in any position of the triple. The specification also endorses replacing rule rdfD1 with the generalised form GrdfD1 shown in Table 4.2: when literals are allowed as subjects, there is no longer a need for surrogate blank nodes.

Table 4.2 Generalised RDF rule

ID	if G matches	then G RDFS$_D$-entails
GrdfD1	?x ?p ?l . (?l a literal with datatype IRI dt(?l) $\in D$)	?l a dt(?l) .

4.4.4 RDF(S) Inference Procedure

Given an input RDF graph G, the process of inference with respect to RDFS semantics suggested by the standard [180] is given in Figure 4.3. The standard proves that all and only the entailments expected according to the RDFS semantics will be derived as inferences by this process [180].

Before we formalise this result, given an RDF graph G, we must first define the *generalised RDFS closure of G* as the result of applying the RDFS inference procedure of Figure 4.3 to G; furthermore, given a second RDF graph G', we define the *generalised RDFS closure of G towards G'* as the result of applying the RDFS inference procedure of Figure 4.3 to G but where the RDFS axiomatic triples for all terms of the form rdf:_n appearing in G' are additionally added in Step 1. These two concepts are important for ensuring the correct handling of entailments that require intermediate triples that are not valid RDF, and entailments that deal with container membership properties, respectively. We now state the result.

Theorem 2. *Let D recognise only* xsd:string *and* rdf:langString. *Let G be an RDF graph that is $RDFS_D$-satisfiable. Let G' be a second RDF graph. Let G^* denote the generalised RDFS closure of G towards G'. Then G $RDFS_D$-entails G' if and only if G^* simple-entails G'* [180].

Remark 4.21   (i)

The result also holds under the more lightweight RDF semantics, replacing RDFS closure, satisfiability and entailment with RDF closure, satisfiability and entailment (D remains the same).

Remark 4.22   (i)

Computing the generalised RDFS closure of G (towards G') always terminates and can be run in polynomial time.

Exercise 4.24

Regarding Remark 4.22, can you argue why the generalised RDFS closure is always guaranteed to terminate (in polynomial steps)?

Theorem 2 only holds when D recognises a minimal set of datatypes: if we add, for example, xsd:boolean to D, although we could use datatype canonicalisation procedures to capture many relevant inferences, the procedure would still miss the sorts of exotic entailments discussed in Remark 4.15. Of course, an implementation may still to choose to support such datatypes and apply incomplete inferencing through, for example, canonicalisation.

4.4.5 Extensional Semantics

Aside from missing exotic inferences involving datatypes, the RDFS inference procedure likewise misses entailments that would result if the standard considered an *if-and-only-if*-style semantics (aka. an *extensional semantics*).

Example 4.41

Let's consider the following triples:

```
ex:hasTopping        rdfs:subPropertyOf    ex:hasIngredient
ex:hasIngredient     rdfs:domain           ex:Recipe
```

Given these two triples and any triple of the form:

```
x                    ex:hasTopping         y
```

We can infer:

```
x                    ex:hasIngredient      y
x                    rdf:type              ex:Recipe
```

Hence, from the last triple, we could likewise think that the original two triples should infer the following triple in the RDFS vocabulary:

```
ex:hasTopping        rdfs:domain           ex:Recipe
```

But we have no such rule to perform this inference in Table 4.1, nor does the addition of the axiomatic triples help us at all.

As a similar example, consider:

```
ex:hasTopping        rdfs:subPropertyOf    ex:hasIngredient
ex:hasIngredient     rdfs:range            ex:Ingredient
```

Following a similar intuition, it seems natural to infer:

```
ex:hasTopping        rdfs:range            ex:Ingredient
```

Exercise 4.25

Consider the following triples:

```
ex:hasTopping        rdfs:range            ex:Topping
ex:Topping           rdfs:subClassOf       ex:Ingredient
```

What "seemingly intuitive" inference not supported by the previously discussed rules and axiomatic triples would seem to follow from these two triples (in the same style as Example 4.41)?

Likewise, consider the following RDF graph:

```
ex:hasMeatTopping    rdfs:domain           ex:MeatRecipe
ex:MeatRecipe        rdfs:subClassOf       ex:Recipe
```

Is there another such inference possible from these two triples?

Though the types of entailments outlined in Example 4.41 seem like they should intuitively hold, they are not mandated by the standard definition of

RDFS-entailment (see Section 4.3) since the pertinent semantic conditions – for `rdfs:domain` and `rdfs:range` in this case – are defined with *if* rather than *if-and-only-if*; in other words, even if we know, for example, that the value of a given property must always be in a given class, the standard semantics do not require us to entail the relevant `rdfs:range` triple.

Conditions on sub-class, sub-property, domain and range are not given as "*if-and-only-if*" because it is more difficult to implement a procedure that captures all entailments possible under such a semantics. In fact, there are quite a number of strange entailment patterns that would arise in trying to infer all possible `rdfs:subClassOf`, `rdfs:subPropertyOf`, `rdfs:domain` and `rdfs:range` triples. We now look at a non-obvious example.

Example 4.42

Take the following two triples:

`rdfs:subClassOf`	`rdfs:subPropertyOf`	`ex:containedWithin`
`ex:containedWithin`	`rdfs:domain`	`ex:Grouping`

If we used a stronger if-and-only-if semantic condition for sub-class in RDFS, then the above two triples would entail:

`rdfs:Class`	`rdfs:subClassOf`	`ex:Grouping`

Though this example is exotic, a complete inference procedure would need to capture this entailment and others likewise.

In the 2004 version of the RDF Semantics [179], an **extensional semantics** was defined with precisely this stronger if-and-only-if semantics on sub-class, sub-property, domain and range. Likewise an informal set of valid inference rules under this semantics was provided in the standard; these rules are enumerated for reference in Table 4.1. However, the standard warned that this set of inference rules was not known to lead to a sound and complete inference procedure for this semantics. Though Franconi et al. [132] later proposed a practical inference procedure for RDFS under an extensional semantics, discussion of such a semantics (including the rules of Table 4.1) was completely dropped from the 2014 version of the RDF Semantics standard [180].

This discussion more generally highlights that although the model theory defines the notion of entailment in a rigorous manner, it does not offer any direct answers on how to compute such entailment. Though the extensional semantics would be easy to define in terms of the model theory – and in fact would be cleaner and more succinct to define – designing a provably sound and complete inference procedure would be more difficult. This issue of computability of what a model theory defines will return again in the next chapter where we discuss OWL: a more complex ontology language defined in terms of a model theory and with the stronger if-and-only-if semantics.

Table 4.3 Extensional RDFS inference patterns

ID	*if* G matches	*then* G extens. RDFS$_D$-entails
ext1	?u rdfs:domain ?v . ?v rdfs:subClassOf ?z .	?u rdfs:domain ?z .
ext2	?u rdfs:range ?v . ?v rdfs:subClassOf ?z .	?u rdfs:range ?z .
ext3	?u rdfs:domain ?v . ?w rdfs:subPropertyOf ?u .	?w rdfs:domain ?v .
ext4	?u rdfs:range ?v . ?w rdfs:subPropertyOf ?u .	?w rdfs:range ?v .
ext5	rdf:type rdfs:subPropertyOf ?w . ?w rdfs:domain ?v .	rdfs:Resource rdfs:subClassOf ?v .
ext6	rdfs:subClassOf rdfs:subPropertyOf ?w . ?w rdfs:domain ?v .	rdfs:Class rdfs:subClassOf ?v .
ext7	rdfs:subPropertyOf rdfs:subPropertyOf ?w . ?w rdfs:domain ?v .	rdf:Property rdfs:subClassOf ?v .
ext8	rdfs:subClassOf rdfs:subPropertyOf ?w . ?w rdfs:range ?v .	rdfs:Class rdfs:subClassOf ?v .
ext9	rdfs:subPropertyOf rdfs:subPropertyOf ?w . ?w rdfs:range ?v .	rdf:Property rdfs:subClassOf ?v .

4.5 Summary

In this chapter, we introduced the RDF Schema (RDFS) standard, used to describe lightweight semantics for classes and properties. Such features are useful to allow publishers to make explicit the semantics of the terms used in RDF data. Combined with a formal process of inference, this can then avoid the need for publishing redundant data or writing redundant patterns in queries, instead allowing the machine to automatically deduce novel data through an inference process; for example, rather than the publisher having to explicitly define that each *red supergiant* in their data is a *star* and an *astronomical body*; or rather than each user interested in entities of type *astronomical body* needing to also ask for instances of all sub-classes like *star*, *red supergiant*, etc.; with RDFS, one can define a class hierarchy and use RDFS inference to automatically conclude the relevant class memberships.

After motivating RDFS, we described the vocabulary it provides, which aside from allowing to define sub-class relations, also allows for specifying sub-properties, classes that are the domain of properties, and classes that are the range of properties. RDFS also defines some auxiliary vocabulary for annotating resources, for dealing with RDF containers, as well as classes to denote, for example, the class of all resources, or the class of all classes.

With the RDFS vocabulary covered, we then looked at how we could provide a rigorous definition of the semantics – the meaning – of such a vocabulary. We discussed how model theory provides a basis for specifying such formal definitions using set theory, and proceeded to use this theory to define notions of satisfiability and entailment for RDF and RDFS; namely we provided model theoretic definitions of simple semantics, D semantics, RDF semantics and RDFS semantics. These formalisms then provide a precise definition of which RDF graphs entail which under the given semantics.

While model theory allows us to define formal notions of entailment, it does not immediately lead us to an inference procedure that can perform computational tasks relating to such entailments. We thus provided details of an inference procedure for RDF(S) based on rules and discussed the manner in which it is sound (identifying only correct entailments) and complete (identifying all correct entailments) with respect to the formal semantics.

4.6 Discussion

Discussion 4.3

FRANK: The model theoretic semantics of Section 4.3 was challenging
  to follow. How are Web developers expected to use the Semantic
  Web standards when they are defined in such a theoretical manner?
AIDAN: While that is a without doubt a valid concern, not everyone
  who wants to work with RDFS needs to understand the model theory semantics – much in the same way that people who programme
  with Python do not necessarily need to understand how the com-
  piler works or what a Turing machine is (though it may help). More
  concretely, folks who wish to define their vocabularies using RDFS,
  for example, often simply need an intuitive understanding of what
  terms like rdfs:subPropertyOf or rdfs:domain mean and how they
  can be used – as discussed in Section 4.2. Other folks who wish
  to develop reasoning systems for RDFS can work directly with the
  rule-based inference procedure discussed in Section 4.4.
FRANK: Who then needs the model theoretic semantics? Why not just
  define the vocabulary and some rules?
AIDAN: The model-theory provides a rigorous definition of RDF(S),
  which of course is a key goal for any standard to avoid incompatibilities arising at a later stage due to different interpretations of
  what the semantics is supposed to be. Such a definition can be
  used to propose novel inferencing algorithms for RDFS and prove
  them to be compliant with the standard semantics, or otherwise
  formalise what entailments they can miss. It allows for studying
  the computational complexity of various problems associated with
  the standard [162]. Furthermore, it allows RDFS to be extended in
  future standards (including OWL, as described next).
ANNE: When discussing the RDFS vocabulary, you mentioned that
  there is some debate about the importance of certain features like
  container-membership properties and meta-classes, where the inference procedure in Section 4.4 is complicated by these features
  – particularly the container-membership properties, which lead to
  a potentially infinite number of axiomatic triples. Why were these
  features included in the standard if they are so controversial?
AIDAN: When the RDF(S) Semantics was first formally standardised in
  2004 [179], it was not yet clear which features of RDF would become
  of most importance in the future. Taking container-membership
  properties, for example, the idea that RDF – based on unordered
  sets of triples – may need standard ways to express ordered lists
  seems quite reasonable. Hence containers were included in the standard RDF model and syntax. Thereafter, being able to query for

any member of such a list seems useful, and hence `rdfs:member` was introduced as a super-property of all the container-membership properties. In retrospect, containers would not become frequently used [144], where collections and other custom methods for representing order became more popular; hence the additional semantic complications are probably not justified for the little adoption they have received. While there was discussion around deprecating them in the updated RDF 1.1 specification, in the end they were not. However, there is no particular reason why an implementation needs to support them, and more minimal inference processes have been proposed for a version of RDFS without such features [286].

JULIE: So RDFS has been around for a while. Is it used in practice?

AIDAN: Yes, studies have shown that the core features of RDFS – sub-class, sub-property, domain and range – have been widely used in published RDF data, though features relating to containers, for example, are less commonly used [144].

JULIE: And again, is RDFS a key ingredient for the Web of Data?

AIDAN: Until (or *unless*) we reach a point where we have strong AI that can emulate an understanding of the Web's content in a similar fashion to how humans can, something *like* RDFS would certainly seem to be a key building block for the Web of Data. RDFS allows us to tell machines, for example, that all *red supergiant*s are *star*s, any pair of entities related by *mother of* are also related by *parent of*, and so forth. If we do not provide such semantics to the machines of the Web and empower them to perform inference over such semantics in a general way, this leaves three alternatives: publishers make redundant data explicit, users write more complex queries, or developers use some ad hoc methods specific to their website to enable such inference locally. Relating to the latter point, aside from RDFS being a Web standard, it is designed to allow publishers to reuse external definitions – which is a major design principle of Linked Data discussed in a later chapter. So it is not the case that every website needs to define the class hierarchy of astronomical bodies, for example, but rather agreement can be reached on one vocabulary and reused by multiple websites to define their data, allowing uniform inference methods to be applied. So in conclusion, yes, while one can reasonably argue over specific details, something like RDFS *is* a key ingredient for a Web of Data. But in fact, there are many semantic definitions that would be useful to specify that are not supported by RDFS; hence the OWL standard – that we will discuss in the following chapter – was proposed.

Chapter 5
Web Ontology Language

In order to realise the full potential of a Web of Data, we need machines to be capable of collecting, interpreting and integrating data from various sources. The RDFS standard described in the previous chapter offers a step in that direction, outlining a well-defined vocabulary that primarily allows us to specify sub-classes, sub-properties, and the domains and ranges of properties, which in turn can be interpreted by machines and used to reason about the data. But in fact, we are still quite limited in what we can express with this vocabulary: more such features would be useful, including, for example, the ability to state that two IRIs refer to the same resource, or to different resources; to state that a user-defined property is transitive; or to state that two classes must be disjoint; or to define a new class as the union of two existing classes, or the intersection of those classes; and so forth.

The **Web Ontology Language (OWL)** aims to provide exactly such a vocabulary: it extends the core RDFS vocabulary with a wide range of new, well-defined terms that allow for saying much *much* more in a machine-readable fashion than would otherwise be possible relying on RDFS alone. Using OWL, a much richer semantics can be made explicit for a given dataset, which in turn can help to automatically integrate data from various sources.

Example 5.1

Let us consider three RDF graphs taken from different websites. The first graph is from a source that talks about winners of Nobel Prizes:

ex1:NLP1983	ex1:awardedTo	ex1:WilliamGolding
ex1:NLP1983	rdf:type	ex1:NobelPrizeLit
ex1:NLP1983	ex1:year	"1982"^^xsd:integer
ex1:WilliamGolding	rdf:type	ex1:Novelist
ex1:WilliamGolding	rdfs:label	"William Golding"

The second source has some biographical data about authors:

© Springer Nature Switzerland AG 2020
A. Hogan, *The Web of Data*, https://doi.org/10.1007/978-3-030-51580-5_5

```
        ex2:WGGolding          rdf:type           ex2:Author
        ex2:WGGolding          ex2:foughtIn       ex2:NormandyInvasion
```

The third source has some data about wars:

```
        ex3:NormandyInvasion   rdf:type           ex3:Conflict
        ex3:NormandyInvasion   ex3:partOf         ex3:OperationOverlord
        ex3:OperationOverlord  ex3:partOf         ex3:WorldWarII
```

All three sources have a high level of semantic heterogeneity: other than some core RDF(S) terms, they use different vocabularies.

Now given these three sources, let's assume that a user – perhaps Julie from Example 1.1 – issues a query in her own vocabulary:

```
        ?x                     rdf:type           ex4:WWIIVeteran
        ?x                     rdf:type           ex4:NobelLaureateLit
        ?x                     rdfs:label         ?y
```

Intuitively we can imagine that the query is asking for the names of people who fought in World War II and are Nobel Laureates in Literature.

To answer this query, we are going to need to bridge the four vocabularies: the three vocabularies used in the data and the fourth used in the query. As discussed previously, in theory at least, we can use explicit semantics to bridge these types of gaps and integrate the data.

With RDFS, we could state, for example:

```
        ex1:Novelist           rdfs:subClassOf    ex2:Author
        ex2:Author             rdfs:subClassOf    ex2:Person
        ex2:foughtIn           rdfs:domain        ex2:Person
        ex2:foughtIn           rdfs:range         ex3:Conflict
        ex2:foughtIn           rdfs:subPropertyOf ex2:involvedIn
```

Here we see various semantics made explicit with respect to several classes and properties. The first and fourth claims are notable because they intuitively connect terms from two different vocabularies: we refer to these claims as semantic mappings, or simply just mappings. While these two mapping triples do help to bridge the vocabularies used in the sources, none of these triples really help us yet to answer the query.

However, with a richer ontology language than RDFS, we could go much further to make the semantics of these data explicit and to specify mappings that better bridge these sources. We could state, for example:

- that ex1:WilliamGolding and ex2:WGGolding refer to the same resource, while ex2:NormandyInvasion and ex3:NormandyInvasion also refer to the same resource;
- that ex3:partOf is transitive, meaning that if x ex3:partOf y and y ex3:partOf z, then x ex3:partOf z;
- that ex1:hasAward is the inverse of ex1:awardedTo, meaning that if x ex1:hasAward y, then y ex1:awardedTo x;
- that given a path where x ex2:foughtIn y and y ex3:partOf z, then x ex2:foughtIn z;
- that the class ex4:WWIIVeteran is the class of all resources with the value ex3:WorldWarII for the property ex2:foughtIn;
- that the class ex4:NobelLaureateLit is the class of all resources with a value from the class ex1:NobelPrizeLit for ex1:hasAward;
- and so forth.

With these semantics made explicit – and assuming an appropriate inference process – from the merge of the above three sources, we could then automatically infer data relevant to the original query:

```
ex1:WilliamGolding      rdf:type       ex4:WWIIVeteran
ex1:WilliamGolding      rdf:type       ex4:NobelLaureateLit
ex1:WilliamGolding      rdfs:label     "William Golding"
```

Thus we could generate (at least) the following answer to the query:

?x	?y
ex1:WilliamGolding	"William Golding"

Such claims (and more besides) can be expressed in a well-defined manner through the richer semantics offered by OWL.

5.1 Overview

In this chapter, we describe the OWL vocabulary, which can be used to express the types of definitions illustrated in Example 5.1. We will first discuss the general notion of ontologies, and how they relate to the Web of Data. We then discuss some preliminaries relating to the model theoretic semantics of OWL before we begin to introduce and define the additional vocabulary that OWL introduces. We then discuss computational issues relating to inference that motivate the need for a variety of restricted sub-languages of OWL.

Historical Note 5.1

Inspired by earlier works on Web ontology languages – including SHOE [252], DAML [183], OIL [125], DAML+OIL [183, 211] – work on the Web Ontology Language (OWL) first began at the W3C in 2001. Subsequently, the first official version of OWL became a W3C Recommendation in February 2004 [266, 363], extending upon the RDFS vocabulary of the same time. OWL 2 – which first became a W3C Recommendation in October 2009 and was revised in December 2012 [149, 190] – added further features and vocabulary to the OWL specification. This chapter reflects the 2012 version of OWL 2.

The remainder of this chapter is structured as follows:

Section 5.2 discusses the core notion of an "ontology" and how it relates to OWL and the Web of Data.

Section 5.3 provides some preliminaries for the model theory that is used to formally define OWL.

Section 5.4 details the OWL vocabulary, including examples, discussion and definitions.

Section 5.5 discusses some of the reasoning tasks that can be performed with respect to OWL ontologies.

Section 5.6 demonstrates why reasoning over ontologies described with the unrestricted OWL language is computationally problematic, further introducing some restricted sub-languages of OWL for which implementations of reasoning tasks become more practical.

Sections 5.7 and 5.8 conclude the chapter with a summary and discussion.

5.2 Ontologies

To begin, we should first give some context with respect to the "O" in OWL.

The notion of *ontology* originates in philosophy, where it refers to the study of the nature of things and how they can be categorised.

More concretely perhaps, ontology deals with *epistemological questions* – questions about knowledge and understanding – such as what characterises an entity, how can entities be grouped or composed into hierarchical classifications (also known as **taxonomies**), what are the *essential* properties of entities (the properties that define what the entity is), what are the *accidental* properties of entities (the properties that the entity could change or not have but still be the same entity), how can properties themselves be grouped or categorised in a hierarchical manner, and so forth.

In the area of computer science, an ontology is a formal representation of knowledge that forms a shared conceptualisation of a given domain. Thus the computer science notion of an ontology, for a given domain, could be seen as an explicit, formal answer to the types of ontological questions posed in philosophy for that domain: what are the entities, how can they be categorised, what are the properties of these entities, what are the essential properties, and so forth. The goal is not to find the "correct" answer to these questions, but to find an answer parties can agree to: if multiple parties working in the same domain can agree, a priori, to the same formal conceptualisation of their domain, then they can then exchange and work collectively on data with higher levels of interoperability and less chance of misunderstanding.

Example 5.2

Let's take the seemingly innocent example of the concept of a *book*. What can we say about a book? What makes a book a book? While these may seem like rather philosophical questions – questions of semantics – their answers do have direct practical consequences.

For a bibliographic database of authors and the books they wrote, we can think that a book has an author or author(s), it has a year when it was first published, it is written in a given language or languages with translations to other languages, it has a unique International Standard Book Number (ISBN), it may have received certain awards or had positions on the best-seller charts of various countries, it may have sequels or prequels, it may have various critical reviews, and so forth.

For a library, much of the above still applies: books have authors and awards and so forth. But in the context of a library, a book can have a Dewey Decimal Code (DDC) code, or a book can have a number of copies available, or a book may have a member currently holding it, or a date when it will be available again, and so forth.

For a bookstore, a book will have a price associated with it, the number of books in stock, it may have various editions and versions available, reviews, staff recommendations and so forth.

For an instructor, a book may have pages and chapters and exercises; it may have certain courses in which it is used, and so forth.

For a reader, a book may have a number of pages read, a number of pages left to read, a review, some annotations, and so forth.

For a publisher, a book may have a particular printing and binding method, a particular royalty agreement or copyright enforcement policy, a particular marketing and pricing strategy, and so forth.

For an online retailer, a book may come in physical or electronic formats, or may even be available as an audiobook, and so forth.

And so forth.

What we can say about a book – what makes a book a *book* – depends on whom you ask. A book means different things in different contexts.

A book can be thought of as the abstract work, or a particular version of that work, or a physical copy of that version of the work, and so on.

Us humans are good at dealing with such ambiguity; for example, if we are holding a book and a passer-by remarks that they've read that book, we will understand that they likely refer to the abstract work and not that particular physical copy of the book. If someone asks if the book is ours, we will understand that they are probably asking about the physical copy and not authorship of the abstract work. We resolve such ambiguities based on shared experience. As a result, when communicating with other humans, we are only as unambiguous as we need to be – and often (thankfully) no more unambiguous than that.

But if we wish to exchange data between different contexts – for example, if we wished to automatically integrate data from bibliographic databases, libraries, bookstores, online retailers, etc., to provide a user with options on how they can read books by a given author – then we will need to more unambiguous about what we mean by a "book".

For example, when exporting bibliographic data, if we define that ISBNs uniquely identify a book (which will be possible in OWL), then we need to be careful that that does not apply to physical copies of a book, where distinct copies may share the same ISBN. Conversely, if we were to define that a copy of a book must have a number of pages (which again will be possible in OWL), then we may have interoperability issues when it comes to the online retailer publishing audiobooks.

Here we could use an ontology – in the computer science sense – to formalise a conceptualisation of "a book" that is shared by the bibliographic database, the library, the bookstore, the reader, etc., facilitating interoperability in the concrete sense of being able to exchange and integrate data across contexts. Ideally the ontology would:

- facilitate data exchange across contexts without loss of information, where all local data in each context can be mapped to the ontology;
- support different ways of expressing analogous data preferable in different contexts and have explicit semantics to align them;
- have a clear semantics that avoids unintended consequences in diverse contexts, including those not originally anticipated;
- be extensible.

Assuming agreement on such an ontology for books, we could then start exchanging data over the Web about books in a much more interoperable manner than if each party simply created a data model (e.g., relational schema) with just their local application in mind.

Project 5.1

Sketch an abstract ontology for books that fits at least the scenarios discussed in Example 5.2. You can sketch the ontology in natural language, with a drawing, as a relational schema, or however you prefer. What classes relating to books are necessary to cover these scenarios? What attributes/properties would these classes have? How do these classes interrelate? How might the ontology be extended in future? How might it connect later with external ontologies?

Another important property of ontologies in the context of computer science is that they facilitate certain inference tasks. For example, if we know that books have unique ISBNs, then we could automatically integrate information on books from different sources with the same ISBNs.

In the context of the Web, creating detailed ontologies – whose definitions a relevant set of parties can agree upon – thus provides a shared, formal conceptualisation under which machines can exchange data.

Discussion 5.1

ANNA: Getting people to agree on definitions for everything on the Web seems like a huge task. How will these ontologies come about?

AIDAN: This idea of shared conceptualisations is not new. For example, libraries use standard classification schemes like the DDC to organise books, which can help increase interoperability across libraries. Such schemes can be seen as a very simple form of ontology that arose out of a very practical need. Ontologies are already used in a variety of walks of life and will continue to emerge as needed.

Example 5.3

A prominent example of the practical use of ontologies comes from the area of health-care, where hospitals often wish to exchange **Electronic Health Records (EHRs):** when a new patient visits a hospital for the first time, an electronic record of their medical history – previous illnesses or treatments, current medication, etc. – may be more reliable than taking a verbal history since the patient may omit or forget important details pertaining to their current care. In such cases, it is vital to avoid ambiguity: for example, the term "cold" in a medical record may refer to the opposite of feeling warm, or may refer to a common cold, or may refer to a chest cold (acute bronchitis), or may refer to chronic obstructive lung disease (with the acronym COLD). Thus a variety of standards have emerged to increase interoperability of EHRs and related clinical and administrative data, the most prominent of which is perhaps **Health Level 7 (HL7)**, which aside from general guidelines and methodologies, also offers well-defined vocabularies and models to facilitate data exchange, which can also be seen as ontologies [301].

Discussion 5.2

ANNA: But these few domains with existing ontologies are just a drop in the ocean of what we would need to exchange data on the Web.

AIDAN: Yes, but detailed ontologies are not necessary to start exchanging data in a given domain. They can be added, adopted, improved, extended, mapped, replaced, etc., as needs arise. A general trend at the moment is towards defining and promoting vocabularies for a given domain in order to first ensure agreement on the terms to use [389]. Such vocabularies are associated with some semantic definitions, forming lightweight ontologies. A prominent example is schema.org[a], proposed by Google, Microsoft, Yahoo and Yandex as a broad-but-lightweight ontology that publishers can use to embed metadata in their webpages about entities from a variety of domains. We will discuss this more in Chapter 8.

---

[a] http://schema.org/

Defining ontologies thus requires shared agreement, which in turn implies a social cost that must be justified by a clear benefit, particularly in terms of data exchange. But ontologies are never "all or nothing": one can start with a relatively simple ontology that can be extended and refined over time. In terms of costs, this is often described as a *"pay-as-you-go"* scenario, where, beginning with a simple and low-cost ontology that serves initial needs, one can "pay" to further extend the ontology as needs be. One can thus also define an ontology that bridges two other existing ontologies, permitting the exchange of data across previously distinct conceptualisations. The overall vision is that ontologies can thus begin to emerge on the Web where they are most in need, and later be extended, merged or bridged – as needs justify.

The next question then is: how should ontologies be represented? In general, any formal representation of knowledge could be called an ontology, including, for example, claims made in RDFS. However, the term "ontology" has the *connotation* of a rich body of formalised knowledge, perhaps richer than what RDFS can express. This is what OWL offers: a rich vocabulary that extends RDFS and allows for expressing much, much more.

As per the case of RDFS, ontologies described in OWL not only serve as documentation of a shared conceptualisation, but also further serve as a machine-readable description of the semantics of a particular domain (or domains), thus permitting automated inference. However, this additional *expressivity* comes at a cost: inference tasks become more computationally expensive – and even **undecidable**, i.e., there exist no sound and complete algorithms for them – when considering reasoning over ontologies described using such an expressive language. Hence we encounter a fundamental trade-off: being able to express more allows for a richer shared conceptualisation, but makes inferencing much more computationally difficult.

The goal of the Web Ontology Language (OWL) – the topic of this chapter – is to provide a rich language with which detailed ontologies can be described in a formal, unambiguous, machine-readable fashion in order to increase interoperability, not only in terms of the exchange and integration of data on the Web, but also the exchange and integration of ontologies themselves. Unfortunately, the resulting language, if left unrestricted, leads to undecidability for common tasks. Hence, OWL also defines restricted versions of the language, called sub-languages, that offer practical guarantees with respect to **decidability** and computational complexity for different tasks.

Exercise 5.1

A zebroid is a cross between a zebra and another (non-zebra) member of the Equus genus (a horse, a donkey, an ass, etc.). Sire is the equine father relation, while dam *is the equine mother relation.*

After this brief lesson on equine breeding, consider the graph:

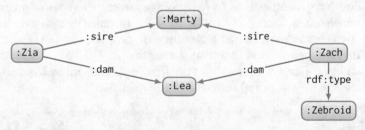

Based on these data – and some background knowledge about how the world works – we, as humans, will probably jump to the conclusion that Zia is also a zebroid. But for a machine on the Web of Data to draw such a conclusion, we would need to make some definitions and assumptions explicit for machines (in a formal language such as OWL). List all of the definitions/assumptions (in natural language) that are required to logically derive the conclusion that Zia is a zebroid.

Further Reading 5.1

This chapter focuses on describing the OWL 2 standard in terms of the features and semantics of its language, how reasoning can be conducted over ontologies using the language, and so forth. We will not cover in detail the methodologies and tools that can be used to design and achieve consensus on an ontology within a particular organisation or community. Such is the subject of the area of *ontology engineering*, on which there already exists considerable literature to which we refer for more details, including the books by Allemang and Hendler [8], Hitzler et al. [189], and Hoeskstra [192]; book chapters by Gangemi and Presutti [137], Pinto et al. [319], and Sure et al. [375]; surveys by Brank et al. [75], Katifori et al. [225], and Simperl [361]; as well as papers by Blomqvist et al. [64], Doran et al. [116], Horridge et al. [206], Peroni [312], Strohmaier et al. [371], and Suárez-Figueroa et al. [373].

5.3 OWL 2 Model Theory

In Section 4.3 we defined a model theoretic semantics for RDFS based on models, interpretations and entailment. Likewise the OWL vocabulary can be defined in terms of model theory [349, 281]. We will use this model theory to more rigorously define the vocabulary introduced in the section that follows, complementing examples. We recall the notion of a simple interpretation I from Definition 9, composed of I_R (a set of resources), I_P (a set of properties), I_{EXT} (which maps a property in I_P to a set of pairs of resources in $I_R \times I_R$), I_S (which maps an IRI to a resource or property in $I_R \cup I_P$), and I_L (which maps a well-formed literal to a resource in I_R). We will further use the notation I_C (the set of classes), and I_{CEXT} (which maps from a class to its members: a subset of I_R) introduced in Definition 20.

Remark 5.1

OWL is defined in two different flavours, with two formal semantics specified through model theory: Direct Semantics [281] and RDF-Based Semantics [349]. When defining the OWL 2 Vocabulary in the following section, we will follow the RDF-Based Semantics because it (1) extends the RDF Semantics discussed in Section 4.3; and (2) it is more concise than the Direct Semantics counterpart. We may simplify some aspects of the model theoretic definitions; for example, we will drop some syntactic conditions that are not essential to understanding the OWL vocabulary. Later in the chapter, we will motivate and discuss the Direct Semantics [281] (defined to maintain decidability).

OWL semantics is generally defined in an if-and-only-if (aka. *extensional*) manner. This is similar to the extended if-and-only-if semantics discussed for RDFS in Section 4.4.5. Such a semantics will allow for additional types of entailments but at the cost of making inference more complex.

Finally, unlike RDFS, certain OWL definitions may involve 3, 4, 5 or even an arbitrary number of domain terms. For example, we may define that the (1) *child* of a (2) *human* is (3) *human*; such definitions involve precisely three domain terms. Or we may define that the class (1) *equus* is the union of (2) *horses*, (3) *zebras*, (4) *donkeys* and (5) *asses*; such definitions may involve an arbitrary number of domain terms. While binary relations can be expressed easily as a single RDF triple, these *n*-ary definitions cannot.

Example 5.4

To represent the OWL definition that the *child* of a *human* is *human*, we use the following RDF triples [153]:

```
:Human        rdfs:subClassOf     _:b
_:b           owl:allValuesFrom   :Human
_:b           owl:onProperty      :child
```

Here we use two triples and a blank node _:b to first define the class of all things whose children (if any) are all members of :Human. With the rdfs:subClassOf relation, we then say that any member of :Human must be in this class. Such a definition is not possible in a single triple.

To represent that *equus* is the union of *asses*, *donkeys*, *horses* and *zebras*, since we can have the union of an arbitrary number of classes, we use an RDF collection (aka. RDF list; see Section 3.5.4):

```
:Equus     owl:equivalentClass   _:u
_:u        owl:unionOf           ( :Ass :Donkey :Horse :Zebra )
```

This expands to ten triples of the following form:

```
:Equus     owl:equivalentClass   _:u
_:u        owl:unionOf           _:b1
_:b1       rdf:first             :Ass
_:b1       rdf:rest              _:b2
...        ...                   ...
_:b4       rdf:rest              rdf:nil
```

Here we use the blank node _:u to represent the class that is the union of *asses*, *donkeys*, *horses* and *zebras*, and say that the class *equus* is precisely equivalent to this union class (which states that any member of class *ass*, *donkey*, *horse* or *zebra* is a member of *equus* and vice versa).

As we will see later, various OWL definitions require multiple triples – possibly even an arbitrary-length collection – to express in RDF [153].

Along these lines, we will write $I_{LIST}(b_1, x_1, \ldots, x_n)$ to represent the boolean condition that there exists $\{b_1, \ldots, b_n, x_1, \ldots, x_n\} \subseteq I_R$ such that:

- $(b_1, x_1) \in I_{EXT}(\text{rdf:first})$; and
- $(b_1, b_2) \in I_{EXT}(\text{rdf:rest})$; and
- ...; and
- $(b_n, x_n) \in I_{EXT}(\text{rdf:first})$; and
- $(b_n, I_S(\text{rdf:nil})) \in I_{EXT}(\text{rdf:rest})$.

In other words, $I_{LIST}(b_1, x_1, \ldots, x_n)$ states that the interpretation I satisfies a collection with the head b_1 and the sequence of elements $(x_1, \ldots, x_n)$.

5.4 OWL 2 Vocabulary

OWL 2 introduces a variety of novel and well-defined terms that greatly extend the terms available from the RDFS vocabulary. In this section, we introduce the OWL 2 vocabulary categorised by how the constituent terms are used: to make claims about the equality and inequality of resources, to make claims about properties, to make claims about classes, to define new classes, and finally, to define new datatypes. Before continuing, we discuss some conventions and abbreviations that we will use in the following section:

1. Rather than first present the OWL 1 vocabulary and then the OWL 2 vocabulary, we will introduce the OWL 1 and OWL 2 vocabulary together. We will mark terms that are new to OWL 2 with an asterisk symbol (*).
2. We will use x, y, z to refer to general resources (from I_R); p, q to refer to properties (from I_P); b, c to refer to classes (from I_C); and n to refer to natural numbers ($n \geq 0$). For an RDF term ex:term, we may use the local name in small-caps TERM to denote its referent (i.e., $I_S(\text{ex:term})$).

5.4.1 Equality and Inequality

As was discussed in Section 4.3.1, RDF does not have a UNA, meaning that multiple (coreferent) IRIs and/or literals may refer to the same resource. Not applying a UNA means that publishers do not need to agree in every case on a specific term for every single resource of interest out there. Coreferent terms are then common in data published on the Web [113, 166, 204]. With the lack of a UNA, while under D semantics we may sometimes know which literals are coreferent, the default case in RDF is that a pair of IRIs *may or may not be* coreferent: they *may or may not* refer to the same resource. In fact, there is no generic way in RDF nor in RDFS to state explicitly whether or not two IRIs are coreferent. However, the OWL vocabulary provides two properties with which we can explicitly specify (non-)coreference:

owl:sameAs: relates two resources that are the same.

$$(x_1, x_2) \in I_{EXT}(I_S(\text{owl:sameAs})) \text{ IF AND ONLY IF } x_1 = x_2$$

- This property is used to denote that two RDF terms are coreferent: that they refer to the same resource.

  - When owl:sameAs is stated between two RDF terms, those terms become interchangeable in the RDF graph.
  - Example 5.5 will demonstrate a typical use.

- On the other hand, as a result of the IF-AND-ONLY-IF semantics, when we know that two RDF terms are coreferent, we can state an owl:sameAs relation between them.

  - Thus, for example, the owl:sameAs relation becomes transitive, symmetric and reflexive.
  - Taking transitivity as an example, given x_1 same-as x_2 and x_2 same-as x_3, we know that $x_1 = x_2$ and $x_2 = x_3$, from which we can conclude that $x_1 = x_3$; from this latter implication in the model theory, the IF-AND-ONLY-IF semantics allows us to conclude that x_1 same-as x_3 on the RDF level.

---

owl:differentFrom: relates two resources that are different.

$$(x_1, x_2) \in I_{EXT}(I_S(\text{owl:differentFrom})) \text{ IF AND ONLY IF } x_1 \neq x_2$$

- This property is used to denote that two RDF terms are not coreferent: that they refer to different resources.

  - For example, if a graph states or entails that x_1 same-as x_2 and x_1 different-from x_2, that graph contains an *inconsistency* (i.e., a *contradiction*) since it implies both $x_1 = x_2$ and $x_1 \neq x_2$.
  - Furthermore, the owl:differentFrom relation becomes **irreflexive** since stating x_1 different-from x_1 would imply $x_1 \neq x_1$.

- On the other hand, when we know that two RDF terms are not coreferent, we entail an owl:differentFrom relation between them.

  - As a result, for example, the owl:differentFrom relation becomes symmetric: given a different-from b, we know that $a \neq b$, which implies $b \neq a$, which in turn gives b different-from a.

Example 5.5

We recall the RDF dataset from Example 3.14 where we represented four RDF graphs found in four different Web documents on three domains: a shopping site, a local profile and a recipe site. We see that the graphs in different domains refer to the same resources using different IRIs where we draw a dashed line between such occurrences. In the case of ex2:TescoTerryland, we highlight that the same IRI is used in two different graphs with a thick grey line.

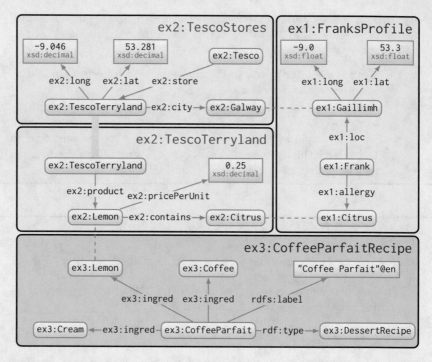

The coreference of the three dashed pairs can be represented using the owl:sameAs property:

ex2:Galway	owl:sameAs	ex1:Gaillimh
ex2:Lemon	owl:sameAs	ex3:Lemon
ex2:Citrus	owl:sameAs	ex1:Citrus

The combination of these three triples and the merge of the four graphs in the dataset above would then entail:

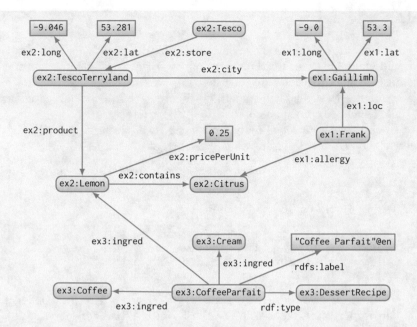

Recall that the coreferent terms are interchangeable: we could equivalently select or duplicate them, e.g., using ex3:Lemon instead of or in addition to ex2:Lemon. By considering coreference across graphs, the result is better connected and easier to process as a whole. Such reasoning thus has many benefits for an automated search process; for example, it would be much easier to find a store close to Jen's location, or to rule out recipes containing her allergies, and so forth.

With respect to owl:differentFrom, this could be used to state, for example, that an IRI referring to another Galway – e.g., the town Galway in New York, U.S. – should not be confused with the location of ex1:Frank, whose referent will probably not wish to go all the way from the West Coast of Ireland to New York just to buy lemons.

Exercise 5.2

How can the OWL features of equality be used in the context of Example 5.1 to (partially) help answer Julie's query?

Remark 5.2   (i)

Since the owl:differentFrom relation is quite prevalent – i.e., it
would likely hold true for the vast majority of pairs of IRIs in a realistic
dataset – such relations are often left implicit: explicitly writing down
every name that refers to something different than every other name
would quickly approach a cumbersome $\binom{n}{2}$ triples.

In cases where a set of **individuals** need to be declared pairwise different, OWL provides a linear-length shortcut syntax as follows:

```
[]                  rdf:type              owl:AllDifferent ;
                    owl:members           ( :m_1 ... :m_n ) .
```

... (using Turtle syntax) which represents ...

```
:m_1                owl:differentFrom     :m_2 , ... , :m_n .
:m_2                owl:differentFrom     :m_3 , ... , :m_n .
...                 ...                   ...
:m_n-1              owl:differentFrom     :m_n .
```

In OWL 1, owl:members was instead written as owl:distinctMembers;
either property can be used in OWL 2 for owl:AllDifferent.

Remark 5.3   (i)

It is not always the case that owl:sameAs and owl:differentFrom
need to be stated explicitly in the data: later we will see a variety of
features from which both such relations can be entailed.

5.4.2 Properties

RDFS allows for defining some basic semantics for properties: their sub-
properties, their domains and their ranges. However, OWL supports further
property **axioms**: claims made about properties that are assumed true in
order to reason over the data. We now begin to describe such axioms.

5.4.2.1 Datatype vs. Object Properties

First, unlike the rdf:Property class previously introduced, OWL introduces
two distinct classes of properties that make a clear distinction between *individuals* (identified by IRIs) and *datatype values* (typically identified by literals). This distinction will later enable certain computational guarantees.

owl:ObjectProperty is the class of all properties that relate individuals to other individuals.

- For example, HASPARENT would be an object property that relates individuals to other individuals.

owl:DatatypeProperty is the class of all properties that relate individuals to datatype values.

- For example, HASAGE would be a datatype property that relates individuals to a datatype value (e.g., an integer).

5.4.2.2 RDFS Property Axioms

OWL recycles some RDFS terms discussed in Section 4.1 that can be used specifically to define the semantics of properties. However, this time the normative semantics for RDFS terms is *if-and-only-if*. To keep the current discussion self-contained, we briefly re-introduce this vocabulary (since sub-class does not relate to properties, it will be discussed later):

rdfs:subPropertyOf relates every pair of properties p_1 and p_2 such that if p_1 holds between a pair of resources, then p_2 holds likewise.

$$(p_1, p_2) \in I_{EXT}(I_S(\text{rdfs:subPropertyOf})) \text{ IF AND ONLY IF}$$
$$p_1 \in I_P, \, p_2 \in I_P \text{ and}$$
$$I_{EXT}(p_1) \subseteq I_{EXT}(p_2)$$

- If p_1 is a sub-property of p_2, then both p_1 and p_2 are properties, and if p_1 relates x_1 to x_2, then p_2 must also relate x_1 to x_2.

    - For example, if HAS-MOTHER is given as a sub-property of HAS-PARENT, and if x_1 HAS-MOTHER x_2, then x_1 HAS-PARENT x_2.

- On the other hand, if we know that p_1 and p_2 are properties, and that p_1 relating x_1 to x_2 implies that p_2 also relates x_1 to x_2, then we can conclude that p_1 is a sub-property of p_2.

    - As a result, for example, the rdfs:subPropertyOf relation becomes transitive and reflexive.
    - Taking transitivity, if HAS-MOTHER is a sub-property of HAS-PARENT, and HAS-PARENT is a sub-property of HAS-ANCESTOR, then HAS-MOTHER is a sub-property of HAS-ANCESTOR.

rdfs:domain relates a property p to a class c if and only if all subjects of p are a member of c.

$$(p,c) \in I_{EXT}(I_S(\texttt{rdfs:domain})) \text{ IF AND ONLY IF}$$
$$p \in I_P,\ c \in I_C, \text{ and for all } x_1, x_2:$$
$$(x_1, x_2) \in I_{EXT}(p) \text{ implies } x_1 \in I_{CEXT}(c)$$

- If p has domain c, then p is a property and c is a class, and if p relates x_1 to x_2, then x_1 must be of type c.

  - For example, if HAS-DAUGHTER were defined with the domain PARENT, and if x_1 HAS-DAUGHTER x_2, then it must hold that x_1 is a member of the class PARENT.

- On the other hand, if we know that any subject x_1 of p must be in the class c, then we conclude that p has domain c.

  - For example, if we know that HAS-CHILD has domain PARENT, and HAS-SON is a sub-property of HAS-CHILD, then we can conclude that HAS-SON also has domain PARENT.

---

rdfs:range relates a property p to a class c if and only if all objects of p are a member of c.

$$(p,c) \in I_{EXT}(I_S(\texttt{rdfs:range})) \text{ IF AND ONLY IF}$$
$$p \in I_P,\ c \in I_C, \text{ and for all } x_1, x_2:$$
$$(x_1, x_2) \in I_{EXT}(p) \text{ implies } x_2 \in I_{CEXT}(c)$$

- If p has range c, then p is a property and c is a class, and if p relates x_1 to x_2, then x_2 must be of type c.

  - For example, if HAS-DAUGHTER were defined with the range FEMALE, and if x_1 HAS-DAUGHTER x_2, then it must hold that x_2 is a member of the class FEMALE.

- On the other hand, if we know that any object x_2 of p must be in the class c, then we conclude that p has range c.

  - For example, if we know that HAS-CHILD has range CHILD, and HAS-DAUGHTER is a sub-property of HAS-CHILD, then we can conclude that HAS-DAUGHTER also has range CHILD.

5.4.2.3 Property Types

OWL introduces a variety of new terms for defining the semantics of properties further than possible with RDFS alone. Some of these terms refer to built-in classes with well-defined meaning, where properties that are members of these classes have certain semantic conditions associated with them. Recall that we will use an asterisk (*) to denote terms new to OWL 2.

---

owl:TransitiveProperty is the class of all transitive properties.

$$p \in I_{CEXT}(\text{owl:TransitiveProperty}) \text{ IF AND ONLY IF}$$
$$p \in I_P \text{ and for all } x_1, x_2, x_3 :$$
$$(x_1, x_2) \in I_{EXT}(p) \text{ and } (x_2, x_3) \in I_{EXT}(p) \text{ imply } (x_1, x_3) \in I_{EXT}(p)$$

- If p is a member of the transitive-property class, then p is a property, and if p relates x_1 to x_2 and x_2 to x_3, then p also relates x_1 to x_3.

  - For example, if we say that HAS-ANCESTOR is a transitive property, and if we know that x_1 HAS-ANCESTOR x_2 and x_2 HAS-ANCESTOR x_3, then x_1 HAS-ANCESTOR x_3 holds.

- Conversely, for a property p, if we know that p relating x_1 to x_2 and p relating x_2 to x_3 implies that p also relates x_1 to x_3, then we can conclude that p is transitive.

  - For example, we can conclude that the properties owl:sameAs and rdfs:subPropertyOf are members of the transitive class.

---

owl:SymmetricProperty is the class of all symmetric properties.

$$p \in I_{CEXT}(\text{owl:SymmetricProperty}) \text{ IF AND ONLY IF}$$
$$p \in I_P \text{ and for all } x_1, x_2 :$$
$$(x_1, x_2) \in I_{EXT}(p) \text{ implies } (x_2, x_1) \in I_{EXT}(p)$$

- If p is a member of the symmetric-property class, then p is a property, and if p relates x_1 to x_2, then p also relates x_2 to x_1.

  - For example, if we say that SIBLING is a symmetric property, and if we have that x_1 SIBLING x_2, then x_2 SIBLING x_1 holds.

- Conversely, if we know that a property p relating x_1 to x_2 implies that p relates x_2 to x_1, then we can conclude that p is symmetric.

  - For example, we can conclude that the properties owl:sameAs and owl:differentFrom are members of the symmetric class.

`owl:AsymmetricProperty`* is the class of all **asymmetric** properties.

$$p \in I_{CEXT}(\texttt{owl:AsymmetricProperty}) \text{ IF AND ONLY IF}$$
$$p \in I_P \text{ and for all } x_1, x_2 :$$
$$(x_1, x_2) \in I_{EXT}(p) \text{ implies } (x_2, x_1) \notin I_{EXT}(p)$$

- If p is a member of the asymmetric-property class, then p is a property, and if p relates x_1 to x_2, then p cannot relate x_2 to x_1; in other words, if p relates x_1 to x_2 and x_2 to x_1, a contradiction arises.

  - For example, if HAS-PARENT is asymmetric, and if we have that x_1 HAS-PARENT x_2, then x_2 HAS-PARENT x_1 cannot hold.

- Conversely, if we know that a property p relating x_1 to x_2 implies p cannot relate x_2 to x_1, then we can conclude that p is asymmetric.

  - No such example seems possible with the vocabulary seen thus far. However, later we will be able to define a class c_1 as disjoint with c_2 if they share no instances. Then, for example, if we have that the class COUNTRY is disjoint with the class PERSON, and if we have a property CITIZEN-OF with domain PERSON and range COUNTRY, we can conclude that CITIZEN-OF is asymmetric: more specifically, x_1 CITIZEN-OF x_2 implies (for example) that x_1 is a PERSON, and thus x_2 CITIZEN-OF x_1 cannot hold as it would imply that x_1 is also a COUNTRY, which would be a contradiction (a similar argument applies for x_2).

Remark 5.4

We briefly highlight the distinction between asymmetric and **antisymmetric** relations. An example of an asymmetric relation might be LESS-THAN, where if a LESS-THAN b, then b LESS-THAN a cannot hold (even if we allow that $a = b$). We can define this in OWL as:

```
:lessThan        rdf:type                owl:AsymmetricProperty
```

However, there is the related notion of an antisymmetric relation; an example might be the property LESS-THAN-OR-EQUALS, where if a LESS-THAN-OR-EQUALS b and b LESS-THAN-OR-EQUALS a, we can conclude that $a = b$ (a same-as b). There is no direct way to express that a relation is antisymmetric in OWL (the author is also not aware of any *indirect* way to express antisymmetric relations in OWL).

owl:ReflexiveProperty* is the class of all reflexive properties.

$$p \in I_{CEXT}(\text{owl:ReflexiveProperty}) \text{ IF AND ONLY IF}$$
$$p \in I_P \text{ and for all } x \in I_R :$$
$$(x,x) \in I_{EXT}(p) \text{ holds}$$

- If p is a member of the reflexive-property class, then p is a property that relates each resource $x \in I_R$ to itself.

  - An example might be the SIMILAR relation since everything is SIMILAR to itself.

- Conversely, if p is a property that must relate all resources $x \in I_R$ to itself, then we can conclude that p is reflexive.

  - For example, we can conclude that owl:sameAs must be reflexive.

It is worth noting that owl:ReflexiveProperty states that a property is reflexive for all resources. Later we will see a feature of OWL that allows for defining reflexive properties on certain classes.

owl:IrreflexiveProperty* is the class of irreflexive properties.

$$p \in I_{CEXT}(\text{owl:IrreflexiveProperty}) \text{ IF AND ONLY IF}$$
$$p \in I_P \text{ and for all } x \in I_R :$$
$$(x,x) \notin I_{EXT}(p) \text{ holds}$$

- If p is a member of the irreflexive-property class, then p is a property that cannot relate any resource to itself; if p does relate a resource x to itself, a contradiction arises.

  - For example, if we say HAS-SISTER is irreflexive, then x HAS-SISTER x cannot hold (for any resource x).

- Conversely, if p is a property that cannot relate any resource to itself, then we can conclude that p is irreflexive.

  - For example, we can conclude that owl:differentFrom must be irreflexive.
  - As a more interesting example, if we state that CITIZEN-OF is asymmetric, we can conclude that it is also irreflexive (being a special case of asymmetry where $x_1 = x_2$).

owl:FunctionalProperty is the class of all properties for which a subject resource can relate to at most one object resource.

$$p \in I_{CEXT}(\text{owl:FunctionalProperty}) \text{ IF AND ONLY IF}$$
$$p \in I_P \text{ and for all } x, y_1, y_2 :$$
$$(x, y_1) \in I_{EXT}(p) \text{ and } (x, y_2) \in I_{EXT}(p) \text{ imply } y_1 = y_2$$

- If p is a member of the **functional**-property class, then p is a property, and if it relates x to y_1 and x to y_2, we conclude that y_1 same-as y_2.

  - For example, if we say HAS-BIOLOGICAL-FATHER is functional, and we know that x HAS-BIOLOGICAL-FATHER y_1 and x HAS-BIOLOGICAL-FATHER y_2, then we can conclude y_1 same-as y_2.

- Conversely, if p is a property that can only take one object resource for each subject, we can conclude that it is functional.

  - For example, we can conclude that owl:sameAs must be functional. (A more interesting example will follow next.)

---

owl:InverseFunctionalProperty is the class of all properties for which an object resource can be related to by at most one subject resource.

$$p \in I_{CEXT}(\text{owl:InverseFunctionalProperty}) \text{ IF AND ONLY IF}$$
$$p \in I_P \text{ and for all } x_1, x_2, y :$$
$$(x_1, y) \in I_{EXT}(p) \text{ and } (x_2, y) \in I_{EXT}(p) \text{ imply } x_1 = x_2$$

- If p is a member of the **inverse-functional**-property class, then p is a property, and if it relates x_1 to y and x_2 to y, we must conclude that x_1 same-as x_2.

  - For example, if we say ELDEST-CHILD-OF is inverse-functional, and we know that x_1 ELDEST-CHILD-OF y and x_2 ELDEST-CHILD-OF y, then we can conclude x_1 same-as x_2.

- Conversely, if p is a property that can only have one subject resource for each object, we can conclude that it is inverse-functional.

  - For example, if we state that HAS-TWIN-SIBLING is functional and symmetric, then we can conclude it is inverse-functional (on the other hand, if it were symmetric and inverse-functional, we could conclude that it is functional).

5.4.2.4 Property Relations

OWL also introduces some novel vocabulary to define semantic relations between various user-defined properties (and classes), as follows:

`owl:equivalentProperty` relates two properties if and only if they relate the same pairs of resources.

$$(p_1,p_2) \in I_{EXT}(I_S(\texttt{owl:equivalentProperty})) \text{ IF AND ONLY IF}$$
$$p_1 \in I_P, p_2 \in I_P \text{ and}$$
$$I_{EXT}(p_1) = I_{EXT}(p_2)$$

- If p_1 is an equivalent property to p_2, then both are properties, and:

  ... if p_1 relates x_1 to x_2, then p_2 also relates x_1 to x_2;
  ... likewise if p_2 relates x_3 to x_4, then p_1 relates x_3 to x_4.
  - An example of equivalent properties might be HAS-CHILD and PARENT-OF, since they express the same relation.

- Conversely, if we know that every pair of resources related by p_1 must be related by p_2 and vice versa, we can conclude that p_1 is an equivalent property to p_2 and vice versa.

  - For example, if p_1 is a sub-property of p_2 and p_2 a sub-property of p_1, we can conclude that p_1 is equivalent to p_2, and vice versa.

Remark 5.5 ⓘ

Using `owl:sameAs` is stronger than `owl:equivalentProperty`: the former will replace equivalent terms in any position, while the latter only concerns the predicate position. Consider, for example:

```
:Sanders         :firstName          "Bernie" .
:firstName       rdfs:label          "First Name" .
```

If we then state the relationship between two properties as follows:

```
:firstName       owl:sameAs          :givenName .
```

... then the following triples hold:

```
:Sanders         :givenName          "Bernie" .
:givenName       rdfs:label          "First Name" .
```

If we rather stated the relationship using `owl:equivalentProperty`, then only the former triple would hold.

`owl:inverseOf` relates two properties if and only if one is the directional inverse of the other.

$$(p_1, p_2) \in I_{EXT}(I_S(\text{owl:inverseOf})) \text{ IF AND ONLY IF}$$
$$p_1 \in I_P, \, p_2 \in I_P, \text{ and}$$
$$I_{EXT}(p_1) = \{(x_1, x_2) \mid (x_2, x_1) \in I_{EXT}(p_2)\}$$

- If p_1 is an inverse property of p_2, then both are properties and:

  ... if p_1 relates x_1 to x_2, then p_2 relates x_2 to x_1;
  ... likewise if p_2 relates x_3 to x_4, then p_1 relates x_4 to x_3.
  - For example, if we state that CHILD-OF is the inverse of PARENT-OF, and we have that x_1 CHILD-OF x_2, then x_2 PARENT-OF x_1 holds; otherwise, if we have that x_3 PARENT-OF x_4, then x_4 CHILD-OF x_3 also holds.

- Conversely, if we know that every pair of resources related by p_1 must be inversely related by p_2 and vice versa, we can conclude that p_1 is an inverse property of p_2, and vice versa.

  - For example, if HAS-SIBLING is a symmetric property, we can conclude that HAS-SIBLING inverse-of HAS-SIBLING.

`owl:propertyDisjointWith`* relates two properties if and only if they never relate the same pair of resources.

$$(p_1, p_2) \in I_{EXT}(I_S(\text{owl:propertyDisjointWith})) \text{ IF AND ONLY IF}$$
$$p_1 \in I_P, \, p_2 \in I_P, \text{ and}$$
$$I_{EXT}(p_1) \cap I_{EXT}(p_2) = \emptyset$$

- If p_1 is property-disjoint-with p_2, and some x_1 and x_2 are related by both p_1 and p_2, then a contradiction arises.

  - An example of disjoint properties might be HAS-TWIN-SIBLING and HAS-CHILD.

- On the other hand, if we know that properties p_1 and p_2 can never relate the same pair of resources, we can conclude that they are disjoint properties.

  - For example, if HAS-PARENT is given as asymmetric, and given HAS-CHILD as the inverse of HAS-PARENT, then we can conclude that HAS-CHILD and HAS-PARENT are disjoint properties.

Remark 5.6

Similar to the syntax discussed in Remark 5.2, we can use the term owl:AllDisjointProperties to declare a list of properties as pairwise disjoint. The property owl:members must be used.

---

owl:propertyChainAxiom* states that a property can be composed of an ordered chain (aka. path) of other properties.

$$I_{LIST}(b,p_1,\ldots,p_n) \text{ and } (p,b) \in I_{EXT}(I_S(\text{owl:propertyChainAxiom}))$$

IF AND ONLY IF

$$\{p,p_1,\ldots,p_n\} \subseteq I_P, \text{ and for all } x_1,\ldots x_{n+1}:$$
$$(x_1,x_2) \in I_{EXT}(p_1) \text{ and } \ldots \text{ and } (x_n,x_{n+1}) \in I_{EXT}(p_n)$$
$$\text{implies } (x_1,x_{n+1}) \in I_{EXT}(p)$$

- If p has the property chain $p_1,\ldots,p_n$, and x_i is related to x_{i+1} by p_i for $1 \leq i \leq n$, then x_1 is related to x_{n+1} by p.

    - A two-hop example might be a HAS-UNCLE relation being defined as having the property chain HAS-PARENT, HAS-BROTHER.
    - A three-hop example might be HAS-GREAT-GRANDFATHER being defined as HAS-PARENT, HAS-PARENT, HAS-FATHER.
    - Example 5.6 illustrates a more detailed use-case.

- On the other hand, if we know that the path $p_1,\ldots,p_n$ relating x_1 to x_{n+1} implies that the property p relates x_1 to x_{n+1}, then we can conclude that p has the property chain $p_1,\ldots,p_n$.

    - For example, if p is transitive, we can conclude that p has the property chains $p, \ldots, p$ of arbitrary length. Indeed, this entails an infinite number of property paths for p!
    - As another (this time finite) example, if p is symmetric, and q is the inverse of p, then p has the property chain p, q.

Remark 5.7

If p has the property chain $p_1,\ldots,p_n$, a triple (x_1,p,x_{n+1}) does *not* entail the existence of a path $(x_1,p_1,x_2),\ldots,(x_n,p_n,x_{n+1})$.

owl:hasKey* states that instances of a given class are uniquely identified by the values for a given set of properties.

$$I_{LIST}(b,p_1,\ldots,p_n) \text{ and } (c,b) \in I_{EXT}(I_S(\text{owl:hasKey}))$$

IF AND ONLY IF

$$\{p_1,\ldots,p_n\} \subseteq I_P,\; c \in I_C, \text{ and for all } x_1,x_2,y_1,\ldots,y_n:$$
$$x_1 \in I_C(c) \text{ and } (x_1,y_1) \in I_{EXT}(p_1)\ldots \text{ and } (x_1,y_n) \in I_{EXT}(p_n)$$
$$\text{and } x_2 \in I_C(c) \text{ and } (x_2,y_1) \in I_{EXT}(p_1)\ldots \text{ and } (x_2,y_n) \in I_{EXT}(p_n)$$

imply $x_1 = x_2$

- If the class c has the complex key $\{p_1,\ldots,p_n\}$, and x_1 and x_2 are both instances of c, and x_1 and x_2 share at least one value for each of $p_1,\ldots,p_n$, then x_1 and x_2 are the same resource.

  - An example might be the combination of the two properties $\{\text{HAS-BIOLOGICAL-MOTHER}, \text{DATE-OF-BIRTH}\}$ for the class SINGLETON (denoting lone-births; i.e., not twins, triplets, etc.).
  - Example 5.7 illustrates a more detailed use-case.

- On the other hand, if we know that any two resources x_1 and x_2 in the class c with shared values for $p_1,\ldots,p_n$ must be the same resource, we can conclude that c has the key $p_1,\ldots,p_n$.

  - For example, if ISBN is inverse-functional, we can conclude that the class RESOURCE ($I_S(\text{rdfs:Resource})$) – or in fact any (even *empty*) sub-class thereof – has the key $\{\text{ISBN}\}$.

Remark 5.8   ⓘ

The terms owl:hasKey and owl:InverseFunctionalProperty act in similar ways. The former defines a complex key (with multiple properties) that acts only on the instances of a specific class, whereas the latter is a simple key (one property) that acts on any resource. In sub-languages of OWL, however, owl:hasKey is restricted to apply only over named individuals, i.e., resources that are explicitly named (as opposed to resources known to exist but that are not named).

Needless to say, the different features for property axioms that we have introduced here can combine to create more complex patterns of entailment, as shown in the following example involving inverse properties and chains.

Example 5.6

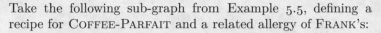

Take the following sub-graph from Example 5.5, defining a recipe for COFFEE-PARFAIT and a related allergy of FRANK's:

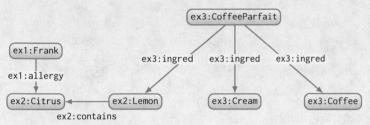

If we add the following OWL property axioms:

ex3:ingred	rdfs:subPropertyOf	ex2:contains
ex2:contains	rdf:type	owl:TransitiveProperty
ex2:foundIn	owl:inverseOf	ex2:contains
ex1:unsuitable	owl:propertyChainAxiom	(ex1:allergy ex2:foundIn)

The above graph and axioms would entail:

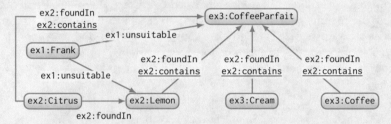

For brevity, we underline properties for the inverse of the edge shown. The entailments now indicate, for example, that the recipe COFFEE-PARFAIT is unsuitable for FRANK – who has an intolerance to CITRUS – as it contains LEMON, which in turn contains CITRUS.

In Remark 5.3, we mentioned that equality (same-as) and inequality (different-from) can be entailed indirectly by other features. Indeed, this includes some of the property axioms we have seen, such as functional properties, inverse-functional properties, complex keys, as well as other axioms that can entail the necessary conditions for such features. Next we provide an example of such entailment of equality involving a combination of features.

Example 5.7

Consider the following graph:

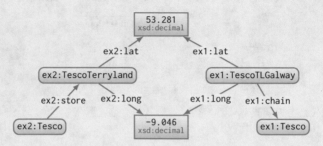

Intuitively, we can see that two of the stores are coreferent, and that two of the store chains are coreferent. To capture the coreference of the stores, we could define a property axiom to state that a store's longitude and latitude are enough to uniquely identify it (here assuming that the latitude and longitude are precise enough to identify a store).

```
ex1:Store      owl:hasKey           ( ex2:long ex2:lat )
```

However, we still cannot infer that both stores are the same. First they must be instances of `ex1:Store` before the axiom can apply. Second, one of the stores uses `ex1:lat` and `ex1:long`, not `ex2:lat` and `ex2:long`; the other store uses `ex2:store`, not `ex1:chain`. Hence we need some more property axioms before the coreference is entailed:

```
ex2:store      rdfs:range              ex1:Store
ex2:store      owl:inverseOf           ex1:chain
ex2:long       owl:equivalentProperty  ex1:long
ex2:lat        owl:equivalentProperty  ex1:lat
```

With these additional property axioms, we could infer:

```
ex1:TescoTLGalway   owl:sameAs      ex2:TescoTerryland
ex2:TescoTerryland  owl:sameAs      ex1:TescoTLGalway
```

What about the two chains? Now that both stores are known to be the same, we can state that a store can belong to at most one chain:

```
ex1:chain          rdf:type         owl:FunctionalProperty
```

Equivalently in this case, we could have stated the following:

```
ex2:store          rdf:type         owl:InverseFunctionalProperty
```

Either axiom combined with the previous axioms and data will entail:

```
ex1:Tesco          owl:sameAs       ex2:Tesco
ex2:Tesco          owl:sameAs       ex1:Tesco
```

In this case, each store effectively acts like a key for each chain: although the chain can have other stores, no other chain can have that store. Hence when we entailed equality of the two stores, this in turn combines the keys needed to entail equality of the two chains.

Remark 5.9ⓘ

The previous example was unrealistic in a way that illustrates an important point: for the original key to work, the latitudes and longitudes had to be exact matches in both sources, which may be unlikely in practice. While datatype reasoning could take care of matching across compatible datatypes, if one source specified a longitude of -9.046 and the other a longitude of -9.05, a match would not occur. OWL is not suitable for expressing approximate matches on keys. We will return to this issue of approximate matching later in Chapter 8.

Exercise 5.3

How can the OWL features for property axioms be used in the context of Example 5.1 to (partially) help answer Julie's query?

5.4.2.5 Top/Bottom Properties

Finally, for the purposes of making more complex definitions (discussed later), OWL introduces two properties with special meaning. The first property (sometimes called the "top property") is assumed to relate all pairs of resources. The second property (sometimes called the "bottom property") is assumed to be empty: to relate no pair of resources. Both of these properties are defined to be members of owl:ObjectProperty.

owl:topObjectProperty relates all possible pairs of resources:
$$I_{EXT}(I_S(\texttt{owl:topObjectProperty})) = I_R \times I_R.$$

owl:bottomObjectProperty relates no pair of resources:
$$I_{EXT}(I_S(\texttt{owl:bottomObjectProperty})) = \emptyset.$$

Example 5.8

Regarding the top property, let us assume the following triple:

```
:Frank          :loves                  :Frank
```

This entails the top relation between all possible pairs of resources:

```
:Frank          owl:topObjectProperty   :Frank
:Frank          owl:topObjectProperty   :loves
:loves          owl:topObjectProperty   :Frank
:loves          owl:topObjectProperty   :loves
```

Why is this useful? The idea is not that a system should materialise all such entailments – which would clearly be a waste of resources. Rather the top property can be used in more complex class definitions discussed later (e.g., to define that "all elephants are bigger than all mice" [337]).

Example 5.9

Regarding the bottom property, in an ontology, one may have a property (perhaps deliberately, perhaps indeliberately) that cannot relate anything without causing an inconsistency. For example:

```
:sibling    rdf:type             owl:IrreflexiveProperty
:sibling    owl:propertyChainAxiom ( :parent :child )
:parent     owl:inverseOf        :child
```

Individually, each definition seems reasonable: that (1) a resource cannot be a SIBLING of itself; (2) if a PARENT b and b CHILD c hold, then a SIBLING c holds; and (3) if a PARENT b holds, then b CHILD a holds.
However, consider for example:

```
:Frank          :parent                 :FrankSr
```

Combined with the aforementioned three axioms, we can infer:

```
:FrankSr    :child              :Frank
:Frank      :sibling            :Frank
```

The latter triple gives an inconsistency as SIBLING is irreflexive. In fact, any PARENT relation will cause such an inconsistency and hence the relation must remain empty. Such relations are sometimes called *unsatisfiable*. Thus we can say that the original three axioms entail that the PARENT relation is equivalent to the bottom relation:

```
:parent     owl:equivalentProperty owl:bottomObjectProperty
```

> **Remark 5.10** ⓘ
>
> OWL also defines top and bottom properties for datatype values: `owl:topDataProperty` and `owl:bottomDataProperty`. Both properties are members of `owl:DatatypeProperty`.

5.4.3 Classes

OWL build upon the RDFS vocabulary for defining classes with new features for stating axioms about classes or to define new classes.

5.4.3.1 Top/Bottom Classes

OWL defines a number of "built-in" classes that can be referenced in more complex definitions discussed later. The first such class is a new class for the class of classes. OWL also introduces a new top class that contains all resources, as well as an empty bottom class that contains no resources.

`owl:Class` is the class of all classes: $I_{CEXT}(I_S(\texttt{owl:Class})) = I_C$.

`owl:Thing` is the class of all resources: $I_{CEXT}(I_S(\texttt{owl:Thing})) = I_R$.

`owl:Nothing` is the empty class: $I_{CEXT}(I_S(\texttt{owl:Nothing})) = \emptyset$.

As per the top and bottom properties seen earlier, the top and bottom classes can be used in more complex definitions discussed later. Furthermore, *unsatisfiable classes* – classes that would cause an inconsistency were they to have any member – are entailed to be equivalent to the bottom class.

> **Remark 5.11** ⓘ
>
> So how do `owl:Class` and `owl:Thing` differ from `rdfs:Class` and `rdfs:Resource` respectively? For now, they do not differ! However, later when we apply restrictions to OWL to ensure decidability, we will restrict what `owl:Class` and `owl:Thing` can contain.

5.4.3.2 Class Axioms

Class axioms are formal claims about classes. The first class axiom supported by OWL (and the most important) is inherited from RDFS:

---

rdfs:subClassOf relates any class c_1 to any class c_2 such that if a resource is a member of c_1, then it must be a member of c_2.

$$(c_1, c_2) \in I_{EXT}(I_S(\text{rdfs:subClassOf})) \text{ IF AND ONLY IF}$$
$$c_1 \in I_C,\ c_2 \in I_C, \text{ and}$$
$$I_{CEXT}(c_1) \subseteq I_{CEXT}(c_2)$$

- If c_1 is a sub-class of c_2 and x is a member of c_1, then x is also a member of c_2.

  – An example of sub-classes might be GORILLA and PRIMATE.

- On the other hand, if we know that x being a member of c_1 implies x being a member of c_2, we can conclude that c_1 and c_2 are sub-classes.

  – For example, if c is a class, we can conclude that c is a sub-class of owl:Thing, and that owl:Nothing is a sub-class of c.

OWL also adds two new terms to relate classes as follows:

---

owl:equivalentClass relates all pairs of classes c_1 and c_2 that have the same set of members.

$$(c_1, c_2) \in I_{EXT}(I_S(\text{owl:equivalentClass})) \text{ IF AND ONLY IF}$$
$$c_1 \in I_C,\ c_2 \in I_C, \text{ and}$$
$$I_{CEXT}(c_1) = I_{CEXT}(c_2)$$

- If c_1 is an equivalent class to c_2 and:

  ... if x is a member of c_1, then x is a member of c_2;
  ... likewise, if y is a member of c_2, then y is a member of c_1.
  – An example might be HUMAN and HOMOSAPIENS

- On the other hand, if we know that x being a member of c_1 implies x being a member of c_2 and vice versa, we can conclude that c_1 and c_2 are equivalent classes.

  – For example, if c_1 is a sub-class of c_2 and c_2 is a sub-class of c_1, we can conclude that c_1 and c_2 are equivalent classes.

---

owl:disjointWith relates all pairs of classes c_1 and c_2 that share no members.

$$(c_1, c_2) \in I_{EXT}(I_S(\text{owl:disjointWith})) \text{ IF AND ONLY IF}$$
$$c_1 \in I_C,\ c_2 \in I_C, \text{ and}$$
$$I_{CEXT}(c_1) \cap I_{CEXT}(c_2) = \emptyset$$

- If c_1 is disjoint with c_2, and any resource x is a member of both c_1 and c_2, then a contradiction arises.

  - An example of disjoint classes might be HUMAN and PLANET: something cannot be both at the same time.

- On the other hand, if we know that no resource x can be a member of both c_1 and c_2, we can conclude that c_1 and c_2 are disjoint classes.

  - For example, any class c is disjoint-with owl:Nothing.

Example 5.10

Taking the following triples:

ex2:TescoTerryland	rdf:type	ex2:Store
ex1:Tesco	rdf:type	ex1:Franchise
ex1:Outlet	owl:equivalentClass	ex2:Store
ex1:Outlet	owl:disjointWith	ex1:Franchise

These would entail:

ex2:TescoTerryland	rdf:type	ex1:Outlet
ex2:TescoTerryland	owl:differentFrom	ex1:Tesco
ex1:Tesco	owl:differentFrom	ex2:TescoTerryland

Exercise 5.4

Which of the following meta-statements universally hold:

1. rdfs:subClassOf   rdf:type   owl:ReflexiveProperty .
2. rdfs:subClassOf   rdf:type   owl:SymmetricProperty .
3. rdfs:subClassOf   rdf:type   owl:TransitiveProperty .
4. owl:equivalentClass   rdf:type   owl:ReflexiveProperty .
5. owl:equivalentClass   rdf:type   owl:SymmetricProperty .
6. owl:equivalentClass   rdf:type   owl:TransitiveProperty .
7. owl:disjointWith   rdf:type   owl:ReflexiveProperty .
8. owl:disjointWith   rdf:type   owl:SymmetricProperty .
9. owl:disjointWith   rdf:type   owl:TransitiveProperty .

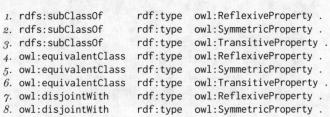

Exercise 5.5

What could we conclude from the following:

```
:A          owl:disjointWith      :B
:A          owl:equivalentClass   :B
```

Remark 5.12

As per `owl:differentFrom` and `owl:propertyDisjointWith`, OWL provides a linear-length shortcut syntax for defining a list of classes as pairwise disjoint using the term `owl:AllDisjointClasses`.

Remark 5.13

As before for the `owl:equivalentProperty` property (see Remark 5.5), an `owl:sameAs` relation between classes is stronger than `owl:equivalentClass` since the former will make the class terms in question replaceable in all positions whereas the latter only makes them replaceable in the object position of triples with the predicate `rdf:type`.

5.4.3.3 Set-based Class Definitions

Aside from class axioms, OWL also contains a rich vocabulary for "defining" new classes in terms of their *extension* (their set of members). To start with, we can define new classes based on set operations – union, intersection or complement – applied over other classes.

Example 5.11

If we define EXO-PLANET to be a sub-class of PLANET that is disjoint with SOLAR-PLANET, we are defining axioms between classes that already exist. But using the OWL vocabulary for class definitions, we can define a new class that is the intersection of PLANET and the complement of SOLAR-PLANET and state that this new class is equivalent to EXO-PLANET. Using such a class definition, we now know that if x is a PLANET and is not a SOLAR-PLANET, then it must be an EXO-PLANET, which would not be possible through class axioms alone.

With respect to defining new classes as the result of set operations over other classes, OWL provides the following options:

owl:intersectionOf is used to define a class whose extension is the intersection of the extensions of a set of other classes.

$$I_{LIST}(b,c_1,\ldots,c_n) \text{ and } (c,b) \in I_{EXT}(I_S(\text{owl:intersectionOf}))$$

IF AND ONLY IF

$$\{c,c_1,\ldots,c_n\} \subseteq I_C, \text{ and}$$

$$I_{CEXT}(c) = I_{CEXT}(c_1) \cap \ldots \cap I_{CEXT}(c_n)$$

- If a class c is defined as the intersection of $\{c_1,\ldots,c_n\}$ and:

  ... if x is a member of c, then x is also a member of all classes in $\{c_1,\ldots,c_n\}$;

  ... on the other hand, if y is a member of all the classes in $\{c_1,\ldots,c_n\}$, then it is also a member of c.

  - An example might be where GIRL is defined to be equivalent to the intersection of {FEMALE, CHILD}. In this case, if x is a member of GIRL, x is also a member of FEMALE and CHILD. Conversely if y if a member of FEMALE and CHILD, it is also a member of GIRL.

- Conversely, if we know that the extension of a class c must be equal to the intersection of the extensions of the classes $c_1,\ldots,c_n$, then we can conclude that c intersection-of $c_1,\ldots,c_n$.

  - For example, we can infer that any class is the intersection of itself (and any super-classes thereof), or that the class owl:Nothing is the intersection of any two disjoint classes.

---

owl:unionOf is used to define a class whose extension is the union of the extensions of a set of other classes.

$$I_{LIST}(b,c_1,\ldots,c_n) \text{ and } (c,b) \in I_{EXT}(I_S(\text{owl:unionOf}))$$

IF AND ONLY IF

$$\{c,c_1,\ldots,c_n\} \subseteq I_C, \text{ and}$$

$$I_{CEXT}(c) = I_{CEXT}(c_1) \cup \ldots \cup I_{CEXT}(c_n)$$

- If a class c is defined as the union of $\{c_1,\ldots,c_n\}$ and:

  ... if x is a member of c, then x is also a member of at least one class in $\{c_1,\ldots,c_n\}$ (though which may not be known);

  ... on the other hand, if y is a member of any class in $\{c_1,\ldots,c_n\}$, then it is also a member of c.

– An example might be where DOCTOR is defined to be equivalent to the union of {MEDICAL-DOCTOR, PHD-HOLDER}. In this case, if x is a member of MEDICAL-DOCTOR or PHD-HOLDER, then it is a member of DOCTOR. Conversely, if y is a member of DOCTOR, then it is also a member of either MEDICAL-DOCTOR or PHD-HOLDER (or both).

- Conversely, if we know that the extension of a class c must be equal to the union of the extensions of the classes $c_1, \ldots, c_n$, then we can conclude that c union-of $c_1, \ldots, c_n$.

  – For example, we can infer that any class is the union of itself (and any sub-classes thereof).

---

owl:complementOf is used to define a class whose extension is the complement (with respect to all resources) of another class.

$$(c_1, c_2) \in I_{EXT}(I_S(\texttt{owl:complementOf})) \text{ IF AND ONLY IF}$$
$$c_1 \in I_C, \ c_2 \in I_C \text{ and}$$
$$I_{CEXT}(c_1) = I_R \setminus I_{CEXT}(c_2)$$

- If a class c_1 is defined as the complement of c_2, and:

  ... if any resource x cannot be a member of c_1, then it must be a member of c_2; on the other hand, if any resource y cannot be a member of c_2, then it must be a member of c_1;

  ... if any resource x is a member of c_1, then it cannot be a member of c_2; on the other hand, if any resource x is a member of c_2, then it cannot be a member of c_1.

  – For example, if we define the class VISIBLE as the complement of INVISIBLE, this means that any resource must be a member of VISIBLE or INVISIBLE but cannot be a member of both.

- Conversely, if we know that the extension of a class c_1 is precisely the set of resources not in c_2, we can conclude c_1 complement-of c_2.

  – For example, if we know that SEEABLE is equivalent to VISIBLE and that VISIBLE is the complement-of INVISIBLE, we can conclude that SEEABLE is the complement-of INVISIBLE.

  – As a meta-example, we could infer that owl:Thing is the complement of owl:Nothing.

While these features define classes by applying set operators over other classes, OWL also allows for defining a class by enumerating its members.

owl:oneOf is used to define a class whose extension is a given set of resources (often called an *enumeration*).

$$I_{LIST}(b, x_1, \ldots, x_n) \text{ and } (c, b) \in I_{EXT}(I_S(\texttt{owl:oneOf}))$$

IF AND ONLY IF

$$c \in I_C \text{ and}$$

$$I_{CEXT}(c) = \{x_1, \ldots, x_n\}$$

- If c is defined as one-of the resources $\{x_1, \ldots, x_n\}$, then each resource $x_1, \ldots, x_n$ is a member of c and if x is a member of c then x must be the same-as at least one element of $\{x_1, \ldots, x_n\}$.

  - As an example, we could define the class US-STATE as equivalent to the class with the extension {ALABAMA, ..., WYOMING}. Aside from stating that ALABAMA, ..., WYOMING, etc., are members of US-STATES, we are saying that that's all the members of that class, effectively "closing" the class. Thus, for example, if we were to later add that COTTON-STATE is a member of US-STATE, but it did not appear in the original enumeration above, it would follow that COTTON-STATE must be the same as one of the members of the enumeration above; figuring out *which* state it was the same-as would require further evidence.

- On the other hand, if we know that the extension of a class c is precisely the set of resources $\{x_1, \ldots, x_n\}$, we can conclude that c is one-of $\{x_1, \ldots, x_n\}$.

  - For example, if we know that the class CANADIAN-REGION is the union of the classes CANADIAN-PROVINCE and CANADIAN-TERRITORY, where the class CANADIAN-PROVINCE is one-of {ALBERTA, ..., SASKATCHEWAN} and CANADIAN-TERRITORY is one-of {NW-TERRITORIES, NUNAVAT, YUKON}, then we can conclude that the class CANADIAN-REGION is one-of the union of both sets of resource: {ALBERTA, ..., YUKON}.

Remark 5.14

To define OWL classes based on intersection, union, and one-of in RDF, collections are used. In Example 5.4, we stated that EQUUS is the union of the classes ASS, DONKEY, HORSE and ZEBRA as follows:

```
:Equus      owl:equivalentClass  _:u
_:u         owl:unionOf          ( :Ass :Donkey :Horse :Zebra )
```

One may then wonder why we did not write it more simply as:

```
:Equus      owl:unionOf          ( :Ass :Donkey :Horse :Zebra )
```

... after all, both correspond to the same semantic definitions. The reason is that the former convention is enforced for restricted sub-languages of OWL introduce later [153]; the rationale is that we have a blank node _:u that represents only the union class and is not used for anything else. We abide by this former convention since it is acceptable in both the restricted and unrestricted OWL languages.

Remark 5.15

As a convenience, OWL (2) defines owl:disjointUnionOf, which, like owl:unionOf, allows for defining that the extension of the class c is the union of the extensions of the classes $\{c_1,...,c_n\}$, but adds the additional constraint that the extensions of $\{c_1,...,c_n\}$ are pairwise disjoint. This means that if x is a member of c, then x must be a member of *precisely one* class in $\{c_1,...,c_n\}$. For example:

```
:Planet     owl:equivalentClass  _:u .
_:u         owl:disjointUnionOf  ( :ExoPlanet :SolarPlanet ) .
```

is equivalent to writing:

```
:Planet     owl:equivalentClass  _:u
_:u         owl:unionOf          ( :ExoPlanet :SolarPlanet ) .
:ExoPlanet  owl:disjointWith     :SolarPlanet .
```

Example 5.12

Henceforth, we will begin to use the concrete Turtle syntax more often since it provides useful shortcuts for representing complex OWL definitions. We show how to represent previous in-line examples in RDF using the Turtle syntax and its abbreviations (see Section 3.8.3).

To represent that GIRL is equivalent to the intersection of FEMALE and CHILD, we will write (using Turtle syntax):

```
:Girl owl:equivalentClass
  [ owl:intersectionOf ( :Female :Child ) ] .
```

To define that DOCTOR is equivalent to the union of MEDICALDOCTOR and PHDHOLDER, we can write:

```
:Doctor owl:equivalentClass
    [ owl:unionOf ( :MedicalDoctor :PhDHolder ) ] .
```

To define that VISIBLE is equivalent to the complement of INVISIBLE, we can write (note that unlike the other definitions, here we do need not to use a collection as only one class is being complemented):

```
:Visible owl:equivalentClass
    [ owl:complementOf :Invisible ] .
```

To define that US-STATE is equivalent to the class with the extension {ALABAMA, ..., WYOMING}, we can write:

```
:USState owl:equivalentClass
    [ owl:oneOf ( :Alabama :Alaska :A :Wyoming ) ] .
```

Exercise 5.6

How does the following class axiom:

```
:Living owl:disjointWith :Deceased .
```

differ from the following class axiom (if at all)?

```
:Living owl:equivalentClass [ owl:complementOf :Deceased ] .
```

In these set-based class definitions, the order of elements does not matter; for example, the intersection of FEMALE and CHILD is the same as the intersection of CHILD and FEMALE, and so forth. Likewise, we can use any class axiom we wish on a class defined in this manner, including sub-class, disjoint-with, or equivalent-class, where we can have a class definition on the left-hand side, on the right-hand side, or on both sides. We could also use class definitions on the right-hand side of domain or range axioms.

Example 5.13

Instead of writing:

```
:Girl owl:equivalentClass
    [ owl:intersectionOf ( :Female :Child ) ] .
```

We could equivalently write the following axiom:

```
[ owl:intersectionOf ( :Female :Child ) ] owl:equivalentClass
    :Girl .
```

Or indeed we could equivalently write the following two axioms:

```
:Girl rdfs:subClassOf
      [ owl:intersectionOf ( :Female :Child ) ] .
[ owl:intersectionOf ( :Female :Child ) ] rdfs:subClassOf
      :Girl .
```

If we were to include just the first sub-class axiom, then we would be stating that any member of GIRL is also a member of FEMALE and CHILD. On the other hand, if we were to include just the second sub-class axiom, then we would be stating that any member of both FEMALE and CHILD is a member of GIRL. Combining both is then equivalent to either of the former two equivalent-class axioms.

Likewise we can consider nesting class definitions.

Example 5.14

We might state, for example, that LIVING-PERSON is equivalent to the intersection of PERSON and the complement of DECEASED as:

```
:LivingPerson owl:equivalentClass
   [ owl:intersectionOf (
       :Person
       [ owl:complementOf :Deceased ]
     ) ] .
```

If we rather wished to use the complement-of DECEASED in multiple definitions, we may define:

```
:NotDeceased owl:equivalentClass [ owl:complementOf :Deceased ] .
```

And then use :NotDeceased where it is required.

Exercise 5.7

Consider a standard set of 52 playing cards with the standard set of 4 suits – CLUB (♣), DIAMOND (◇), HEART (♡), and SPADE (♠) – times the standard set of 13 values – TWO (2), ..., TEN (10), JACK (J), QUEEN (Q), KING (K) and ACE (A). (Assume no jokers.)

We will assume an RDF graph that lists each card as follows:

```
:Ac            rdf:type            :Card .
:Ad            rdf:type            :Card .
:Ah            rdf:type            :Card .
:As            rdf:type            :Card .
:Kc            rdf:type            :Card .
. . .          rdf:type            :Card .
:2s            rdf:type            :Card .
```

where :Ac *refers to* A♣, *etc.*

Given a card (e.g., 8♣), we wish to create an ontology that will classify that card as being a member of various playing-card classes (e.g., EIGHT, CLUB, FACE-CARD, BLACK-CARD, etc.).

(In the following questions, you can use Turtle syntax.)

- *Define the class* CLUB *as being all cards* 2♣, ..., A♣.
- *Define the class* EIGHT *as being all cards* 8♣, 8◇, 8♡, 8♠.
- *Assuming enumerations for all four suits (like* CLUB*), use those classes to define a class* STANDARD-CARD *that includes all 52 cards.*
- *Assuming enumerations for all card values (like* EIGHT*), define the class* FACE-CARD *as containing all (and only) the cards in* JACK, QUEEN, KING *or* ACE.
- *Define the class* BLACK-CARD *as containing all (and only) the cards in either* CLUB *or* SPADE.
- *Define* RED-CARD *as all (and only) the cards in* STANDARD-CARD *that are not a* BLACK-CARD.
- *Define* RED-FACE-CARD *as all (and only) the cards in both* RED-CARD *and* FACE-CARD.

5.4.3.4 Restriction-based Class Definitions

Referring back to Example 5.11, while we can now state that a PLANET must be either an EXO-PLANET or a SOLAR-PLANET (and cannot be both) – for example, by stating that PLANET is the disjoint union of EXO-PLANET and SOLAR-PLANET – we have yet to see features that would allow us to define that SOLAR-PLANET contains precisely those planets that ORBIT our SUN. Along these lines, OWL also provides features to define new classes by defining restrictions on the members that it may contain, including restrictions on the value that is taken for a given property, on the class to which a value on a given property belongs, on the number of values taken for a given property, etc. Such features enable increasingly complex class definitions.

Along these lines, OWL first defines a meta-class:

---

owl:Restriction is the class of all classes defined using one of the restrictions discussed in the following.

$$I_{CEXT}(I_S(\texttt{owl:Restriction})) \subseteq I_C$$

OWL then provides vocabulary to express a variety of flavours of "restrictions" that can be used to define new classes.

Remark 5.16

Unlike the IF-AND-ONLY-IF semantic definitions for the vocabulary discussed this far, the OWL 2 RDF-Based Semantics [349] defines
the following vocabulary under a weaker IF–THEN semantics. Under
the weaker IF–THEN semantics, we thus cannot (always) infer new restriction classes when the corresponding semantic conditions are met.
Without going into further detail, there are three main reasons for the
two different semantics: backwards compatibility with earlier versions
of the standard, conciseness, and alignment with the semantics of restricted flavours of OWL discussed later. These reasons relate more to
convention than anything of general technical interest to us, and hence
we refer to the standard [349, Section 5] for more details.

`owl:someValuesFrom` defines a restriction class whose members have
some value for a given property from a given class.

$$\text{IF } (b,c) \in I_{EXT}(I_S(\texttt{owl:someValuesFrom})) \text{ and}$$
$$(b,p) \in I_{EXT}(I_S(\texttt{owl:onProperty}))$$
$$\text{THEN } b \in I_C, c \in I_C, p \in I_P \text{ and}$$
$$I_{CEXT}(b) = \{x \in I_R \mid \exists y : (x,y) \in I_{EXT}(p) \text{ and } y \in I_{CEXT}(c)\}$$

- If b is defined to have some values from c on a property p and:

  ... if x_1 has a value for p that is a member of the class c, then x_1
  is a member of the restriction class b.

  ... otherwise, if x_2 is a member of the restriction class b, it is known
  that x_2 has at least one value for the property p that is a member
  of the class c.

  - For example, we may state that the class EU-CITIZEN is equiv-
    alent to the class having some values from the class EU-STATE
    on the property CITIZEN-OF. If there is a resource y such that
    x_1 CITIZEN-OF y and y is a EU-STATE, then we know that x_1 is
    a EU-CITIZEN (x_1 may be a citizen of other states that are not
    EU states; this does not affect their status as an EU citizen).
    On the other hand, if we know that x_2 is a EU-CITIZEN, we
    know it must have some value for CITIZEN-OF that is a member
    of EU-STATE, even if we cannot name that value (we could, for
    example, represent that value as a blank node).

owl:allValuesFrom defines a restriction class whose members only have values from a given class on a given property.

$$\text{IF } (b,c) \in I_{EXT}(I_S(\texttt{owl:allValuesFrom})) \text{ and}$$
$$(b,p) \in I_{EXT}(I_S(\texttt{owl:onProperty}))$$
$$\text{THEN } b \in I_C, \ c \in I_C, \ p \in I_P \text{ and}$$
$$I_{CEXT}(b) = \{x \in I_R \mid \forall y : (x,y) \in I_{EXT}(p) \text{ implies } y \in I_{CEXT}(c)\}$$

- If b is defined to have all values from c on a property p and:

  ... if x is a member of b and has a value for the property p, that value must be a member of c;

  ... on the other hand, if all values for x on a property p must be in the class c, then x is a member of b.

- As an example, we could define the class MASSLESS as equivalent to the class having all values from MASSLESS for the property PART. Then, if x_1 is a member of MASSLESS and has the value y for PART, we can conclude that y is also MASSLESS. On the other hand, if we know that all possible values of PART for x_2 must be MASSLESS (including those not specified yet in the data) then we can conclude that x_2 is a member of MASSLESS; this also holds for the vacuous case where we know that x_2 cannot have any value at all for PART, in which case we can still conclude that it is MASSLESS!

- Such vacuous cases make it difficult to define a direct, equivalent, practical example for all-values-from since if a class does not have the property p, it vacuously satisfies the condition. It is, however, more straightforward to define practical examples using sub-class. An example would be to state that the class HUMAN is a *sub-class* of the class having all values from HUMAN for the property HAS-CHILD; this states that any child of a human must be human, or equivalently, that humans cannot have non-human children. Importantly, we cannot state *equivalence* in this case since otherwise classes of resources that we know have no children (e.g., LAWNMOWER) would vacuously satisfy the restriction of "having all values from HUMAN for the property HAS-CHILD"; any members of such classes would then be implied to be a member of HUMAN!

- When used with equivalent-class axioms, all-values restrictions can also be combined with other restrictions to avoid vacuous cases. For example, we can say that HUMAN is an equivalent-class of the intersection of (1) the class having all values from HUMAN for the property HAS-CHILD, and (2) the class having some value (from HUMAN or even THING) for the property HAS-CHILD.

---

owl:hasValue defines a restriction class whose members have a given value on a given property.

$$\text{IF } (b,y) \in I_{EXT}(I_S(\text{owl:hasValue})) \text{ and}$$
$$(b,p) \in I_{EXT}(I_S(\text{owl:onProperty}))$$
$$\text{THEN } b \in I_C, \, p \in I_P \text{ and}$$
$$I_{CEXT}(b) = \{x \in I_R \mid (x,y) \in I_{EXT}(p)\}$$

- If b is defined as the class that has the value y on property p and ...

  ... if x_1 is a member of c, then x_1 must have the value y for p;
  ... on the other hand, if x_2 has the value y for p, then x_2 must be a member of c.

- For example, we may state that a JOVIAN-MOON is equivalent to the class having the value JUPITER on the property ORBITS (note that JUPITER is a resource, not a class). In this case, if x is a member of JOVIAN-MOON, then it must have the value JUPITER on the property ORBITS. On the other hand, if y has the value JUPITER on the property ORBITS, it must be a member of JOVIAN-MOON.

---

owl:hasSelf defines a restriction class whose members are reflexive for a given property.

$$\text{IF } (b,\text{TRUE}) \in I_{EXT}(I_S(\text{owl:hasSelf})) \text{ and}$$
$$(b,p) \in I_{EXT}(I_S(\text{owl:onProperty}))$$
$$\text{THEN } b \in I_C, \, p \in I_P \text{ and}$$
$$I_{CEXT}(b) = \{x \mid (x,x) \in I_{EXT}(p)\}$$

- If c is defined to have self on property p and:

  ... if x is a member of b, then p must relate x to itself;
  ... on the other hand, if y is related to itself by p, then y is a member of b.

- An example might be stating that the class NARCISSIST is equivalent to the class having self on the property LOVES. If x is a member of NARCISSIST, it must have the value x for the property LOVES. On the other hand, if y has itself as a value for the property LOVES, it must be a member of NARCISSIST (note that y may love other things, which does not affect its membership of NARCISSIST).

Before we continue, we give some concrete examples of the RDF representations of some of the inline examples we have seen in the above descriptions.

Example 5.15

To represent in RDF that the class EU-CITIZEN is equivalent to the class having some values from EU-STATE on the property CITIZEN-OF, we can write (in Turtle):

```
:EUCitizen owl:equivalentClass
  [ a owl:Restriction ;
    owl:someValuesFrom :EUState ;
    owl:onProperty :citizenOf ] .
```

To represent that the class HUMAN is a sub-class of the class having all values from HUMAN for the property HAS-CHILD, we can write:

```
:Human rdfs:subClassOf
  [ a owl:Restriction ;
    owl:allValuesFrom :Human ;
    owl:onProperty :hasChild ] .
```

To represent that the class JOVIAN-MOON is equivalent to the class having the value JUPITER on the property ORBITS, we can write:

```
:JovianMoon owl:equivalentClass
  [ a owl:Restriction ;
    owl:hasValue :Jupiter ;
    owl:onProperty :orbits ] .
```

To represent that the class NARCISSIST is equivalent to the class having self on the property LOVES, we write:

```
:Narcissist owl:equivalentClass
  [ a owl:Restriction ;
    owl:hasSelf true ;
    owl:onProperty :loves ] .
```

Exercise 5.8

How might we use all-values-from to state that members of the class LAWNMOWER have no value for the property HAS-CHILD?

Remark 5.17

Per Remark 5.16, owl:someValuesFrom was defined using a weaker IF–THEN semantics. So what sort of inference do we miss when compared with an IF-AND-ONLY-IF semantics? Let us assume that we have the following statements:

```
:BeneluxCitizen owl:equivalentClass
  [ a owl:Restriction ;
    owl:someValuesFrom :BeneluxState ;
    owl:onProperty :citizenOf ] .
:BeneluxState rdfs:subClassOf :EUState .

:RobertCailliau :citizenOf :Belgium .
:Belgium a :BeneluxState .
```

Under both an IF-AND-ONLY-IF semantics and an IF–THEN semantics), we can then infer:

```
:RobertCailliau a :BeneluxCitizen .
```

Only under an IF-AND-ONLY-IF semantics (and not an IF–THEN semantics) could we infer:

```
:RobertCailliau rdf:type
  [ a owl:Restriction ;
    owl:someValuesFrom :EUState ;
    owl:onProperty :citizenOf ] .
```

Though we know that a Robert must be in the class having citizenship of an EU state, we cannot create a *new* restriction class that represents that conclusion under the IF–THEN semantics chosen by OWL.

Remark 5.18

For `owl:someValuesFrom` and `owl:allValuesFrom`, OWL also provides an optional abbreviation `owl:onProperties` to specify multiple properties at once, where one can state, for example:

```
:Human rdfs:subClassOf
  [ a owl:Restriction ;
    owl:allValuesFrom :Human ;
    owl:onProperties ( :mother :father ) ] .
```

Without the abbreviation, this could also be represented as:

```
:Human rdfs:subClassOf
  [ owl:intersectionOf (
      [ a owl:Restriction ;
        owl:allValuesFrom :Human ;
        owl:onProperty :mother ]
      [ a owl:Restriction ;
        owl:allValuesFrom :Human ;
        owl:onProperty :father ] ) ] .
```

Remark 5.19 ⓘ

In Remark 5.8, we mentioned that the top property owl:topObjectProperty can be used in more complex definitions, where we mentioned the example of defining that "all elephants are bigger than all mice" [337]. Towards seeing this example in action, we assume two classes :Elephant and :Mouse, where we wish to infer that every member of the former class has the relation :biggerThan to every member of the latter class. In fact, this definition is quite tricky.

We start with the following step sometimes called "*rolification*" [241]:

```
:Elephant rdfs:subClassOf
  [ a owl:Restriction ; owl:hasSelf true ; owl:onProperty :e ] .
:Mouse rdfs:subClassOf
  [ a owl:Restriction ; owl:hasSelf true ; owl:onProperty :m ] .
```

This defines a self-loop labelled :e or :m on each member of :Elephant or :Mouse respectively. Now we can define:

```
:biggerThan owl:propertyChainAxiom ( :e owl:topObjectProperty :m ) .
```

This will entail that every ELEPHANT is BIGGER-THAN every MOUSE. Here the properties :e and :m are used in a path to verify the class of the current resource, so the above path can be read as *check that the resource is an elephant (:e), if so, move to any resource (owl:topObjectProperty) and check that it is a mouse (:m).*

Next, the following list of OWL vocabulary terms allow for defining number-based restrictions on members of a class. In the following, we will use the notation $\#S$ to denote the cardinality (number of elements) of the set S, and we will use n to refer to a natural number (i.e., $n \in \mathbb{N}, n \geq 0$).

---

owl:minCardinality defines a restriction class based on a property having *at least* a given number of values.

$$\text{IF } (b,n) \in I_{EXT}(I_S(\text{owl:minCardinality})) \text{ and}$$
$$(b,p) \in I_{EXT}(I_S(\text{owl:onProperty}))$$
$$\text{THEN } b \in I_C, \ p \in I_P \text{ and}$$
$$I_{CEXT}(b) = \{x \mid \#\{y \mid (x,y) \in I_{EXT}(p)\} \geq n\}$$

- If b is a cardinality class with at least n values (a natural number including zero) for property p and:

  ... if x_1 is a member of the cardinality class b, then x_1 is entailed to have at least n (distinct) values for property p;

... on the other hand, if it is known that x_2 has at least n values for the property p, then x_2 is entailed to be a member of b.

- Any such definition for ≥ 0 creates a class to which every resource vacuously belongs (i.e., equivalent to owl:Thing). For example, if we state that the class CLIENT is equivalent to the class with zero or more values for FAX, then any resource x_1 will be a member of CLIENT, no matter whether or not it has a value for FAX. Conversely, if x_2 is known to be a member of CLIENT, we cannot conclude anything about x_2 from that.
- As an example for ≥ 1, we could state that the class DECEASED is equivalent to the class having at least one value for PLACE-OF-DEATH. If we know that x_1 is a member of DECEASED, we can conclude it has some (possibly existential) value for PLACE-OF-DEATH. On the other hand, if x_2 has any value for PLACE-OF-DEATH, we can conclude that it is a member of DECEASED.
- As an example for ≥ 2, we could state that a POLYGLOT is equivalent to the class having at least two values for SPEAKS-LANGUAGE. If we know that x_1 has values y_1 and y_2 for SPEAKS-LANGUAGE and that y_1 different-from y_2, then we can conclude that x_1 is a member of POLYGLOT. On the other hand, if we know that x_2 is a member of POLYGLOT, we can infer that it has at least two values for SPEAKS-LANGUAGE (possibly existentials) that are different-from each other; however, it is worth remarking that if x_2 already had two stated values for SPEAKS-LANGUAGE, we *could not* infer that these values are different-from each other since other values may exist.

---

owl:maxCardinality defines a restriction class based on a property having *at most* a given number of values.

$$\text{IF } (b,n) \in I_{EXT}(I_S(\text{owl:maxCardinality})) \text{ and}$$
$$(b,p) \in I_{EXT}(I_S(\text{owl:onProperty}))$$
$$\text{THEN } b \in I_C,\ p \in I_P \text{ and}$$
$$I_{CEXT}(b) = \{x \mid \#\{y \mid (x,y) \in I_{EXT}(p)\} \leq n\}$$

- If b is a cardinality class with at most n values (a natural number including zero) for property p and:

... if x_1 is a member of the cardinality class b, then x_1 is entailed to have at most n (distinct) values for property p;

... on the other hand, if it is known that x_2 has at most n values for the property p, then x_2 is entailed to be a member of b.

- As an example for ≤ 0, we could state that the class INVISIBLE is equivalent to the class that has at most zero values for COLOUR. If x is a member of INVISIBLE and has a value of COLOUR, a contradiction arises. On the other hand, if we know x cannot have any value for COLOUR, then we could conclude that x is a member of INVISIBLE.
- As an example for ≤ 1, we could state that a COUNTRY is a *sub-class* of the class with at most one value for HEAD-OF-STATE. If we know that x is a member of COUNTRY and we find that it has two values for HEAD-OF-STATE, we conclude that they must be the same. Here we must avoid the trap of saying that COUNTRY is equivalent to such a class since otherwise anything without a HEAD-OF-STATE – including perhaps members of LAWNMOWER – could be inferred to be a member of COUNTRY.
- As an example for ≤ 2, we could state that the class PERSON is a *sub-class* of the class with at most two values for BIOLOGICAL-PARENT. If x has three stated values for BIOLOGICAL-PARENT, we know that at least two such values must be same-as.

---

owl:cardinality defines a restriction class based on a property having *exactly* a given number of values.

$$\text{IF } (b,n) \in I_{EXT}(I_S(\texttt{owl:cardinality})) \text{ and}$$
$$(b,p) \in I_{EXT}(I_S(\texttt{owl:onProperty}))$$
$$\text{THEN } b \in I_C, \, p \in I_P \text{ and}$$
$$I_{CEXT}(b) = \{x \mid \#\{y \mid (x,y) \in I_{EXT}(p)\} = n\}$$

- If b is a cardinality class with exactly n values (a natural number including zero) for property p and:

  ... if x_1 is a member of the cardinality class b, then x_1 is entailed to have exactly n (distinct) values for property p;
  ... on the other hand, if it is known that x_2 has exactly n values for the property p, then x_2 is entailed to be a member of b.

- Defining exact cardinality $= 0$ is equivalent to defining max-cardinality ≤ 0. Thus we could again state that the class INVISIBLE is equivalent to the class that has exactly zero values for COLOUR. This has the same semantics as the equivalent max-cardinality definition.

- As an example for $= 1$, we could state that the class MONOLIN-GUAL is equivalent to the class having exactly one value for SPEAKS-LANGUAGE. If x_1 is a member of MONOLINGUAL, we know it must have one value for speaks language (possibly existential), and if it has two or more stated values for SPEAKS-LANGUAGE, we know they must all be same-as. On the other hand, if we know that x_2 must have precisely one value for SPEAKS-LANGUAGE, we can conclude it to be a member of MONOLINGUAL.

- An an example for $= 2$, we could state that the class TERNARY-STAR is equivalent to the class having exactly 2 values for the property ORBITS-STAR. If x_1 is a member of TERNARY-STAR with no defined value for ORBITS-STAR, then two can be entailed to exist; otherwise if x_1 is given three values for ORBITS-STAR in the data, then we must know that at least two of those values are same-as. On the other hand, if we know that x_2 must have precisely two values for ORBITS-STAR, we can conclude it to be a member of TERNARY-STAR.

Remark 5.20 ⓘ

One may have guessed that `owl:cardinality` is a shortcut for the intersection of `owl:maxCardinality` and `owl:minCardinality`. For example, we could state that the class TERNARY-STAR is equivalent to the class of things that orbit two stars (in Turtle syntax) as follows:

```
:TernaryStar owl:equivalentClass
  [ a owl:Restriction ;
    owl:onProperty :orbitsStar ;
    owl:cardinality 2 ] .
```

We could also write it more verbosely as:

```
:TernaryStar owl:equivalentClass
  [ owl:intersectionOf (
      [ a owl:Restriction ;
        owl:onProperty :orbitsStar ;
        owl:maxCardinality 2 ]
      [ a owl:Restriction ;
        owl:onProperty :orbitsStar ;
        owl:minCardinality 2 ] ) ] .
```

Both forms are semantically equivalent (with the syntactic exception that the latter introduces two additional anonymous classes).

> **Remark 5.21**   (i)
>
> In the previous discussion, we mentioned that if we know that
> a resource x has at most n values for a given property, we may be able
> to conclude that it is a member of a max- or exact-cardinality class.
> But under the OWA, how could we ever hope to establish an upper
> bound on the number of properties that x has? Such upper bounds are
> most often established when we know x to be a member of another
> stricter cardinality class, or when we know x to have all values from a
> bounded enumeration on a property p. Admittedly, however, non-trivial
> conclusions involving such upper bounds are rare under the OWA.
>
> Likewise if we know that a resource x has at least n values for a
> property p, we may be able to conclude that it is a member of a min-
> or exact-cardinality class. But again, putting a *lower*-bound (greater
> than one) on the number of values that x takes for a property p is
> complicated by the UNA since even if x is stated in the data to have
> several values for p, unless these values are known to be different-from
> each other, then all we can conclude is that x has at least one value. To
> find a lower-bound greater than one for the number of values x takes
> for p, again one possibility is that the lower-bound is established by
> a stricter cardinality class; another possibility is that we know that n
> values are distinct (either by direct different-from statements or as can
> be inferred from, e.g., disjointness constraints).

The previous vocabulary definitions apply restrictions on the number of
values a property can take; however, they do not consider from which class
those values are taken. OWL (2) thus also offers *qualified* cardinality restrictions that only count values from a particular class.

---

owl:minQualifiedCardinality* defines a restriction class based on a
   property having *at least* a given number of values *that are members
   of a given class.*

$$\text{IF } (b,n) \in I_{EXT}(I_S(\texttt{owl:minQualifiedCardinality})) \text{ and}$$
$$(b,p) \in I_{EXT}(I_S(\texttt{owl:onProperty})) \text{ and}$$
$$(b,c) \in I_{EXT}(I_S(\texttt{owl:onClass}))$$
$$\text{THEN } b \in I_C, \, c \in I_C, \, p \in I_P \text{ and}$$
$$I_{CEXT}(b) = \{x \mid \#\{y \in I_{CEXT}(c) \mid (x,y) \in I_{EXT}(p)\} \geq n\}$$

- If b is a qualified cardinality class with at least n values for property
  p in class c, and:

... if x_1 is a member of b, then x_1 is entailed to have at least n values for property p that are a member of c;

- on the other hand, if x_2 is known to have at least n values on property p in class c, then x_2 is entailed to be a member of b.

- An example of a qualified min-cardinality might be stating that the MULTI-STAR class is equivalent to the class of all resources having at least 2 values for the property ORBITED-BY in the class STAR. In this case, if we know that x_1 is a member of MULTI-STAR, we know that it must be ORBITED-BY (at least) two distinct resources that are members of STAR. On the other hand, if we know that x_2 is ORBITED-BY two distinct members of STAR, we can conclude that it is a member of MULTI-STAR. Note that a MULTI-STAR may be orbited by resources that are not members of STAR (e.g., members of PLANET), which are ignored by the qualified restriction.

---

owl:maxQualifiedCardinality* defines a restriction class based on a property having *at most* a given number of values *that are members of a given class.*

$$\text{IF } (b,n) \in I_{EXT}(I_S(\text{owl:maxQualifiedCardinality})) \text{ and}$$
$$(b,p) \in I_{EXT}(I_S(\text{owl:onProperty})) \text{ and}$$
$$(b,c) \in I_{EXT}(I_S(\text{owl:onClass}))$$
$$\text{THEN } b \in I_C, \ c \in I_C, \ p \in I_P \text{ and}$$
$$I_{CEXT}(b) = \{x \mid \#\{y \in I_{CEXT}(c) \mid (x,y) \in I_{EXT}(p)\} \leq n\}$$

- If b is a qualified max-cardinality class with at most n (distinct) values for property p in class c, and:

  ... if x_1 is a member of b, then x_1 can have at most n values for property p that are a member of c;

  ... on the other hand, if x_2 is known to have at most n values on property p in class c, then x_2 is entailed to be a member of b.

- For example, we may state that the class REPUBLIC is a *sub-class* of the class having at most zero values for HEAD-OF-STATE from the class MONARCH. If x_1 is a member of REPUBLIC where x_1 HEAD-OF-STATE y_1, then we can conclude that y_1 cannot be a member of MONARCH; furthermore, if x_2 is a member of REPUBLIC and y_2 a member of MONARCH, we know x_2 HEAD-OF-STATE y_2 cannot hold. We use *sub-class* since we do not wish to infer resources that cannot have a HEAD-OF-STATE from the class MONARCH (e.g, members of LAWNMOWER) to be members of REPUBLIC.

- Taking an example for ≤ 1, we can state that MOON is a *sub-class* of the class having at most 1 value for the property ORBITS in the class PLANEMO. If x is a member of MOON, and it ORBITS two members of PLANEMO, then we can infer those two resources to be same-as. This definition does not affect resources that a MOON orbits that are not known to be PLANEMOs (e.g., a STAR).

---

owl:qualifiedCardinality* defines a restriction class based on a property having *exactly* a given number of values *that are members of a given class*.

$$\text{IF } (b,n) \in I_{EXT}(I_S(\texttt{owl:qualifiedCardinality})) \text{ and}$$
$$(b,p) \in I_{EXT}(I_S(\texttt{owl:onProperty})) \text{ and}$$
$$(b,c) \in I_{EXT}(I_S(\texttt{owl:onClass}))$$
$$\text{THEN } b \in I_C,\ c \in I_C,\ p \in I_P \text{ and}$$
$$I_{CEXT}(b) = \{x \mid \#\{y \in I_{CEXT}(c) \mid (x,y) \in I_{EXT}(p)\} = n\}$$

- If b is a qualified cardinality class with exactly n values for property p in class c, and:

  ... if x_1 is a member of b, then x_1 is entailed to have exactly n values for property p that are a member of c;
  ... on the other hand, if x_2 is known to have exactly n values on property p in class c, then x_2 is entailed to be a member of b.

- For example, we may state that the class ZEBROID is equivalent to the class of resources having precisely one value for PARENT from the class ZEBRA. If x_1 is a member of ZEBROID, we know it must have precisely one PARENT from the class ZEBRA; thus if no such parent is current known, we can infer the existence of such a resource; otherwise if two or more values of PARENT from the class ZEBRA are known, we can infer that they are same-as. On the other hand, if we know that x_2 has precisely one PARENT from the class ZEBRA, we know that it must be a ZEBROID.

Remark 5.22 (i)

Analogous to Remark 5.20, owl:qualifiedCardinality n on class c and property p can be alternatively expressed as the intersection of owl:maxQualifiedCardinality n and owl:minQualifiedCardinality n on class c and property p.

We now give concrete examples of the RDF representations of some of the inline examples we have seen for cardinality restrictions.

Example 5.16

To represent that the class POLYGLOT is equivalent to the class having at least 2 values for the property SPEAKS-LANGUAGE, we write:

```
:Polyglot owl:equivalentClass
   [ a owl:Restriction ;
     owl:minCardinality 2 ;
     owl:onProperty :speaksLanguage ] .
```

To represent that the class COUNTRY is a sub-class of the class having at most 1 value for the property HEAD-OF-STATE, we write:

```
:Country rdfs:subClassOf
   [ a owl:Restriction ;
     owl:maxCardinality 1 ;
     owl:onProperty :headOfState ] .
```

To represent that the class ZEBROID is equivalent to the class having exactly 1 value for the property PARENT in the class ZEBRA, we write:

```
:Zebroid owl:equivalentClass
   [ a owl:Restriction ;
     owl:qualifiedCardinality 1 ;
     owl:onProperty :parent ;
     owl:onClass :Zebra ] .
```

Exercise 5.9

For `owl:someValuesFrom`, *we gave an example where the class EU-CITIZEN is defined as equivalent to the class having some values from the class EU-STATE on the property CITIZEN-OF. How could we express this using (qualified) cardinality restrictions instead?*

As before, we can use whatever axiom involving classes we like, where restriction classes can appear on the left-hand side or right-hand side (or both) of equivalence, sub-class and disjointness axioms, or on the right-hand side of domain and range axioms. We can also consider nesting class definitions, including arbitrary mixes of set-based classes and restriction-based classes.

Example 5.17

To represent that the class ZEBROID is equivalent to the class having exactly 1 value for the property PARENT in the class ZEBRA and exactly 1 value for the property PARENT in the class of EQUUS that are not ZEBRA, we write:

```
:Zebroid owl:equivalentClass
   [ owl:intersectionOf (
      [ a owl:Restriction ;
         owl:qualifiedCardinality 1 ;
         owl:onProperty :parent ;
         owl:onClass :Zebra ]
      [ a owl:Restriction ;
         owl:qualifiedCardinality 1 ;
         owl:onProperty :parent ;
         owl:onClass [
            owl:intersectionOf ( :Equus [ owl:complementOf :Zebra ] )
         ] ] ) ] .
```

Of course, we could also create some named classes to "unnest" this structure, such as to first define:

```
:EquusNotZebra owl:equivalentClass
   [ owl:intersectionOf ( :Equus [ owl:complementOf :Zebra ] ) ] .
```

which then helps us to simplify the definition (a little):

```
:Zebroid owl:equivalentClass
   [ owl:intersectionOf (
      [ a owl:Restriction ;
         owl:qualifiedCardinality 1 ;
         owl:onProperty :parent ;
         owl:onClass :Zebra ]
      [ a owl:Restriction ;
         owl:qualifiedCardinality 1 ;
         owl:onProperty :parent ;
         owl:onClass :EquusNotZebra ] ) ] .
```

Discussion 5.3

FRANK: This seems to have gotten pretty complicated. Does the Web of Data really need ways to make these sorts of definitions?

AIDAN: What sort of Web of Data would it be if the machines were not able to automatically reason about Zebroids?

Exercise 5.10

Examples 5.16 and 5.17 provide two alternative definitions for the class ZEBROID. *But which definition is weaker/stronger in terms of the entailments they permit about* ZEBROIDs?

Exercise 5.11

How can the OWL features for class definitions and axioms be used in the context of Example 5.1 to help answer Julie's query?

Remark 5.23

With respect to `owl:someValuesFrom` and the min-cardinality and exact-cardinality features, note that in certain circumstances, we can define classes that have an infinite extension. An example might be stating that the class HUMAN is equivalent to the class having some value(s) from HUMAN on the property BIOLOGICAL-MOTHER: every human must have a human biological mother and anything with a human biological mother must be human. Thus we create a class HUMAN where if we have one member of that class, we must have infinite members with an infinite chain of BIOLOGICAL-MOTHER relations.

Of course this idea of infinite humans is inaccurate. We have created a chicken-and-egg situation: the first "true human" could not have had a human mother. Arguably, definitions creating an infinite chain of existential individuals in this manner do not reflect the material world.

On the other hand, we could state, for example, that the class NATURAL-NUMBER is equivalent to the class that has some value(s) from NATURAL-NUMBER on the property SUCCESSOR. This would accurately reflect if not the real world, a mathematical abstraction thereof.

In fact, here we have a hint as to why reasoning tasks in OWL may be undecidable: why there is no possible implementation that covers all inferences. We will discuss this issue further in Section 5.5.

Exercise 5.12

This extended exercise offers a challenging test of various aspects of the OWL vocabulary discussed thus far.

We will extend Exercise 5.7 to consider some hands in poker. First of all, consider the following format of data:

```
:PokerRound42 a :PokerRound ;
   :hasDeal :FranksDeal42 , :JuliesDeal42 , :AnnasDeal42 .

:FranksDeal42 a :PokerDeal ; :hasPlayer :Frank ; :hasHand :2c7c8c9cAc .
:JuliesDeal42 a :PokerDeal ; :hasPlayer :Julie ; :hasHand :3h3s6c6d6h .
:AnnasDeal42  a :PokerDeal ; :hasPlayer :Anna  ; :hasHand :JsKcKdKhKs .

:2c7c8c9cAc a :PokerHand ; :hasCard :2c , :7c , :8c , :9c , :Ac .
:3h3s6c6d6h a :PokerHand ; :hasCard :3h , :3s , :6c , :6d , :6h .
:JsKcKdKhKs a :PokerHand ; :hasCard :Js , :Kc , :Kd , :Kh , :Ks .
```

From these data, we would like to entail, for example:

```
:2c7c8c9cAc a :Flush       ; :beatenBy :3h3s6c6d6h , :JsKcKdKhKs .
:3h3s6c6d6h a :FullHouse    ; :beatenBy :JsKcKdKhKs .
:JsKcKdKhKs a :FourOfAKind .

:Frank :loses :PokerRound42 .
:Julie :loses :PokerRound42 .
```

In the following, you can assume that the basic definitions of Exercise 5.7 are given and that we thus know the following enumerations:

```
:StandardCard owl:equivalentClass [ owl:oneOf ( :2c ... :As ) ] .

:Club      owl:equivalentClass [ owl:oneOf ( :2c ... :Ac ) ] .
:Diamond   owl:equivalentClass [ owl:oneOf ( :2d ... :Ad ) ] .
:Heart     owl:equivalentClass [ owl:oneOf ( :2h ... :Ah ) ] .
:Spade     owl:equivalentClass [ owl:oneOf ( :2s ... :As ) ] .

:Ace       owl:equivalentClass [ owl:oneOf ( :Ac :Ad :Ah :As ) ] .
...
:Two       owl:equivalentClass [ owl:oneOf ( :2c :2d :2h :2s ) ] .
```

with 52 members for STANDARD-CARD; *13 members for each suit class* CLUB, . . . , SPADE; *and 4 members for each value class* :TWO, . . . :ACE. *You can further assume that all 52 cards are defined pairwise different and all players are also defined as pairwise different (see Remark 5.2):*

```
[] a owl:AllDifferent ; owl:members ( :2c ... :As ) .
[] a owl:AllDifferent ; owl:members ( :Anna :Frank :Julie ) .
```

The following questions may require use of a mix of property axioms, class axioms, class definitions, etc. We mark particularly challenging parts with "⚠" and even more formidable parts with "♣♣". You may assume solutions for previous parts as given.

- Define that all values for the property HAS-PLAYER are in the class POKER-PLAYER.
- Define that the property HAS-CARD for members of the class POKER-HAND takes values only from the class STANDARD-CARD.

- *Define that each POKER-DEAL has exactly one value on the property HAS-PLAYER and exactly one value on the property HAS-HAND.*
- *Define that each POKER-HAND has exactly five values on the property HAS-CARD.*
- *Define that each member of POKER-DEAL is the value of exactly one HAS-DEAL relation (i.e., it is part of one and only one round).*
- *Define that any POKER-ROUND has at least two and at most ten values (inclusive) for the property HAS-DEAL.*
- *Define any POKER-HAND having all CLUB cards as a CLUB-FLUSH.*
- *Assuming DIAMOND-FLUSH, HEART-FLUSH and SPADE-FLUSH are defined likewise, define any POKER-HAND where all five cards have the same suit as a FLUSH.*
- *Define any POKER-HAND having four cards of a particular value as a FOUR-OF-A-KIND.*
- *Define any poker hand having three cards of one value and two cards of a different value as a FULL-HOUSE.*
- ⚠ *Define that the POKER-HANDs in different POKER-DEALs of the same POKER-ROUND cannot share a card.*
- *Define that no two POKER-DEALs in the same POKER-ROUND can have the same player.*
- ⚠ *Define that any two POKER-HANDs that do not share all five values for HAS-CARD are different.*
- *Define that BEATEN-BY is transitive.*
- ⚠ *Define that any member of FLUSH is BEATEN-BY any member of FULL-HOUSE and that any member of FULL-HOUSE is BEATEN-BY any member of FOUR-OF-A-KIND.*
- ⚠ *Define that the player of any POKER-DEAL in a given round that has a hand BEATEN-BY by the hand of any other POKER-DEAL in that round LOSES that round (i.e., that in the example above Frank and Julie lose round 42).*
- ☢ *Define that any two POKER-HANDs with the same five values for HAS-CARD are the same.*

Project 5.2

Extend Exercise 5.12 to create an ontology that can classify other types of poker hands in a similar manner and to entail which poker hands beat which. You may wish to add some further triples to annotate individual standard cards, for example, to state that all cards in TWO are followed-by all cards in THREE, and so forth, to capture the notion of a STRAIGHT (five cards with sequential values). Another

> challenge may be to define which player(s) wins a round, which is much more challenging than entailing player(s) who lose!
>
> Creating an ontology that fully captures the classification and ordering of poker hands is an exceptionally challenging task (also you may have to learn the rules of poker beforehand), so rather than aiming for a complete ontology, see how far you can go. You may wish to feed your axioms and definitions into an OWL reasoning system such as Protégé; however, be aware that performance will likely be a major issue.[a]
>
> ---
>
> [a] http://protege.stanford.edu/

5.4.4 Negation

OWL supports negation where one can state that something does not hold. Such *negative property* **assertions** are expressed in RDF using something similar to reification (see Section 3.5.3).

---

owl:NegativePropertyAssertion* is the class of negation statements.
owl:sourceIndividual* denotes the subject of the negated statement.
owl:assertionProperty* denotes the property of the negated statement.
owl:targetIndividual* denotes the object of the negated statement in the case that the assertion property is an object-property.
owl:targetValue denotes the object of the negated statement in the case that the assertion property is a datatype-property.

$$(b,x) \in I_{EXT}(I_S(\texttt{owl:sourceIndividual})) \text{ and}$$
$$(b,p) \in I_{EXT}(I_S(\texttt{owl:assertionProperty})) \text{ and}$$
$$((b,y) \in I_{EXT}(I_S(\texttt{owl:targetIndividual})) \text{ or}$$
$$(b,y) \in I_{EXT}(I_S(\texttt{owl:targetValue})))$$
$$\text{IF AND ONLY IF } \{b,x,y\} \subseteq I_R, p \in I_P \text{ and}$$
$$(x,y) \notin I_{EXT}(p)$$

- The semantics is given as IF-AND-ONLY-IF; note that an existential (blank node) is introduced for b to represent the entailment on an RDF level if the model theoretic condition holds.
- We illustrate the use of these terms in Examples 5.18 and 5.19.

Example 5.18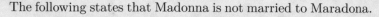

The following states that Madonna is not married to Maradona.

```
[] rdf:type owl:NegativePropertyAssertion ;
  owl:sourceIndividual :Madonna ;
  owl:assertionProperty :spouse ;
  owl:targetIndividual :Maradona .
```

If the object of the relation is a literal, then a slightly different syntax is required. The following example states that Madonna is not, in fact, 27.4 metres tall. Note that since the value is a datatype, the property `owl:targetIndividual` is replaced with `owl:targetValue`.

```
[] rdf:type owl:NegativePropertyAssertion ;
  owl:sourceIndividual :Madonna ;
  owl:assertionProperty :heightInMetres ;
  owl:targetValue 27.4 .
```

Such negated statements can also be entailed.

Example 5.19

Let us assume the following definitions:

```
:Married owl:disjointWith :Single .
:spouse rdfs:domain :Married ; rdfs:range Married .
```

Now given:

```
:Madonna a :Single .
:Maradona a :Single .
```

We could entail (creating a fresh blank node):

```
[] rdf:type owl:NegativePropertyAssertion ;
  owl:sourceIndividual :Madonna ;
  owl:assertionProperty :spouse ;
  owl:targetIndividual :Maradona .
```

5.4.5 Datatypes

Like in RDF(S), OWL also supports datatypes through the definition of a datatype map. As in RDF(S), a datatype in OWL is identified by an IRI and is defined in terms of a mapping from a lexical space (e.g., the string "2") to a value space (e.g., the number two). OWL supports the following primitive XML Schema datatypes (introduced previously in Section 3.2.2): xsd:decimal, xsd:double, xsd:float, xsd:string, xsd:boolean, xsd:base64binary, xsd:hexBinary, xsd:anyURI, xsd:dateTime, xsd:date-TimeStamp. All standard datatypes derived from these primitive datatypes are also supported, including, for example, xsd:integer, xsd:byte, etc., derived from xsd:decimal. Likewise rdf:PlainLiteral is also supported. Other primitive datatypes – xsd:date, xsd:time xsd:duration, the Gregorian datatypes like xsd:gYear, and syntactic XML datatypes like xsd:QName – are omitted.

On the other hand, OWL adds two new primitive datatypes: owl:rational and owl:real referring to rational and real numbers, respectively.

---

owl:rational[*] denotes the datatype of all rational numbers: numbers that can be expressed as the fraction of two whole numbers.

- This datatype thus extends the value space of xsd:decimal with values like $\frac{1}{3}$ that are inexpressible as a finite decimal string.
- OWL defines a lexical mapping for this datatype based on the syntax [numerator]'/'[denominator], where both [numerator] and [denominator] are replaced by valid xsd:integer lexical strings and where the denominator is non-zero (e.g., "3/-7"). As a result, some lexical strings that are valid for xsd:decimal (e.g., "13.4") are not valid for owl:rational, though a lexical string exists for any decimal value (e.g., "134/10").

---

owl:real[*] denotes the datatype of all real numbers, which includes all values on the continuous number line, consisting of the union of the set of rational numbers and irrational numbers.

- This datatype thus extends the value space of owl:rational with irrational values like $\sqrt{2}$ or π that cannot be expressed as a fraction of two whole numbers.
- OWL does not define a lexical mapping for this datatype since such a mapping would necessarily be incomplete: the set of real values is *uncountably* infinite, meaning that one would need strings of infinite length (or with an uncountably infinite alphabet) to capture a lexical string for all such values.

Unlike RDF(S), each datatype in OWL is additionally associated with a *facet space*, which allows for deriving new datatypes by restricting facets of old datatypes; for example, one can define a new datatype TEEN-AGE by restricting the existing INTEGER datatype by the facets of minimum-value inclusive (13) and maximum-value inclusive (19). Formally, a *facet space* is a set of pairs of the form (F, v) where F is an IRI that identifies the *constraining facet* and v is the *constraining value*. The constraining facets supported by

OWL are taken from the XML Schema Definition specification [313]. The
facets that OWL supports vary according to the datatype in question; we
first discuss numeric/temporal facets, and then later string-based facets.

For the datatypes xsd:decimal, xsd:double, xsd:float, owl:rational,
owl:real, xsd:dateTime, and xsd:dateTimeStamp, the *normative facets* – the
facets that a compliant OWL implementation must support – are as follows:

---

xsd:minInclusive The minimum value in the derived datatype taken
    from the base datatype.

---

xsd:maxInclusive The maximum value in the derived datatype taken
    from the base datatype.

---

xsd:minExclusive The maximum value in the base datatype that is less
    than all the values in the derived datatype.

---

xsd:maxExclusive The minimum value in the base datatype that is
    greater than all the values in the derived datatype.

Like RDF(S), OWL then considers datatypes to be classes. As such, the
OWL vocabulary for class axioms and definitions can be applied to datatypes.

Example 5.20

Let us assume the age of a MINOR to be between 0 (inclusive)
and 18 (exclusive). We can state that MINOR-AGE is equivalent to the
datatype with precisely these numeric values, as follows:

```
:MinorAge a rdfs:Datatype ; owl:equivalentClass
  [ a rdfs:Datatype ;
    owl:onDatatype xsd:integer ;
    owl:withRestrictions (
      [ xsd:minInclusive  0 ].
      [ xsd:maxExclusive  18 ] ) ] .
```

This defines MINOR-AGE as having the values (such as 14) from the
base datatype that satisfy the facets; it excludes values (such as 18)
that are in the base datatype but do not satisfy the facets, and values
(such as 14.5) that satisfy the facets but are not in the base datatype.

We could then define a MINOR as follows:

```
:age a owl:FunctionalProperty .

:Minor owl:equivalentClass
  [ owl:intersectionOf (
     :Person
     [ a owl:Restriction ;
       owl:someValuesFrom :MinorAge ;
       owl:onProperty :age ] ) ] .
```

First we define that a resource has at most one AGE. Second we define that a PERSON with an AGE value from MINOR-AGE is a MINOR.

Remark 5.24

The definitions in Example 5.20 do not directly enforce that the age is written as a literal in the :MinorAge lexical space. For example:

```
:Fred a :Minor ; :age :fourteen .
```

These data are not problematic in unrestricted versions of OWL: the entailment is rather that :fourteen must refer to a value in MINOR-AGE. However, in restricted flavours of OWL, properties need to be declared as either object-properties or datatype-properties; if :age were thus defined as an datatype-property, this example would become problematic.

On the other hand, if one were to write:

```
:Fred a :Minor ; :age "14" .
```

This would lead to an inconsistency, since "14" is simply shorthand for "14"^^xsd:string, and the value space of the xsd:string and xsd:integer datatypes are disjoint, and thus by definition, "14" cannot be in the value space of MINOR-AGE.

Remark 5.25

It is not recommendable to explicitly write down literals like "14"^^:MinorAge in RDF data. Many tools may not be able to understand this datatype (for example, they may be agnostic to OWL definitions). Likewise the literal only makes sense when accompanied with the definition(s) for MINOR-AGE. In the interest of generality, it would seem much safer to write "14"^^xsd:integer. Later, an OWL implementation provided with the pertinent definitions can, if needed, infer that such a literal is in the value space for MINOR-AGE.

Remark 5.26

One may recall from Section 3.2.2 that date-times do
not have a natural total ordering due to time-zones being optional: how would a date-time such as `2015-06-29T20:00:00` and
`2015-06-30T04:00:00+01:00` be compared? The latter date-time may
have occurred before or after the former, depending on the omitted
time-zone of the former. Unchecked, this would leave some ambiguity
with respect to which date-times would fall under which facet bounds.

The solution used by OWL is to conservatively only include values
that are *certain* to fall in the required range assuming that the omitted
time-zone(s) are between `+14:00` and `-14:00`, inclusive. Thus, for example, if `2015-06-29T20:00:00` were specified as the max-inclusive value
for a datatype facet, since there are time-zones between `+14:00` and
`-14:00` for which the facet would exclude `2015-06-30T04:00:00+01:00`,
the latter date-time is excluded from the derived datatype. A similar
argument holds if the former date-time is used for any of the other
facets: the latter date-time would be excluded. Likewise, if the **roles**
were reversed and the latter date-time were used in a facet, in all cases,
the former date-time would be excluded.

Given that OWL views datatypes as classes, we may also create new
datatypes through standard class definitions.

Example 5.21

Take MINOR-AGE as defined in Example 5.20, and a new
datatype TEEN-AGE, derived as integers in the interval of 13 (inclusive) to 19 (inclusive). Say we now wish to define CHILD-AGE as ages
in MINOR-AGE not in TEEN-AGE. We can do that as follows:

```
:ChildAge owl:equivalentClass
  [ owl:intersectionOf ( :MinorAge [ owl:complementOf :TeenAge ] ) ] .
```

Next, for datatypes derived from the `xsd:string` datatype, and for the
`xsd:anyURI` datatype, only the following facets are supported:

> `xsd:length` An exact number of characters.

> `xsd:minLength` A minimum number of characters.

`xsd:maxLength` A maximum number of characters.

`xsd:pattern` A regular expression the string must match.

For the `rdf:PlainLiteral` datatype, the above normative facets for string are supported, as well as an additional RDF-specific facet:

`rdf:langRange` A restriction on the language of the plain literal.

Remark 5.27

The `rdf:langRange` facet is defined in terms of the basic profile for matching language tags defined in RFC 4647 [315]. This defines language range strings that match a range of specific language tags. A more general range string will match more specific language variants. The asterisk symbol ('*') acts as a wild-card. Matching is case insensitive. Beyond that, it suffices to get the gist with some examples:

- "en" or "en-*" would match "en-US", "en-UK";
- "nan-hant" would match "nan-Hant-TW";
- "en-UK" would not match "en-US".

Example 5.22

We could define a datatype WEEKENDEN – referring to the strings of the names of the days of the weekend in English, including proper- and lower-case variations – as follows:

```
:WeekendEN a rdfs:Datatype ; owl:equivalentClass
  [ a rdfs:Datatype ;
    owl:onDatatype rdf:PlainLiteral ;
    owl:withRestrictions (
      [ xsd:pattern "^[Ss](atur|un)day$" ]
      [ rdf:langRange "en-*" ] ) ] .
```

The pattern `^[Ss](atur|un)day` is a regular expression that matches strings starting with "S" or "s", followed by "atur" or "un", followed by "day". The language range "en-*" matches English language tags.

Example 5.23

We can also define a datatype by means of an enumeration. For instance, instead of messing around with regular expressions to define the English strings referring to days of the weekend as per Example 5.22, we could instead consider defining the following:

```
:WeekendEN owl:oneOf (
  "Saturday"@en "saturday"@en "Sunday"@en "sunday"@en
) .
```

This definition varies from that given in Example 5.22 on language tags; for example, the current definition excludes "Saturday"@en-IE while the previous pattern-based definition includes it.

Regarding the xsd:hexBinary and xsd:base64binary datatypes, only the xsd:length, xsd:minLength and xsd:maxLength facets are normative in OWL (the xsd:pattern facet is not normative).

Finally, no normative facets are listed for the xsd:boolean datatype.

5.4.6 Annotations

OWL allows for annotating elements of an ontology with (meta-)information. The most important of these annotations are:

> rdfs:label provides a human-readable name for something, be it a class, a property, a resource, etc.
> rdfs:comment provides a human-readable description of something.

Terms are also provided to annotate an ontology: a collection of OWL axioms and definitions found within a document. In particular, OWL allows for providing links to dependencies and to previous versions of ontologies.

> owl:Ontology denotes the class of ontologies.
> owl:imports links an ontology to the location of one that it imports.
> owl:priorVersion links to a previous version of the ontology.
> owl:backwardCompatibleWith links to a previous version of the ontology with which the current version is compatible.
> owl:incompatibleWith links to a previous version of the ontology with which the current version is incompatible.

Example 5.24

We give an example of some human-readable annotations and
some imports statements and version statements of different flavours:

```
:RelationshipV21.4 rdf:type owl:Ontology ;
  rdfs:label "Relationship ontology"@en ;
  rdfs:comment "V-21.4 of the Relationship ontology now ..."@en ;
  owl:imports :PeopleV7.6 ;
  owl:priorVersion :RelationshipV21.3 ;
  owl:backwardCompatibleWith :RelationshipV21.3 ;
  owl:incompatibleWith :RelationshipV21.1 .

:loves rdf:type owl:ObjectProperty ;
  rdfs:label "loves"@en , "ama"@es ;
  rdfs:comment "directed form of hysteria caused by hormones"@en .
```

Labels and comments are crucial to provide where possible.

Remark 5.28

The idea of (in)compatibility is not formally defined. It is left
to the discretion of the ontology creator to decide such cases.

Remark 5.29

OWL offers other custom, non-RDF-based syntaxes within
which other forms of annotations can be provided, such as on axioms.
Given that this book is set in the broader context of the Web of Data
and assumes RDF as a core data model, we do not discuss these syntaxes or annotations here, but refer the interested reader to the OWL 2
Primer for more information [190].

5.4.7 Features Not Supported by OWL 2

Having gone through an extensive list of all the language features supported
by OWL 2, one may be left wondering what sorts of entailments *cannot* be
supported within the language. In general, many sorts of entailments and
ontological claims can be – either directly or indirectly – modelled with the
OWL 2 language, and it is difficult to provide a full characterisation of what
is not supported. However, we mention a number of "prominent" entailment
patterns that cannot be modelled in OWL 2.

Firstly, while OWL supports class intersection, OWL does not support *property intersection* in an analogous manner. What we mean by "property intersection" is best explained with an intuitive example.

Example 5.25

Let's take the following two RDF triples:

```
:Sally :youngerThan :Jim ; :siblingOf :Jim .
```

Now assume we wish to define an entailment whereby if two resources are related by both YOUNGERTHAN and SIBLINGOF, they are also related by YOUNGERSIBLINGOF. In other words, using some ontological definition(s), we would like the above data to entail the following:

```
:Sally :youngerSiblingOf :Jim .
```

OWL 2 provides no way to effect a property-intersection entailment of this form where X P_1 Y and X P_2 Y entail X P_3 Y (i.e., we have no way to define that $I_{EXT}(p_3) = I_{EXT}(p_1) \cap I_{EXT}(p_2)$).

Generalising this example, OWL does support entailments that intuitively involve "cycles" in the data; while property intersections involve a cycle of length 2, we also cannot express such cases for length n.

Example 5.26

Consider the following flight information:

```
:EZE :flight :COR .
:EZE :country :Argentina .
:COR :country :Argentina .
```

We see that the triples form an undirected cycle between :EZE, :COR and :Argentina. Say that we wish to infer from this cyclic pattern that:

```
:EZE :domesticFlight :COR .
```

Such entailments cannot be expressed in OWL 2.

We could, however, classify airports with at least one domestic flight using a has-self definition on a chain of FLIGHT, COUNTRY, and inverse of COUNTRY. Though we can entail classes for resources that are involved in a cyclic pattern (either directed or undirected), we cannot entail arbitrary relations between two resources based on such patterns.

Remark 5.30

To cover such "blind spots" of OWL, there are a number of proposals for rule languages that can be combined with OWL ontologies.

Around the same time as the release of the original OWL standard, the **Semantic Web Rule Language (SWRL)** [210] was proposed as a way to extend ontologies with rules. For example, in human-readable syntax, one could capture the inference of Example 5.26 as:

$$:\texttt{flight}(?x,?y) \wedge :\texttt{country}(?y,?z) \wedge :\texttt{country}(?x,?z)$$
$$\Rightarrow :\texttt{domesticFlight}(?x,?y)$$

where $?x$, $?y$, $?z$, are variables that can be mapped to elements of the domain. If these variables can only be mapped to named elements of the domain (i.e., not existentials), the rules are considered *DL-safe* [284]: a condition that ensures decidability when used in conjunction with certain decidable sub-languages of OWL (discussed in Section 5.6).

Other similar proposals exist, one of the more prominent being *nominal schemas* [242], whereby – sketching the idea – one can use a version of the `owl:hasValue` feature, but where the value in question is a variable that is bound to named elements of the domain.

Another rule language – standardised by the W3C [66, 107] – is the **Rule Interchange Format (RIF)**, which aims to provide a standard, well-defined syntax for exchanging various forms of logical rules and production rules. A specification has also been standardised defining the compatibility of RIF with and OWL [107].

Note that here we have discussed how OWL can be *extended* with rules; a number of proposals have also been made to implement OWL with rules. We will discuss one such proposal later in Section 5.6.

Aside from not supporting such cyclic patterns, due to the assumptions upon which it is designed (in particular the OWA and the lack of a UNA), OWL is (*by design*) not well-suited for:

- Specifying and enforcing database-like integrity constraints, such as checking the (in)completeness of data, for example, to ensure that all people in the data have a name specified.
- Specifying entailments based on missing data, for example that any person without a sibling is an only child; in OWL, it is not sufficient that no sibling is known, rather it must be known that no such sibling *can* exist;
- Checking that too many values have been defined for a property; without a unique name assumption, OWL is more likely to entail same-as relations from maximum-cardinality restrictions than to flag a problem – for example, even if we state in OWL that a person can have at most two biological parents, a person in the data can still have three parents

defined, where it is assumed that these are three names referring to two parents (only if it is known that these three parents are pairwise different will a problem be detected);

- Axiomatising non-crisp claims, such as associating claims with a probability – e.g., *it is 37% probable* that there is life on Mars – or modelling exceptions – e.g., all mammals are flightless, *except for bats.*

Remark 5.31

An active area of research is in extending OWL towards supporting more of these closed-world/defeasible style features (see, for example, [283, 70, 68, 253]).

5.5 OWL 2 Reasoning Tasks

As we have seen, OWL 2 has many features that together allow for making very specific, machine-readable claims. But what can we use these claims for? We now demonstrate the use of a combination of multiple types of OWL axioms using a variety of OWL vocabulary terms to model inferences.

Example 5.27

Take the following three RDF graphs: some data from a recipe for lemon tart, and some data about the allergies of two people.

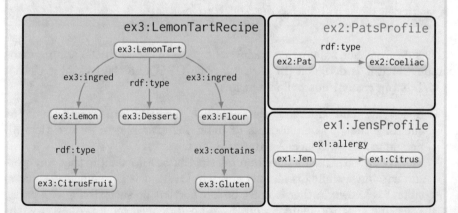

Intuitively as humans, we can see that the recipe on the left is not suitable for the two people on the right. However, a machine would not be able to make that assessment since it does not have enough background knowledge to know what terms like ex2:Coeliac might mean. However, we can use OWL to instruct the machine on some of the semantics of these terms in a formal manner.

Per Example 5.6, let us start with the following property axioms:

```
ex3:ingred rdfs:subPropertyOf ex3:contains .
ex3:contains rdf:type owl:TransitiveProperty .
ex4:containedIn owl:inverseOf ex3:contains .
ex4:unsuitable owl:propertyChainAxiom ( ex1:allergy ex4:containedIn ) .
```

Now the machine would know that LEMON-TART would not be suitable for someone allergic to LEMON or FLOUR or GLUTEN.

However, PAT does not state an allergy directly, and JEN does not state an allergy to a substance that the recipe is known to contain. There is still a little more work to do.

In the case of JEN, we still need to inform the machine that anything of type CITRUS-FRUIT will contain CITRUS:

```
ex3:CitrusFruit rdfs:subClassOf
  [ a owl:Restriction ;
    owl:hasValue ex1:Citrus ;
    owl:onProperty ex3:contains ] .
```

Note here the use of the sub-class relation: although all citrus fruits contain citrus, not everything that contains citrus is a citrus fruit.

At this point we know that: LEMON CONTAINS CITRUS, and that LEMON-TART contains LEMON, and thus that LEMON-TART contains CITRUS. We also know that JEN has an ALLERGY to CITRUS, and thus we can entail that the LEMON-TART recipe is unsuitable for her:

```
ex1:Jen ex4:unsuitable ex3:LemonTart .
```

Returning to PAT, we can tell the machine, in a formal manner, that all members of COELIAC have an ALLERGY to GLUTEN (and indeed anyone with an ALLERGY to GLUTEN is a COELIAC):

```
ex2:Coeliac owl:equivalentClass
  [ a owl:Restriction ;
    owl:hasValue ex3:Gluten ;
    owl:onProperty ex1:allergy ] .
```

Now the machine finally has enough pieces of the semantic puzzle to make the assessment that:

```
ex2:Pat ex4:unsuitable ex3:LemonPudding .
```

It is crucial to note that the OWL axioms we have provided are much more general than the specific example, and could be applied to

many other people than Jen and Pat across the Web, or indeed many
other types of allergies, or even many other types of entailment pattern.
Thus the purpose of the aforementioned OWL axioms is not solely to
help the machine conclude that the Lemon Tart recipe is not suitable
for Jen and Pat – otherwise it would be much easier to just tell the
machine that directly – but rather to describe the semantics of terms
in the domain independently of a particular application. Since such
definitions are described using a Web standard, they can be published
on the Web for other machines to reuse for other applications.

A second point to again highlight is our use of OWL to bridge the
different vocabulary of multiple sources. Other than generic terms like
rdf:type, the original three sources did not reuse any vocabulary terms.
However, once the previous OWL axioms are defined, we can see that
entailments are possible using a mix of different vocabulary, effectively
integrating the vocabulary used in the three graphs.

The integrated graph resulting from entailment is illustrated in the
following, where entailed triples have their edge labels shown in bold.

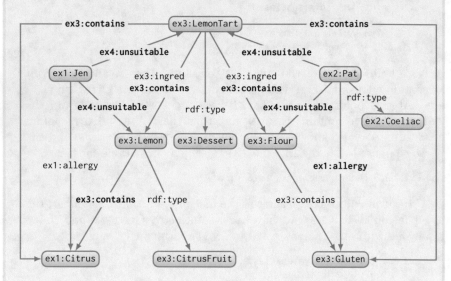

Clearly this enriched graph would facilitate many new queries and
applications not possible over the (disconnected) base data sources.

In order for machines to make use of OWL definitions, we need algorithms that implement various reasoning tasks with respect to the semantics
of such definitions. However, defining concrete algorithms that enable sound
and complete reasoning over ontologies described in OWL is a non-trivial
task. Given an OWL ontology, the first task is to define: what precisely do
we want a machine to do over this ontology? Along these lines, OWL 2 is

associated with a set of standard reasoning tasks [281] whose theoretical properties are considered when designing languages from the full set of features. Often these tasks are defined as **decision problems** – where the output is either true or false – to facilitate the study of their theoretical properties.

Ontology Consistency: Given an OWL ontology O as input, is the ontology satisfiable? In other words, does it permit a valid model?

Ontology Entailment: Given two OWL ontologies O_1 and O_2 as input, does O_1 entail O_2? In other words, is every model of O_1 a model of O_2?

Ontology Equivalence: Given two OWL ontologies O_1 and O_2 as input, does O_1 entail O_2 and O_2 entail O_1? In other words, do they permit the same models?

Class Satisfiabilty: Given a class c defined in an ontology O, is there a valid model of O in which c has a member? In other words, could c have a member without causing an inconsistency?

Class Subsumption: Given two classes c_1 and c_2 defined in an ontology O, is c_1 entailed by O to be a sub-class of c_2? In other words, must any member of c_1 be entailed to be a member of c_2?

Instance Checking: Given a resource x and a class c in an ontology O, is x entailed by O to be a member of c?

A final task involves considering a conjunctive query as input. In OWL, a conjunctive query can be considered as a set of triples where predicates must be kept constant, but where subjects or objects can be variables. If these variables can be matched against the data/ontology/entailments, the query is satisfied. Conjunctive queries will be discussed in more detail in Chapter 6; for now we sketch the idea with an example.

Example 5.28

Consider the following conjunctive query:

$$Q := \{(\_:p, ex1:allergy, ?a), (\_:p, ex4:unsuitable, ?u)\}$$

Here we denote by $\_:p$ an existential variable and by $?a$ and $?u$ *distinguished* (or *free*) variables that are projected as part of the results. Applying this query over the raw data in Example 5.27 would return no answers. However, applying this conjunctive query over the entailments of the data would provide the following solutions:

?a	?u
ex3:Gluten	ex3:Flour
ex3:Gluten	ex3:LemonTart
ex1:Citrus	ex3:Lemon
ex1:Citrus	ex3:LemonTart

A *boolean conjunctive query* is one with no distinguished variables, where the answer is true or false. Consider the following query:

$$Q' := \{(\_\!:\!p, ex1\!:\!allergy, \_\!:\!a), (\_\!:\!p, ex4\!:\!unsuitable, \_\!:\!u)\}$$

Intuitively this query "matches" against the entailments of O: we know that by mapping $\_\!:\!p$ to $ex2\!:\!Pat$, $\_\!:\!a$ to $ex3\!:\!Gluten$ and $\_\!:\!u$ to $ex3\!:\!Flour$, we have at least one mapping from Q' to a graph entailed by O; i.e., Q' returns true if and only if a solution for Q is entailed by O, in which case we say that Q' is an *answer* for O [281].

Remark 5.32   ⓘ

In the relational database setting, conjunctive queries can be thought of as selection–projection–join queries – or in terms of SQL, SELECT–FROM–WHERE queries – only allowing equality conditions. Unlike in the relational database setting, however, conjunctive queries over graphs have relations of fixed arity.

The final reasoning task considered by the OWL standard [281] is then:

Boolean Conjunctive Query Answering: Given an ontology O and a boolean conjunctive query Q, is Q an answer for O?

Remark 5.33   ⓘ

All of these tasks are decision problems, meaning that the output is true or false. For example, in the case of conjunctive queries, the goal is to return a boolean value indicating if some answer exists, not to return the answers. Intuitively in many practical cases, *enumerating* answers would be more desirable: for example, users of an ontology would want to get all answers rather than just knowing that an answer exists. The focus on decision problems may thus seem a bit strange, but the goal is to help simplify theoretical analysis. The associated **enumeration problem** can sometimes be reduced to a decision problem; e.g., one could (perhaps naively) put all pairs of classes into the class satisfiability procedure to enumerate all sub-class relations in the ontology.

Note that in terms of enumerating all entailments, these may be infinite. Say we have a definition that PERSON is a sub-class of the class with cardinality 2 on property HASBIOLOGICALPARENT from the class PERSON. Then any instance of PERSON will be entailed to have an infinite chain of biological parents.

Remark 5.34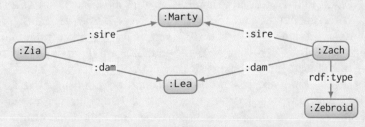

Some of the above tasks can intuitively be reduced to other tasks. For example, if one has an algorithm for Boolean Conjunctive Query Answering, then one can trivially use that algorithm to solve Ontology Entailment, Class Subsumption and Instance Checking since one can simply write a boolean conjunctive query to test each such case. For example, to check if ex1:Jen is an instance of ex2:Coeliac, one can see if the following boolean conjunctive query returns true:

$$Q := \{(\text{ex1:Jen}, \text{rdf:type}, \text{ex2:Coeliac})\}$$

Let us assume that we allow all OWL features to be used without restriction and we wish to write an algorithm to implement each of the above decision problems. What sort of procedure should we implement?

In the case of RDFS, we already saw that reasoning can be implemented in the style of recursive IF-THEN rules (see Section 4.4.1). It may then seem natural to apply a similar strategy for reasoning over OWL: define an extended set of rules that encode the semantics of the OWL vocabulary and then recursively apply those rules over the data to make entailments explicit (aka. *materialisation* of entailments). However, OWL presents a number of complications that make such a rule-based procedure less effective.

The first such issue relates to disjunctions, where certain class definitions – in particular union, disjoint-union, one-of, max-cardinality definitions, etc. – create multiple possibilities where at least one possibility must be true. Disjunctions can give rise to complex entailments whereby various possibilities are narrowed down to one that yields certain conclusions, or where a particular conclusion holds no matter which possibility is considered.

Example 5.29

Returning to the case of Zebroids, consider the following graph:

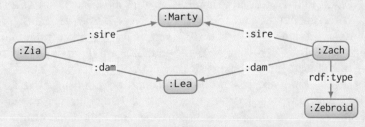

It may be helpful to recall that in the world of equine breeding, sire is the equine form of father, dam the equine form of mother. What class might we then intuitively guess :Zia to belong to?

Let us first consider the following domain definitions:

```
:Stallion rdfs:subClassOf :MaleEquus .
:Mare rdfs:subClassOf :FemaleEquus .

:Equus owl:equivalentClass
  [ owl:disjointUnionOf ( :FemaleEquus :MaleEquus ) ] .

:sire rdfs:domain :Equus ; rdfs:range :Stallion ;
   rdfs:subPropertyOf :parent .
:dam rdfs:domain :Equus ; rdfs:range :Mare ;
   rdfs:subPropertyOf :parent .

:Equus rdfs:subClassOf
  [ a owl:Restriction ;
    owl:cardinality 2 ;
    owl:onProperty :parent ] .

:NonZebraEquus owl:equivalentClass
  [ owl:intersectionOf ( :Equus [ owl:complementOf :Zebra ] ) ] .

:Zebroid owl:equivalentClass
  [ owl:intersectionOf (
     [ a owl:Restriction ;
       owl:someValuesFrom :Zebra ;
       owl:onProperty :parent ]
     [ a owl:Restriction ;
       owl:someValuesFrom :NonZebraEquus ;
       owl:onProperty :parent ] ) ] .
```

Here we state that a STALLION is a MALE-EQUUS and a MARE is a FEMALE-EQUUS, that an EQUUS must be a FEMALE-EQUUS or a MALE-EQUUS but not both, that SIRE and DAM are PARENT relations for EQUUS, that SIRE points to a STALLION and DAM to a MARE, that each EQUUS has precisely two PARENTs, that a NON-ZEBRA-EQUUS is an EQUUS that is not a ZEBRA, and that a ZEBROID has (at least) one PARENT a ZEBRA and (at least) one a NON-ZEBRA-EQUUS (in this latter definition, since an EQUUS has precisely two PARENTs and ZEBRA and NON-ZEBRA-EQUUS are disjoint, this implies that one PARENT of a ZEBROID is a ZEBRA and the other is a NON-ZEBRA-EQUUS).

These definitions generate a *disjunction*: two distinct possibilities. More specifically, given that MARTY and LEA are distinct PARENTs of ZACH (a ZEBROID), the first possibility is that MARTY is a ZEBRA and LEA a NON-ZEBRA-EQUUS, while the second possibility is that LEA is a ZEBRA and MARTY a NON-ZEBRA-EQUUS. Only one such possibility can hold true; by definition, neither parent can be both a ZEBRA and NON-ZEBRA-EQUUS. But from the provided data and definitions, we do not have enough information to figure out *which* possibility holds.

Despite this, no matter which – and not knowing which – possibility reflects "reality", we still should entail that ZIA is a ZEBROID! We do not need to know which of ZIA's PARENTs is the ZEBRA and which is the NON-ZEBRA-EQUUS to arrive at this conclusion; under both possibilities, we are certain that ZIA must be a ZEBROID.

But how should we implement an algorithm that would – given the above data and definitions – capture the desired entailment? We could consider a rule that captures this one specific case:

$$:\mathsf{parent}(?x, ?y) \wedge :\mathsf{parent}(?x, ?z) \wedge \mathsf{rdf:type}(?x, :\mathsf{Zebroid}) \wedge$$
$$:\mathsf{parent}(?w, ?y) \wedge :\mathsf{parent}(?w, ?z) \wedge \mathsf{owl:differentFrom}(?y, ?z)$$
$$\Rightarrow \mathsf{rdf:type}(?w, :\mathsf{Zebroid})$$

However, this rule does not use the OWL definitions to derive that conclusion: rather it is a domain-specific rule defined independently of OWL. A rule that implements the semantics of the OWL definitions would rather need to avoid using domain terms like :parent, :Zebroid, etc., and rather only use terms from the RDF/S, OWL vocabulary. More likely in the case of OWL, we should define a set of rules to capture the semantics of parts of the vocabulary. However, what rule could we use to capture the crucial disjunction? Such a rule that would capture this specific entailment – though possible – would be nightmarishly complex! This rule would have to capture an argument of the form

"IF x is a member of a class c_1 defined to have precisely two values for a property p, and x is a member of a class c_2 defined as having at least one value for p from the class d_1 and another from the class d_2, and x has the values y and z for p, and y is different-from z, and w is also a member of the class c_1, and w also has values y and z for p, then w is a member of c_2."

And in any case, even with such a rule, we would still only have captured one particular way of proving that ZIA is a ZEBROID!

The previous example focuses on a central disjunction formed by cardinality constraints (a some-values-from constraint can be seen as an at-least-one qualified cardinality constraint). Other forms of disjunction may arise from class definitions based on enumerations, unions, complements, etc. As the number of independent disjunctions increases, the number of different combinations of possibilities to be considered during reasoning grows exponentially, which in turn increases the complexity of the aforementioned reasoning tasks.

Aside from the problem of disjunction, a rule-based procedure similar to what we used in the case of RDF(S) would support existential knowledge, which may also lead to concrete entailments being missed.

Example 5.30

Returning to ZIA and ZACH from Example 5.29, let us change
the data slightly such that we know both are twins, but do not know
specifically which mare is their dam:

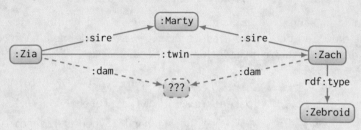

The dashed edges and nodes are not (yet) given; rather we will add
definitions to entail that since ZIA and ZACH are TWINS, they must have
the same DAM. We will start as follows:

```
:twin a owl:SymmetricProperty .
:dam owl:propertyChainAxiom ( :twin :dam ) .
:dam a owl:FunctionalProperty .
```

This states that the DAM of a resource's TWIN is also the resource's
DAM, and that a resource can have at most one DAM.

Now we can reuse the definitions of Example 5.29, but we additionally need to be more specific on one particular point, namely that each
EQUUS has precisely one DAM:

```
:Equus rdfs:subClassOf
  [ a owl:Restriction ;
    owl:cardinality 1 ;
    owl:onProperty :dam ] .
```

Now − as per the original graph − we have enough information to
entail that ZIA and ZACH have a DAM, and that it is the same DAM,
even if we do not know the identity of that DAM; in other words, this
DAM becomes an existential value. But even not knowing explicitly who
the DAM is, the fact that ZIA is a ZEBROID is still entailed!

To support this entailment, we could consider using rules that can
"create" new existential resources that satisfy the conditions of other
rules. However, this introduces a more general problem. In the current
example, we know that the existential DAM is a MARE, which is in turn
known to be an EQUUS, which is known to have a DAM that is a MARE,
and so if not careful, we could begin to entail an arbitrary number of
DAM relations to existential MAREs:

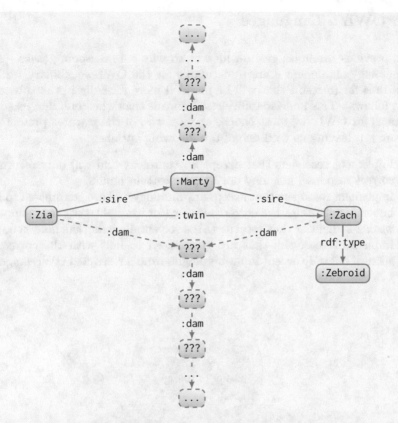

Intuitively it appears useless to continue generating such resources after a certain period of time, but we know we must generate at least one such existential resource to entail that ZIA is a ZEBROID in this particular case. Thus a general problem arises: how do we know when to stop a rule from generating existential resources? How do we know or how can we define which existentials are "useful" to consider towards finding concrete entailments and which are not?

With these examples, we see that complications such as the presence of disjunctions, existentials, etc., make the implementation of the aforementioned reasoning tasks much more complicated for OWL than, e.g., in the case of RDFS. In fact, we will soon see that all of the aforementioned reasoning tasks are undecidable for ontologies that allow use of OWL 2 vocabularies without restriction; in other words, it is known that there does not exist any algorithm for any of the reasoning tasks previously mentioned that is guaranteed to terminate with the correct true/false answer for all valid inputs [280] (this will be discussed in Section 5.6.1). For this reason, the OWL standard defines a variety of restricted sub-languages for which decidable algorithms are known to exist. These are discussed in the following section.

5.6 OWL 2 Languages

The previous examples give an idea as to why core reasoning tasks – such as ontology entailment – are undecidable for the OWL vocabulary we have seen thus far (a result that will be justified more formally in the subsection that follows). This undecidability result means that when building reasoning systems for OWL, we must choose at most two of the features presented in Figure 5.1, leaving us with one of the following options:

1. Implement reasoners that accept any ontology and will only return the correct response, but may not halt for certain inputs.
2. Implement reasoners that accept any ontology and are guaranteed to halt, but may not return the correct answer (for example, they may support a weaker semantics that returns false for entailments that hold true).
3. Implement reasoners that are guaranteed to halt with the correct response, but only accept input ontologies from a restricted OWL language.

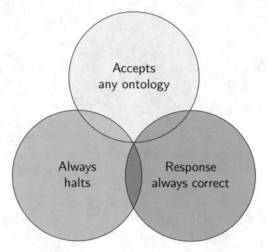

Fig. 5.1 "Choose two": The options for implementing an algorithm for deciding entailment over OWL ontologies according to the RDF-based Semantics defined previously: the intersection of all three options is empty as such entailment is undecidable

The first and second options are applicable for the OWL vocabulary used without restriction, while the third option requires the definition of restricted sub-languages for which reasoning tasks become decidable. The OWL standard itself does not suppose one type of reasoning or another; however, it does define standard decidable sub-languages along the lines of the third option that particular reasoning implementations may choose to adopt.

In this section, we will first discuss the unrestricted OWL language – called OWL 2 Full – and in particular, why reasoning tasks over this language are undecidable. We will then discuss the OWL 2 DL language, which aims to restore the decidability of reasoning tasks while preserving as much **expressivity** as possible. However, reasoning over the OWL 2 DL language remains computationally costly; hence, we will thereafter motivate and introduce three standard sub-languages – often called *profiles* – that have been defined in the OWL 2 standard to permit more efficient reasoning implementations, each with their own desiderata and applications in mind.

5.6.1 OWL 2 Full

The OWL 2 Full language allows use of all of the vocabulary discussed in Section 5.4 without restriction, which is to say that any RDF graph is a valid OWL 2 Full ontology no matter how it uses the RDF(S)/OWL vocabulary. The following example gives just some ideas of what is thus permitted.

Example 5.31

Under the OWL 2 Full language, we can use the OWL vocabulary to generate further "meta-vocabulary"; for example:

```
:EquivalenceRelationProperty owl:equivalentClass
  [ owl:intersectionOf
    ( owl:TransitiveProperty
      owl:SymmetricProperty
      owl:ReflexiveProperty ) ] .
```

This provides a new class of properties – equivalence properties – that are reflexive, transitive and symmetric. We could then state that:

```
:hasSameMassAs a :EquivalenceRelationProperty .
```

This property is then reflexive, transitive and symmetric.

We could further use the OWL vocabulary to "redefine" the OWL vocabulary itself; for example, we could state that:

```
owl:TransitiveProperty rdfs:subClassOf owl:IrreflexiveProperty .
```

This states that in our ontology, all of the transitive properties that we define are also irreflexive properties.

Some such definitions may lead to a contradiction; for example:

```
owl:Thing rdfs:subClassOf owl:Nothing .
```

would mean that we can not have any instance of THING (it is unsatisfiable), but even the class THING itself must be a member of the class THING, and hence we arrive at a contradiction.

Example 5.32

In OWL 2 Full, we can further forget about the syntactic conventions we have seen previously, and make statements such as:

```
:Equus owl:hasQualifiedCardinality 1 ;
  owl:onProperty :sire , :dam ;
  owl:onClass :Equus .
```

Here we drop the convention of using an anonymous class, and qualify the cardinality of two properties in one definition. Again, any RDF graph is permitted in OWL 2 Full, so this is permitted. Furthermore, any RDF graph is well-defined under the RDF-based Semantics of OWL [349]. Taking the latter definition, recall the model theoretic definition of the semantics of qualified cardinality:

$$\text{IF } (b,n) \in I_{EXT}(I_S(\texttt{owl:qualifiedCardinality})) \text{ and}$$
$$(b,p) \in I_{EXT}(I_S(\texttt{owl:onProperty})) \text{ and}$$
$$(b,c) \in I_{EXT}(I_S(\texttt{owl:onClass}))$$
$$\text{THEN } b \in I_C,\ c \in I_C,\ p \in I_P \text{ and}$$
$$I_{CEXT}(b) = \{x \mid \#\{y \in I_{CEXT}(c) \mid (x,y) \in I_{EXT}(p)\} = n\}$$

We see that the latter OWL definitions satisfy the IF condition for two values of p, and hence the definition is similar to intersecting two individual definitions for :sire and :dam. However, if we were to say:

```
:Equus owl:hasQualifiedCardinality 1 ;
  owl:onProperty :sire , :dam .
```

The condition is not satisfied; the incomplete definition is "ignored".

In the OWL 2 Full language, users can thus potentially "redefine" the OWL semantics to better suit their needs, or use syntactic tricks to make definitions more concise. However, such definitions may not be considered good practice as they may break compatibility with other ontologies or reasoners, and could naively lead to a variety of undesired consequences.

A more general problem with OWL 2 Full relates to the question of *computability*: do there exist algorithms for common reasoning tasks (as previously discussed) that are guaranteed to eventually terminate with the correct answer for any input(s) in the OWL 2 Full language? In fact, the answer is negative: no such algorithms exist. For example, there does not exist an algorithm that – given two ontologies O_1 and O_2 (i.e., two RDF graphs) – can decide whether or not O_1 entails O_2 under the RDF-based Semantics of OWL 2 Full; in more succinct terms, the problem is undecidable.

Discussion 5.4

JULIE: Okay, but maybe we will discover such algorithms in future?
AIDAN: Impossible! We are saying that such algorithms *cannot exist* ...
JULIE: But how can we know that?
AIDAN: We discuss this next.

How can we know that such reasoning tasks are undecidable for ontology in the OWL 2 Full language? Or more generally, how can we know that any problem is undecidable? Towards answering these questions, we must begin by being more precise on certain key aspects of what undecidability means.

First we must define what we mean by an "algorithm", which requires a notion of "machine" on which that algorithm will run. Here we thus assume a *Turing machine*: an abstract model of computation that captures the capabilities of current computational machines (assuming an arbitrary amount of memory can be made available to that hardware). We then define an algorithm to be something that can be executed as a Turing machine.

Second, we must define what we mean as a "problem", where we define a problem to be a decision problem: a question with a well-defined yes/no answer on a set of inputs (e.g., is n a prime? does O_1 entail O_2?, etc.).

Next, we say that an algorithm is an **effective algorithm** for a problem if and only if it halts with the correct answer for all valid inputs to the problem.

Finally, a problem is called undecidable if and only if there does not exist an effective algorithm for that problem.

One of the first problems known to be undecidable was the Halting Problem, which, given an algorithm and an input for that algorithm, returns true if the algorithm halts on that input, or false otherwise (if it will run forever). It was proven that no effective algorithm for the Halting Problem can exist (i.e., no effective algorithm exists that can take an arbitrary algorithm and an arbitrary input and say whether that algorithm halts on that input).

Remark 5.35

To sketch the main idea of how the undecidability of the Halting Problem can be proved, let us assume an algorithm $H(A, i)$ that implements the Halting Problem, and thus given a representation of an algorithm A and an input i, it will halt and return true if $A(i)$ halts; otherwise it will halt and return false. What we can show is that the existence of such an algorithm H would allow us to construct an "adversarial algorithm" that, for some input, halts when H says it should not, and does not halt when H says it should. The following suffices:

```
B(C): if H(C,C) then loop forever; otherwise return
```

This accepts an algorithm C as input and loops forever if and only if the algorithm C should halt given itself as input.[a] Observe that B is a valid algorithm if and only if H is a valid algorithm (as assumed previously); in simpler terms, assuming H were already implemented as a function in a given (Turing-complete) programming language, then B could easily be implemented in that language using H's implementation. However, we now ask, what should $B(B)$ return? If $H(B,B)$ returns true then $B(B)$ should halt, but instead it will run forever; on the other hand, if $H(B,B)$ returns false then $B(B)$ should run forever, but instead it halts; a contradiction! We are forced to conclude that H cannot exist since it would permit creating the impossible algorithm B. Since the algorithm H does not exist, the Halting Problem must be undecidable.

The core idea here is that H claims it can always predict whether or not an algorithm will halt on a given input, but an adversarial algorithm like B can ask H to predict what it thinks B will do and then do the opposite. Hence we must conclude that H's claim is false: it cannot predict what some algorithms (like the adversarial B) are going to do.

---

[a] The idea of an algorithm that runs on "itself" may seem a bit strange, but we may consider, for example, an algorithm $C(s)$ that accepts a string s and returns its length in characters: "$C(s)$: return s.length()". If we run $C(C)$, we would expect it to halt with a value of (e.g.) 24; and thus $H(C,C)$ would return true, and $B(C)$ should loop forever. If we rather defined an algorithm "$C(s)$: if s.contains('con') then loop forever; otherwise return", then $C(C)$ would not halt, $H(C,C)$ would return false, and $B(C)$ should halt.

Once we have a problem we know to be undecidable, this gives us a direct strategy – called a *reduction* – for proving other problems to be undecidable: given a problem P, if we can show that there exists an effective algorithm B that converts an instance of an undecidable problem (e.g., the Halting Problem) to an instance of P, then we know P must be undecidable as well! In more detail, if we assume an effective algorithm A for P, and design an effective algorithm B that converts any valid input i_Q of an undecidable problem Q to an input i_P of the problem P such that $P(i_P) = Q(i_Q)$, then $A(B(i_Q))$ would be an effective algorithm for the undecidable problem Q: a contradiction! Hence, given P, if we can find a reduction from any known undecidable problem to P, we must conclude that P is undecidable.

Given the OWL 2 Full entailment problem of deciding whether or not ontology O_1 entails ontology O_2 under the RDF-based Semantics, we could then prove this problem to be undecidable if we find a reduction from the Halting Problem – or any other undecidable problem – to this entailment problem. Along these lines, we present a proof of the undecidability of the OWL 2 Full entailment problem involving a reduction to a different undecidable problem than the Halting Problem, namely the *Domino Problem*.

Remark 5.36

We will show the undecidability of the OWL 2 Full entailment problem based on a reduction from the *Domino Problem*, which is
known to be undecidable (by reduction from the Halting Problem [44]).
Reduction from the Domino Problem has been used by several authors
for undecidability results relating to OWL (e.g., [212, 279], etc.). The
Domino Problem is best illustrated with an example:

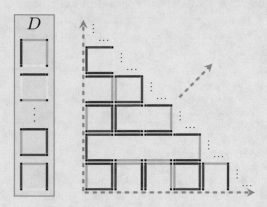

On the left, we have a finite set of dominos D (sometimes known as
Wang dominos or Wang tiles [44]). Each domino is associated with a
bottom, top, left and right colour. We now want to know whether or
not we can *tile* the plane using these dominos: using each domino as
many times as we want, can we cover an infinite space using these
tiles in the manner illustrated above such that the top/bottom colours
and left/right colours of all adjacent dominos coincide? The Domino
Problem thus takes a set of dominos D as input and returns true if an
infinite such tiling exists, or false otherwise. Clearly for some inputs –
such as a set D that contains a domino with the same colour on all four
sides – the problem is easy! However, for other inputs the problem looks
considerably more challenging. In fact, as aforementioned, the problem
is undecidable: it has no effective algorithm [44].

To show the undecidability of entailment for OWL 2 Full, we will
need to reduce an instance of the Domino Problem to entailment of two
ontologies in the corresponding semantics. We thus need to model the
Domino Problem with OWL. What precisely do we need to model?

First, we shall model the dominos themselves. Given $D = \{d_1, \ldots, d_n\}$
as input to the reduction, we should keep in mind that each domino
$d_1, \ldots, d_n$ can be used multiple times in the tiling: for that reason, we
will consider *each* $d_1, \ldots, d_n$ to be a class, and define the class of all
dominos as the disjoint union of $d_1, \ldots, d_n$, as follows:

```
:D owl:equivalentClass
[ owl:disjointUnionOf ( :D1 ... :Dn ) ] .
```

For brevity, we will call an instance of a domino (used in the tiling) a *tile*. In this case a tile is a member of the class :D, and each tile must be a member of precisely one of the classes :D1 ... :Dn. We highlight that the above definition, as well as later definitions, encode the input D as well as the general restrictions of the Domino Problem for that input (and since D is finite, the above definition will also be finite).

Second, we define the basic structure of the infinite tiling itself, wherein each tile has a tile above, and a tile to the right:

```
:D owl:equivalentClass
[ owl:intersectionOf
   ( [ a owl:Restriction ;
       owl:someValuesFrom :D ;
       owl:onProperty :above ]
     [ a owl:Restriction ;
       owl:someValuesFrom :D ;
       owl:onProperty :right ] ) ] .
```

These restrictions are general to the Domino Problem; i.e., they do not encode any details about the specific input D given to the reduction.

Third, we should define that neighbouring tiles match colours on their adjacent sides. One option would be to define top, bottom, left and right colours for each domino and then check compatibility of neighbouring tiles, but since we are given a finite set of dominos D as input, we can model these colour restrictions more "directly" as:

```
:D1 owl:equivalentClass
[ owl:intersectionOf
   ( [ a owl:Restriction ;
       owl:allValuesFrom [ owl:unionOf D1A ] ;
       owl:onProperty :above ]
     [ a owl:Restriction ;
       owl:allValuesFrom [ owl:unionOf D1R ] ;
       owl:onProperty :right ] ) ] .


   ...


:Dn owl:equivalentClass
[ owl:intersectionOf
   ( [ a owl:Restriction ;
       owl:allValuesFrom [ owl:unionOf DnA ] ;
       owl:onProperty :above ]
     [ a owl:Restriction ;
       owl:allValuesFrom [ owl:unionOf DnR ] ;
       owl:onProperty :right ] ) ] .
```

where we denote by $\boxed{\text{D1A}}$ an RDF list of the dominos from :D1 ... :Dn
that :D1 can have above it (i.e., the dominos in D that have the same
bottom colour as the top colour of :D1), by $\boxed{\text{D1R}}$ an RDF list of the
dominos from :D1 ... :Dn that :D1 can have to its right, and so forth.
This thus models the colour restrictions that are given by the input D
without having to explicitly model the colours of each domino.

Thus far we have modelled that each tile must have at least one tile
above it and one to its right, and that such neighbouring tiles must
satisfy the colour restrictions specified by D. But we are not done yet
since these definitions could still be satisfied by a tree of compatible tiles:
we have not yet enforced that the tiling be a grid! More specifically, if
tile t_2 is to the right of t_1 and t_4 is above t_2, and if tile t_3 is above t_1
and t_4' is to the right of t_3, we are left to enforce that $t_4 = t_4'$. Thus, as
a fourth step, we state the following:

```
:rightAbove owl:propertyChainAxiom ( :right :above ) .
:rightAbove owl:propertyChainAxiom ( :above :right ) .
:rightAbove a owl:FunctionalProperty .
```

This states that a tile can only have one tile above and to the right of
it, thus enforcing the grid that should be formed by a valid tiling.

There is one remaining subtlety we should consider: all these definitions could be satisfied by cycles of compatible tiles rather than an
infinite tiling. To illustrate this, consider the following interpretation,
where nodes are tiles and their domino types are illustrated inside the
node (we assume the input D to contain at least these three dominos):

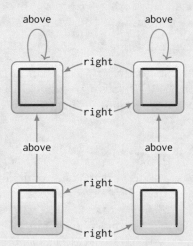

Let us assume we have created the above OWL ontology encoding conditions for a valid tiling on D. Observe that each tile (1) is an instance
of precisely one domino, (2) has a tile to the right and a tile above,

(3) has compatible tiles to the right and above, (4) has the same tile going right then above as going above then right. Though we do not have an infinite tiling, this is a complete model of the restrictions in the ontology! If we so desired, we could force an infinite tiling by defining:

```
:right rdfs:subPropertyOf :successor .
:above rdfs:subPropertyOf :successor .
:successor a owl:TransitiveProperty , owl:AsymmetricProperty .
```

This would ban such cycles (note: if we directly defined `:right` and `:above` to be asymmetric, for example, we would only ban cycles with one or two nodes). However these restrictions are not necessary to add since, as the above example suggests, cyclic models of this form are sufficient to prove the existence of an infinite tiling: intuitively speaking we can "unravel" the cycles to produce a valid infinite tiling.

Now let O denote the ontology with all previous definitions (we can exclude the latter definitions to prevent cycles amongst tiles); this ontology encodes the input D and all of the relevant restrictions.

To finish the reduction, we need to state an entailment problem that tells us whether or not there exists a valid tiling for D. Note that in O, the class `:D` can always be empty! However, if this class has even one member (i.e., if there exists even one tile), then to satisfy the definitions of O, that tile must have a tile to the right and a tile above, and each of those tiles must have a tile to the right and a tile above, and so on, such that the neighbouring tiles satisfy the aforementioned restrictions of a tiling; in other words, the class `:D` is satisfiable – i.e., the class `:D` can have a member – if and only if there exists a valid infinite tiling! Hence we can consider a second ontology O' stating that `:D` is unsatisfiable:

```
:D owl:equivalentClass owl:Nothing .
```

If O entails O', this implies that `:D` is unsatisfiable, and D does not permit an infinite tiling. If O does not entail O', it implies that `:D` is satisfiable, and D permits an infinite tiling. The reduction is complete.

In summary, given D as input, to decide if D permits an infinite tiling per the Domino Problem, we can generate O as above and then check whether or not O entails that the class of dominos is unsatisfiable. Given that creating O from D is decidable following the above steps, and that the Domino Problem is undecidable, we are forced to conclude that the entailment problem is undecidable for OWL 2 Full: there does not exist any effective algorithm to decide such entailments. (Otherwise, with the above reduction, we would have an effective algorithm for the Domino Tiling problem and, in turn, the Halting Problem!)

Following the proof in Remark 5.36, we know that deciding entailment between OWL 2 Full ontologies under the RDF-Based Semantics is undecidable. Furthermore, it is possible to adapt the given argument to show that the other reasoning tasks defined previously are analogously undecidable.

> **Exercise 5.13**
>
> *Following the proof in Remark 5.36 for ontology entailment, argue why the problems of ontology consistency, ontology equivalence, class satisfiability, class subsumption, instance checking and boolean conjunctive query answering must also all be undecidable for OWL 2 Full. (You may reuse O as constructed in Remark 5.36.)*

In practice, this undecidability result means we cannot implement effective algorithms for common reasoning tasks over OWL 2 Full considering the full RDF-Based Semantics. Faced with this fact, in the introduction to Section 5.6 we discussed three high-level options: (1) implement algorithms that only give correct answers but may not halt on certain inputs, (2) implement algorithms that will halt but may not always give the correct answer according to the full semantics, (3) restrict the ontology language so that effective algorithms can be implemented for inputs in the restricted language.

Regarding the first option, a similar result exists for first-order logic (FOL), where analogous reasoning tasks are likewise undecidable. Despite this negative result, there are a variety of *first-order theorem provers* that implement algorithms for such tasks that, if they halt, will give the correct solution. Even though these provers may not halt on certain inputs, they do provide the solution for many inputs (and many of those "decidable cases" are very useful indeed for applications such as proof assistance, programme verification, integrated circuit design, etc.). Much of the RDF-Based Semantics of OWL 2 Full can be defined in terms of FOL, where there has been work on implementing reasoning for OWL 2 Full by translating ontologies to FOL and using off-the-shelf first-order theorem provers (e.g., [350]).

However, not knowing if (or for which inputs) a reasoner will halt is a deal-breaker for certain applications. Imagine a group of health-care organisations using the Web to exchange patient data according to a collection of agreed-upon, well-defined ontologies. Guaranteeing that the reasoning system will be able to return an answer to a question such as *"is this prescription drug contraindicated for the given patient history?"* may indeed be a crucial requirement. Thus, although there are proposals for reasoning systems that forsake guarantees that they will halt in order to support the full semantics over unrestricted ontologies, the more general trend is towards implementing OWL reasoners that are guaranteed to halt. Along these lines, the OWL standard defines a variety of restricted sub-languages that permit effective algorithms for common reasoning task, as discussed in the following.

5.6.2 OWL 2 DL

The first standard sub-language of OWL that we discuss is OWL 2 DL, which aims to be an expressive sub-language of OWL for which common reasoning tasks over ontologies in the language become decidable. This language supports all of the OWL vocabulary introduced in Section 5.4, but places restrictions on how this vocabulary is used to ensure decidability.

5.6.2.1 Design Goals

In order to understand the design of OWL 2 DL, we first ask: how can we know which language restrictions are required to ensure decidability?

Referring back to the undecidability result outlined in Remark 5.36, we used a relatively small subset of the OWL 2 Full vocabulary in the reduction from the undecidable Domino Problem. This means that the corresponding entailment problem for ontologies using even just this small subset of the vocabulary must be undecidable! Thus to maintain decidability, we must avoid that OWL 2 DL allows a reduction from the Domino Problem: we must (at least) restrict some aspect of the OWL language as used in the ontology O of Remark 5.36. As it happens, OWL 2 DL chooses to enforce the restriction that functional properties must be *simple*, meaning that they cannot also be involved or entailed from a property-chain or from transitivity, their inverses must also be *simple*, amongst other restrictions [208]. Most importantly, in the reduction from the Domino Problem, this restriction prevents us from defining a crucial step (that :rightAbove is functional), which again gives us hope of returning to the terra firma of decidable entailment.

However, we are far from done yet: there may be other ways of achieving a similar reduction – using other vocabulary – from the Domino Problem! And even if we cannot find a reduction from the Domino Problem – or from the Halting Problem, or from some other undecidable problem – to a reasoning problem for OWL 2 DL, this does not guarantee decidability, nor (crucially) would it tell us how we could implement an effective algorithm for that reasoning problem. Instead, when we define OWL 2 DL, not only should we know that reasoning tasks are decidable, we should also know of effective algorithms for those tasks (whose existence, in turn, imply decidability). Thus the design of OWL 2 DL is predicated on having effective algorithms for reasoning tasks over ontologies defined within that language.

In practice, it may not be sufficient for certain reasoning tasks to be merely decidable, nor for there to exist merely effective algorithms, as guaranteed for OWL 2 DL. Rather when dealing with lots of data, we need *efficient* algorithms. However, OWL 2 DL paves the way for further sub-languages that provide guarantees of efficiency, which will be discussed later.

Discussion 5.5

ANNA: I find it a bit strange that OWL 2 DL restricts which properties can be functional when the more glaring issue seems to be that we can create infinite chains of existentials in OWL.

AIDAN: Well, there is a large space of *possible* sub-languages for OWL for which reasoning becomes decidable, and indeed some of those sub-languages restrict existentials rather than which properties can be functional. Others still might restrict disjunctions, for example.

ANNA: Why, then, the decision to restrict functional properties?

AIDAN: OWL 2 DL is a particular language whose design is largely influenced by decidability results in the **Description Logics (DL)** community. We will discuss this further in the following, but existentials are part of even the most foundational DL language. One might argue that this is then mostly for historical reasons. However many members of the logic community would argue that existentials are a foundational – and very important – feature used in many ontologies. The typical example cited by proponents of existentials is the SNOMED Clinical Terms (SNOMED-CT) ontology [115], which formalises the semantics of a huge collection of medical terms. The SNOMED-CT ontology makes heavy use of existentials, such as to state that *influenza* is caused by *some* virus. In ontologies such as these – that really focus on formally defining a terminology – existentials do appear like a very useful feature! But for just regular Web data – like to describe movies or recipes or what have you – we will rather discuss such issues in more detail in Chapter 8.

5.6.2.2 Description Logics

The question of which ontology languages permit effective reasoning algorithms is not a trivial one. Hence the design of OWL 2 DL is largely informed by theoretical studies in an area known as **Description Logics (DL)** from which the language takes its name. We previously mentioned how FOL entailment is undecidable. The motivating goal of the DL community is then to study restricted sub-languages of FOL for which reasoning tasks become decidable, as well as to define concrete, effective algorithms by which such reasoning tasks can be implemented in real-world systems. As such, DLs are a family of languages for which reasoning is decidable. In fact, certain DLs may even go beyond what can be expressed in FOL while maintaining decidability guarantees (e.g., supporting transitive closure).

> **Historical Note 5.2**
>
> DL had been studied for decades before the standardisation
> of OWL: the DL area dates back to works from the 80's on Knowl-
> edge Representation (KR) systems, such as the seminal KL-ONE sys-
> tem proposed in 1985 [74]. Works on early ontology languages such as
> DAML+OIL [183, 211] were influential in terms of creating a bridge
> from DLs to OWL and the design of ontology languages for the Web.

> **Further Reading 5.2**
>
> DL is a deep area of study. Rather than aiming at a complete
> treatment, our goal is to provide context for the design of the OWL 2 DL
> language, where we can refer the reader looking for a more in-depth
> discussion on DL to the various books [22, 24] and primers [336, 360,
> 243] on this topic, as well as the more general textbook by Hitzler et
> al. [191].

DL Syntax

Like any language based on logic, DL defines a syntax for making claims. In
Table 5.1, we refer to some of the main syntactic constructs used in a variety
of DLs and how they correspond with the OWL language. In the first column
we denote the typical name provided to that construct. In the second column,
we provide the DL syntax of that construct. In the third column, we denote a
key-term indicating the OWL definition to which the construct most closely
corresponds.[1] In the fourth column, we provide a key that indicates to which
DL family the construct belongs (these keys will be discussed later).

With respect to the DL syntax itself, we note that Table 5.1 is divided
into six parts. First, we distinguish **concepts**, **roles** and **assertions**, where
concepts refer to classes, roles to properties, and assertions involve individuals.[2] Second, we distinguish definitions from axioms: definitions allow for
referencing or defining new concepts/roles/individuals, while axioms make a
formal claim about those concepts/roles/individuals. In a DL ontology, con-

---

[1] In the third column, `owl:*cardinality` and `owl:*qualifiedCardinality` refer to
the various exact/max/min alternatives defined in OWL, while `owl:*Property` and
`owl:top*Property` refer to their datatype-property and object-property alternatives.

[2] Again the DL terminology pre-dates OWL, while the OWL terminology was based on
its RDF(S) origins: hence perhaps the reason why two parallel terminologies exist.

Table 5.1 Description Logic syntax

Name	Syntax	OWL key-term	DL
CONCEPT DEFINITIONS			
Atomic Concept	A	owl:Class	$\mathcal{ALC}$
Top Concept	$\top$	owl:Thing	$\mathcal{ALC}$
Bottom Concept	$\bot$	owl:Nothing	$\mathcal{ALC}$
Concept Negation	$\neg C$	owl:complementOf	$\mathcal{ALC}$
Concept Intersection	$C \sqcap D$	owl:intersectionOf	$\mathcal{ALC}$
Concept Union	$C \sqcup D$	owl:unionOf	$\mathcal{ALC}$
Nominal	$\{a_1, ..., a_n\}$	owl:oneOf	$\mathcal{O}$
Existential Restriction	$\exists R.C$	owl:someValuesFrom	$\mathcal{ALC}$
Universal Restriction	$\forall R.C$	owl:allValuesFrom	$\mathcal{ALC}$
Self Restriction	$\exists R.\mathsf{Self}$	owl:hasSelf	$\mathcal{R}$
Number Restriction	$\leq n R, \geq n R, = n R$	owl:*cardinality	$\mathcal{N}$
Qualified Number Restriction	$\leq n R.C, \geq n R.C, = n R.C$	owl:*qualifiedCardinality	$\mathcal{Q}$
CONCEPT AXIOM (T-Box)			
Concept Inclusion	$C \sqsubseteq D$	rdfs:subClassOf	$\mathcal{ALC}$
ROLE DEFINITIONS			
Role	R	owl:*Property	$\mathcal{ALC}$
Inverse Role	R^-	owl:inverseOf	$\mathcal{I}$
Universal Role	U	owl:top*Property	$\mathcal{R}$
ROLE AXIOM (R-Box)			
Role Inclusion	$R \sqsubseteq S$	rdfs:subPropertyOf	$\mathcal{H}$
Complex Role Inclusion	$R_1 \circ ... \circ R_n \sqsubseteq S$	owl:propertyChainAxiom	$\mathcal{R}$
Transitive Roles	$\mathsf{Trans}(R)$	owl:TransitiveProperty	$\mathcal{S}$
Functional Roles	$\mathsf{Func}(R)$	owl:FunctionalProperty	$\mathcal{F}$
Reflexive Roles	$\mathsf{Ref}(R)$	owl:ReflexiveProperty	$\mathcal{R}$
Irreflexive Roles	$\mathsf{Irref}(R)$	owl:IrreflexiveProperty	$\mathcal{R}$
Symmetric Roles	$\mathsf{Sym}(R)$	owl:SymmetricProperty	$\mathcal{I}$
Asymmetric Roles	$\mathsf{Asym}(R)$	owl:AsymmetricProperty	$\mathcal{R}$
Disjoint Roles	$\mathsf{Disj}(R, S)$	owl:propertyDisjointWith	$\mathcal{R}$
ASSERTIONAL DEFINITIONS			
(Named) Individual	a	*(RDF IRI or Literal)*	$\mathcal{ALC}$
ASSERTIONAL AXIOM (A-Box)			
Role Assertion	$R(a, b)$	*(RDF triple)*	$\mathcal{ALC}$
Negative Role Assertion	$\neg R(a, b)$	owl:NegativePropertyAssertion	$\mathcal{ALCO}$
Concept Assertion	$C(a)$	rdf:type	$\mathcal{ALC}$
Equality	$a = b$	owl:sameAs	$\mathcal{ALCO}/\mathcal{F}$
Inequality	$a \neq b$	owl:differentFrom	$\mathcal{ALCO}$

cept axioms form the **Terminological Box (T-Box)**, role axioms form the **Role Box (R-Box)**, while assertional axioms form the **Assertional Box (A-Box)**.[3]

Many constructs that may at first glance appear "missing" from Table 5.1 can in fact be modelled using the provided syntax; for example, class equivalence (sometimes written with the shortcut $C \equiv D$) can be expressed as $C \sqsubseteq D$, $D \sqsubseteq C$. On the other hand, some constructs that are provided in Ta-

---

[3] Some literature reserves the term "axioms" for concept and role axioms, referring to assertional axioms as simply "assertions". We preserve a dichotomy of definitions/axioms.

ble 5.1 are not necessary to include as they are covered by other constructs; for example, $\mathsf{Sym}(R)$ can be written equivalently as $R \sqsubseteq R^-$.

Remark 5.37 🛈

There are other constructs sometimes studied in the DL literature that are not expressible by the constructs in Table 5.1; one such example is role intersection – $R \sqcap S$ – which, per Example 5.25, we could use to define YOUNGERTHAN $\sqcap$ SIBLING $\sqsubseteq$ YOUNGERSIBLING. We omit this feature (and other such features) since it is not supported in OWL.

Before we discuss DL semantics and languages, we will first illustrate the syntax with an example involving a variety of definitions and axioms.

Example 5.33 ⚙

Referring back to Example 5.29, we shall model the definitions provided there about ZEBROIDS, this time using DL syntax. We can start by modelling some *assertions* about the individuals involved:

$$\text{SIRE}(\text{ZIA}, \text{MARTY}) \qquad \text{SIRE}(\text{ZACH}, \text{MARTY})$$
$$\text{DAM}(\text{ZIA}, \text{LEA}) \qquad \text{DAM}(\text{ZACH}, \text{LEA})$$
$$\text{ZEBROID}(\text{ZACH})$$

These assertions form what is called the "*assertional knowledge*" or "*A-Box*" of the ontology. The A-Box describes data about individuals. Note that all individuals mentioned in the A-Box must be named: we cannot make assertions about existential individuals directly in the A-Box (like we could with blank nodes in RDF graphs).

Aside from the A-Box, a DL ontology also may contain "*terminological knowledge*" or a "*T-Box*", which defines the semantics of concepts. The definitions that follow would thus form part of the T-Box.

First we state that the concept STALLION is contained in the concept MALEEQUUS, while MARE is contained in FEMALEEQUUS:

$$\text{STALLION} \sqsubseteq \text{MALEEQUUS} \qquad \text{MARE} \sqsubseteq \text{FEMALEEQUUS}$$

Here STALLION, MALEEQUUS and FEMALEEQUUS are known as *atomic concepts*: they are base concepts used to define other concepts. Statements such as "STALLION $\sqsubseteq$ MALEEQUUS" are known as axioms: rather than defining a new (complex) concept, they make a formal *claim*.

Second, we define that EQUUS is equivalent to the disjoint union of FEMALEEQUUS and MALEEQUUS:

$$\text{EQUUS} \sqsubseteq \text{MALEEQUUS} \sqcup \text{FEMALEEQUUS}$$
$$\text{MALEEQUUS} \sqcup \text{FEMALEEQUUS} \sqsubseteq \text{EQUUS}$$
$$\text{MALEEQUUS} \sqcap \text{FEMALEEQUUS} \sqsubseteq \bot$$

Definitions such as MALEEQUUS ⊔ FEMALEEQUUS are used to create complex concepts that can be involved in axioms. Although not used here, ≡ is often used as a shortcut to denote symmetric concept inclusions (concept equivalence), or sometimes ≐ can be used to name a complex concept. Though Table 5.1 offers us no syntax to specifically express disjoint-union or even disjoint concepts, per the latter axiom above, we can equivalently use the bottom concept to state that the intersection of the two concepts in question is empty.

Third, we assert the domain and range of SIRE and DAM:

$$\top \sqsubseteq \forall \text{SIRE}^-.\text{EQUUS} \qquad \top \sqsubseteq \forall \text{SIRE}.\text{STALLION}$$
$$\top \sqsubseteq \forall \text{DAM}^-.\text{EQUUS} \qquad \top \sqsubseteq \forall \text{DAM}.\text{MARE}$$

Again, although Table 5.1 does not provide specific syntax for domain and range axioms, we can still state a range axiom as "all individuals ($\top$) have all values from a class C on a role R ($\forall R.C$)". Domain axioms then follow precisely the same idea but on the inverse role R^-.

Fourth, we define that the class EQUUS has two values for PARENT:

$$\text{EQUUS} \sqsubseteq\, = 2\,\text{PARENT}$$

Though not present in the original OWL example, if desired, we could further define the qualified number restriction that the class EQUUS has two values for PARENT from the class EQUUS as follows:

$$\text{EQUUS} \sqsubseteq\, = 2\,\text{PARENT}.\text{EQUUS}$$

It is worth highlighting that neither axiom is redundant here: the former states that EQUUS has precisely two parents of any type (we could also write it as EQUUS $\sqsubseteq\, = 2\,\text{PARENT}.\top$), while the latter states that EQUUS has precisely two parents of type EQUUS (but may have more parents of other types). If we combine the two, we know that all parents of EQUUS must be EQUUS (in fact, given EQUUS $\sqsubseteq\, = 2\,\text{PARENT}$, we could have replaced the latter definition with EQUUS $\sqsubseteq \forall \text{PARENT}.\text{EQUUS}$).

Fifth, we define the concept NONZEBRAEQUUS as equivalent to the intersection of EQUUS and not ZEBRA:

$$\text{NONZEBRAEQUUS} \equiv \text{EQUUS} \sqcap \neg \text{ZEBRA}$$

This time for brevity we use the ≡ shortcut to denote symmetric $\sqsubseteq$.

Sixth, we define that a ZEBROID has (at least) one PARENT from ZEBRA, and (at least) one parent from NONZEBRAEQUUS:

$$\text{ZEBROID} \equiv \exists \text{PARENT.ZEBRA} \sqcap \exists \text{PARENT.NONZEBRAEQUUS}$$

The observant reader may have noticed that we skipped one important definition: that SIRE and DAM are both sub-properties of PARENT. In fact, such axioms defined (purely) on roles are considered part of the "*Role Box*", or "*R-Box*". We can state these axioms simply as:

$$\text{DAM} \sqsubseteq \text{PARENT} \qquad\qquad \text{SIRE} \sqsubseteq \text{PARENT}$$

We use the same symbol ($\sqsubseteq$) for concept and role inclusion, which is understood from context; more specifically, we assume distinguished sets of individual names (MARTY, LEA, ZACH, ZIA, ...), concept names (EQUUS, FEMALEEQUUS, MALEEQUUS, MARE, ...) and role names (DAM, SIRE, PARENT, ...), which provides the necessary context.

Exercise 5.14

Define the DL T-Box and R-Box corresponding to the OWL definitions in Example 5.27.

DL Semantics

Similar to the semantics of RDF(S) and OWL, the semantics of the DL syntax – as listed in Table 5.2 and illustrated in Example 5.33 – is defined in terms of model theory. An interpretation I in a DL setting is typically defined as a pair $(\Delta^I, \cdot^I)$, where Δ^I is the domain, and $\cdot^I$ is the interpretation function. The interpretation domain contains a set of individuals. The interpretation function accepts a definition of either an individual, a concept, or a role, mapping them, respectively, to an element of the domain, a subset of the domain, or a set of pairs from the domain. On the other hand, axioms are interpreted as semantic conditions. Such interpretations can then be used to define a model theoretic semantics for DL in the usual way; for reference, Table 5.2 defines the semantics for the DL syntax seen previously.

The semantics of DL then gives rise to the usual notion of entailment between DL ontologies, namely ontology O_1 entails ontology O_2 ($O_1 \models O_2$) if and only if each interpretation that satisfies O_1 also satisfies O_2.

Example 5.34

The DL axioms defined in Example 5.33 entail ZEBROID(ZIA).

Remark 5.38

There are direct correspondences between the interpretations for OWL seen previously and those for DL syntax. Specifically, I_R generalises Δ^I, while $I_S(\cdot)$ generalises $\cdot^I$ on individuals, $I_{CEXT}(I_S(\cdot))$ corresponds with $\cdot^I$ on classes, and $I_{EXT}(I_S(\cdot))$ corresponds with $\cdot^I$ on roles. We say that I_R *generalises* Δ^I since I_R also contains classes and properties, not just individuals. We further say that $I_S(\cdot)$ *generalises* $\cdot^I$ since likewise I_S is defined for classes and properties, not just individuals. For this reason, DL interpretations can be defined more succinctly: in DL, we assume that individual, concept and role names can be distinguished, while in OWL 2 Full this is not the case. Furthermore, in DL we have a set of reserved symbols and functions (e.g., $\exists$, $\sqsubseteq$, Trans), while in OWL 2 Full, such symbols are simply vocabulary used in an RDF graph, where we can define axioms over the vocabulary of the OWL language itself; for example, while in OWL (2 Full) we can state

```
owl:equivalentProperty rdfs:subPropertyOf rdfs:subPropertyOf .
```

in DL we cannot state

$$\equiv\ \sqsubseteq\ \sqsubseteq$$

Since OWL interpretations must, under RDF-Based Semantics, be well-defined for any RDF graph, they are more liberal in what they interpret.

DL Languages

The core design goal of DL languages is the decidability of reasoning tasks. Beyond that, the DL community further emphasises the importance of understanding the complexity of reasoning tasks with respect to DL ontologies in a given language, as well as the formulation of effective algorithms for reasoning within such languages. While the DL community began with relatively inexpressive languages known to be decidable, these languages were continuously extended over time with more and more features to allow for expressing richer and richer ontologies while staying in the realm of decidability (and indeed sometimes without changing the complexity of reasoning).

Table 5.2 Description Logic semantics

Name	Syntax	Semantics $(\cdot^I)$
	CONCEPT DEFINITIONS	
Atomic Concept	A	A^I (a subset of Δ^I)
Top Concept	$\top$	Δ^I
Bottom Concept	$\bot$	$\emptyset$
Concept Negation	$\neg C$	$\Delta^I \setminus C^I$
Concept Intersection	$C \sqcap D$	$C^I \cap D^I$
Concept Union	$C \sqcup D$	$C^I \cup D^I$
Nominal	$\{a_1,...,a_n\}$	$\{a_1^I,...,a_n^I\}$
Existential Restriction	$\exists R.C$	$\{x \mid \exists y : (x,y) \in R^I \text{ and } y \in C^I\}$
Universal Restriction	$\forall R.C$	$\{x \mid \forall y : (x,y) \in R^I \text{ implies } y \in C^I\}$
Self Restriction	$\exists R.\mathsf{Self}$	$\{x \mid (x,x) \in R^I\}$
Number Restriction	$\star n\,R$ (where $\star \in \{\geq,\leq,=\}$)	$\{x \mid \#\{y : (x,y) \in R^I\} \star n\}$
Qualified Number Restriction	$\star n\,R.C$ (where $\star \in \{\geq,\leq,=\}$)	$\{x \mid \#\{y : (x,y) \in R^I \text{ and } y \in C^I\} \star n\}$
	CONCEPT AXIOM (T-Box)	
Concept Inclusion	$C \sqsubseteq D$	$C^I \subseteq D^I$
	ROLE DEFINITIONS	
Role	R	R^I (a subset of $\Delta^I \times \Delta^I$)
Inverse Role	R^-	$\{(y,x) \mid (x,y) \in R^I\}$
Universal Role	U	$\Delta^I \times \Delta^I$
	ROLE AXIOM (R-Box)	
Role Inclusion	$R \sqsubseteq S$	$R^I \subseteq S^I$
Complex Role Inclusion	$R_1 \circ ... \circ R_n \sqsubseteq S$	$R_1^I \circ ... \circ R_n^I \subseteq S^I$
Transitive Roles	$\mathsf{Trans}(R)$	$R^I \circ R^I \subseteq R^I$
Functional Roles	$\mathsf{Func}(R)$	$\{(x,y),(x,z)\} \subseteq R^I \text{ implies } y = z$
Reflexive Roles	$\mathsf{Ref}(R)$	for all $x \in \Delta^I : (x,x) \in R^I$
Irreflexive Roles	$\mathsf{Irref}(R)$	for all $x \in \Delta^I : (x,x) \notin R^I$
Symmetric Roles	$\mathsf{Sym}(R)$	$R^I = (R^-)^I$
Asymmetric Roles	$\mathsf{Asym}(R)$	$R^I \cap (R^-)^I = \emptyset$
Disjoint Roles	$\mathsf{Disj}(R,S)$	$R^I \cap S^I = \emptyset$
	ASSERTIONAL DEFINITIONS	
Individual	a	a^I (an element of Δ^I)
	ASSERTIONAL AXIOM (A-Box)	
Role Assertion	$R(a,b)$	$(a^I,b^I) \in R^I$
Negative Role Assertion	$\neg R(a,b)$	$(a^I,b^I) \notin R^I$
Concept Assertion	$C(a)$	$a^I \in C^I$
Equality	$a = b$	$a^I = b^I$
Inequality	$a \neq b$	$a^I \neq b^I$

Of course, from the features of Table 5.1, it would be unreasonable to consider every possible language that arises from all possible combinations of features. For example, some features, (such as Trans, Func, Ref, Sym, etc.), are covered by other features (respectively, $R_1 \circ ... \circ R_n \sqsubseteq S, \leq n\,R, \exists R.\mathsf{Self}, R^-$). Hence DL considers some conventional groupings of features that allow, loosely speaking, for extending the expressivity of a language.

Most DLs are founded on one of the following base languages:

$\mathcal{ALC}$ (*Attributive Language with Complement* [348]), supports atomic concepts, the top and bottom concepts, concept intersection, concept union, concept negation, universal restrictions and existential restrictions; role and concept assertions are also supported (see Table 5.1).

$\mathcal{S}$ extends $\mathcal{ALC}$ with transitive closure.

These base languages can be extended as follows:

$\mathcal{H}$ adds role inclusion.

$\mathcal{R}$ adds (limited) complex role inclusion (subsuming $\mathcal{H}$), as well as role reflexivity, role irreflexivity, role disjointness and the universal role.

$\mathcal{O}$ adds (limited) nomimals.

$\mathcal{I}$ adds inverse roles.

$\mathcal{F}$ adds (limited) functional properties.

$\mathcal{N}$ adds (limited) number restrictions (subsuming $\mathcal{F}$ given $\top$).

$\mathcal{Q}$ adds (limited) qualified number restrictions (subsuming $\mathcal{N}$ given $\top$).

Thus DLs are typically named per the following scheme, where $[a|b]$ denotes an alternative between a and b and $[c][d]$ denotes a concatenation cd:

$$[\mathcal{ALC}|\mathcal{S}][\mathcal{H}|\mathcal{R}][\mathcal{O}][\mathcal{I}][\mathcal{F}|\mathcal{N}|\mathcal{Q}]$$

Examples include $\mathcal{ALCO}$, $\mathcal{ALCHI}$, $\mathcal{SHIF}$, $\mathcal{SROIQ}$, etc.[4] The alternatives to the right are more expressive, and hence the most expressive DL possible from this scheme is $\mathcal{SROIQ}$ [208], which supports every feature in Table 5.1.

However, such DL languages often apply further restrictions on the features they support; for example, although $\mathcal{SROIQ}$ supports every feature in Table 5.1, it does restrict the usage of some features, which is necessary to ensure the decidability of entailment [208] per the following example.

Example 5.35

Let us extend the DL axioms in Example 5.33 following the definitions in Example 5.30. We define that TWIN is a symmetric role, that DAM has a chain of TWIN and DAM, and that DAM is functional:

$$\mathsf{Sym}(\text{TWIN}) \qquad \text{TWIN} \circ \text{DAM} \sqsubseteq \text{DAM} \qquad \mathsf{Func}(\text{DAM})$$

These three axioms would form part of the R-Box of the ontology. (As a side note, we could equivalently have written Sym(TWIN) as TWIN $\sqsubseteq$ TWIN⁻.) However, a key design goal of DL is to ensure decidability, where functional properties entailed by chains (and other such "complex roles") allow us to complete a reduction from the undecidable

---

[4] Some naming combinations permitted by this pattern may not make sense. For example, since transitivity $\mathsf{Trans}(R)$ can be expressed as the complex role inclusion $R \circ R \sqsubseteq R$, it would not make such sense to speak of $\mathcal{ALCR}$; rather this would be called $\mathcal{SR}$.

Domino Problem (see Remark 5.36 and in particular the definition of :rightAbove). Rather than remove features entirely (e.g., disallow Func(R)) DLs often enforce syntactic restrictions to ensure decidability. Such a restriction, in this case, is to not allow the definition of a functional role entailed by a chain, as per the axioms on DAM above.

Thus, although the above definitions are valid per the DL syntax of Table 5.1, they would not be permitted as part of a $\mathcal{SROIQ}$ ontology.

Remark 5.39

The precise restrictions enforced by $\mathcal{SROIQ}$ are quite technical to define, but can be summarised as follows:

- the universal role cannot be used on the left-hand-side of complex role inclusions;
- while $R \circ R \sqsubseteq R$, $R \circ S_1 \circ ... \circ S_n \sqsubseteq R$, $S_1 \circ ... \circ S_n \circ R \sqsubseteq R$, $R^- \circ R$ are allowed, other cycles in (complex) role inclusions are disallowed; for example, $Q \circ R \sqsubseteq S$, $R \circ T \sqsubseteq Q$, $T \sqsubseteq S$, would be disallowed since S "depends on" Q, Q depends on T, T depends on S, forming a cycle;
- intuitively speaking, a role R is *simple* if and only if an assertion for R cannot be entailed (possibly indirectly) from a complex role inclusion (including transitivity); Disj, Asym, Irref, Func axioms and (qualified) number restrictions can only involve simple roles.

We refer to [208] for a more formal definition of $\mathcal{SROIQ}$.

5.6.2.3 Reasoning over $\mathcal{SROIQ}$

There are a variety of possible techniques for reasoning over DL ontologies. For deciding the satisfiability of ontologies from more expressive DLs – such as $\mathcal{SROIQ}$ – a common technique used is that of constructing a **tableau** [28].

Tableau refers to a general technique that can be used in a variety of logics to check the satisfiability of a set of formulae. The core idea is to try to explore the space of possibilities that may satisfy a given set of formulae: possibilities that lead to contradictions are ruled out, and if all possibilities are ruled out, then the formulae are considered unsatisfiable. In the case of DL ontologies, for example, the tableau will search through various possibilities for a (representation of a) model of the ontology – an interpretation satisfying the ontology – asserting that the ontology is satisfiable if such a model is found, otherwise asserting that it is unsatisfiable if no such model is found. Thereafter, we can use this technique for any reasoning task that can be reduced to checking satisfiability (in the case of $\mathcal{SROIQ}$, this includes ontology entailment, class satisfiability, class subsumption and instance checking).

We will give the main ideas of the tableau method with the following example. We highlight that this example is for the purposes of illustration and skips some technical details that we will rather summarise afterwards.

Example 5.36

Taking the definitions from Example 5.33, let us consider the following $\mathcal{SROIQ}$ ontology, which we shall denote O (note that to keep things a little more concise, rather than provide definitions that entail MARTY $\neq$ LEA, we assume it to be asserted in the A-Box):

A-Box		
DAM(ZACH,LEA)[A1]	SIRE(ZACH,MARTY)[A2]	ZEBROID(ZACH)[A3]
DAM(ZIA,LEA)[A4]	SIRE(ZIA,MARTY)[A5]	MARTY $\neq$ LEA[A6]

T-Box	
$\top \sqsubseteq \forall$SIRE$^-$.EQUUS	[T1]
$\top \sqsubseteq \forall$SIRE.EQUUS	[T2]
$\top \sqsubseteq \forall$DAM$^-$.EQUUS	[T3]
$\top \sqsubseteq \forall$DAM.EQUUS	[T4]
EQUUS $\sqsubseteq$ $=2$PARENT	[T5]
NONZEBRAEQUUS $\equiv$ EQUUS $\sqcap \neg$ZEBRA	[T6]
ZEBROID $\equiv$ $\exists$PARENT.ZEBRA $\sqcap$ $\exists$PARENT.NONZEBRAEQUUS	[T7]

R-Box	
DAM $\sqsubseteq$ PARENT[R1]	SIRE $\sqsubseteq$ PARENT[R2]

Now assume we wish to check whether or not O entails the assertion ZEBROID(ZIA). We can do so by checking whether or not the ontology $O' := O \cup \{\neg$ZEBROID(ZIA)$\}$ is satisfiable; more specifically, the entailment holds if and only if the ontology O' is unsatisfiable.

To decide the satisfiability of O', the tableau method tries to search for an interpretation that satisfies O', or otherwise determine that no such interpretation is possible. This is done by by "expanding" the assertions of the A-Box of O' until all axioms are satisfied, potentially creating "branches" that represent multiple possibilities. If a branch reaches a contradiction, the branch is rejected and the algorithm moves to the next branch. If a branch is fully expanded and contains no contradictions (aka. "*clashes*"), then that branch represents a valid interpretation for O'; in other words, the ontology is satisfiable. Otherwise if all possible branches are found to have contradictions, the algorithm concludes that O' is unsatisfiable. We now see this in action.

We start with A': the A-Box of O' (with the negated goal [A0]).

A'		
DAM(ZACH,LEA)[A1]	SIRE(ZACH,MARTY)[A2]	ZEBROID(ZACH)[A3]
DAM(ZIA,LEA)[A4]	SIRE(ZIA,MARTY)[A5]	MARTY $\neq$ LEA[A6]
¬ZEBOID(ZIA)[A0]		

However A' does not yet satisfy all the axioms of the T-Box and the R-Box. For example, to satisfy [T2] and [A5], we would need to add EQUUS(MARTY). Likewise given [R1] and [A4], we would need to add PARENT(ZIA, LEA). With respect to [T1-4], [R1-2] and A', let us add:

EQUUS(LEA)[A7]	PARENT(ZIA,LEA)[A8]	PARENT(ZACH,LEA)[A9]
EQUUS(MARTY)[A10]	PARENT(ZIA,MARTY)[A11]	PARENT(ZACH,MARTY)[A12]
EQUUS(ZACH)[A13]	EQUUS(ZIA)[A14]	

That leaves us to satisfy [T5-7]. Let us first consider [T5]. The individuals ZACH and ZIA have two distinct PARENTs and thus satisfy [T5]. On the other hand, MARTY and LEA are both members of EQUUS but have no parents and thus do not satisfy [T5]. Furthermore, we have no way to confirm if their parents are one of the existing individuals seen thus far. Hence we must create fresh individuals – denoted here by mp_1, mp_2, lp_1, lp_2 – to represent their (respectively distinct) parents.

$mp_1 \neq mp_2$[A15]	PARENT(MARTY,mp_1)[A16]	PARENT(MARTY,mp_2)[A17]
$lp_1 \neq lp_2$[A18]	PARENT(LEA,lp_1)[A19]	PARENT(LEA,lp_2)[A20]

Now we satisfy [T5]: all members of EQUUS have two (distinct) parents.

Moving onto [T6], we are fine for now since we have no members of NONZEBRAEQUUS nor members in the intersection of EQUUS and ¬ZEBRA. Now let us consider [T7]. Currently ZACH does not satisfy this condition since neither of its parents is of type ZEBRA nor NONZEBRAEQUUS. Hence let us create some fresh individuals as before to satisfy [T7] on ZACH (since we do not know which existing parent of ZACH is a ZEBRA and which is a NONZEBRAEQUUS).

PARENT(ZACH, zap_1)[A21]	ZEBRA(zap_1)[A22]
PARENT(ZACH, zap_2)[A23]	NONZEBRAEQUUS(zap_2)[A24]

Now, returning to [T6], we see that [A24] requires us to add:

EQUUS(zap_2)[A25]	¬ZEBRA(zap_2)[A26]

At this point, we have two problems with [T5]: first, zap_2 is now an EQUUS but does not have two parents, were we should add:

$$\mathsf{zap}_{2,1} \neq \mathsf{zap}_{2,2}{}^{[\text{A27}]} \quad \text{PARENT}(\mathsf{zap}_2,\mathsf{zap}_{2,1})^{[\text{A28}]} \quad \text{PARENT}(\mathsf{zap}_2,\mathsf{zap}_{2,2})^{[\text{A29}]}$$

Second, [T5] requires that ZACH has two parents, but we currently mention four. We do not have a clash yet, but rather we thus know that some of the following equalities must hold: (1) MARTY = LEA; (2) zap_1 = MARTY; (3) zap_2 = MARTY; (4) zap_1 = LIA; (5) zap_2 = LEA; (6) zap_1 = zap_2. To explore these possibilities, we are forced to branch.

Let A_0' denote A' extended with the assertions seen thus far. This is the "base branch" meaning that we know A_0' *must* "hold" based on O'. Furthermore observe that A_0' is maximal in that sense: we could not have extended A_0' any further before reaching the first branch. Now, based on the above possible equalities, let us start to branch as follows:

A_0'

B_1	MARTY = LEA	clash MARTY = LEA, MARTY $\neq$ LEA
B_2	zap_1 = MARTY	
	$B_{2,1}$ zap_2 = MARTY	clash ZEBRA(MARTY), $\neg$ZEBRA(MARTY)
	$B_{2,2}$ zap_1 = LEA	clash MARTY = LEA, MARTY $\neq$ LEA
	$B_{2,3}$ zap_2 = LEA	clash ZEBROID(ZIA), $\neg$ZEBROID(ZIA)
	$B_{2,4}$ zap_1 = zap_2	clash ZEBRA(MARTY), $\neg$ZEBRA(MARTY)
B_3	zap_2 = MARTY	
	$B_{3,1}$ zap_1 = LEA	clash ZEBROID(ZIA), $\neg$ZEBROID(ZIA)
	$B_{3,2}$ zap_2 = LEA	clash MARTY = LEA, MARTY $\neq$ LEA
	$B_{3,3}$ zap_1 = zap_2	clash ZEBRA(MARTY), $\neg$ZEBRA(MARTY)
B_4	zap_1 = LEA	
	$B_{4,1}$ zap_2 = LEA	clash ZEBRA(LEA), $\neg$ZEBRA(LEA)
	$B_{4,2}$ zap_1 = zap_2	clash ZEBRA(LEA), $\neg$ZEBRA(LEA)
B_5	zap_2 = LEA	
	$B_{5,1}$ zap_1 = zap_2	clash ZEBRA(LEA), $\neg$ZEBRA(LEA)

Let us take the example of the B_2 branch where we speculate that zap_1 = MARTY. We start with the single axiom on which we branched:

$$B_2$$

$$\mathsf{zap}_1 = \text{MARTY}^{[\text{B}(2)1]}$$

We expand on this branch additionally considering the information from all ancestors of the branch. Given [A22] and [B(2)1], we add:

$$\text{ZEBRA}(\text{MARTY})^{[\text{B}(2)2]}$$

We still have three possible parents for ZACH, and hence we still have further possible equalities between the remaining three individuals: MARTY, LEA and zap_2. We can rule out the case that MARTY = LEA since this was ruled out on the higher-level branch B_1 (i.e., it was ruled out on the sibling of an ancestor branch). Now let us try branch $B_{2,1}$:

$$B_{2,1}$$

$$\mathsf{zap}_2 = \text{Marty}^{[B(2,1)1]}$$

Expanding on $[B(2,1)1]$ with $[A24]$, $[A25]$, $[A26]$, we add:

$$\text{NonZebraEquus(Marty)}^{[B(2,1)2]} \qquad \neg\text{Zebra(Marty)}^{[B(2,1)3]}$$
$$\text{Equus(Marty)}^{[B(2,1)4]}$$

We have a clash: $\text{Zebra(Marty)}^{[B(2)2]}$, $\neg\text{Zebra(Marty)}^{[B(2,1)3]}$! Hence the tableau method will "backtrack" to B_2 and check what other possibilities are available on that branch. If the algorithm tries $B_{2,2}$ next, it will similarity find a clash, and eventually proceed to branch $B_{2,3}$. Let us consider the $B_{2,3}$ branch, which constitutes a more notable case:

$$B_{2,3}$$

$$\mathsf{zap}_2 = \text{Lea}^{[B(2,3)1]}$$

Expanding on $[B(2,3)1]$ with $[A24]$, $[A25]$, $[A26]$:

$$\text{NonZebraEquus(Lea)}^{[B(2,3)2]} \qquad \neg\text{Zebra(Lea)}^{[B(2,3)3]}$$
$$\text{Equus(Lea)}^{[B(2,3)4]}$$

Further expanding on $[B(2,3)2]$ with $[T7]$, $[A8]$, $[A11]$, $[B(2)2]$:

$$\text{Zebroid(Zia)}^{[B(2,3)5]}$$

A clash since $[A0]$ states $\neg\text{Zebroid(Zia)}$! This branch is notable because it requires $[A0]$ – the negation of the entailment being checked – to derive unsatisfiability. Were we to check the satisfiability of O (rather than O') using this tableau method, in expanding this branch we would not find a clash and thus the tableau would conclude, without continuing any further, that O is satisfiable (where $A'_0 \cup B_2 \cup B_{2,3}$ represents a Herbrand interpretation satisfying O). However, given O' at the input, since we find a clash, we must continue to the next branch.

In the end, as shown previously, in all possible branches we find a clash, and hence we conclude that O' is unsatisfiable, and, in turn, that the original ontology O indeed entails the axiom Zebroid(Zia).

While Example 5.36 provides an idea of how a tableau-based algorithm can be used to implement a reasoning algorithm over an expressive DL such as $\mathcal{SROIQ}$, there are some technical details that we glossed over, such as the order of expansion and branching, the order in which branches are navigated, the detection of redundant branches, the prior application of normal forms to the ontology, branching on concept inclusion axioms (where $C \sqsubseteq D$ gives the disjunction $(\neg C \sqcap D)(a)$ for all individuals a), checking the entailment of an ontology with multiple axioms [209], and so forth [28, 208].

Example 5.37

In the previous tableau example, we very conveniently omitted a T-Box axiom from Example 5.33, specifying that all EQUUS have two parents *who are members of EQUUS*. To see why it was convenient to omit this axiom, let us consider the following $\mathcal{SROIQ}$ ontology O, which this time includes the problematic missing axiom [T⋆]:

A-Box		
DAM(ZACH,LEA)[A1]	SIRE(ZACH,MARTY)[A2]	ZEBROID(ZACH)[A3]
DAM(ZIA,LEA)[A4]	SIRE(ZIA,MARTY)[A5]	MARTY $\neq$ LEA[A6]

T-Box	
$\top \sqsubseteq \forall\text{SIRE}^-.\text{EQUUS}$	[T1]
$\top \sqsubseteq \forall\text{SIRE}.\text{EQUUS}$	[T2]
$\top \sqsubseteq \forall\text{DAM}^-.\text{EQUUS}$	[T3]
$\top \sqsubseteq \forall\text{DAM}.\text{EQUUS}$	[T4]
$\text{EQUUS} \sqsubseteq\ = 2\,\text{PARENT}$	[T5]
$\text{EQUUS} \sqsubseteq\ = 2\,\text{PARENT}.\text{EQUUS}$	[T⋆]
$\text{NONZEBRAEQUUS} \equiv \text{EQUUS} \sqcap \neg\text{ZEBRA}$	[T6]
$\text{ZEBROID} \equiv \exists\text{PARENT}.\text{ZEBRA} \sqcap \exists\text{PARENT}.\text{NONZEBRAEQUUS}$	[T7]

R-Box	
DAM $\sqsubseteq$ PARENT[R1]	SIRE $\sqsubseteq$ PARENT[R2]

Consider again checking the satisfiability of O (the same applies likewise for O') as before in Example 5.36, but this time with the [T⋆] axiom included. Let us assume we now wish to ensure that MARTY satisfies [T⋆]. Again we need to add fresh individuals, but, unlike before, we should now add that these new parents are also members of EQUUS:

A		
...		
$mp_1 \neq mp_2$	PARENT(MARTY,mp_1)	PARENT(MARTY,mp_2)
EQUUS(mp_1)	EQUUS(mp_2)	...

But now we should make mp_1 and mp_2 satisfy [T⋆]:

$mp_{1,1} \neq mp_{1,2}$	PARENT(mp_1,$mp_{1,1}$)	PARENT(mp_1,$mp_{1,2}$)
	EQUUS($mp_{1,1}$)	EQUUS($mp_{1,2}$)
$mp_{2,1} \neq mp_{2,2}$	PARENT(mp_2,$mp_{2,1}$)	PARENT(mp_2,$mp_{2,2}$)
	EQUUS($mp_{2,1}$)	EQUUS($mp_{2,2}$)

And so forth for their parents, and their parents' parents, and their parents' parents' parents, and .... Naively if we attempt to fully satisfy [T⋆], we could end up in an infinite loop creating fresh individuals.

> **Discussion 5.6**
>
> JULIE: But not all equines have parents who are equines. Go back far
>   enough and they evolved from something else! Do definitions like
>   all equines have two parents who are equines really make sense?
> AIDAN: It is certainly fair to question how well a definition satisfied
>   by an infinite trail of equines reflects reality, but we should note
>   that this is not the only way that such a definition can be satisfied.
>   Using the same form of definition, we might say, for example, that
>   TRINARY-STAR ⊑= 2 ORBITS.TRINARY-STAR, which intuitively is
>   satisfied by trinary stars that orbit each other! We saw a similar
>   example in Remark 5.36, where a cycle of finite tiles could satisfy
>   the ontology encoding the Domino Problem. Unfortunately though,
>   in $\mathcal{SROIQ}$ – for the reasons of decidability discussed previously –
>   we cannot add to this the axioms needed – e.g., Trans(ORBITS) – to
>   force the trinary stars to form a finite cycle.

Left unaddressed, the case highlighted by Example 5.37 would under-
mine the termination guarantees of tableau-based algorithms for DLs such
as $\mathcal{SROIQ}$. However, by the definition (and design) of $\mathcal{SROIQ}$, we do not
need to materialise the "full" interpretation to demonstrate that it exists;
rather we need only materialise enough fresh individuals to ensure that all
axioms could be satisfied if we continued "unravelling" an infinite number
of fresh individuals in this manner. In this case, the tableau searches for a
representation that could be unravelled straightforwardly into a model for
the ontology, rather than for a full representation of the model itself.

This unravelling argument does not hold in the general case: we may not
always be able to construct a finite tableau that establishes for certain the
existence (or non-existence) of a model for any ontology/DL by such an unravelling! However, it has been proven for the case of $\mathcal{SROIQ}$ [208]. Without
venturing too much into the details, the general idea is that ontologies described by $\mathcal{SROIQ}$ only have models where existential/fresh individuals do
not form cycles, but rather continue to branch outward like trees (known as
the *forest-model property*). If we did not apply restrictions on role axioms in
$\mathcal{SROIQ}$, on the other hand, we could create ontologies that are only satisfied by interpretations that have complex graph structures on these fresh
individuals, such as creating the infinite grid needed to satisfy the Domino
Problem (see Remark 5.36); in such cases, the unravelling trick no longer
works, and more generally, we may not be able to generate a finite tableau
to decide satisfiability/unsatisfiability for some ontologies.

In practice, to ensure they will always halt, tableau algorithms dealing with
existentials in decidable DLs (like $\mathcal{SROIQ}$) thus often need to implement a
"blocking" policy, which will block the creation of fresh individuals after
they reach a certain distance from the individuals named in the original on-

tology [212]; for example, blocking may allow for generating fresh individuals to represent (parents-of-)parents of named individuals in the style of Example 5.37, but will block the creation of fresh individuals thereafter. Depending on the DL in use, different blocking conditions need to be implemented to ensure that the partial/blocked branch can be unravelled straightforwardly into a model for the ontology, or indeed, that every ontology has at least one model that can be unravelled from such a partial/blocked branch.

While tableaux are often seen as the "reference implementation" for expressive DLs like $\mathcal{SROIQ}$, there are other approaches by which reasoning can be implemented for such DLs, including (hyper)resolution [228], hypertableau [285, 145], disjunctive datalog [213, 338], automata [23, 146], and so forth. Amongst the most prominent systems implementing reasoning for expressive DLs, we can mention FaCT++ [381], HermIT [145], KAON2 [213], Pellet [362], and RacerPro [165]. These systems – amongst others – are accessible through the OWL API [205], the Protégé ontology editor [140], etc.

5.6.2.4 From $\mathcal{SROIQ}$ to OWL 2 DL

The $\mathcal{SROIQ}$ DL described previously – being expressive while permitting effective algorithms for entailment – thus offers a compelling basis upon which to form the OWL 2 DL language; furthermore, it offers a natural extension of the previous OWL 1 standard based on on the $\mathcal{SHOIN}$ DL. Along these lines, OWL 2 DL is designed to be compatible with $\mathcal{SROIQ}$: with the exception of some extensions beyond $\mathcal{SROIQ}$ (that we will discuss momentarily), an OWL 2 DL ontology, expressed in RDF, should be directly translatable to a $\mathcal{SROIQ}$ ontology and be interpretable with an analogous semantics. Maintaining such a close correspondence to $\mathcal{SROIQ}$ ensures that OWL 2 DL benefits from the theoretical decidability guarantees of – and effective algorithms designed for – entailment under $\mathcal{SROIQ}$ [208].

To enforce this correspondence between $\mathcal{SROIQ}$ and OWL 2 DL necessitates various syntactic restrictions on which RDF graphs constitute a valid OWL 2 DL ontology (unlike OWL 2 Full, where any RDF graph is considered a valid OWL 2 Full ontology). These restrictions in OWL 2 DL disallow, for example, definitions of the style presented in Example 5.31 for OWL 2 Full, which use the built-in OWL vocabulary in unusual ways that could not be translated to the $\mathcal{SROIQ}$ syntax outlined in Table 5.1 (and which are known to quickly lead to undecidability [279]). Furthermore, OWL 2 DL's restrictions also enforce the restrictions that $\mathcal{SROIQ}$ places on complex role inclusions (property chains) to ensure decidability (see Remark 5.39; otherwise the reduction of Remark 5.36 to the Domino Problem would still be possible in OWL 2 DL, implying undecidability of entailment!).

However, while OWL 2 DL is closely based on $\mathcal{SROIQ}$'s syntax and semantics, a number of practical extensions were added to OWL 2 DL that go

beyond the $\mathcal{SROIQ}$ DL; these extensions preserve decidability guarantees
and compatibility between OWL 2 DL and $\mathcal{SROIQ}$ for ontologies not using
extended features. The most notable of these extensions to OWL 2 DL are:

1. support for complex keys were added;
2. support for datatypes were added (the corresponding DL is sometimes
   referred to as $\mathcal{SROIQ}^{(D)}$ denoting $\mathcal{SROIQ}$ with datatypes);
3. support for *metamodelling* (aka. *"punning"*) was added, whereby an IRI
   in OWL can refer simultaneously to a property, class and individual.

By complex keys, we refer to the OWL construct `owl:hasKey`, which allows
us to state that members of a particular class are uniquely identified by a
combination of properties (see Example 5.7). However, the semantics of such
keys will be restricted slightly such that they only apply to named individuals
(we will discuss this restriction later with an example in Remark 5.41).

Support for datatypes refers precisely to the features that were previously
discussed in Section 5.4.5. However, restrictions are applied with respect to
the use of datatype properties (e.g., `:dateOfBirth` taking a date value) versus
object properties (e.g., `:placeOfBirth` taking an IRI value); for example, we
cannot define the inverse of a datatype property, nor can we define a datatype
property to be inverse-functional (for reasons we now justify).

Example 5.38

We just mentioned that in OWL 2 DL, datatype properties cannot be inverse-functional; in fact, this would be quite a useful feature
to have! Consider datatype properties like ISBN, BARCODE, etc. Indeed
it would be useful to define that such properties are inverse-functional,
serving as simple keys. But allowing inverse-functional datatype properties creates some non-obvious complications for reasoning, in particular
by requiring (sound and complete) implementations to be able to count
how many elements a datatype can have, which may be non-trivial.

Assume we wish to assign the following ordinals to the days of the
week so we know which follow which: MONDAY (1) ... FRIDAY (5). We
can define a datatype for the numbers 1–5 in OWL as follows:

```
:WeekDayOrdinal a rdfs:Datatype; owl:equivalentClass
  [ a rdfs:Datatype ;
    owl:onDatatype xsd:integer ;
    owl:withRestrictions (
      [ xsd:minInclusive 1 ]
      [ xsd:minInclusive 5 ] ) ] .
```

Next we can state that a WEEK-DAY must have an ordinal and that an
ordinal uniquely defines that WEEK-DAY:

```
:hasOrdinal a owl:DatatypeProperty , owl:InverseFunctionalProperty .

:WeekDay rdfs:subClassOf
  [ a owl:Restriction ;
    owl:someValuesFrom :WeekDayOrdinal ;
    owl:onProperty :hasOrdinal ] .
```

We can now finally recognise – formally, in OWL, so the machines can appreciate it too – the dedication of all those hardworking employees of our company who work on at least six days of the week:

```
:HardWorkingEmployee a owl:Class ; owl:equivalentClass
  [ a owl:Restriction ;
    owl:minCardinality 6 ;
    owl:onProperty :worksOnWeekday ] .

:worksOnWeekday a owl:ObjectProperty ;
  rdfs:domain :Employee ; rdfs:range :WeekDay .
```

Finally we can recognise Jane's hard work:

```
:Jane a :HardWorkingEmployee .
```

But in so doing, we create an inconsistent (OWL 2 Full) ontology! By defining the ordinals as a key on WEEK-DAY, and stating that every WEEK-DAY has an ordinal and that there are five possible ordinals, we entail that WEEK-DAY has at most five members. Hence an employee cannot have six WEEK-DAYs to work on, and hence no employee can be hardworking, and hence Jane cannot be hardworking by our impossible standards (the class HARD-WORKING-EMPLOYEE is unsatisfiable)!

Note that instead of defining ordinals as keys for week-days, and defining ordinal values as a datatype with five possible values, we could have created a similar situation by rather defining:

```
:WeekDay owl:equivalentClass
  [ owl:oneOf ( :Monday :Tuesday :Wednesdsay :Thursday :Friday ) ] .
```

This states that WEEK-DAY has at most five members (we say "at most" because some of the five individuals mentioned might be the same-as others). Such a definition could thus likewise be used to make a class like HARD-WORKING-EMPLOYEE unsatisfiable but without needing inverse-functional datatype properties. The real problem comes when we consider a definition like (adapted from Example 5.22):

```
:WeekendEN a rdfs:Datatype ; owl:equivalentClass
  [ a rdfs:Datatype ;
    owl:onDatatype xsd:string ;
    owl:withRestrictions (
      [ xsd:pattern "^[Ss](atur|un)day$" ] ) ] .
```

As before, if we defined that members of the class WEEKEND-DAY must have a value for an inverse-functional datatype property HAS-NAME from this datatype, we would again be limiting the number of members that WEEKEND-DAY can have, in this case to four based on the four possible values (saturday, Saturday, sunday, Sunday). Hence to correctly decide entailment (and recognise that nobody could work on five WEEKEND-DAYs), we would need to deduce how many values such datatypes can take, which would add major complications for reasoning implementations when supporting even the standard datatypes.

Disallowing inverse-functional datatype properties helps to avoid such complications relating to having to count datatype values. However, we could also achieve similar examples by defining inverses of datatype properties that are functional, or defining (qualified) cardinality restrictions involving inverses of datatype properties. For these reasons, OWL 2 DL does not allow inverse datatype properties either.

However, datatype properties *can* be used in cardinality restrictions or keys. We will discuss datatype properties in keys in Remark 5.41.

Metamodelling refers to the idea that we can simultaneously view a particular term as referring to a property, a class, or an individual, depending on the context [279]. This is not well-supported by $\mathcal{SROIQ}$.

Example 5.39

Consider the following statements in OWL:

```
:Kanzi          rdf:type          :Bonobo
:Bonobo         rdfs:subClassOf   :Chimpanzee
:Chimpanzee     rdf:type          :Genus .
```

Observe that CHIMPANZEE takes a dual role here as a class to which KANZI (a specific chimp) is entailed to belong, while also itself being an individual: a member of GENUS. The RDFS and OWL 2 Full semantics are well-defined for such statements. However, OWL 2 DL is based on $\mathcal{SROIQ}$, where one cannot immediately simply state:

$$\text{BONOBO(KANZI)} \quad \text{BONOBO} \sqsubseteq \text{CHIMPANZEE} \quad \text{GENUS(CHIMPANZEE)}$$

Here CHIMPANZEE is used both as an individual name (in the concept assertion GENUS(CHIMPANZEE)) and a concept name (in the concept axiom BONOBO $\sqsubseteq$ CHIMPANZEE). Now, for an interpretation I of these $\mathcal{SROIQ}$ axioms, what should PRIMATE^I give? An individual or a set of individuals from the domain? PRIMATE^I is not well-defined!

On the other hand, OWL 2 DL supports these types of axioms, and indeed axioms where the same term is used as a property and an individual/class (though admittedly such examples are less natural than metamodelling on classes/individuals). It supports this by defining more complex interpretations, where different interpretation functions are applied to terms depending on the type of axiom (see Remark 5.38). However, it does not allow "punning" datatype/object properties, nor "punning" classes with datatypes, since there are special restrictions that apply to each case; for example, we briefly mentioned that datatype properties cannot be inverse-functional, and hence punning datatype properties with inverse-functional object properties would create a "back-door" to circumvent this restriction.

(We note that such metamodelling was not allowed in OWL 1 DL.)

In summary, OWL 2 DL restricts OWL 2 Full to correspond more closely to $\mathcal{SROIQ}$, but extends $\mathcal{SROIQ}$ to include the restricted forms of complex keys, datatypes, and metamodelling as previously discussed.

The restrictions of OWL 2 DL are defined in terms of a custom syntax [282] that enforces such restrictions. Thereafter, a mapping between an RDF graph and an ontology in the OWL 2 DL syntax is defined [153]. While any OWL 2 DL ontology can be represented as an RDF graph, not all RDF graphs can be mapped to an OWL 2 DL ontology.

Remark 5.40 (i)

The details of the OWL 2 DL restrictions are quite tedious, so rather than go into details, we summarise the key points:

- The syntax of RDF graphs used to define OWL axioms must be well-formed according to the defined mapping of RDF graphs to OWL 2 DL ontologies [153].

  – For example, lists must be well-formed and complete (e.g., they must be terminated with no branching or loops). This prevents definitions like were given in Example 5.32, simplifying the mapping from RDF graphs to OWL 2 DL ontologies [153].

- The use of built-in RDF(S) and OWL terms is greatly restricted.

  – This prevents the types of axioms given in Example 5.31 – which quickly lead to undecidability [279] and could not be translated into $\mathcal{SROIQ}$ – from being defined.

- Any property used must be explicitly typed as a datatype property (owl:DatatypeProperty) or object property (owl:ObjectProperty).

  – This allows particular restrictions and interpretations to be applied to a property depending on which it is; for example, an

OWL 2 DL tool can ensure that any inverse-functional properties are declared to be object properties.

- All classes and datatypes used in axioms must be explicitly typed
  accordingly (as `owl:Class` or `rdfs:Datatype`).

  - This allows novel datatypes to be defined using OWL's vocab-
    ulary for set-based definitions of classes (intersection, union,
    complement, one-of; see Example 5.23) but not other restric-
    tions on classes (existential, universal, cardinality, etc.).

- Restrictions on $\mathcal{SROIQ}$ roles are enforced (see Remark 5.39).

  - These restrictions help ensure decidability of entailment.

- Restrictions on datatype properties are enforced (see Example 5.38).

  - These restrictions avoid having to count datatype values.

We refer to the standard for full details [153, 282].

Thereafter, the semantics of OWL 2 DL ontologies are defined in a model
theoretic manner by the standard [281]. These semantics are compatible with
the RDF-Based Semantics of OWL 2 Full discussed previously, as well as the
semantics of $\mathcal{SROIQ}$ (see Table 5.2). The resulting semantics is called the
Direct Semantics [281], and is defined only for valid OWL 2 DL ontologies.

Remark 5.41   (i)

In Example 5.38, we mentioned that while OWL 2 DL disallows
inverse-functional datatype properties, it allows datatype properties on
keys. What, one may then ask, is the difference between:

```
:hasOrdinal a owl:DatatypeProperty , owl:InverseFunctionalProperty .
```

which is disallowed in OWL 2 DL, and

```
:hasOrdinal a owl:DatatypeProperty .
owl:Thing owl:hasKey ( :hasOrdinal ) .
```

which is allowed in OWL 2 DL? The answer is that while both definitions are analogous in OWL 2 Full under the RDF-Based Semantics, in
the Direct Semantics of OWL 2 DL, keys are interpreted in a restricted
way (unlike inverse-functional properties) so that they only apply to
named individuals [281]. This "trick" avoids the sorts of complications
mentioned by Example 5.38, where we avoid having to speculate on
how many existentials could be generated by keys on datatype properties (including the unnamed members of a class like WEEK-DAY), which
avoids having to compute how many values a datatype can take.

5.6.3 OWL 2 Profiles

Alongside OWL 2 Full (the unrestricted but undecidable language) and OWL 2 DL (the restricted but still highly expressive and decidable language), the OWL 2 standard defines a novel set of three sub-languages – called *profiles* – that further restrict the OWL 2 DL language. These profiles are called OWL 2 EL, OWL 2 QL, and OWL 2 RL, where each is associated with particular reasoning algorithms and use-cases. Additionally, a valid ontology in any of these languages is also a valid OWL 2 DL ontology. But before we discuss these profiles further, we first give some rationale for defining further sub-languages of OWL 2 DL in the first place.

5.6.3.1 Rationale: Problems with OWL 2 DL

While OWL 2 DL restricts OWL 2 Full in such a manner that permits effective algorithms for reasoning tasks like ontology entailment, ontology satisfiability, class subsumption, etc., OWL 2 DL has two fundamental limitations (that is, aside from the limitation of restricting the language).

First, there is the issue of *complexity*: while we can implement effective entailment algorithms for OWL 2 DL that are guaranteed to halt in theory, there is no guarantee that they will halt before the heat-death of the universe on any conceivable machine – even for reasonably small inputs. We perhaps got a sense of the complexity of reasoning over $\mathcal{SROIQ}$/OWL 2 DL ontologies in Example 5.36, where we illustrated a tableau procedure. In particular, we saw how the procedure must branch on disjunctive possibilities, and must invent fresh individuals to satisfy existential axioms. While methods like hyperresolution [228] or hypertableau [285, 145] can help to optimise a naive tableau method by reducing the non-deterministic possibilities explored and thus guide the process more quickly towards a refutation, no matter how clever the algorithm, there are only so many optimisations possible.

More formally, the problems of ontology entailment, ontology satisfiability, class subsumption, class satisfiability, and instance checking over OWL 2 DL ontologies with respect to the standard Direct Semantics is N2EXPTIME-complete in taxonomic complexity [280]. We will discuss complexity classes in more detail in Remark 5.43, but in summary, the problem is doubly-exponential – in the number of input T-Box and R-Box axioms – on a non-deterministic machine, in the worst case. Given that we do not have a working non-deterministic machine (or know that P = NP), this means that current algorithms running on a conventional (deterministic) machine, in the worst case, will require $O(2^{2^{2^n}})$ steps to halt. Being glib, for an ontology with $n = 3$ T-Box and R-Box axioms, this number of steps would exceed even ambitious estimates for the number of atoms in the observable universe.

Discussion 5.7

FRANK: Doesn't this complexity make OWL 2 DL impractical?

AIDAN: Not necessarily. Here we speak of worst-case complexity. The fact there exist inputs for which reasoning will not finish in the life-time of our universe does not preclude the possibility of there being a lot of useful inputs for which reasoning will take no more than a few seconds. Indeed, there are various practical reasoners supporting OWL 2 DL [381, 145, 213, 362, 165] that work fine for many real-world ontologies, deriving useful conclusions.

FRANK: But ...

AIDAN: In general, worst-case complexity offers a limited perspective of a problem. Much of the digital world runs on relational databases, for example, but deciding if a basic SQL query with joins even has *some* answer on a given database is exponential based on known algorithms! Should we conclude that relational databases and SQL are impractical? No! Even without the precedent we see around us, this complexity result is measured by the size of the query; many real-world queries tend to be simple; and so forth.

ANNA: But why, then, go to all the bother to restrict the language in this complicated way – functional properties must be "simple", etc. – to guarantee a purely theoretical notion of decidability? What pragmatic difference is there between a language whose reasoning tasks will not halt in theory for some inputs and a language whose reasoning tasks will not halt in our physical reality for some inputs? Why not just let the people use whatever features they want and if reasoning halts it halts, and if it doesn't, it doesn't?

AIDAN: Well OWL 2 Full is that latter option. But in terms of why OWL 2 DL is useful to also have, the short answer is that decidable procedures have sound and complete algorithms that halt, where people do implement and use OWL 2 DL reasoners in practice. More generally, studying complexity allows us to understand what makes a problem difficult and based on that, we can make a more informed decision about which features of a language we want to keep, bringing us closer to a practical ontology language. This has led, for example, to the OWL 2 profiles that we will discuss later.

Indeed, the expressivity of the OWL 2 DL and $\mathcal{SROIQ}$ languages comes at a high cost, as evidenced by such a high computational complexity.

The second (related) issue is the decidability of OWL 2 DL. We already stated that tasks like ontology entailment, ontology satisfiability, class subsumption, etc., are decidable for OWL 2 DL, sketching an effective algorithm. But what about tasks such as query answering over OWL 2 DL ontologies? What if we wish to run queries and have the solutions extended by all valid entailments from the ontology? The corresponding decision problem studied in theory – *(boolean) conjunctive query answering*, which simply checks if a query has an answer or not with respect to the ontology and its entailments – is not known to be decidable: despite positive results for weaker DLs [147], decidability for $\mathcal{SROIQ}$ (and even $\mathcal{SHOIN}$) remains open [280].

These issues impede use-cases for OWL involving large (but relatively simple) ontologies (like SNOMED-CT [115]), or use-cases requiring query-answering capabilities. The three profiles defined in the following are designed to target precisely such use-cases, permitting simpler, more efficient, reasoning implementations, including for tasks such as query answering. Hence, **tractability** of reasoning is the key design goal for the following profiles.

Remark 5.42   ⓘ

What precisely do we mean by "tractability"? In general speech, it can be interpreted to mean *feasible, easy to handle*, etc. However, in the context of Computer Science, often is it interpreted to mean problems for which effective algorithms exist that are guaranteed to run in polynomial time (that are in PTIME; aka. simply P), by which we mean (deterministic) algorithms that will run in $O(n^k)$ steps for n the size of the input and k a fixed constant, even in the worst case; these include algorithms that run in $O(n)$, $O(n^2)$, $O(n^{500})$, etc. One may then reasonably think: in what way should problems whose best algorithms run in $O(n^{500})$, for example, be considered "easy to handle"?

The (partial) answer is that it is assumed by Cobham's thesis (aka. Cobham–Edmonds' thesis), from 1965, which states that only algorithms that run in polynomial time are those feasible to execute on a particular machine. This thesis has been historically adopted by the theoretical community as the yardstick of tractability. Proponents may argue that the exponential increase in computational capacity predicted by Moore's Law lends strength to the thesis since exponential growth outstrips polynomial increases in time complexity. Furthermore they may point to the trend that where an algorithm runs in $O(n^k)$, experience has shown that k very often tends to be low (loosely, the k can be thought of as the number of nested loops required). Detractors may point to the fact that $O(n^{500})$ is considered tractable while $O(2^{0.001n})$ is considered intractable. As a more general weakness of worst-case complexity studies, in an algorithm with a worst-case of $O(n^2)$, all cases may require n^2 steps, while for an algorithm with a worst-case of $O(2^n)$, all but a few constructed cases may run in n, etc.

In general, worst-case complexity analysis – though necessarily an incomplete perspective, or perhaps even at times an oversimplification – has proven useful to understand the feasibility of implementation, and the expectation of scaling characteristics, for a variety of problems.

Remark 5.43

Later in this section, we will encounter a variety of complexity classes, where we give a brief overview of how these classes can be interpreted. In the following description, n refers to the size of the input, while $p(n)$ refers to any polynomial function on n (i.e., functions that sum terms involving n raised to a constant power, possibly with constant factors, such as n, n^5, $3n^4 + 6$, $\pi n^{-\sqrt{2}}$, but not $3n!$, 2^n, etc.).

N2EXPTIME: The class of problems solvable by non-deterministic algorithms in double exponential time ($\leq 2^{2^{p(n)}}$ time).

NEXPTIME: The class of problems solvable by non-deterministic algorithms in exponential time ($\leq 2^{p(n)}$ time).

EXPTIME: The class of problems solvable by deterministic algorithms in exponential time ($\leq 2^{p(n)}$ time).

PSPACE: The class of problems solvable by deterministic algorithms in polynomial space ($\leq p(n)$ space).

NP: The class of problems solvable by non-deterministic algorithms in polynomial time ($\leq p(n)$ time).

PTIME: The class of problems solvable by deterministic algorithms in polynomial time ($\leq p(n)$ time).

NLOGSPACE: The class of problems solvable by non-deterministic algorithms in logarithmic space ($\leq \log(n)$ space).

LOGSPACE: The class of problems solvable by deterministic algorithms in logarithmic space ($\leq \log(n)$ space).

AC^0: The class of problems solvable with a family of circuits with constant depth and polynomial size ($\leq p(n)$). The size of the circuit refers to the number of gates, where k-fanin AND and OR gates ($k \geq 2$) are allowed anywhere on the circuit, while NOT gates are allowed at the input only. Intuitively this refers to the class of problems that can be solved in constant time assuming a number of processors polynomial in the size of n; i.e., it is often seen as the class of problems that can be efficiently parallelised.

We add the following explanatory/clarifying remarks:

- PTIME is also known as P, NLOGSPACE is also known as NL, and LOGSPACE is also known as L.
- $2^{2^{p(n)}}$ is common shorthand for $2^{(2^{p(n)})}$ (different from $(2^2)^{p(n)}$)
- N2EXPTIME, NEXPTIME and NP are assumed to run on theoretical non-deterministic machines, which are machines that can compute multiple possibilities at once and then select the result of the best possibility (if such a possibility exists), all with the same cost that a deterministic machine would have were it to somehow

get lucky and "guess" one of the right possibilities leading to a solution.[a] Conventional machines are deterministic, and hence (unless PTIME = NP), N2EXPTIME, NEXPTIME and NP will have an extra exponential factor in practice; for example, NEXPTIME on a non-deterministic machine running in time $2^{p(n)}$ can be expected to run in time $2^{2^{p(n)}}$ on a conventional deterministic machine.

- PSPACE, NLOGSPACE and LOGSPACE are slightly different in that they put a bound on space rather than time. The $\log(n)$ space that these algorithms can use is additional to the n space required for the input. For NLOGSPACE, which assumes a non-deterministic machine, there exist equivalent algorithms running on a deterministic machine that take (at worst) quadratically more space $(\log^2(n))$.

- The above classes are presented in order of "hardness". However, a problem that is in PTIME, for example, will also be in NP since if a problem can be solved in time $\leq p(n)$ on a deterministic machine (PTIME), it can surely be solved in time $\leq p(n)$ on a non-deterministic machine (NP). Considering PTIME and NP as sets of problems, we can thus write PTIME $\subseteq$ NP, where, in this particular case, it is an open problem whether or not there exists problems in NP that are not in PTIME (possibly the classes are the same). In other cases however, like $AC^0 \subsetneq$ LOGSPACE, we know the containment to be strict, denoted by "$\subsetneq$". Along these lines, for the above classes, the following inclusions are known:

$$AC^0 \subsetneq \text{LOGSPACE} \subseteq \text{NLOGSPACE} \subseteq \text{PTIME} \subseteq \text{NP} \subseteq$$
$$\text{PSPACE} \subseteq \text{EXPTIME} \subseteq \text{NEXPTIME} \subsetneq \text{N2EXPTIME}$$

We further know some other strict inclusions, such as

$$\text{NLOGSPACE} \subsetneq \text{PSPACE, NP} \subsetneq \text{NEXPTIME, etc.}$$

- As mentioned, a problem in PTIME is in NP. However, problems known to be in PTIME are not the "hardest" problems for NP: there are problems in NP not known to be in PTIME. We say that the "hardest problems" for a given class X are X-complete; formally this is defined in terms of reductions that preserve identity of that class. For example, there exists a polynomial-time reduction from every NP-complete problem to any other NP-complete problem (hence if we knew that any NP-complete problem were in PTIME, by such reductions, we would immediately know that PTIME = NP).

- Conversely, we may say that a problem is X-hard, which indicates that we know it is at least as hard as the hardest problems in class X, though we may not know if it is in X. For example, a problem that is EXPTIME-hard may be in EXPTIME (in which case it is EXPTIME-complete), or it may be NEXPTIME-complete, or it may even be UNDECIDABLE; it cannot, however, be in PTIME.

- What do we mean by the size of the input? Do we mean the size of the T-Box? The R-Box? The A-Box? In the case of conjunctive query answering, do we include the size of the query as well? The answer depends on the problem and the type of complexity considered, where the following discussion considers four options:

  Combined Complexity: Considers the size of everything given as input, including all axioms in the T-Box/R-Box/A-Box, the query (in the specific case of query answering), and the expression being checked (in the case of class satisfiability, class subsumption, or instance checking).

  Taxonomic Complexity: Considers the size of only the T-Box/R-Box axioms of the ontology.

  Data Complexity: Considers the size of only the A-Box axioms (aka. assertions) of the ontology.

  Query Complexity: Considers the size of the query (only applicable in the case of query answering).

- Finally, when considering the complexity of query answering with respect to ontologies, we highlight that the non-emptiness problem for query answering – which asks, does this conjunctive query have any solution over these data? – is NP-complete in query/combined complexity, even without any ontology (i.e., just considering explicit data). In data complexity, the same problem is in AC^0. Hence, we should expect that with ontologies, the complexity of the problem will not be better than these results without ontologies.

To conclude, here we are limited to a "crash course" on complexity theory for the uninitiated, dealing with some of the complexity classes that are mentioned in the following discussion. For a more general and rigorous treatment, we refer to, e.g., the book by Papadimitriou [305].

---

[a] For instance, given as input a finite non-empty set of integers S, the *Subset Sum Problem* asks: is there any subset of S that sums to zero? For example, for $S_1 = \{-1, 4, 8, -12\}$, a yes solution is proven by $S'_1 = \{4, 8, -12\}$, while for $S_1 = \{-1, 4, 10, -12\}$, the solution is no. The problem is NP-complete, meaning that only non-deterministic algorithms for the problem are known to run in polynomial time. A non-deterministic machine can check all candidate subsets at the same time and find one whose sum is zero with the same cost a deterministic algorithm would incur if it simply "guessed" the right subset. In practice, known deterministic algorithms take exponential time. The question of PTIME = NP (aka. P = NP) then relates to the fact that we do not know whether or not there is a clever way to find a solution on a deterministic machine in polynomial time.

5.6.3.2 OWL 2 EL

The first OWL 2 profile that we shall discuss – called OWL 2 EL – targets reasoning over large but relatively inexpressive terminologies, such as SNOMED-CT [115], where ontology satisfiability, class satisfiability and instance checking tasks are of most importance. In particular, these tasks are tractable for OWL 2 EL, meaning they can be solved in polynomial time (versus N2EXPTIME-complete for OWL 2 DL and undecidable for OWL 2 Full).

To achieve this (major) improvement in the efficiency of reasoning tasks, OWL 2 EL applies a variety of restrictions, inspired by the $\mathcal{EL}++$ DL [25] from which it gets its name. In terms of nomenclature, $\mathcal{EL}$ does not follow the previous DL naming conventions, but rather refers to a novel base language, called the $\mathcal{E}$xistential $\mathcal{L}$anguage, which, in terms of concept definitions and axioms, supports the top concept, concept intersection, existential restriction, and concept inclusion; in other words, support for concept union and universal restrictions is dropped and no support is assumed for role axioms. With these previous restrictions, the aforementioned reasoning tasks become tractable, while terminologies such as SNOMED-CT can still be expressed.

The $\mathcal{EL}++$ extension then adds back in a variety of features – such as the bottom concept, domain/range restrictions, nominals with one element, and some limited role axioms – that do not affect tractability of reasoning [25]. OWL 2 EL is based on $\mathcal{EL}++$, but additionally maintains a handful of additional features from $\mathcal{SROIQ}$, such as self-restrictions, that likewise do not affect the tractability of reasoning.[5] The DL syntax of $\mathcal{EL}++$ is summarised in Table 5.3. Features of OWL 2 DL beyond $\mathcal{SROIQ}$, such as complex keys and limited datatype support, are also kept for OWL 2 EL.

To highlight what is not supported, OWL 2 EL drops features such as concept negation, concept union, universal restrictions (aside from domain/range axioms), number restrictions (qualified or not), nominals with more than one individual, disjoint roles, irreflexive roles, inverse roles, functional and inverse-functional roles (functional datatype properties are allowed), symmetric and asymmetric roles. The typical restrictions of OWL 2 DL are also considered: every valid OWL 2 EL ontology is a valid OWL 2 DL ontology. A number of more specific restrictions are also applied, summarised as follows [280]:

- Anonymous individuals are not allowed in assertions.
- If the ontology defines axioms of the form $R_1 \circ \ldots R_n \sqsubseteq R$, $\mathsf{ran}(R) \sqsubseteq C$, then the ontology must also state $\mathsf{ran}(R_n) \sqsubseteq C$.
- Datatypes with a finite value space are not supported, nor are datatypes whose intersection with a supported datatype is non-empty and finite. In summary, the datatypes that are disallowed are xsd:boolean, xsd:double, xsd:float and all datatypes derived from xsd:integer other than xsd:nonNegativeInteger (for example, the datatypes xsd:short, xsd:positiveInteger, etc., are disallowed).

---

[5] $\mathcal{EL}++$ supports reflexive roles, but not in concept definitions [25].

Table 5.3 $\mathcal{EL}{+}{+}$ syntax and semantics
(additional features of $\mathcal{SROIQ}$ kept by OWL 2 EL denoted by †)

Name	Syntax	Semantics $(\cdot^I)$	Note
		CONCEPT DEFINITIONS	
Atomic Concept	A	A^I (a subset of Δ^I)	
Top Concept	$\top$	Δ^I	
Bottom Concept	$\bot$	$\emptyset$	
Concept Intersection	$C \sqcap D$	$C^I \cap D^I$	
Nominal	$\{a\}$	$\{a^I\}$	Singleton only
Existential Restriction	$\exists R.C$	$\{x \mid \exists y : (x,y) \in R^I \text{ and } y \in C^I\}$	
Self Restriction†	$\exists R.\mathsf{Self}$	$\{x \mid (x,x) \in R^I\}$	Added by OWL 2 EL
		CONCEPT AXIOM (T-Box)	
Concept Inclusion	$C \sqsubseteq D$	$C^I \subseteq D^I$	
Domain Axiom	$\mathrm{dom}(R) \subseteq C$	$R^I \subseteq C^I \times \Delta^I$	Alternatively: $\exists R.\top \sqsubseteq C$
Range Axiom	$\mathrm{ran}(R) \subseteq C$	$R^I \subseteq \Delta^I \times C^I$	Weakening universal res.
		ROLE DEFINITIONS	
Role	R	R^I (a subset of $\Delta^I \times \Delta^I$)	
Universal Role†	U	$\Delta^I \times \Delta^I$	
Bottom Role†	B	$\emptyset$	Weakening disjoint roles
		ROLE AXIOM (R-Box)	
Role Inclusion	$R \sqsubseteq S$	$R^I \subseteq S^I$	
Complex Role Inclusion	$R_1 \circ ... \circ R_n \sqsubseteq S$	$R_1^I \circ ... \circ R_n^I \subseteq S^I$	
Transitive Roles	$\mathrm{Trans}(R)$	$R^I \circ R^I \subseteq R^I$	
Functional Roles†	$\mathrm{Func}(R)$	$\{(x,y),(x,z)\} \subseteq R^I \text{implies } y = z$	Datatype roles only
Reflexive Roles	$\mathrm{Ref}(R)$	for all $x \in \Delta^I : (x,x) \in R^I$	
		ASSERTIONAL DEFINITIONS	
Named Individual	a	a^I (an element of Δ^I)	No existentials
		ASSERTIONAL AXIOM (A-Box)	
Role Assertion	$R(a,b)$	$(a^I, b^I) \in R^I$	
Negative Role Assertion†	$\neg R(a,b)$	$(a^I, b^I) \notin R^I$	
Concept Assertion	$C(a)$	$a^I \in C^I$	
Equality	$a = b$	$a^I = b^I$	
Inequality	$a \neq b$	$a^I \neq b^I$	

- Facets on datatypes are also not supported: however, one can define the
  intersection of supported datatypes, or a datatype with a single element
  through a nominal.

We refer the reader to [280] for more details.

The benefit of all these restrictions is tractable reasoning: more specifically, ontology satisfiability, class satisfiability, class subsumption and instance checking become PTIME-complete in the size of the T-Box and R-Box axioms [280]. Along these lines, a number of efficient reasoning systems have been proposed for $\mathcal{EL}{+}{+}$/OWL 2 EL, including CEL [27] and ELK [227]. These reasoners generally work by first applying normal forms to the ontology, and thereafter materialising relevant concept inclusions using rules; we refer the reader to the respective papers for details [27, 227], but here we will provide an overview of the core reasoning algorithm of ELK [227].

Example 5.40

The ELK reasoner [227] supports an $\mathcal{EL}$ variant called $\mathcal{EL}_\perp^+$, which from OWL 2 EL (see Table 5.3) does not support range axioms, nominals, self restrictions, universal/bottom roles, functional roles, reflexive roles, negative role assertions, equality, inequality; conversely, it adds complex role inclusions, and the top and bottom concept, to $\mathcal{EL}$.

ELK applies the following rules to compute concept inclusions for $\mathcal{EL}_\perp^+$ ontologies; the premise above the line, when matched by the ontology or inferred inclusions, implies the inclusion below the line:

$$R_0 \; \frac{}{C \sqsubseteq C} \qquad\qquad R_\top \; \frac{}{C \sqsubseteq \top}$$

$$R_\perp \; \frac{E \sqsubseteq \exists R.C \quad C \sqsubseteq \perp}{E \sqsubseteq \perp} \qquad R_\exists \; \frac{E \sqsubseteq \exists R.C \quad C \sqsubseteq D}{E \sqsubseteq \exists R.D}$$

$$R_\sqcap^- \; \frac{C \sqsubseteq D_1 \sqcap D_2}{C \sqsubseteq D_1 \quad C \sqsubseteq D_2} \qquad R_\sqcap^+ \; \frac{C \sqsubseteq D_1 \quad C \sqsubseteq D_2}{C \sqsubseteq D_1 \sqcap D_2}$$

$$R_\sqsubseteq \; \frac{C \sqsubseteq D \quad D \sqsubseteq E}{C \sqsubseteq E} \qquad R_H \; \frac{E \sqsubseteq \exists R.C \quad R \sqsubseteq S}{E \sqsubseteq \exists S.C}$$

$$R_\circ \; \frac{E \sqsubseteq \exists R_1.C \quad C \sqsubseteq \exists R_2.D \quad R_1 \circ R_2 \sqsubseteq S}{E \sqsubseteq \exists S.D}$$

Note that a complex role inclusion $R_1 \circ ... \circ R_n \sqsubseteq S$ can be rewritten as $n-1$ pairwise inclusions of the form $R_1 \circ R_2 \sqsubseteq S_{1,2}$, $S_{1,2} \circ R_3 \sqsubseteq S_{1,3}$, $S_{n-2,n-1} \circ R_n \sqsubseteq S$, introducing fresh roles $S_{1,2}, ..., S_{n-2,n-1}$ [27].

These rules then form the basis for reasoning in ELK, where the system further applies a range of optimisations, including the identification of non-recursive parts of rule premises, identification of possible redundancies where rules need not be applied, goal-directed rule applications (to check only a given concept inclusion for subsumption checking, or only a given concept assertion for instance checking), as well as procedural optimisations including indexing, parallelisation, and so forth. We refer the reader to the paper for further details [227].

On the other hand, while there have been works on reasoners for $\mathcal{EL}$ based on query rewriting [167], more generally, the complexity of conjunctive query answering under $\mathcal{EL}++$ entailment escalates: data complexity jumps from AC^0 to PTIME-complete, while combined complexity is PSPACE-hard [280].

5.6.3.3 OWL 2 QL

In many scenarios, being able to answer queries with respect to an ontology – rather than just check subsumptions or satisfiability – becomes the key task. But as discussed in the previous section, query answering becomes more complex in data complexity when considering OWL 2 EL entailments. The second profile of OWL that we discuss – called OWL 2 QL – thus aims to support efficient query answering under OWL entailment. More formally, the core design goal of OWL 2 QL is to maintain the complexity of query answering versus the base case where no ontology/entailment is considered.

To achieve this goal, considerable restrictions are required. OWL 2 QL is based on a family of description logics called *DL-Lite* [84, 20], whose aim is to maintain tractable query answering in data complexity. The foundational DL-Lite variant is called DL-Lite$_{core}$, which allows limited existential restrictions ($\exists R.\top$ where R is an atomic role or its inverse), concept negation, concept inclusion, inverse roles, and negated roles; the T-Box contains limited concept inclusions ($C \sqsubseteq D$ where C is $\exists R.\top$ or an atomic concept A); the A-Box contains positive concept and role assertions; no R-Box (role inclusion) axioms are permitted. Thereafter DL-Lite$_\mathcal{R}$ extends DL-Lite$_{core}$ with role inclusions (which indirectly allows for expressing a number of other features, such as $\exists R.C$ on the right-hand-side of concept inclusions), while DL-Lite$_\mathcal{F}$ extends DL-Lite$_{core}$ with functional role axioms (including on inverse roles).

A major difference between the DL-Lite family and the OWL languages discussed thus far is that DL-Lite considers a UNA: in other words, it assumes that one name points to one individual. Hence, for example, in DL-Lite$_\mathcal{F}$, functional roles act as constraints rather than implying equality. Admitting a UNA would make OWL 2 QL semantically incompatible with other OWL languages, and hence DL-Lite$_\mathcal{R}$ – which does not *rely* on a UNA and supports limited role inclusions (no chains) – was chosen as the basis for OWL 2 QL. In Table 5.4, we provide an overview of the syntax and semantics of DL-Lite$_{core}$, DL-Lite$_\mathcal{R}$ and OWL 2 QL, where the latter preserves a number of additional features from $\mathcal{SROIQ}$ that do not cause issues for the complexity of query answering, such as reflexive roles and irreflexive roles, as well as the top and bottom concepts/roles. Limited datatype support is also provided.

Summarising what is not supported, OWL 2 QL drops features such as concept intersection[6], concept union, nominals, universal restrictions, self restrictions, number restrictions (qualified or not), general concept inclusions (only A or $\exists R.\top$ are allowed on the right-hand-side), chains in complex role inclusions, transitive roles, functional and inverse functional roles, negative assertions, and equality assertions. Complex keys are also dropped since equality is not supported in OWL 2 QL. The restrictions of OWL 2 DL are also considered: every valid OWL 2 QL ontology is a valid OWL 2 DL ontol-

---

[6] OWL 2 QL actually allows intersection on the right-hand-side of concept inclusions, but $C \sqsubseteq D_1 \sqcap \ldots \sqcap D_n$ is just an alternative syntax for $C \sqsubseteq D_1, \ldots, C \sqsubseteq D_n$.

Table 5.4 DL-Lite$_{core}$ and DL-Lite$_R$ syntax and semantics

Additional features of $\mathcal{SROIQ}$ kept by OWL 2 QL denoted by $\dagger$
R.H.S. indicates features restricted to right-hand-side of inclusion axioms

Name	Syntax	Semantics $(\cdot^I)$	Note
		CONCEPT DEFINITIONS	
Atomic Concept	A	A^I (a subset of Δ^I)	
Top Concept	$\top$	Δ^I	OWL 2 QL only
Bottom Concept	$\bot$	$\emptyset$	OWL 2 QL only
Concept Negation	$\neg C$	$\Delta^I \setminus C^I$	R.H.S only
Existential Participation	$\exists R.\top$	$\{x \mid \exists y : (x,y) \in R^I\}$	Weakens existential res.
Existential Restriction	$\exists R.C$	$\{x \mid \exists y : (x,y) \in R^I \text{ and } y \in C^I\}$	DL-Lite$_R$/R.H.S only
		CONCEPT AXIOM (T-Box)	
Concept Inclusion	$C \sqsubseteq D$	$C^I \subseteq D^I$	C Atomic or $\exists R.\top$
		ROLE DEFINITIONS	
Role	R	R^I (a subset of $\Delta^I \times \Delta^I$)	
Inverse Role	R^-	$\{(y,x) \mid (x,y) \in R^I\}$	
Universal Role†	U	$\Delta^I \times \Delta^I$	OWL 2 QL only
		ROLE AXIOM (R-Box)	
Role Inclusion	$R \sqsubseteq S$	$R^I \subseteq S^I$	DL-Lite$_R$ only
Reflexive Roles†	$\mathsf{Ref}(R)$	for all $x \in \Delta^I : (x,x) \in R^I$	OWL 2 QL only
Irreflexive Roles†	$\mathsf{Irref}(R)$	for all $x \in \Delta^I : (x,x) \notin R^I$	OWL 2 QL only
Symmetric Roles	$\mathsf{Sym}(R)$	$R^I = (R^-)^I$	DL-Lite$_R$ only
Asymmetric Roles	$\mathsf{Asym}(R)$	$R^I \cap (R^-)^I = \emptyset$	OWL 2 QL only
Disjoint Roles	$\mathsf{Disj}(R,S)$	$R^I \cap S^I = \emptyset$	DL-Lite$_R$ only
		ASSERTIONAL DEFINITIONS	
Named Individual	a	a^I (an element of Δ^I)	No existentials
		ASSERTIONAL AXIOM (A-Box)	
Role Assertion	$R(a,b)$	$(a^I, b^I) \in R^I$	Atomic role only
Concept Assertion	$C(a)$	$a^I \in C^I$	Atomic concept only
Inequality	$a \neq b$	$a^I \neq b^I$	OWL 2 QL only

ogy. Finally, the following restrictions (a subset of those applied in the case of OWL 2 EL) are also enforced for OWL 2 QL:

- Anonymous individuals are not allowed in assertions.
- Datatypes with a finite value space are not supported, nor are datatypes whose intersection with a supported datatype is non-empty and finite. In summary, the datatypes that are disallowed are xsd:boolean, xsd:double, xsd:float and all datatypes derived from xsd:integer other than xsd:nonNegativeInteger (for example, the datatypes xsd:short, xsd:positiveInteger, etc., are disallowed).
- Facets on datatypes are also not supported: however, one can define the intersection of supported datatypes. Furthermore, $\exists R.D$, where D is a datatype, can be used in the left-hand-side of concept inclusions (possibly defined as the intersection of datatypes).

We again refer to the standard for further details [280].

> ### Remark 5.44
>
> There is a very strong relation between RDFS and DL-Lite$_\mathcal{R}$/OWL 2 QL, where sub-classes are expressed as $C \sqsubseteq D$, sub-properties as $R \sqsubseteq S$, domain as $\exists R.\top \sqsubseteq C$, and range as $\exists R^-.\top \sqsubseteq C$. In fact, the standard notes that, in relation to OWL 2 QL:
>
> > [...] this profile contains the intersection of RDFS and OWL 2 DL. [280]
>
> However, OWL 2 QL does add a number of features that go beyond RDFS, including disjointness ($C \sqsubseteq \neg D$, $\mathsf{Disj}(R,S)$), existential particiation ($\exists R.\top$), symmetric and asymmetric roles ($\mathsf{Sym}(R)$, $\mathsf{Asym}(R)$), inverse roles (R^-), and inequalities ($a \neq b$). On the other hand, unlike OWL 2 QL, any RDF graph can be interpreted under RDFS semantics. Furthermore, some syntactic RDFS features, like container membership properties, are not supported under OWL 2 QL (nor OWL 2 DL).

The purpose of all these restrictions, again, is to maintain tractable query answering. More specifically, the data complexity of conjunctive query answering is AC^0, while the query complexity is NP-complete (see Remark 5.43). Importantly, this is precisely the complexity of query answering without ontologies, and in a practical sense is thus "the best one could hope for" in terms of complexity for query answering under ontologies. The DL-Lite family aims to be maximal while not escalating the complexity of conjunctive query answering. The original paper proposing DL-Lite proves a number of results showing that adding further features will escalate complexity [84].

A further advantage is that query answering under OWL 2 QL can be implemented by *query rewriting* [84]: given a database, an OWL 2 QL ontology and a query (in a language such as SQL or SPARQL), one can "extend" the query according to the ontology and answer that extended query over the database to capture the entailments of the ontology. This query rewriting strategy can then be used not only to see if some answer to a query is entailed, but also to generate the answers that are entailed. The query rewriting strategy further works for input queries that are unions of conjunctive queries, supporting select (with equalities), project, join and union. This strategy can then be implemented as follows: (1) given an ontology, index the A-Box in a database offline; (2) when a query is received, rewrite it according to the T-Box and R-Box; (3) run the rewritten query over the database. Hence, in practice all that needs to be implemented is method (2), where (1) and (3) can rely on off-the-shelf (highly-optimised) database engines.

The fact that OWL 2 QL entailments can be supported in a sound and complete fashion through query rewriting – requiring only a single, extended SQL/SPARQL query to be evaluated for a given input query – is a non-trivial property of the language, and one that obviates the need to materialise and maintain indexes over entailments. This property (called *first-order rewritability*) has made OWL 2 QL the language of choice for **Ontology-Based Data Access (OBDA)** systems [404], which rewrite a high-level input query using the vocabulary of an ontology to low-level queries that can be evaluated over an underlying database, or set of databases, with solutions having entailments. For technical details of OWL 2 QL/DL-Lite query rewriting, we refer to [84]; here we will rather illustrate the main idea with an example.

Example 5.41

Consider the following DL-Lite$_\mathcal{R}$/OWL 2 QL ontology:

A-Box	
PLANET(KAPTEYNB)[A1]	TWINSTAR(SIRIUSA,SIRIUSB)[A2]
COLLAPSAR(CYGNUSX1)[A3]	ORBITS(HDE226868,CYGNUSX1)[A4]

T-Box		
COLLAPSAR ⊑ BLACKHOLE [T1]	COLLAPSAR ⊑ COMPACTSTAR [T2]	
COMPACTSTAR ⊑ STAR [T3]	∃TWINSTAR.⊤ ⊑ STAR [T4]	
PLANET ⊑ ∃ORBITS.STAR [T5]		

R-Box	
Sym(TWINSTAR)[R1]	TWINSTAR ⊑ ORBITS[R2]

Now consider the following query, asking for bodies that orbit stars:

$$Q(b) \leftarrow \exists s \big(\text{ORBITS}(b,s) \land \text{STAR}(s) \big)$$

Running this query over the base A-Box gives empty results.

Instead, considering query rewriting under OWL 2 QL, let us begin by extending the STAR(s) atom of this query according to [T3]:

$$Q'(b) \leftarrow \exists s \Big(\big(\text{ORBITS}(b,s) \land \text{STAR}(s) \big)$$
$$\lor \big(\text{ORBITS}(b,s) \land \text{COMPACTSTAR}(s) \big) \Big)$$

Observe that by [T4], we should consider anything with a value for TWINSTAR as a star as well (for which we add a new existential variable):

$$Q'(b) \leftarrow \exists s,t \Big(\big(\text{ORBITS}(b,s) \land \text{STAR}(s) \big)$$
$$\lor \big(\text{ORBITS}(b,s) \land \text{COMPACTSTAR}(s) \big)$$
$$\lor \big(\text{ORBITS}(b,s) \land \text{TWINSTAR}(s,t) \big) \Big)$$

Next we expand $\text{COMPACTSTAR}(s)$ according to [T2]:

$$Q'(b) \leftarrow \exists s, t \Big(\big(\text{ORBITS}(b,s) \wedge \text{STAR}(s)\big)$$
$$\vee \big(\text{ORBITS}(b,s) \wedge \text{COMPACTSTAR}(s)\big)$$
$$\vee \big(\text{ORBITS}(b,s) \wedge \text{TWINSTAR}(s,t)\big)$$
$$\vee \big(\text{ORBITS}(b,s) \wedge \text{COLLAPSAR}(s)\big) \Big)$$

Continuing recursively, we end up with the following expanded query:

$$Q'(b) \leftarrow \exists s, t \Big(\big(\text{ORBITS}(b,s) \wedge \text{STAR}(s)\big)$$
$$\vee \big(\text{ORBITS}(b,s) \wedge \text{COMPACTSTAR}(s)\big)$$
$$\vee \big(\text{ORBITS}(b,s) \wedge \text{TWINSTAR}(s,t)\big)$$
$$\vee \big(\text{ORBITS}(b,s) \wedge \text{COLLAPSAR}(s)\big)$$
$$\vee \big(\text{ORBITS}(b,s) \wedge \text{TWINSTAR}(t,s)\big)$$
$$\vee \big(\text{TWINSTAR}(b,s) \wedge \text{STAR}(s)\big)$$
$$\cdots$$
$$\vee \big(\text{TWINSTAR}(b,s) \wedge \text{TWINSTAR}(t,s)\big)$$
$$\vee \big(\text{TWINSTAR}(s,b) \wedge \text{STAR}(s)\big)$$
$$\cdots$$
$$\vee \big(\text{TWINSTAR}(s,b) \wedge \text{TWINSTAR}(t,s)\big)$$
$$\vee \text{PLANET}(b) \Big)$$

The results to this query would give KAPTEYNB, SIRIUSA, SIRIUSB and HDE226868 as results for the variable b.

The rewritten query takes the form of a union of conjunctive queries with unions of joins (in fact, it would be much more succinct to make a join over unions for query languages that allow this, however, the standard algorithm outputs a union of conjunctive queries [84]). We highlight that this query contains redundancy; for example, the clause $\text{TWINSTAR}(b,s) \wedge \text{TWINSTAR}(t,s)$ is equivalent to $\text{TWINSTAR}(b,s)$ since the existential variable b can always be mapped to t; furthermore, the clause $\text{TWINSTAR}(b,s) \wedge \text{STAR}(s)$ is redundant since the results it generates would always be contained in the aforementioned (less-specific) clause. In the original proposal of the query rewriting algorithm, the authors delegate the process of minimisation to the database engine [84].

We recall that the core of query languages such as SQL is based on first-order logic as used above to represent the input query Q and extended query Q'. Assuming the A-Box were indexed, for example, in a relational database with schema `Orbits(o1,o2)`, `Star(s)`, `TwinStar(t1,t2)`, etc., Q' could be written in SQL as follows:

```
SELECT o1 AS b FROM Orbits
  JOIN Star ON Orbits.o2 = Star.s
UNION SELECT o1 AS b FROM Orbits
  JOIN CompactStar ON Orbits.o2 = CompactStar.c
...
UNION SELECT p AS b FROM Planet
```

Running this query on the base data will give the expected solutions. We highlight that query rewriting aims to return unique solutions, and will not maintain multiplicities of solutions as allowed in SQL. This is implicit in the above example, where SQL's `UNION` applies set union. We further highlight that one could achieve the same result using the SPARQL query language for RDF (described in Chapter 6).

Remark 5.45 ⓘ

Though the complexity of query answering under OWL 2 QL does not escalate, and it can be implemented by means of query rewriting over existing optimised database engines, it is certainly not the case that OWL 2 QL entailment comes for "free" in terms of query answering. Indeed there is an fundamental caveat: the rewritten query may potentially be much larger than the input query (depending on the taxonomy). Furthermore, in database theory, data complexity [390] – considering only the size of the data in the input, not the query – is often studied under the rationale that queries, in practice, are somehow fixed as part of an application, or that they tend to be relatively simple with, for example, a fixed number of joins. Under that assumption, it is then reasonable to consider the input query as "fixed" since in practice, queries grow only so complex. In the case of DL-Lite, while it is a positive result that data complexity remains AC^0 (a necessary condition to allow query rewriting strategies, for example), this result "hides" the size and complexity of rewritten queries, whose growth depends on the T-Box and R-Box. On a more positive note, the combined complexity of query answering under OWL 2 QL – considering the A-Box (data), T-Box and R-Box (taxonomy) and the query – remains NP-complete.

5.6.3.4 OWL 2 RL

The third OWL 2 profile – called OWL 2 RL – is designed such that reasoning within the profile can be conducted using rule engines (such as Datalog-style systems) in a similar manner to which RDFS entailments can be supported using rules (see Section 4.4.1). The OWL 2 RL profile is inspired by a number of related proposals, key of which are Description Logic Programs (DLP) [156], and pD* [379]. The main design goal of OWL 2 RL is to define a sub-language of OWL 2 DL whose entailments can be captured by a succinct set of rules, such that the rule-based inferences of valid OWL 2 RL ontologies precisely capture entailments under the Direct Semantics. A set of such rules – called OWL 2 RL/RDF rules – is proposed by the standard. A major advantage of such rules is that they can be applied over any RDF graph, enabling sound but incomplete inferencing with respect to the RDF-Based Semantics of OWL. However, when applied on graphs that are not valid OWL 2 RL ontologies, this semantic correspondence with the Direct Semantics is lost, with reasoning being sound but now incomplete.

Where such a correspondence is considered important, ontologies should stay within the OWL 2 RL profile, which supports almost all of the OWL 2 vocabulary, but with the following restrictions to concept inclusions [280]:

- The left-hand-side of concept inclusions do not permit the top concept, nominals other than has-value ($\exists R.\{a\}$ is allowed), concept negation, universal restrictions, self-restrictions, nor (qualified) number restrictions.
- The right-hand-side of concept inclusions do not permit the top concept, concept union, nomimals and existential restrictions other than has-value, self restriction, nor (qualified) number restrictions other than at most 0/1.
- The top and bottom roles are not permitted.
- All OWL 2 DL datatypes, except `owl:real` and `owl:rational`, are supported. However, only intersection is supported for datatypes: one cannot define enumerations of datatypes nor facet restrictions in OWL 2 RL.

Example 5.42

To give an intuition of why these restrictions are thusly defined, consider, for example, $\forall R.C \sqsubseteq D$. To check if $D(a)$ holds, we may need to make sure that all possible values for a on the role R are from the class C, which is not possible to support by rules where we do not have a universal quantifier (or negation). On the other hand, for the definition $D \sqsubseteq \forall R.C$, this states that if we have $D(a)$ and $R(a,b)$, then it follows that $C(b)$, which is straightforward to support by a rule. For this reason, class restrictions of the form $\forall R.C$ are only allowed on the "easy" side of concept inclusions in OWL 2 RL, namely the right-hand-side.

Conversely, taking existential restrictions, consider $\exists R.C \sqsubseteq D$. This is relatively straightforward to support since if we have $R(a,b)$ and $C(b)$, we can then infer $D(a)$: so long as no other feature can entail existential individuals, this can be easily supported by a rule. Now consider $D \sqsubseteq \exists R.C$. For this case, we would need to consider existential individuals in the reasoning process. Hence existential restrictions are considered on the left-hand-side, but not the right-hand-side of OWL 2 RL.

Finally, taking has-value restrictions of the form $\exists R.\{b\}$, consider $\exists R.\{b\} \sqsubseteq C$; if we have $R(a,b)$, we can infer $C(a)$. On the other hand, consider $C \sqsubseteq \exists R.\{b\}$; if we have $C(a)$ we can infer $R(a,b)$. Inferences in both directions are straightforward to support with rules, and hence OWL 2 RL supports has-value restrictions on both sides.

Again the benefit of these restrictions is that they permit OWL 2 RL entailments to be captured by rule-based engines. Along these lines, the standard proposes the OWL 2 RL/RDF rules, which can be applied directly over any RDF graph. These rules are presented for reference in Tables 5.5 and 5.6 using a Turtle-style syntax, where we use ?u, ?v, etc., to denote variables. The term FALSE indicates a contradiction: the graph is inconsistent.

Remark 5.46 ⓘ

We write rules in an informal syntax for reasons of space. However, these rules (aside from rules dt-*) can be represented as Horn clauses/FOL implications/Datalog rules, or any such rule language.

The standard proposes, for example, to use a single ternary predicate $T(s,p,o)$ to represent triples. Taking prp-dom, for example:

$$\text{?p rdfs:domain ?c . ?x ?p ?y . } \rightarrow \text{ ?y a ?c .}$$

This rule could be more formally represented as an FOL implication:

$$T(y, \text{rdf:type}, c) \leftarrow \exists x, p \big(T(x,p,y) \wedge T(p, \text{rdfs:domain}, c) \big)$$

With respect to this rule-set, we make the following remarks:

- The identifiers for rules indicate six groupings of rules:

  eq-* prefixes rules for equality and inequality;
  prp-* prefixes rules for property/role axioms;
  cls-* prefixes rules for class/concept definitions;
  cax-* prefixes rules for class/concept axioms;
  dt-* prefixes rules for datatypes;
  scm-* prefixes rules for schema (IF-AND-ONLY-IF) inferences.

- A number of rules (e.g., eq-diff2, prp-key, prp-key, cls-uni, etc.) involve arbitrary-length lists in their premises. These can be supported as multiple rules with fixed-arity predicates (see Remark 5.47).
- Rule prp-ap is simply a shortcut for axiomatic triples declaring the built-in properties rdfs:label, rdfs:comment, owl:priorVersion, etc., to be annotation properties (see Section 5.4.6).

- Rules cls-thing and cls-nothing1 have empty premises: again they can be thought of as adding axiomatic triples that always hold.
- Rules dt-* supporting datatypes are different from other rules. These rules suppose a datatype-map that can reason about which values are contained/not contained in which supported datatypes, which values are same-as/different-from each other, etc. Given a datatype with infinite values, such as xsd:integer, it suffices to apply these rules considering only the (finite set of) literals that appear in the ontology/graph [280].
- To support equality/inequality of datatype values (dt-eq, dt-diff), an efficient strategy is to "canonicalise" literals appearing in the data by mapping various lexical strings with the same value to one canonical form; for example, literals such as "+001"^^xsd:integer, "1"^^xsd:byte, "+1.000"^^xsd:decimal, etc., can all be mapped to "1"^^xsd:decimal. This then permits syntactic (in)equality to be (passively) applied.
- As in the case of RDFS (see Section 4.4.3), some rules may produce triples with literals in the subject position, or blank nodes or literals in the predicate position; in other words, some OWL 2 RL/RDF rules may produce invalid RDF triples. Application of OWL 2 RL/RDF rules should allow generalised RDF triples as part of the intermediate conclusions as they may later lead to the inference of valid RDF triples.
- These rules are not minimal; for example, eq-trans is covered by eq-rep-s, while prp-eqp1 and prp-eqp2 are both covered by a combination of prp-spo1 and scm-eqp1. On the other hand, the rules are not maximal; for example, no rule covers the symmetry of owl:differentFrom or owl:inverseOf. More generally, the schema rules that entail concept and role axioms are largely incomplete. The OWL 2 RL/RDF rules are, however, sufficient to cover A-Box entailments of role, concept and equality assertions for OWL 2 RL ontologies as mandated by the Direct Semantics [280].

Remark 5.47   (i)

Rules containing arbitrary-length lists can also be codified using rules with fixed-arity predicates. For example, take rule cls-uni, which is written informally in Table 5.5 with the shorthand:

  ?c owl:unionOf (?c$_1$ ... ?c$_n$) . ?y a ?c$_i$. $(1 \leq i \leq n) \rightarrow$?y a ?c .

In order to traverse the list, we can first write rules as follows:

$$T(l, \texttt{:contains}, f) \leftarrow T(l, \texttt{rdf:first}, f)$$
$$T(l_1, \texttt{:contains}, f) \leftarrow \exists l_2 \big(T(l_1, \texttt{rdf:rest}, l_2)$$
$$\wedge\, T(l_2, \texttt{:contains}, f) \big)$$

This populates the new relation :contains, which gives all elements of a list (including recursive sub-lists). Then cls-uni can become:

$$T(y, \texttt{rdf:type}, c) \leftarrow \exists c_i, l \big(T(c, \texttt{owl:unionOf}, l)$$
$$\wedge T(l_2, \texttt{:contains}, c_i)$$
$$\wedge T(y, \texttt{rdf:type}, c_i) \big)$$

Such a pattern can be applied to any rule that applies an inference for each element of a list. However, note that rules eq-diff2, eq-diff3, prp-adp and cax-adc are applied over pairs of distinct list members, which may be done by syntactic inequality, or by another rule of the form:

$$T(f_1, \texttt{:diff}, f_2) \leftarrow \exists l_1, l_2 \big(T(l_1, \texttt{rdf:first}, f_1)$$
$$\wedge T(l_1, \texttt{rdf:rest}, l_2)$$
$$\wedge T(l_2, \texttt{:contains}, f_2) \big)$$

Distinct pairs of list members can now be matched with the pattern:

$$\ldots \wedge T(l, \texttt{:contains}, f_1) \wedge T(l, \texttt{:contains}, f_2) \wedge T(f_1, \texttt{:diff}, f_2) \ldots$$

Next rule cls-int1 requires checking that an individual is a member of all elements of a list. This can be done with multiple rules as follows:

$$T(y, \texttt{:fills}, l) \leftarrow \exists f \big(T(l, \texttt{rdf:first}, f)$$
$$\wedge T(l, \texttt{rdf:rest}, \texttt{rdf:nil})$$
$$\wedge T(y, \texttt{rdf:type}, f) \big)$$
$$T(y, \texttt{:fills}, l_1) \leftarrow \exists f_1, l_2 \big(T(l_1, \texttt{rdf:first}, f_1)$$
$$\wedge T(l_1, \texttt{rdf:rest}, l_2)$$
$$\wedge T(y, \texttt{:fills}, l_2)$$
$$\wedge T(y, \texttt{rdf:type}, f_1) \big)$$

Here the relation :fills states that the subject has all the types mentioned recursively in the object (sub-)list. Thereafter, rule cls-int1 can be straightforwardly expressed as:

$$T(y, \texttt{rdf:type}, c) \leftarrow \exists l \big(T(c, \texttt{owl:unionOf}, l)$$
$$\wedge T(y, \texttt{:fills}, l) \big)$$

However, in the case of prp-spo2, some way to represent higher-arity information – be it a different ternary predicate, or the ability to generate new (existential) nodes – is needed since we must remember three elements: the source node, the target node, and the (sub-)list whose chain is satisfied by a path from the source to the target. Likewise prp-key requires remembering three elements: the two candidate individuals who are same-as and the sub-list of properties they satisfy as a complex key. Higher arity features are available in many rule-based formalisms.

The above rules assume, in some sense, that the collections are well-formed. Another option is to develop custom procedural methods to pre-process collections (possibly prior to using an existing rule engine).

Ultimately, the OWL 2 RL/RDF rules can then be applied recursively to any RDF graph to materialise inferences in a similar style to how RDFS reasoning is conducted. Thus, OWL 2 RL/RDF rules offer a standard rule-set for systems that wish to extend RDFS-style reasoning to cover a broad range of features of OWL. A major benefit of such an approach is that it is applicable to arbitrary RDF graphs, not only those that meet the syntactic restrictions of the OWL 2 RL profile. This can be particularly useful when working, for example, with Web data, where documents may not always meet the (sometimes complex) restrictions imposed by OWL for the purposes of decidability. In this setting, OWL 2 RL/RDF rules offer incomplete reasoning – where not all entailments are covered by the inferencing procedure – but where all inferences produced are entailed according to the OWL semantics.

Along these lines, a number of systems have been proposed that support OWL 2 RL/RDF-based inference, including DLEJena [267], QueryPIE [387] and Oracle [238]. Other systems supporting Datalog-style reasoning – such as RDFox [287] – can also be leveraged for OWL 2 RL/RDF-based inferencing.

Remark 5.48 (**i**)

One may be wondering what is the difference between the OWL 2 RL/RDF rules and the rule-based languages – such as SWRL and RIF – discussed in Section 5.4.7. The short answer is that OWL 2 RL/RDF rules are designed specifically to (partially) cover inferencing with respect to OWL semantics, while proposals such as SWRL and RIF allow for expressing general rules that may go beyond what can be expressed in OWL. However, OWL 2 RL/RDF rules could be expressed in such rule languages, where, for example, an encoding of the OWL 2 RL/RDF rules in RIF Core has been published such that OWL 2 RL reasoning can be done in RIF-compliant engines [332].

In terms of complexity, OWL 2 RL is PTIME-complete for all standard tasks in taxonomic and data complexity (including conjunctive query answering); however, class satisfiability, class subsumption and instance checking become intractable in combined complexity (co-NP-complete).

Table 5.5 OWL 2 RL/RDF rules (Part I)

ID	if G matches	then G OWL-entails
eq-ref	?s ?p ?o .	?s owl:sameAs ?s . ?p owl:sameAs ?p . ?o owl:sameAs ?o .
eq-sym	?x owl:sameAs ?y .	?y owl:sameAs ?x .
eq-trans	?x owl:sameAs ?y . ?y owl:sameAs ?z .	?x owl:sameAs ?z .
eq-rep-s	?s owl:sameAs ?s' . ?s ?p ?o .	?s' ?p ?o .
eq-rep-p	?p owl:sameAs ?p' . ?s ?p ?o .	?s ?p' ?o .
eq-rep-o	?o owl:sameAs ?o' . ?s ?p ?o .	?s ?p ?o' .
eq-diff1	?x owl:sameAs ?y ; owl:differentFrom ?y .	FALSE
eq-diff2	?x a owl:AllDifferent ; owl:members (?y_1 ... ?y_n) . ?y_i owl:sameAs ?y_j . $(1 \leq i < j \leq n)$	FALSE
eq-diff3	?x a owl:AllDifferent ; owl:distinctMembers (?y_1 ... ?y_n) . ?y_i owl:sameAs ?y_j . $(1 \leq i < j \leq n)$	FALSE
prp-ap	[?p a built-in annotation property]	?p a owl:AnnotationProperty .
prp-dom	?p rdfs:domain ?c . ?x ?p ?y .	?x a ?c .
prp-rng	?p rdfs:range ?c . ?x ?p ?y .	?y a ?c .
prp-fp	?p a owl:FunctionalProperty . ?x ?p ?y_1 . ?x ?p ?y_2 .	?y_1 owl:sameAs ?y_2 .
prp-ifp	?p a owl:InverseFunctionalProperty . ?x_1 ?p ?y . ?x_2 ?p ?y .	?x_1 owl:sameAs ?x_2 .
prp-irp	?p a owl:IrreflexiveProperty . ?x ?p ?x .	FALSE
prp-symp	?p a owl:SymmetricProperty . ?x ?p ?y .	?y ?p ?x .
prp-asyp	?p a owl:AsymmetricProperty . ?x ?p ?y . ?y ?p ?x .	FALSE
prp-trp	?p a owl:TransitiveProperty . ?x ?p ?y . ?y ?p ?z .	?x ?p ?z .
prp-spo1	?p_1 rdfs:subPropertyOf ?p_2 . ?x ?p_1 ?y .	?x ?p_2 ?y .
prp-spo2	?p owl:propertyChainAxiom (?p_1 ... ?p_n) . ?a_1 ?p_1 ?a_2 . ... ?a_n ?p_n ?a_{n+1} .	?a_1 ?p ?a_{n+1} .
prp-eqp1	?p_1 owl:equivalentProperty ?p_2 . ?x ?p_1 ?y .	?x ?p_2 ?y .
prp-eqp2	?p_1 owl:equivalentProperty ?p_2 . ?x ?p_2 ?y .	?x ?p_1 ?y .
prp-pdw	?p_1 owl:propertyDisjointWith ?p_2 . ?x ?p_1 ?y . ?x ?p_2 ?y .	FALSE
prp-adp	?x a owl:AllDisjointProperties ; owl:members (?p_1 ... ?p_n) . ?y ?p_i ?z ; ?p_j ?z . $(1 \leq i < j \leq n)$	FALSE
prp-inv1	?p_1 owl:inverseOf ?p_2 . ?x ?p_1 ?y .	?y ?p_2 ?x .
prp-inv2	?p_1 owl:inverseOf ?p_2 . ?y ?p_2 ?x .	?x ?p_1 ?y .
prp-key	?c owl:hasKey (?p_1 ... ?p_n) . ?x a ?c ; ?p_1 ?z_1 ; ... ; ?p_n ?z_n . ?y a ?c ; ?p_1 ?z_1 ; ... ; ?p_n ?z_n .	?x owl:sameAs ?y .
prp-npa1	?x owl:sourceIndividual ?s ; owl:assertionProperty ?p ; owl:targetIndividual ?o . ?s ?p ?o .	FALSE
prp-npa2	?x owl:sourceIndividual ?s ; owl:assertionProperty ?p ; owl:targetValue ?o . ?s ?p ?o .	FALSE
cls-thing		owl:Thing a owl:Class .
cls-nothing1		owl:Nothing a owl:Class .
cls-nothing2	?x a owl:Nothing .	FALSE
cls-int1	?c owl:intersectionOf (?c_1 ... ?c_n) . ?y a ?c_1 , ..., ?c_n .	?y a ?c .
cls-int2	?c owl:intersectionOf (?c_1 ... ?c_n) . ?y a ?c .	?y a ?c_1 , ..., ?c_n .
cls-uni	?c owl:unionOf (?c_1 ... ?c_n) . ?y a ?c_i . $(1 \leq i \leq n)$	?y a ?c .
cls-com	?c_1 owl:complementOf ?c2 . ?x a ?c_1 , ?c_2 .	FALSE
cls-svf1	?x owl:someValuesFrom ?y ; owl:onProperty ?p . ?u ?p ?v . ?v a ?y .	?u a ?x .
cls-svf2	?x owl:someValuesFrom owl:Thing ; owl:onProperty ?p . ?u ?p ?v .	?u a ?x .
cls-avf	?x owl:allValuesFrom ?y ; owl:onProperty ?p . ?u ?p ?v ; a ?x .	?v a ?y .
cls-hv1	?x owl:hasValue ?y ; owl:onProperty ?p . ?u a ?x .	?u ?p ?y .
cls-hv2	?x owl:hasValue ?y ; owl:onProperty ?p . ?u ?p ?y .	?u a ?x .
cls-maxc1	?x owl:maxCardinality 0 ; owl:onProperty ?p . ?u a ?x ; ?p ?y .	FALSE
cls-maxc2	?x owl:maxCardinality 1 ; owl:onProperty ?p . ?u a ?x ; ?p ?y_1 , ?y_2 .	?y_1 owl:sameAs ?y_2 .
cls-maxqc1	?x owl:maxQualifiedCardinality 0 ; owl:onProperty ?p ; owl:onClass ?c . ?u a ?x ; ?p ?y . ?y a ?c .	FALSE
cls-maxqc2	?x owl:maxQualifiedCardinality 0 ; owl:onProperty ?p ; owl:onClass owl:Thing . ?u a ?x ; ?p ?y .	FALSE
cls-maxqc3	?x owl:maxQualifiedCardinality 1 ; owl:onProperty ?p ; owl:onClass ?c . ?u a ?x ; ?p ?y_1 , ?y_2 . ?y_1 a ?c . ?y_2 a ?c .	?y_1 owl:sameAs ?y_2 .
cls-maxqc4	?x owl:maxQualifiedCardinality 1 ; owl:onProperty ?p ; owl:onClass owl:Thing . ?u a ?x ; ?p ?y_1 , ?y_2 .	?y_1 owl:sameAs ?y_2 .
cls-oo	?c owl:oneOf (?y_1 ... ?y_n) .	?y_1 a ?c . ... ?y_n a ?c .

Table 5.6 OWL 2 RL/RDF rules (Part II)

ID	if G matches	then G OWL-entails
cax-sco	$?c_1$ rdfs:subClassOf $?c_2$. $?x$ a $?c_1$.	$?x$ a $?c_2$.
cax-eqc1	$?c_1$ owl:equivalentClass $?c_2$. $?x$ a $?c_1$.	$?x$ a $?c_2$.
cax-eqc2	$?c_1$ owl:equivalentClass $?c_2$. $?x$ a $?c_2$.	$?x$ a $?c_1$.
cax-dw	$?c_1$ owl:disjointWith $?c_2$. $?x$ a $?c_1$, $?c_2$.	FALSE
cax-adc	$?x$ a owl:AllDisjointClasses ; owl:members $(?c_1 \dots ?c_n)$. $?y$ a $?c_i$, $?c_j$. $(1 \le i < j \le n)$	FALSE
dt-type1	[$?dt$ a supported datatype]	$?dt$ a rdfs:Datatype .
dt-type2	[$?lt$ a literal in supported datatype $?dt$]	$?lt$ a $?dt$.
dt-eq	[$?lt_1$ same data value as $?lt_2$]	$?lt_1$ owl:sameAs $?lt_2$.
dt-diff	[$?lt_1$ different data value to $?lt_2$]	$?lt_1$ owl:differentFrom $?lt_2$.
dt-not-type	$?lt$ a $?dt$. [$?lt$ not a value in $?dt$]	FALSE
scm-cls	$?c$ a owl:Class .	$?c$ rdfs:subClassOf $?c$. $?c$ owl:equivalentClass $?c$. $?c$ rdfs:subClassOf owl:Thing . owl:Nothing rdfs:subClassOf $?c$.
scm-sco	$?c_1$ rdfs:subClassOf $?c_2$. $?c_2$ rdfs:subClassOf $?c_3$.	$?c_1$ rdfs:subClassOf $?c_3$.
scm-eqc1	$?c_1$ owl:equivalentClass $?c_2$.	$?c_1$ rdfs:subClassOf $?c_2$. $?c_2$ rdfs:subClassOf $?c_1$.
scm-eqc2	$?c_1$ rdfs:subClassOf $?c_2$. $?c_2$ rdfs:subClassOf $?c_1$.	$?c_1$ owl:equivalentClass $?c_2$.
scm-op	$?p$ rdf:type owl:ObjectProperty .	$?p$ rdfs:subPropertyOf $?p$. $?p$ owl:equivalentProperty $?p$.
scm-dp	$?p$ rdf:type owl:DatatypeProperty .	$?p$ rdfs:subPropertyOf $?p$. $?p$ owl:equivalentProperty $?p$.
scm-spo	$?p_1$ rdfs:subPropertyOf $?p_2$. $?p_2$ rdfs:subPropertyOf $?p_3$.	$?p_1$ rdfs:subPropertyOf $?p_3$.
scm-eqp1	$?p_1$ owl:equivalentProperty $?p_2$.	$?p_1$ rdfs:subPropertyOf $?p_2$. $?p_2$ rdfs:subPropertyOf $?p_1$.
scm-eqp2	$?p_1$ rdfs:subPropertyOf $?p_2$. $?p_2$ rdfs:subPropertyOf $?p_1$.	$?p_1$ owl:equivalentProperty $?p_2$.
scm-dom1	$?p$ rdfs:domain $?c_1$. $?c_1$ rdfs:subClassOf $?c_2$.	$?p$ rdfs:domain $?c_2$.
scm-dom2	$?p_2$ rdfs:domain $?c$. $?p_1$ rdfs:subPropertyOf $?p_2$.	$?p_1$ rdfs:domain $?c$.
scm-rng1	$?p$ rdfs:range $?c_1$. $?c_1$ rdfs:subClassOf $?c_2$.	$?p$ rdfs:range $?c_2$.
scm-rng2	$?p_2$ rdfs:range $?c$. $?p_1$ rdfs:subPropertyOf $?p_2$.	$?p_1$ rdfs:range $?c$.
scm-hv	$?c_1$ owl:hasValue $?x$; owl:onProperty $?p_1$. $?c_2$ owl:hasValue $?x$; owl:onProperty $?p_2$. $?p_1$ rdfs:subPropertyOf $?p_2$.	$?c_1$ rdfs:subClassOf $?c_2$.
scm-svf1	$?c_1$ owl:someValuesFrom $?d_1$; owl:onProperty $?p$. $?c_2$ owl:someValuesFrom $?d_2$; owl:onProperty $?p$. $?d_1$ rdfs:subClassOf $?d_2$.	$?c_1$ rdfs:subClassOf $?c_2$.
scm-svf2	$?c_1$ owl:someValuesFrom $?d$; owl:onProperty $?p_1$. $?c_2$ owl:someValuesFrom $?d$; owl:onProperty $?p_2$. $?p_1$ rdfs:subPropertyOf $?p_2$.	$?c_1$ rdfs:subClassOf $?c_2$.
scm-avf1	$?c_1$ owl:allValuesFrom $?d_1$; owl:onProperty $?p$. $?c_2$ owl:allValuesFrom $?d_2$; owl:onProperty $?p$. $?d_1$ rdfs:subClassOf $?d_2$.	$?c_1$ rdfs:subClassOf $?c_2$.
scm-avf2	$?c_1$ owl:allValuesFrom $?d$; owl:onProperty $?p_1$. $?c_2$ owl:allValuesFrom $?d$; owl:onProperty $?p_2$. $?p_1$ rdfs:subPropertyOf $?p_2$.	$?c_1$ rdfs:subClassOf $?c_2$.
scm-int	$?c$ owl:intersectionOf $(?c_1 \dots ?c_n)$.	$?c$ rdfs:subClassOf $?c_1$, $\dots$, $?c_n$.
scm-uni	$?c$ owl:unionOf $(?c_1 \dots ?c_n)$.	$?c_1$ rdfs:subClassOf $?c$. $\dots$ $?c_n$ rdfs:subClassOf $?c$.

5.6.4 Complexity

For reference, in Table 5.7, we summarise the complexity of two tasks – namely Ontology Satisfiability (O.S.) and Conjunctive Query Answering (Q.A.) – for the OWL 2 languages and profiles discussed thus far. For comparison, we also present the complexity of OWL 1 DL [280]. These complexity classes and categorisations are discussed in more detail in Remark 5.43. However, for ease of understanding, we also shade the cells in terms of possible difficulty, with lighter cells indicating lesser computational complexity.[7] We further make the following clarifying remarks:

- Query complexity applies to Conjunctive Query Answering; N/A denotes that query complexity is not applicable for Ontology Satisfiability.
- OWL 2 Full is interpreted under the RDF-Based Semantics, while all other languages are interpreted under the Direct Semantics.
- We denote problems that are complete for that class with the suffix -C, while in cases where no such result is given, we use ∈ to denote memberships of the given complexity class as an upper-bound.
- Some problems are denoted as DECIDABILITY OPEN meaning that it is not yet known whether or not the problem is decidable.
- In almost all cases, the tasks of class satisfiability, class subsumption and instance checking have the same complexity as ontology satisfiability; the lone exception is OWL 2 RL, which is co-NP-complete for these additional tasks under combined complexity.[8]

Visually, this table helps to motivate the definition of the OWL 2 Profiles discussed previously: namely, we see that these profiles are associated with a number of lightly-coloured cells indicating that tractable reasoning is possible (with classes within PTIME being considered tractable, per convention).

5.7 Summary

In this chapter, we discussed the Web Ontology Language (OWL 2) standard, and how it extends RDFS with a broad range of novel, well-defined vocabulary. This vocabulary allows Web publishers to make claims under an expressive semantics, and in so doing, to create, reuse, extend and/or map ontologies. These ontologies then offer a machine-readable understanding of domain terms that, where agreed-upon, can be used for the principled exchange of data over the Web – within or across domains – further supported

---

[7] We consider possible difficulty, meaning that we shade, for example, NP-complete darker than PTIME-complete although it is not known whether or not PTIME = NP.

[8] We cannot reduce such tasks to ontology satisfiability since we cannot negate concept inclusions or concept assertions in OWL 2 RL.

Table 5.7 Summary of complexity of Ontology Satisfiability (O.S.) and Conjunctive Query Answering (Q.A.) for the OWL 2 Languages and OWL 1 DL [280]

Language	Task	Complexity			
		Taxonomy	*Data*	*Query*	*Combined*
OWL 2 Full	O.S.	UNDECIDABLE	UNDECIDABLE	N/A	UNDECIDABLE
	Q.A.	UNDECIDABLE			
OWL 2 DL	O.S.	N2EXPTIME-c	∈ N2EXPTIME	N/A	N2EXPTIME-c
	Q.A.	DECIDABILITY OPEN			
OWL 2 EL	O.S.	PTIME-c	PTIME-c	N/A	PTIME-c
	Q.A.	∈ EXPTIME	PTIME-c	NP-c	∈ EXPTIME
OWL 2 QL	O.S.	NLOGSPACE-c	AC^0	N/A	NLOGSPACE-c
	Q.A.	NLOGSPACE-c	AC^0	NP-c	NP-c
OWL 2 RL	O.S.	PTIME-c	PTIME-c	N/A	PTIME-c
	Q.A.	PTIME-c	PTIME-c	NP-c	NP-c
OWL 1 DL	O.S.	NEXPTIME-c	∈ NEXPTIME	N/A	NEXPTIME-c
	Q.A.	DECIDABILITY OPEN			

by automated reasoning methods. The semantics of OWL thus (largely) subsumes and far surpasses that defined for RDFS, capturing equality and inequality of individuals, novel axioms about properties (e.g., that CONTAINS is transitive, that ISBN is a key), complex class definitions and axioms (e.g., that the class NOBEL LAUREATE has WON something that is a member of the class NOBEL PRIZE), as well as definitions of novel datatypes (e.g., that CELCIUS is a datatype derived from decimal with a minimum value of -273.15).

However, we also discussed how this added expressivity comes at the high cost of undecidability for reasoning tasks interpreting the OWL 2 language without restriction. In practice, this undecidability result means that any reasoning algorithm for the unrestricted language will, on some inputs, be forced to return an incorrect/incomplete answer, or to run forever. To restore decidability of reasoning, the OWL standards thus draw upon theoretical results from the Description Logics community, which focuses on defining expressive but restricted languages for which reasoning tasks become decidable. These results thus guide the definition of the OWL 2 DL language, aiming to apply just enough restrictions to reinstate the decidability of reasoning.

Still, although with OWL 2 DL the decidability of some reasoning tasks is restored, these tasks still incur a very high computational cost. Furthermore, decidability remains open for applications requiring query answering over OWL 2 DL. Hence OWL 2 defines three profiles – sub-languages that further restrict OWL 2 DL – targeting specific use-cases where it may be desirable to trade expressivity for more efficient reasoning. As its main use-case,

OWL 2 EL targets class-based reasoning for large but relatively inexpressive ontologies that formalise domain-specific taxonomies. On the other hand, OWL 2 QL focuses on efficient query answering, defining a language that allows reasoning to be implemented using existing database systems through query rewritings. Finally, OWL 2 RL enables reasoning to be implemented using rule-based systems that can be applied for sound but incomplete reasoning on arbitrary RDF graphs, which is useful in scenarios where data may use the OWL vocabulary without restriction. These three profiles greatly reduce the complexity burden of reasoning, but at the cost of expressivity.

5.8 Discussion

Discussion 5.8

JULIE: Does the Web of Data really require OWL?

AIDAN: Data – in whatever format they may find themselves – are described using various terms, be they the names of columns, the values of cells, the keys of a dictionary, the elements of an array. If we want machines to be able to collect and combine data from multiple sources in intelligent ways, those machines need to "understand" how these terms relate to one another, both within a single dataset, and across datasets. The more profoundly the machine understands the relations between such terms, the more "intelligently" it can combine and repurpose data for novel applications. A pragmatic way to have machines "understand" such relations between terms is to simply tell them such relations using machine-readable (formal) languages. Machines can then process and draw conclusions from the relations between terms using reasoning algorithms.

JULIE: And OWL is one such language we can use.

AIDAN: Yes, but when we consider modelling more and more complex relations between terms – like that a PERSON *has* 2 PARENTs, or that INFLUENZA is a DISEASE caused by *some* VIRUS, or that whatever a PLANET ORBITS *must be* a STAR – while this allows machines to draw seemingly even more intelligent, automated conclusions from data using those terms, we quickly reach a limit where reasoning becomes intractable and eventually undecidable: for some inputs, no matter how powerful a machine or how clever an implementation we may imagine, reasoning can never completely finish.

JULIE: So then ...

AIDAN: So then we are faced with three options: we can build reasoners that stop with some incomplete conclusions, or we can limit the language so as to allow reasoning to become decidable/tractable again,

or we can simply accept that reasoners will in some cases run forever. We will always face these options when creating increasingly-
detailed, formal descriptions of the world for machines to deductively reason about. There are limits to what machines can do.
These options are then also fundamental to OWL, and also part of
the reason why it makes for a complex standard: different languages
of OWL take different stances with respect to these three options,
pushing the limits of expressivity and complexity in different ways.

ANNA: But what about OWL as a *Web* Ontology Language? ...

FRANK: ... yes, in practice, doesn't OWL somehow assume that ontologies will always be correctly described? What happens when
OWL reasoners are faced with erroneous definitions and incorrect
claims? If something like OWL really began to take off on the Web,
what would stop people from creating spam to force reasoners to
make erroneous conclusions that may be beneficial for some scam
or another? Would OWL not become a victim of its own success?

AIDAN: OWL does not take a stance on the "correctness" of the definitions and axioms it can be used to describe. OWL rather allows
publishers to make *claims* backed by a formal semantics. Like any
information we may find on the Web, claims made in OWL should
not be taken as facts: we should take into consideration the source
of data, how well-linked the ontology is, and so on.

ANNA: But the OWL standard appears to be very complex. Doesn't
this create a barrier to adoption, particularly on the Web?

AIDAN: That is a valid concern and it is probably fair to say that the
OWL standard is not celebrated for its conciseness. But the general
idea is that people can cherry-pick and focus on the parts of the
standard that are of most value for whatever they want to achieve.
For example, if someone is interested in efficient query answering
under OWL entailment, they may choose to focus on OWL 2 QL
and not worry about the rest of the standard. Or if they are interested in rule-based reasoning, they might take (some of) the
OWL 2 RL/RDF rules and apply them. OWL is complex, in part,
because it offers various options as to how it is implemented and
how it is used to describe ontologies. As we will see later in Chapter 8, many of the most frequently used ontologies currently on the
Web use only a small subset of the full range of OWL features – for
defining same-as relations, inverse properties, disjoint classes, etc.
– avoiding complex class definitions, for example.

Chapter 6
SPARQL Query Language

Given a collection of RDF data, a user may naturally have some questions that they would like to answer over that collection, such as *"which Nobel Literature laureates have fought in wars?"*. However, machines struggle to interpret complex questions posed in natural language [249]. Hence a query language allows clients – be they human or machine – to express questions in a machine-readable format, where the solutions that the resulting query shall return for a given data collection are unambiguous and well-defined by the language. The **SPARQL Protocol And RDF Query Language (SPARQL)** is then the W3C-recommended query language for RDF [169].

Example 6.1

Considering the graph shown in Figure 6.1, assume that we are interested in finding the Nobel Laureates in Literature that have fought in wars, returning the IRI for the winner, the year of the award and the year the war ended. We may express this query in SPARQL as:

```
PREFIX : <http://ex.org/>
SELECT ?nplWinner ?nplYear ?warEndYear
WHERE {
  ?npl a :NobelPrizeLiterature ; :year ?nplYear ; :winner ?nplWinner .
  ?war :combatant ?nplWinner ; :end ?warEndYear .
}
```

SPARQL query syntax is inspired by the Turtle RDF syntax, where terms beginning with '?' (or '$') indicate variables that match any term in the graph. Running this query over the aforementioned graph returns:

?nplWinner	?nplYear	?warEndYear
:SPrudhomme	"1901"^^xsd:gYear	"1871"^^xsd:gYear

Further details of the query will be explained later in the chapter.

© Springer Nature Switzerland AG 2020
A. Hogan, *The Web of Data*, https://doi.org/10.1007/978-3-030-51580-5_6

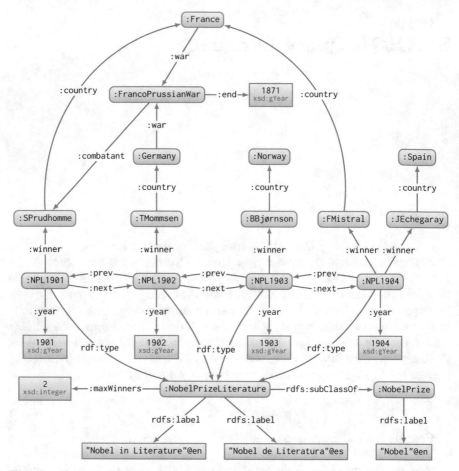

Fig. 6.1 Example RDF graph describing winners of Nobel Prizes for Literature

---

Remark 6.1   (i)

A reader familiar with the SQL language used for querying (and
managing) relational databases may recognise some of the syntactic
keywords used in the SPARQL query of Example 6.1 (in particular,
SELECT and WHERE). Many features of SPARQL are inspired by SQL,
both in terms of syntax and semantics. Much like in SQL, the most
popular form of query in SPARQL returns tables of results. However,
SPARQL offers a number of graph-specific features not supported in
SQL, such as the ability to return graphs, to reference paths of arbitrary
length, etc. We discuss such features later in the chapter.

6.1 Overview

In this chapter, we discuss the SPARQL Protocol and RDF Query Language (SPARQL), used to express queries over RDF as illustrated in Example 6.1. We will first discuss details of the query language, including: patterns that allow for matching sub-graphs, various relational-style operators that can be used to express more complex queries, expressions that allow to capture arbitrary-length paths, as well as features that allow for querying multiple RDF graphs and external datasets. We then provide formal definitions for the language. Later we cover features to update data, support for entailment, the protocol by which SPARQL queries can be executed over the Web, as well as a vocabulary to describe SPARQL services on the Web.

Historical Note 6.1

SPARQL was preceded by various proposals for RDF query languages [30], including RQL [82], SquishQL [274] and RDQL [354], amongst others. SPARQL first became a W3C Recommendation in 2008 [328], with the extended SPARQL 1.1 standard finalised in 2013 [169]. This chapter reflects the SPARQL 1.1 standard [169]; we will use the marker '†' to denote features new to SPARQL 1.1.

The remainder of this chapter is structured as follows:

Section 6.2 discusses the SPARQL query language.
Section 6.3 formally defines the core of the SPARQL query language and discusses issues relating to semantics and complexity.
Section 6.4 discusses SPARQL Federation for querying external services.
Section 6.5 describes the SPARQL Update language for modifying data.
Section 6.6 discusses the SPARQL Entailment Profiles, designed to extend query results according to various notions of semantic entailment.
Section 6.7 describes the SPARQL Protocol for querying over the Web, along with a vocabulary for describing SPARQL services.
Sections 6.8 and 6.9 conclude the chapter with a summary and discussion.

6.2 SPARQL Query Language

We now discuss the cornerstone of the SPARQL standard: the SPARQL query language. By means of examples, we will illustrate the syntax and various features supported by the language, starting with the most elemental features, building towards more and more powerful expressions. Later in Section 6.3 we will provide a more formal treatment of the core of the language.

In Figure 6.2, we represent the anatomy of a SPARQL query, which is inspired by Turtle syntax (see Section 3.8.3) and composed of six parts:

1. *Base and prefix declarations*: Similar to the Turtle syntax for RDF, base and prefix IRIs can be declared and later used to abbreviate IRIs.
2. *Dataset construction*: Rather than being defined on a single RDF graph, SPARQL is defined on datasets composed of multiple graphs, where a custom dataset can be composed for a particular query.
3. *Query type and solution modifiers*: SPARQL supports four query types:

   SELECT: Returns a table as the result.
   ASK: Returns true if there exists any result; false otherwise.
   CONSTRUCT: Returns an RDF graph as the result.
   DESCRIBE: Returns an RDF graph describing terms or solutions.

   In the case of SELECT, solution modifiers allow for controlling whether or not duplicate solutions can (REDUCED) or must (DISTINCT) be removed.
4. *Where clause*: specifies the patterns to be matched in the graph(s) being queried in order to generate solutions.
5. *Aggregation*: indicates variables or other expressions by which results should be grouped, which allow aggregate functions (SUM, MAX, MIN, etc.) to be applied within each group, and further allows solutions to be filtered depending on the result of the aggregation function.
6. *Solution modifiers*: states how the solutions should be ordered, how many solutions to return and how many to skip.

These parts of a SPARQL query will be discussed in further detail in this chapter. The most elemental (and most commonly used [342]) query type is the SELECT type; the following discussion initially focuses on SELECT queries, where other query types will be discussed later in Section 6.2.12.

Remark 6.2 ⓘ

Although the anatomy of a SPARQL query shown in Figure 6.2 captures the most commonly used syntax, it is intended to be illustrative rather than exhaustive. For simplicity, some types of queries and shortcuts are not shown. For example, the following is a valid query in SPARQL though it is not captured by Figure 6.2:

```
DESCRIBE <http://ex.org/Norway>
```

The query requests a description of the resource identified by the given IRI. Other abbreviations, such as omitting the WHERE keyword in certain queries, omitting the CONSTRUCT pattern when it is the same as that specified in the WHERE clause, etc., are not shown for brevity. For the official SPARQL grammar, we refer to the specification [169].

```
###### (1) base and prefix declarations
[BASE i]?
[PREFIX i]*

###### (2) dataset construction
[FROM i]*
[FROM NAMED i]*

###### (3) query type and solution modifiers
[SELECT S :: [DISTINCT|REDUCED]? [v|(e AS v)]+|ASK|DESCRIBE v|CONSTRUCT {B}]

###### (4) where clause
WHERE {
  P :: [
      B' |
      {P} [.|UNION|OPTIONAL|MINUS|FILTER EXISTS|FILTER NOT EXISTS] {P} |
      P FILTER (e) |
      BIND (e AS v) |
      VALUES ([v]+) {[([x|UNDEF]+)]*} |
      GRAPH [v|i] {P} |
      SERVICE [SILENT]? i {P} |
      { SELECT S }
    ] :: P
}

###### (5) aggregation
[GROUP BY [v|e]+]?
[HAVING e]?

###### (6) solution modifiers
[ORDER BY [[v|e]|ASC([v|e])|DESC([v|e])]+]?
[LIMIT n]?
[OFFSET n]?
:: S
```

Fig. 6.2 Anatomy of a SPARQL query, where '|' is used to separate alternatives; '[]*' is used to indicate multiplicities (default is precisely one, '?' indicates zero-or-one, '*' indicates zero-or-more, '+' indicates one-or-more); 'i', 'v', 'x', 'e', 'B', 'B'', 'n' indicate, respectively, terminals for IRIs, variables, RDF terms, expressions, basic graph patterns, basic graph patterns with property paths, and natural numbers; '::' indicates the start and end of capture groups used for recursive definitions; in cases where multiple elements are allowed they should be separated by whitespace (space, tab or newline)

6.2.1 Basic Graph Patterns

A foundational notion in the SPARQL query language is that of a **triple pattern**: an RDF triple (s, p, o) that further permits a (query) variable in any position. As such, triple patterns consist of a tuple containing IRIs, literals, blank nodes and query variables. IRIs and literals in triple patterns will match (only) themselves in the RDF graph being queried, while blank nodes and query variables can match any term in the RDF graph. Terms matched by query variables can be returned as part of the results of the query, while terms matched by blank nodes cannot be returned.

Example 6.2

The following SPARQL query consists of a single triple pattern:

```
SELECT *
WHERE {
  ?s <http://www.w3.org/2000/01/rdf-schema#label> "Nobel"@en
}
```

Posed against the graph of Figure 6.1, the query returns:

?s
<http://ex.org/NobelPrize>

In SPARQL, one may use Turtle-style shortcuts to abbreviate IRIs, where, for example, we may equivalently write the above query as:

```
PREFIX rdfs: <http://www.w3.org/2000/01/rdf-schema#>
SELECT *
WHERE {
  ?s rdfs:label "Nobel"@en
}
```

which will return the same results as above. In the following discussion, we will often present both queries and results using abbreviated IRIs, omitting prefix declarations for brevity.

Remark 6.3

By default, matching is done in SPARQL by matching RDF terms, not their corresponding values or referents. Consider, for example, the following SPARQL query posed against the RDF graph of Figure 6.1, asking for prizes that have at most 2 winners:

```
SELECT *
WHERE {
  ?s :maxWinners "2"^^xsd:nonNegativeInteger .
}
```

According to the SPARQL standard, no result is returned: although
:NobelPrizeLiterature is assigned "2"^^xsd:integer for :maxWinners,
and though this is equal to the value of "2"^^xsd:nonNegativeInteger,
they are different RDF terms. Later we will discuss expressions and (optional) entailments under which matching-by-value becomes possible.

In the previous examples – which use SELECT * – results for all query
variables are returned. However, we can opt to *project* certain variables.

Example 6.3

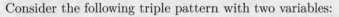

Consider the following triple pattern with two variables:

```
SELECT ?prize
WHERE {
  ?prize :winner ?person
}
```

The SELECT clause requests only the terms matched for ?person, and
hence the following results would be given over the graph of Figure 6.1.

?prize
:NPL1901
:NPL1902
:NPL1903
:NPL1904
:NPL1904

Note that by default, a SPARQL query may return solutions in any order (in Section 6.2.8 we will discuss features for ordering solutions). The
solution :NPL1904 is returned twice since there are two triples matching the triple pattern for that prize (:NPL1904 has two winners in the
graph). If we prefer distinct results, we may specify SELECT DISTINCT.

```
SELECT DISTINCT ?prize
WHERE {
  ?prize :winner ?person
}
```

This returns the same results, but removing duplicate rows.

We previously mentioned that blank nodes serve as variables that match any term but will not be returned as part of the query solutions. Hence the previous query could be equivalently written as:

```
SELECT DISTINCT *
WHERE {
  ?prize :winner _:b
}
```

This can be read as *return terms in the graph that have some value for* :winner; in this case, * will only return query variables (?prize).

Remark 6.4   (i)

When DISTINCT is specified in a SPARQL query, only unique solutions are returned; this is sometimes referred to as **set semantics** [310], meaning that a set of solutions are returned (not permitting duplicates). By default, when DISTINCT is not specified, this is referred to as **bag semantics** (aka. multiset semantics [11]), where duplicates are returned corresponding to the number of pattern matches in the data. SPARQL further supports a REDUCED keyword, which allows the engine to optionally remove some duplicates (typically if deemed more efficient).

A **basic graph pattern** is then a set of triple patterns, which forms a SPARQL **graph pattern** analogously to how a set of RDF triples forms an RDF graph. The triple patterns of the basic graph pattern are joined, which is equivalent to finding solutions that map the basic graph pattern (replacing variables per the solution) to a sub-graph of the RDF graph being queried.

Example 6.4

Assume we wish to find the IRIs of the *winners of the Nobel Prize in Literature in the year 1904*. To do so, we must match multiple triple patterns, which we can do as follows:

```
SELECT ?winner ?prize
WHERE {
  ?prize rdf:type :NobelPrizeLiterature .
  ?prize :year "1904"^^xsd:gYear .
  ?prize :winner ?winner .
}
```

This query is interpreted as a *join* of the three triple patterns; over the graph of Figure 6.1, the query will thus return:

?winner	?prize
:FMistral	:NPL1904
:JEchegaray	:NPL1904

To make the query more concise, we may use Turtle-style abbreviations:

```
SELECT ?winner ?prize
WHERE {
  ?prize a :NobelPrizeLiterature ;
    :year "1904"^^xsd:gYear ;
    :winner ?winner .
}
```

This query is equivalent and returns the same results (for any graph).

The prior example illustrates a join on a subject variable; however variables in arbitrary positions of triple patterns can be joined in a basic graph pattern.

Example 6.5

Consider the introductory query given in Example 6.1:

```
SELECT ?nplWinner ?nplYear ?warEndYear
WHERE {
  ?npl a :NobelPrizeLiterature ; :year ?nplYear ; :winner ?nplWinner .
  ?war :combatant ?nplWinner ; :end ?warEndYear .
}
```

The variables ?nplWinner joins object to object. Much like we can consider a set of RDF triples as forming a graph, we can also consider a set of triple patterns as forming (basic) graph patterns, where we could represent the above WHERE clause graphically as:

```
?npl ——rdf:type→ :NobelPrizeLiterature           ?warEndYear

  :year        :winner                                  :end

?nplYear                  ?nplWinner ←—:combatant—— ?war
```

We then wish to map this "query graph" to the RDF "data graph" such that the constant (grey) nodes match to themselves, the variable (white) nodes match any node, and the edges in the query graph are preserved by the mapping to the data graph. Such mappings form the initial solutions for the query, which may be further refined or combined by other query operators (e.g., using SELECT to project variables, etc.).

Basic graph patterns can also contain arbitrary cycles. Consider for example the following query looking for combatants of wars of their home countries that have won a Nobel Prize in Literature:

```
SELECT *
WHERE {
  ?war :combatant ?combatant .
  ?combatant :country ?country .
  ?country :war ?war .
  ?npl a :NobelPrizeLiterature ; :winner ?combatant .
}
```

The WHERE clause encodes the following basic graph pattern:

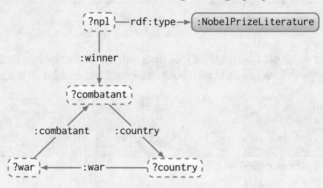

The results for the graph in Figure 6.1 are given as:

?npl	?combatant	?war	?country
:NPL1901	:SPrudhomme	:FrancoPrussianWar	:France

Finally, it is important to note that more than one variable (and/or blank node) in the query may match to the same node in the data.

Example 6.6

Consider the following query asking for pairs of winners of the Nobel Prize in Literature from the same country:

```
SELECT ?winner1 ?winner2 ?country
WHERE {
  ?npl1 a :NobelPrizeLiterature ; :winner ?winner1 .
  ?npl2 a :NobelPrizeLiterature ; :winner ?winner2 .
  ?winner1 :country ?country .
  ?winner2 :country ?country .
}
```

The following results will be given for the running example:

?winner1	?winner2	?country
:FMistral	:SPrudhomme	:France
:SPrudhomme	:FMistral	:France
:SPrudhomme	:SPrudhomme	:France
:TMommsen	:TMommsen	:Germany
:BBjørnson	:BBjørnson	:Norway
:FMistral	:FMistral	:France
:JEchegaray	:JEchegaray	:Spain

In each of the latter five results, variables ?winner1 and ?winner2 (as well as ?npl1 and ?npl2) are mapped to the same node in the data.

Exercise 6.1

Given the RDF graph of Figure 6.1, write a SPARQL query to find wars in which Nobel Laureates in Literature were combatants.

Remark 6.5

SPARQL queries with basic graph patterns, projection and set semantics correspond to conjunctive queries as discussed in the context of OWL in Section 5.5. However, SPARQL does not consider semantic entailment by default; rather this forms parts of an optional extension that will be discussed later in Section 6.6.

6.2.2 Unions of Graph Patterns

Certain queries may require matching various alternatives patterns in the RDF graph that will yield solutions. In this case, SPARQL allows for defining the union of two graph patterns, which will return solutions that are in the solutions for either (or both) of the graph patterns.

UNION: Takes the union of solutions for two query patterns.

Multiples unions can further be combined to capture three or more alternatives. The results of unions can also be joined with basic graph patterns, or query patterns using other features of SPARQL.

Example 6.7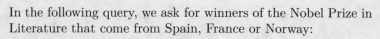

In the following query, we ask for winners of the Nobel Prize in Literature that come from Spain, France or Norway:

```
SELECT ?winner
WHERE {
  { ?npl a :NobelPrizeLiterature ; :winner ?winner .
    ?winner :country :Spain . }
  UNION
  { ?npl a :NobelPrizeLiterature ; :winner ?winner .
    ?winner :country :France . }
  UNION
  { ?npl a :NobelPrizeLiterature ; :winner ?winner .
    ?winner :country :Norway . }
}
```

This query applies a union of the solutions of the three basic graph patterns, where the solutions map the ?winner variable to :JEchegaray, :SPrudhomme, :FMistral and and :BBjørnson.

The previous query features repetition of some query patterns. We could equivalently express the query without such repetition as:

```
SELECT ?winner
WHERE {
  ?npl a :NobelPrizeLiterature ; :winner ?winner .
  { ?winner :country :Spain . }
  UNION
  { ?winner :country :France . }
  UNION
  { ?winner :country :Norway . }
}
```

This query joins winners of Nobel Prizes in Literature with the union of winners from Spain, France and Norway, yielding the same solutions.

(A reader familiar with logic may note that the first query corresponds to a disjunctive normal form (DNF) – a disjunction of conjunctions – while the second query corresponds to a conjunctive normal form (CNF) – a conjunction of disjunctions – with both being equivalent.)

Exercise 6.2

With respect to the RDF graph of Figure 6.1, write a SPARQL query to find Nobel Laureates in Literature that came either directly before (:prev) or after (:next) a win by :BBjørnson.

Remark 6.6 ⓘ

A reader familiar with SQL may be reminded of similar UNION
and UNION ALL features from that query language, where the former
returns a set of solutions and the latter a bag of solutions. SPARQL
UNION corresponds more closely to UNION ALL, meaning that it adds the
multiplicity of duplicate solutions. For example:

```
SELECT ?winner
WHERE {
  { ?npl a :NobelPrizeLiterature ; :winner ?winner .
    ?winner :country :Spain . }
  UNION
  { :NPL1904 :winner ?winner . }
}
```

would return :FMistral once and :JEchegaray twice, with the latter
solution being returned (once) on both sides of the union. More generally, the UNION in SPARQL will – under the default bag semantics –
add the multiplicities of a given solution from both sides.

Furthermore, unlike SQL, SPARQL allows unions of patterns with
different sets of variables. Thus, for example, we may write:

```
SELECT DISTINCT ?npl ?spainWinner ?franceWinner ?norwayWinner
WHERE {
  { ?npl a :NobelPrizeLiterature ; :winner ?winner .
    ?spainWinner :country :Spain . }
  UNION
  { ?npl a :NobelPrizeLiterature ; :winner ?winner .
    ?franceWinner :country :France . }
  UNION
  { ?npl a :NobelPrizeLiterature ; :winner ?winner .
    ?norwayWinner :country :Norway . }
}
```

This would return the following result:

?npl	?spainWinner	?franceWinner	?norwayWinner
:NPL1904	:JEchegaray		
:NPL1904		:FMistral	
:NPL1901		:SPrudhomme	
:NPL1903			:BBjørnson

After applying the union, variables in a solution that are not defined are
left blank, generating what are called UNBOUND terms in SPARQL. (In
SQL, a query involving UNION or UNION ALL requires that the attributes
on both sides are the same; otherwise an error would be thrown.)

6.2.3 Optional Graph Patterns

In scenarios where data may be heterogeneous and/or incomplete (as per the Web), an important feature of SPARQL is the ability to specify optional patterns where data matched by the pattern, if available, are returned as part of the solution; otherwise, where no match is found, the solution is preserved and the variables specific to the optional pattern are left blank.

OPTIONAL: Extends solutions for the left query pattern with solutions
  from the right query pattern where available.

Example 6.8

Assume we wish to find winners of the Nobel Prize in Literature and their predecessors and successors. However, we would still like to return the first winner(s), which will not have a predecessor, and the last winner(s), which will not have a successor. In SPARQL, we could thus rather use optional graph patterns to find the predecessors and successors of such winners, which would result in the following query:

```
SELECT ?predecessor ?winner ?successor
WHERE {
  ?npl a :NobelPrizeLiterature ; :winner ?winner .
  OPTIONAL { ?npl :prev ?prev . ?prev :winner ?predecessor }
  OPTIONAL { ?npl :next ?next . ?next :winner ?successor }
}
```

For the RDF graph of Figure 6.1, this query would return:

?predecessor	?winner	?successor
	:SPrudhomme	:TMommsen
:SPrudhomme	:TMommsen	:BBjørnson
:TMommsen	:BBjørnson	:FMistral
:TMommsen	:BBjørnson	:JEchegaray
:BBjørnson	:FMistral	
:BBjørnson	:JEchegaray	

Solutions with winners for which no predecessor or successor exist are preserved in the results and the corresponding variable is left blank (an UNBOUND in SPARQL). This is in contrast to a join in a basic graph pattern where the "incomplete" solution would be dropped.

It is also possible to combine optional graph patterns with other features of SPARQL (such as UNION). In fact, it is even possible to have nested optional graph patterns. Consider for example:

```
SELECT ?predecessor ?winner ?successor
WHERE {
  ?npl a :NobelPrizeLiterature ; :winner ?winner .
  OPTIONAL {
    ?npl :prev ?prev . ?prev :winner ?predecessor
    OPTIONAL { ?npl :next ?next . ?next :winner ?successor }
  }
}
```

This query asks for winners and if available their predecessor; furthermore, if a predecessor is available, their successor, if available, is also returned. The results are the same as before, save for the first solution, which now rather has two UNBOUND values:

?predecessor	?winner	?successor
	:SPrudhomme	
...	...	...

Given that the optional successor pattern is now nested, when no predecessor for :SPrudhomme is found, a successor is not sought.

Exercise 6.3

In SPARQL, it is also allowed to nest unions and optionals as desired. Following on from the previous examples, can you figure out what the solutions to the following SPARQL query might be?

```
SELECT ?predecessor ?winner
WHERE {
  ?npl a :NobelPrizeLiterature ; :winner ?winner .
  OPTIONAL {
    { ?npl :prev ?prev . ?prev :winner ?predecessor }
    UNION
    { ?prev :next ?npl . ?prev :winner ?predecessor }
  }
}
```

Remark 6.7

A reader familiar with relational queries may note that optional patterns in SPARQL correspond with left-outer-joins in SQL. Right-outer-joins can be expressed by simply swapping the operands while full-outer-joins can also be expressed by additionally using union.

6.2.4 Filtering and Binding Values

The query features we have seen thus far interpret RDF terms as opaque symbols that are checked for equality against a given triple pattern. But what if we wish to define solutions that depend on the value that a term represents? For example, what if we wish to find Nobel Prize Laureates within a given range of years, or descriptions in a particular language, or labels containing the string "Nobel"? Furthermore, what if we wish to compute a new value based on a given solution, such as the gap between two years?

SPARQL offers a variety of operators and functions that can be used to filter or assign new values to variables in. Here we first provide examples using expressions to filter results, and then later present examples where the result of an expression is bound to a fresh variable. Finally we enumerate all of the operators and expressions that SPARQL provides for such purposes.

6.2.4.1 Filtering Solutions: FILTER

SPARQL expressions can be used to filter solutions that do not satisfy some criteria, as we will see in Example 6.9 where prizes after 1903 are removed.

> FILTER: Given an expression, removes solutions for which the expression evaluates to false or an error.

Example 6.9

The following query finds winners of the Nobel Prize in Literature since the year 1903, inclusive:

```
SELECT ?winner
WHERE {
  ?npl a :NobelPrizeLiterature ; :winner ?winner ; :year ?year .
  FILTER (xsd:integer(str(?year)) >= 1903)
}
```

The query will return :BBjørnson, :FMistral and :JEchegaray as solutions for ?winner. Note that SPARQL, by default, does not support comparisons on datatypes of xsd:gYear, and hence we must first call str to return the string value of the literal, converting it to xsd:integer.

Each filter is associated with a scope delimited by braces ({ . . . }), where the placement of a filter within a query may thus affect the solutions.

Example 6.10

Consider the following query, seeking winners of the Nobel Prize in Literature from France or Spain since 1903, where the filter condition checking the value for year is placed outside of the union:

```
SELECT ?winner
WHERE {
  { ?npl a :NobelPrizeLiterature ; :winner ?winner ; :year ?year .
    ?winner :country :France }
  UNION
  { ?npl a :NobelPrizeLiterature ; :winner ?winner ; :year ?year .
    ?winner :country :Spain }
  FILTER (xsd:integer(str(?year)) >= 1903)
}
```

This query would return :FMistral and :JEchegaray for the RDF graph of Figure 6.1, with the filter applied to the results of the union.

Now compare the previous query with the following query where the filter is now placed inside the second operand of the union:

```
SELECT ?winner
WHERE {
  { ?npl a :NobelPrizeLiterature ; :winner ?winner ; :year ?year .
    ?winner :country :France }
  UNION
  { ?npl a :NobelPrizeLiterature ; :winner ?winner ; :year ?year .
    ?winner :country :Spain .
    FILTER (xsd:integer(str(?year)) >= 1903) }
}
```

This time the filter on year is scoped to the winners from Spain, so the query would return :SPrudhomme, :FMistral and :JEchegaray. (We remark that it does not matter if the filter comes before or after the triple patterns matching winners from Spain; what matters is the group – delimited by braces – in which it is present).

6.2.4.2 Binding Values: BIND AS

Aside from using expressions to filter solutions, we may wish to return solutions that – rather than simply return selected terms from the graph – apply an expression to compute some new value based on the current solution, binding the result of the expression to a particular variable.

BIND/AS[†]: Used to bind the result of an expression to a fresh variable.

Example 6.11

The following query returns winners of the Nobel Prize in Literature, along with how many years ago they won the prize:

```
SELECT ?winner ?yearsAgo
WHERE {
  ?npl a :NobelPrizeLiterature ; :winner ?winner ; :year ?year .
  BIND (year(now()) - xsd:integer(str(?year)) AS ?yearsAgo)
}
```

Since the variable `?yearsAgo` is not referenced elsewhere in the WHERE clause, we could alternatively write this query as follows:

```
SELECT ?winner (year(now()) - xsd:integer(str(?year)) AS ?yearsAgo)
WHERE {
  ?npl a :NobelPrizeLiterature ; :winner ?winner ; :year ?year .
}
```

Assuming that the query is run in 2020, the results returned would be:

?winner	?yearsAgo
:SPrudhomme	"119"^^xsd:integer
:TMommsen	"118"^^xsd:integer
:BBjørnson	"117"^^xsd:integer
:FMistral	"116"^^xsd:integer
:JEchegaray	"116"^^xsd:integer

Remark 6.8

A similar feature for binding tuples of static solutions to variables – using VALUES – will be discussed later in Section 6.2.10.

6.2.4.3 Operators and Functions

SPARQL provides a wide range of operators and functions to support filtering solutions and binding new values; these operators are summarised in Table 6.1 while the functions are summarised in Table 6.2. Recall that we use '†' as shorthand to denote features new to SPARQL 1.1. Both tables indicate the supported types of both arguments and return values, as follows; TERM: RDF term, unbound or error; SUB: sub-query; IRI: IRI; LIT: literal; BNODE: blank node; BOOL: boolean; STR: string (or plain literal); NUM: numeric; INT: integer; DT: date-time; DTD: day-time-duration. Table 6.1 further uses the type COM, which refers to types for which value-based comparison is supported by

Table 6.1 Summary of built-in SPARQL operators

$I_L(\cdot)$ denotes the value interpretation of a datatype literal

A	**Op** B	**Return type and value**
	! BOOL b	BOOL true if $I_L(b)$ is false; false otherwise
BOOL b_1	|| BOOL b_2	BOOL true if $I_L(b_1)$ or $I_L(b_2)$; false otherwise
BOOL b_1	&& BOOL b_2	BOOL true if $I_L(b_1)$ and $I_L(b_2)$; false otherwise
TERM* t_1	= TERM* t_2	BOOL true if t_1 same term as t_2; false otherwise
TERM* t_1	!= TERM* t_2	BOOL true if t_1 not same term as t_2; false otherwise
COM v_1	= COM v_2	BOOL true if $I_L(v_1) = I_L(v_2)$; false otherwise
COM v_1	!= COM v_2	BOOL true if $I_L(v_1) \neq I_L(v_2)$; false otherwise
COM v_1	< COM v_2	BOOL true if $I_L(v_1) < I_L(v_2)$; false otherwise
COM v_1	> COM v_2	BOOL true if $I_L(v_1) > I_L(v_2)$; false otherwise
COM v_1	<= COM v_2	BOOL true if $I_L(v_1) \leq I_L(v_2)$; false otherwise
COM v_1	>= COM v_2	BOOL true if $I_L(v_1) \geq I_L(v_2)$; false otherwise
	+ NUM n	NUM $I_L(n)$
	- NUM n	NUM $-I_L(n)$
NUM n_1	+ NUM n_2	NUM $I_L(n_1) + I_L(n_2)$
NUM n_1	- NUM n_2	NUM $I_L(n_1) - I_L(n_2)$
NUM n_1	* NUM n_2	NUM $I_L(n_1) \times I_L(n_2)$
NUM n_1	/ NUM n_2	NUM $\frac{I_L(n_1)}{I_L(n_2)}$

SPARQL, including NUM, STR, BOOL and DT; conversely, the type TERM* then refers to any term that is not of one of these comparable types.

We will not discuss the precise details of each operator and function listed in these tables (for which we rather refer to the SPARQL standard [169]); rather here we will present a list of key considerations and clarifications. For brevity, we will henceforth refer to operators and functions generically as functions (in any case, the distinction between operators and functions is merely a convention based on their syntax [226]; both operators and functions accept some input arguments and return some output value). We refer to a particular function call used in a query generically as an expression.

- All functions accept variables as arguments; for a given solution, the term to which a variable is mapped will be given as the function argument.
- The types BOOL, STR, NUM, INT, DT and DTD are expressed as XML datatype values, such as xsd:boolean, xsd:string, etc. For STR, typically a plain literal (a lexical string without a datatype) or a datatyped string (xsd:string) can be considered. The type NUM includes all standard datatypes derived from xsd:decimal, as well as the "imprecise" floating-precision types xsd:double and xsd:float. Many of the SPARQL functions that take arguments from these XML types are defined following analogous functions in the XPath/XQuery standard [226].
- SPARQL permits "Effective Boolean Values", where the BOOL type interprets invalid numeric and boolean literals (e.g., "yes"^^xsd:boolean) as

Table 6.2 Summary of built-in SPARQL functions

[A] indicates optional argument; A|B indicates alternative arguments.

Function		Return type and value
bound($\text{TERM }t$)	BOOL	true if t is bound; false if unbound
if($\text{BOOL }b$,$\text{TERM }t_1$,$\text{TERM }t_2$)[†]	TERM	t_1 if b is true; t_2 otherwise
coalesce($\text{TERM }t_1$,...,t_n)[†]	TERM	first t_i $(1 \le i \le n)$ that is not an error or unbound
not exists($\text{SUB }Q$)[†]	BOOL	true if Q has any solution; false otherwise
exists($\text{SUB }Q$)[†]	BOOL	true if Q has no solution; false otherwise
sameTerm($\text{TERM }t_1$, $\text{TERM }t_2$)	BOOL	true if t_1 same term as t_2; false otherwise
$\text{TERM }t$ in($\text{TERM }t_1$,...,t_n)[†]	BOOL	true if t=t_i for any $t_i \in \{t_1,...,t_n\}$; false otherwise
$\text{TERM }t$ not in($\text{TERM }t_1$,...,t_n)[†]	BOOL	true if t!=t_i for all $t_i \in \{t_1,...,t_n\}$; false otherwise
isIRI($\text{TERM }t$)	BOOL	true if t is an IRI; false otherwise
isBlank($\text{TERM }t$)	BOOL	true if t is a blank node; false otherwise
isLiteral($\text{TERM }t$)	BOOL	true if t is a literal; false otherwise
isNumeric($\text{TERM }t$)[†]	BOOL	true if t is a numeric value; false otherwise
str($\text{LIT }l$|$\text{IRI }i$)	STR	lexical value of l | string of i
lang($\text{LIT }l$)	STR	language tag string of l
datatype($\text{LIT }l$)	IRI	datatype IRI of l
iri($\text{STR }s$|$\text{IRI }i$)[†]	IRI	s resolved against the in-scope base IRI | i
bnode([$\text{STR }s$])[†]	BNODE	fresh blank node [unique to s]
strdt($\text{STR }s$,$\text{IRI }i$)[†]	LIT	$"s"\text{^^}<i>$
strlang($\text{STR }s$,$\text{STR }l$)[†]	LIT	$"s"@l$
uuid()[†]	IRI	fresh IRI (from UUID URN scheme)
struuid()[†]	STR	fresh string (from UUID URN scheme)
strlen($\text{STR }s$)[†]	INT	length of string s
substr($\text{STR }s$,$\text{INT }b$,[$\text{INT }l$])[†]	STR	substring of s from index b [of length l]
ucase($\text{STR }s$)[†]	STR	uppercase s
lcase($\text{STR }s$)[†]	STR	lowercase s
strstarts($\text{STR }s$,$\text{STR }p$)[†]	BOOL	true if s starts with p; false otherwise
strends($\text{STR }s$,$\text{STR }p$)[†]	BOOL	true if s ends with p; false otherwise
strbefore($\text{STR }s$,$\text{STR }p$)[†]	STR	string before first match for p in s
strafter($\text{STR }s$,$\text{STR }p$)[†]	STR	string after first match for p in s
encode_for_uri($\text{STR }s$)[†]	STR	s percent-encoded
concat($\text{STR }s_1$,...,s_n)[†]	STR	$s_1,...,s_n$ concatenated
langMatches($\text{STR }s$,$\text{STR }l$)	BOOL	true if s a language tag matching l; false otherwise
regex($\text{STR }s$,$\text{STR }p$[,$\text{STR }f$])	BOOL	true if s matches regex p [with flags f]; false otherwise
replace($\text{STR }s$,$\text{STR }p$,$\text{STR }r$[,$\text{STR }f$])[†]	STR	s with matches for regex p [with flags f] replaced by r
abs($\text{NUM }n$)[†]	NUM	absolute value of n
round($\text{NUM }n$)[†]	NUM	round to nearest whole number (towards $+\infty$ for $*.5$)
ceil($\text{NUM }n$)[†]	NUM	round up (towards $+\infty$) to nearest whole number
floor($\text{NUM }n$)[†]	NUM	round down (towards $-\infty$) to nearest whole number
rand($\text{NUM }n$)[†]	NUM	random double between 0 (inclusive) and 1 (exclusive)
now()[†]	DT	current date-time
year($\text{DT }d$)[†]	INT	year of d (as an integer)
month($\text{DT }d$)[†]	INT	month of d (as an integer)
day($\text{DT }d$)[†]	INT	day of d (as an integer)
hours($\text{DT }d$)[†]	INT	hours of d (as an integer)
minutes($\text{DT }d$)[†]	INT	minutes of d (as an integer)
seconds($\text{DT }d$)[†]	INT	seconds of d (as an integer)
timezone($\text{DT }d$)[†]	DTD	time-zone of d (as day-time-duration)
tz($\text{DT }d$)[†]	STR	time-zone of d (as a string)
md5($\text{STR }s$)[†]	STR	MD5 hash of s
sha1($\text{STR }s$)[†]	STR	SHA1 hash of s
sha256($\text{STR }s$)[†]	STR	SHA256 hash of s
sha384($\text{STR }s$)[†]	STR	SHA384 hash of s
sha512($\text{STR }s$)[†]	STR	SHA512 hash of s

false, strings as false when they have zero-length and true otherwise, numeric literals as false when they equal 0 or NaN and true otherwise.

- Unbound terms may arise as a result of an OPTIONAL pattern for which no match is found, a UNION pattern where a given variable appears on one side of the union but not the other, or a variable that is out-of-scope or otherwise never bound to a value in the query.
- Errors commonly arise from passing incompatible arguments to a function; for example, the expression ?str < 1 will return an error for any solution where ?str is mapped to an IRI or string term. Some functions are well-defined for errors; for example, coalesce can be used to find the first argument that is not an error or unbound, and hence may return a non-error value though some of its arguments are errors. Additionally, boolean operators are defined such that they may return a result when the value that an error would take does not affect the outcome; more specifically, denoting by ε an expression giving an error: $!\varepsilon$ returns ε; ε || true returns true, while ε || false and ε || ε return ε; finally, ε && false returns false, while ε && true and ε && ε return ε.
- When expressions are used in a FILTER clause, the solution is kept if the expression evaluates to true (including Effective Boolean Values), whereas the solution is removed if the expression evaluates to false or error.
- When expressions whose results are bound to a variable (using AS) give an error, the solution is kept but the variable is left unbound.
- As seen in Example 6.9, casting is allowed using the datatype IRI as the name of the function (e.g., xsd:integer("14.0")), returning an error if the result is an invalid datatype (e.g., xsd:integer("14.5")).

Beyond these general remarks, we clarify aspects of particular functions:

- SPARQL offers two forms of equality/inequality checks : term-based and value-based. Under the former, 2 (a shortcut for "2"^^xsd:integer) and 2.0 (a shortcut for "2.0"^^xsd:decimal) would be considered unequal, while under the latter they would be considered equal. Matching in basic graph patterns always assumes term-based equality. On the other hand, the = operator applies value-based equality if both terms have comparable values (e.g., xsd:decimal and xsd:int, but not xsd:decimal and xsd:dateTimeStamp); otherwise, term-based equality is applied. The != operator is then the negation of =. To apply term-based equality for all cases, the sameTerm function can instead be used.
- Inequality operators – <, >, <=, >= – assume that both arguments have comparable values. Otherwise the expression will return an error.
- Numeric operators attempt to "preserve" the most specific input datatype possible from xsd:integer, xsd:decimal, xsd:float and xsd:double. For example, the product of an xsd:byte and xsd:int will result in a value of type xsd:integer, while their division will be an xsd:decimal.
- The functions not exists and exists take sub-queries as arguments. We will discuss these features further in Section 6.2.5.

- The functions in and not in are defined using value-based equality; for example, the expression 116 in (116.0) would return true even though 116 is parsed as an xsd:integer and 116.0 as an xsd:decimal.
- Functions like str and lang return strings without term delimiters; for example, str(<http://ex.org/>) returns "http://ex.org/".
- The function lang returns an empty string if no language is defined.
- The function datatype returns the datatype IRI xsd:string for a plain literal (a literal without a datatype or language tag) and the datatype IRI rdf:langString for a literal with a language tag.
- The function bnode returns a fresh blank node for the current solution (not appearing in the dataset or any other solution). When the function is used without arguments, it generates a unique blank node every time it is called. When used with a string argument, it will generate a blank node unique to that string, outputting the same blank node each time the same argument is given within the same solution.
- The string functions strstarts, strends, strbefore, strafter, and contains accept strings with language tags, but only where both arguments have the same language tag (otherwise an error is returned).
- When all arguments to concat have the same language tag or datatype (xsd:string), the language tag or datatype is preserved in the output.
- The function langMatches compares language ranges to language tags; for example, langMatches("*","en-UK"), langMatches("en","en-UK"), and langMatches("en-UK","en-UK") return true, while langMatches("*",""), langMatches("en","es"), and langMatches("en-UK","en") return false.
- The functions regex and replace match standard regular expression patterns (the second argument p); flags offer options for escaping special characters, or case insensitivity; for example, regex("hi","^h") returns true since the first argument starts with h, while regex("hi","^H","i") also returns true since the "i" flag indicates case insensitivity.
- The function timezone returns a time-zone as a day-time-duration; for example, both timezone("2001-01-01T01:01:01Z"^^xsd:dateTime) and timezone("2001-01-01T01:01:01+00:00"^^xsd:dateTime) will return the time-zone as "PT0S"^^xsd:dayTimeDuration. On the other hand, the tz function returns the time-zone string, namely "Z" and "+00:00" in the previous cases. The former function returns an error when the time-zone is not given; the latter returns the empty string.

For reasons of space and brevity we refer to the standard for further details on these SPARQL functions [169]. We will now rather provide a succinct example that combines three such functions in order to specify preferences on languages, illustrating the use of such functions both for the purposes of filtering results, and for extending results with additional values. Later examples will also make use of other operators and functions.

Example 6.12

In this example, we show how the `coalesce` feature can be used to express a common pattern where one specifies preferences in the solutions generated. More specifically, we will ask for the labels of the types of prizes won by :SPrudhomme, preferring a French label, but if not available, we will accept a Spanish or (in turn) an English label:

```
SELECT (coalesce(?lFr,?lEs,?lEn) AS ?l)
WHERE {
  ?prize :winner :SPrudhomme ; a ?type .
  OPTIONAL {
    ?type rdfs:label ?lEn .
    FILTER (langMatches(lang(?lEn),"en"))
  }
  OPTIONAL {
    ?type rdfs:label ?lEs .
    FILTER (langMatches(lang(?lEs),"es"))
  }
  OPTIONAL {
    ?type rdfs:label ?lFr .
    FILTER (langMatches(lang(?lFr),"fr"))
  }
}
```

Given that no French label is available in the RDF graph depicted in Figure 6.1, the query will return the next available option, namely the label "Nobel de Literatura"@es in Spanish.

Remark 6.9

SPARQL provides the possibility to extend the built-in functions with custom functions. For example, we may directly define a custom function :yearsAgo that accepts an xsd:gYear value and directly returns the corresponding interval of years from the current year:

```
SELECT ?winner (:yearsAgo(?year) AS ?yearsAgo)
WHERE {
  ?npl a :NobelPrizeLiterature ; :winner ?winner ; :year ?year .
}
```

A particular SPARQL engine must then support the required logic to implement the custom function; otherwise if it does not recognise a given custom function, an error is returned.

> **Exercise 6.4**
>
> With respect to the RDF graph of Figure 6.1, write SPARQL queries to respond to the following:
>
> 1. Find pairs of Nobel Laureates in Literature whose countries have participated in the same war, filtering solutions where both winners are the same or are from the same country.
> 2. Find pairs of distinct Nobel Laureates from the same country along with the gap in years between the corresponding prizes; the first winner should precede or be in the same year as the second winner.

> **Remark 6.10**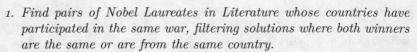
>
> While we could consider using functions such as `contains` or `regex` to perform keyword search, such functions are often applied as a filter rather than being supported by indexes, meaning that they may be inefficient if the query without the filter generates a lot of results. For this reason, SPARQL implementations often provide custom extensions for efficient keyword search using inverted indexes over text.

> **Discussion 6.1**
>
> FRANK: What about other functions that are often used in practice, like counting, computing averages, and so forth?
>
> AIDAN: The expressions discussed thus far are applied for a single solution, so we could compute, for example, the average of three values in the same solution by applying ?v1 + ?v2 + ?v3 / 3. However, the operations you mention are typically done over multiple solutions; this requires aggregation features that can apply operations over groups of solutions, as will be discussed later in Section 6.2.7.

6.2.5 Negation of Graph Patterns

In SPARQL, we may express queries that involve the negation of graph patterns, meaning that from the results of one graph pattern, we may remove solutions based on the results for a second graph pattern. There are three main ways this can be achieved, where the first relies on use of optional patterns and filters, while the other two are as follows:

> MINUS[†]: Removes solutions from the left pattern that join with some
> solution for the right pattern.
> FILTER (NOT) EXISTS[†]: Removes solutions from the left pattern for which
> the right pattern – substituted with the left-hand solution – has a
> solution (or in the case of NOT, does not have a solution).

In most (though not all) cases, these two options for negation will yield the
same results. We will discuss their differences in detail momentarily, further
comparing them with the alternative of using optional patterns with filters.
First, however, we illustrate the three options with an extended example
involving a more typical case where negation is required.

Example 6.13

Assume we wish to find the first winner of the Nobel Prize in
Literature; we may think of this query as finding winners of such a prize
for which there was no previous prize. There are three main alternatives
by which we may express such a query in SPARQL.

The first alternative uses an optional graph pattern, subsequently
applying a filter to ensure that no optional matches are found:

```
SELECT ?winner
WHERE {
  ?npl a :NobelPrizeLiterature ; :winner ?winner .
  OPTIONAL { ?npl :prev ?prev . }
  FILTER (!bound(?prev))
}
```

This will filter any solution for which ?prev is matched to some term,
leaving only :SPrudhomme as a solution.

The second alternative we may use is FILTER NOT EXISTS.

```
SELECT ?winner
WHERE {
  ?npl a :NobelPrizeLiterature ; :winner ?winner .
  FILTER NOT EXISTS { ?npl :prev ?prev . }
}
```

This feature removes any solution from the outer graph pattern for
which there exists a corresponding match for the inner graph pattern,
leaving us (again) with :SPrudhomme as the only solution for ?winner.

A third (as of yet unseen) alternative is to instead use MINUS, which
specifies that any solutions of the outer graph pattern that join with
the solutions of the inner graph pattern should be removed.

```
SELECT ?winner
WHERE {
  ?npl a :NobelPrizeLiterature ; :winner ?winner .
  MINUS { ?npl :prev ?prev . }
}
```

To the left we show the solutions of the outer graph pattern, and to the right the solutions of the inner (minus) graph pattern:

?npl	?winner
:NPL1901	:SPrudhomme
:NPL1902	:TMommsen
:NPL1903	:BBjørnson
:NPL1904	:FMistral
:NPL1904	:JEchegaray

?npl	?prev
:NPL1902	:NPL1901
:NPL1903	:NPL1902
:NPL1904	:NPL1903

Removing all solutions from the left that join on the ?npl variable with solutions from the right and then projecting ?winner, we are left with :SPrudhomme as the only solution. We highlight that although :NPL1904 appears twice on the left and only once on the right, both solutions on the left are removed from the results of the MINUS operator.

Remark 6.11

The reader may be wondering why SPARQL offers three seemingly redundant options for negation. With respect to the first option – combining OPTIONAL and a !BOUND filter – this was present since SPARQL 1.0, but was a rather indirect and unintuitive way to express negation. SPARQL 1.1 thus introduced the latter two options – MINUS and FILTER NOT EXISTS – the difference between which is rather subtle, as illustrated by the following two (slightly unusual) queries:

```
SELECT ?winner
WHERE {
  ?npl a :NobelPrizeLiterature .
  FILTER NOT EXISTS { :Germany :war ?war . }
}
```

```
SELECT ?winner
WHERE {
  ?npl a :NobelPrizeLiterature .
  MINUS { :Germany :war ?war . }
}
```

The two queries are identical except the first uses FILTER NOT EXISTS while the second uses MINUS. We say that the queries are "slightly unusual" because there is no variable in common between the inner and outer graph patterns. In the case of FILTER NOT EXISTS, no matter what the solution for the outer graph pattern, a solution always exists for the inner graph pattern (:FrancoPrussianWar), and hence all outer solutions are removed, leaving empty results. In the case of MINUS, since no join variable exists between the inner and outer patterns, no results are removed and all winners of a Nobel Prize in Literature are returned.

A second difference relates to the scoping of filters. For example, consider the following two queries asking for winners of the Nobel Prize in Literature in the year(s) after :TMommsen won the prize:

```
SELECT ?winner
WHERE {
  ?npl a :NobelPrizeLiterature ; :winner ?winner ; :year ?year .
  FILTER NOT EXISTS {
    ?ntm a :NobelPrizeLiterature ; :winner :TMommsen ; :year ?ytm .
    FILTER (xsd:integer(str(?year)) > xsd:integer(str(?ytm)))
  }
}
```

```
SELECT ?winner
WHERE {
  ?npl a :NobelPrizeLiterature ; :winner ?winner ; :year ?year .
  MINUS {
    ?ntm a :NobelPrizeLiterature ; :winner :TMommsen ; :year ?ytm .
    FILTER (xsd:integer(str(?year)) > xsd:integer(str(?ytm)))
  }
}
```

The first query gives :BBjørnson, :FMistral and :JEchegaray, while the second gives :SPrudhomme, :TMommsen :BBjørnson, :FMistral and :JEchegaray. This difference is due to how the variables are scoped in both queries: because filter clauses do not affect variable scope, the variable ?year is still in-scope within the FILTER NOT EXISTS clause while it is out-of-scope within the MINUS clause. Hence, in the latter case, the variable ?year will always be unbound, generating an error for each solution inside the MINUS clause, leaving nothing to be removed from the outer pattern, and ultimately returning all winners as a result.

Exercise 6.5

Following Remark 6.11, does the SPARQL 1.0 form of negation using OPTIONAL/!bound act like MINUS or FILTER NOT EXISTS?

Thus far we have focused on features for negation, but SPARQL also supports a positive FILTER EXISTS, which checks for the existence of a match for a pattern. This is not frequently used as it is ultimately very similar to a standard join in a basic graph pattern. The main differences are that variables used only in FILTER EXISTS clause cannot be projected, and that the multiplicity of results under bag semantics is not affected by such variables.

Remark 6.12

Consider the following query using FILTER EXISTS:

```
SELECT ?npl
WHERE {
  ?npl a :NobelPrizeLiterature .
  FILTER EXISTS { ?npl :winner ?winner }
}
```

This asks for Nobel Prizes in Literature that have been won by somebody. Compare this with a standard basic graph pattern:

```
SELECT ?npl
WHERE {
  ?npl a :NobelPrizeLiterature .
  ?npl :winner ?winner .
}
```

The main difference is that FILTER EXISTS will not affect the number of times a solution is returned; in other words, the first query returns :NPL1904 once, while the second query returns :NPL1904 twice. Another minor difference is that ?winner is not bound in the second query (e.g., SELECT * for the first query would return solutions only for ?npl while in the second query, both variables would be returned).

Exercise 6.6

Call a country not associated with any war a "neutral country". For the purposes of this exercise we shall assume that each winner is from a single country. With respect to the running example, write SPARQL queries to return all Nobel Prizes in Literature, where:

1. some winner is from a neutral country;
2. all winners are from a neutral country;
3. no winner is from a neutral country.

(Each query will give a different result over the running example.)

Exercise 6.7

Consider the following queries:

```
SELECT DISTINCT ?npl
WHERE {
  ?npl a :NobelPrizeLiterature ; :winner ?winner .
  ?winner :country ?country .
  FILTER (?country != :France)
}
```

```
SELECT DISTINCT ?npl
WHERE {
  ?npl a :NobelPrizeLiterature ; :winner ?winner .
  FILTER NOT EXISTS {
    ?winner :country :France .
  }
}
```

```
SELECT DISTINCT ?npl
WHERE {
  ?npl a :NobelPrizeLiterature .
  FILTER NOT EXISTS {
    ?npl :winner ?winner .
    ?winner :country :France .
  }
}
```

Will these queries return the same solutions for the running example?

6.2.6 Property Paths

Given that SPARQL is a query language for graphs, we may wish to query pairs of nodes connected by arbitrary-length paths in the graph. The features we have seen thus far would not support such queries since they are bounded. Along these lines, SPARQL 1.1 introduced **property paths**.

Remark 6.13

Unlike the features seen thus far, path expressions are not directly expressible in languages such as SQL (though they can be supported indirectly using WITH RECURSIVE). Querying paths is characteristic of SPARQL and other graph query languages [10].

Table 6.3 SPARQL property paths syntax

† All bar the first expression were introduced in SPARQL 1.1.

The following are path expressions	
p	a predicate IRI
$!p$	any predicate IRI that is not p
$!(p_1 \mid \ldots \mid p_k \mid {^\wedge}p_{k+1} \mid \ldots \mid {^\wedge}p_n)$	any (inverse) predicate IRI not listed

and if e, e_1, e_2 are path expressions **the following are also path expressions:**	
${^\wedge}e$	an inverse path
e_1/e_2	a path of e_1 followed by e_2
$e_1 \mid e_2$	a path of e_1 or e_2
$e\star$	a path of zero or more e
$e{+}$	a path of one or more e
$e?$	a path of zero or one e
(e)	brackets used for grouping

Example 6.14

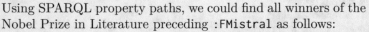

Using SPARQL property paths, we could find all winners of the Nobel Prize in Literature preceding `:FMistral` as follows:

```
SELECT ?before
WHERE {
  ?nfm a :NobelPrizeLiterature ; :winner :FMistral .
  ?nfm :prev+ ?nbefore .
  ?nbefore :winner ?before .
}
```

The expression `:prev+` represents a property path that will match a path of one or more edges labelled `:prev`. The running example will yield three results: `:SPrudhomme`, `:TMommsen`, `BBjørnson`.

Table 6.3 enumerates the syntax of property paths. The base case is a path consisting of a simple predicate. On top of this base case, one can (recursively) define inverse paths, concatenation of paths, alternative paths, arbitrary-length paths, and optional paths. Finally, one can also specify the negation of simple predicates, or the negation of a list of simple and inverse predicates (though one cannot specify the negation of a complex path). Property paths can then be used with either variable or constant subject/object terms.

Example 6.15

As a more complex example, consider looking for pairs of compatriots who have won Nobel Prizes, where the first winner should precede or be in the same year as the second winner.

```
SELECT ?w1 ?w2
WHERE {
  ?np1 a/rdfs:subClassOf* :NobelPrize  ; ?winner ?w1 .
  ?np2 a/rdfs:subClassOf* :NobelPrize  ; ?winner ?w2 .
  ?np1 :next* ?np2 .
  ?w1 :country/^:country ?w2 .
  FILTER (?w1 != ?w2)
}
```

The property path `a/rdfs:subClassOf*` allows us to recursively traverse the class hierarchy, finding all instances of a class that is (transitively) a sub-class of `:NobelPrize` (as well as direct instances of `:NobelPrize`). The property path `:next*` will match ?np2 to the prizes that came after ?np1 and to ?np1 itself (we assume here that `:next` only connects prizes of the same type); by stating `:next*` rather than `:next+`, if two compatriot winners share a prize in the same year, they will be included in the results. Finally, the property path `:country/^:country` will ensure that the winners matched in the query are from the same country. The running example will yield `:SPrudhomme` (?w1) and `:FMistral` (?w2).

Discussion 6.2

ANNA: So SPARQL does not support sub-class entailment?

AIDAN: There is a standard for supporting entailments in SPARQL that we will discuss in Section 6.6, but support is not widespread. Instead users often manually extend their queries with property paths, such as `a/rdfs:subClassOf*`. The types of entailments that can be captured by property paths is limited, however.

Exercise 6.8

Assume an extended version of the graph in Figure 6.1 with analogous data for all Nobel Prizes in Literature and their winners. Note that Romain Rolland (:RRolland) – a French author – won in 1915. How could we rewrite the query of Example 6.15 to only consider most recent predecessors (e.g., returning the pairs :SPrudhomme/:FMistral and :FMistral/:RRolland, but not :SPrudhomme/:RRolland)?

Remark 6.14

Of the property path expressions in Table 6.3, those not involving * and + can be expressed otherwise in SPARQL. For example:

```
SELECT *
WHERE {
  ?x a/rdfs:subClassOf ?y .
}
```

can be rewritten equivalently as:

```
SELECT *
WHERE {
  ?x a [ rdfs:subClassOf ?y ] .
}
```

(recalling that blank nodes in queries act as variables not returned as
part of the solutions). However, the following query:

```
SELECT *
WHERE {
  ?x a/rdfs:subClassOf* ?y .
}
```

cannot be expressed by other means in SPARQL since it may match
arbitrary-length paths of rdfs:subClassOf edges.

Where * and + are not used, a default bag semantics is considered
(as if the property path were rewritten to its equivalent form without
using a property path expression). On the other hand, sub-expressions
involving * or + are evaluated under set semantics, meaning that nodes
connected by a matching path are only returned once. For example:

```
SELECT *
WHERE {
  ?x (:prev|:next)* ?y .
}
```

This query will return each pair of prizes only once (even though there
are multiple distinct paths connecting each pair):

?x	?y
:NPL1901	:NPL1901
:NPL1901	:NPL1902
...	...
:NPL1904	:NPL1904

This set semantics is applied to reduce computational complexity. More specifically, if we define a "distinct path" as one that visits a unique set of nodes/edges, we may say that there are infinite edges between each prize that match the property path expression in the previous query, meaning that under bag semantics, we would need to return an infinite number of results! An earlier draft of the SPARQL 1.1 standard rather proposed to evaluate property paths under a more "reasonable" definition of a "distinct path" as one where the same node is not visited twice (aka. a "simple path"); however, even under this definition, the number of distinct paths can be factorial in the number of nodes, and hence it was observed that bag semantics would still be prohibitively costly [15, 250]. The final SPARQL 1.1 standard thus switched to defining the evaluation of * and + expressions in terms of set semantics.

6.2.7 Aggregation

The expressions that we previously discussed in Section 6.2.4 are applied at the level of individual solutions, but what if we wish to apply a sum, count, average, etc., over multiple solutions? For example, what if we wished to count the number of Nobel Prizes in Literature over the years? For such queries, SPARQL provides aggregation features that allow for applying functions over multiple solutions, for grouping solutions, and for filtering solutions according to the result of an aggregate function; we now discuss each in turn.

6.2.7.1 Aggregate Functions

SPARQL defines seven aggregate functions that apply over bags (multisets) of solutions, which we enumerate in Table 6.4. We begin with illustrative examples for the first (and most popular) such function: count.

Example 6.16

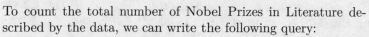

To count the total number of Nobel Prizes in Literature described by the data, we can write the following query:

```
SELECT (count(*) AS ?num)
WHERE {
  ?npl a :NobelPrizeLiterature .
}
```

This will return the value 4 over the running example. The aggregate function count(*) invokes a count of the current solutions. Where necessary, we may also request a count of the solutions for a given variable.

```
SELECT (count(?npl) AS ?num)
WHERE {
  ?npl a :NobelPrizeLiterature .
}
```

This will also return the value 4 for ?num.

Table 6.4 SPARQL aggregate functions
† All expressions were introduced in SPARQL 1.1.

Function	Result
count†	Counts the number of solutions
sum†	Sums numeric values across solutions
avg†	Averages numeric values across solutions
min†	Returns the minimum solution
max†	Returns the maximum solution
groupConcat†	Concatenates strings from the solutions
sample†	Samples one solution (possibly non-deterministically)

Remark 6.15

Based on the previous example, one may ask: what precisely is the difference between counting the current solutions (count(*)) and counting the solutions for a given variable (e.g., count(?npl))?

First note that counting on a variable will only count solutions for which that variable is bound, so in the case of optional patterns, unions, etc., counting on variables may return fewer results than counting the entire solution tuples with * (assuming another variable may be bound).

Second, in the case of duplicate bindings for ?npl, note that the returned count will reflect these duplicates. For example, if we consider:

```
SELECT (count(?npl) AS ?num)
WHERE {
  ?npl a :NobelPrizeLiterature ; :winner ?winner .
}
```

This query returns 5 (as it would if we had specified count(*)), counting :NPL1904 twice (since it has two winners). To avoid this, we might be tempted to add the DISTINCT keyword as follows:

```
SELECT DISTINCT (count(?npl) AS ?num)
WHERE {
  ?npl a :NobelPrizeLiterature ; :winner ?winner .
}
```

However, this DISTINCT will remove duplicate solutions; since the only solution returned is 5, no solutions are removed. Instead what we wish to specify is an inner distinct clause:

```
SELECT (count(distinct ?npl) AS ?num)
WHERE {
  ?npl a :NobelPrizeLiterature ; :winner ?winner .
}
```

This removes the duplicate :NPL1904 result before applying the count function, thus giving the expected result of 4. On the other hand:

```
SELECT (count(distinct *) AS ?num)
WHERE {
  ?npl a :NobelPrizeLiterature ; :winner ?winner .
}
```

This query would return 5 since the two solutions for :NPL1904 are unique when considering both variables. In summary, counting on variables further allows to count distinct terms bound to that variable.

We further provide an example of a numeric aggregation function.

Example 6.17

Consider the following query looking for the average of the years in which a person from France won the Nobel Peace Prize in Literature:

```
SELECT (avg(?yearInt) AS ?avgYear)
WHERE {
  ?npl a :NobelPrizeLiterature ; :winner ?winner ; :year ?year .
  ?winner :country :France .
  BIND (xsd:integer(str(?year)) AS ?yearInt)
}
```

The running example would return "1902.5"^^xsd:decimal (taking the average of the years 1901 and 1904 in which a French person won).

6.2.7.2 Grouping Solutions: GROUP BY

What then if we wished to count winners per country? For this, we would need to group solutions by country before applying an aggregation function.

> GROUP BY[†]: Groups solutions according to a set of variables bound to the same tuple of terms.

We illustrate the use of GROUP BY in the following example.

Example 6.18

To count the number of winners of the Nobel Prize in Literature per country, we can write the following query using GROUP BY:

```
SELECT ?country (count(?winner) AS ?num)
WHERE {
  ?npl a :NobelPrizeLiterature ; :winner ?winner.
  ?winner :country ?country .
}
GROUP BY ?country
```

This query groups solutions by their binding for the ?country variable, applies the aggregate function to each group, and returns:

?country	?num
:Spain	"1"^^xsd:integer
:France	"2"^^xsd:integer
:Germany	"1"^^xsd:integer
:Norway	"1"^^xsd:integer

Remark 6.16

We can only directly project variables used in the GROUP BY clause; for example, the following query is invalid (otherwise ?winner would have a bag of terms for each ?country and thus each solution):

```
SELECT ?country ?winner (count(?winner) AS ?num)
WHERE {
  ?npl a :NobelPrizeLiterature ; :winner ?winner.
  ?winner :country ?country .
}
GROUP BY ?country
```

Exercise 6.9

Write a query that, for each winner of the Nobel Prize in Literature, returns the number of winners in previous years from the same country, returning zero in the case that no such winner exists (rather than omitting the solution for that winner).

We can further group solutions by a set of variables.

Example 6.19

Assuming we wished to count winners per country and decade, we could write this query as follows:

```
SELECT ?country ?decade (count(?winner) AS ?num)
WHERE {
  ?npl a :NobelPrizeLiterature ; :winner ?winner ; :year ?year .
  ?winner :country ?country .
  BIND (concat(substr(str(?year),1,3),"0") AS ?decade)
}
GROUP BY ?country ?decade
```

To make the results more interesting, let us cheat and assume that the graph includes the fact that Romain Rolland (:RRolland) from France won the prize in 1915. In this case, the results would be as follows:

?country	?decade	?num
:Spain	"1900"	"1"^^xsd:integer
:France	"1900"	"2"^^xsd:integer
:Germany	"1900"	"1"^^xsd:integer
:Norway	"1900"	"1"^^xsd:integer
:France	"1910"	"1"^^xsd:integer

Syntactically, we could also write the above query as:

```
SELECT ?country ?decade (count(?winner) AS ?num)
WHERE {
  ?npl a :NobelPrizeLiterature ; :winner ?winner ; :year ?year .
  ?winner :country ?country .
}
GROUP BY ?country (concat(substr(str(?year),1,3),"0") AS ?decade)
```

We continue by providing examples using other aggregate functions. The first example illustrates the use of max and min.

Example 6.20

Assume we wished to find the interval between the first time a country won the Nobel Prize in Literature and the last time they won; we could write this as the following query:

```
SELECT ?country (max(?yearInt) - min(?yearInt) AS ?interval)
WHERE {
  ?npl a :NobelPrizeLiterature ; :winner ?winner ; :year ?year .
  ?winner :country ?country .
  BIND (xsd:integer(str(?year)) AS ?yearInt)
}
GROUP BY ?country
```

Evaluated on the running example, this would return an interval of 0 for :Germany, :Norway and :Spain, while returning 3 for :France.

Remark 6.17

Like the expressions discussed in Section 6.2.4, when an aggregation function throws an error, the solution is preserved and an unbound is returned as a result for the function. For example, consider:

```
SELECT ?country (avg(?year) AS ?average)
WHERE {
  ?npl a :NobelPrizeLiterature ; :winner ?winner ; :year ?year .
  ?winner :country ?country .
}
GROUP BY ?country
```

Since each year in the data is of type xsd:gYear while avg is defined for numeric types, each call to the function will return an error. However, rather than return empty solutions, the following will be returned:

?country	?avg
:Spain	
:France	
:Germany	
:Norway	

All countries are returned, even though the corresponding aggregate function will throw an error in each case. Rather than discarding the solution, the variable storing the aggregation result is left unbound.

The next example illustrates the use of group_concat and sample.

Example 6.21

In Remark 6.16, we mentioned that we can only project variables used in a GROUP BY clause (unless part of an aggregate function); hence we cannot write, for example:

```
SELECT ?country ?winner (count(?winner) AS ?num)
WHERE {
  ?npl a :NobelPrizeLiterature ; :winner ?winner.
  ?winner :country ?country .
}
GROUP BY ?country
```

However, the aggregate functions group_concat and sample provide two options to still project data from variables such as ?winner above.

```
SELECT ?country (group_concat(?winner) AS ?wins)
  (count(?winner) AS ?num)
WHERE {
  ?npl a :NobelPrizeLiterature ; :winner ?winner.
  ?winner :country ?country .
}
GROUP BY ?country
```

This returns the following result, where multiple winners within a given group winners are concatenated and returned as a single string (in reality, this string would contain full IRI strings for the winners):

?country	?wins	?num
:Spain	":JEchegaray"	"1"^^xsd:integer
:France	":SPrudhomme :FMistral"	"2"^^xsd:integer
:Germany	":TMommsen"	"1"^^xsd:integer
:Norway	":BBjørnson"	"1"^^xsd:integer

By default, the concatenation uses a space separator, but this can be changed by specifying – for example – (?winner;separator="|").

Rather than concatenate all of the winners, we might prefer to see an example of one such winner. For this we can use sample.

```
SELECT ?country (sample(?winner) AS ?ex)
  (count(?winner) AS ?num)
WHERE {
  ?npl a :NobelPrizeLiterature ; :winner ?winner.
  ?winner :country ?country .
}
GROUP BY ?country
```

This randomly samples a winner from each group, returning (e.g.):

?country	?wins	?num
:Spain	:JEchegaray	"1"^^xsd:integer
:France	:FMistral	"2"^^xsd:integer
:Germany	:TMommsen	"1"^^xsd:integer
:Norway	:BBjørnson	"1"^^xsd:integer

Replacing :FMistral with :SPrudhomme would also give a valid result.

6.2.7.3 Aggregate Filters: HAVING

Consider a query for countries with two or more winners of the Nobel Prize in Literature. Though it may be tempting to use a FILTER over count, the filters we have seen thus far inhabit the WHERE clause, while count resides outside the WHERE clause. Hence we need a special filter:

> HAVING[†]: Filters a solution based on an expression that requires using an aggregate function.

Example 6.22

To find countries with two or more winners, we can write:

```
SELECT ?country (count(?winner) AS ?num)
WHERE {
  ?npl a :NobelPrizeLiterature ; :winner ?winner.
  ?winner :country ?country .
}
GROUP BY ?country
HAVING (count(?winner) >= 2)
```

A HAVING clause resides outside the WHERE clause and allows for filtering solutions based on the result of an aggregate function. Functions allowed in standard FILTER clauses can likewise be used in a HAVING clause. The aggregate functions used in the HAVING clause do not necessarily need to correspond to those appearing in the projection of the query. The running example will yield the result :France (?country) and 2 (?num).

> *Exercise 6.10*
>
> *Write a query to count the number of winners of the Nobel Prize in Literature after the year 1902 (exclusive).*

6.2.8 Solution Modifiers

Solution modifiers in SPARQL transform the solutions returned to the user. In fact, we have already seen a number of these solution modifiers in action:

SELECT: Project certain variables.
  DISTINCT: Remove duplicate solutions.
  REDUCED: Permit duplicate solutions to be (optionally) removed.

However, there are three important solution modifiers we have not yet seen. By default, the solutions to a SPARQL query are unordered, but in many circumstances, users may wish to view results ordered by some criteria. Furthermore, they may wish to only return a subset of results, such as to specify top-k queries. For such operations, SPARQL provides a number of features to modify the final set of solutions. These include:

ORDER BY: Allows for ordering solutions by one or more variables; order
  can be ascending (by default) or descending.
OFFSET: Allows for skipping a given number of solutions.
LIMIT: Allows for returning (at most) a given number of solutions.

Example 6.23

The following query returns the second and third Nobel Prizes in Literature:

```
SELECT ?npl
WHERE {
  ?npl a :NobelPrizeLiterature ; :year ?year .
  BIND (xsd:integer(?year) AS ?yearInt)
}
ORDER BY ?yearInt
LIMIT 2
OFFSET 1
```

The ORDER BY clause specifies that solutions should be sorted in ascending order of the ?yearInt term; the OFFSET clause will then skip the first result, while the LIMIT clause specifies that at most 2 results should be returned. The result is thus :NPL1902 and :NPL1903.

We can also order over multiple columns, specify ascending or descending order, and order the result of aggregation functions.

Example 6.24

We illustrate a more advanced `ORDER BY` clause on multiple attributes, with descending order and an aggregation function:

```
SELECT ?country (count(?winner) AS ?num)
WHERE {
  ?npl a :NobelPrizeLiterature ; :winner ?winner.
  ?winner :country ?country .
}
GROUP BY ?country
ORDER BY (count(?winner)) DESC(?country)
```

This gives results ordered by ?num, then by ?country (descending).

?country	?num
:Spain	"1"^^xsd:integer
:Norway	"1"^^xsd:integer
:Germany	"1"^^xsd:integer
:France	"2"^^xsd:integer

Remark 6.18

SPARQL does not define a total ordering of all terms; however, it does fix the following high-level ordering that must be followed by a compliant implementation (starting with the lowest elements):

1. Unbound
2. Blank nodes
3. IRIs
4. Literals
   a. Simple literals (no language tag)
   b. String literals (with datatype xsd:string)

Furthermore, IRIs must be ordered following UTF-8 codepoint ordering, and datatypes compatible with a comparison operator (e.g., <) must follow the ordering of that operator, meaning that, for example, "2"^^xsd:integer must come before "3.0"^^decimal. However, SPARQL does not define an order for literals with language tags, literals across different (primitive) datatypes, literals with unsupported datatypes, etc. Thus a SPARQL implementation may implement whatever ordering it so chooses over pairs of such terms, so long as the ordering does not conflict with what the standard does define.

Casting xsd:gYear to xsd:integer in Example 6.23 is thus "safer", since the latter datatype has a total ordering.

Remark 6.19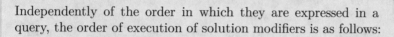

The aggregate functions min/max are defined in terms of ORDER
BY and so the results of, for example, ORDER BY/LIMIT 1 correspond with
those given for the aggregate function min while the results of ORDER BY
DESC/LIMIT 1 correspond with those for max.

Remark 6.20

Independently of the order in which they are expressed in a
query, the order of execution of solution modifiers is as follows:

1. ORDER BY
2. SELECT
3. DISTINCT / REDUCED
4. OFFSET
5. LIMIT

Hence, for example, solutions can be ordered based on unprojected variables, duplicates are removed from projected solutions, offsets and limits
apply after duplicate solutions have been removed (if specified), etc.

6.2.9 Sub-Select Queries

In a typical query, aggregation functions and solution modifiers can only be
used outside the WHERE clause. But what if we wish to use them inside the
WHERE clause, for example, to join their results with other parts of the data?
In this case, we can use a sub-select query (introduced in SPARQL 1.1).

Example 6.25

Consider a query looking for the highest number of people
awarded the Nobel Prize in Literature in a given year:

```
SELECT (count(?winner) AS ?num)
WHERE {
  ?npl a :NobelPrizeLiterature ; :winner ?winner .
}
GROUP BY ?npl
ORDER BY DESC(count(?winner))
LIMIT 1
```

But what if we wished to return the years in which the highest number of people were awarded? We could consider a query such as:

```
SELECT ?year (count(?winner) AS ?num)
WHERE {
  ?npl a :NobelPrizeLiterature ; :winner ?winner ; :year ?year .
}
GROUP BY ?npl ?year
ORDER BY DESC(count(?winner))
LIMIT 1
```

We add ?year to the GROUP BY clause to be able to project it (assuming that each prize has precisely one year, this will not affect the grouping of solutions). However, in the case of ties, this query will only return one year in which the highest number of people were awarded – the year that happens to be returned by the LIMIT 1 clause.

If we wished to account for years with ties, a better way to express this query would be using two sub-queries as follows:

```
SELECT ?year ?num
WHERE {
  ?npl :year ?year .
  FILTER(?num = ?maximum)
  {
    SELECT (count(?winner) AS ?maximum)
    WHERE {
      ?npl a :NobelPrizeLiterature ; :winner ?winner .
    }
    GROUP BY ?npl
    ORDER BY DESC(count(?winner))
    LIMIT 1
  }
  {
    SELECT ?npl (count(?winner) AS ?num)
    WHERE {
      ?npl a :NobelPrizeLiterature ; :winner ?winner .
    }
    GROUP BY ?npl
  }
}
```

The first sub-query finds the highest number of winners of a given prize, while the second sub-query computes the counts of winners in each year. SPARQL defines a "bottom-up" style of evaluation, where the sub-queries are evaluated first and their solutions are fed to the outer query, where the outer query then finds the year of the prize returned by the second sub-query and ensures that its count of winners equals the highest value found by the first sub-query. This returns one solution, namely "1904"^^xsd:gYear with a count of "2"^^xsd:integer.

Due to the "bottom-up" evaluation of sub-queries, the outer query can only see the variables projected from a sub-query. Hence for example, the variable ?npl in the outer query will be joined with the same variable projected from the second sub-query, but not with the unprojected variable in the first sub-query; in other words, we could rename ?npl to some other variable in the first sub-query without affecting the results as it has no correspondence with the ?npl variable elsewhere. Likewise the ?winner variables in both sub-queries do not correlate.

> **Exercise 6.11**
>
> Write a query to find the average number of Nobel Prizes in Literature per country (with some winner). If a country has multiple winners for a prize in the same year, count that prize once.

> **Exercise 6.12**
>
> Building on Exercise 6.11, find countries that have won more Nobel Prizes in Literature than average.

> **Exercise 6.13**
>
> Write a query to find winners of the Nobel Prize in Literature with the same number of predecessors as successors for the prize (i.e., the query should return :BBjørnson over the running example).

6.2.10 In-line Values

In cases where a user wishes to match against a static list of values, SPARQL offers the expression in (and its negation not in); however, this expression only allows for matching a single variable and does not allow for binding new values. Hence SPARQL also offers a VALUES feature, which can bind specific tuples of terms to tuples of variables – effectively creating an initial set of solutions – that can be used elsewhere in the query.

VALUES[†]: Provides in-line solutions for a tuple of variables.

Unlike the BIND/AS feature seen previously – which allows for extending each solution either with a constant or the result of a function applied over the solution – the VALUES feature allows for defining a set of tuples that will be joined over all the solutions. Thus the VALUES feature can be thought of as an alternative to sub-select queries, where instead of providing a query expression, one may directly give static solutions.

Example 6.26

Assume we are interested in a linguistic analysis of the Nobel Prizes in Literature, where in particular we are interested in associating winners with a particular language family. Unfortunately in the data we do not have information available about languages, but we could give at least a crude distribution of winners per language family by associating countries to language families using VALUES as follows.

```
SELECT ?family (count(distinct ?winner) AS ?num)
WHERE {
  ?npl a :NobelPrizeLiterature ; :winner ?winner .
  ?winner :country ?country .
  VALUES (?country ?family) {
    (:France :Romance)
    (:France :Celtic)
    (:Spain :Romance)
    (:Norway :Germanic)
    (:Germany :Germanic)
  }
}
GROUP BY ?family
```

The VALUES clause constructs a set of initial solutions that are joined with the results of the outer query, returning a count of 2 for the :Celtic and :Germanic families and a count of 3 for the :Romance family.

A particular setting in which this feature may be useful is as an optimisation for SPARQL Federation, where a query engine can invoke and return results from an external SPARQL service over the Web. In this setting, the client can send a list of local results to the remote service using VALUES [12]. In order to facilitate this use-case, SPARQL supports appending a VALUES clause to the end of a query; this avoids the client having to parse a query to insert the VALUES clause within the WHERE clause (see Remark 6.22 for an example). We will discuss more about SPARQL Federation later in Section 6.4.

In some cases, there may be no information available for a particular variable in a tuple that we wish to include as part of the in-line values. For such cases, SPARQL introduces the UNDEF keyword to leave a variable undefined.

Example 6.27

We now wish to perform a more fine-grained analysis of the languages of the winners of the Nobel Prize in Literature, where this time we are armed with the principal language of the countries of the winners and – in the case of some winners – the principal language of their works. In cases where we do not directly have a language associated with an author we can use UNDEF in the VALUES clause and resort to using the primary language of their country as a fall-back language.

```
SELECT ?language (count(distinct ?winner) AS ?num)
WHERE {
  ?npl a :NobelPrizeLiterature ; :winner ?winner .
  ?winner :country ?country .
  VALUES (?country ?cLang) {
    (:France :French)
    (:Spain :Spanish)
    (:Norway :Norwegian)
    (:Germany :German)
  }
  VALUES (?winner ?wLang) {
    (:SPrudhomme UNDEF)
    (:TMommsen UNDEF)
    (:BBjørnson UNDEF)
    (:FMistral :Provençal)
    (:JEchegaray :Spanish)
  }
  BIND (coalesce(?wLang,?cLang) AS ?language)
}
GROUP BY ?language
```

This query would return a count of one for each language: :French, :Spanish, :Norwegian, :German and :Provençal. Note that if we were to remove, for example, the tuple (:BBjørnson UNDEF), we would lose :Norwegian as a result since the winners generated by the outer query would not join with the solutions specified by the second VALUES clause.

Remark 6.21

When VALUES is defined for one variable:

```
... VALUES (?winner) {  (:SPrudhomme) (:TMommsen) (UNDEF) } ...
```

SPARQL permits the following abbreviated syntax:

```
... VALUES ?winner {  :SPrudhomme :TMommsen UNDEF) } ...
```

Remark 6.22   (i)

One can put the VALUES clause after the query, in which case
the specified solutions join with the query solutions after aggregation,
but before solution modifiers (e.g., SELECT) are applied. For example:

```
SELECT ?p ?l
WHERE {
 ?p :country ?c .
}
VALUES ( ?c ?l ) { (:Spain :Spanish) }
```

returns :JEchegary, :Spanish; although ?c is not projected from the
query, it is joined with the VALUES before the projection is applied.

6.2.11 Querying Multiple Graphs

Our trusty running example of Figure 6.1 has served us well – if perhaps a
bit repetitively – until now. But in fact, the SPARQL standard is defined
not over a single graph, but rather over a collection of graphs. Consider, for
example, a SPARQL engine indexing RDF data collected from thousands of
sources on the Web. Storing all this data as one giant RDF graph would mean
that we may lose the ability to recall which RDF triples came from which
source; this may be problematic, for example, if there are certain sources we
trust more (or less) than other sources. For such a scenario where we wish
to track the source of data – amongst others – SPARQL offers the ability
to manage and query multiple graphs. Thus, in a particular query, we may
choose to return solutions from a particular combination of sources, and/or
return the sources of data used as part of the solutions. Furthermore, we will
later be able to update selected graphs from their original sources.

Along these lines, SPARQL offers support for indexing multiple graphs, for
restricting which query patterns access which graphs, as well as for selecting
which graphs will be used for a particular query. We now discuss these aspects.

6.2.11.1 Dataset: Named Graphs and Default Graph

Rather than being defined over a single RDF graph (as exemplified in
Figure 6.1), SPARQL is defined over an RDF dataset as previously discussed in Section 3.6. We recall that an RDF dataset is defined as follows:
$D := \{G, (x_1, G_1), \ldots, (x_n, G_n)\}$, where each $G, G_1, \ldots, G_n$ is an RDF graph,
where each $x_1, \ldots, x_n$ is either a blank node or an IRI, where G is called the
default graph, and where $(x_1, G_1), \ldots, (x_n, G_n)$ are called named graphs. In

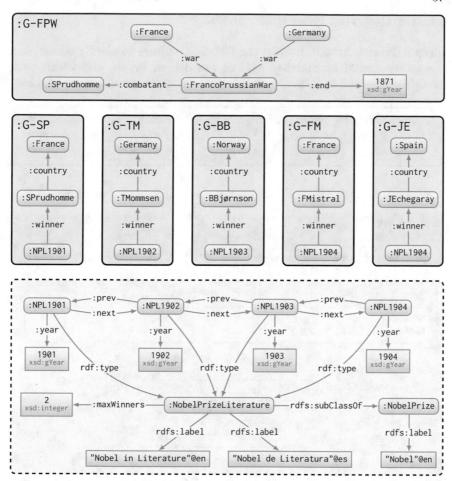

Fig. 6.3 Example SPARQL dataset describing winners of Nobel Prizes for Literature; named graphs are bordered with solid lines and their name is given in the top-left corner; the default graph is bordered with a dashed line

the case of SPARQL, however $x_1, \ldots, x_n$ are all IRIs (blank nodes cannot be used as names). In Figure 6.3, we provide an example of an RDF dataset, consisting of a default graph and six named graphs. The default graph contains high-level data about all of the Nobel Prizes for Literature, five of the named graphs contain information about the winners of the prizes, while a sixth named graphs represents background data about the Franco-Prussian War. The features that we discuss in this section will allow for selectivity querying specific graphs or specific combinations of graphs; furthermore, they allow for finding the (names of) graphs that match given graph patterns.

6.2.11.2 Querying Named Graphs: GRAPH

Given a dataset, SPARQL offers the following feature to specify which parts of a query should be matched against the default graph, and which parts should be matched against a particular named graph or all named graphs:

> GRAPH: Allows to match data from a specific named graph (when given an IRI), or named graphs (when given a variable). Where GRAPH is not specified, results are generated from the default graph only.

We illustrate the GRAPH clause by means of an extended example.

Example 6.28

First we consider the case where no FROM, FROM NAMED or GRAPH clause is specified; the following query asks for available information about the Nobel Prize in Literature in 1904:

```
SELECT *
WHERE { :NPL1904 ?p ?o }
```

When executed over Figure 6.3, the results are:

?p	?o
:year	"1904"^^xsd:gYear
:prev	:NPL1903
rdf:type	:NobelPrizeLiterature

The results do not reflect the fact that :FMistral and :JEchegaray won the prize though present in the dataset: since no GRAPH clause is specified, results are generated only from the default graph, where the winners are rather given in the graphs named :G-FM and :G-JE.

If we wanted to fetch data about :NPL1904 from only the graph named :G-FM, we would use a GRAPH clause as follows:

```
SELECT *
WHERE { GRAPH :G-FM { :NPL1904 ?p ?o } }
```

This returns only results from that named graph:

?p	?o
:winner	:FMistral

If we would rather return the data about :NPL1904 from the default graph and *all* named graphs, we would write:

```
SELECT *
WHERE {
  { :NPL1904 ?p ?o }
  UNION
  { GRAPH ?g { :NPL1904 ?p ?o } }
}
```

Since the graph clause is specified with a variable, it will match all named graphs; furthermore, the name of the graph is projected from the query as ?g, generating the following results:

?p	?o	?g
:year	"1904"^^xsd:gYear	
:prev	:NPL1903	
rdf:type	:NobelPrizeLiterature	
:winner	:FMistral	:G-FM
:winner	:JEchegaray	:G-JE

Solutions generated from the default graph leave the ?g variable unbound, per the usual application of a union in SPARQL.

Next, assume we wished to find prizes shared by winners from France and Spain considering data from all named graphs; we could write:

```
SELECT ?prize
WHERE {
  GRAPH ?g {
    ?prize :winner ?winner1 . ?winner1 :country :France .
    ?prize :winner ?winner2 . ?winner2 :country :Spain .
  }
}
```

But this query will not generate any results since the pattern inside the graph can match at most one graph at-a-time: no single graph contains data that satisfies the pattern. What we should rather write is:

```
SELECT ?prize
WHERE {
  GRAPH ?g1 { ?prize :winner ?winner1 . ?winner1 :country :France . }
  GRAPH ?g2 { ?prize :winner ?winner2 . ?winner2 :country :Spain . }
}
```

This time the query allows the information about French and Spanish winners to be contained in different graphs. With these changes, the query now generates :NPL1904 as a solution.

Finally, we remark that a graph variable acts like any other, and can be filtered, joined, aggregated, and so forth, accordingly. Consider:

```
SELECT ?winner
WHERE {
  GRAPH ?g {
    ?prize :winner ?winner .
    ?winner :country :France .
  }
  VALUES ?g { :G-SP :G-TM :G-BB }
}
```

This query will return :SPrudhomme.

Exercise 6.14

*Based on Figure 6.3, write a query to find the winners of
the Nobel Prize in Literature that have fought in wars (returning
:SPrudhomme). You should not assume to know which parts of the data
are in named graphs and which parts are in the default graph.*

Remark 6.23

Many SPARQL systems can be configured to create a "virtual"
default graph that is the union (not distinguishing blank nodes across
graphs) or the merge (distinguishing blank nodes across graphs) of all
named graphs and the defined default graph, meaning that a query
without a GRAPH clause will access all triples in the dataset; this pre-
cludes the need to "copy" all data from the named graphs to the default
graph in cases where such a behaviour is desired.

Remark 6.24

The previous examples against the original RDF graph in Figure 6.1 have implicitly assumed it to be the default graph of the dataset.

6.2.11.3 Constructing a Query Dataset: FROM/FROM NAMED

Example 6.28 showed how the GRAPH clause can be used to access data from
named graphs, and how when it is absent, solutions are generated with respect
to the default graph. All such queries are defined with respect to the base
dataset shown in Figure 6.3 without modification. However, to provide more
flexibility in how various graphs are queried, SPARQL further allows to define

a query-specific dataset by constructing a new default graph (using FROM) and a set of named graphs (using FROM NAMED) from the base dataset; solutions are then generated with respect to the query-specific dataset.

FROM: Specifies the names of graphs that will be (RDF) merged to create the default graph of the query dataset.

FROM NAMED Specifies the names of graphs that will be added as named graphs to the query dataset.

Example 6.29

Let us consider the query:

```
SELECT *
FROM :G-FM
WHERE { :NPL1904 ?p ?o }
```

The FROM clause defines that the default graph for the query is defined with the data from :G-FM, and so the results are:

?p	?o
:winner	:FMistral

Importantly, the data in the base default graph – the year of the prize, the previous prize, and its type – are not returned: when we use a FROM or FROM NAMED clause, a fresh query-specific dataset is defined that "clears" the rest of the data from the base dataset.

We can also define a FROM clause that generates a default graph from multiple named graphs; consider, for example, the query:

```
SELECT *
FROM :G-FM
FROM :G-JE
WHERE { :NPL1904 ?p ?o }
```

This generates the following results:

?p	?o
:winner	:FMistral
:winner	:JEchegaray

(Though not shown, when multiple FROM graphs are specified, an RDF merge is applied to generate the default graph, meaning that any shared blank nodes will be distinguished before taking the union of triples.)

Next, let us combine GRAPH and FROM as follows:

```
SELECT *
FROM :G-FM
FROM :G-JE
WHERE { GRAPH ?g { :NPL1904 ?p ?o } }
```

This returns empty results: when we use FROM (or FROM NAMED) we start a fresh dataset, where in this case, we have not defined any named graphs for the query. Compare this with the following query:

```
SELECT *
FROM :G-FM
FROM NAMED :G-JE
WHERE { GRAPH ?g { :NPL1904 ?p ?o } }
```

The FROM NAMED clause loads :G-JE as a named graph, returning:

?p	?o	?g
:winner	:JEchegaray	:G-JE

We recall that the GRAPH clause only accesses data in named graphs.

Finally, we consider a more complex example that combines FROM, FROM NAMED and GRAPH clauses in one query:

```
SELECT *
FROM :G-FPW
FROM :G-SP
FROM NAMED :G-SP
FROM NAMED :G-TM
FROM NAMED :G-BB
FROM NAMED :G-FM
FROM NAMED :G-JE
WHERE {
  GRAPH ?g {
    ?prize :winner ?winner .
  }
  OPTIONAL {
    ?war :combatant ?winner .
    ?country :war ?war .
    ?winner :country ?country .
  }
}
```

We highlight the appearance of the graph name :G-SP in both a FROM and FROM NAMED clause such that the corresponding graph will be kept as a named graph and will also added to the default graph for the query. The dataset used for this query will then be as follows:

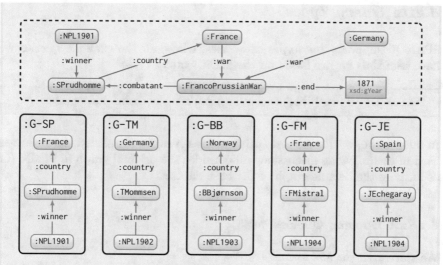

The dataset constructed for the query contains five named graphs (one for each FROM NAMED graph in the query) and a default graph (composed of the merge of the two FROM graphs in the query). The results for the query over the constructed dataset will then be as follows:

?g	?prize	?winner	?country	?war
:G-SP	:NPL1901	:SPrudhomme	:France	:FrancoPrussianWar
:G-TM	:NPL1902	:TMommsen		
:G-BB	:NPL1903	:BBjørnson		
:G-BB	:NPL1904	:FMistral		
:G-BB	:NPL1904	:JEchegaray		

Exercise 6.15

Use FROM/FROM NAMED *(but not* GRAPH*) to find prizes shared by winners from France and Spain (returning* :NPL1904 *from Figure 6.3).*

Remark 6.25

Using FROM/FROM NAMED, there is no way to reference the data in the default graph of the base dataset; furthermore, once we use FROM/FROM NAMED, this default graph is not considered by the query. Hence if we wish to query data that (only) resides in the default graph of the base dataset, we must avoid using FROM/FROM NAMED (however, we may still use GRAPH clauses, as required, for parts of the query).

6.2.12 Query Types

SPARQL supports four types of queries, where all the example queries we have seen thus far are based on the SELECT query type:

SELECT Returns a table of results (a multiset of solution mappings)

In this section, we discuss three other query types; for simplicity, the examples used in the following discussion will consider the original graph in Figure 6.1 as forming the default graph of the base dataset.

6.2.12.1 Boolean Queries: ASK

We start with the ASK form.

ASK Returns a boolean indicating whether the query has some result(s) (true) or not (false).

Example 6.30

Has anyone from France ever won the Nobel Prize in Literature? We can pose this query as follows:

```
ASK
WHERE {
  ?npl a :NobelPrizeLiterature ; :winner ?winner .
  ?winner :country :France .
}
```

This query returns true indicating that some solution is present. If we were to change :France to :Argentina the query would return false.

6.2.12.2 Creating Graphs: CONSTRUCT

Next we illustrate usage of CONSTRUCT queries, which can be used to transform from RDF graphs to RDF graphs.

CONSTRUCT Returns an RDF graph based on a specified template whose variables are instantiated with solutions from the query.

Example 6.31

Consider the following example query, which aims to construct a more concise graph that directly indicates which laureates of the Nobel Prize in Literature are successors/predecessors of which laureates:

```
CONSTRUCT {
  ?w1 :succ ?w2 .
  ?w2 :pred ?w1 .
}
WHERE {
  ?npl1 a :NobelPrizeLiterature ; :winner ?w1 .
  ?npl2 a :NobelPrizeLiterature ; :winner ?w2 .
  ?npl1 :next ?npl2 .
}
```

This query would result in the following RDF graph:

Remark 6.26

SPARQL offers an abbreviated syntax for queries with identical CONSTRUCT and WHERE clauses; for example, we could abbreviate:

```
CONSTRUCT { ?p :winner ?w. ?w :country :France . }
WHERE { ?p :winner ?w. ?w :country :France . }
```

as follows:

```
CONSTRUCT WHERE { ?p :winner ?w. ?w :country :France . }
```

In cases where a solution to a query would generate an invalid RDF triple – placing a literal as a subject or predicate, a blank node as a predicate, or an unbound in any position – the CONSTRUCT clause will simply omit that triple, while other valid triples for the solution will be kept.

Example 6.32

Returning to Example 6.31, what if we wished to add to the resulting graph a shared relation in case that two people from the same year win the prize? We could extend the above query as follows:

```
CONSTRUCT {
  ?w1a :succ ?w2 .
  ?w2 :pred ?w1a .
  ?w1b :shared ?w1c .
}
WHERE {
  ?npl1 a :NobelPrizeLiterature ; :winner ?w1a .
  OPTIONAL {
    ?npl2 a :NobelPrizeLiterature ; :winner ?w2 .
    ?npl1 :next ?npl2 .
  }
  OPTIONAL {
    ?npl1 :winner ?w1b , ?w1c . FILTER(?w1b != ?w1c)
  }
}
```

The WHERE clause generates the following solutions:

?npl1	?npl2	?w1a	?w1b	?w1c	?w2
:NPL1901	:NPL1902	:SPrudhomme			:TMommsen
:NPL1902	:NPL1903	:TMommsen			:BBjørnson
:NPL1903	:NPL1904	:BBjørnson			:FMistral
:NPL1903	:NPL1904	:BBjørnson			:JEchegaray
:NPL1904		:FMistral	:FMistral	:JEchegaray	
:NPL1904		:FMistral	::JEchegaray	:FMistral	
:NPL1904		:JEchegaray	:FMistral	:JEchegaray	
:NPL1904		:JEchegaray	:JEchegaray	:FMistral	

For the solutions that generate an unbound for a variable in a triple pattern in the CONSTRUCT clause, the corresponding triple is omitted from the result graph. Hence the above query solutions will be used to generate the following RDF graph, adding the shared relation:

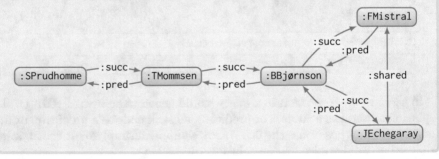

Exercise 6.16

Exercise 6.16

Following Example 6.32, provide a CONSTRUCT *query to generate the predecessors and successors of Nobel Laureates in Literature from the same country (e.g.,* :SPrudhomme *should be the predecessor of* :FMistral *and* :FMistral *the successor of* :SPrudhomme*), adding a shared relation in case two people from the same country share the prize in the same year. The resulting graph should only contain most recent predecessors/-successors by this definition, such that, for example, if A is a predecessor of B and B a predecessor of C, then A should not be represented as a predecessor of C. Laureates who do not share a country with another laureate should not be included in the resulting graph.*

Example 6.33

In the previous example, the nodes in the result graph were generated from existing terms in the base dataset. But a common requirement is to also generate new nodes for each solution. The more direct way to achieve this is by putting a blank node in the CONSTRUCT clause. Consider for example a query that, for each country, aims to summarise its achievements in the Nobel Prize in Literature, counting the number of years in which the award was won:

```
CONSTRUCT {
  _:x :country ?c .
  _:x :prize :NobelPrizeLiterature .
  _:x :won ?n .
}
WHERE {
  { SELECT (count(distinct ?npl) AS ?n ) ?c
    WHERE {
      ?npl a :NobelPrizeLiterature ; :winner ?w .
      ?w :country ?c .
    }
    GROUP BY ?c
  }
}
```

We require a sub-query here to state that we wish to count the results of the aggregation. In this case, the blank node _:x will generate a fresh blank node once for each solution (for a given solution, the same blank node will be generated for each appearance of _:x). Thus the above query will generate an RDF graph as follows:

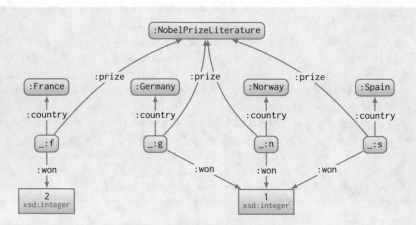

A fresh blank node is generated for each solution in the resulting graph (the blank node labels may vary modulo RDF isomorphism).

If we wished to instead generate fresh IRIs for each solution, we may consider using an expression as follows in the WHERE clause:

```
BIND (iri(concat(str(?c),"_NPL")) AS ?x)
```

... replacing the blank node _:x with the variable ?x in the CONSTRUCT clause; this returns the same graph replacing _:f with :France_NPL, etc. Note that such functions may generate the same IRI across multiple solutions (which may be indeed a useful feature for some queries).

6.2.12.3 Describing Resources: DESCRIBE

The final form of SPARQL query is the DESCRIBE query.

> DESCRIBE Given an IRI, or a list of variables, returns an RDF graph describing the IRI, or the terms (IRIs or blank nodes) returned as solutions for the specified variables.

Intuitively, the DESCRIBE form allows users to succinctly ask for relevant RDF triples for a given term or set of terms. What precisely constitutes "relevant triples" is left for a particular implementation to define, but typically will include all triples where the given term appears as subject, possibly all triples where the term appears as object, and perhaps some other triples as well, such as those connected by a path of blank nodes to the described term (sometimes called a "Concise Bounded Description" (CBD); see [370]).

We first illustrate use of DESCRIBE with a constant IRI.

Example 6.34

The following query:

```
DESCRIBE :NPL1901
```

May return an RDF graph such as:

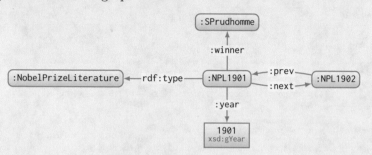

This assumes that the implementation has chosen to return, for example, all triples where the term appears as subject and object. Other implementations may choose to return other graphs, such as only the triples where the term appears as subject, all triples where the term appears, triples connecting blank nodes in the graph to the term, etc.

This feature is often used to support Linked Data with SPARQL engines, as will be described in more detail in Chapter 8.

Aside from requesting RDF sub-graphs describing particular constants, we can also use the DESCRIBE feature to request a sub-graph describing the terms matched by a given WHERE clause, as illustrated in the following.

Example 6.35

We use DESCRIBE to return an RDF graph about Nobel Prizes:

```
DESCRIBE ?np ?type
WHERE {
  ?np a ?type .
  ?type rdfs:subClassOf :NobelPrize .
}
```

(Since we request a description for all in-scope variables, we could equivalently have written DESCRIBE *.) The DESCRIBE query takes the union of terms bound to each variable and returns a graph containing relevant triples for each term; the following graph is returned if we consider all triples where the described term appears as subject or object:

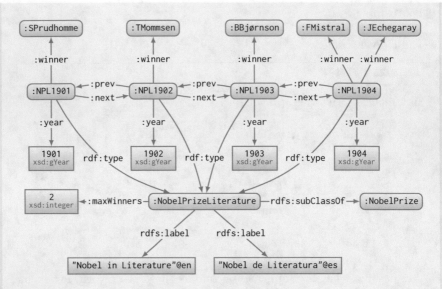

Any literal or unbound terms given by a variable will be ignored; however, literal terms may be included in the results when they describe an IRI or blank node (for example, the labels for :NobelPrizeLiterature).

Remark 6.27

Since an ASK query returns a boolean value indicating the existence of a solution, and CONSTRUCT and DESCRIBE queries return a set of triples (without order or duplicates), such queries are insensitive to duplicate solutions and to order (unless combined with an offset or limit).

6.2.13 In Practice

Since its standardisation, the SPARQL query language has been implemented in various systems, including, for example, 4store [168], Blazegraph (formerly BigData) [380], GraphDB (formerly (Big)OWLIM) [57], Jena TDB [401], RDF4J (formerly Sesame) [82] and Virtuoso [120]. Such implementations have been used to publish a variety of SPARQL query services – often called "SPARQL endpoints" – on the Web, where hundreds of such services have emerged in recent years, indexing RDF datasets extending into the billions of triples, offering open access to users [13]. Some of these SPARQL endpoints receive thousands or even millions of queries per day [342, 72, 255]. One such endpoint is that hosted for the Wikidata knowledge graph [255].

Project 6.1

The Wikidata knowledge graph offers a public SPARQL end-point at `https://query.wikidata.org/`. *The data in the knowledge graph cover a wide variety of topics including – you guessed it – Nobel Prizes! To put your new-found SPARQL knowledge into practice, consider writing SPARQL queries on the Wikidata query service to answer the following questions. Note that some questions may leave some ambiguity – for example, regarding what precisely to project as return variables, whether to return labels or IRIs, whether countries that no longer exist should be filtered, etc. – where the reader is encouraged to make their own interpretation as interests them personally. We also recommend the reader to understand the autocompletion services and other tools that the Wikidata service provides to assist users when writing queries; a number of example queries are further provided by the query service that may help to get started (we do not detail these here as the interface and/or RDF modelling may change after publication).*

Write SPARQL queries to return:

- *The types of Nobel Prize (Peace, Literature, etc.).*
- *Laureates who have won two or more Nobel Prizes.*
- *Laureates who have won two or more types of Nobel Prize.*
- *Organisations who have won Nobel Prizes.*
- *People who have won a Nobel Prize and an Academy Award.*
- *Pairs of siblings who have won Nobel Prizes.*
- *The most populated country without a Nobel Prize in Literature.*
- *The top-10 universities ordered by Nobel Laureate alumni.*
- *The top-10 countries with the highest number of Nobel Laureates per capita (dividing winners from that country by its population).*
- *The number of winners of Nobel Prizes by continent.*
- *Pairs of Nobel Laureates where the first laureate was (recursively) influenced by the second laureate.*
- *For each type of Nobel Prize, the ratio of female laureates.*
- *The ratio of female Nobel Laureates per decade.*
- *For each type of Nobel Prize, the average no. of laureates per year.*
- *For each type of Nobel Prize, the count of laureates per profession.*
- *People nominated at least once for a Nobel Prize but without winning a Nobel Prize, ordered by the number of nominations.*
- *For each person, a count of nominations and wins of Nobel Prizes; the results should not count a win as a nomination, should return zero in the case that a person has not won or been nominated without winning, and should only return results where one value is non-zero.*
- *Winners of the Nobel Prize in Literature that fought in wars, the year they won the prize, and the year the war ended.*

> *Owing to its nature as an extensive, collaboratively-edited knowledge graph, Wikidata may be incomplete or indeed inaccurate for some facts pertinent to these questions; however, by the same token, the reader may also choose to add or revise such facts in the knowledge graph such that the results will improve for the reader that follows!*
>
> *Of the above questions, which could have been easily answered using Google? (... assuming a previous reader has not published the results of the above questions online already, of course.)*

6.3 SPARQL Semantics and Complexity

While Section 6.2 introduced all features supported by the SPARQL query language, it did so in an informal way through illustrative examples. However, these examples leave some ambiguity in terms of what, precisely, the results for certain queries should be over a dataset. A good example of such ambiguity was highlighted in Remark 6.11, where we discussed the two main differences between MINUS and FILTER NOT EXISTS; these features were not defined in sufficient detail for such differences to follow as a consequence, and hence we were left to give yet more examples to approach a better fit of their semantics.

While the SPARQL standard [169] provides in-depth definitions that aim to be unambiguous and complete – including a formal grammar outlining valid queries, definitions of how expressions and other query features should be evaluated, and so forth – these definitions are complex, not self-contained (relying on other standards such as XML Schema [313]), and mix set-theoretic style definitions with more imperative pseudo-code and informal clarifications. Hence we will not delve into the full details of how SPARQL is defined in the standard – which are perhaps of most relevance to those who wish to implement the standard, and for which we refer to the standard itself [169].

Still, it would be useful to have a more formal definition of the query language, not only to understand precisely what results should be given by what queries, but also to understand its expressivity (for example, *how does SPARQL relate to existing languages like SQL?*), and to understand the complexity of tasks involving the language (for example, *which features of the query language are the most computationally costly to support?*).

Various authors have already formalised and studied core aspects of the query language, including features such as basic graph patterns, optional patterns, unions of patterns, negation, property paths, amongst others [310, 250, 11]. Here, we will likewise define a high-level syntax and semantics for SPARQL, which will help us to characterise the language according to some interesting theoretical properties. However, rather than studying isolated features, our goal will be to define as much of the language as possible.

Remark 6.28

We emphasise that the definitions that follow should not be considered normative. Our objective in this section is a difficult one: to define the meaning of SPARQL queries in as clean a manner as possible while staying as faithful to the standard as possible. We claim that our objective is difficult since there are various issues in the standard – relating to the scoping of variables and filters; the interpretation of blank nodes; the multiplicity of results; the handling of unbounds and errors; converting between ordered lists, bags of solutions, and grouped solutions; etc. – that complicate things considerably and that are often overlooked (for simplicity) in the definitions of SPARQL found in the research literature. Many of the definitions we provide here are – to the best of our knowledge – novel. Despite some considerable efforts to remain faithful to the standard, there are likely to be some differences between what we define here and what the standard recommends. In such cases, of course, the standard takes precedence [169].

6.3.1 SPARQL Solutions and Abstract Syntax

We begin by defining a query solution, which is a mapping from variables to terms (IRIs, blank nodes, literals, or unbound). Such solutions are returned by SELECT queries, and are used to generate results for other query types.

Definition 21 (SPARQL solution). Let u denote an unbound value. A *solution* μ is a mapping from variables **V** to terms $\mathbf{IBL} \cup \{u\}$.[a] We denote by $\mathrm{dom}(\mu)$ the set of variables that μ does not map to u.

[a] We recall that we use, e.g., **IBL** as a shortcut for $\mathbf{I} \cup \mathbf{B} \cup \mathbf{L}$.

Example 6.36

We define the first solution from Example 6.32:

?npl1	?npl2	?w1a	?w1b ?w1c ?w2
:NPL1901	:NPL1902	:SPrudhomme	:TMommsen

as a mapping μ such that $\mu(\text{?npl1}) = $:NPL1901, $\mu(\text{?npl2}) = $:NPL1902, $\mu(\text{?w1a}) = $:SPrudhomme, $\mu(\text{?w1b}) = \mu(\text{?w1c}) = u$, and $\mu(\text{?w2}) = $:TMommsen.

Next we define an abstract syntax for the SPARQL language. This defines what sorts of queries can be written down, but simplifies the real-world syntax (e.g., it does not contain certain shortcuts, prefix statements, etc.).

Definition 22 (SPARQL abstract syntax). Let $\mathbf{V}$ denote a set of query variables disjoint with $\mathbf{IBL}$. Given a set of terms $X \subset \mathbf{VIBL}$,[a] we denote by $\mathrm{vars}(X) := X \cap \mathbf{V}$ a function giving the variables that X contains. We define the abstract syntax of a SPARQL query as follows:

1. A **triple pattern** (s, p, o) is an element of $\mathbf{VIBL} \times \mathbf{VI} \times \mathbf{VIBL}$ (i.e., an RDF triple allowing variables in any position).
2. A **basic graph pattern** B is a set of **triple patterns**.

   - A **basic graph pattern** is a **query pattern** on
     $\bigcup_{(s,p,o) \in B} \mathrm{vars}(\{s, p, o\})$.

3. A **path pattern** (s, e, o) is a member of the set $\mathbf{VIBL} \times \mathbf{E} \times \mathbf{VIBL}$, where $\mathbf{E}$ is the set of all path expressions defined by Table 6.3.
4. A **navigational graph pattern** N is a set of **paths patterns** and **triple patterns**.

   - A **navigational graph pattern** is a **query pattern** on
     $\bigcup_{(s,x,o) \in N} \mathrm{vars}(\{s, x, o\})$.

5. If Q_1 and Q_2 are **query patterns** on V_1 and V_2 then:

   - $[Q_1 \, \mathrm{AND} \, Q_2]$ is a **query pattern** on $V_1 \cup V_2$;
   - $[Q_1 \, \mathrm{UNION} \, Q_2]$ is a **query pattern** on $V_1 \cup V_2$;
   - $[Q_1 \, \mathrm{OPTIONAL} \, Q_2]$ is a **query pattern** on $V_1 \cup V_2$;
   - $[Q_1 \, \mathrm{MINUS} \, Q_2]$ is a **query pattern** on V_1.

6. Let R be a *function expression*, built from the operators and functions of Tables 6.1 and 6.2, that takes a tuple of elements from $\mathbf{VIBL}$ as input and returns a value in $\mathbf{IBL} \cup \{u, \varepsilon\}$ where ε is an error. If Q is a **query pattern** on V and $v \in \mathbf{V} \setminus V$, then:

   - $\mathrm{FILTER}_R(Q)$ is a **query pattern** on V;
   - $\mathrm{BIND}_{R,v}(Q)$ is a **query pattern** on $V \cup \{v\}$.

7. Let M denote a bag of solutions on V_M (i.e., $V_M := \bigcup_{\mu \in M} \mathrm{dom}(\mu)$). If Q is a **query pattern** on V, then:

   - $\mathrm{VALUES}_M(Q)$ is a **query pattern** on $V \cup V_M$.

8. Let x denote an IRI and v a variable. If Q is a **query pattern** on V, then:

   - $\mathrm{GRAPH}_x(Q)$ is a **query pattern** on V.
   - $\mathrm{GRAPH}_v(Q)$ is a **query pattern** on $V \cup \{v\}$.

9. Let A denote an *aggregation expression* – using aggregation functions from Table 6.4[b] and functions from Tables 6.1 and 6.2[c] – that takes a tuple of elements in **VIBL** and returns a value in $\mathbf{IBL} \cup \{u, \varepsilon\}$;

   - If Q is a **query pattern** on V then:
     - Q is a **group pattern** on (V,V).
   - If Q is a **query pattern** on V and V' is a non-empty set of variables (called the *group key*), then:
     - GROUP$_{V'}(Q)$ is a **group pattern** on (V',V).
   - If Q is a **group pattern** on (V',V), then:
     - HAVING$_A(Q)$ is a **group pattern on** (V',V).
   - If Q is a **group pattern** on (V',V) and v is a fresh variable not appearing in $V \cup V'$, then:
     - AGG$_{A,v}(Q)$ is a **group pattern** on $(V' \cup \{v\}, V \cup \{v\})$.
   - If Q is a **group pattern** on (V',V) then:
     - FLATTEN(Q) is a **query pattern** on V'.

10. Let $\pm$ denote an element of $\{+, -\}$ (denoting ascending or descending order) and let $v_1, ..., v_n$ denote variables. Let Δ denote a boolean value (set to true for distinct results; false otherwise) and i and j denote natural numbers (for offset and limit, respectively).

    - If Q is a **query pattern** on V, then:
      - ORDER$_{(v_1, \pm_1), ..., (v_n, \pm_n)}(Q)$ is an **order pattern** on V.
    - If Q is a **query pattern** or **order pattern** on V; then:
      - SLICE$_{\Delta,i}(Q)$ is a **slice pattern** on V.
      - SLICE$_{\Delta,i,j}(Q)$ is a **slice pattern** on V.

11. Let Q denote a **query pattern**, **order pattern** or **slice pattern** on V; further let V' denote a set of variables; B a basic graph pattern; $X \subset \mathbf{IBV}$ a set of IRIs, blank nodes and variables; and $Y \subset \mathbf{IB}$ a set of IRIs and blank nodes. Then:

    - SELECT$_{V'}(Q)$ is a **query** and a **query pattern** on V'.
    - ASK(Q) is a **query**.
    - CONSTRUCT$_B(Q)$ is a **query**.
    - DESCRIBE$_X(Q)$ is a **query**.
    - DESCRIBE$_Y()$ is a **query**.

12. Let Q be a **query** and X and X' be a set of IRIs such that $X \cup X' \neq \emptyset$; then:

    - DATASET$_{X,X'}(Q)$ is a **query**.

---

[a] We say $X \subset \mathbf{VIBL}$ rather than $X \subseteq \mathbf{VIBL}$ since X is a finite set.

[b] For simplicity, we will assume distinct variants of aggregation functions (e.g., count(distinct . . .))) to be separate functions.

[c] Only aggregation functions from Table 6.4 will accept non-group-key variables.

This abstract syntax brings us a step closer to being able to formalise what a SPARQL query really means, and what solutions it should give over a particular dataset. In particular, it provides a simpler (though not simple!) abstraction of what can be expressed in a SPARQL query. In practice, the first step that a SPARQL implementation will follow upon receiving a query is to parse and convert it to an abstract syntax/structure similar to what we have defined, clearly denoting the sequence of operators that are to be applied to generate the result, allowing each operator to be defined and implemented individually. The abstract syntax serves as a similar purpose for us, but rather than implementing each operator, we will later define what each operator does. Ideally, in the interests of being thorough, we would now discuss conversion of the concrete SPARQL syntax into this abstract syntax, but that would require defining the precise grammar of the concrete syntax and a sequence of tedious syntactic conversions that we will not go into. Rather we will give an idea of such a translation with an example:

Example 6.37

Consider the following query:

```
SELECT (count(?winner) AS ?num)
WHERE {
  ?npl a :NobelPrizeLiterature ; :winner ?winner .
}
GROUP BY ?npl
ORDER BY DESC(count(?winner))
LIMIT 1
```

Letting B_0 denote the basic graph pattern $\{(?npl, :winner, ?winner), (?npl, a, :NobelPrizeLiterature)\}$, we could translate this query into the abstract syntax of Definition 22 as follows:

$$
\text{SELECT}_{\{?num\}}(
$$
$$
\quad \text{SLICE}_{false,0,1}(
$$
$$
\quad\quad \text{ORDER}_{(?num,-)}(
$$
$$
\quad\quad\quad \text{FLATTEN}(
$$
$$
\quad\quad\quad\quad \text{AGG}_{count(?winner),?num}(
$$
$$
\quad\quad\quad\quad\quad \text{GROUP}_{\{?npl\}}(B_0))))))
$$

One may observe some similarities but also some differences between the concrete syntax and the abstract syntax, where for example AGG, FLATTEN and SLICE appear only in the latter; these operations will make defining the semantics of the abstract syntax a little more concise. Defining precisely what each step does towards generating the final solutions is the subject of the discussion that follows.

Remark 6.29 ⓘ

Definition 22 defines two notions of a "join". The first is implicit in the definition of a basic graph pattern, which will be defined as a join of triple patterns. The second is given by $[Q_1 \text{ AND } Q_2]$, which is intended as the join of higher level operators. For example, consider:

```
SELECT ?winner
WHERE {
  { ?winner :country :Germany . }    # t1
  UNION
  { ?winner :country :France .  }    # t2
  ?prize :winner ?winner .           # t3
  ?prize a :NobelPrizeLiterature .   # t4
}
```

This query is represented in the abstract syntax as:

$$\text{SELECT}_{\{?winner\}}([[\{t_1\} \text{ UNION } \{t_2\}] \text{ AND } \{t_3, t_4\}])$$

The join between t_3 and t_4 is expressed as a basic graph pattern. The join between the union of t_1 and t_2 and this basic graph pattern is expressed with AND. The reason why we define two separate ways to express a join relates to how blank nodes in the query are mapped to terms in the graph: in SPARQL, the same blank node in two different basic graph patterns (e.g., on two sides of a union) can be mapped to two different terms in a single solution. We will provide more details in Remark 6.34 after defining the evaluation of such query patterns.

Note that there is no explicit term AND in the SPARQL concrete syntax: AND serves as an implicit (default) operator in SPARQL.

Remark 6.30 ⓘ

The reader may wonder why, in certain cases, the abstract syntax does not restrict variables to appear in the domain of the sub-pattern. For example, the abstract syntax defines the function $\text{GROUP}_{V'}(Q)$ but it does not restrict V' to be a subset of the domain of Q. This is in fact the case for the SPARQL standard, where one can put a "fresh" variable in a GROUP BY (or a SELECT, DESCRIBE, etc.); these variables will then map to unbound (u). On the other hand, given a group pattern on (V', V) where V' is the group key and V the domain, SPARQL does restrict usage of $V \setminus V'$ since each such variable may map to a bag of terms. In particular, these variables cannot be projected in SELECT, cannot be used for ORDER, cannot be used in non-aggregation functions, etc.; these restrictions are reflected in the abstract syntax.

6.3.2 SPARQL Algebra and Evaluation

Finally, we can start to define the semantics of queries in the abstract syntax; in other words, what results the query provides for that dataset.

We shall consider two semantics for evaluation: set semantics and bag semantics (the default semantics). In each case, we will first define the set semantics, where each solution appears at most once; thereafter we will define the *multiplicity* of each solution – the number of times it appears – under bag semantics. Throughout all definitions, when a solution is not given under set semantics, it will have a multiplicity of 0 under set semantics. Given a set X, we denote by $\#X$ the number of elements of X. Given a bag Y, we denote by $Y(a)$ the multiplicity of a in Y.

6.3.2.1 Basic Graph Pattern Matching

We begin by defining the elemental notion of basic graph pattern matching (aka. basic graph pattern evaluation), which defines the solutions that a basic graph pattern – a set of triple patterns – generates with respect to a graph.

We begin by defining the evaluation of a basic graph pattern under set semantics, where duplicates are not preserved.

Definition 23 (Basic graph pattern evaluation (set)). Let B denote a basic graph pattern; $\text{vars}(B)$ the set of variables used in B; and $\text{bnodes}(B)$ the set of blank nodes used in B. Further let α denote a partial mapping of blank nodes to terms in **IBL**, and let $\alpha(B)$ denote the result of replacing each blank node b in B by $\alpha(b)$. Let μ be a solution (Definition 21) and let $\mu(B)$ be the result of replacing each variable v in B by $\mu(v)$. Finally let $\text{dom}(\alpha)$ denote the set of blank nodes for which α is defined, and $\text{dom}(\mu)$ the set of variables for which μ is defined. We define the evaluation of a basic graph pattern under set semantics as:

$$B(G) := \{\mu \mid \exists \alpha : \mu(\alpha(B)) \subseteq G \text{ and}$$
$$\text{dom}(\mu) = \text{vars}(B) \text{ and}$$
$$\text{dom}(\alpha) = \text{bnodes}(B)\}$$

Next we define the evaluation of a basic graph pattern under bag semantics, where duplicates are now preserved. We remark that duplicates can only arise from a basic graph pattern in the presence of blank nodes, which may match multiple terms in the graph, but are "projected away" during evaluation. The multiplicity of a given solution is then the number of distinct blank node mappings that "complete" that solution over the graph.

Definition 24 (Basic graph pattern evaluation (bag)). Given a basic graph pattern B, let μ denote a solution such that $\mathrm{dom}(\mu) = \mathrm{vars}(B)$. The multiplicity of μ for B evaluated over the graph G under bag semantics – denoted by $B(G)(\mu)$ – is defined as:

$$B(G)(\mu) := \#\{\alpha \,|\, \mu(\alpha(B)) \subseteq G \text{ and } \mathrm{dom}(\alpha) = \mathrm{bnodes}(B)\}$$

Otherwise if $\mathrm{dom}(\mu) \neq \mathrm{vars}(B)$, then $B(G)(\mu) := 0$.

Example 6.38

Consider the query posed against the graph G of Figure 6.1:

```
SELECT *
WHERE {
  ?npl a :NobelPrizeLiterature .
  ?npl :winner [ :country :Spain ] .
}
```

The basic graph pattern B is then as follows:

$$\{(?\mathsf{npl}, \mathsf{rdf:type}, \mathsf{:NobelPrizeLiterature})$$
$$(?\mathsf{npl}, \mathsf{:winner}, \_\mathsf{:b})$$
$$(\_\mathsf{:b}, \mathsf{:winner}, \mathsf{:Spain})\}$$

If we consider the solution μ such that $\mathrm{dom}(\mu) = \{?\mathsf{npl}\} = \mathrm{vars}(B)$ and $\mu(?\mathsf{npl}) = \mathsf{:NPL1904}$, then there exists a blank node mapping α such that $\alpha(\_\mathsf{:b}) = \mathsf{:JEchegaray}$, giving rise to the RDF graph $\mu(\alpha(B))$:

$$\{(\mathsf{:NPL1904}, \mathsf{rdf:type}, \mathsf{:NobelPrizeLiterature})$$
$$(\mathsf{:NPL1904}, \mathsf{:winner}, \mathsf{:JEchegaray})$$
$$(\mathsf{:JEchegaray}, \mathsf{:winner}, \mathsf{:Spain})\}$$

where $\mu(\alpha(B)) \subseteq G$. Hence μ is a solution: $\mu \in B(G)$.
On the other hand consider the query:

```
SELECT *
WHERE {
  ?npl a :NobelPrizeLiterature ; :year "1904"^^xsd:gYear .
  ?npl :winner [] .
}
```

This will return $\mathsf{:NPL1904}$ twice: letting $\_\mathsf{:w}$ denote the blank node for $\mathsf{:winner}$, then there are two mappings α_1 and α_2 that generate a solution with $\mathsf{:NPL1904}$ – $\alpha_1(\_\mathsf{:w}) = \mathsf{:FMistral}$ and $\alpha_2(\_\mathsf{:w}) = \mathsf{:JEchegaray}$.

Remark 6.31

There is no way in SPARQL to query for a blank node with a given label. Furthermore, given a bag of solutions M that result from the evaluation $Q(G)$, one can rewrite the blank nodes in M in a one-to-one manner such that the result is also valid for the evaluation of $Q(G)$; in other words, solutions are defined modulo blank node labels.

Remark 6.32

When DISTINCT is used, duplicates are removed from the solutions under bag semantics. Consider, for example:

```
SELECT DISTINCT (count(*) AS ?c) { { ?s ?p ?o } UNION { ?s ?p ?o } }
```

This query would return twice the number of triples in the graph.

6.3.2.2 Paths

Next we define the evaluation of a path expression under set semantics.

Definition 25 (SPARQL path algebra (set)). For an RDF graph G, let $\mathrm{so}(G) := \{(x,x) \mid \exists y, \exists z : (x,y,z) \in G \text{ or } (z,y,x) \in G\}$ return the set of subject and object terms in G. We now define the evaluation of a path expression (see Table 6.3) under set semantics as follows:

$$p(G) := \{(s,o) \mid (s,p,o) \in G\}$$
$$!p(G) := \{(s,o) \mid \exists q : (s,q,o) \in G \text{ and } q \neq p\}$$
$$!(p_1 \mid \ldots \mid p_k)(G) := \{(s,o) \mid \exists q : (s,q,o) \in G \text{ and } q \notin \{p_1, \ldots, p_k\}\}$$
$$!({}^\wedge p_{k+1} \mid \ldots \mid {}^\wedge p_n)(G) := \{(s,o) \mid \exists q : (o,q,s) \in G \text{ and } q \notin \{p_{k+1}, \ldots, p_n\}\}$$
$$^\wedge e(G) := \{(s,o) \mid (o,s) \in e(G)\}$$
$$e_1/e_2(G) := \{(x,z) \mid \exists y : (x,y) \in e_1(G) \text{ and } (y,z) \in e_2(G)\}$$
$$e_1 \mid e_2(G) := e_1(G) \cup e_2(G)$$
$$e{+}(G) := \{(y_1, y_{n+1}) \mid \text{ for } 1 \leq i \leq n : \exists(y_i, y_{i+1}) \in e(G)\}$$
$$e{\star}(G) := e{+}(G) \cup \mathrm{so}(G)$$
$$e?(G) := e(G) \cup \mathrm{so}(G)$$

We can then define the evaluation $!(p_1 \mid \ldots \mid p_k \mid {}^\wedge p_{k+1} \mid \ldots \mid {}^\wedge p_n)(G)$ as the union $!(p_1 \mid \ldots \mid p_k)(G) \cup !({}^\wedge p_{k+1} \mid \ldots \mid {}^\wedge p_n)(G)$.

We can now define the evaluation of a path expression under bag semantics.

Definition 26 (SPARQL path algebra (bag)). We define the evaluation of a path expression under bag semantics as follows:

$$!p(G)(s,o) := \#\{q \mid (s,q,o) \in G \text{ and } q \neq p\}$$

$$!(p_1 \mid \ldots \mid p_k)(G)(s,o) := \#\{q \mid (s,q,o) \in G \text{ and } q \notin \{p_1,\ldots,p_k\}\}$$

$$!({}^\wedge p_{k+1} \mid \ldots \mid {}^\wedge p_n)(G)(s,o) := \#\{q \mid (o,q,s) \in G \text{ and } q \notin \{p_{k+1},\ldots,p_n\}\}$$

$${}^\wedge e(G)(s,o) := e(G)(o,s)$$

$$e_1/e_2(G)(x,z) := \sum_{y \in \mathbf{IBL}} e_1(G)(x,y) \cdot e_2(G)(y,z)$$

$$e_1 \mid e_2(G)(x,y) := e_1(G)(x,y) + e_2(G)(x,y)$$

The multiplicity of $!(p_1 \mid \ldots \mid p_k \mid {}^\wedge p_{k+1} \mid \ldots \mid {}^\wedge p_n)(G)(x,y)$ is then defined as $!(p_1 \mid \ldots \mid p_k)(G)(x,y) + !({}^\wedge p_{k+1} \mid \ldots \mid {}^\wedge p_n)(G)(x,y)$.

For all other path expressions $e(G)$ not shown – namely those of the form $p(G)$, $e{+}(G)$, $e{*}(G)$ and $e?(G)$ – the multiplicity of a pair (x,y) is defined as 1 if $(x,y) \in e(G)$ under set semantics, and 0 otherwise.

Remark 6.33

One may ask why some path expressions are defined under bag semantics (where $e(G)(x,y)$ can be greater than 1) and some are defined under set semantics (where $e(G)(x,y)$ is at most 1). First note that $p(G)(x,y)$ must be 1 by definition since it checks that $(x,p,y) \in G$ (and (x,p,y) can only appear at most once in G). Expressions that are evaluated under bag semantics are those that can be translated to other query features, where their multiplicity follows from that translation:

- $(s,{}^\wedge e,o)$ is translated to (o,e,s);
- $(s,e_1/e_2,o)$ is translated to a join between (s,e_1,v) and (v,e_2,o) for a fresh intermediate variable $v \in \mathbf{V}$;
- $(s,e_1 \mid e_2,o)$ is translated to a union between (s,e_1,o) and (s,e_2,o);

On the other hand, the patterns $(s,e{+},o)$ and $(s,e{*},o)$ cannot be directly translated. In these cases – and in the related case of $(s,e?,o)$ – set semantics is applied; otherwise, the cost of evaluating such paths under bag semantics would increase considerably as it would require generating a potentially factorial number of repeated results representing all the possible (simple) paths between two nodes [15].

We next define an RDF graph enriched with paths, which will make the definition of the evaluation of navigational graph patterns more concise.

Definition 27 (Path graph). Given an RDF graph G and a set of path expressions E, we denote by $E(G) \subseteq \mathrm{so}(G) \times E \times \mathrm{so}(G)$ the path graph of G with respect to E. Under set semantics, we define $E(G)$ as:

$$E(G) := \{(s,e,o) \mid e \in E \text{ and } (s,o) \in e(G)\}$$

Under bag semantics we define $E(G)$ as the following bag:

$$E(G)(s,e,o) := e(G)(s,o)$$

Next we define the evaluation of a navigational graph pattern N under set semantics. The evaluation of N is analogous to the evaluation of a basic graph pattern – per Definition 23 – except that evaluation is conducted on the path graph of G rather than on G directly. In the definitions that follow, for any path expression e, we assume that $\mu(e) = e$ and $\alpha(e) = e$.

Definition 28 (Navigational graph pattern evaluation (set)). We evaluate a navigational graph pattern N under set semantics as:

$$
\begin{aligned}
N(G) := \{\mu \mid \exists \alpha : {}&\mu(\alpha(N)) \subseteq E(G) \text{ and} \\
&\mathrm{dom}(\mu) = \mathrm{vars}(N) \text{ and} \\
&\mathrm{dom}(\alpha) = \mathrm{bnodes}(N)\}
\end{aligned}
$$

where $E := \{e \mid \exists s, o : (s,e,o) \in N \text{ or } (s,e,o) \in G\}$ denotes path expressions used in N and predicates used in G.

For evaluating a navigational graph pattern N under bag semantics, we must consider duplicates not only arising from blank nodes, but also from paths with a multiplicity greater than one in the path graph.

Definition 29 (Navigational graph pattern evaluation (bag)). We evaluate a navigational graph pattern N under bag semantics as:

$$N(G)(\mu) := \sum_{\alpha \in A} \prod_{(s,e,o) \in \mu(\alpha(N))} E(G)(s,e,o)$$

where E denotes path expressions used in N and predicates used in G, while A denotes the set $\{\alpha \mid \mu(\alpha(N)) \subseteq E(G)\}$. As a special case, note that if $\mu \notin N(G)$ (under set semantics), then $N(G)(\mu) := 0$.

6.3.2.3 Core Algebra

Extending basic graph pattern matching, we now construct an algebra that allows us to capture a "core" of the SPARQL standard.

Definition 30 (SPARQL core algebra (set)). Given two solutions μ_1 and μ_2 and a set of variables V, let $\mu_1 \sim_V \mu_2$ denote that μ_1 and μ_2 are *compatible* under V, meaning that for all $v \in V$, it holds that $\mu_1(v) = \mu_2(v)$. If μ_1 and μ_2 are compatible under $\mathrm{dom}(\mu_1) \cap \mathrm{dom}(\mu_2)$, we say that they are *join compatible*, denoted $\mu_1 \sim \mu_2$. Letting M, M_1 and M_2 denote bags of solutions; and R a function expression, we define the *SPARQL core algebra* under set semantics as follows:

$$M_1 \bowtie M_2 := \{\mu_1 \cup \mu_2 \mid \mu_1 \in M_1, \mu_2 \in M_2, \text{ and } \mu_1 \sim \mu_2\}$$
$$M_1 \cup M_2 := \{\mu \mid \mu \in M_1 \text{ or } \mu \in M_2\}$$
$$M_1 \triangleright M_2 := \{\mu_1 \in M_1 \mid \nexists \mu_2 \in M_2 : \mu_1 \sim \mu_2\}$$
$$M_1 ⟕ M_2 := (M_1 \bowtie M_2) \cup (M_1 \triangleright M_2)$$
$$\sigma_R(M) := \{\mu \in M \mid \mu \models R\}$$
$$\pi_V(M) := \{\mu \mid \mathrm{dom}(\mu) \subseteq V \text{ and } \exists \mu' \in M : \mu \sim_V \mu'\}$$

where $\mu \models R$ denotes that R returns true for variables assigned by μ.

Definition 31 (SPARQL core algebra (bag)). We define the multiplicity of a solution μ for the core algebra under bag semantics as:

$$(M_1 \bowtie M_2)(\mu) := \sum_{\mu_1 \cup \mu_2 = \mu} M_1(\mu_1) \cdot M_2(\mu_2)$$
$$(M_1 \cup M_2)(\mu) := M_1(\mu) + M_2(\mu)$$
$$(M_1 \triangleright M_2)(\mu) := M_1(\mu) \text{ if } \nexists \mu' \in M_2 : \mu \sim \mu'; \text{ else } 0$$
$$(M_1 ⟕ M_2)(\mu) := (M_1 \bowtie M_2)(\mu) + (M_1 \triangleright M_2)(\mu)$$
$$(\sigma_R(M))(\mu) := M(\mu) \text{ if } \mu \models R; \text{ else } 0$$
$$(\pi_V(M))(\mu) := \sum_{\mu \sim_V \mu'} M(\mu') \text{ if } \mathrm{dom}(\mu) \subseteq V; \text{ else } 0$$

Now we can begin to define the semantics of some of the features of the abstract syntax in terms of *query evaluation*: what results are returned by what queries. We first define the evaluation of core features, which can evaluate the algebra under set semantics or bag semantics as appropriate:

Definition 32 (SPARQL core evaluation). We define the evaluation of the following core query patterns as follows:

$$[Q_1 \text{ AND } Q_2](G) := Q_1(G) \bowtie Q_2(G)$$
$$[Q_1 \text{ UNION } Q_2](G) := Q_1(G) \cup Q_2(G)$$
$$[Q_1 \text{ OPTIONAL } Q_2](G) := Q_1(G) \mathbin{⟕} Q_2(G)$$
$$[Q_1 \text{ MINUS } Q_2](G) := Q_1(G) \triangleright Q_2(G)$$
$$\text{FILTER}_R(Q)(G) := \sigma_R(Q(G))$$
$$\text{SELECT}_V(Q)(G) := \pi_V(Q(G))$$

Remark 6.34   (i)

Referring back to Remark 6.29, we can now clarify the difference between $\{t_1, t_2\}(G)$ and $[\{t_1\} \text{ AND } \{t_2\}](G)$. Considering the graph G from Figure 6.1, define the two triple patterns t_1 and t_2 as:

$$t_1 := (\_{:}b, {:}\text{winner}, ?\text{country})$$
$$t_2 := (\_{:}b, {:}\text{winner}, {:}\text{France})$$

asking for countries who shared a prize with :France. For the basic graph pattern evaluation $\{t_1, t_2\}(G)$, the blank node _:b must be mapped to the same term in each solution (in this case :NPL1904), mapping the variable ?country to :France and :Spain. On the other hand, for the join $[\{t_1\} \text{ AND } \{t_2\}](G)$, the blank node _:b appears in two basic graph patterns, and so can be mapped to different terms, leading to ?country being mapped to :France, :Germany, :Norway and :Spain.

If on the other hand we replaced _:b with ?b, there would be no difference between $\{t_1, t_2\}(G)$ and $[\{t_1\} \text{ AND } \{t_2\}](G)$.

6.3.2.4 Binding Values

Next we define evaluation of features that bind values to variables. We begin by defining some notation for extending a solution.

Definition 33 (Solution extension). Letting μ denote a solution, v a variable not in $\text{dom}(\mu)$ and x a term in $\mathbf{IBL} \cup \{u\}$, we denote by $\mu[v \to x]$ the extension of μ such that $\mu[v \to x](v') = \mu(v')$ for $v \neq v'$, and $\mu[v \to x](v) = x$. Letting M denote a bag of solutions, we denote by $M[v \to x]$ the extension of every solution in M accordingly.

Definition 34 (Binding evaluation). Let R denote a function expression, $R(\mu)$ the result of applying R replacing variables according to the solution μ, and v a variable. Further let M denote a bag of solution mappings. We now define the evaluation of the following two operators:

$$\text{BIND}_{R,v}(Q)(G) := Q(G)[v \to R(\mu)]$$
$$\text{VALUES}_{M}(Q)(G) := Q(G) \bowtie M$$

In case that $R(\mu)$ gives an error, then v is mapped to unbound.

Remark 6.35

$(\mathbf{i})$

We highlight that in the definition of $\text{BIND}_{R,v}(Q)$ in the abstract syntax (Definition 22), the variable v must not be in the domain of Q.

6.3.2.5 Datasets and Graphs

Next we define the evaluation of features for selecting graphs from a dataset:

Definition 35 (Dataset and graph evaluation). Given the base RDF dataset $D = \{G, (x_1, G_1), \ldots, (x_n, G_n)\}$, let $\overline{D}$ denote the default graph G of D. Further let $\overline{D}(x_i)$ denote G_i if $(x_i, G_i) \in D$ or $\emptyset$ otherwise, and let $D(x_i)$ denote (x_i, G_i) if $(x_i, G_i) \in D$ or $(x_i, \emptyset)$ otherwise. Next, for a set of IRIs X, let $\overline{D}(X) := +_{x \in X}\{\overline{D}(x)\}$ denote the RDF merge of all graphs named from X in D, and let $D(X) := \{(D, x) \mid x \in X\}$ select all graphs from D named from X. Finally, let $D(X, X') := \{\overline{D}(X)\} \cup D(X')$ define a new dataset with a new default graph merging graphs from X and selecting a set of named graphs from X'. We now define the evaluation of the following SPARQL features for selecting graphs:

$$\text{DATASET}_{X,X'}(Q)(D, \overline{D}) := Q(D(X, X'), D(X))$$
$$\text{GRAPH}_x(Q)(D, G) := Q(D, \overline{D}(x))$$
$$\text{GRAPH}_v(Q)(D, G) := \biguplus_{(x_i, G_i) \in D} Q(D, G_i)[v \to x_i]$$

where x denotes an IRI, v a variable, and $\uplus$ a bag union such that the multiplicities of solutions are summed across the respective bags in the union (under set semantics a standard set union can be applied).

Remark 6.36   (i)

The reader may notice a clear abuse of notation in Definition 35: whereas previously we defined query patterns with one argument – $Q(G)$ – in this definition we call query patterns with two arguments $Q(D, G)$, the first argument being a dataset and the second a graph. Strictly speaking, we should define all query patterns with two arguments, e.g., $B(D, G)$, $[Q_1 \text{ AND } Q_2](D, G)$, etc., where the additional dataset argument is passed along to the sub-patterns; for example:

$$[Q_1 \text{ AND } Q_2](D, G) := Q_1(D, G) \bowtie Q_2(D, G)$$
$$\ldots := \ldots$$

Acknowledging this abuse of notation, we leave the additional dataset argument as implicit throughout since the only internal query pattern that requires knowledge of the dataset is GRAPH.

Remark 6.37   (i)

The above definitions permit nested graph patterns to access other graphs from the dataset; for example, we could express $\text{GRAPH}_{x_2}(\text{GRAPH}_{x_1}(Q))(D, G)$, written in SPARQL as:

```
... GRAPH :x2 { GRAPH :x1 { Q } } ...
```

The inner graph pattern will be called with $\text{GRAPH}_{x_1}(Q)(D, \overline{D}(x_2))$, leading to the call $Q(D, \overline{D}(x_1))$; i.e., the inner graph can still "see" the graph named x_1. Hence the above expression could be written as:

```
... GRAPH :x1 { Q } ...
```

6.3.2.6 Aggregation

We define the evaluation of aggregation features, starting with the group-by operator, which gathers solutions with common values for a set of variables.

Definition 36 (Group-by algebra). Given a bag of solutions M, we define the following group-by operator:

$$\gamma_V(M) := \{(\mu, \{\!\{\mu' \in M \mid \pi_V(\{\mu'\}) = \{\mu\}\}\!\}) \mid \mu \in \pi_V(M)\}$$

Example 6.39

Assume a bag of solutions M:

?a	?b	?c	?d
1	1	2	3
1	1	2	4
1	1	2	4
2	1	2	4
	1	3	4
		4	5

Let $V = \{?a, ?b\}$. Then $\gamma_V(M)$ gives the following:

$$
\begin{aligned}
\{(\{a \to 1, b \to 1\}, &\{\!\{ \{a \to 1, b \to 1, c \to 2, d \to 3\}, \\
&\quad \{a \to 1, b \to 1, c \to 2, d \to 4\}, \\
&\quad \{a \to 1, b \to 1, c \to 2, d \to 4\} \}\!\}), \\
(\{a \to 2, b \to 1\}, &\{\!\{ \{a \to 2, b \to 1, c \to 2, d \to 4\} \}\!\}), \\
(\{b \to 1\}, &\{\!\{ \{b \to 1, c \to 3, d \to 4\} \}\!\}), \\
(\{\}, &\{\!\{ \{c \to 4, d \to 5\} \}\!\})\}
\end{aligned}
$$

We now define the evaluation of aggregation operators in the abstract syntax. These operators can be used to group solutions, to apply aggregation functions over solution groups, to apply aggregation filters over solution groups, and to "flatten" solution groups back to a bag of solutions.

Definition 37 (Aggregation evaluation). Letting A be an aggregation expression, we define the evaluation of the following features:

$$\text{GROUP}_V(Q)(G) := \gamma_V(Q(G))$$

$$\text{HAVING}_A(Q)(G) := \{(\mu, M) \mid A \models M\}$$

$$\text{AGG}_{A,v}(Q)(G) := \bigcup_{(\mu, M) \in Q(G)} \{(\mu[v \to A(M)], M[v \to A(M)])\}$$

$$\text{FLATTEN}(Q)(G) := \{\mu \mid \exists M : (\mu, M) \in Q(G)\}$$

where $A \models M$ denotes that the function A evaluates to true on the bag of solutions M, and $A(M)$ denotes the result of applying A over M (in the latter case an error may arise from the evaluation of $A(M)$, where any solution with an error will be removed).

Remark 6.38

In some cases, an aggregation can be applied without grouping; take, for example, the following SPARQL query:

```
SELECT (count(distinct ?s)) WHERE { ?s ?p ?o }
```

In such cases, given a solution mapping M, and letting $\mu_\emptyset$ denote the empty mapping $\{\emptyset\}$, we define the trivial group-by operator $\gamma_\emptyset(M) := \{(\mu_\emptyset, M)\}$, which can be (implicitly) applied when a non-grouped solution mapping M is passed to an aggregate function.

On the other hand, in Definition 22, a group pattern is not defined as a query pattern; the results must pass through a FLATTEN to ensure that the grouped solutions are "flattened" before being passed to other query operators that expect a simple bag of solutions as input. Along these lines, we can define that $\text{FLATTEN}(Q)(G) := M$ when $Q(G) = M$.

6.3.2.7 Solution Modifiers

We now define the evaluation of the solution modifiers.

Definition 38 (Modifier evaluation). Given a bag of solution modifiers, let $\text{list}(M)$ return a list M containing all elements of M in some (arbitrary order) preserving duplicates. Given a list M, let $\text{list}(\mathsf{M}) := \mathsf{M}$ and define $\text{sort}(\mathsf{M}, \omega)$ as a function that orders the list M according to the criteria specified in ω. Further let Δ denote a boolean value and let M^Δ denote M when Δ is false, or M with duplicate entries removed when Δ is true. Also let $\text{len}(\mathsf{M})$ denote the length of the list M, let $\mathsf{M}[i]$ denote the sub-list of M starting at position i whose length is $\max(\text{len}(\mathsf{M}) - i, 0)$, and let $\mathsf{M}(j)$ denote the sub-list of M whose length is $\min(\text{len}(\mathsf{M}), j)$. We now define the evaluation of the following solution modifiers:

$$\text{ORDER}_\omega(Q)(G) := \text{sort}(\text{list}(Q(G)), \omega)$$
$$\text{SLICE}_{\Delta,i}(Q)(G) := \text{list}(Q(G))^\Delta[i]$$
$$\text{SLICE}_{\Delta,i,j}(Q)(G) := \text{list}(Q(G))^\Delta[i](j)$$

Remark 6.39

$\text{SLICE}_{\Delta,0,j}(Q)(G)$ expresses a LIMIT without OFFSET.

Remark 6.40

We do not formalise the REDUCED feature – which allows duplicates to optionally be removed – since it is not a deterministic function.
Furthermore, we do not formalise how order criteria are used to sort,
where we rather refer to Section 6.2.8 for more details. Finally, SELECT
is considered a solution modifier by the standard, but to keep the definitions a little more clean, we will define this in the following section.

6.3.2.8 Query Types

Finally, we can define the four types of queries supported by SPARQL.

Definition 39 (Query evaluation). Given a solution $\mu \in M$, let
$\mu_\alpha(s,p,o)$ replace any variable (s,p,o) by its mapping in μ and rewrite
any blank node in (s,p,o) according to a one-to-one mapping $\alpha : \mathbf{B} \to \mathbf{B}$
such that for two blank nodes b and b', $\mu_\alpha(b) = \mu'_{\alpha'}(b')$ if and only
if $\mu = \mu'$ and $b = b'$. Furthermore, for a set of tuples T, let $\mathrm{rdf}(T) :=$
$T \cap (\mathbf{IB} \times \mathbf{I} \times \mathbf{IBL})$ return any tuples in T that are valid RDF triples. We
now define the evaluation of the following three query types in SPARQL:

$$\textsc{select}_V(Q)(G) := \pi_V(\mathrm{list}(Q(G)))$$
$$\textsc{construct}_B(Q)(G) := \mathrm{rdf}(\{\mu_\alpha(s,p,o) \mid \mu \in Q(G) \text{ and } (s,p,o) \in B\})$$
$$\textsc{ask}(Q)(G) := \mathsf{true} \text{ if } Q(G) \text{ is not empty; } \mathsf{false} \text{ otherwise}$$

Remark 6.41

SPARQL defines query evaluation modulo blank node labels,
so letting G' denote any RDF graph isomorphic to G ($G \cong G'$; see
Definition 6), we may return $\textsc{select}_V(Q)(G')$ or $\textsc{construct}_B(Q)(G')$
as results for $\textsc{select}_V(Q)(G)$ or $\textsc{construct}_B(Q)(G)$, respectively.

Remark 6.42

We do not formalise DESCRIBE since it is not well-defined;
rather, we refer to the discussion provided in Section 6.2.

6.3.3 SPARQL Complexity

Now that we have defined more formally what a SPARQL query Q means in terms of evaluation – what solutions Q gives over an input dataset D – we can begin to consider questions of computational complexity that ask, for example: *how hard is it to evaluate a SPARQL query Q on a dataset?*

Obviously the answer to that question depends on the particular Q in question, so to arrive at a more general answer, we will define some general problems and study the worst-case complexity for queries that use particular features of SPARQL. The first such problem is that of query evaluation.

> **Remark 6.43** (i)
>
> For simplicity, we will consider queries posed over an RDF graph G, rather than a dataset D. However, the complexity results discussed will not change when talking about datasets.

6.3.3.1 Query Evaluation

When we study computational complexity, traditionally theoreticians like to study decision problems with a true/false answer. Hence, in the theoretical literature, the complexity of QUERY EVALUATION is often framed in terms of the following decision problem: given a query Q, a graph G, and a solution μ, is μ a solution to Q over G (i.e., is $\mu \in Q(G)$)?

Let us restrict the query Q that we allow and say that we only allow basic graph patterns, and nothing more (say, with all query variables projected: SELECT $\star$). Now, for an RDF graphs G, given a solution μ, deciding if $\mu \in Q(G)$ is NP-complete! This is because Q can contain blank nodes, where even after applying $\mu(Q)$ (replacing all variables in Q with those given in the solution μ), we are still left to decide the RDF entailment $G \models \mu(Q)$, which is NP-complete (since we are still left to decide a version of the graph homomorphism problem mapping blank nodes in Q to terms in G [162])!

What about if Q is a basic graph pattern, but it does not contain blank nodes? Then assuming all variables are projected as the final results, $\mu(Q)$ would give us a valid RDF graph, and we are left to check whether or not it is a sub-graph of G, which we can do efficiently [310].[1] However, if some variables are not projected, then the solution μ may not provide a mapping for those variables, and we are again left to find a homomorphism from $\mu(Q)$ to G – this time for query variables rather than blank nodes. Hence if some variables are not projected, deciding if $\mu \in Q(G)$ is again NP-complete [310]!

---

[1] If we assume ideal hashing, we can do it in $O(n)$ for $n := |Q| + |G|$ by hashing all triples of G and then checking membership in G of each triple in $\mu(Q)$.

Returning to the case where Q is a basic graph pattern with blank nodes and/or projection, then query evaluation is NP-complete. If we add UNION and AND, the problem remains NP-complete [310]. In fact, if we add path expressions on top of these features, the query evaluation problem still remains NP-complete [240] since (per Definition 27) we can pre-compute all pairs of nodes connected by each path expression in the query, and add "virtual edges" to G between each pair with a unique predicate for that expression, replacing the path expressions in the query likewise with their unique predicate; this rewriting is feasible in polynomial time, where applying query evaluation on the extended path graph and rewritten query no longer involves any path expressions, so the problem remains NP-complete.

On the other hand, once we add OPTIONAL, or any features that permit negation, then query evaluation jumps to PSPACE-complete [347, 310].[2]

To the best of our knowledge, no complexity study has been done on the entire SPARQL 1.1 language, though other features have been studied in isolation, such as the complexity of counting solutions for queries expressed in sub-fragments of SPARQL [318] (relevant for aggregates).

Remark 6.44 ⓘ

The choice of set (SELECT DISTINCT) or bag semantics does not affect the query evaluation problem since checking if $\mu \in Q(G)$ is not concerned with duplicates (or the lack thereof) in $Q(G)$.

Remark 6.45 ⓘ

The previous discussion considers combined complexity, which considers both Q and G to be part of the input. In general, the complexity of query evaluation is heavily dependent on the complexity of Q. Given that queries in the real-world tend to be relatively simple, another measure of complexity that is often considered is that of data complexity, which considers Q as constant and thus is only concerned with the size of G. In this case, query evaluation drops from PSPACE-complete for the aforementioned fragment to AC^0 (see Section 5.6.3.1), which intuitively speaking is the class of problems that can be parallelised efficiently. This result indicates that although the complexity of query evaluation is quite high in the general case, much of that complexity is dependent on the query, rather than the data. In summary, if queries remain relatively small and simple, then query evaluation can be decided efficiently, even for complex data.

---

[2] ... which is the same complexity as one gets for the relational algebra.

Remark 6.46

$$\large\textcircled{\textbf{i}}$$

As previously mentioned, theoreticians often work with decision problems. But a reader may rightly wonder how relevant is it to study the problem of deciding if $\mu \in Q(G)$. After all, how often will a user wish to propose a solution and see if it is an answer to a query over a graph? In practice, a user will often require all solutions for Q over G, and in fact, there may be an exponential number of such solutions! Hence the related enumeration problem – specifically QUERY ENUMERATION – is sometimes studied in the literature, for which guarantees in the *delay* between computing solutions can be proposed; indeed, some related results have been proven for the case of SPARQL [32].

6.3.3.2 Query Equivalence and Containment

There are many ways to write the same query in SPARQL. Indeed, some ways to write the query may be more efficient to execute, in practice, than others, even though the same answers will be returned! Along these lines, given two queries Q and Q', we may be interested to more formally study certain relations between these queries. Do they give the same solutions for any dataset? Perhaps one always gives a subset of the solutions of the other? More importantly, can we design algorithms to decide these relations between two queries? And if so, what is the complexity of such algorithms?

Such questions are often studied formally in the area of *static analysis*, so-called because it is independent of a particular dataset. Formally, we can define two important static relations between queries: **query containment** and **query equivalence**. We define these relations with respect to RDF graphs for simplicity, though the definitions could be extended to cover RDF datasets.

Definition 40 (Query containment). Given two queries Q and Q', we say that Q is contained in Q' – denoted $Q \sqsubseteq Q'$ – if and only if, for any RDF graph G, it holds that $Q(G) \subseteq Q'(G)$.

Definition 41 (Query equivalence). Given two queries Q and Q', we say that Q is equivalent to Q' – denoted $Q \equiv Q'$ – if and only if, for any RDF graph G, it holds that $Q(G) = Q'(G)$.

Note that $Q \equiv Q'$ if and only if $Q \sqsubseteq Q'$ and $Q' \sqsubseteq Q$.

Example 6.40

Let us consider the following two SPARQL queries – which we denote Q_1 and Q_1' respectively – looking for winners of the Nobel Prize in Literature from either France or Germany:

```
SELECT DISTINCT ?winner
WHERE {
  { ?winner :country :Germany . }
  UNION
  { ?winner :country :France . }
  ?npl a :NobelPrizeLiterature ; :winner ?winner .
}
```

```
SELECT DISTINCT ?winner
WHERE {
  { ?winner :country :Germany .
    ?npl a :NobelPrizeLiterature ; :winner ?winner . }
  UNION
  { ?winner :country :France .
    ?npl a :NobelPrizeLiterature ; :winner ?winner . }
}
```

Both queries will return the same results over any RDF graph; hence we say that they are equivalent: $Q_1 \equiv Q_1'$.

Consider the following query Q_1'':

```
SELECT DISTINCT ?winner
WHERE {
  ?npl a :NobelPrizeLiterature ; :winner ?winner ; :winner ?winner2 .
  { ?winner :country :Germany . }
  UNION
  { ?winner :country :France . }
}
```

In fact, this query is also equivalent to Q_1 and Q_1' since the ?winner2 variable is not projected and can always be mapped to the same term as ?winner: the ?winner2 variable is redundant.

Finally consider the following query Q_2 seeking German winners:

```
SELECT DISTINCT ?winner
WHERE {
  ?npl a :NobelPrizeLiterature . ?winner :country :Germany .
}
```

The results of Q_2 are contained in the results for Q_1, Q_1' and Q_1'': $Q_2 \sqsubseteq Q_1$, $Q_2 \sqsubseteq Q_1'$, $Q_2 \sqsubseteq Q_1''$. Furthermore, note that, for example, $Q_1 \equiv Q_1'$ if and only if $Q_1 \sqsubseteq Q_1'$ and $Q_1' \sqsubseteq Q_1$.

Detecting query equivalence may help an engine to ensure that two query plans – two ways to execute a query – are indeed equivalent; for example, we may use such a procedure to perform *minimisation* of a query, removing redundant patterns that do not affect the solutions. Likewise containment (and equivalence) may help to implement a **caching** system that reuses the solutions of previously executed queries that are more general than (or equivalent to) the current query. Unfortunately, however, these are hard problems [341].

Beginning with set semantics – where SELECT DISTINCT is specified – the problem of deciding query containment or query equivalence for basic graph patterns (with projection; aka. conjunctive queries) is NP-complete [91]; effectively, we can confirm containment by finding a homomorphism from one query to the other (and vice versa in the case of equivalence) that maps blank nodes and variables to query terms. If we add UNION but disallow AND, meaning that we can only apply UNION over basic graph patterns – like query Q' in Example 6.40; aka *unions of conjunctive queries* – then these problems remain NP-complete [340]. However, if we allow AND over UNION – like query Q in Example 6.40; aka. *monotone queries* [340] – then the problem increases in difficulty, jumping to a complexity class called Π_2^P-complete [340]. Indeed, once we add more features, equivalence and containment quickly become undecidable; for example, for queries using only OPTIONAL and projection, these problems become undecidable [318]. Effectively this rules out the possibility of having a sound and complete algorithm for deciding query containment and query equivalence between two SPARQL queries under set semantics.

What about under bag semantics, where duplicate solutions are preserved according to the "unique ways" in which they can be generated (i.e., SELECT without DISTINCT)? Interestingly, query equivalence between basic graph patterns (with projection; aka. conjunctive queries) is easier in the case of bag semantics than in the case of set semantics, falling into the complexity class GI-complete [93], meaning that the problem is "as hard" as deciding graph isomorphism, a problem not known to be NP-complete nor in P; intuitively, this is because under bag semantics, no patterns can be redundant, and hence it suffices to check a flavour of isomorphism between two queries, mapping query terms to query terms in a one-to-one manner. On the other hand, the decidability of *containment* for basic graph patterns relates to a long-open problem [93], where adding UNION [216] or even FILTER with inequalities [220] is known to make containment under bag semantics undecidable. Again, other than for the most basic flavours of SPARQL queries, this rules out the possibility of a sound and complete algorithm for deciding query containment (and, to a lesser extent, query equivalence) under bag semantics.

Though the aforementioned problems are hard, again, in practice, queries are often much simpler than the types of worst cases considered in theory. Thus even an NP-complete problem, such as query containment, is often feasible – even efficient – for the vast majority of practical queries. Along these lines, efficient algorithms have been proposed to decide query containment [248] and query equivalence [341] for SPARQL (in decidable cases).

Discussion 6.3

ANNE: So in summary, these theoretical results imply that SPARQL is a difficult query language to optimise?

AIDAN: Well we need to be more careful. First, there is nothing particular to SPARQL here; most of the results quoted above were developed for relational databases (SQL) but apply equally for SPARQL. Second, we are always studying worst-case complexities here: the queries considered for such worst-cases are not the most "natural". Third, most engines do not need a general procedure for query equivalence or containment to optimise their query plans; instead, they simply need to know that specific "rewriting strategies" will not change the query results. Referring back to Example 6.40, for instance, an engine may benefit from knowing that rewriting Q_1 to Q_1' by a fixed rule such as $(A \cup B) \bowtie C \equiv (A \bowtie B) \cup (A \bowtie C)$ (or vice versa) will not change the answers. Engines can still apply specific rewriting/optimisation rules proven to preserve equivalence even though the general problem is hard/undecidable. And again, the same applies for relational databases optimising SQL.

FRANK: What about queries that are equivalent except that the variable names are different? Wouldn't this be useful for caching?

AIDAN: There is a notion of *query congruence* in the literature, which states that two queries are congruent if and only if we can rewrite the variables (in a one-to-one manner) such that both queries are then equivalent [341]. In general, it is no harder than query equivalence – or at least it is in the same complexity class.

FRANK: What about containment with partial results? Like where one query gives unbounds that are "filled in" by the second query?

AIDAN: There's a notion of *query subsumption* in the literature as well that covers precisely such a case for set semantics [310]. In general, there's quite a lot of theoretic work on such problems in various settings that we cannot cover here, including work on query containment considering path expressions under set semantics [240], or under Description Logics entailment [85], and so forth. Here our goal was to introduce some of the main concepts and results.

6.4 SPARQL Federation

When we think of the Web of Data, we should be careful to avoid thinking about all data as being in one place – as being in one index, on one server, hosted by one website, etc. Rather, to avoid losing generality, we should think

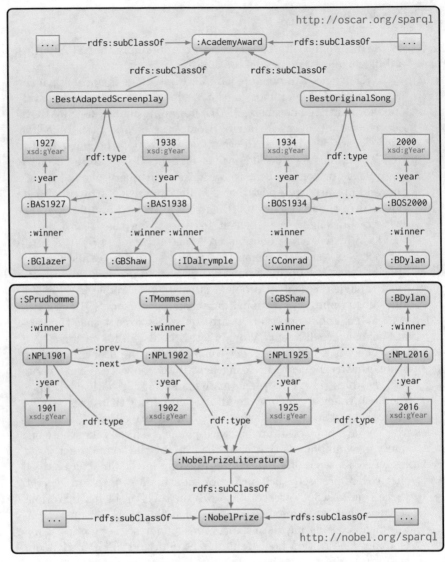

Fig. 6.4 Example of two SPARQL services on the Web: the first hosts data about Academy Awards while the second hosts data about Nobel Prizes

of data as being *decentralised*: spread across the entire Web. But how can we answer queries over data spread across various websites?

The SPARQL standard provides one possible solution to this question: SPARQL **federation** [326]. The goal of SPARQL federation is to enable running sub-queries over remote SPARQL services on the Web; the solutions returned are then joined with the solutions from the rest of the query.

Example 6.41

In Figure 6.4, we provide a sample of data hosted by two (fictitious) SPARQL services: the first at location `http://oscar.org/sparql`
hosting RDF data about Academy Awards; the second at location
`http://nobel.org/sparql` hosting RDF data about Nobel Prizes. We
can use SPARQL Federation to query both services in unison. For example, we could send to the first service the query:

```
SELECT DISTINCT ?winner
WHERE {
  ?aa a/rdfs:subClassOf* :AcademyAward ; :winner ?winner .
  SERVICE <http://nobel.org/sparql> {
    ?np a/rdfs:subClassOf* :NobelPrize ; :winner ?winner .
  }
}
```

The sub-query in the SERVICE clause is executed on the SPARQL service
for Nobel Prizes. The remote results are joined with the local query
pattern seeking all winners of Academy Awards. The result is thus a
list of winners of both a Nobel Prize and an Academy Award, where
`:GBShaw` and `:BDylan` will be returned.

We could also run the following query on the second SPARQL service:

```
SELECT DISTINCT ?winner
WHERE {
  ?np a/rdfs:subClassOf* :NobelPrize ; :winner ?winner .
  SERVICE <http://oscar.org/sparql> {
    ?aa a/rdfs:subClassOf* :AcademyAward ; :winner ?winner .
  }
}
```

This should return the same results as the previous query, where this
time the SERVICE sub-query is sent to the query service hosting data
about Academy Awards and joined with local results for Nobel Prizes.

If the SPARQL service is unavailable, the query will throw an error unless
SERVICE SILENT is specified, which will rather return the empty solution $\{\mu_\emptyset\}$
(the join identity) from a service call that fails.

We can now extend the abstract syntax of Definition 22, as follows:

Definition 42 (SPARQL federated syntax).

- If Q is a **query pattern** on V, x an IRI (service location), and Δ
  a boolean value (true for silent operation; false otherwise), then:

  – $\text{SERVICE}_{x,\Delta}(Q)$ is a query pattern on V.

Definition 43 (Service evaluation). Given a query pattern Q on V and x an IRI, let $\mathrm{SELECT}_V(Q)(x)$ denote the evaluation of the query $\mathrm{SELECT}_V(Q)$ on the remote service at location x, which may return a list of solutions M or an error ε. We now define a service evaluation as:

$$\mathrm{SERVICE}_{x,\Sigma}(Q) := \begin{cases} \mathrm{SELECT}_V(Q)(x) & \text{if } \mathrm{SELECT}_V(Q)(x) \neq \varepsilon \\ \{\mu_\emptyset\} & \text{if } \mathrm{SELECT}_V(Q)(x) = \varepsilon \text{ and } \Delta \\ \varepsilon & \text{otherwise} \end{cases}$$

Where ε is returned, it invokes a runtime query-level error.

The SERVICE clause can be combined with other query features. As per Remark 6.29, when a SERVICE operation is written sequentially before/after another operation in the concrete syntax, a join (AND) connects them.

Example 6.42

Consider the following query run with respect to the first SPARQL service illustrated in Figure 6.4:

```
SELECT DISTINCT ?winner ?wa1 ?wn1
WHERE {
    ?aa a/rdfs:subClassOf* :AcademyAward ; :winner ?winner .
    OPTIONAL { ?aa :winner ?wa1, ?wa2 . FILTER (?wa1 != ?wa2) }
    FILTER(!bound(?wa1) || ?wa1 != ?winner)
    SERVICE <http://nobel.org/sparql> {
        ?np a/rdfs:subClassOf* :NobelPrize ; :winner ?winner .
        OPTIONAL { ?np :winner ?wn1 , ?wn2 . FILTER (?wn1 != ?wn2) }
        FILTER(!bound(?wn1) || ?wn1 != ?winner)
    }
}
```

The query asks for winners of both an Academy Award and a Nobel Prize, and optionally the people with whom they shared one or the other prize. The results for this query will be:

?winner ?wa1	?wn1
:GBShaw :IDalrymple	
:BDylan	

The results of the SERVICE call are joined with the results for the rest of the query. If the above SERVICE call fails (e.g., there is no SPARQL service listening at the above location), then the query throws an error. If, however, we were to add SERVICE SILENT and the call fails, the following results would be returned:

?winner	?wa	?wn
:BGlazer		
:GBShaw	:IDalrymple	
:IDalrymple	:GBShaw	
:BDylan		
...		

Along the same lines, we can even nest SERVICE clauses.

Example 6.43

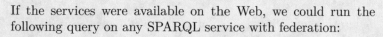

If the services were available on the Web, we could run the
following query on any SPARQL service with federation:

```
SELECT ?winner
WHERE {
  SERVICE <http://oscar.org/sparql> {
    ?aa a/rdfs:subClassOf* :AcademyAward ; :winner ?winner .
    SERVICE <http://nobel.org/sparql> {
      ?np a/rdfs:subClassOf* :NobelPrize ; :winner ?winner .
    }
  }
}
```

This requests the first service to call the second service and perform the
join, returning the solutions to the service on which the query is run.
Another option, for example, would be to call the services "in parallel":

```
SELECT ?winner
WHERE {
  SERVICE <http://oscar.org/sparql> {
    ?aa a/rdfs:subClassOf* :AcademyAward ; :winner ?winner .
  }
  SERVICE <http://nobel.org/sparql> {
    ?np a/rdfs:subClassOf* :NobelPrize ; :winner ?winner .
  }
}
```

The service on which this query is run will send the sub-queries (possibly, but not necessarily, in parallel) to both services.

Remark 6.47

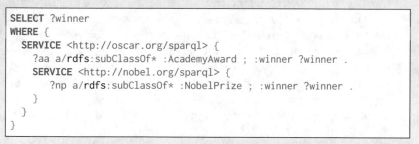

How can a query be run on a remote service over the Web? This
is discussed in Section 6.7, which describes the SPARQL protocol.

Remark 6.48

The SPARQL Federated Query standard [326] also provides some informative notes on how SERVICE can be invoked with a variable, with the intuition that such a variable should be bound (e.g., by a query on a local default graph) to the IRIs of remote services, which are then invoked, and where UNION is applied over the solutions of all services. However, precise details are not formalised by the standard.

Discussion 6.4

JULIE: Federating querying looks interesting on paper, but in Figure 6.4, isn't it convenient that both sources agree on the same identifiers, the same properties and the same classes? Because if the sources don't agree, then it seems like federation will not work.

AIDAN: True! Here we have laid one possible foundation for answering queries over multiple sources on the Web. But for this to work, indeed we either need the sources to agree on how things should be named, or we need a way to map the naming schemes – and vocabulary – of both sources. This is far from trivial, but we will discuss ways forward in Chapter 8 on Linked Data.

JULIE: Also doesn't it assume that all sources have RDF data indexed with SPARQL? What about data in other formats on the Web?

AIDAN: Yes. We also discuss other formats in Chapter 8.

FRANK: But even assuming the ideal case that all sources use RDF, and all sources use the same terms in their data, what about the performance? Some of these federated queries expect the remote service to return a list of all winners of Academy Awards over the Web. Doesn't that seem unrealistic? What about bandwidth?

AIDAN: In terms of bandwidth, watching a high-definition movie on Netflix will probably equate to streaming a couple of billion IRIs of Academy Award winners, so bandwidth should rarely be a technical problem, except perhaps for applications that require low latency.

6.5 SPARQL Update

Thus far in the chapter, we have discussed features for querying RDF datasets. But what if we wish to modify the underlying data? The SPARQL Update language [139] – recommended as part of the SPARQL 1.1 specification – provides a standard, declarative way to perform updates on the underlying RDF dataset. This section details the SPARQL Update language.

Recall that SPARQL queries are defined over an RDF dataset $D :=$ $\{G, (x_1, G_1), \ldots, (x_n, G_n)\}$, where G is the default graph, and where each (x_i, G_i) for $1 \leq i \leq n$ is a named graph. SPARQL updates are likewise defined over an RDF dataset, where in the following we will introduce features that allow for inserting or removing static triples to/from individual graphs, inserting or removing triples based on the results of a query pattern, loading triples from RDF documents on the Web into the local dataset, as well as applying operations (clear, drop, create, copy, move, add) on graphs.

> **Remark 6.49**
>
> Security concerns arise when considering a SPARQL service that provides write access to clients over the Web. The SPARQL Update specification [139] does not discuss such issues in detail, but rather mentions that standard access and authentication methods – specifically HTTPS – should be used. They also warn of the dangers of injection-style attacks in services that accept both queries and updates.

6.5.1 Inserting/Deleting Triples

SPARQL Update provides two features for directly inserting/deleting triples.

> INSERT DATA: Insert specified triples into a graph (or graphs).
> DELETE DATA: Delete specified triples from a graph (or graphs).

We begin with an example of inserting data.

> **Example 6.44**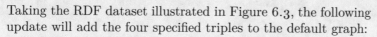
>
> Taking the RDF dataset illustrated in Figure 6.3, the following update will add the four specified triples to the default graph:
>
> ```
> INSERT DATA {
>   :NPL1905 :year "1905"^^xsd:gYear ; :prev :NPL1904 ;
>     a :NobelPrizeLiterature .
>   :NPL1904 :next :NPL1905 .
> }
> ```
>
> If we wish to insert data into a named graph, we can use a graph clause:

```
INSERT DATA {
  GRAPH :G-FPW { :FrancoPrussianWar :start "1870"^^xsd:gYear . }
}
```

If the graph does not exist, it should be created. We can also combine
insertions into multiple graphs; as follows:

```
INSERT DATA {
  GRAPH :G-HS {
    :NPL1904 :winner :HSienkiewicz .
    :HSienkiewicz :country :Poland .
  }
  :NPL1905 :year "1905"^^xsd:gYear ; :prev :NPL1904 ;
    a :NobelPrizeLiterature .
  :NPL1904 :next :NPL1905 .
}
```

This will create a new graph :G-HS containing the two triples and insert
the latter four triples into the default graph (if not already present).

No variables are permitted in an INSERT DATA clause. Any blank nodes
inserted will be distinguished from any existing blank nodes in the dataset.

We can also delete triples directly from a graph or set of graphs.

Example 6.45

The following deletes all triples for the node :NPL1904 from the
dataset (from the default graph and from the graphs :G-FM and :G-JE):

```
DELETE DATA {
  GRAPH :G-FM { :NPL1904 :winner :FMistral . }
  GRAPH :G-JE { :NPL1904 :winner :JEchegaray . }
  :NPL1904 :year "1904"^^xsd:gYear ; :prev :NPL1903 ;
    a :NobelPrizeLiterature .
  :NPL1903 :next :NPL1904 .
}
```

Blank nodes are not allowed in a DELETE DATA update. When all data from
a named graph are deleted, an empty graph is kept with that name. Furthermore, multiple DELETE DATA and INSERT DATA updates can be concatenated
into one update request, which will be executed in sequential order.

6.5.2 Inserting/Deleting with Queries

Rather than explicitly writing all of the triples we wish to insert or delete, we can also insert and/or delete triples based on solutions for a query pattern.

DELETE / INSERT / WHERE: Deletes and/or inserts data based on the solutions generated by the query pattern in the WHERE clause. Either a DELETE or INSERT clause (or both) must be specified.

Example 6.46

For each Nobel Prize that was the first of its kind, the following SPARQL update will add the type :InauguralNobelPrize.

```
INSERT { ?prize a :InauguralNobelPrize }
WHERE {
  ?prize a/rdfs:subClassOf* :NobelPrize .
  MINUS { ?prize :prev ?prior }
}
```

We can also combine insertions and deletions in one update, in which case:

- The solutions M for the query pattern are generated.
- The deletions corresponding to M are applied.
- The insertions corresponding to M are applied.

Example 6.47

The following update will add :next triples for which there exists an inverse :prev triple:

```
INSERT { ?prize1 :next ?prize2 }
WHERE  { ?prize2 :prev ?prize1 }
```

The following update will delete :prev triples for which there already exists a :next triple.

```
DELETE { ?prize2 :prev ?prize1 }
WHERE  { ?prize1 :next ?prize2 }
```

We can combine these as follows to only keep :next triples in the graph where previously there was a :next triple or inverse :prev triple:

```
DELETE { ?prize2 :prev ?prize1 }
INSERT { ?prize1 :next ?prize2 }
WHERE  {
  { ?prize1 :next ?prize2 }
  UNION
  { ?prize2 :prev ?prize1 }
}
```

First, the results for the query pattern will be generated. Second, the deletions will be performed. Third, the insertions will be performed. Thus, deletions and insertions cannot affect the results from the query pattern; furthermore, triples may be reinserted after they are deleted.

Remark 6.50

SPARQL offers a shortcut for cases where the DELETE and WHERE clauses are the same, such that:

```
DELETE { ?prize1 :next ?prize2 }
WHERE  { ?prize1 :next ?prize2 }
```

can be written more succinctly as:

```
DELETE WHERE { ?prize1 :next ?prize2 }
```

If the query pattern in the WHERE clause produces a triple in an INSERT or DELETE clause that is not a valid RDF triple, that particular triple will be ignored (though other valid triples generated by the same solution will be acted upon). Blank nodes are not permitted in a DELETE clause. On the other hand, blank nodes in the INSERT clause will act like they do for CONSTRUCT clauses, meaning that a fresh blank node will be generated for each solution, and no generated blank node will already exist in the dataset D.

All previous updates are applied over the default graph. We can use the WITH keyword with an IRI (variables are not allowed) to select a named graph that will be used by DELETE, INSERT and WHERE in place of the default graph.

> WITH: Specifies the IRI of a single named graph that will be used as a fall-back default graph for the DELETE / INSERT / WHERE clauses.

Example 6.48

We will remodel the graph :G-FPW of Figure 6.3 to take into consideration that future wars may have opposing factions composed of multiple countries, creating a fresh blank node for each faction:

```
WITH :G-FPW
DELETE { ?country :war ?war }
INSERT { ?war :faction [ :country ?country ] . }
WHERE  { ?country :war ?war }
```

The above update is equivalent to:

```
DELETE { GRAPH :G-FPW { ?country :war ?war } }
INSERT { GRAPH :G-FPW { ?war :faction [ :country ?country ] . } }
WHERE  { GRAPH :G-FPW { ?country :war ?war } }
```

We can also specify an explicit GRAPH clause to override WITH.

Example 6.49

The following update additionally assigns :SPrudhomme to the faction of the country which he is from in Figure 6.3:

```
WITH :G-FPW
DELETE {
  ?country :war ?war .
  ?war :combatant ?combatant .
}
INSERT {
  ?war :faction [ :country ?country ; :combatant ?combatant ] .
}
WHERE {
  ?country :war ?war .
  OPTIONAL { GRAPH :G-SP { ?combatant :country ?country . } }
}
```

Again note that triples containing unbounds will be ignored; in this case, the German faction will still be created, but without a combatant. The final graph will be as follows (other graphs will remain unchanged):

```
:G-FPW
[:France] ◄─ :country ─ [_:b1]              [_:b2] ─ :country ► [:Germany]
            :combatant   :faction        :faction
   [:SPrudhomme]        [:FrancoPrussianWar] ─── :end ► [1871 xsd:gYear]
```

Like for INSERT DATA, if INSERT tries to insert at least one triple into a graph that does not exist, that graph will be created automatically.

Updates may also specify the dataset that the WHERE clause will use with USING and USING NAMED. These features are analogous to FROM and FROM NAMED for queries and will override WITH specifically in the WHERE clause.

USING: Specifies the IRI(s) of (a) named graph(s) whose content will be merged to form the default graph queried by the WHERE clause.

USING NAMED: Specifies the IRI(s) of (a) named graph(s) that will be added to the dataset queried by the WHERE clause.

Example 6.50

The update in Example 6.49 could also be written as:

```
WITH :G-FPW
DELETE {
  ?country :war ?war .
  ?war :combatant ?combatant .
}
INSERT {
  ?war :faction [ :country ?country ; :combatant ?combatant ] .
}
USING :G-FPW
USING :G-SP
WHERE {
  ?country :war ?war .
  OPTIONAL { ?combatant :country ?country . }
}
```

The DELETE and INSERT clauses again apply to the WITH-specified graph; however, the WHERE clause now generates solutions over a default graph created from the merge of :G-FPW and :G-SP (the WITH clause is ignored). If we were to replace USING :G-SP with USING NAMED :G-SP, the query would be run on the default graph of :G-FPW and the single named graph of :G-SP (thus requiring an explicit GRAPH clause to access :G-SP).

Finally, we note that the graphs from which triples are deleted or to which they are inserted can also be selected by the solutions to the query. More specifically, given a GRAPH clause with a variable in a DELETE or INSERT, for each solution generated by the WHERE clause mapping that variable to an IRI, the corresponding operation will be applied for that graph. Any graph patterns for which a variable is bound to a non-IRI term in a solution will be ignored for that solution. Again, if at least one triple is inserted to a named graph that does not exist, that named graph will be created automatically.

Example 6.51

The following update will remove combatant triples from their
current graphs (in this case :G-FPW) and add them to the individual
graphs for winners of Nobel Prizes (in this case :G-SP).

```
DELETE {
  GRAPH ?g1 { ?war :combatant ?combatant }
}
INSERT {
  GRAPH ?g2 { ?war :combatant ?combatant }
}
WHERE {
  GRAPH ?g1 { ?war :combatant ?combatant }
  GRAPH ?g2 { ?prize :winner ?combatant }
  ?prize a :NobelPrizeLiterature .
}
```

Exercise 6.17

*Write a SPARQL update to add all triples from all named
graphs to the default graph and remove all triples from named graphs.*

Exercise 6.18

*Write a SPARQL update over Figure 6.3 to create new named
graphs for each country with a Nobel Laureate in Literature, adding all
the winners from that country and the prize(s) they won to that graph;
the named graph can be named after the country (e.g., :France).*

6.5.3 Loading Triples from the Web

Thus far we have discussed managing a local dataset with update operations.
But on the Web of Data, we may wish to draw together multiple sources of
information on the Web to subsequently perform queries. SPARQL Update
provides a step in that direction with its LOAD feature.

LOAD: Perform a (HTTP) lookup on an IRI and if it resolves to an RDF
    document, loads the RDF triples into the dataset

There are two main options that can be specified with LOAD:

SILENT: If not specified, by default the LOAD operation will return an
error if no RDF triples could be parsed from the given location
(e.g., no document could be found at that location, or the document
does not contain RDF); the local dataset remains unmodified. If
specified, the operation will return without error; an implementation
may choose what modifications to make to the local dataset, if any.

INTO GRAPH: If not specified, any RDF triples retrieved from the specified location will be loaded into the default graph. If specified with
an IRI, retrieved triples will be loaded into a named graph.

Example 6.52

The following update will load the RDF triples described by the
document at location http://oscars.org/winners.ttl (if any) into the
default graph of the local dataset:

```
LOAD <http://oscars.org/winners.ttl>
```

If the document does not exist, by default, an error will return. To avoid
an error being thrown, the SILENT keyword can be specified (useful if
the update is part of a sequence of operations):

```
LOAD SILENT <http://oscars.org/winners.ttl>
```

To load the triples into a named graph (rather than the default graph),
INTO GRAPH can be specified with the IRI of the named graph:

```
LOAD SILENT <http://oscars.org/winners.ttl> INTO GRAPH :Oscars
```

(INTO GRAPH can be specified with or without SILENT.)

6.5.4 Managing Graphs

SPARQL Update provides six further features for managing the local graphs
– and the data they contain – in the dataset. We provide an informal gram-
mar for these features, where '($\cdot$)?' indicates an optional keyword, '($\cdot$|...|$\cdot$)'
indicates alternatives from which one is chosen, GRAPH i and GRAPH j denote
named graphs (where i and j are IRIs), DEFAULT denotes the default graph,
NAMED denotes all named graphs, and ALL denotes all graphs (the default and
named graphs). Finally, SILENT denotes that errors should be suppressed.

CLEAR (SILENT)? (GRAPH i | DEFAULT | NAMED | ALL):
- Removes all triples from the specified graph(s) leaving them empty

CREATE (SILENT)? GRAPH i:
- Creates an empty named graph

DROP (SILENT)? (GRAPH i | DEFAULT | NAMED | ALL):
- Deletes the specified graph(s) and their content (if the default graph is dropped, an empty default graph must be created)

COPY (SILENT)? (GRAPH i | DEFAULT) TO (GRAPH j | DEFAULT):
- Copies one graph to another, creating or replacing the target graph, leaving the source graph unmodified

MOVE (SILENT)? (GRAPH i | DEFAULT) TO (GRAPH j | DEFAULT):
- Moves one graph to another, creating or replacing the target graph, dropping the source graph

ADD (SILENT)? (GRAPH i | DEFAULT) TO (GRAPH j | DEFAULT):
- Merges the data from the source graph to the target graph (created if necessary), leaving the source graph unmodified

---

Example 6.53

Referring back to Figure 6.3, we can move all triples to the default graph and remove all named graphs as follows:

```
ADD GRAPH :G-FPW TO DEFAULT;
ADD GRAPH :G-SP TO DEFAULT;
ADD GRAPH :G-TM TO DEFAULT;
ADD GRAPH :G-BB TO DEFAULT;
ADD GRAPH :G-FM TO DEFAULT;
ADD GRAPH :G-JE TO DEFAULT;
DROP NAMED;
```

Remark 6.51

By default, such operations may throw errors, for example, when a particular graph does not exist, or when it cannot be created, etc. The details of when such errors must be thrown or may be thrown is not easily summarised, where the standard leaves certain cases to be decided by a particular implementation [139]. To avoid errors being thrown (e.g., when the update is part of a sequence of operations), the SILENT keyword is used (e.g., COPY SILENT ..., MOVE SILENT ..., etc.).

6.6 SPARQL Entailment Regimes

In Chapters 4 and 5, we discussed the importance of having well-defined vocabulary (RDF, RDFS, OWL) with a formal semantics, in particular for enabling automated entailments through inference procedures. The discussion thus far on SPARQL has not explicitly addressed the topic of entailment.

Example 6.54

Thus far, to find instances of Nobel Prizes with a SPARQL query over the data in Figure 6.1, we have used a path expression to traverse the sub-class hierarchy as follows (see, e.g., Example 6.15):

```
SELECT ?np
WHERE {
  ?np a/rdfs:subClassOf* :NobelPrize .
}
```

The path expression looks for an edge labelled `rdf:type` (denoted by the shortcut "a"), followed by zero or many edges labelled `rdfs:subClassOf`, thus effectively traversing the class hierarchy.

Under RDFS or OWL entailment, such a path expression would not be necessary; under such entailments, we could rather ask:

```
SELECT ?np
WHERE {
  ?np a :NobelPrize .
}
```

where any instance of a sub-class of the class `:NobelPrize` – for example, `:NobelPrizeLiterature` – would be automatically entailed to be an instance of `:NobelPrize`. With an appropriate entailment procedure to interpret the special vocabulary (e.g., `rdfs:subClassOf`) used in the data, we could find more solutions for more concise queries.

In order to support such entailments, SPARQL 1.1 introduces **entailment regimes** [148], which define a standard behaviour for evaluating queries under different types of entailments (including RDF, RDFS, OWL, and more). The standard addresses the following key questions (amongst others) that naturally arise when evaluating SPARQL queries under entailments:

- How should we handle infinite entailments (e.g., the infinite number of axiomatic triples under the RDF semantics)?
- How should we handle inconsistency (e.g., something being an instance of two disjoint classes in OWL)?

- How should we handle restrictions on RDF graphs (e.g., RDF graphs that do not express valid OWL 2 DL ontologies)?

We will now introduce the various entailment regimes supported by SPARQL, which include simple entailment, RDF/RDFS/D entailment, various forms of OWL entailment, as well as RIF entailment.

6.6.1 Extending Simple Entailment

In fact, SPARQL is already implicitly defined in terms of one entailment regime, namely simple entailment, which formalises the existential semantics of blank nodes in RDF (see Section 4.3.1).

Example 6.55

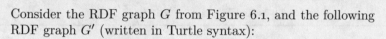

Consider the RDF graph G from Figure 6.1, and the following RDF graph G' (written in Turtle syntax):

```
[] a :NobelPrizeLiterature ;
   :winner [ :country :France ] ;
   :winner [ :country :Spain ] .
```

This graph encodes the claims that there exists a Nobel Prize in Literature for which there exists a winner from Spain and a winner from France. In terms of simple entailment, we see that $G \models G'$ with the first blank node mapping to :NPL1904, the second to :FMistral and the third to :JEchegaray. In fact, to check $G \models G'$, we could also use the following SPARQL query encoding G' as an ASK query:

```
ASK {
  [] a :NobelPrizeLiterature ;
     :winner [ :country :France ] ;
     :winner [ :country :Spain ] .
}
```

Posed against G, this query returns true if and only if $G \models G'$ under simple entailment. Hence we see that one entailment regime we have seen previously – simple entailment – is already at the heart of SPARQL.

To formalise the relation between simple entailment and basic graph pattern matching – and to extend basic graph pattern matching towards more expressive forms of entailment – we provide the following definition.

Definition 44 (Basic graph pattern eval. under entailment). Extending Definition 23, we define the *possible solutions* of B for an RDF graph G under entailment regime R as follows:

$$B_R^*(G) := \{\mu \mid \exists \alpha : G \models_R \mu(\alpha(B)) \text{ and}$$
$$\text{dom}(\mu) = \text{vars}(B) \text{ and}$$
$$\text{dom}(\alpha) = \text{bnodes}(B)\}$$

such that $\models_R$ denotes entailment under R.

Next, for an RDF graph G, let bnodes(G) denote the blank nodes mentioned in G. Further define $R'(G)$ to be the maximal (and possibly infinite) RDF graph such that $G \models R'(G)$, $G \subseteq R'(G)$, and bnodes(G) = bnodes($R'(G)$) hold; in other words, $R'(G)$ extends G with all possible entailments under R without generating new blank nodes or renaming existing blank nodes. Finally, we define the *restricted solutions* of B for an RDF graph G under entailment regime R – denoted $B_R(G)$ – as $B(R'(G))$, i.e., the standard evaluation of B over $R'(G)$.

Remark 6.52 ⓘ

As per the base SPARQL semantics, the multiplicity of a solution to a basic graph pattern under entailment is also defined to be the number of distinct α mappings that satisfy the corresponding condition.

Remark 6.53 ⓘ

We highlight that since $R'(G)$ is defined to be an RDF graph, entailments involving generalised triples (e.g., triples with literals in the subject position, etc.) cannot lead to restricted solutions.

The definition of restricted solutions helps to ensure (under some entailment regimes) that queries do not generate infinite solutions. In particular, given a basic graph pattern B and an RDF graph G, if we let R denote simple entailment (see Definition 14), then the base solutions $B(G)$ and restricted solutions $B_R(G)$ coincide (per the standard semantics for basic graph pattern evaluation). However, the set of possible solutions is infinite.

Example 6.56

Consider the following select query Q consisting of a single basic graph pattern $B := \{(?s, ?p, ?o)\}$:

```
SELECT * WHERE { ?s ?p ?o }
```

Further consider an RDF graph $G := \{(:X, :Y, \_:b)\}$. The *base solutions* $B(G)$ are then given as follows:

?s	?p	?o
:X	:Y	_:b

(*Note*: when the SELECT operator is applied, _:b can be replaced with any blank node, as implied by the end of Definition 39.)

On the other hand, the *possible solutions* $B_R^*(G)$ under simple entailment are infinite, including:

?s	?p	?o
:X	:Y	_:b
_:a	:Y	_:b
_:b	:Y	_:a
...		

Each such solution corresponds to a triple that is (individually) simple-entailed by G; more formally, for each such solution μ, $G \models_R \mu(\alpha(B))$ holds (for α the empty mapping since B contains no blank nodes).

On the other hand, the *restricted solutions* under simple entailment do not allow arbitrary blank nodes to be generated (nor blank nodes to be renamed); hence only the first possible solution would be a restricted solution. In fact, under simple entailment, the restricted solutions always correspond to the base solutions (since $R'(G) = G$).

When we consider more expressive notions of entailment for evaluating SPARQL queries, in effect, we will consider extensions of basic graph pattern matching beyond simple entailment [148]. This approach offers us an elegant "hook" for augmenting SPARQL with entailment since we do not need to (re)define the evaluation of every operator in the (abstract) SPARQL syntax, but rather can focus on what notion of entailment to use for basic graph pattern matching (per Definition 23), which then "feeds" the other operators.

More specifically, each entailment regime is based on two notions [148]:

1. a subset of RDF graphs called *well-formed* for the regime;
2. an *entailment relation* from well-formed graphs to well-formed graphs.

The well-formedness condition is useful when, for example, we consider OWL entailment under Direct Semantics, where only a subset of RDF graphs are well-formed OWL 2 DL ontologies (see Section 5.6.2). Note that the well-formedness condition applies not only to the graph from which solutions are generated, but also any instances of the basic graph pattern after replacing blank nodes and query variables with RDF terms. This gives rise to the notion of *legal graphs* (well-formed graphs) and *legal queries* (queries for which all instances of all basic graph patterns are well-formed graphs), which vary depending on the entailment regime considered. Finally, each entailment regime must define what happens when an inconsistent graph is considered, and should define restrictions to avoid entailing infinite solutions.

Along these lines, we can now define the Simple Entailment Regime, which as aforementioned, is equivalent to standard basic graph pattern matching. This definition – and the definition of entailment regimes that follow – are based on Definition 44 for basic graph pattern evaluation under entailment.

Simple Entailment Regime

Entailment R: Simple entailment (Definition 14)
Legal Graphs: Any valid RDF graph G
Legal Queries: Any valid SPARQL basic graph pattern B
Inconsistency: Cannot occur
Solutions for B(G): All restricted solutions $B_R(G)$.

6.6.2 RDF/RDFS/D Entailment

We now extend simple entailment according to the (other) entailment regimes defined in the RDF (1.1) Semantics standard [180]. We first consider RDF entailment and RDFS entailment with support only for strings (i.e., the datatypes rdf:langString and xsd:string, as required by the standard [180]). We then consider D entailment, with support for arbitrary datatypes.

We start by defining the RDF Entailment Regime.

RDF Entailment Regime

Entailment: RDF entailment [180] (Section 4.3.3)
Legal Graphs: Any valid RDF graph G
Legal Queries: Any valid SPARQL basic graph pattern B
Inconsistency: Cannot occur
Solutions for B(G): A restricted solution $\mu \in B_R(G)$ is a solution if and only if μ does not map any variable to a term x of the form rdf:_n (for $n \in \mathbb{N}$) where x does not appear in $B \cup G$.

The additional constraint on the set of solutions ensures finiteness.

Example 6.57

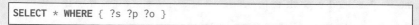

Consider the select query Q:

```
SELECT * WHERE { ?s ?p ?o }
```

Under the RDF Entailment regime, no matter to which graph the above query is applied, the *restricted solutions* include infinite tuples pertaining to axiomatic triples about container-membership properties:

?s	?p	?o
rdf:_1	rdf:type	rdf:Property
rdf:_2	rdf:type	rdf:Property
...		

The set of restricted solutions is thus infinite, where the entailment regime adds additional constraints to restore finiteness. More concretely, let G denote the following RDF graph:

```
_:b1 rdf:_1 :X .
_:b1 rdf:_1 _:b2 .
_:b3 rdf:_3 _:b1 .
```

The solutions for $Q_R(G)$ under the RDF Entailment Regime will include the previous type triples for rdf:_1 and rdf:_3, but not for rdf:_2, etc.

Next we define the RDFS Entailment Regime.

RDFS Entailment Regime

Entailment: RDFS entailment [180] (Section 4.3.4)
Legal Graphs: Any valid RDF graph G
Legal Queries: Any valid SPARQL basic graph pattern B
Inconsistency: An error may be raised
Solutions for $B(G)$: A restricted solution $\mu \in B_R(G)$ is a solution if and only if μ does not map any variable to a term x of the form rdf:_n (for $n \in \mathbb{N}$) where x does not appear in $B \cup G$.

The definition of a solution is the same as for the RDF Entailment Regime, but note that it also constrains triples where properties of the form rdf:_n are typed as rdfs:ContainerMembershipProperty. With respect to inconsistency[3], recall that an inconsistent graph entails all possible triples. An implementation may choose to throw an error, or to provide results for a consistent subset of the graph, or to return solutions for all (finite) triples using the vocabulary of the graph and the RDF(S) vocabulary. With the RDFS Entailment Regime, we now cover the entailments needed by Example 6.54: we no longer need a path expression to traverse the class hierarchy.

Next, we define the D Entailment Regime.

D Entailment Regime

Entailment: D entailment [180] (Section 4.3.2)
Legal Graphs: Any valid RDF graph G
Legal Queries: Any valid SPARQL basic graph pattern B
Inconsistency: An error may be raised
Solutions for $B(G)$: A restricted solution $\mu \in B_R(G)$ is a solution if and only if μ does not map any variable to a literal l that is not the *canonical form* of a literal appearing in $B \cup G$.

We are left to define what is meant by a literal being in "canonical form". Intuitively, we may have multiple syntactic ways to represent the same value with a literal; for example, if D supports `xsd:decimal`, `xsd:integer` and `xsd:byte`, we may represent the numeric value 42 as `"42.0"^^xsd:decimal`, `"42"^^xsd:integer`, or `"+42"^^xsd:byte`. The Entailment Regimes standard assumes that D includes a canonical mapping from a particular value – like 42 – to a canonical lexical string and datatype. A natural choice of canonical form would be to select a minimal lexical string and the primitive (most general) datatype, which in the previous case would give `"42"^^xsd:decimal`; this is defined in the XML Schema Datatypes 1.1 standard [313], and recommended by the Entailment Regimes standard [148]. Literals appearing in non-canonical form will be mapped to canonical form by D entailment, with non-canonical literals being filtered by the above restrictions. The Entailment Regimes standard suggests that a convenient way to support D entailment is to consider rewriting all literals to canonical form directly in the data [148].

Example 6.58

Assume the following RDF graph:

```
:Molybdenum :atomicNumber "42"^^xsd:positiveInteger .
:Calcium-42 :atomicMass "+42.0"^^xsd:decimal .
:Silicon-42 :atomicMass "+42.0"^^xsd:decimal .
```

---

[3] This may occur in RDFS when an ill-typed literal such as `"/"^^rdf:XMLLiteral` is combined with a range definition (though `rdf:XMLLiteral` is optional in RDF 1.1).

Assume the following query looking for isotopes with the same atomic mass as the atomic number of Molybdenum.

```
SELECT ?isotope ?iam
WHERE {
  :Molybdenum :atomicNumber ?man .
  ?isotope :atomicMass ?iam .
  FILTER (?iam = ?man)
}
```

Without entailment, this will return the results:

?isotope	?iam
:Calcium-42	"+42.0"^^xsd:decimal
:Silicon-42	"+42.0"^^xsd:decimal

However, consider the query:

```
SELECT ?isotope ?man
WHERE {
  :Molybdenum :atomicNumber ?man .
  ?isotope :atomicMass ?man .
}
```

Without entailment, this will return no results! While the "=" operator applies value equality (where possible), joins use RDF term equality.

However, assuming that D contains the standard XSD numeric datatypes, note that the original RDF graph D-entails an infinite set of triples of the following form:

```
:Molybdenum :atomicNumber "42"^^xsd:decimal .
:Molybdenum :atomicNumber "42.0"^^xsd:decimal .
:Molybdenum :atomicNumber "42.00"^^xsd:decimal .
...
:Molybdenum :atomicNumber "42"^^xsd:byte .
:Molybdenum :atomicNumber "+42"^^xsd:byte .
:Molybdenum :atomicNumber "42"^^xsd:integer .
...
:Calcium-42 :atomicMass "42"^^xsd:decimal .
...
:Silicon-42 :atomicMass "42"^^xsd:decimal .
...
```

If we were to consider running the second query over the graph extended by D-entailment, the restricted answers would include an infinite number of solutions of the form:

?isotope	?iam
:Calcium-42	"42"^^xsd:decimal
:Calcium-42	"42.0"^^xsd:decimal
:Calcium-42	"42.00"^^xsd:decimal
...	...
:Calcium-42	"42"^^xsd:byte
:Calcium-42	"+42"^^xsd:byte
...	...
:Silicon-42	"42"^^xsd:decimal
...	...

Hence in the Entailment Regimes standard, solutions are restricted to only include canonical literals. If we take the minimal lexical string and most general (derived) datatype as the canonical form – per the recommendation of the XML Schema Datatypes 1.1 standard [313] – we end up with the following two solutions:

?isotope	?iam
:Calcium-42	"42"^^xsd:decimal
:Silicon-42	"42"^^xsd:decimal

These solutions would likewise have been achieved had we simply rewritten the literals in the original data to their canonical form.

Remark 6.54

The previous example raises another implicit question: what happens to the multiplicity of results under entailment?

Take for example the graph:

```
:Molybdenum :atomicNumber "42"^^xsd:positiveInteger .
:Calcium-42 :atomicMass "42.0"^^xsd:decimal , "42"^^xsd:integer .
:Silicon-42 :atomicMass "42.0"^^xsd:decimal .
```

And the following query:

```
SELECT ?isotope ?iam
WHERE {
  :Molybdenum :atomicNumber ?iam .
  ?isotope :atomicMass ?iam .
}
```

Under D entailment, the question now is: will the "duplicate" value on :Calcium-42 in the input data affect the multiplicity of the result?

> The answer is no: for each valid solution, the multiplicity is defined in the standard way over the graph extended with entailment, in which the triple that generates the final (canonical solution) appears once:
>
> ```
> :Calcium-42 :atomicMass "42"^^xsd:decimal .
> ```
>
> In fact, this single solution would have also been given had we rewritten the literals in the original data to their canonical form: this rewriting strategy would require removing the "duplicate" atomic mass.
>
> More generally, multiplicity under entailment does not capture the number of ways in which something can be entailed; rather it captures the number of solutions over the entailed graph. This holds more generally for entailment regimes other than D entailment.

6.6.3 OWL Entailment

Having covered entailment regimes relating to the RDF 1.1 Semantics standard [180], we now discuss support for regimes relating to the OWL 2 standard, covering OWL 2 RDF-Based entailment [349], OWL 2 Direct entailment [281], and entailment under the OWL 2 Profiles [280].

We start with the most expressive regime: OWL 2 RDF-Based Entailment.

OWL 2 RDF-Based Entailment Regime

Entailment: OWL 2 Full/RDF-Based entailment [349] (Section 5.6.1)
Legal Graphs: Any valid RDF graph G
Legal Queries: Any valid SPARQL basic graph pattern B
Inconsistency: An error may be raised
Solutions for $B(G)$: A restricted solution $\mu \in B_R(G)$ is a solution if and only if μ does not map any variable to a literal l that is not the *canonical form* of a literal appearing in $B \cup G$ and μ does not map any variable to a term x of the form rdf:_n (for $n \in \mathbb{N}$) where x does not appear in $B \cup G$.

The OWL 2 RDF-Based entailment is thus a straightforward extension of the RDF, RDFS and D entailment regimes, where the set of solutions defined is finite along the same lines as seen before. However, OWL 2 RDF-Based entailment is undecidable (see Remark 5.36), and hence there does not exist an algorithm that guarantees to enumerate all solutions in finite steps; in practice, this means that any implementation of the OWL 2 RDF-Based entailment regime will return an incomplete set of solutions for some inputs.

Remark 6.55   ⓘ

For μ to be a solution under OWL 2 RDF-Based entailment,
any literal it maps to must be the canonical form of a literal in the
graph or the basic graph pattern. This may sometimes lead to missing
solutions. For example, consider the following graph G and query Q:

```
:Jane a :Sophomore .
:Sophomore owl:equivalentClass
  [ a owl:Restriction ;
    owl:onProperty :year ;
    owl:someValuesFrom
      [ a rdfs:Datatype ;
        owl:onDatatype xsd:integer ;
        owl:withRestrictions (
          [ xsd:minExclusive  1 ]
          [ xsd:maxExclusive  3 ] ) ] ] .
```

```
SELECT * WHERE { ?student :year ?year }
```

Although the graph entails that Jane must be in year 2, the query would
return empty results under OWL 2 RDF-Based Entailment since the
literal value 2 does not appear anywhere in the graph or the query.

However, if we were to consider the following query Q':

```
SELECT * WHERE { ?student :year 2 }
```

Jane would be given as a result for the query Q' since a literal corresponding to the value 2 now appears in the query. Alternatively, if the
graph had contained a datatype literal such as "2"^^xsd:int, then Jane
would have been returned by the original query.

Next we cover the OWL 2 Direct Entailment Regime.

OWL 2 Direct Entailment Regime

Entailment: OWL 2 DL/Direct entailment [281] (Section 5.6.2)
Legal Graphs: An OWL 2 DL-compatible graph G
Legal Queries: An OWL 2 DL-compatible basic graph pattern B
Inconsistency: An error must be raised
Solutions for $B(G)$: A restricted solution $\mu \in B_R(G)$ is a solution if and
    only if μ does not map any variable to a literal l that is not the
    canonical form of a literal appearing in $B \cup G$ and μ does not map
    any variable to a term x of the form rdf:_n (for $n \in \mathbb{N}$) where x
    does not appear in $B \cup G$.

A key difference from previous regimes is that only OWL 2 DL-compatible graphs and basic graph patterns are accepted as input, which means that the graph being queried must be a well-formed OWL 2 DL ontology, and each basic graph pattern in the query must also follow the OWL 2 DL restrictions, with some alterations to allow for query variables to appear [153]. We omit the precise details of which basic graph patterns are considered OWL 2 DL-compatible; instead we capture the gist with some concrete examples.

Example 6.59

Let us consider the following query:

```
SELECT * WHERE { ?s ?p ?o }
```

This query contains a single basic graph pattern that is not considered to be OWL 2 DL compatible: OWL 2 DL requires type statements to distinguish object properties from datatype properties, etc., where, in order for the query to be OWL 2 DL compatible – allowing entailment checking between the graph and the basic graph pattern under a given solution – we would need to add, for example:

```
SELECT * WHERE {
  ?s ?p ?o .
  ?p a owl:DatatypeProperty .
}
```

Next, consider a query:

```
SELECT * WHERE { ?s :winner ?o }
```

Although :winner is not typed in the query as a datatype/object property, if it is typed in the graph being queried, this query would be OWL 2 DL compatible: in other words, elements typed as object/datatype properties, etc., in the data do not need to be typed again in the query.

Even if well-typed, queries may not be OWL 2 DL compatible if they contain basic graph patterns that break restrictions of the OWL 2 DL language intended to maintain certain computational guarantees for tasks such as entailment checking. For example, consider asking:

```
SELECT * WHERE {
  ?p a owl:InverseFunctionalProperty , owl:DatatypeProperty
}
```

In OWL 2 DL, datatype properties cannot be inverse-functional (see Example 5.38), and hence this query is not OWL 2 DL compatible.

Finally, consider a query such as:

```
SELECT * WHERE {
  :Human rdfs:subClassOf
  [ a owl:Restriction ;
    ?quantifier :Human ;
    owl:onProperty :hasParent ] .
}
```

This query effectively asks what quantifier holds on the parents of humans that are human: are *all* parents of humans human, are *some* parents of humans human, etc. However, for a basic graph pattern to be OWL 2 DL compatible, its variables can only appear in positions where a class, an object/datatype property, an individual or a literal may appear; in the case of the above query, the variable ?quantifier does not appear in such a position, but rather in the position of a logical quantifier in the language – hence the query is not OWL 2 DL compatible.

A number of entailment regimes are further defined for the OWL 2 EL, OWL 2 QL and OWL 2 RL profiles (see Section 5.6.3).

OWL 2 EL Entailment Regime

Entailment: OWL 2 EL/Direct entailment [280] (Section 5.6.3.2)
Legal Graphs: An OWL 2 EL-compatible graph G
Legal Queries: An OWL 2 EL-compatible basic graph pattern B
Inconsistency: An error must be raised
Solutions for B(G): A restricted solution $\mu \in B_R(G)$ is a solution if and only if μ does not map any variable to a literal l that is not the *canonical form* of a literal appearing in $B \cup G$ and μ does not map any variable to a term x of the form rdf:_n (for $n \in \mathbb{N}$) where x does not appear in $B \cup G$.

OWL 2 QL Entailment Regime

Entailment: OWL 2 QL/Direct entailment [280] (Section 5.6.3.3)
Legal Graphs: An OWL 2 QL-compatible graph G
Legal Queries: An OWL 2 QL-compatible basic graph pattern B
Inconsistency: An error must be raised
Solutions for B(G): A restricted solution $\mu \in B_R(G)$ is a solution if and only if μ does not map any variable to a literal l that is not the *canonical form* of a literal appearing in $B \cup G$ and μ does not map any variable to a term x of the form rdf:_n (for $n \in \mathbb{N}$) where x does not appear in $B \cup G$.

The OWL 2 RL profile is defined differently, accepting any graph and any query, applying OWL 2 RL/RDF rules to capture entailments.

OWL 2 RL Entailment Regime

Entailment: OWL 2 RL/RDF rule entailment [280] (Section 5.6.3.4)
Legal Graphs: Any valid RDF graph G
Legal Queries: Any valid SPARQL basic graph pattern B
Inconsistency: An error must be raised
Solutions for $B(G)$: A restricted solution $\mu \in B_R(G)$ is a solution if and
   only if μ does not map any variable to a literal l that is not the
   canonical form of a literal appearing in $B \cup G$ and μ does not map
   any variable to a term x of the form rdf:_n (for $n \in \mathbb{N}$) where x
   does not appear in $B \cup G$.

6.6.4 RIF Entailment

Rather than using ontologies defined in OWL, it may sometimes be more straightforward to represent entailments using rules; for example, as discussed in Section 5.4.7, some patterns of entailment cannot be captured in OWL. One way in which custom rules can be expressed over RDF graphs is using the RIF Core standard [66, 107]; though a detailed treatment of RIF Core is out-of-scope for our purposes, we give an example to sketch the idea.

Example 6.60

Referring back to Example 5.25, we mentioned that "property intersection" (aka. "role intersection") cannot be directly expressed in OWL, meaning that for example, given an RDF graph G:

```
:Sally :youngerThan :Jim ; :siblingOf :Jim .
```

we cannot (straightforwardly) capture an entailment of the form in OWL:

```
:Sally :youngerSiblingOf :Jim .
```

On the other hand, capturing such entailments with rules is straightforward. Using RIF Core [66] for example, we can represent this entailment with the following rule-based pattern:

```
Forall ?X ?Y (
    ?X [ :youngerSiblingOf -> ?Y ] :- And( ?X [ :siblingOf -> ?Y ]
                                            ?X [ :youngerThan -> ?Y ] )
)
```

The RIF standard then defines a variety of entailment regimes that combine RDF/OWL entailment with rule-based entailment under RIF [107]. The SPARQL Entailment Regimes specification supports one such form of entailment – called RIF–Simple entailment – which combines simple entailment with RIF-Core rules. We refer to the SPARQL specification for details [148].

6.6.5 Beyond Basic Graph Patterns

Entailment regimes are directly over basic graph patterns, with entailment applied over the active graph. However, the solutions generated for a basic graph pattern through entailment over the active graph may serve as input for other query operators (analogous with the base SPARQL semantics).

Example 6.61

Consider the following graph from Example 6.58:

```
:Molybdenum :atomicNumber "42"^^xsd:positiveInteger .
:Calcium-42 :atomicMass "+42.0"^^xsd:decimal .
:Silicon-42 :atomicMass "+42.0"^^xsd:decimal .
```

Further consider the following query:

```
SELECT (count(?isotope) AS ?num)
WHERE {
    :Molybdenum :atomicNumber ?man .
    ?isotope :atomicMass ?man .
}
```

The basic graph pattern under D entailment will produce the solutions:

?isotope	?man
:Calcium-42	"42"^^xsd:decimal
:Silicon-42	"42"^^xsd:decimal

The count operator is applied as in the base SPARQL case over these solutions, generating an answer of "2"^^xsd:integer for ?num.

Thus assuming that individual basic graph patterns meet the restrictions required by a particular entailment regime, defining the solutions given for a query that users other query operators – like FILTER, UNION, GRAPH, COUNT, ORDER BY, etc. – follows straightforwardly, for the most part.

Exercise 6.19

Consider the graph G from Remark 6.55, and the following two SPARQL queries:

```
SELECT ?student WHERE {
  ?student :year ?year .
  FILTER(?year > 1)
}
```

```
SELECT ?student WHERE {
  ?student :year ?year .
  FILTER(?year >= 2)
}
```

What solutions would be returned for these two queries under OWL 2 RDF-Based Entailment? What solutions would be returned if we were to add the following triple to the graph?

```
:Bill :year "2"^^xsd:int
```

One complication does arise, on the other hand, when considering property paths. We recall that in Definition 44, we laid the foundations for all entailment regimes by defining that a solution μ is a possible solution for a basic graph pattern B over a graph G under entailment R if the image of B under μ is R-entailed by G. But this entailment is only well-defined when B consists of triple patterns: what would it mean for a graph G to R-entail a path pattern of the form ":x :y* :z"? The Entailment Regimes standard thus defines the following with respect to supporting property paths [148]:

- Property paths that can be rewritten to triple patterns without paths – meaning non-recursive patterns like `:p/:q`, `:p|:q`, etc. – should be supported by rewriting them to triple patterns without paths.
- For property paths that cannot be rewritten to triple patterns without paths, the standard gives two options: (1) reject queries with these path patterns; (2) evaluate these path patterns without entailment.

Another complication arising from more expressive entailment regime – beyond simple entailment, and perhaps D-entailment – is their cost to implement and support in a SPARQL query service. As discussed previously, for example, entailment for OWL 2 Full is undecidable. Even for decidable fragments, entailment regimes may incur prohibitive costs. Partly for this reason, although entailment regimes would undoubtedly be a useful feature, few public SPARQL services support such functionality at the time of writing (beyond simple entailment and D-entailment with literal canonicalisation).

6.7 SPARQL Service

Having discussed the main features of the SPARQL standard – the query language and its semantics, the update language, and the entailment regimes it defines – we now discuss how such features can be used to host a SPARQL service invokable over the Web. We first discuss the output formats that SPARQL supports [178, 97, 355] before describing the protocol by which agents can interact with a SPARQL service over the Web [124]. Finally, we describe the SPARQL Service Description vocabulary [402], which allows a SPARQL service to describe and advertise its capabilities in RDF.

6.7.1 Output Formats

Depending on the query form used, SPARQL offers a variety of output formats used to serialise solutions to a client application. For SELECT and ASK queries, the following formats are supported:

XML [178] was the first format released for SPARQL 1.0 and subsequently updated for the SPARQL 1.1 standard.

JSON [97] was added to SPARQL 1.1, reflecting the increasing popularity of the JSON syntax for Web development.

CSV and TSV [355] was added to SPARQL 1.1, offering a plain-text tabular-style formats that can easily be opened, e.g., as a spreadsheet.

We refer the reader to the respective standards for more details [178, 97, 355].

Example 6.62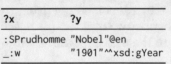

Consider the following results for a SELECT query:

?x	?y
:SPrudhomme	"Nobel"@en
_:w	"1901"^^xsd:gYear

The simplest output format for SPARQL 1.1 is CSV[355]:

```
x,y
http://ex.org/SPrudhomme,"Nobel"@en
_:w,"1901"^^<http://www.w3.org/2001/XMLSchema#gYear>
```

While the above results are comma-separated (CSV), one may also choose to return results as tab-separated (TSV) [355].

In the XML format [178], these results would be written:

```xml
<?xml version="1.0"?>
<sparql xmlns="http://www.w3.org/2005/sparql-results#">
  <head>
    <variable name="x"/>
    <variable name="y"/>
  </head>
  <results>
    <result>
      <binding name="x">
        <uri>http://ex.org/SPrudhomme</uri>
      </binding>
      <binding name="y">
        <literal xml:lang="en">Nobel</literal>
      </binding>
    </result>
    <result>
      <binding name="x">
        <bnode>w</bnode>
      </binding>
      <binding name="y">
        <literal datatype="http://www.w3.org/2001/XMLSchema#gYear">
            ↪ 1901</literal>
      </binding>
    </result>
  </results>
</sparql>
```

In the JSON format [97], these results would be written:

```json
{ "head": { "vars": [ "x" , "y" ] } ,
  "results": {
    "bindings": [
      { "x": {
          "type": "uri" , "value": "http://ex.org/SPrudhomme"
        } ,
        "y": {
          "type": "literal" , "value": "Nobel" , "xml:lang": "en"
        }
      } ,
      { "x": {
          "type": "bnode" , "value": "w"
        } ,
        "y": {
          "type": "literal" ,  "value": "1901",
          "datatype": "http://www.w3.org/2001/XMLSchema#gYear"
        }
      }
    ]
  }
}
```

> **Example 6.63**
>
> We show the true response for ASK queries in CSV/TSV:
>
> ```
> true
> ```
>
> ...in XML:
>
> ```
> <?xml version="1.0"?>
> <sparql xmlns="http://www.w3.org/2005/sparql-results#">
>   <head></head>
>   <boolean>true</boolean>
> </sparql>
> ```
>
> ...in JSON:
>
> ```
> {
>   "head" : { } ,
>   "boolean" : true
> }
> ```
>
> ...and
> False results are given analogously (replacing true with false).

On the other hand, CONSTRUCT and DESCRIBE queries return RDF graphs, and thus their output is serialised as an RDF syntax (see Section 3.8). A client can then choose the output format that they find most convenient.

6.7.2 SPARQL Protocol

The SPARQL Protocol [124] defines how queries and updates may be sent to a SPARQL service via HTTP and what responses should be returned. In terms of queries, three parameters are supported:

query (1 value): the query string;
default-graph-uri (0 or more values): the IRIs of the graphs with which to form the default graph of the query (analogous to FROM);
named-graph-uri (0 or more values): the IRIs of the named graphs over which to apply the query (analogous to FROM NAMED);

An agent may send a query request with the aforementioned parameters by HTTP GET or POST; values must be appropriate encoded (e.g., using percent-encoding). If the request can be answered, results should be returned in an appropriate format as described in Section 6.7.1; an agent may use content negotiation to select a preferred output format (or output formats).

Updates can likewise be sent via HTTP with the following parameters:

update (1 value): the update string;

using-graph-uri (0 or more values): the default graph to use for matching the WHERE clause (analogous to USING);

using-named-graph-uri (0 or more values): the named graphs to use for matching the WHERE clause (analogous to USING NAMED);

An agent may only send an update request with the aforementioned parameters by HTTP POST (GET is not allowed for updates).

Discussion 6.5

JULIE: It seems a bit naive to allow updates over the Web?

AIDAN: Updates though the HTTP protocol are usually disabled or restricted. There may be use-cases however where restricted updates may be allowed over the Web in combination with authentication and access-control methods; we will discuss these use-cases further in the context of "Read–Write Linked Data" in Chapter 8.

The service should respond with a HTTP response code indicating the outcome of the request: a 2xx code (typically 200), or a 3xx code should be returned if the request succeeds (i.e., the query was successfully parsed and solutions – possibly empty – are returned); otherwise if there is a problem with the request (such as an invalid query string), a 4xx code should be returned; finally if the request is valid but the server encounters an error (e.g., the service is overloaded), a 5xx code should be returned.

We refer to the standard for further details and examples [124].

6.7.3 SPARQL Service Description

Different SPARQL services may support different parts of the standard: while it is expected that such a service should at least support the query language, it may, for example, not support other features such as federation, updates, entailment regimes, and so forth. The SPARQL Service Description standard provides a vocabulary – a set of RDF(S) classes and properties – that can be used to describe the capabilities of a service.

Remark 6.56

We use the prefix nb: to denote the namespace:

```
http://www.w3.org/ns/sparql-service-description#
```

We begin by enumerating the classes and their standard instances:

---

sd:Service denotes SPARQL services.

sd:Feature denotes features a service can support. Five standard instances are defined by the specification:

  sd:DereferencesURIs: A feature whereby if an IRI is used in a FROM, FROM NAMED, USING or USING NAMED clause that does not appear in the local dataset, the service can try to retrieve an RDF document from the Web at that location

  sd:UnionDefaultGraph: A feature whereby the default graph of the base dataset is defined to be the union of all named graphs.

  sd:RequiresDataset: A feature whereby the current service requires a dataset to be explicitly defined using FROM, FROM NAMED, USING, USING NAMED or the parameters default-graph-uri, named-graph-uri, using-graph-uri, or using-named-graph-uri

  sd:EmptyGraphs: A feature whereby the service allows empty graphs (for example, if all triples are removed from a graph, the empty graph will be preserved rather than begin removed)

  sd:BasicFederatedQuery: A feature for federated query support

sd:Language denotes SPARQL languages. Three standard instances are defined by the specification:

  sd:SPARQL10Query: The SPARQL 1.0 Query Language [328]

  sd:SPARQL11Query: The SPARQL 1.1 Query Language [169]

  sd:SPARQL11Update: The SPARQL 1.1 Update Language [139]

sd:Function A function (e.g., +, &&, coalesce, etc.)

sd:Aggregate An aggregate function (e.g., count, max, etc.)

sd:EntailmentRegime An entailment regime (e.g., D, OWL 2 Direct)

sd:EntailmentProfile An entailment profile (e.g., OWL 2 EL/QL/RL)

sd:Graph An RDF graph

sd:NamedGraph A named graph

sd:GraphCollection A collection of zero or more named graphs

sd:Dataset An RDF dataset with a default (RDF) graph and zero or more named graphs (a sub-class of sd:GraphCollection)

Remark 6.57   (i)

Though not defined by the Service Description specification, a list of IRIs to refer to standard entailment regimes[a] (instances of sd:EntailmentRegime) and OWL 2 profiles[b] (instances of sd:EntailmentProfile) is recommended for use by the specification.

---

[a] https://www.w3.org/ns/entailment/

[b] https://www.w3.org/ns/owl-profile/

Next we enumerate the properties provided in the vocabulary:

---

sd:endpoint relates a service to the URL to which requests can be sent via the SPARQL protocol

sd:feature relates a service to a supported feature

sd:defaultEntailmentRegime relates a service to the entailment regime supported by default

sd:entailmentRegime relates a specific named graph to a particular entailment regime applied over that graph

sd:defaultSupportedEntailmentProfile relates a service to the entailment profile supported by default

sd:supportedEntailmentProfile relates a specific named graph to a particular entailment profile applied over that graph

sd:extensionFunction relates a service with a function it supports

sd:extensionAggregate relates a service to an aggregate function it supports

sd:supportedLanguage relates a service to a supported language

sd:languageExtension relates a service to a supported extension of the SPARQL Query or Update language

sd:propertyFeature relates a service to a supported extension of the SPARQL Query or Update language that is accessed using the given property

sd:resultFormat relates a service to an output format supported for serialising results

sd:inputFormat relates a service to an input RDF format supported for, e.g., loading RDF graphs from the Web

sd:defaultDataset relates a service to its default dataset

sd:availableGraphs relates a service to a graph collection that indicates named graphs that can be used in a query

sd:defaultGraph relates a dataset to its default graph

sd:namedGraph relates a graph collection (or dataset) to a named graph it contains

sd:name relates a named graph to its name

sd:graph relates a named graph to its graph

Remark 6.58   ⓘ

Though not defined by the Service Description specification, a list of file format IRIs[a] is recommended for use, covering typical values for sd:resultFormat and sd:inputFormat.

---
[a] https://www.w3.org/ns/formats/

This vocabulary can then be used to describe the capabilities of a SPARQL service in RDF. The next question is then: how should an agent find the SPARQL service description of a given service? The specification provides a simple solution: when the service endpoint URL is looked up in HTTP without any parameters, the result should be a document containing the service's description in RDF (possibly RDFa embedded in (X)HTML).

Example 6.64

We give an example description of a fictitious SPARQL service:

```
@base <http://nobel.org/sparql/> .
@prefix sd: <http://.../ns/sparql-service-description#> .
@prefix ent: <http://www.w3.org/ns/entailment/> .
@prefix profile: <http://www.w3.org/ns/owl-profile/> .
@prefix formats: <http://www.w3.org/ns/formats/> .
@prefix rdfs: <http://www.w3.org/2000/01/rdf-schema#> .

<this> a sd:Service ;
  sd:endpoint <> ;
  rdfs:label "Nobel Prize SPARQL Service"@es ;
  rdfs:comment "SPARQL service with data about Nobel Prizes"@en ;
  sd:feature sd:EmptyGraphs , sd:BasicFederatedQuery ;
  sd:defaultEntailmentRegime ent:OWL-RDF-Based ;
  sd:defaultSupportedEntailmentProfile profile:RL ;
  sd:supportedLanguage sd:SPARQL11Query , sd:SPARQL11Update ;
  sd:resultFormat formats:Turtle , formats:SPARQL_Results_XML ;
  sd:inputFormat formats:Turtle , formats:RDF_XML ;
  sd:extensionFunction <KeywordSearch> ;
  sd:defaultDataset [
    a sd:Dataset ;
    sd:defaultGraph [
      a sd:Graph ;
      rdfs:comment "Types of prizes won"@en
    ] ;
    sd:namedGraph [
      a sd:NamedGraph ;
      sd:name <literature/> ;
      sd:graph [
        a sd:Graph ;
        rdfs:comment "Winners for literature"@en
      ]
    ]
  ] .
```

The service description provides a summary of the features, entailments, languages and formats supported by the service, as well as providing details on the default dataset, which is defined to be composed of a default graph and a single named graph, with comments for both.

6.8 Summary

We began this chapter by introducing the cornerstone of the SPARQL standard: the query language. We discussed a variety of features in the query language that allow for increasingly complex queries to be expressed, starting with basic graph patterns, then looking at unions of graph patterns, optional graph patterns, filtering, negation, and so forth. Though many such features can be found in other query languages such as SQL, we also discussed some features that are more particular to graph query languages, such as being able to query multiple graphs, arbitrary-length paths, etc. Next we formally defined the query language and presented discussion on the complexity of tasks such as deciding query evaluation, equivalence and containment. We then discussed the federation feature, which supports calling external SPARQL services through sub-queries. We discussed the update language that allows for adding or deleting RDF data, as well as applying operations – such as copy, move, delete, etc. – over named graphs. We discussed entailment regimes that extend the solutions for basic graph patterns according to the standards previously discussed in other chapters – namely RDF(S) and OWL – that allow for defining the semantics of terms. Finally, we discussed how SPARQL services can be hosted on the Web, describing the output formats supported, the HTTP-based protocol for invocation over the Web, as well as a vocabulary for describing and advertising the capabilities of a particular service.

6.9 Discussion

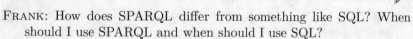

Discussion 6.6

FRANK: How does SPARQL differ from something like SQL? When should I use SPARQL and when should I use SQL?

AIDAN: While fundamentally there are a lot of similarities between SPARQL and SQL – and indeed queries in one can often be rewritten to the other, and vice versa – there are also key practical differences. First, being based on RDF, SPARQL is a query language for graphs, and offers some graph-specific features such as querying multiple graphs, querying arbitrary-length paths in graphs, etc. Likewise, SPARQL offers a more flexible way to manage data, foregoing the need to design and maintain a relational schema: instead, triples can be added or removed from graphs, graphs can be added or removed from datasets, and so forth, on the fly. Furthermore,

SPARQL offers standard mechanisms for reasoning, where additional solutions can be inferred from the explicit semantics (defined in RDF(S)/OWL) through the provision of entailment regimes. Finally, the SPARQL standard defines a variety of "webby" features, such as the ability to host SPARQL services invocable via HTTP, the ability to call external SPARQL services in federated sub-queries, the ability to load new RDF graphs from the Web, etc.

FRANK: So when should I use SPARQL and when should I use SQL?

AIDAN: Probably you should use SQL and relational databases when you have a fixed (relational) schema that rarely changes, you are not really interested in integrating new data "on-the-fly" and are mostly interested in doing queries in a local setting over tabular data; these assumptions hold in many commercial applications, such as for data management inside banks, hospitals, etc. However, if the schema is difficult to define *a priori*, the schema often changes, you often wish to integrate new data on the fly, you want to make your data public on the Web for others to use, etc., then SPARQL may fit better.

FRANK: And how does SPARQL relate to NoSQL stores?

AIDAN: SPARQL fits within the "Not only SQL" philosophy. However, unlike the majority of query languages for NoSQL, SPARQL is fully featured – with operators like joins, unions, etc. – and has been standardised and implemented by several engines. SPARQL can be considered as a language for querying graph databases, similar to the Cypher language used by Neo4j [10]. However, SPARQL has uniquely "webby" features (federation, etc.) while most NoSQL stores focus on centralised data residing on a cluster of machines.

JULIE: But in the context of the Web of Data, will it be expected that users learn SPARQL to be able to answer complex queries?

AIDAN: No. Users can write SPARQL queries if they so wish, but the idea is that the majority of traffic to SPARQL services will be through applications that users interact with.

FRANK: But what about the costs of hosting such services?

AIDAN: This is certainly a concern, and indeed many public SPARQL services must make practical compromises, such as limiting the maximum number of results that can be returned, rate-limiting the volume of requests from individual clients, disabling entailments, implementing configurable timeouts to suspend costly queries, and so forth [13]. Still, SPARQL services such as that hosted by Wikidata – which, in 2018, answered on average 3.8 million queries per day, free-of-charge, over a dataset with several billion triples, with update latencies of less than a minute and timeout rates of less than 0.05% [255] – are testament to the fact that SPARQL can be implemented in practice, at large scale, on the Web (of Data).

Chapter 7
Shape Constraints and Expressions

The RDFS and OWL standards allow publishers to define the semantics of terms used in an RDF graph; however, the capabilities of these standards for validating RDF graphs are limited to checking for logical inconsistency. While in RDFS we can use a domain axiom to state that any entity defined with an ISBN code must be a book, we cannot enforce that a particular RDF graph provide an ISBN code on all books. While in OWL we can use a cardinality restriction to state that a football match has precisely two teams participating, we cannot enforce that a particular RDF graph name two teams – and no more than two teams – on each football match it describes. Such limitations are a feature of RDFS and OWL rather than a bug: the purpose of these standards is to derive new knowledge from incomplete RDF data rather than to validate the completeness and structure of a given RDF graph.

Still, however, it may be useful to have such validation mechanisms for RDF graphs: to be able to state, for example, that the RDF graphs accepted by a particular application must define an ISBN code on every book described, or that any football match described must name the two teams (and only two teams) that participate. Along these lines, two languages have recently been proposed for validating RDF graphs in this manner: the **Shapes Constraint Language (SHACL)** [236] and the **Shape Expressions Language (ShEx)** (ShEx) [325]. This chapter describes these two languages in turn.

> **Example 7.1**
>
> In Figure 7.1, we provide a motivating example for SHACL/ShEx based on a quite messy RDF graph describing Nobel Prizes in Physics. The comments embedded in the data indicate the main issues that should be cleaned up before the data are consumed.
>
> Using RDFS and OWL, we could define axioms that would raise inconsistencies for (1), (6), (7), (8) and (10) – which we shall leave as Exercise 7.1 for the reader. With respect to (2), we could define that

© Springer Nature Switzerland AG 2020
A. Hogan, *The Web of Data*, https://doi.org/10.1007/978-3-030-51580-5_7

d:PZeeman must be a person and must have some name and some country, but we could not enforce – under the OWA – that these names
and countries be given in the RDF graph. The situation is similar for
(4), where we could define that each prize has a year, but we could not
enforce that an RDF graph give the year. With respect to (3) we could
entail that the two values for :next must refer to the same thing, but
we could not enforce – without a UNA, or without otherwise indicating that the names refer to different elements of the domain (e.g, using
owl:differentFrom) – that duplicate identifiers of this form be avoided
in the RDF graph. Regarding (5), we could require that a name have
a particular number of values from a particular language range (using
datatype facets), but distinguishing between @en or @en-US, or generically stating that there should be only one name per language (no matter what the language) is not direct, and may require listing all possible
languages. With respect to (9), we could attempt to perhaps convert
the o:winners count to an exact cardinality constraint on the instance,
but this would again involve some quite messy OWL 2 Full definitions
and would again not ensure that the number of winners corresponds
with those specified (due to the OWA and the lack of a UNA).

On the other hand, we may consider using SPARQL queries to detect
such issues in an RDF graph [235]. In some cases, however, this might
not be so easy. Regarding (1), consider using a SPARQL ASK query to
encode the check that each Nobel Prize in Physics has precisely one
year, which must be an xsd:gYear value; the query should return true
if there is a violation and false otherwise:

```
ASK {
  ?npp a o:NobelPrizePhysics .
  OPTIONAL { ?npp o:year ?year1 , ?year2 . }
  FILTER(!bound(?year1) || ?year1 != ?year2 || !isLiteral(?year1)
     || datatype(?year1) != xsd:gYear)
}
```

This query requires some careful consideration to ensure that it correctly captures the required constraint. Further complications would be
introduced if we were to consider more complex constraints, for example, requiring between one and three winners for each Nobel Prize in
Physics, with all winners defined as people and not as any other type –
we shall leave this problem as Exercise 7.2 for the reader.

Compared to RDFS and OWL, the shapes languages described in this
chapter allow for validating the completeness of resources described in
RDF and for ensuring that redundant identifiers are not present. These
languages were designed specifically for validating RDF graphs, offering
a higher-level alternative to SPARQL .

```
@prefix d: <http://nobel.org/data#> .
@prefix o: <http://nobel.org/ont#> .
@prefix rdfs: <http://www.w3.org/2000/01/rdf-schema#> .
@prefix xsd: <http://www.w3.org/2001/XMLSchema#> .

d:NPP1901 a o:NobelPrizePhysics ;
  o:name "Nobelpriset i fysik 1901"@sv ;
  o:name "Nobel Prize in Physics 1901"@en ;
  o:year "1901"^^xsd:gYear ;
  o:winner d:WCRöntgen ;
  o:winners 1 ;
  o:number 1 ;
  o:next d:NPP1902 .

d:NPP1902 a o:NobelPrizePhysics ;
  o:name "Prix Nobel de physique 1902"@fr ;
  o:name "Nobel Prize in Physics 1902"@en ;
  o:name "Nobel Prize for Physics 1902"@en-US ;
  o:year "1902"^^xsd:gYear , 1902 ;           # (1) two values for year
  o:winner d:HLorentz , d:PZeeman ;           # (2) no data for PZeeman
  o:winners 2 ;
  o:number 2 ;
  o:prev d:NPP1901 ;
  o:next d:NPP1903 , d:npp1903 .              # (3) two values for next

d:NPP1903 a o:NobelPrizePhysics ;            # (4) no o:year
  o:name "Nobel Prize in Physics 1903"@en ;
  o:name "Nobel Prize for Physics 1903"@en ; # (5) two names, same lang
  o:winner d:France , d:Poland ;              # (6) winners are countries
  o:number 2 , 3 ;                            # (7) two values
  o:prev d:NPP1903 ;                          # (8) has itself as previous
  o:winners 3 .                               # (9) number does not match

d:WCRöntgen a o:Person ;
  o:name "Wilhelm C. Röntgen" ;
  o:country d:Germany .

d:HLorentz a o:Person ;
  o:name "" ;                                 # (10) name is blank
  o:country d:Netherlands .

d:France a o:Country .
d:Poland a o:Country .

o:NobelPrizePhysics rdfs:subClassOf o:NobelPrize .
o:NobelPrize rdfs:subClassOf o:Prize .
```

Fig. 7.1 RDF graph in Turtle syntax describing Nobel Prizes in Physics (to be used as a running example), listing a number of data issues highlighted as comments

Though the following exercises (mentioned in the previous example) do not directly use shapes, they do help to motivate these languages.

Exercise 7.1

With respect to Figure 7.1, provide the RDFS/OWL axioms needed to generate inconsistencies for issues (1), (6), (7), (8) and (10):

(1) Any entity can only have one value for year: a value in xsd:gYear.
(6) Winners must be people (and cannot be countries).
(7) Nobel Prizes can only have one number: a value in xsd:integer.
(8) No entity can have itself as a previous value.
(10) Name must take a non-blank string as value.

Exercise 7.2

With respect to Figure 7.1, provide a SPARQL ASK query to check that each Nobel Prize in Physics has between one and three winners (inclusive) and that all winners are declared as persons and not any other type. Following the convention of Figure 7.1, the ASK query should return true in case of a violation, and false otherwise.

In this chapter, we describe languages for shape expressions and constraints that can be used to validate RDF graphs. We will begin with SHACL, where constraints are themselves modelled in RDF. We then describe ShEx, which rather uses a custom, concise syntax for expressing constraints. Thereafter we provide a comparison of both languages to help understand why these two specifications were developed in parallel.

Historical Note 7.1

A number of proposals have been made down through the years for validating RDF graphs. One such approach was to allow RDFS/OWL to be interpreted under CWA and/or UNA (see, for example [378]), allowing existing ontologies to be used to validate RDF graphs in the manner previously discussed. Under such assumptions, an OWL cardinality restriction of n on a property would mean that precisely n values would have to be specified in an RDF graph.

An orthogonal approach was to rather use SPARQL for validation, as per the **SPARQL Inferencing Notation (SPIN)** specification – proposed as a W3C Member Submission in 2011 [235] – for expressing both rules and constraints on top of RDF, which can then be compiled and executed as SPARQL queries. The SPIN approach has the benefit of being able to leverage existing SPARQL implementations. A similar proposal using SPARQL for validating RDF graphs was that of RDFUnit [239]: a unit-test framework for improving and verifying the quality of RDF data with individual tests expressed in SPARQL. However, not all constraints are easily expressed as SPARQL queries.

Aside from validation frameworks based on RDFS, OWL or SPARQL, a number of novel languages were further proposed, including the RDF Data Descriptions (RDD) language [130], which allows for mixing Closed World and Open World semantics for defining constraints; and the Resource Shape (2.0) language [339], which rather proposed a custom vocabulary for describing RDF constraints in RDF.

The SHACL and ShEx languages can be traced back to an RDF Validation Workshop held in 2013. In 2014, the first proposals for ShEx were published [327] and the W3C Data Shapes Working Group convened. In 2017, SHACL was recommended by the W3C [236]; the SHACL-SPARQL dialect was heavily inspired by SPIN. In the same year ShEx version 2 was published as a Draft Community Group Report, with an update (ShEx v.2.1) released in 2019 [325]. This chapter is based on the SHACL W3C Recommendation [236] and on ShEx v.2.1 [325].

The remainder of this chapter is structured as follows:

Section 7.1 discusses SHACL and its two dialects: SHACL-Core and SHACL-SPARQL, which extends SHACL-Core with SPARQL features.
Section 7.2 discusses ShEx and the custom syntaxes it proposes for defining shapes and validating RDF graphs.
Section 7.3 briefly compares SHACL and ShEx.
Section 7.4 outlines an abstract syntax for shapes that generalises SHACL and ShEx, further defining a formal semantics.
Sections 7.5 and 7.6 conclude the chapter with a summary and discussion.

7.1 Shape Constraints Language (SHACL)

SHACL allows for specifying constraints on an RDF graph, where these constraints are themselves expressed in an RDF graph. The SHACL standard thus centres on the definition of a vocabulary for specifying constraints on an RDF graph, the target of those constraints, as well as options for how RDF graphs should be validated with respect to those constraints. SHACL itself is broken down into two dialects: SHACL-Core and SHACL-SPARQL. SHACL-Core provides a vocabulary for defining constraints in a high-level (declarative) manner, while SHACL-SPARQL extends this dialect to allow the use of SPARQL queries to specify constraints that may not be expressible in SHACL-Core. In this section we will start by describing the SHACL-Core standard, including shapes graphs, the shapes that they describe, the constraints that can be placed on shapes, as well as options for controlling how these shapes and constraints are used to validate RDF graphs. Later we will discuss SHACL-SPARQL and the additional expressivity it allows, before briefly summarising some non-standard extensions proposed for SHACL.

> **Discussion 7.1**
>
> FRANK: You have mentioned that SHACL and ShEx are declarative languages. But isn't SPARQL a declarative language too?
>
> AIDAN: Yes, SPARQL is a declarative query language; declarative here means that the user declares what they want to do and an interpreter decides how best to do it. For the purposes of validation, we can argue that SHACL and ShEx are *more* declarative: they do not require the user to reason about how to express their constraints as a concrete query, for example, but rather provide a higher-level language where constraints can be expressed more abstractly.

7.1.1 Shapes Graph

The SHACL standard distinguishes two important classes of RDF graph:

Data graph: an RDF graph to be validated;
Shapes graph: an RDF graph describing the validation constraints.

In fact, as we discuss later, a shapes graph can be used for purposes other than validation, such as building user interfaces, automatically generating forms to populate an RDF dataset, optimising queries, and so forth. However, such use-cases will typically assume that the underlying data graph is valid with respect to the shapes graph, where validation thus underpins such use-cases.

We begin our discussion of SHACL with an example that gives a flavour of how shapes graphs are defined, illustrating some of the main features of SHACL-Core that will be described in more detail later in the section.

> **Example 7.2**
>
> We take again the data graph provided in Figure 7.1, describing Nobel Prizes in Physics, but exhibiting various issues that we would like to constrain in SHACL and detect through validation. Along these lines, we will define a shapes graph in SHACL-Core, where we shall start by constraining the properties that instances of the Nobel Prize in Physics

can take, and the type and number of values that these properties can take. We begin by defining a *node shape* targeting the desired class:

```
@prefix rdf: <http://www.w3.org/1999/02/22-rdf-syntax-ns#> .
@prefix xsd: <http://www.w3.org/2001/XMLSchema#> .
@prefix sh: <http://www.w3.org/ns/shacl#> .
@prefix d: <http://nobel.org/data#> .
@prefix o: <http://nobel.org/ont#> .
@prefix v: <http://nobel.org/val#> .

v:NobelPrizePhysicsShape a sh:NodeShape ;
  sh:targetClass o:NobelPrizePhysics ;
  [...] # continued
```

As a convention, we shall use the prefix v: for terms used for validation, the prefix d: for instances, and the prefix :o for properties and classes; the sh: prefix refers to the SHACL vocabulary itself.

To this node shape, we now associate a *property shape* stating that instances of the Nobel Prize in Physics should have precisely one value for year, and it should have the datatype xsd:gYear:

```
v:NobelPrizePhysicsShape a sh:NodeShape ;
  [...]
  sh:property [
    sh:path o:year ;
    sh:maxCount 1 ;
    sh:minCount 1 ;
    sh:datatype xsd:gYear
  ] ;
  [...] # continued
```

Constraints are applied independently of each other; for example, d:NPP1902 in Figure 7.1 violates the max-count constraint on o:year even though only one of the two values has the datatype xsd:gYear.

Next we require that each such prize have at least one and at most three winners, and that each winner be identified with an IRI and be an instance of the o:Person class:

```
v:NobelPrizePhysicsShape a sh:NodeShape ;
  [...]
  sh:property [
    sh:path o:winner ;
    sh:maxCount 3 ;
    sh:minCount 1 ;
    sh:class o:Person ;
    sh:nodeKind sh:IRI ;
  ] ;
  [...] # continued
```

We require that each such prize have zero or one values for o:next, and
that the value (if present) be identified by an IRI and be an instance of
the o:NobelPrizePhysics class:

```
v:NobelPrizePhysicsShape a sh:NodeShape ;
  [...]
  sh:property [
    sh:path o:next ;
    sh:maxCount 1 ;
    sh:class o:NobelPrizePhysics ;
    sh:nodeKind sh:IRI ;
  ] ;
  [...] # continued
```

We end by closing the node shape, thus stating that such a prize
should not be defined with any properties other than those for which
we have defined property shapes (o:year, o:winner, o:next) and other
properties listed as exceptions (namely the properties o:name, o:next,
o:number, o:prev, o:winners, rdf:type):

```
v:NobelPrizePhysicsShape a sh:NodeShape ;
  [...]
  sh:closed true ;
  sh:ignoredProperties
    ( o:name o:next o:number o:prev o:winners rdf:type ) .
  [...] # continued
```

This ends the node shape for Nobel Prizes in Physics.

We may continue in the shapes graph, this time by by defining a
node shape for people (i.e., instances of the class o:Person):

```
v:PersonShape a sh:NodeShape ;
  sh:targetClass o:Person ;
  [...] # continued
```

We require that a person have one name and that not be blank:

```
v:PersonShape a sh:NodeShape ;
  [...]
  sh:property [
    sh:path o:name ;
    sh:maxCount 1 ;
    sh:minCount 1 ;
    sh:datatype xsd:string ;
    sh:minLength 1
  ] .
```

This time, rather than close the shape, we leave it open such that additional properties can be defined for people (such as country).

Finally, if we validate the data graph of Figure 7.1 with respect to this shapes graph, we will receive a validation report as follows:

```
@prefix sh: <http://www.w3.org/ns/shacl#> .

[] a sh:ValidationReport ;
  sh:conforms false ;
  sh:result
    [ a sh:ValidationReport ;
      sh:resultSeverity sh:Violation ;
      sh:focusNode d:NPP1902 ;
      sh:resultPath o:next ;
      sh:sourceConstraintComponent sh:MaxCountConstraintComponent ;
    ] ,
    ...
```

Here we show a snippet of the report, which will list each violation in the data graph of the constraints specified in the shapes graph, following the same format. Details of each violation are provided to help debug the data graph, including the instance of the target graph on which the violation occurs (the *focus node*), the property (or path) for which the violation is found, as well as the type of constraint violated. Other details can also (optionally) be provided, such as the value causing the violation, the identifier for the shape that is violated, and so forth.

Having given a flavour of SHACL-Core, we continue by describing its features in more detail, starting with the central notion of shapes and how they may interconnect, next describing the specific constraints supported by the language, before discussing in more detail features relating to validation.

7.1.2 Shapes

There are two types of shape that may be defined in a SHACL shapes graph:

sh:Shape the class of all shapes, with two sub-classes:

> sh:NodeShape a shape that targets nodes in the data graph and defines constraints directly on the nodes it targets
>
> sh:PropertyShape a shape that targets nodes in the data graph and for each node targeted, defines constraints on the nodes reachable from it via a specified path

A node refers to a term appearing in the subject or object position of some triple(s) in the data graph. We will first describe how shapes target nodes in the data graph. Thereafter we discuss node shapes and property shapes.

Note that in the following we will introduce a variety of built-in SHACL properties, some that can be used only on property shapes (P), some that can be used only on node shapes (N), some that can be used on either type of shape (S), some that can be defined zero-or-one times on a shape (?), some that can be defined zero-to-many times on a shape (*), and some that must be defined one time on a shape (1). Rather than discuss these restrictions for each term, we introduce a syntactic convention where, for example, N^* refers to a property that can only be used on node shapes and can be used zero-to-many times, while $S?$ refers to a property that can be used on both property shapes and node shapes but only zero-or-one times per shape.

Our examples use some simple constraints for illustration purposes. Specifically we will use sh:nodeKind, sh:class, sh:maxCount and sh:minCount, which restrict the type of term a node uses (IRI, literal or blank node), the class of which a node is an instance, and the maximum and minimum (inclusive) number of values a node can be associated with, respectively. Details of these and further constraints will be discussed in Section 7.1.4.

7.1.2.1 Targets and Focus Nodes

Both node shapes and property shapes may target specific nodes in the data graph. More specifically, a shape may define its target nodes using one of the following built-in properties from the SHACL vocabulary:

---

sh:targetClass^{S*} targets the instances of a given class
sh:targetObjectsOf^{S*} targets the objects of a given property
sh:targetSubjectsOf^{S*} targets the subjects of a given property
sh:targetNode^{S*} targets a given node

The nodes in the data graph targeted by the shape are called *focus nodes*. Where multiple such targets are defined on one shape, the focus nodes become the union of the set of focus nodes for all targets. We will see various examples of targets – and how they can be combined – in the following discussion.

7.1.2.2 Node Shapes

A node shape can be used to define constraints directly on the focus nodes that match its target. We start with an example of a simple such node shape.

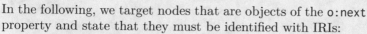

Example 7.3

In the following, we target nodes that are objects of the o:next property and state that they must be identified with IRIs:

```
v:NextObjectShape a sh:NodeShape ;
  sh:targetObjectsOf o:next ;
  sh:nodeKind sh:IRI .
```

This shape *targets* nodes that are the object of a triple with the predicate o:next. We call the matching nodes in the data graph (d:NPP1902, d:NPP1903, and d:npp1903 in Figure 7.1) the *focus nodes*.

When targeting a class, SHACL can take into account instances of sub-classes so long as sub-class triples are explicitly declared in the data graph (or if entailment is enabled during validation, which we shall discuss later).

Example 7.4

Consider a node shape targeting the class :NobelPrize:

```
v:NobelPrizeShape a sh:NodeShape ;
  sh:targetClass o:NobelPrize ;
  ...
```

Noting that o:NobelPrizePhysics is defined in the data graph to be a sub-class of o:NobelPrize, the question then is: would all the instances of the former class also be targeted by the aforementioned node shape?

As we will discuss later, a specific entailment regime can be specified for the purposes of validation, where, in summary, any nodes entailed to meet the targeted criteria will be considered as targeted. Additionally, entailed triples suffice to satisfy (or violate) any constraints that have been defined. Enabling entailment regimes is, however, optional.

On the other hand, SHACL makes an exception for rdfs:subClassOf: node shapes targeting a class c will target any nodes connected by a path rdf:type/rdfs:subClassOf* to c in the data graph, even if no entailment regime is specified; hence the answer to our present question is *yes*: given the rdfs:subClassOf triple present in the data graph, instances of Nobel Prizes in Physics will be targeted by the aforementioned node shape (even without entailment enabled). But for instances of sub-classes to be targeted without entailment, the corresponding rdfs:subClassOf triples must be made explicit in the data graph.

Shapes can also target classes implicitly (without sh:targetClass) by using the same IRI to identify the targeted class and the node shape.

Example 7.5

Referring back to Example 7.4, we could similarly have created a node shape targeting the class o:NobelPrize by declaring o:NobelPrize to be both an RDFS class and a node shape in the shapes graph:

```
o:NobelPrize a sh:NodeShape , rdfs:Class ;
  ...
```

To implicitly target a class c in this manner, the same IRI must be used for the shape and the class (using a blank node will not suffice) and c must be declared as an instance of rdfs:Class in the shapes graph (declaring the class in the data graph does not suffice).

As aforementioned, a shape may combine targets, where the focus nodes of the shape will then be the union of the sets of focus nodes for each target.

Example 7.6

The following node shape targets nodes in the data graph that are explicitly stated to be instances of the class o:Country, as well as nodes that are the object of triples with the predicate o:country:

```
v:CountryShape a sh:NodeShape ;
  sh:targetClass o:Country ;
  sh:targetObjectsOf o:country ;
  ...
```

Considering the data graph of Figure 7.1, the focus nodes for this node shape will be d:Germany, d:Netherlands, d:France and d:Poland.

Finally, a shape does not need to explicitly define a target, in which case explicit focus nodes may be specified during validation.

Example 7.7

The following node shape, which requires that the required nodes be IRIs or blank nodes, does not define a target:

```
v:SubjectNodeShape a sh:NodeShape ;
  sh:nodeKind sh:BlankNodeOrIRI .
```

We may later request to validate specific nodes (e.g.,"1902"^^xsd:gYear and d:NPP1903) against this shape; the former will fail, being a literal.

Table 7.1 Mapping from SHACL paths to SPARQL property paths

SHACL (Turtle)	SPARQL	Remark
p	p	Predicate IRI
[sh:inversePath e]	$\hat{}e$	Inverse of path e
(e_1 e_2)	e_1/e_2	Path e_1 followed by path e_2
[sh:alternativePath (e_1 e_2)]	$e_1 \vert e_2$	Path e_1 or e_2
[sh:zeroOrMorePath e]	$e\star$	Zero or more of path e
[sh:oneOrMorePath e]	$e{+}$	One or more of path e
[sh:zeroOrOnePath e]	$e?$	Zero or one of path e

> ### Exercise 7.3
>
> *Define a node shape to target (only) the nodes* d:HLorentz *and* d:PZeeman *in the data graph of Figure 7.1.*

7.1.2.3 Property Shapes

Property shapes are specified by a target and a path. The target matches a set of focus nodes in the data graph and is defined precisely as seen for node shapes. For each focus node, the path then matches the set of nodes that are connected to the focus node in the data graph via the path; we call this set of nodes the *value nodes* of the focus node. For each focus node, a property shape can then specify constraints on its value nodes per the specified path.

A property shape must then be defined with one path (and only one path):

> sh:path^{P1} denotes a path connecting the focus nodes to the value nodes
> that are constrained by the property shape

For a focus node s, a property shape defined with the path expression e then matches all values o such that the path (s, e, o) is satisfied by the data graph. Paths in SHACL are similar to property paths in SPARQL (see Section 6.2.6) but using an alternative RDF-based syntax. The correspondences between both syntaxes are shown in Table 7.1, where e, e_1 and e_2 denote any valid path expression in the corresponding syntax. All SHACL paths can be translated to SPARQL property paths, but SPARQL's negated property paths ($!p$ or $!(p_1 \vert \ldots \vert p_k \vert \hat{}p_{k+1} \vert \ldots \vert \hat{}p_n)$) cannot be expressed in SHACL.

Example 7.8

The following property shape defines as its target all prizes and
all objects of a o:winner triple, stating that each such node must have
at least one name, and that the name must be a literal:

```
v:PrizeAndWinnerNameShape a v:PropertyShape ;
  sh:targetClass o:Prize ;
  sh:targetObjectsOf o:winner ;
  sh:path o:name ;
  sh:nodeKind sh:Literal ;
  sh:minCount 1 .
```

With respect to Figure 7.1, the focus nodes targeted by this shape are
the union of the sets of focus nodes for both the class and objects-
of targets, namely d:NPP1901, d:NPP1902, d:NPP1903, d:WCRöntgen,
d:HLorentz, d:PZeeman, d:France, and d:Poland. The value nodes for
each focus node are then their set of names; for example, the value
nodes of focus node d:NPP1901 are "Nobelpriset i fysik 1901"@sv and
"Nobel Prize in Physics 1901"@en. The focus nodes failing the constraint are those with no value nodes: d:PZeeman, d:France, d:Poland.

Example 7.9

We now illustrate a property shape stating that Nobel Prizes
can have at most one prize reachable from a path o:prev|^o:next:

```
v:NobelPrizePrevInvNext a v:PropertyShape ;
  sh:targetClass o:NobelPrize ;
  sh:path [
    sh:alternativePath (
      o:prev
      [ sh:inversePath o:next ]
    )
  ] ;
  sh:maxCount 1 .
```

With respect to Figure 7.1, the focus nodes are d:NPP1901, d:NPP1902
and d:NPP1903. Node d:NPP1901 has no value nodes: it has no outgoing
o:prev triples nor incoming o:next triples. Node d:NPP1902 has one
value node: d:NPP1901 is reachable as both an outgoing o:prev triple
and an incoming o:next triple. Node d:NPP1903 has two value nodes:
d:NPP1902 reachable from an incoming o:next triple and d:NPP1903
reachable from an outgoing o:prev triple. Focus nodes d:NPP1901 and
d:NPP1902 thus pass the constraint, having zero and one value nodes
respectively, while d:NPP1903 fails, having two value nodes.

> **Exercise 7.4**
>
> *Define a property shape that requires the winners of something to have at least one country defined.*

Remark 7.1

Assume that we wanted users to help populate our RDF graph, and that we consider creating an online form through which they can submit data. SHACL property shapes could potentially be used not only to generate such forms automatically – with each property shape corresponding to a particular field in the form – but also to validate inputs. But we are missing (informal) metadata about property shapes that could help us generate better forms: a human-readable label and description of the field, how the fields could be grouped by theme, in what order the groups and fields should go, etc. Along these lines, SHACL provides the following vocabulary for property shapes:

sh:name^{P*} provides a human-readable name for the shape;
sh:description^{P*} provides a human-readable description of the shape;
sh:group^{P*} allows to group property shapes by theme;
sh:defaultValue$^{P?}$ indicates a default value for a property;
sh:order$^{P?}$ indicates an ordinal value for groups and property shapes.

We make the following remarks with respect to these properties:

- A property shape may have multiple names and descriptions, though only one name and one description should be given per language.
- With respect to groups, SHACL defines the additional class:

  sh:PropertyGroup the class for groups of property shapes;

  Taking a brief example, a name property group might group first name and last name property shapes into a name section of a form.
- The default value, on the other hand, may be used to assign the default value for a field; taking a brief example, in a movie form, English may be suggested as the default language.
- Finally, order is a decimal value, with lower values indicating precedence; groups can be assigned order, as well as shapes within groups.

This vocabulary is introduced by the standard without any fixed semantics and is not intended for validation purposes; rather the vocabulary is intended to guide applications that aim to build human-friendly forms – or display human-friendly data – using SHACL shapes. We refer to the standard for more details on this vocabulary [236].

7.1.2.4 Generalising Node and Property Shapes

Many (though not all) of the SHACL features that we will discuss can be applied to both node shapes and property shapes. In fact, we have already seen this for targets, which can be defined analogously on both node shapes and property shapes; and for the sh:nodeKind constraint, which can be used to validate focus nodes on node shapes and value nodes on property shapes.

Before we proceed, it is thus important to clarify how node shapes and property shapes differ, and more importantly, what they have in common.

- As previously discussed, both node and property shapes can have a *target* defined (possibly itself the union of multiple targets). Targets are defined in the same way for node and property shapes. The targets in both cases induce a set of *focus nodes* in the data graph.
- Property shapes are distinguished from node shapes by the definition of a path. A property shape must have precisely one path defined, while a node shape cannot have a path defined. This path then gives rise to the notion of *value nodes* for property shapes. We may speak of the *value nodes for a focus node*, which are the nodes connected to that focus node by the path; or of the *value nodes for a property shape*, which are the nodes connected to any focus node by the path.

Constraints are then defined on the focus nodes of node shapes and the value nodes of property shapes. This language quickly becomes tedious, where – following the convention of the standard [236] – we will also speak of the *focus nodes of a node shape* as being the *value nodes of a node shape*: we consider focus nodes and value nodes as being synonymous for node shapes. In this perspective, a node shape is a special type of property shape: one with a zero-length path that maps focus nodes to themselves as value nodes. This finally allows us to talk more generally about shapes: we say the *focus nodes of a shape* to mean the focus nodes of a property shape or the focus/value nodes of a node shape, and we say the *value nodes of a shape* to mean the value nodes of a property shape or the value/focus nodes of a node shape.

> **Remark 7.2** (i)
>
> Shapes do not need to be explicitly declared as instances of sh:NodeShape or sh:PropertyShape. Instances of sh:PropertyShape can always be inferred from the domain of the sh:path property: precisely one path must be defined for a property shape and only property shapes can have paths defined. On the other hand, instances of sh:NodeShape can be inferred from any property that has sh:Shape as its domain or range, combined with the absence of a sh:path definition.

Remark 7.3

Shapes do not need to be identified by an IRI. In general, we will prefer naming shapes with IRIs for clarity; however, Example 7.2 shows an abbreviated style using blank nodes for property shapes.

Remark 7.4

Shapes can be deactivated using the following property:

sh:deactivated can be assigned "true"^^xsd:boolean to stop a shape being used for validation; if assigned "false"^^xsd:boolean or omitted, the shape will be used for validation.

Remark 7.5

Shapes can be assigned one of three priority levels:

sh:severity assigns at most one priority to a shape:

    sh:Info indicates a non-critical informative violation.
    sh:Warning indicates a non-critical warning violation.
    sh:Violation indicates a critical violation.

The default severity is sh:Violation if omitted from a shape. For simplicity, we will use the term "violation" to indicate any severity.

Remark 7.6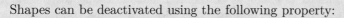

Shapes can be associated with messages to generate human-readable explanations:

sh:message provides a human-readable explanation of a violation.

To illustrate, consider the shape v:PrizeAndWinnerNameShape from Example 7.8. We may add messages to this shape to explain violations:

```
v:PrizeAndWinnerNameShape sh:message
  "must have a name; names must be literals"@en ,
  "debe tener un nombre; los nombres deben ser literals"@es .
```

A shape can have at most one message with a given language tag.

7.1.2.5 Validation Reporting

Shapes are used to validate data graphs. SHACL provides a standard vocabulary for validation reports that describe validation results.

---

sh:ValidationReport the class of validation reports

A validation report must first indicate whether or not the graph conforms to the shapes graph. The graph is considered as conforming to the shapes graph if and only if the report contains no validation results (note that non-critical informative and warning violations also generate validation results).

---

sh:conforms takes the value "true"^^xsd:boolean when the data graph
conforms to the shapes graph, or "false"^^xsd:boolean otherwise

---

Next, a validation report may list zero or more validation results.

---

sh:result associates a validation report with a validation result
sh:ValidationResult is the class of validation results

Validation results describe violations. Each validation result must have precisely one value for each of the following properties:

---

sh:focusNode indicates the focus node causing the result
sh:resultSeverity indicates the severity of the result
sh:sourceConstraintComponent indicates the constraint violated

---

The severity of the result is defined as the priority of the shape whose constraint is violated. The source constraint components can either be built-in constraints (SHACL-CORE), or custom ones defined using SPARQL or another language (SHACL-SPARQL); such constraints will be discussed later. Each validation result can have at most one value for the following:

---

sh:resultPath indicates the SHACL path of the property shape
sh:value indicates the value node causing a violation
sh:sourceShape indicates the shape applied to the focus node

Each validation result can have zero or more values for the following:

> sh:detail links to a validation result with more details
> sh:resultMessage provides a human-readable violation description
> sh:sourceShape indicates the shape applied to the focus node

A result message must be generated for each message on the shape violated (see Remark 7.6); additional result messages may also be generated.

Example 7.10

We provide a sample of the validation report for the shapes graph of Example 7.8 as applied to the data graph of Figure 7.1. We assume the shape messages of Remark 7.6 are also given.

```
[] a sh:ValidationReport ;
  sh:conforms false ;
  sh:result [
    a sh:ValidationResult ;
    sh:resultSeverity sh:Violation ;
    sh:focusNode d:PZeeman ;
    sh:resultPath o:name ;
    sh:resultMessage
      "must have a name; names must be literals"@en ,
      "debe tener un nombre; los nombres deben ser literals"@es .
    sh:sourceConstraintComponent sh:MinCountConstraintComponent ;
    sh:sourceShape v:PrizeAndWinnerNameShape
  ] ,
  ... .
```

7.1.3 Connecting and Combining Shapes

In the same sense that an RDF graph consists of edges connecting various nodes, it also makes sense in the context of SHACL to connect shapes: thus data graphs can be validated by graphs of shapes. The simplest pattern involves passing the value nodes of one shape to serve as the focus nodes for validation in another shape. Another pattern supported by SHACL is to combine the results of multiple shapes using boolean operations. Finally, SHACL also supports qualified constraints, which establish bounds on the number of value nodes in one shape that pass the constraints of another shape. We will look at each of these three patterns for connecting shapes in turn.

7.1.3.1 Connecting Shapes

The first pattern for connecting shapes is to pass the value nodes of a parent shape as the focus nodes of a child shape for further validation.

There are two properties for connecting shapes in this manner, depending on whether the child shape is a node shape or a property shape.

---

sh:node[N*] connects a shape to a node shape where the value nodes of
    the former become the focus/value nodes of the latter
sh:property[N*] connects a shape to a property shape where the value
    nodes of the former become the focus nodes of the latter

Example 7.11

Referring back to Example 7.9, we could rather have separated
this into two shapes, targeting Nobel Prizes with a node shape and then
passing these nodes as focus nodes to a separate property shape.

```
v:NobelPrizeShape a sh:NodeShape ;
  sh:targetClass o:NobelPrize ;
  sh:property v:NobelPrizePrevInvNextShape .

v:NobelPrizePrevInvNextShape a v:PropertyShape ;
  sh:path [
    sh:alternativePath (
      o:prev
      [ sh:inversePath o:next ]
    )
  ] ;
  sh:maxCount 1 .
```

Validation would then be performed as discussed in Example 7.9.

Connecting shapes to one another in this fashion thus creates a shapes graph, with shapes connected to the shapes upon which they depend for validation. Passing nodes from one shape to another may lead to cycles in this graph, which in turn may sometimes require recursive validation of nodes. In order to ensure termination of the validation process, such cycles must be detected by an implementation in order to avoid naively checking conformance of the same nodes to the same shapes over and over.

Example 7.12

In this example, we illustrate passing nodes to node shapes, as well as having cycles between shapes.

```
v:NobelPrizeShape a sh:NodeShape ;
  sh:nodeKind sh:IRI .

v:NobelPrizePhysicsShape a sh:NodeShape ;
  sh:targetClass o:NobelPrizePhysics ;
  sh:node v:NobelPrizeShape ;
  sh:property v:NobelPrizePhysicsNextShape .

v:NobelPrizePhysicsNextShape a v:PropertyShape ;
  sh:path o:next ;
  sh:maxCount 1 ;
  sh:class o:NobelPrizePhysics ;
  sh:node v:NobelPrizePhysicsShape .
```

The first shape requires that nodes be identified with IRIs. The second shape targets Nobel Prizes in Physics and passes these nodes to the first shape and to the third shape. The third shape checks, for each focus node, that it has at most one value node for o:next and that the value (if present) is a Nobel Prize in Physics; this shape further passes its value nodes back to the second shape. The following graph then illustrates the interactions between these shapes, and how they pass (novel) nodes between each other with respect to the data graph of Figure 7.1:

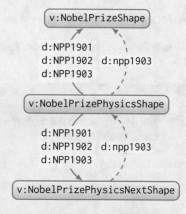

To ensure termination during validation, it is of course important that in the presence of cycles, shapes block nodes they have already seen, as shown. Only the second shape defines a target: instances of Nobel Prizes in Physics; this shape then passes its nodes to the first and third shapes; the third shape advances along the o:next path and

passes further (novel) nodes – like d:npp1903, not targeted at first –
back to the second shape, which passes them on to the first shape.

Note that in this example, we could have modelled the same abstract
validation process without using sh:node or sh:property by duplicating
the sh:nodeKind constraint of the first constraint on the second shape,
and by duplicating the target of the second shape on the third shape.

The previous example shows how sh:property and sh:node can be used as
shortcuts to avoid repeating constraints across shapes, thus helping to modu-
larise a shapes graph. The question then is: are such features purely syntactic
sugar, or do they allow for expressing forms of validation that could not otherwise be expressed? In fact, the sh:property feature is not just syntactic
sugar: since a property shape can further pass its value nodes to be the focus nodes of another property shape, this pattern can be used to "navigate"
through the data graph, applying validation to nodes at each step.

Example 7.13

Relating to Exercise 7.4, assume we wished to more specifically
require that winners of Nobel Prizes in Physics be people, and that each
such person have at least one country defined in the data. For this, we
will need to pass nodes between property shapes as follows:

```
v:NobelPrizePhysicsWinnerShape a v:PropertyShape ;
  sh:targetClass o:NobelPrizePhysics ;
  sh:path o:winner ;
  sh:class o:Person ;
  sh:property v:NobelPrizePhysicsWinnerCountryShape .

v:NobelPrizePhysicsWinnerCountryShape a v:PropertyShape ;
  sh:path o:country ;
  sh:minCount 1 .
```

The value nodes of the former property shape (the winners) then become the focus nodes of the latter property shape.

Note the difference with this shapes graph:

```
v:NobelPrizePhysicsWinnerShape a v:PropertyShape ;
  sh:targetClass o:NobelPrizePhysics ;
  sh:path o:winner ;
  sh:class o:Person .

v:NobelPrizePhysicsWinnerCountryShape a v:PropertyShape ;
  sh:targetClass o:NobelPrizePhysics ;
  sh:path ( o:winner o:country ) ;
  sh:minCount 1 .
```

The former shapes graph requires one country per winner (failing d:PZeeman in Figure 7.1, for example), while the latter shapes graph requires one country per prize (passing d:NPP1902 for country in Figure 7.1, though d:PZeeman still fails for not being a o:Person). We see that connecting property shapes in this manner offers a way to navigate the graph and apply validation at each step, allowing to define constraints that may not be possible with a "one shot" path expression.

As before, if multiple source targets are specified, a given shape will take as focus nodes the union of all targets and nodes passed to it.

Example 7.14

Consider the following node shape and connected property shape; the node shape targets explicit instances of the class o:Country while the property shape targets values of the property o:country:

```
v:CountryShape a sh:NodeShape ;
  sh:targetClass o:Country ;
  sh:property v:CountryNameShape .

v:CountryNameShape a sh:PropertyShape ;
  sh:targetObjectsOf o:country ;
  sh:path o:name ;
  sh:maxCount 1 ;
  sh:minCount 1 .
```

The property shape requires that both explicit instances of o:Country (d:France and d:Poland), as well as values of o:country (d:Germany and d:Netherlands), have precisely one name.

Exercise 7.5

Provide shapes to ensure that any country – be it an instance of o:Country and an object of o:country – is the country (only) of people that have won something, and is the country of at least one such winner.

7.1.3.2 Combining Shapes

SHACL also allows a parent shape to pass its value nodes for validation to one of four boolean combinations of child shapes, as follows:

---

sh:not^{N*} negates a single shape
sh:and^{N*} forms a conjunction of a list of shapes
sh:or^{N*} forms a disjunction of a list of shapes
sh:xone^{N*} requires that precisely one shape from a list be satisfied

---

The first constraint takes a single shape as its operand; the others take a list of shapes as their operands. Each such property can be defined on a parent node shape or property shape; the value nodes of the parent shape are then passed as the focus nodes of each operand shape, where the results of all operand shapes are combined with the given boolean operation.

Example 7.15

Consider the following shapes graph, which intuitively attempts to capture the idea that a Nobel Prize must have precisely one value for a previous prize (applicable to the most recent prize), or precisely one value for a next prize (applicable to the inaugural prize), or possibly both (applicable to all the prizes in between):

```
v:NobelPrizeShape a sh:NodeShape ;
  sh:targetClass o:NobelPrize ;
  sh:or (
    v:NobelPrizeHasOneNextShape
    v:NobelPrizeHasOnePrevShape
  ) .

v:NobelPrizeHasOneNextShape a sh:PropertyShape ;
  sh:path o:next ;
  sh:minCount 1 ;
  sh:maxCount 1.

  v:NobelPrizeHasOnePrevShape a sh:PropertyShape ;
    sh:path o:prev ;
    sh:minCount 1 ;
    sh:maxCount 1 .
```

However, in Figure 7.1, the node d:NPP1902 will pass the constraints in this shape graph since – although it has two next prizes – it passes the constraint on having only one previous prize, and thus passes the disjunctive sh:or. Hence we see we need to be a little more detailed to ensure that a case like d:NPP1902 does not pass validation.

A better alternative would be as follows:

```
v:NobelPrizePhysicsShape a sh:NodeShape ;
  sh:targetClass o:NobelPrize ;
  sh:xone (
    [ sh:and (
        v:NobelPrizeHasOneNextShape
        v:NobelPrizeHasOnePrevShape ) ]
    [ sh:and (
        v:NobelPrizeHasOneNextShape
        [ sh:not v:NobelPrizeHasPrevShape ] ) ]
    [ sh:and (
      v:NobelPrizeHasOnePrevShape
      [ sh:not v:NobelPrizeHasNextShape ] ) ]
  ) .

v:NobelPrizeHasNextShape a sh:PropertyShape ;
  sh:path o:next ;
  sh:minCount 1 .

v:NobelPrizeHasOneNextShape a sh:PropertyShape ;
  sh:path o:next ;
  sh:minCount 1 ;
  sh:maxCount 1 .

v:NobelPrizeHasPrevShape a sh:PropertyShape ;
  sh:path o:prev ;
  sh:minCount 1 .

v:NobelPrizeHasOnePrevShape a sh:PropertyShape ;
  sh:path o:prev ;
  sh:minCount 1 ;
  sh:maxCount 1 .
```

This shapes graph states that each Nobel Prize must satisfy one of the following: (1) have precisely one next prize and one previous prize; (2) have precisely one next prize and no previous prize; (3) have precisely one previous prize and no next prize. This time, d:NPP1901 will pass, as will d:NPP1903; however, d:NPP1902 will fail.

Exercise 7.6

Provide a more concise way to capture the constraint of the previous example, requiring that each prize have (1) precisely one next prize and one previous prize; or (2) precisely one next prize and no previous prize; or (3) precisely one previous prize and no next prize.

Remark 7.7   (i)

The sh:xone combination is syntactic sugar. Requiring precisely
one of $X_1, \ldots, X_n$ boolean variables to be true can be expressed as :

$$\bigvee_{1 \leq i \leq n} (\neg X_1 \wedge \ldots \wedge X_i \wedge \ldots \wedge \neg X_n)$$

where sh:and ($\wedge$) sh:or ($\vee$) and sh:not ($\neg$) are thus sufficient to capture sh:xone. However clearly using sh:xone is more succinct, and the
pattern is sufficiently common to warrant a shortcut. A common pattern for which it is used is to ensure that the instances of a super-class
follow the shape for one of a disjoint set of sub-classes; for example, we
may say that instances of o:NobelPrize should satisfy precisely one of
the shapes for o:NobelPrizePhysics, o:NobelPrizePeace, etc.

Furthermore, per De Morgan's laws, either sh:or or sh:and can be
considered syntactic sugar assuming we also have sh:not. More specifi-
cally, given that $X_1 \vee X_2 \equiv \neg(\neg X_1 \wedge \neg X_2)$ – i.e., X_1 or X_2 holds if and
only if X_1 and X_2 are not both false – we can express any sh:or using
sh:and and sh:not. Conversely, given that $X_1 \wedge X_2 \equiv \neg(\neg X_1 \vee \neg X_2)$ –
i.e., X_1 and X_2 hold if and only if neither X_1 nor X_2 is false – we can
express any sh:and using sh:or and sh:not.

7.1.4 Core Constraints

We have already seen a variety of constraints applied to shapes in the examples previously presented – be they to limit the properties defined on a focus
node, or to limit how many values a focus node can take on a given property
or path, or to limit what types of such values it can take. In this section we
will provide more details on the constraints supported by SHACL-Core. Some
of these constraints are specific to node shapes, others to property shapes,
and others still can be used on either.

7.1.4.1 Type Constraints

SHACL offers three features for constraining the types of value nodes on both
node shapes and property shapes. The first pair of type constraints indicate
the class or datatype of which the corresponding nodes must be an instance:

sh:class[S*] states that nodes must be instances of a class
sh:datatype[S?] states that nodes must be instances of a datatype

The former constraint is satisfied not only in the case that the node is explicitly declared to be an instance of the specified class, but more generally if there is a path matching `rdf:type/rdfs:subClassOf*` from the value to the specified class. On the other hand, the latter constraint requires an exact match on the datatype IRI (i.e., derived datatypes are not considered).

The third and final constraint in this category rather restricts the type of RDF term – blank node, IRI or literal – that values can be:

`sh:nodeKind`[S?] states that value nodes must be a particular type of RDF term; the range of this property is the class `sh:NodeKind`, which has six instances representing the different options for defining this constraint: `sh:BlankNode`, `sh:IRI`, `sh:Literal`, `sh:BlankNodeOrIRI`, `sh:BlankNodeOrLiteral` or `sh:IRIOrLiteral`

Example 7.16

Consider the following node shape:

```
v:NobelPrizeShape a sh:NodeShape ;
   sh:targetClass o:NobelPrize ;
   sh:nodeType sh:BlankNodeOrIRI ;
   sh:class o:NobelPrizeChemistry ;
   sh:property v:NobelPrizeNextShape , v:NobelPrizeWinnersShape .
   ...
```

With respect to Figure 7.1, the value nodes for the node shape will be `d:NPP1901`, `d:NPP1902` and `d:NPP1903` since `o:NobelPrizePhysics` is declared to be a sub-class of `o:NobelPrize` in the data graph. A node-type constraint is then applied to these value nodes, where all three pass since all are either blank nodes or IRIs. Next a class constraint is defined requiring that all value nodes (instances of `o:NobelPrize`) are also instances of `o:NobelPrizeChemistry` – stating that any Nobel Prize the graph describes must be a Nobel Prize in Chemistry and not in another discipline – where all three value nodes will fail this constraint.

The node shape links to two property shapes, the first being:

```
   ...
v:NobelPrizeNextShape a sh:PropertyShape ;
   sh:path o:next ;
   sh:class o:NobelPrize .
```

This property shape defines that any value for `o:next` on an instance of `o:NobelPrize` must be an instance of `o:NobelPrize`. Focus node `d:NPP1901` passes because `d:NPP1902` is declared to be an instance of `o:NobelPrize`. Focus node `d:NPP1902` fails since the value `d:npp1903` is not declared to be an instance of a sub-class of `o:NobelPrize`. Focus node `d:NPP1903` trivially passes since it has no value for `o:next`.

The second property shape is defined in the following:

```
 ⋯ 
v:NobelPrizeWinnersShape a sh:PropertyShape ;
  sh:path o:winners ;
  sh:datatype xsd:decimal .
```

This property shape defines that any value for `o:winners` must have the datatype IRI `xsd:decimal`. Recall that in Turtle syntax, integers without quotes will be parsed as an `xsd:integer`. Athough `xsd:integer` is derived from `xsd:decimal`, all focus nodes will fail this test since the constraint requires a match on the datatype IRI (if the property shape rather defined the datatype as `xsd:int`, which is derived *from* `xsd:integer`, all focus nodes would also fail for the same reason).

7.1.4.2 Cardinality Constraints

Given a property shape, SHACL also supports cardinality constraints on the maximum and minimum number of value nodes that should be reachable from an individual focus node following the path expression.

`sh:maxCount`[P?] states the maximum number of value nodes that can be reached from an individual focus node following the path expression

`sh:minCount`[P?] states the minimum number of value nodes that can be reached from an individual focus node following the path expression

---

Both cardinality limits are considered inclusive. For validating these cardinality constraints, all values nodes are counted, no matter whether or not they conform to the other constraints specified in the shapes graph.

> **Remark 7.8**   (i)
>
> Unlike cardinality definitions in OWL, which restrict the number of resources in the interpretation of an RDF graph (under the OWA and without a UNA), cardinality constraints in SHACL restrict the number of terms in an RDF graph. In other words, while SHACL applies restrictions directly to an RDF graph at the data level (similar to counting in SPARQL), OWL applies restrictions to the possible interpretations of an RDF graph at the semantic level.

Example 7.17

The following property shape states that a Nobel Prize in
Physics must have one year, and that (as an independent constraint)
the value of year must be an instance of the datatype xsd:gYear.

```
v:NobelPrizeYearShape a sh:PropertyShape ;
  sh:targetClass o:NobelPrizePhysics ;
  sh:path o:year ;
  sh:datatype xsd:gYear ;
  sh:maxCount 1 ;
  sh:minCount 1 .
```

Of the three focus nodes in Figure 7.1 – d:NPP1901, d:NPP1902, and
d:NPP1903 – only d:NPP1901 passes this constraint. The node d:NPP1902
fails as constraints are applied independently: the property shape should
not be read as stating that there is one xsd:gYear value for o:year
(ignoring values of other datatypes), but rather should be understood
as stating that there is one value for o:year and that it must be an
xsd:gYear value. On the other hand, d:NPP1903 has no value for o:year,
and thus violates the minimum count constraint.

7.1.4.3 Qualified Cardinality Constraints

While the previous cardinality constraints are unconditional – counting each
value node irrespective of its characteristics – SHACL also supports qualified
cardinality constraints, which sets limits on the number of value nodes that
a focus node can have conforming to a specified shape. Like the previous
cardinality constraints, qualified constraints are defined on property shapes:

sh:qualifiedValueShape[P?] connects a property shape to another shape
 that qualifies the following cardinality constraints on values nodes
sh:qualifiedMaxCount[P?] specifies the maximum number of value nodes
 on a focus node that can conform to the qualifying shape
sh:qualifiedMinCount[P?] specifies the minimum number of value nodes
 on a focus node that can conform to the qualifying shape
sh:qualifiedValueShapesDisjoint[P?] specifies a boolean flag that if set
 to true, will not count values conforming to "sibling shapes"

> **Remark 7.9**   (i)
>
> If any property sh:qualifiedMaxCount, sh:qualifiedMinCount or sh:qualifiedValueShapesDisjoint is specified on a shape, then sh:qualifiedValueShape must also be specified on that shape.

With respect to the sh:qualifiedValueShapesDisjoint boolean flag, for a property shape with ID n connected to a qualifying shape with ID n', the sibling shapes of n are the qualifying shapes defined by the IDs reachable from n through the SPARQL property path expression:

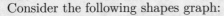

^sh:property/sh:property/sh:qualifiedValueShape

in the shapes graph, excluding n' itself. We will provide an example to clarify this notion and give an intuition of how it can be used, but we start with a simpler example that involves only the first three features.

> **Example 7.18**   ⚙
>
> Consider the following shapes graph:
>
> ```
> v:NobelPrizePhysicsPrevShape a sh:PropertyShape ;
>   sh:targetClass o:NobelPrizePhysics ;
>   sh:path [ sh:zeroOrMorePath o:prev ] ;
>   sh:qualifiedMinCount 1 ;
>   sh:qualifiedMaxCount 1 ;
>   sh:qualifiedValueShape v:InauguralNobelPrizeShape .
>
> v:InauguralNobelPrizeShape a sh:PropertyShape ;
>   sh:path o:prev ;
>   sh:maxCount 0 .
> ```
>
> Intuitively these shapes state that each Nobel Prize in Physics must be connected through a path o:prev* to precisely one Nobel Prize in Physics that has no value for o:prev (the inaugural such prize). Of the three focus nodes in Figure 7.1, only d:NPP1903 fails the constraint since it is not connected to any node by such a path without a previous value (it is connected to itself and has itself as a previous prize). On the other hand, focus node d:NPP1902 passes since although it has two value nodes (d:NPP1901 and d:NPP1902), only d:NPP1901 passes the qualifying shape, not having a previous prize. Finally focus node d:NPP1901 also passes since its only value node (itself) has no previous prize.

Next we provide two examples illustrating disjoint qualifying shapes.

Example 7.19

Consider the following shapes graph, which requires that each
Nobel Prize in Physics be connected to precisely one such prize (the
most recent one) by a path o:next* that has at least one value for
o:prev but not o:next, and conversely, that it be connected to precisely
one such prize (the inaugural one) by a path o:prev* that has at least
one value for o:next but not o:prev.

```
v:NobelPrizePhysicsShape a sh:NodeShape ;
  sh:targetClass o:NobelPrizePhysics ;
  sh:property v:ZeroOrMoreNextShape ;
  sh:property v:ZeroOrMorePrevShape .

v:ZeroOrMoreNextShape a sh:PropertyShape ;
  sh:path [ sh:zeroOrMorePath o:next ] ;
  sh:qualifiedMinCount 1 ;
  sh:qualifiedMaxCount 1 ;
  sh:qualifiedValueShapesDisjoint true ;
  sh:qualifiedValueShape v:HasPrevShape .

v:ZeroOrMorePrevShape a sh:PropertyShape ;
  sh:path [ sh:zeroOrMorePath o:prev ] ;
  sh:qualifiedMinCount 1 ;
  sh:qualifiedMaxCount 1 ;
  sh:qualifiedValueShapesDisjoint true ;
  sh:qualifiedValueShape v:HasNextShape .

v:HasNextShape a sh:PropertyShape ;
  sh:path o:next ;
  sh:minCount 1 .

v:HasPrevShape a sh:PropertyShape ;
  sh:path o:prev ;
  sh:minCount 1 .
```

In this case, note that the parent shapes of the qualifying shapes both
set the disjointness constraint, which means that value nodes that conform to a sibling shape will not be counted. In the case above, considering the path ^sh:property/sh:property/sh:qualifiedValueShape, the
sibling shape of v:ZeroOrMoreNextShape is v:HasNextShape while the
sibling shape of v:ZeroOrMorePrevShape is v:HasPrevShape.

To understand the validation results for this shapes graph, let us first
consider the nodes that conform to v:HasNextShape and v:HasPrevShape.

Shape	Conforming
v:HasNextShape	d:NPP1901, d:NPP1902
v:HasPrevShape	d:NPP1902, d:NPP1903

When checking the qualified count constraint, those conforming to a sibling shape will be ignored. For v:ZeroOrMoreNextShape, whose qualifying shape is v:HasPrevShape, only value node d:NPP1903 will be counted since d:NPP1902 conforms to a sibling shape; hence the focus nodes d:NPP1901, d:NPP1902 and d:NPP1903 will pass since they all have only one value node on a path o:next* matching the given qualifying constraint and no other sibling constraint (namely d:NPP1903). On the other hand, for v:ZeroOrMorePrevShape, whose qualifying shape is v:HasNextShape, only the value node d:NPP1901 will be counted; this time focus node v:NPP1903 will fail as it is not connected to d:NPP1901 on a path o:prev*; meanwhile d:NPP1901 and d:NPP1902 will pass. In other words, when counting nodes with a o:next value, or nodes with a o:prev value, nodes with values for both will not be counted.

If the disjointness flag were set to false – or omitted entirely – then d:NPP1902 would be included in the count both for v:HasNextShape and v:HasPrevShape. In this case, v:ZeroOrMoreNextShape would fail focus nodes d:NPP1901 and d:NPP1902 for having two conforming values: d:NPP1902 and d:NPP1903. On the other hand, v:ZeroOrMorePrevShape would additionally fail focus node d:NPP1902 for having two conforming values: d:NPP1901 and d:NPP1902. This time, nodes with a o:next value and a o:prev value are counted in both qualifying shapes.

Given that the previous example may admittedly be difficult to comprehend, we present a second – hopefully clearer – example in a different domain to reinforce the idea of how qualified disjoint shapes operate.

Example 7.20

Consider the following data graph describing a course:

```
d:WebOfData a o:Course ;
  o:enrolled d:Julie , d:Frank , d:Anna , d:Aidan .

d:Julie a o:Student .
d:Frank a o:Student .
d:Anna a o:TeachingAssistant .
d:Aidan a o:Professor .

o:Professor rdfs:subClassOf o:Instructor .
o:TeachingAssistant rdfs:subClassOf o:Instructor , o:Student .
```

Now we state that a course must have at least three students and at most one instructor enrolled:

```
v:CourseShape a sh:NodeShape ;
  sh:targetClass o:Course ;
  sh:property v:EnrolledInstructorShape ;
  sh:property v:EnrolledStudentShape .

v:EnrolledInstructorShape a sh:PropertyShape ;
  sh:path o:enrolled ;
  sh:qualifiedMaxCount 1 ;
  sh:qualifiedValueShapesDisjoint true ;
  sh:qualifiedValueShape v:InstructorShape .

v:InstructorShape a sh:NodeShape ;
  sh:class o:Instructor .

v:EnrolledStudentShape a sh:PropertyShape ;
  sh:path o:enrolled ;
  sh:qualifiedMinCount 3 ;
  sh:qualifiedValueShapesDisjoint true ;
  sh:qualifiedValueShape v:StudentShape .

v:StudentShape a sh:NodeShape ;
  sh:class o:Student .
```

Intuitively speaking, we can use the disjointness constraints to specify whether or not a teaching assistant like :Anna will count as only a student, or as only an instructor, or as none, or as both, when validating the course according to the respective qualified cardinality constraints.

- With the disjointness constraints both enabled – as shown – then d:Anna would not count for the instructor cardinality nor the student cardinality: the course d:WebOfData in the data graph thus fails v:EnrolledStudentShape having only 2 students but passes v:EnrolledInstructorShape having 1 instructor.
- With the disjointness constraints both disabled – set to false or omitted – then d:Anna would count for both the instructor cardinality and the student cardinality: the aforementioned course thus fails v:EnrolledInstructorShape having 2 instructors but passes v:EnrolledStudentShape having 3 students.
- With the first disjointness constraint disabled and the second enabled, then d:Anna would count only for instructor cardinality: the aforementioned course thus fails v:EnrolledInstructorShape with 2 instructors and v:EnrolledStudentShape with 2 students.
- With the second disjointness constraint disabled and the first enabled, then d:Anna would count only for student cardinality: the aforementioned course thus passes v:EnrolledInstructorShape having 1 instructor and v:EnrolledStudentShape having 3 students.

7.1.4.4 Range Constraints

SHACL allows for constraining the range of values that a (literal) value node can take on both node shapes and property shapes.

---

sh:maxInclusive$^{S?}$ states the maximum value that a node can take
sh:minInclusive$^{S?}$ states the minimum value that a node can take

---

The value for both properties must be a literal. Comparisons are defined per SPARQL (see Table 6.1) where incomparable values – including datatypes not supported by a SPARQL implementation – will violate the constraint.

Example 7.21

The following exemplifies typical usage of range constraints:

```
v:NobelPrizeWinnersShape a sh:PropertyShape ;
  sh:targetClass o:NobelPrizePhysics ;
  sh:path o:winners ;
  sh:maxInclusive 3 ;
  sh:minInclusive 1 .
```

This property shape states that the property o:winners on instances of o:NobelPrizePhysics should take a value between 1 and 3 inclusive. All three such focus nodes in Figure 7.1 pass this constraint. Furthermore, consider a property shape with analogous constraints as follows:

```
v:NobelPrizeWinnersShape a sh:PropertyShape ;
  sh:targetClass o:NobelPrizePhysics ;
  sh:path o:winners ;
  sh:maxInclusive 3.0 ;
  sh:minInclusive 1.0 .
```

Although the range constraints are defined with a different datatype (xsd:decimal) than the values used in the data graph, SPARQL comparisons can compare between numeric datatypes, and thus the two range constraints are equivalent (all three focus nodes again pass).

Though the most common pattern will be defining range constraints on the value nodes of property shapes, SHACL also allows for defining range constraints on a node shape. We provide an example usage.

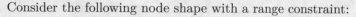

Example 7.22

Consider the following node shape with a range constraint:

```
v:WinnersObjectShape a sh:NodeShape ;
  sh:targetObjectsOf o:winners ;
  sh:maxInclusive 3 ;
  sh:minInclusive 1 .
```

With respect to Figure 7.1, the focus nodes given by target of the node shape are "1"^^xsd:integer, "2"^^xsd:integer, and "3"^^xsd:integer. The associated range constraints are then applied on the focus nodes, where all three pass both constraints, being within the range.

Remark 7.10

The SPARQL standard requires that the comparisons listed in Table 6.1 be supported, but also allows an implementation to define further comparisons not explicitly listed by the standard. For example, it may be tempting to define a range as follows:

```
v:NobelPrizeYearShape a sh:PropertyShape ;
  sh:targetClass o:NobelPrizePhysics ;
  sh:path o:year ;
  sh:maxInclusive "2100"^^xsd:gYear ;
  sh:minInclusive "1901"^^xsd:gYear .
```

However, referring back to Table 6.1, observe that comparing two xsd:gYear values is not required of a SPARQL implementation (though it may be optionally supported). Hence while the above constraint will always be passed by d:NPP1903 since it has no year, it may or may not fail for d:NPP1901 and d:NPP1902, depending on the comparisons supported by a particular SHACL implementation.

7.1.4.5 Lexical Constraints

Other constraints can be defined on the lexical values of literals or IRI:

> sh:minLength[S?] states the minimum length (inclusive) of a string
> sh:maxLength[S?] states the maximum length (inclusive) of a string
> sh:pattern[S*] gives a regular expression that a string must match
> sh:flags[S?] sets optional flags for the regular expression(s)

We first provide examples of constraints on string length.

Example 7.23

Consider the following node shape defining restrictions on the objects of the sh:year property:

```
v:NobelPrizePhysicsShape a sh:NodeShape ;
  sh:targetClass o:NobelPrizePhysics ;
  sh:minLength 29 ;
  sh:maxLength 29 .
```

The lexical values matched in Figure 7.1 will be as follows:

> "http://nobel.org/data#NPP1901"
> "http://nobel.org/data#NPP1901"
> "http://nobel.org/data#NPP1903"

All will pass having an exact length of 29 characters.

Regular expressions are applied as defined in SPARQL, which in turn is based on XPath. Options for flags include s: the dot symbol matches newlines and carriage returns; m: start and end symbols match the start/end of each line; i: matches are case insensitive; x: removes (most) whitespace before matching; q: all characters are interpreted as themselves. Where multiple patterns are defined on a node shape, the flags will apply to all patterns.

Example 7.24

Consider the following node shape defining restrictions on the objects of the sh:year property:

```
v:YearObjectShape a sh:NodeShape ;
  sh:targetObjectsOf o:year ;
  sh:pattern "(19|20).*" ;
  sh:pattern "[0-9]*" ;
  sh:minLength 4 ;
  sh:maxLength 4 .
```

The value nodes will be "1901"^^xsd:gYear, "1902"^^xsd:gYear and "1902"^^xsd:integer. The first pattern states that the lexical value must start with "19" or "20"; the second pattern further requires that the lexical value contain only numeric digits; the third and fourth patterns state that the length of the lexical value must be precisely 4.

Ultimately all three value nodes will pass all constraints.

Example 7.25

Consider the following node shape defining restrictions on the objects of the sh:next property on the data graph of Figure 7.1:

```
v:NameObjectShape a sh:NodeShape ;
  sh:targetObjectsOf o:next ;
  sh:pattern ".+npp(19|20)[0-9][0-9]" ;
  sh:flags "i" .
```

The pattern states that the lexical values of the nodes should end in /nppYYYY for YYYY a year in the 20th or 21st century. The flag "i" further indicates case sensitivity. Without the flag, only d:npp1903 would pass; with the flag, d:NPP1902, d:NPP1903 and d:npp1903 all pass.

Remark 7.11

Blank nodes will always generate a violation for a string constraint, even for a trivially satisfied condition. Consider, for example, the following data graph with the year given as a blank node:

```
d:NPP1904 a o:NobelPrizePhysics ;
  o:year [] .
```

Further consider the following node shape:

```
v:YearObjectShape a sh:NodeShape ;
  sh:targetObjectsOf o:year ;
  sh:minLength 0 .
```

Though any IRI or literal would pass, the blank node fails.

7.1.4.6 Language Constraints

The next two constraints apply on the language tags of a literal. If an IRI or blank node is matched the constraint will be violated.

sh:languageIn$^{S?}$ gives a list of permitted languages for a literal
sh:uniqueLang$^{P?}$ if set to true, states that a property cannot have two values with the same language tag

The former constraint applies a range match on the language tag, analogous to SPARQL's langMatches($\cdot,\cdot$) function. The latter constraint considers exact language tags and can only be applied to a property shape since the notion of uniqueness is with respect to a focus node of such a shape.

Example 7.26

Consider the following data graph:

```
d:NPP1901 a o:NobelPrizePhysics ;
  o:name "Nobelpriset i fysik 1901"@sv ;
  o:name "Nobel Prize in Physics 1901"@en-IE ;
  o:name "Nobel Prize in Physics 1901"@en .

d:NPP1902 a o:NobelPrizePhysics ;
  o:name "Prix Nobel de physique 1902"@fr ;
  o:name "Nobel Prize in Physics 1902"@en .

d:NPP1903 a o:NobelPrizePhysics ;
  o:name "Nobel Prize in Physics 1903"@en ;
  o:name "Nobel Prize for Physics 1903"@en .
```

Now consider the following shape(s):

```
v:NobelPrizePhysicsShape a sh:NodeShape ;
  sh:targetClass o:NobelPrizePhysics ;
  sh:property [
    sh:path o:name ;
    sh:languageIn ( "en" "sv" ) ;
    sh:uniqueLang true
  ] .
```

The focus node d:NPP1901 passes both tests since @en-IE matches with the language-in range "en", while the unique-lang constraint considers @en-IE and @en to be different language tags. On the other hand d:NPP1902 fails the language-in constraint since @fr does not match with any range. Finally d:NPP1903 fails the unique-lang constraint due to having two values for o:name with the same language tag.

7.1.4.7 Value Constraints

SHACL offers two features that require the set of value nodes of a shape to contain either a specified RDF term, or one of a list of specified RDF terms.

sh:hasValue[N*] specifies a term that must be in the set of value nodes
sh:in[N*] specifies a list of terms that each value node must appear in

Example 7.27

Consider the following constraint, which ensures that the inaugural Nobel Prize in Physics (namely d:NPP1901) is in the list of (recursive) previous prizes for all Nobel Prize in Physics:

```
v:NobelPrizePhysicsShape a sh:NodeShape ;
  sh:targetClass o:NobelPrizePhysics ;
  sh:property v:NobelPrizePhysicsTransitivePrevShape .

v:NobelPrizePhysicsTransitivePrevShape a sh:PropertyShape ;
  sh:path [ sh:zeroOrMorePath o:prev ] ;
  sh:hasValue d:NPP1901 .
```

With respect to Figure 7.1, focus node d:NPP1901 passes with the zero-length path to itself; focus node d:NPP1902 passes with the direct path to d:NPP1901 (even though d:NPP1902 is also a value node); on the other hand, focus node d:NPP1903 fails since its only value node is d:NPP1903.

Example 7.28

We now say that each Nobel Prize in Physics must have the value 1 or 2 for the property o:number (which does not make much sense, but we take some artistic licence to give a better example):

```
v:NobelPrizePhysicsShape a sh:NodeShape ;
  sh:targetClass o:NobelPrizePhysics ;
  sh:property v:NobelPrizeNumberShape .

v:NobelPrizeNumberShape a sh:PropertyShape ;
  sh:path o:number ;
  sh:in ( 1 2 ) .
```

With respect to Figure 7.1, focus nodes d:NPP1901 and d:NPP1902 pass with flying colours. But what about focus node d:NPP1903? In fact d:NPP1903 fails the specified constraint since sh:in requires that each value node appear in the list (where value node 3 does not appear).

7.1.4.8 Property-Pair Constraints

SHACL supports four different types of property-pair constraints, which allow for comparing sets of value nodes to a particular value or set of values.

sh:equals^{S*} for each focus node, its set of value nodes must be equal
to the set of values it has for the given property

sh:disjoint^{S*} for each focus node, its set of value nodes must be disjoint from the set of values it has for the given property

sh:lessThan^{P*} for each focus node, each value node must be less than
every value for the property on the focus node

sh:lessThanOrEquals^{P*} for each focus node, each value node must be
less than or equals every value for the property on the focus node

The first two constraints – sh:equals and sh:disjoint – specify a property
and apply set-based comparisons between the set of value nodes and values
for the property. Both constraints can be applied to node shapes or property
shapes. As per the previous cases, when these constraints are used on a node
shape, the set of value shapes contains (only) the current focus node itself.
We now illustrate the first two constraints by way of an example.

Example 7.29

Consider the following shapes graph applied to Figure 7.1:

```
v:NobelPrizePhysicsShape a sh:NodeShape ;
  sh:targetClass o:NobelPrizePhysics ;
  sh:disjoint o:next ;
  sh:disjoint o:prev ;
  sh:property [
    sh:path ( o:next o:prev o:next ) ;
    sh:equals o:next
  ] ;
  sh:property [
    sh:path [ sh:zeroOrMorePath :next ] ;
    sh:disjoint o:prev
  ] .
```

The first disjointness constraint specifies that Nobel Prizes in Physics
cannot have themselves as a value for o:next; all focus nodes in Figure 7.1 then pass this particular constraint (including d:NPP1903, which
has no value for o:next and thus trivially passes). The second disjointness constraint analogously specifies that Nobel Prizes in Physics cannot
have themselves as a value for o:prev; this time d:NPP1903 will fail.

The equality constraint on the first property shape states that for
a given focus node (one of d:NPP1901, d:NPP1902 or d:NPP1903 in this
case), the set of value nodes (reachable on a path o:next/o:prev/o:next
from the focus node) should be the same as the set of values for o:next
on the focus node; the focus node d:NPP1901 passes this constraint since
the set of value nodes on the path and the set of values for o:next is in

both cases {d:NPP1902}. On the other hand, the focus node d:NPP1902 fails this constraint since the set of value nodes generated by the path is empty {}, while o:next has one value generating the set {d:NPP1903}. Finally, the focus node d:NPP1903 passes since both the path and the equals property generate the same (empty) set of values.

The disjointness constraint on the second property shape states that a given focus node cannot have a value for o:prev that is also reachable on a path of zero or more :next. Focus node d:NPP1901 trivially passes since it has no value for o:prev. Focus node d:NPP1902 passes as its value for o:prev (d:NPP1901) is not reachable through zero-or-many o:next triples. Finally, d:NPP1903 fails because its value for o:prev (d:NPP1903) is reachable from zero o:next triples (the node d:NPP1903 itself).

The next two property-pair constraints – more specifically, sh:lessThan and sh:lessThanOrEquals – again indicate a property whose values are compared with the current value nodes, but this time a pairwise comparison is applied. We again illustrate their behaviour with the following example.

Example 7.30

Consider the following shapes graph applied to Figure 7.1:

```
v:NobelPrizePhysicsShape a sh:NodeShape ;
  sh:targetClass o:NobelPrizePhysics ;
  sh:property [
    sh:path ( [ sh:oneOrMorePath o:prev ] o:number ) ;
    sh:lessThan o:number
  ] .
```

Intuitively this shapes graph states that all previous such prizes must have a lower number. The focus nodes are again d:NPP1901, d:NPP1902 and d:NPP1903. Focus node d:NPP1901 passes this constraint since it has no previous prizes. Focus node d:NPP1902 also passes since its only value node is "1"^^xsd:integer, which is less than its value for o:number: "2"^^xsd:integer. Finally, focus node d:NPP1903 fails, where its set of value nodes is the same as the set of values it takes for o:number: {"2"^^xsd:integer,"3"^^xsd:integer}; hence not all value nodes are less than every value for o:number, and the focus node fails.

If we were to change the constraint to sh:lessThanOrEquals, nodes d:NPP1901 and d:NPP1902 would pass as before. However, d:NPP1903 would fail as one of the focus nodes ("3"^^xsd:integer) is not less than or equals one of the values on the property o:number ("2"^^xsd:integer).

> **Remark 7.12**   (i)
>
> SHACL does not support greater-than or greater-than-or-equals variants. It may thus be tempting to define a greater-than constraint, for example, by using sh:not on a less-than-or-equals constraint, but as we will see in the following, care must be taken.
>
> Consider trying to define the "dual" of the constraints shown in Example 7.30: that all (transitive) next prizes must have a strictly higher number. For this we will consider negation. Let's start with a property shape, which states that all (transitive) next prizes must have a lower or equal number. The idea we will explore later is negating this shape.
>
> ```
> v:NobelPrizePhysicsShape a sh:NodeShape ;
>   sh:targetClass o:NobelPrizePhysics ;
>   sh:property [
>     sh:path ( [ sh:oneOrMorePath o:next ] o:number ) ;
>     sh:lessThanOrEquals o:number
>   ] .
> ```
>
> Let us consider the results of this shape on the focus nodes of Figure 7.1. First, d:NPP1901 will fail, since there exists a value node (either 2 or 3) that is greater than its own number 1. Second, d:NPP1902 will fail, since there is a value node (namely 3) that is not less than or equals its own number 2. Finally d:NPP1903 will pass since it has no value nodes.
>
> Now consider negating this property shape as follows:
>
> ```
> v:NobelPrizePhysicsShape a sh:NodeShape ;
>   sh:targetClass o:NobelPrizePhysics ;
>   sh:not [
>     sh:path ( [ sh:oneOrMorePath o:next ] o:number ) ;
>     sh:lessThanOrEquals o:number
>   ] .
> ```
>
> This negated version of the shape will pass any focus node failed by the positive shape, and fail any focus node passed by the positive shape. So now, of the focus nodes, we will pass d:NPP1901 and d:NPP1902, which previously failed, and fail d:NPP1903, which previously passed. This is not the same as one might expect of a greater-than constraint, where although one would expect d:NPP1901 to pass, one would also expect d:NPP1902 to fail (since the next prize has an equal number), and d:NPP1903 to pass (since it has no next prize). This result is due to the fact that property-pair constraints act on (possibly empty) sets of values, wherein negating less-than-or-equals does not yield greater-than.

7.1.4.9 Closed Constraints

SHACL-Core allows to close a shape, not allowing properties other than those directly used on a shape, and an optional list of exceptions. More specifically, yhe properties directly used on a shape are those whose IRIs can be found on a path sh:property/sh:path from the shape.

---

sh:closed[N?] when set to true, this constraint closes a shape, only allowing properties directly used on a shape

    sh:ignoredProperties[N?] specifies a list of properties that are also allowed on a closed shape (aside from those directly used)

Example 7.31

We illustrate closing various shapes relating to Nobel Prizes:

```
v:NobelPrizeShape a sh:NodeShape ;
  sh:targetClass o:NobelPrize ;
  sh:property v:NobelPrizeYearShape , v:NobelPrizeWinnerShape ;
  sh:closed true ;
  sh:ignoredProperties ( rdf:type o:winners o:number ) .

v:NobelPrizeYearShape a sh:PropertyShape ;
  sh:path o:year ;
  sh:nodeKind sh:Literal .

v:NobelPrizeWinnerShape a sh:PropertyShape ;
  sh:path ( o:winner ) ;
  sh:nodeKind sh:IRI ;
  sh:property v:NobelPrizeWinnerCountryShape ;
  sh:closed true .

v:NobelPrizeWinnerCountryShape a sh:PropertyShape ;
  sh:path o:country ;
  sh:nodeKind sh:IRI .
```

For v:NobelPrizeShape, the allowed properties are o:year, rdf:type, o:winners and o:number (the latter three being exceptions). Note that o:winner is not allowed since it is contained in a path expression and is no longer connected to the closed shape by sh:property/sh:path.

We also close v:NobelPrizeWinnerShape, which limits the properties used on the value nodes: the winners of Nobel Prizes. Since the shape is connected to the property IRI o:country by a path sh:property/sh:path, the only property permitted by this shape on winners of Nobel Prizes is o:country. No exceptions are defined.

7.1.5 *SHACL-SPARQL Constraints*

Extending SHACL-Core is the SHACL-SPARQL variant, which allows for defining constraints using SPARQL queries.

7.1.5.1 SPARQL Constraints

In SHACL-SPARQL, SELECT queries can be used to define constraints over the focus nodes of a shape and to return details of violations (if any).

---

sh:SPARQLConstraint is the class of SPARQL constraints

Both node and property shapes can be connected to SPARQL constraints.

---

sh:sparql^{S*} connects a node/property shape to a SPARQL constraint

---

Finally, SPARQL constraints are defined based on precisely one SPARQL SELECT query string and (optionally) a set of pre-defined prefixes.

---

sh:select provides a SPARQL SELECT query template whose results indicate violations for a given focus node

 sh:prefixes gives pre-defined prefixes used by the SPARQL query (Remark 7.13 will describe how prefixes can be pre-defined)

Remark 7.13

In the upcoming examples, we use sh:prefixes to define prefixes that would be included in the SPARQL query. Such prefix labels must be declared in the shapes graph for each such prefix. For example, to use the prefix o:, we must include the following in the shapes graph:

```
o: sh:declare [
   sh:prefix "o" ;
   sh:namespace "http://nobel.org/ont#"^^xsd:anyURI
] .
```

We will exclude these prefix declarations for brevity.

We first illustrate a SPARQL constraint for a node shape.

Example 7.32

The following shape uses a SPARQL query to check that each Nobel Prize has at most one value for year, and if such a value exists, that it is a literal value with the xsd:gYear datatype:

```
v:HasOneYear a sh:NodeShape ;
  sh:targetClass o:NobelPrize ;
  sh:sparql [
    a sh:SPARQLConstraint ;
    sh:prefixes o: , xsd: , d: ;
    sh:select """
      SELECT $this (o:year AS ?path) ?value {
        $this o:year ?value , ?value2 .
        FILTER(?value != ?value2 || !isLiteral(?value)
          || datatype(?value) != xsd:gYear)
      }
    """
  ] .
```

The focus nodes of the shape are passed as bindings to the SPARQL query through the $this placeholder variable. Any result returned by the query is then considered a constraint violation; for example, if we pass the focus node d:NPP1902 to the query, it will be as follows:

```
PREFIX d: <http://nobel.org/data#>
PREFIX o: <http://nobel.org/ont#>
PREFIX xsd: <http://www.w3.org/2001/XMLSchema#>
SELECT (o:year AS ?path) ?value {
  d:NPP1902 o:year ?value , ?value2 .
  FILTER(?value != ?value2 || !isLiteral(?value)
      || datatype(?value) != xsd:gYear)
}
```

The results for this query will be as follows:

?path ?value
o:year "1902"^^xsd:gYear
o:year "1902"^^xsd:integer

A violation is then generated on :NPP1902 for each result.

Only :NPP1902 violates the constraint. In the case of the focus node d:NPP1901, the value "1901"^^xsd:gYear will be filtered, and no result or violation is detected. In the case of d:NPP1903, no result is generated (it has no value for o:year), and hence no violation is detected.

SPARQL constraints can also be defined for property shapes, where a special placeholder is used to represent the path.

Example 7.33

We now define a similar constraint to that shown in Example 7.32 but this time using a property shape, as follows:

```
v:HasOneYear a sh:PropertyShape ;
  sh:targetClass o:NobelPrize ;
  sh:path o:year ;
  sh:sparql [
    a sh:SPARQLConstraint ;
    sh:prefixes o: , xsd: , d: ;
    sh:select """
      SELECT d:NPP1902 ?value {
        $this $PATH ?value , ?value2 .
        FILTER(?value != ?value2 || !isLiteral(?value)
           || datatype(?value) != xsd:gYear)
      }
      """
  ] .
```

The $PATH placeholder variable will be replaced with the path specified for the parent property shape. If the path is a SHACL path, then the corresponding SPARQL property path will be used; for this reason, $PATH can only be used in the predicate position of a triple pattern. For d:NPP1902, the same query (minus the projected ?path) variable) and the same violations will be returned as seen in Example 7.14.

Remark 7.14

Like $this, SHACL defines two other "pre-bound" variables that are replaced by an external value before the query is executed:

$shapesGraph: Passes the name of a graph that contains the current shapes graph, accessible through GRAPH $shapesGraph { ... } .
$currentShape: The current shape.

Unlike $this, support of these variables is optional. Intuitively, both such variables allow for a constraint query to retrieve information from the shapes graph and the current shape for use within the query.

Given the manner in which variables are replaced in the SPARQL template string, a number of restrictions are applied to the SELECT queries that are permitted. First, queries are not permitted to use MINUS, SERVICE and/or VALUES. Second, queries cannot use AS $var where $var is a "pre-bound variable" such as $this, and any sub-query must return all pre-bound variables that appear within it.

7.1.5.2 Constraint Components

When defining potentially many constraints using SPARQL queries, we may end up repetitively expressing similar patterns. In Examples 7.32 and 7.33, we showed how SPARQL constraints can be used to define that a each Nobel Prize has at most one value for o:year, and if such a value exists, that it must be a literal value with the xsd:gYear datatype. Imagine we now wished to define that each Nobel Prize has at most one value for o:number, and if such a value exists, that it must be a literal value with the xsd:integer datatype. While we could express this as a second query analogous to the o:year case – replacing xsd:gYear with xsd:integer – this would obviously lead to considerable redundancy. For such cases, SHACL-SPARQL allows us to break down constraints into reusable components. Specifically, each such component is again a SPARQL constraint, but one that can accept and use values for custom parameters defined by the component.

SPARQL constraint components are instances of the following class.

---

sh:ConstraintComponent is the class of constraint components

Constraint components may be assigned zero or more parameters.

---

sh:parameter assigns a parameter to a constraint component
sh:Parameter is the class of parameters

    sh:path defines a property for the parameter
    sh:optional takes the value "true"^^xsd:boolean to indicate that
        a parameter is optional; otherwise – if it rather takes the value
        "false"^^xsd:boolean or is omitted – the parameter is required

---

While the constraint component defines the parameters that it accepts, the actual constraint check is defined by a validator. There are two types of validator: one based on ASK queries and another based on SELECT queries. Each validator has precisely one query string defined for it.

---

sh:SPARQLAskValidator is the class of ASK validators

    sh:ask defines the ASK query string of an ASK validator

sh:SPARQLSelectValidator is the class of SELECT validators

    sh:select defines the SELECT query string of a SELECT validator

---

Finally, constraint components are connected to validators.

sh:nodeValidator defines a SELECT validator for a node shape
sh:propertyValidator defines a SELECT validator for a property shape
sh:validator defines an ASK validator for a shape

We first illustrate a SELECT constraint component.

Example 7.34

We will define a constraint component to check that all values
for a given path have a given datatype, and (optionally) lie between a
given maximum and minimum value.

First we will define the parameters that the constraint component
accepts and then link it with the validator. In this case, we will assume
that the validator is used with a property shape.

```
v:HasMaxMinDatatypeValueComponent a sh:ConstraintComponent ;
  sh:parameter [
    sh:path v:dt
  ] ;
  sh:parameter [
    sh:path v:min ;
    sh:optional true
  ] ;
  sh:parameter [
    sh:path v:max ;
    sh:optional true
  ] ;
  sh:propertyValidator v:HasMaxMinDatatypeSelectValidator .
```

Next we define the validator referenced by the last triple.

```
v:HasMaxMinDatatypeSelectValidator a sh:SPARQLSelectValidator ;
  sh:select """
    SELECT DISTINCT $this ?value
    WHERE {
      $this $PATH ?value
      FILTER (!isLiteral(?value) || datatype(?value) != $dt
        || coalesce(?value < $min,false)
        || coalesce(?value > $max,false) )
    }
  """ .
```

This SELECT validator works similarly as a SPARQL constraint where
a query is generated for each focus node by replacing $this with the
focus node (and $PATH with the path if called from a property shape).
Additional parameters can be defined in this case, however, where the

above query uses $dt, $max, and $min, which correspond to the local names of the paths of the parameters in the constraint component.

Finally, we can call the constraint component from a property shape by referencing at least its required parameters. Here we call the component to ensure that a Nobel Prize has at most one number, and that it is a literal with datatype xsd:integer and a value of at least 1:

```
v:HasPositiveNumber a sh:PropertyShape ;
  sh:targetClass o:NobelPrize ;
  sh:path o:number ;
  v:dt xsd:integer ;
  v:min 1 .
```

We do not use the optional parameter v:max. The variable $max will thus be left unbound in the query generated for the constraint:

```
PREFIX o: <http://nobel.org/ont#>
PREFIX xsd: <http://www.w3.org/2001/XMLSchema#>

SELECT DISTINCT $this ?value
WHERE {
  $this o:number ?value
  FILTER (!isLiteral(?value) || datatype(?value) != xsd:integer
    || coalesce(?value < 1,false)
    || coalesce(?value > $max,false) )
}
```

As before, the variable $this will further be replaced by each focus node, where each result for the query will be considered as a constraint violation. Recalling that the function coalesce(...) accepts a list of arguments and returns the first that does not evaluate as an error or unbound, the expression coalesce(?value > $max,false) will skip its first argument since $max (an unspecified optional parameter) is UNBOUND and thus ?value > $max will give an error/UNBOUND; coalesce will subsequently return its second argument: false.

Validators may also be based on ASK queries. Furthermore, constraint components can have more than one validator, where a validator is chosen based on the shape that is calling the component with the following priority:

1. For node shapes, a value for sh:nodeValidator is used, if present.
2. For property shapes, a value for sh:propertyValidator is used, if present.
3. For any shape, a value for sh:validator is used, if present.

If no suitable validator is available, the component is ignored.

Example 7.35

We will extend the constraint component of Example 7.34 in order to include an analogous ASK validator.

```
v:HasMaxMinDatatypeValueComponent a sh:ConstraintComponent ;
  sh:parameter [
    sh:path v:dt
  ] ;
  sh:parameter [
    sh:path v:min ;
    sh:optional true
  ] ;
  sh:parameter [
    sh:path v:max ;
    sh:optional true
  ] ;
  sh:propertyValidator v:HasMaxMinDatatypeSelectValidator ;
  sh:validator v:HasMaxMinDatatypeAskValidator .
```

We assume v:HasMaxMinDatatypeSelectValidator to have been defined as before. We now rather define v:HasMaxMinDatatypeAskValidator.

```
v:HasMaxMinDatatypeAskValidator a sh:SPARQLAskValidator ;
  sh:ask """
    ASK WHERE {
      FILTER (isLiteral($value) && datatype($value) = $dt
        && (coalesce(?value >= $min,true))
        && (coalesce(?value <= $max,true))  )
    }
  """ .
```

This time (perhaps confusingly) the ASK returns true for conformance; hence we must "negate" the conditions when compared with the SELECT constraint, which returns results for non-conformant nodes. Also, rather than accept a focus node and a value node, the ASK query rather only accepts a value node. This additionally means that ASK validators can be used on either node or property shapes. Based on the validator selection rules, note that the property shape v:HasPositiveNumber from Example 7.34 will continue to use v:HasMaxMinDatatypeSelectValidator. Conversely, if we were to define a node shape as follows:

```
v:IsPositiveInteger a sh:NodeShape ;
  sh:targetObjectsOf o:number ;
  v:dt xsd:integer ;
  v:min 1 .
```

Now v:HasMaxMinDatatypeAskValidator will be used instead.

Remark 7.15 ⓘ

In Remark 7.1, we mentioned properties used to document shapes. An additional property is defined for constraint components:

sh:labelTemplate describes a template for a constraint component.

A label template can call parameters that will be replaced by their values. For example, we may define a label template for the component v:HasMaxMinDatatypeValueComponent from Example 7.35 as follows:

```
v:HasMaxMinDatatypeValueComponent sh:labelTemplate
  "literal with datatype {$dt}, max {$max} and min {$min}"@en .
```

which when called from v:IsPositiveInteger should generate:

```
  "literal with datatype xsd:integer, max 1 and min UNBOUND"@en .
```

Remark 7.16 ⓘ

Parameters of validators are also considered to be property shapes that define constraints on – and thereafter can be used to validate – the values passed to the validator by the shapes calling them. We illustrate this idea for the component defined in Example 7.35.

```
v:HasMaxMinDatatypeValueComponent a sh:ConstraintComponent ;
  sh:parameter [
    sh:path v:dt ;
    sh:nodeKind sh:IRI          # new constraint
  ] ;
  sh:parameter [
    sh:path v:min ;
    sh:optional true ;
    sh:datatype xsd:integer     # new constraint
  ] ;
  ...
```

Now each parameter can be used to validate the input given by the shape calling the component. For example, if we were to define:

```
v:IsPositiveInteger a sh:NodeShape ;
  sh:targetObjectsOf o:number ;
  v:dt "integer" ;
  v:min 1 .
```

This shape violates the v:dt parameter, which should take an IRI value.

> **Remark 7.17**
>
> The restrictions of Remark 7.14 also apply for validators.

> **Remark 7.18**
>
> The SHACL standard mentions that the same mechanism can be used to define constraint components using other (possibly imperative) languages. Though details are only provided for SPARQL in the standard itself, a separate note was published for defining constraint components in Javascript [237]. The SHACL standard provides a list of IRIs for the built-in constraint components of SHACL-Core, where for example sh:DatatypeConstraintComponent identifies the constraint defined by sh:datatype. We refer to the standard for more details [236].

7.1.6 SHACL Compact Syntax

Though the SHACL standard is based on RDF [236], an alternative and more compact syntax has been proposed for SHACL-Core called **SHACL Compact Syntax (SHACLC)** [233]. At the time of writing, the syntax remains in draft stage; however, we will provide an example to give a flavour of the syntax.

> **Example 7.36**
>
> We provide the shapes graph of Example 7.31 in the compact syntax (this time leaving nested shapes anonymous):
>
> ```
> PREFIX o: <http://nobel.org/ont#>
> PREFIX v: <http://nobel.org/val#>
>
> shape v:NobelPrizeShape -> o:NobelPrize {
>   closed=true ignoredProperties=[rdf:type o:winners o:number] .
>   o:year Literal [0..*] .
>   o:winner IRI [0..*] {
>     closed=true .
>     o:country IRI [0..*] .
>   } .
> }
> ```

SHACLC can be automatically mapped to SHACL-Core, and is quite similar to the compact syntax used for ShEx, as discussed presently.

7.1.7 SHACL Advanced Features

Alongside the official SHACL standard, an additional note was published, entitled SHACL Advanced Features [234], which defines a number of non-standard extensions to the SHACL specification, including:

Custom Targets provides additional mechanisms for defining a shapes target, such as using SPARQL queries.
Annotation Properties allows for declaring custom properties that are used to enrich validation reports.
SHACL Functions permits defining functions in SHACL, modelling inputs, outputs, etc., providing further modularity.
Node Expressions defines ways to capture focus nodes in a graph, through functions, paths, taking the union or intersection of two sets, etc.
Expression Constraints allows for using custom vocabulary – potentially SHACL functions – for specifying constraints on shapes.
SHACL Rules allows for defining inference rules on focus nodes.

We refer to the respective note for more details of these extensions [234].

7.2 Shape Expressions Language (ShEx)

In parallel with SHACL, an alternative language called ShEx was developed, with ShEx 2.1 published as a W3C Community Group Report in 2019 [325]. Like SHACL, ShEx is used for validating RDF graphs. ShEx was initially based on a custom syntax, called the **ShEx Compact Syntax (ShExC)**. A second ShEx syntax has since been defined, namely **ShEx JSON Syntax (ShExJ)**, which is compatible with JSON-LD [366] and thus with RDF. In this section, we will first provide examples of defining shapes and constraints in ShExC. Thereafter we motivate and provide an example for ShExJ.

7.2.1 ShEx Compact (ShExC) Syntax

ShExC is designed to be a compact, human-readable syntax for encoding shapes and their constraints. At the top level, shapes are declared:

```
:Shape1 { ⋯ }
:Shape2 CLOSED { ⋯ }
:Shape3 EXTRA :prop { ⋯ }
:Shape4 IRI :prop { ⋯ }
```

Shapes can be closed to indicate that conforming nodes cannot have properties associated with them that are not mentioned within the shape. The

EXTRA keyword can be used to denote that a given property can take further values than those specified by the shape (i.e., the shape defines the values that a property should *at least* take). Shapes can also be given node constraints that the conforming nodes must satisfy (e.g., they must be an IRI).[1]

Triple constraints can be declared within a shape, structured as follows:

$$\boxed{\text{PATH}}\;\boxed{\text{NODE CONSTRAINT}}\;[\,\boxed{\text{MULTIPLICITY}}\,]$$

A $\boxed{\text{PATH}}$ can be a property (e.g. o:winner) or its inverse (e.g., ^o:winner).
A $\boxed{\text{NODE CONSTRAINT}}$ can be:

- a *node kind* that the node must be: IRI|LITERAL|BNODE|NONLITERAL;
- a *datatype* that the node must have: e.g., xsd:integer, xsd:boolean;
- a *literal facet* that the node must conform to, which may be for a:
  - *number*: MININCLUSIVE|MAXINCLUSIVE|TOTALDIGITS|FRACTIONDIGITS;[2]
  - *string*: LENGTH|MINLENGTH|MAXLENGTH|/$\boxed{\text{PATTERN}}$/;[3]
- a *value set* that the node (or its language) must match, which may invoke:
  - a list of terms, e.g., [:NobelPrize "NPP"], where terms can be IRIs (e.g., :NobelPrize), literals (e.g., "NPP") or language tags (e.g., @en);
  - a wildcard for prefix matching using "~", e.g., [:Nobel~ @~ "a"~];
  - exclusions using "-", e.g., [:Nobel~ -:NobelPrize];
  - a match on all nodes using ".", e.g., [. -:NobelPrize];
- a *value shape* that the node must conform to, which may:
  - reference a shape by name; e.g., @:ShapeA;
  - define a nested (anonymous) shape containing triple constraints.

The special node constraint '.' can be used to accept any value. Boolean combinations of node constraints can be defined using AND, OR, NOT.

Finally, an optional $\boxed{\text{MULTIPLICITY}}$ can be given using * for zero-or-more, + for one-or-more, ? for at-most-one, {m} for exactly m, and {m,n} for between m and n values (inclusive). If omitted, the default multiplicity is {1,1}.

Multiple triple constraints can be defined within a node constraint, separated by ';'. These triple constraints are considered to be a conjunction (all must be satisfied). However, in the case that two triple constraints mention the same property, a special rule is applied, where a node conforms if the values that the node has for that property in the data can be partitioned such that there exists a one-to-one mapping from each triple constraint with that property to an element of the partition satisfying the constraint (see Remark 7.20 for examples). One can also define a disjunction of triple constraints using the following syntax (where each c_i denotes a triple constraint):

$$(\;\boxed{c_1}\;;\;\ldots\;;\;\boxed{c_m}\;|\;\boxed{c_{m+1}}\;;\;\ldots\;;\;\boxed{c_n}\;)$$

---

[1] Here we can use node-kind constraints IRI|BNODE|NONLITERAL and/or string facets.

[2] FRACTIONDIGITS defines the maximum number of digits after the decimal.

[3] $\boxed{\text{PATTERN}}$ defines a regular expression; e.g., /[0-9]*/.

This states that a conforming node must satisfy all of the triple constraints $\boxed{c_1}$, ..., $\boxed{c_m}$ or all of the triple constraints $\boxed{c_{m+1}}$, ..., $\boxed{c_n}$. Note that disjunctions can further be nested to create multiple options.

Finally, ShExC supports shortcuts that allow for naming a group (i.e., conjunction or disjunction) of triple constraints and reusing them across multiple shapes. To name a group, the syntax $:Group { $\boxed{\cdots}$ } can be used. To recall that group elsewhere, &:Group is used. Groups can also be recalled from external ShExC documents that have been imported (using IMPORT).

Example 7.37

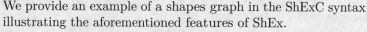

We provide an example of a shapes graph in the ShExC syntax illustrating the aforementioned features of ShEx.

```
PREFIX d: <http://nobel.org/data#>
PREFIX o: <http://nobel.org/ont#>
PREFIX v: <http://nobel.org/val#>
PREFIX xsd: <http://www.w3.org/2001/XMLSchema#>
PREFIX rdfs: <http://www.w3.org/2000/01/rdf-schema#>

v:NobelPrizeShape IRI
  /^http:\/\/nobel\.org\/data#NPP(19|20)[0-9][0-9]/ {
  $v:NobelPrizeConstraints (
    o:name MINLENGTH 1 + ;
    o:year xsd:gYear AND /(19|20)[0-9][0-9]/ ;
    o:winner . * ;
    o:winners MININCLUSIVE 1 MAXINCLUSIVE 4 ;
    o:number MININCLUSIVE 1 ;
    ( o:next @v:NobelPrizeShape | o:prev @v:NobelPrizeShape );
    ( ^o:next @v:NobelPrizeShape | ^o:prev @v:NobelPrizeShape )
  );
  a [ o:NobelPrize~ - o:NobelPrize ]
    AND { rdfs:subClassOf [ o:NobelPrize ] }
}

v:NobelPrizePhysicsShape CLOSED {
  &v:NobelPrizeConstraints ;
  a [ o:NobelPrizePhysics ] ;
  o:winner @v:PersonShape {1,4}
}

v:NobelPrizePeaceShape CLOSED {
  &v:NobelPrizeConstraints ;
  a [ o:NobelPrizePeace ] ;
  o:winner @v:PersonShape OR @v:OrganisationShape {1,4}
}

v:OrganisationShape EXTRA a { a [ o:Organisation ] }

v:PersonShape EXTRA a { a [ o:Person ] }
```

This shapes graph defines five shapes, which we will now describe. Beforehand, we note that counts are not qualified by the constraint, so when we write "*one or more value for* o:name *with at least one character*", this should be understood as "*one or more value for* o:name, *where all values for* o:name *have at least one character*"; in other words, all values are counted, not just those satisfying the constraint.

v:NobelPrizeShape: must be an IRI that matches the given pattern; also must have one or more value for o:name with at least one character, have precisely one value for o:year with the datatype xsd:gYear matching the given pattern, have zero or more values for o:winner, have precisely one value for o:winners with a value between 1 and 4 (inclusive), have precisely one value for o:number with a value of at least 1, have precisely one value for o:next or o:prev that conforms to v:NobelPrizeShape, have precisely one node linking to it with o:next or o:prev that conforms to v:NobelPrizeShape, and have precisely one value for rdf:type that starts with v:NobelPrize but is not v:NobelPrize and that has the value (and only the value) v:NobelPrize for rdfs:subClassOf.

v:NobelPrizePhysicsShape: must conform to all of the constraints listed in the v:NobelPrizeConstraints group, must have the value (and only the value) o:NobelPrizePhysics for rdf:type, must have between one and four values for o:winner with all conforming to v:PersonShape, and cannot have properties other than o:name, o:year, o:winner, o:winners, o:number, o:next, o:prev, rdf:type.

v:NobelPrizePeaceShape: must conform to all of the constraints listed in the v:NobelPrizeConstraints group, must have the value (and only the value) o:NobelPrizePeace for rdf:type, and must have between one and four values for o:winner with all conforming to v:PersonShape or v:OrganizationShape, and cannot have properties other than o:name, o:year, o:winner, o:winners, o:number, o:next, o:prev, rdf:type, as mentioned on the shape.

v:OrganisationShape must have at least the value o:Organisation for rdf:type but may have further values for the property.

v:PersonShape must have at least the value o:Person for rdf:type but may have further values for the property.

Remark 7.19   (i)

Unlike SHACL, ShEx does not provide a direct mechanism for defining the targets of shapes. Rather ShEx focuses on defining shapes and their constraints and assumes targets are defined externally.

Remark 7.20

Earlier we mentioned that triple constraints separated by ';' form a conjunction, unless the same property (or the same inverse property) is mentioned in more than one triple constraint, in which case we must check to see if there exists a partition of the corresponding values in the data such that we can map triple constraints to distinct elements of the partition satisfying them in a one-to-one manner. Consider, for example, the following shape repeating o:name:

```
v:NobelPrizeShape {
  o:name [ @en~ ] ;
  o:name [ @sv~ ]
}
```

Here, '@' invokes a language tag check. If this were a plain conjunction, we would require that each prize have precisely one name with a language tag matching the prefix en and sv – no such conforming nodes are possible. Instead, ShEx tries to find a partition of values for o:name on the node being validated such that each triple constraint with the property o:name is satisfied by a distinct element of the partition (and all elements of the partition are "covered" by a distinct triple constraint). Taking the graph of Figure 7.1, for example, d:NPP1901 conforms to this shape, having precisely one Swedish name and precisely one English name. On the other hand, d:NPP1902 does not conform to this shape, as it has a French name and two English names. Finally, d:NPP1902 does not conform either, as it has two English names.

Compare this with the following shape:

```
v:NobelPrizeShape {
  o:name [ @en~ ] ;
  o:name [ @sv~ ] ;
  o:name . {2}
}
```

Now d:NPP1901 no longer conforms to the shape since the new triple constraint requires the node to have precisely two values for o:name, but where we have already "used up" the English and Swedish names (in other words, we cannot use one data value to help satisfy multiple triple constraints). If we were to change the latter multiplicity to (for example) {0}, {0,2}, or *, then d:NPP1901 would satisfy the shape.

If we wished to define a standard conjunctive constraint for a property, we could do so in a single triple constraint using the AND keyword.

Remark 7.21

In ShEx, closed shapes consider outgoing properties only; inverses are thus ignored. However, disjunctions are considered; for instance, in the v:NobelPrizePhysicsShape shape of Example 7.37, a conforming node must have a value for o:next or o:prev (or both).

Remark 7.22

ShEx supports a number of additional features not mentioned here, relating to *semantic actions*, which allow for embedding procedural code into shapes, and *annotations*, which allow for describing shapes using custom properties (e.g., rdfs:label, rdfs:comment). We refer to the standard for further details [325]).

Remark 7.23

If we use ShEx features without restriction, we may end up with paradoxical situations. For example, consider the following shape:

```
:Barber { :shaves NOT :Barber + }
```

Along with a data graph:

```
:Bob :shaves :Bob .
```

We may then ask: does :Bob conform with :Barber? Let us assume the answer must be true or false. If true, then :Bob does not shave any nodes not conforming to :Barber, so the answer must be false. If false, then :Bob shaves a node not conforming to :Barber, so the answer must be true. Whichever answer we choose, a contradiction arises. Hence the definition is paradoxical. To avoid such paradoxes, the ShEx specification places some restrictions on the shape graphs that are permitted, which includes a restriction that shapes cannot have a negated reference to themselves (neither directly on the same shape, nor indirectly through a cycle of dependencies with a negation). We refer to the ShEx standard for more details on these restrictions [325].

In fact, similar situations can also arise in SHACL, but the specification does not define any restrictions or semantics for such cases [101]. However, Corman et al. [101] propose alternative semantics for recursive shape definitions based on 3-valued logics and stratification.

Exercise 7.7

Taking the data graph of Figure 7.1, define two (open) shapes
v:NobelLaureate *and* v:Country *in ShExC, such that nodes conforming*
to v:NobelLaureate *must be identified with an IRI and have:*

- *precisely one string value for* o:name, *or precisely one string value*
  for o:firstname *and one string value for* o:lastname;
- *one or more values for* o:country *that satisfy the shape* v:Country;
- *one type that is either* o:Person *or* o:Organisation;
- *one or more nodes with at least the type* o:NobelPrize *(but possibly*
  having other types) linking to it through the property o:winner;

while nodes conforming to v:Country *must have:*

- *one or more values for* o:name, *with at least one in English;*
- *the type (and only the type)* o:Country.

7.2.2 ShEx JSON (ShExJ) Syntax

While ShExC is a compact syntax, it is not compatible with RDF. As an
alternative, the ShExJ syntax is based on JSON-LD [366] and can express
the same features as ShExC. We now give a brief flavour of ShExJ.

Example 7.38

We describe the last shape of Example 7.37 in the ShExJ syntax. The result is a JSON-LD document compatible with RDF.

```
{ "type": "Schema",
  "shapes": [
    { "type": "Shape",
      "id": "http://nobel.org/val#PersonShape",
      "expression": {
        "type": "TripleConstraint",
        "predicate":
            "http://www.w3.org/1999/02/22-rdf-syntax-ns#type",
        "valueExpr": {
          "type": "NodeConstraint",
          "values": [ "http://nobel.org/ont#Person" ]
        }
      },
      "extra": [ "http://www.w3.org/1999/02/22-rdf-syntax-ns#type" ]
    }
  ],
  "@context": "http://www.w3.org/ns/shex.jsonld"
}
```

7.3 Comparing SHACL and ShEx

We now highlight some of the key differences between SHACL and ShEx specifications [244], both of which can be used for validating RDF:

Standardisation: SHACL is published as a W3C standard. ShEx is rather published as a W3C report and is not on the standardisation track.

Syntax: SHACL was initially based on RDF and ShEx on a compact syntax. Now however, SHACL has a compact syntax and ShEx an RDF syntax.

Multiplicity: The default multiplicities are zero-to-many for SHACL open shapes, and precisely one for properties mentioned in ShEx open shapes.

Semantics: The SHACL semantics is defined based on SPARQL features. The ShEx semantics is defined independently of SPARQL.

Paths: SHACL supports property paths (without negation). ShEx only supports properties and their inverses.

Repeated properties: SHACL applies conjunctions on constraints. ShEx applies a partitioning strategy for repeated properties (see Remark 7.20).

Closed shapes: SHACL only considers direct properties for closing shapes. ShEx also considers properties in disjunctions (see Remark 7.21).

Validation: SHACL allows for defining shapes and their targets. ShEx only allows for defining shapes where targets must be defined externally.

Inference: SHACL supports limited inference on sub-classes by default. ShEx does not support built-in mechanisms for inference.

Recursion: SHACL does not define a semantics for recursive cases. ShEx defines validation for restricted recursive cases.

Comparisons: SHACL supports comparing the values on two paths (see Section 7.1.4.8). ShEx does not support such mechanisms.

Further Reading 7.1

For further reading on validating RDF – including SHACL and ShEx – we refer to the book by Labra Gayo et al. [244].

7.4 Shapes Definitions

Both the SHACL [236] and ShEx [325] specifications provide different definitions of their constraints, with SHACL being based on SPARQL, and ShEx being based on custom definitions. Furthermore, as noted by Corman et al. [101], SHACL does not provide a complete semantics for recursive cases. With this in mind, following in the footsteps of Labra Gayo et al. [244], Corman et al. [101], etc., we provide abstract definitions of shapes that generalise SHACL-Core and ShEx. We start with the core notion of a *shape*.

Definition 45 (Shape). A shape ϕ is defined according to the following recursive grammar:

$$\phi := \top \mid @s \mid \in N \mid \uparrow P \mid e_1 \star_f e_2 \mid \geq_n e.\phi \mid \phi_1 \wedge \phi_2 \mid \neg\phi$$

where s is an IRI or blank node; N is a set of RDF terms; P is a set of IRIs; e, e_1, e_2 are property paths; $f : 2^{\mathbf{I} \cup \mathbf{L} \cup \mathbf{B}} \times 2^{\mathbf{I} \cup \mathbf{L} \cup \mathbf{B}} \to \{0,1\}$ is a function that maps a pair of sets of RDF terms to either 0 or 1; n is a number; and ϕ, ϕ_1, ϕ_2 are shapes. Other symbols are terminals.

In summary, $\top$ is a shape to which all nodes conform; $@s$ is a shape reference; $\in N$ captures restrictions relating to node types, datatypes, language tags, facet restrictions, etc.; $\uparrow P$ is used to close shapes; $e_1 \star_f e_2$ captures property-pair constraints (see Section 7.1.4.8), as well as the unique language tag constraint; $\geq_n e.\phi$ captures general and qualified cardinality restrictions; $\phi_1 \wedge \phi_2$ captures conjunctions of shapes; and $\neg\phi$ captures the negation of shapes. One may define other syntactic features from this grammar, e.g., $=_n e.\phi \equiv \geq_n e.\phi \wedge \neg \geq_{n+1} e.\phi$, or $\phi_1 \vee \phi_2 \equiv \neg(\neg\phi_1 \wedge \neg\phi_2)$, etc. In Table 7.2 we present some examples of shapes definitions in SHACL, ShExC and abstract syntax. The semantics of abstract shapes will be defined later.

Remark 7.24 ⓘ

With respect to Definition 45, we remark that N can be an infinite set, where SHACL and ShEx both support defining sets based on node type, datatypes, language tags, facet restrictions, etc. The shape $e_1 \star_f e_2$ is used to capture property-pair constraints (Section 7.1.4.8) where, in the case of SHACL, e_2 is restricted to be a simple IRI, and $f(S_1, S_2)$ is restricted to check either set equality ($S_1 = S_2$), disjointness ($S_1 \cap S_2 = \emptyset$), less than ($\max(S_1) < \min(S_2)$), or less than or equals ($\max(S_1) \leq \min(S_2)$); in addition, we can use a shape of this form to ensure that language tags are unique (we need only one path/set for this, which we use to retrieve all value nodes and check uniqueness with f). On the other hand, ShEx does not support such comparisons.

Remark 7.25 ⓘ

If we allow SPARQL property paths, which support negated property sets, then the closed shape $\uparrow P$ is syntactic and could be expressed as $\neg \geq_1 !(p_1 | \ldots | p_n).\top$, where $P = \{p_1, \ldots, p_n\}$ [101]. Since SHACL does not support negated property sets, we add the $\uparrow P$ shape.

Table 7.2 Examples of shapes in SHACL, SheXC and abstract syntax; we denote by $=_1^0$ a function that accepts two sets and returns 1 if they are equals, 0 otherwise

SHACL	ShEx	Abstract ($\lambda(:S)$)
`:S sh:nodeKind sh:IRI .`	`:S IRI { }`	$\in \mathbf{I}$

`:S sh:closed true ;`
`  sh:property [`
`    sh:path :p .`
`] , [`
`    sh:path :q .`
`] .`
	`:S CLOSED {`
	`  :p . * ;`
	`  :q . *`
	`}`
		$\uparrow\{:p,:q\}$

`:S sh:path :p ;` `  sh:minCount 1 .`	`:S { :p . + }`	$\geq_1 :p.\mathsf{T}$

`:S sh:path [`
`    sh:inversePath :p`
`] ;`
`  sh:minCount 1 .`
	`:S { ^:p . + }`	$\geq_1 \text{^}:p.\mathsf{T}$

`:S sh:path :p ;` `  sh:maxCount 1 .`	`:S { :p . ? }`	$\neg \geq_2 :p.\mathsf{T}$

`:S sh:path :p ;`
`  sh:nodeKind sh:Literal ;`
`  sh:minCount 1 .`
	`:S {`
	`  :p LITERAL + ;`
	`}`
		$\geq_1 :p.\in\mathbf{L} \wedge \neg \geq_1 :p.\in\mathbf{B}\cup\mathbf{I}$

`:S sh:path :p ;`
`  sh:qualifiedMinCount 1 ;`
`  sh:qualifiedValueShape :Q .`
	`:S {`
	`  :p @:Q + ;`
	`  :p . *`
	`}`
		$\geq_1 :p.@:Q$

`:S sh:path :p ;`
`  sh:qualifiedMinCount 1 ;`
`  sh:qualifiedValueShape [`
`    sh:and ( :Q :R )`
`] .`
	`:S {`
	`  :p @:Q AND @:R + ;`
	`  :p . *`
	`}`
		$\geq_1 :p.(@:Q \wedge @:R)$

`:S sh:path :p ;`
`  sh:qualifiedMinCount 1 ;`
`  sh:qualifiedValueShape [`
`    sh:or ( :Q :R )`
`] .`
	`:S {`
	`  :p @:Q OR @:R + ;`
	`  :p . *`
	`}`
		$\geq_1 :p.(\neg(\neg @:Q \wedge \neg @:R))$

`:S sh:path :p ;` `  sh:equals :q .`	—	$:p \star_{=_1^0} :q$

Next we define a *shapes schema* that allows for naming shapes.

Definition 46 (Shapes schema). A *shapes schema* is defined as a triple $\Sigma := (S, \Phi, \lambda)$, where $S \subseteq \mathbf{I} \cup \mathbf{B}$ is a set of shape names, Φ is a set of shapes, and $\lambda : S \to \Phi$ maps the shape names S to shapes Φ.

Given a set of shape names S and an RDF graph G, we now define a *shapes assignment*, which assigns either 0 or 1 to each pair of shape name and graph node (we recall the notation $\mathrm{so}(G)$ to refer to all subject and object terms in G, which we refer to as the set of nodes in the graph G).

Definition 47 (Shapes assignment). Given a set of shape names S and an RDF graph G, we call a mapping $\sigma : S \times \mathrm{so}(G) \to \{0,1\}$ a *shapes assignment* for S over G.

Intuitively a shapes assignment represents a possible "solution" to the validation problem in terms of which nodes in the graph conform to (and are targetted by) which shapes named in the shapes schema. Henceforth we assume that the shapes assignments are *total*, i.e., that each pair in $S \times \mathrm{so}(G)$ is assigned a score of either 0 or 1.[4] The semantics of a shape can then be defined in terms of the *evaluation* of that shape over a node of a graph. Note that in the following, given a graph G, an RDF term x, and a property path e, we use $e(G,x)$ to denote the set of nodes in G returned for the variable $v \in \mathbf{V}$ by the evaluation $(x,e,v)(G)$ (see Section 6.3.2.2); in other words, $e(G,n)$ denotes the set of nodes reachable from x in G though e.

Definition 48 (Shape evaluation). The semantics of a shape $\phi \in \Phi$ is defined in terms of the *shape evaluation* $[\![\phi]\!]^{G,x,\sigma} \in \{0,1\}$ for an RDF graph G, a node $x \in \mathrm{so}(G)$, and a shapes assignment σ, such that:

$$[\![\top]\!]^{G,x,\sigma} = 1$$
$$[\![@s]\!]^{G,x,\sigma} = \sigma(s,x)$$
$$[\![\in N]\!]^{G,x,\sigma} = 1 \text{ iff } x \in N$$
$$[\![\uparrow P]\!]^{G,x,\sigma} = 1 \text{ iff } \{p \mid \exists o : (x,p,o) \in G)\} \subseteq P$$
$$[\![e_1 \star_f e_2]\!]^{G,x,\sigma} = f(e_1(G,x), e_2(G,x))$$
$$[\![\geq_n e.\phi]\!]^{G,x,\sigma} = 1 \text{ iff } |\{y \in e(G,x) \mid [\![\phi]\!]^{G,y,\sigma} = 1\}| \geq n$$
$$[\![\phi_1 \wedge \phi_2]\!]^{G,x,\sigma} = \min\{[\![\phi_1]\!]^{G,x,\sigma}, [\![\phi_2]\!]^{G,x,\sigma}\}$$
$$[\![\neg\phi]\!]^{G,x,\sigma} = 1 - [\![\phi]\!]^{G,x,\sigma}$$

If $[\![\phi]\!]^{G,x,\sigma} = 1$, we say that x in G *conforms* to ϕ under σ.

For the purposes of validating an RDF graph, typically a target is defined, requiring specified nodes to conform to specified shapes.

---

[4] A 3-valued semantics is proposed by Corman et al. [101], which could be encoded by allowing partial assignments, or by introducing a third value. See also Remark 7.23.

> **Definition 49 (Shapes target).** Given an RDF graph G and a set of shape names S, a *shapes target* T for S over G is a set of pairs of shape names from S and nodes from G, i.e., $T \subseteq S \times \text{so}(G)$.

In practice, there are potentially many ways in which the shapes target may be defined; for example, for each shape $s \in S$, we may define a SPARQL SELECT query Q_s with a single variable such that s is said to target $Q_s(G)$.

Finally, we can define the notion of a valid graph.

> **Definition 50 (Valid graph).** Given a shapes schema $\Sigma = (S, \Phi, \lambda)$, an RDF graph G, and a shapes target T (for S over G), we say that G is *valid* under Σ and T if and only if there exists a shapes assignment σ (for S over G) such that, for all $s \in S$ and $x \in \text{so}(G)$, the following hold:
>
> - $\sigma(s, x) = [\![\lambda(s)]\!]^{G, x, \sigma}$; and
> - if $(s, x) \in T$, then $\sigma(s, x) = 1$.

Intuitively, the shapes assignment indicates which nodes in the graph conform to which shapes in the shapes schema, and ensures that nodes targetted by a shape conform to that shape. If there exists such a shapes assignment, then the graph is valid under the shapes schema and target. The *validation problem* then accepts a shapes schema Σ, a graph G and a target T and aims to find a shapes assignment that validates G under Σ and T. This problem is intractable in the general case. Corman et al. [101] propose approximations to the validation problem based on minimal fixpoints; in later work they propose to combine a SPARQL engine with a SAT solver to run validation [100].

7.5 Summary

In this chapter, we have discussed the validation of RDF graphs, introducing the key concept of shapes, which capture constraints that can be applied to particular nodes of an RDF graph. We introduced two shapes languages: Shapes Constraint Language (SHACL) and Shape Expressions Language (ShEx). We first discussed SHACL-Core, which provides a vocabulary for defining shapes and constraints in RDF, and then discussed SHACL-SPARQL, which allows for defining constraints using SPARQL. ShEx, on the other hand, was originally based on a more concise, non-RDF syntax. We illustrated the definition of shapes using the ShExC syntax and the ShExJ syntax, highlighting some key differences between SHACL and ShEx. We then introduced an abstract syntax that generalises both SHACL and ShEx, formalised the validation problem, and briefly discussed some implementation strategies for validating RDF graphs in practice.

7.6 Discussion

Discussion 7.2

ANNE: Why were SHACL and ShEx both defined? Wouldn't one of these shapes languages not have sufficed for the Web of Data?

AIDAN: Both emerged from the same community, where there were some differences in opinion in terms of how best to define such a language for RDF. One of the key early differences was on the issue of whether or not it would be better to base the shapes language on RDF (SHACL) or a more concise syntax (ShEx). However, with the advent of the SHACL Concise Syntax and the ShEx JSON Syntax, it is quite clear that this disagreement was primarily a syntactic issue. Both SHACL and ShEx are both being used in practice. For example, Wikidata has begun using ShEx to define constraints on nodes in their graph[a], while SHACL have been used for validating models of Electronic Health Records (EHR) [260].

FRANK: What about the efficiency and scalability of validation? You mentioned at the end of the chapter that the validation problem is intractable. Doesn't that make these languages impractical?

AIDAN: Not necessarily. First, the problem is intractable in the worst case, where such cases involve a high degree of cyclical references. Being intractable in the worst case does not necessarily imply that validation cannot be performed efficiently and/or at large scale for typical graphs and shapes; for example, ShEx is currently being used at large-scale on Wikidata. Second, even if there are hard cases encountered in practice, approximate methods can be employed [101]. Furthermore, SPARQL engines can be used at the core of validation implementations, which allows the optimisations developed for query answering to also be leveraged for validation [100].

JULIE: It would seem like a lot of work manually defining shapes for a large, heterogeneous RDF graph. Are there any works that help to automate this process or make it easier?

AIDAN: Indeed there are two relevant lines of work in this direction. The first line of work aims to develop (semi-)automatic methods in order to extract shapes that best "describe" a given RDF graph [388, 71]. The second line of work aims to offer interfaces for developing and working with shapes [71]. Such works help to reduce the barriers to entry for using shapes, and in turn to help improve the quality of RDF data published on the Web.

---

[a] See, e.g., https://www.wikidata.org/wiki/EntitySchema:E42

Chapter 8
Linked Data

While RDF, RDFS, OWL, SPARQL, SHACL and ShEx define models, languages and semantics by which data on the Web can be described, defined, queried and validated – and while they all offer built-in support for Web identifiers in the form of IRIs – they alone are insufficient to realise a Web of Data. In particular, these standards do not address the key question of how data from different websites published using these standards can be *linked* together to form a coherent Web of Data. **Linked Data** provides an answer to this question based on four core principles that outline a conceptual blueprint for building a Web of Data on top of these standards.

Example 8.1

Extending the dataset introduced in Example 3.14, in Figure 8.1 we present an example of six documents from five websites publishing individual RDF graphs, where for example ex1:FranksProfile is the location of the document with RDF data (mostly) about Frank, identified by the IRI ex1:Frank. This example illustrates a set of challenges yet to be overcome, first and foremost of which is:

- How can we find RDF data on the Web about a given entity?

For example, given the IRI ex1:Frank identifying Frank, how can we establish a *link* from that identifier to the location of the document – ex:FranksProfile – that describes him in RDF?

  Second, we see that the documents in Example 3.14 are not linked or connected in any way. Needless to say, we cannot have a *Web* of Data without links between documents; this introduces the second question:

- How can we link from one RDF document to another on the Web?

© Springer Nature Switzerland AG 2020
A. Hogan, *The Web of Data*, https://doi.org/10.1007/978-3-030-51580-5_8

For example, how can we link from ex3:CoffeeParfaitRecipe – an RDF document describing a recipe that contains lemon – to ex5:LemonFruit – an RDF document that contains further data about lemons?

Third, even assuming we can track down the relevant information on the Web, if we take the merge of all the individual graphs, the resulting graph would be highly disconnected due to diversity in how data are described by different websites. On the one hand, entities are identified using different IRIs in different websites (e.g., Galway is identified by ex1:Gaillimh on Frank's website based on the Irish name and local namespace, while it is identified by ex2:Galway on the Tesco website based on the English name and local namespace). On the other hand, different vocabularies are used to describe analogous data in different ways, where, for example, the recipe website describing ex3:CoffeeParfait defines its type as ex3:DessertRecipe, while the recipe website describing ex4:GrapeSorbet defines its type as ex4:Recipe additionally denoting the course in a separate triple as ex4:Dessert. Hence, even if we could locate the relevant data we need on the Web, this diversity would greatly complicate being able to query or otherwise exploit these data in a given application. A third major question underlying Linked Data is then:

- How can we address the diversity of data on the Web?

While RDFS and OWL provide means to define mappings between different ways of expressing equivalent information (see Example 5.5) that can in principle help to deal with diverse data, defining such mappings can be a costly process. An alternative approach may be to encourage different publishers on the Web to use the same vocabulary and the same patterns when describing analogous data.

Linked Data then addresses these three questions. The Linked Data principles address the first and second challenges by describing how to establish links between the identifiers for entities and the documents that describe them, and thus, implicitly, how to link various documents containing RDF data. A set of Linked Data best practices further aim to mitigate the diversity of data published on the Web with the goal of making such data easier to integrate and consume.

8.1 Overview

In this chapter, we discuss topics relating to Linked Data, where we start by defining four foundational Linked Data principles that state how entities can be described on the Web, and how such descriptions of entities can be re-

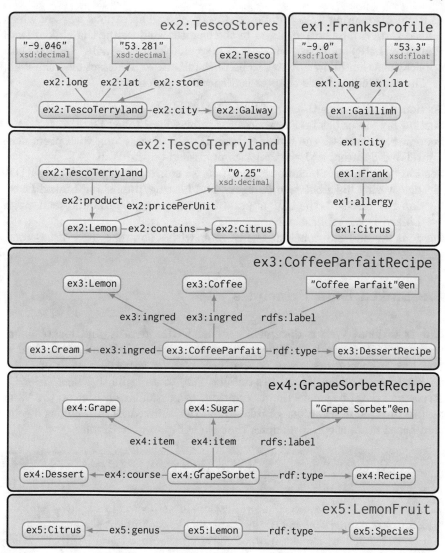

Fig. 8.1 Six example documents from five websites publishing RDF graphs

trieved and interlinked on the Web. We then discuss best practices that guide
Linked Data publishers towards improving the interoperability of their local
data with related data on the broader Web. We subsequently introduce the
Linking Open Data project, which has overseen the publication of hundreds of
datasets on the Web following Linked Data principles and best practices; we
discuss some of the most prominent of these datasets and the most prominent
vocabularies used in these datasets. We then discuss techniques and tools for
producing and publishing Linked Data, including conversion of legacy data

to RDF, discovering links between datasets, as well as various ways in which Linked Data can be hosted. Later in the chapter we describe the **Linked Data Platform (LDP)** standard, whose goal is to enable "read–write" Linked Data applications that allow updates to be pushed back to a dataset over the Web.

The remainder of this chapter is structured as follows:

Section 8.2 describes the core Linked Data principles.
Section 8.3 describes best practices for publishing Linked Data.
Section 8.4 discusses the Linking Open Data project, along with prominent
    related datasets and vocabularies published on the Web.
Section 8.5 discusses techniques and tools for converting legacy data to RDF,
    discovering links between datasets, and hosting/publishing Linked Data.
Section 8.6 discusses the LDP standard that can be used to build read–write
    Linked Data applications.
Sections 8.7 and 8.8 conclude the chapter with a summary and discussion.

8.2 Linked Data Principles

The traditional Web is document-centric: URLs identify and locate documents, HTTP is used to retrieve documents, and HTML allows to format and link from one document to another. Moving towards a Web of Data, we need ways to identify entities on the Web, to describe these entities with structured data, to locate the descriptions of particular entities on the Web, and to link the descriptions of related entities. Linked Data provides a solution based on four core principles that we will presently discuss.

Historical Note 8.1

Berners-Lee published the initial W3C Design Issues document outlining Linked Data principles, rationale and some examples in July 2006 [46]. Some changes were made to this document down through the years, such as the addition of the 5-Star Data criteria in 2010 (discussed in Section 8.4.1). The original document was preceded by similar proposals, such as a W3C Working Note from March 2006 entitled "Best Practice Recipes for Publishing RDF Vocabularies" [272], which described URI naming schemes for vocabulary terms and the HTTP mechanisms that should be used to return information upon lookup of those URIs. Such best practices aligned with the Web Architecture W3C Recommendation [218] and with what was partially seen in practice on the Web when publishing RDF data.

8.2.1 The Four Principles

The four Linked Data principles are as follows:

1. *use IRIs* as names for entities;
2. *use HTTP IRIs* so those names can be looked up (aka. **dereferencing**);
3. *return useful information* (in RDF) upon lookup of those IRIs;
4. *include links* by using IRIs that dereference to remote documents.

—paraphrased from Berners-Lee [46]

Under these principles, the Web is still used to publish documents, but rather than assuming that documents contain human-readable hypertext described in HTML, documents may now also contain machine-readable structured data described in RDF; rather than only identifying documents with URLs, entities can be identified with IRIs; rather than only being able to retrieve HTML documents by that document's URL, RDF documents describing an entity can be retrieved by that entity's IRI; rather than only being able to link from one HTML document to another using hyperlinks, entity IRIs can be used to link from one RDF document to another.

Though concise, these four principles are key to realising the Web of Data.

Remark 8.1   (i)

The Linked Data principles refer to URIs not IRIs as they predate the use of the latter in RDF 1.1 [103]. We refer to IRIs to reflect the modern standards. Also there is some debate as to whether RDF is necessary for Linked Data: in theory, other standard data models with built-in support for IRIs could be used, though use of RDF is recommended. Finally, when we refer to "entities" – such as in the first principle *"use IRIs as names for entities"* – we also generically refer to classes and properties, for which the Linked Data principles also apply.

Example 8.2

In Figure 8.2, we provide a more concise example of two different (fictitious) websites – `nobel.org` and `wiki.org` – publishing five Linked Data documents, where each document contains an RDF graph. The Web location of each document is shown above the graph. By using RDF, the principal entities are identified with IRIs – `nv:Poetry`, `w:FrancoPrussianWar`, `nv:Nobel` – etc. The main additional requirement of Linked Data is that when those IRIs are looked up (on the Web using HTTP), that they dereference to structured data in RDF about the entity. These dereferencing relations are annotated in Figure 8.2; note that we only include such relations when the targets are one of the documents shown (in reality, for example, standard terms such as rdf:type and rdfs:label also dereference to RDF documents hosted by the W3C). In addition to the documents, we enumerate the example namespaces used (see Table 3.1 for the standard prefixes) and summarise the links between documents formed by dereferenceable IRIs.

Using this example, we can make the following observations with respect to the Linked Data principles:

- IRIs in any position of a triple can be dereferenced; for example, the predicate IRI nv:winner dereferences to a document describing the domain and range of that property.
- Multiple IRIs may dereference to a single document; this is the case for IRIs such as nv:winner, nv:NobelLiterature, etc., which all dereference to the n:voc.ttl document.
- Documents may contain IRIs that dereference to external documents; for example, nd:L1.ttl mentions IRIs that dereference to nd:SP.ttl and n:voc.ttl. These IRIs then constitute links to external documents; as such, no explicit linking mechanism is required for Linked Data: mentioning external IRIs – i.e., IRIs that dereference to RDF elsewhere on the Web – in an RDF document suffices.
- It is not expected that the document to which an entity IRI dereferences contains *all* relevant information about that entity; in fact, it is rather expected that many more documents on the Web contribute complementary data about that entity. What is expected is that the dereferenced document contains some "useful" data about that entity. In practice, a site hosting Linked Data will often return all triples from the local dataset where that entity IRI appears as the subject, and potentially further data, such as local triples where the IRI also appears as the object [203].
- RDF can be serialised in a wide variety of standard syntaxes – N-Triples, RDF/XML, Turtle, etc. (see Section 3.8) – where Linked Data is agnostic to the syntax used; all such syntaxes can be parsed into the same RDF data model.For brevity, the example in Figure 8.2 shows each IRI dereferencing to a document in one concrete syntax, indicated by the file extension (.nt for N-Triples, .ttl for Turtle). In practice, when dereferencing a given IRI, a server may offer a choice of documents expressing the same RDF content in different syntaxes; this is implemented using HTTP-level content negotiation and will be discussed later in Section 8.2.3.

It is worth mentioning that neither website yet offers links to the other in this example. We will later return to this issue.

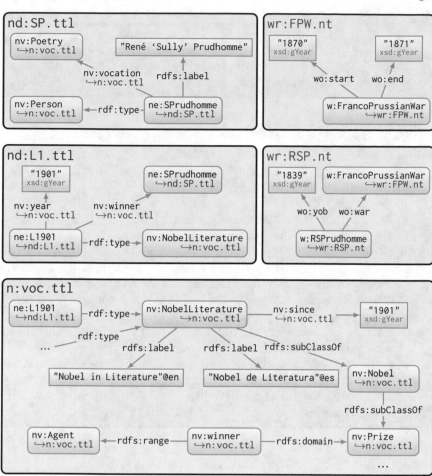

(a) Five Linked Data documents

(b) Example namespaces used

Namespaces (fictitious)
n: http://nobel.org/
nd: http://nobel.org/data/
ne: http://nobel.org/ent/
nv: http://nobel.org/voc.ttl#
w: http://wiki.org/entity/
wo: http://wiki.org/ontology/
wr: http://wiki.org/rdf/

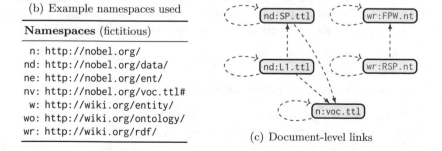

(c) Document-level links

Fig. 8.2 Five example documents from two websites, where dereferencing is shown for the available documents (other IRIs may dereference to documents not shown)

Remark 8.2

Prior to Linked Data, it was common to use `rdfs:seeAlso` to link an entity IRI to a document describing it. The Linked Data principles now offer an implicit linking mechanism based on dereferencing.

Discussion 8.1

FRANK: But to get data about an entity using Linked Data, we need to know that entity's IRI, right?

AIDAN: Right.

FRANK: But how should we know that `ne:L1901` is the IRI that refers to the first Nobel Prize in Literature, for example?

AIDAN: Conceptually the problem is very similar to the question of how you find (the URLs of) documents on the Web that contain a particular keyword. Web search engines solve this by **crawling** the Web and creating an "inverted index" that maps words to document URLs (so-called because usually the Web maps URLs to words in a document, whereas these indexes invert this mapping); this then allows users to perform keyword searches. Likewise in cases where we don't know an entity IRI, we may need a service that crawls Linked Data and builds an inverted index that maps keywords (e.g., extracted from labels) to IRIs like `ne:L1901`. A number of such services have been proposed for Linked Data [73, 299, 94, 200, 105].

8.2.2 Recipes for Dereferencing

The next question is: *how*, precisely, do we establish this dereferencing relation between an entity IRI and an RDF document describing that entity? There are three "recipes" we may consider for implementing dereferencing:

1. use the same entity IRI as the document URL ("**URL recipe**");
2. use a fragment identifier ("**hash recipe**");
3. use a see-other redirect ("**slash recipe**").

We will discuss each principle in turn. In fact, as we soon discuss, the first option is *not* recommended unless the entity *is* actually a document.

8.2.2.1 URL recipe

The first recipe is also the simplest: use the URL of the (RDF) document that describes an entity to identify the entity. Hence when the entity identifier is looked up, the document is returned; this is a trivial form of dereferencing. However, the URL recipe is not recommended unless the entity is actually the document itself; we justify this with a concrete example.

Example 8.3

Let us return to the (more complex) example illustrated in Figure 8.1. We see that `ex2:TescoTerryland` is used both as the location of a document and the identifier for a store that sells lemons. This configuration trivially satisfies the third Linked Data principle in that when one looks up the entity identifier `ex2:TescoTerryland` one gets back a document with RDF describing that entity. However, the problem comes when we consider, for example, the following additional data:

```
@prefix formats: <http://www.w3.org/ns/formats/> .
@prefix dc: <http://purl.org/dc/elements/1.1/> .
@prefix xsd: <http://www.w3.org/2001/XMLSchema#> .

ex2:TescoTerryland dc:hasFormat formats:Turtle ;
    dc:modified "2018-08-08"^^xsd:date .
```

Clearly – to a human – this describes the format of the document and the date it was last modified rather than the format and modification date of the store. And clearly – to a human – it is the store that stocks lemons, not the document. Still, we have created some unnecessary ambiguity that may not be straightforward for a machine to disambiguate.

Possible ambiguities of this form is why it is not recommended to use document URLs as IRIs for entities that are not documents. Even if the URL is only used to describe an entity in that document (e.g., to say that it stocks lemons), a client that reads the document may wish to record some metadata about when the document was retrieved, etc.; thus in the context of Linked Data, a document URL should be seen as "globally reserved" for identifying itself and only itself.

8.2.2.2 Hash Recipe

For the second recipe, we recall from Figure 3.1 that we can use a hash symbol ("#") to append an optional fragment identifier to an IRI, which can be used to identify (and jump to) specific sections of HTML documents. In the context of Linked Data, fragments can also be used to distinguish a document identifier (e.g., "`http://nobel.org/voc.ttl`") from the identifiers

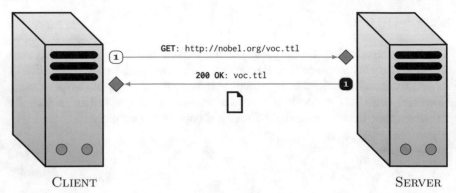

Fig. 8.3 Hash recipe for dereferencing http://nobel.org/voc.ttl#winner

of the entities that it describes (e.g., "http://nobel.org/voc.ttl#winner").
Using this recipe, we can easily have multiple fragment identifiers referencing
multiple entities described by the same document.

Example 8.4

In Figure 8.2, the n:voc.ttl term expands to:

http://nobel.org/voc.ttl

This is the location of a Turtle (.ttl) document defining some vocabulary used to describe Nobel prizes and their winners; two such vocabulary terms defined in this Turtle document are nv:winner and nv:Prize,
which respectively expand to the IRIs:

http://nobel.org/voc.ttl#winner
http://nobel.org/voc.ttl#Prize

We see that these terms – and the other terms defined by the document
– use the "hash recipe" for dereferencing. When these terms are looked
up via HTTP, they will return the Turtle document defining them.

The process of dereferencing via the hash recipe is illustrated in Figure 8.3. On the HTTP level, fragment identifiers are solely seen on the
client-side; for example, when putting http://nobel.org/home.html#Peace
into a browser address bar, the browser will issue a HTTP request for
http://nobel.org/home.html, and assuming the document is returned successfully, will jump to the section marked in the HTML source code with the
identifier peace; hence the remote servers handling the request do not see the
fragment identifier. The same happens in Linked Data: when a HTTP request

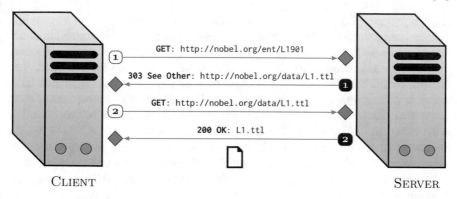

Fig. 8.4 Slash recipe for dereferencing `http://nobel.org/ent/L1901`

for `http://nobel.org/voc.ttl#winner` is performed, remotely speaking, this is the same as directly requesting the document `http://nobel.org/voc.ttl`.

Though relatively simple and easy to implement, the hash recipe necessitates that the entity IRI encodes the location of the document that describes it. In some cases it may rather be beneficial to separate the location of the document from the entity IRI; this observation leads to the third recipe.

8.2.2.3 Slash Recipe

The third recipe allows entity IRIs to be defined independently of the location of the document to which they dereference; this is implemented using a HTTP redirect (`303 See Other`) from the entity IRI to the document. This recipe is frequently called the "slash recipe" since often – though not necessarily – it results in a namespace that ends with a slash ("/") rather than a hash ("#").

Example 8.5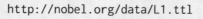

In Figure 8.2, the `nd:L1.ttl` prefix expands to:

$$\text{http://nobel.org/data/L1.ttl}$$

This is the location of a Turtle (`.ttl`) document defining data about the first Nobel Prize in Literature, which is identified by the IRI `ne:L1901`; expanding this latter IRI (noting that `ne:` ends with slash), we get:

$$\text{http://nobel.org/ent/L1901}$$

When a HTTP lookup is performed on the latter IRI, a server implementing the "slash recipe" should offer a `303 See Other` redirect to the location of the corresponding Turtle document (the former URL).

The process of dereferencing by the slash recipe is illustrated in Figure 8.4. Unlike the hash recipe, two separate requests must be sent, doubling the number of messages between the client and the server. Thus, dereferencing content through the slash recipe can lead to considerable considerable overhead. The benefit versus the hash strategy is that the entity IRI and the document URL are now decoupled, where if the corresponding documents move, rather than having to change entity IRIs – which may potentially break interoperability with external data and applications using those IRIs – the redirects can be rewritten (more easily than in the case of the hash recipe) to target the new locations of the respective documents. Whether or not the additional flexibility offered by the slash recipe justifies the overhead of the additional requests it requires has been the subject of an unusual amount of debate, where the most general answer is that it depends on a variety of factors.

Remark 8.3   ⓘ

In practice, there is a trend of using the slash recipe when dealing with, say, thousands or millions of entity IRIs, whereby each IRI redirects to its own individual document; and using the hash recipe with dealing with, say, tens or hundreds of entity IRIs, whereby all IRIs redirect to the same document. Having one document describing millions of entity IRIs would be wasteful: an agent interested in one such entity would have to download and parse a lot of irrelevant data.

However, the slash recipe can be used to redirect multiple entity IRIs to one document, and the hash recipe can be used to redirect entity IRIs to their own individual document; with respect to the latter, consider a hash IRI for identifying the first Nobel Prize in Literature:

http://nobel.org/data/L1.ttl#this

This entity IRI dereferences to its own document. However, a practical complication under this scheme comes when using prefixes to refer to such IRIs in Turtle, either requiring a separate namespace for each entity/document, or leading to the slightly awkward nd:L1.ttl#this.

Remark 8.4   ⓘ

A 303 See Other redirect should generally be used for the slash recipe since other common forms of HTTP redirect (e.g., 301 Moved Permanently or 302 Found) are generally considered to redirect from one document to another document rather than from an entity to a document. Since a 303 redirect marks the transition from entity to document it may be followed by other types of redirects.

Table 8.1 Media types for RDF syntaxes

Syntax	Media Type
JSON-LD	application/ld+json
N-Triples	application/n-triples
RDF/XML	application/rdf+xml
Turtle	text/turtle

Remark 8.5 (i)

On the server side, redirects will commonly be implemented with a simple rewriting engine, where, for example, the entity IRI:

http://nobel.org/ent/L1901

would be "rewritten" to a redirect like:

http://nobel.org/data/L1901.ttl

by a rule that replaces "resource" with "data" and affixes ".ttl". This saves the server having to store the entire 303 redirect relation, which may potentially involve millions of entity IRIs.

8.2.3 Content Negotiation

As discussed in Section 3.8, there are now several standard syntaxes available for serialising RDF graphs (N-Triples, RDF/XML, Turtle, etc.), where a server may offer a choice of syntaxes. A client can then use HTTP-level **content negotiation** to specify which syntax(es) they prefer. Content negotiation should only be used to select the format in which content is returned: the abstract content – in this case, the RDF graph – should not vary across different content negotiation choices for a single IRI.

On a technical level, clients can request specific formats by listing the media types of the corresponding syntaxes in the HTTP Accept header of the request. The media types for a selection of RDF syntaxes are shown in Table 8.1; note that RDFa does not have a specific media type, but rather inherits the type of the HTML document in which the data are embedded. The server should then interpret this Accept header and return the best available syntax; furthermore, the server should indicate the media type of the document returned in the HTTP Content-type header of the response.

When content negotiation is implemented under the hash recipe, entity IRIs will often not contain a file extension indicating a particular syntax, where typically the server will use a Content-location header to indicate

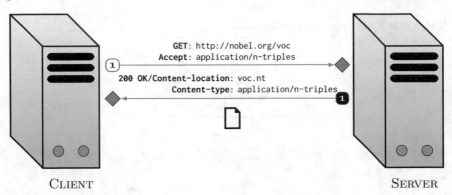

Fig. 8.5 Dereferencing `http://nobel.org/voc#winner` with content negotiation (hash)

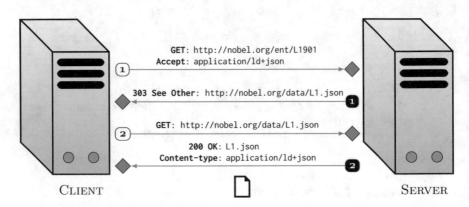

Fig. 8.6 Dereferencing `http://nobel.org/ent/L1901` with content negotiation (slash)

the location of the resource returned (e.g., with the appropriate file extension). Figure 8.5 shows an example of content negotiation for the IRI `http://nobel.org/voc#winner` requesting that N-Triples be returned. For the slash recipe, content negotiation will redirect the entity IRI to a document best corresponding with the requested format(s); Figure 8.6 shows how the IRI `http://nobel.org/ent/L1901` is dereferenced with content negotiation, this time requesting that JSON-LD be returned.

In certain cases, the client may be willing to accept a number of formats. In such cases, in the Accept header of the request, clients may specify a variety of media types with preferences using q weights; for example:

Accept: application/rdf+xml, text/turtle;q=0.8, */*;q=0.1

This indicates that the client prefers RDF/XML, then Turtle, but otherwise, if these are not available, is willing to accept any format. The server should then respond to the client with the most preferred format available.

8.3 Linked Data Best Practices

At the outset of this chapter, Example 8.1 discussed three key questions that Linked Data primarily aims to address, namely:

- How can we find RDF data on the Web about a given entity?
- How can we link from one RDF document to another on the Web?
- How can we address the diversity of data on the Web?

The Linked Data principles focus on the first and second question, laying the groundwork for a *Web* of (RDF) Data by establishing links from entity IRIs to RDF documents and, simultaneously, links from RDF documents to RDF documents. These principles do not, however, address the third question of coping with diverse data on the Web. In fact, this third question is by far the hardest of the three, and relates to one of the longest-standing challenges faced in the area of Computer Science: that of *data integration*.

Example 8.6

Figure 8.1 offers a concrete example of the data integration problem. While we can combine all RDF data into one graph, we will not have fully integrated the data until we can determine that `ex1:Gaillimh` on Frank's site refers to the same entity as `ex2:Galway` on the supermarket site, that being of type `ex3:DessertRecipe` on the first recipe site is equivalent to being a `ex4:Recipe` whose `ex4:course` is `ex4:Dessert` on the second recipe site, and so forth. Without understanding the relations between terms on different websites, we would either require very complex queries that capture the diverse ways in which equivalent information can be represented, or miss results. While a variety of techniques can be brought to bear in terms of addressing the challenges of data integration (some of which we shall discuss later in this chapter), automatically integrating diverse data of this form in a complete and error-free manner is beyond what current techniques are capable of, requiring an almost human-level understanding of the datasets.

Linked Data does not offer a magic bullet for the data integration problem *per se*, but does offer some pragmatic ways in which the problem can be mitigated by leveraging the Web itself. In summary, the goal of the Linked Data best practices is to – whenever and wherever possible – avoid data integration problems in the first place by fostering agreement between publishers on the Web, both on a technical level as well as a social level, so as to reduce the diversity of the data they publish. Where data integration problems do arise, Linked Data offers (semi-)automated techniques to help, and importantly, espouses that the results of integration efforts should be published on the

Web – as links and mappings described using the Semantic Web standards, such as RDFS and OWL – so that they can be reused elsewhere.

In this section, we discuss some of the best practices commonly promoted in the context of Linked Data. Some of these best practices are designed to ensure compliance with the Linked Data principles, while others intend to improve the usability and interoperability of data published following them. All are practically motivated. We divide the discussion of these best practices into four sections: naming, modelling, linking, and vocabularies.

Historical Note 8.2

The Linked Data best practices we describe here originate in a document published by Bizer et al. [60] in 2007, which was superseded by the book of Bizer & Heath [181] published in 2011. Further best practices were later defined in a W3C Working Group Note published in 2014 by Hyland et al. [214]. The following discussion is a synthesis of these contributions, but also varies in some aspects.

8.3.1 Naming

The first and second Linked Data principles state that HTTP IRIs should be used to name entities. We now discuss four best practices that provide further direction on what kinds of HTTP IRIs to use as names for entities:

Mint IRIs in a namespace you control: When creating new IRIs for entities, create them in a namespace for a domain you control. For example, do not create new IRIs like `http://nobel.org/ent/L1901` unless you have access to the `nobel.org` domain to be able to implement suitable dereferencing for such IRIs. (This follows from the Linked Data principles.)

Maintain stable IRIs (aka. use "Cool IRIs" [344]): It is important that Linked Data IRIs remain stable for a long period of time. First, IRIs should be used consistently to refer to the same entity over time; otherwise external data using those IRIs may become incoherent. Second, IRIs should continue to dereference to useful data about that entity over time; otherwise external data using those IRIs will contain dead links. This best practice discourages "recycling" disused IRIs for new entities, as well as creating IRIs in domains that may not be sustainable.

Abstract away implementation deals in IRIs: This best practice discourages minting IRIs with implementation-specific details. For example, parameters like `http://nobel.org/api?type=Lit&year=1901` should be avoided, even if used internally to dynamically generate the required data; instead, concise surface IRIs like `http://nobel.org/Lit1901` should be used (which may, of course, be rewritten or redirect to implementation-specific requests). Aside from conciseness, maintaining the stability of IRIs with implementation-specific details is more difficult: the former IRI would generate the same data if the parameters are swapped, and may be difficult to maintain if the underlying service changes.

Base IRIs on natural keys: Rather than basing IRIs on internal identifiers, it is better – where possible – to use externally recognised or otherwise "natural" keys. For example, rather than using internally generated IDs to identify research papers, a better option might be to base IRIs on Digital Object Identifiers (DOIs). Using natural keys can help external datasets to generate links to a Linked Dataset; for example, any Linked Dataset with IRIs generated algorithmically from DOIs can be linked to by any external data with DOI information using the same algorithm.

Example 8.7

Consider minting the following IRI for a book in Linked Data:

http://book.org/search?page=2&result=4

There are several reasons this might be a bad choice of IRI: if we do not control the book.org domain, we will not be able to implement dereferencing; the IRI may not refer to the same book if the result ordering or results-per-page setting changes; the IRI contains unnecessary implementation details and may break if the underlying service changes; and the IRI uses internal identifiers. Assuming we can register the domain mybook.org, a better IRI (using the slash recipe) for a book would be:

http://mybook.org/book/978-0649030507/

where 978-0649030507 is the International Standard Book Number 13 (ISBN13) code for the book being identified.

Example 8.8

Publishing "Cool IRIs" [344] – i.e., IRIs that do not go offline and do not change their meaning over time – can be challenging for small-scale publishers: domains may go offline, researchers may change institutions, etc. To address this issue, **Persistent Uniform Resource Locator (PURL)** services [359] offer centralised redirection of URLs (or URIs) from their domain, such that the entity is named with a URI on the PURL domain, but the target of the redirect is an external resource and can be changed over time (e.g., if a domain goes offline).

These best practices should be considered as guidelines rather than laws: there may sometimes be good justification for not following (some of) them.

Example 8.9

As an example of a case where not following the guideline of basing IRIs on natural keys is justified: the Linked Data exports of Wikidata [121, 255] use internal identifiers (Q-codes and P-codes) to generate IRIs for entities rather than natural keys. Hence, for example, though Wikidata knows of several identifiers for the book "Slaughterhouse-Five" (including ISBN codes), the IRI used for the book is:

`http://www.wikidata.org/entity/Q265954`

Given the wide variety of entities that Wikidata describes, for many entities there is simply no natural key, other than perhaps using the name with a disambiguation string (as per Wikipedia):

`http://www.wikidata.org/entity/Slaughterhouse-Five_(book)`

But such a scheme presupposes a "preferred" language for generating keys, which Wikidata avoids. Hence, Wikidata chooses to base entity IRIs on internal identifiers, avoiding preference for a language, and keeping identification of different types of entities consistent. On the other hand, Wikidata associates entities with various known identifiers in the data, facilitating linking to and from external datasets.

8.3.2 Modelling

The third Linked Data principle states that useful RDF data should be returned about an entity when its IRI is looked up. We now discuss five best practices that provide additional guidance for modelling RDF in Linked Data:

Minimise use of blank nodes: Blank nodes are locally-scoped terms and cannot be dereferenced or reused in external data. Hence it is recommended to minimise use of blank nodes and prefer IRIs where possible.

Use strings only for strings: String literals in RDF should only be used to represent strings, be they labels, comments or text in natural language, barcode identifiers for products, and so forth. Rather than assigning the string value `"Poetry"` to the property `nv:vocation`, we should assign an IRI like `nv:Poetry` and give it the label `"Poetry"@en`; even if we do not define other data about `nv:Poetry` , having an IRI allows us to add further data in future, and allows for links to/from external datasets.

Minimise use of reification, collections and containers: Where possible, features for modelling reification, collections and containers should be avoided as they complicate using such data. Reification can sometimes be avoided by remodelling the data to view n-ary relations as entities (e.g., using a node in the RDF graph to model a marriage, an event, a prize, a presidency, etc.). Similarly, where order is not important, collections and containers can be avoided by simply giving multiple values for a property.

Comprehensively describe the entities: The Linked Data principles require that "useful data" be returned about an entity when its IRI is looked up. The Linked Data best practices suggest that these "useful data" should generally include the triples from the local dataset where the entity IRI appears as the subject or object, as well as some key triples about the related entities mentioned (for example the types and labels of the other entities mentioned in the aforementioned triples).

Describe the document: Given an entity IRI referring to, say, a person, when that IRI is dereferenced, the RDF document that is returned should not only describe the person, but also the document itself. Key information may include a licence for the document, indicating the terms under which the data it contains may be used; the last time the document was modified, to help clients know, for example, if it should be reindexed in their local cache; the creator(s) of the document; etc.

Example 8.10

Take the IRI we defined in Example 8.7:

http://mybook.org/book/9781439501634/

Assume we implement the slash recipe of dereferencing with content negotiation such that when a client performs a lookup on this IRI requesting RDF in Turtle syntax, they are redirected to a document at:

http://mybook.org/data/9781439501634.ttl

Further assume that based on our initial modelling of RDF data about books and related entities, the above document returns:

```
@prefix mbb: <http://mybook.org/book/> .
@prefix mbd: <http://mybook.org/data/> .
@prefix mbv: <http://mybook.org/voc#> .

mbb:9781439501634 mbv:authors ( "Sully Prudhomme" ) .

_:r1 rdf:subject mbb:9781439501634 ;
    rdf:predicate mbv:rating ;
    rdf:object 3 ;
    mbv:user [ mbv:username "frank" ] .
```

These data contravene a number of best practices defined previously: we use an unnecessary blank node for the user named "frank"; we give the author as a string value; we use unnecessary reification for the review; we do not give the name of the book nor its type; and we do not offer any metadata about the document itself. We could also argue that the use of the RDF collection for authors is unnecessary, depending on how important it is to record the order in which multiple authors appear.

A better RDF model for such data would be, for example:

```
@base <http://mybook.org/data/9781439501634.ttl> .
@prefix mbb: <http://mybook.org/book/> .
@prefix mbp: <http://mybook.org/per/> .
@prefix mbl: <http://mybook.org/lic/> .
@prefix mbr: <http://mybook.org/rev/> .
@prefix mbu: <http://mybook.org/user/> .
@prefix mbv: <http://mybook.org/voc#> .
@prefix xsd: <http://www.w3.org/2001/XMLSchema#> .

<> mbv:licence mbl:CCBYSA2 ;
   mbv:lastModified "2018-08-08T20:20:20Z"^^xsd:dateTimeStamp .

mbb:9781439501634 a mbv:Book ;
  mbv:isbn13 "978-1439501634" ;
  mbv:title "Les Vaines Tendresses"@fr ;
  mbv:authors ( mbp:SPrudhomme ) ;
  mbv:author mbp:SPrudhomme .

mbp:SPrudhomme a mbv:Person ;
  mbv:name "Sully Prudhomme" .

mbr:frank9781439501634 a mbv:Rating ;
  mbv:user mbu:frank ;
  mbv:subject mbb:9781439501634 ;
  mbv:score 3 .

mbu:frank a mbv:User ;
  mbv:username "frank" .
```

This time, the user called "frank" is assigned an IRI, the author is assigned an IRI and a separate label, we represent a review as an entity rather than using reification, we provide at least a label and a type for the book, and we provide some metadata for the document itself (namely a licence and last-modified timestamp). Furthermore, we express authorships in two ways: we use an RDF collection on the mbv:authors property to preserve order in the case of multiple authors, and we use a "flat" mbv:author property that relates the book directly to each author; a client who requires knowledge of the author order can use the former data, while a client who is not interested in author order may find it easier to use the latter data; more generally, the publisher may exercise judgement regarding how author order is handled. Finally note that some basic information – namely types and labels – are defined for some related entities, making the document more self-contained.

As previously argued, there is no unique "correct solution" here: one may consider a variety of alternative RDF modellings, each with their own inherent advantages and disadvantages. But in general, being aware of the Linked Data best practices for modelling – as exemplified above – will result in data that is easier for clients to consume, with more self-contained documents, RDF that is easier to query, offering more possibilities for external datasets to link to the local data, and so forth.

Exercise 8.1

The top four Linked Data documents in Figure 8.2 only include triples where the main entity is in the subject position. How would the document-level links (Figure 8.2(c)) change if triples with the entity in the object position were added to the corresponding documents?

Again, these best practices do not prescribe a unique "correct" way to model RDF in a Linked Data context, but leave room for judgement.

Example 8.11

As an example requiring some judgement for the fourth guideline, assume a large dataset describing people with their citizenships. Returning all triples for an entity denoting a large country – with all its citizens – may create a prohibitively large and wasteful RDF document (e.g., imagine an agent only interested in the capital of the country throwing away the millions of triples for its citizens). In such cases, it would make sense to only include a subset of potentially relevant triples in the corresponding dereferenced document(s). Similar exceptional cases exist for other best practices above. Still, having such best practices in mind when modelling the RDF data should help to produce Linked Data that is easier for clients to process and consume.

8.3.3 Linking

The fourth Linked Data principle requires that links are provided to external datasets by using IRIs that dereference to documents in such datasets. We discuss two guidelines regarding two different ways to represent external links:

Use same-as links for core entities: We refer to the "core entities" as those for which the local dataset currently provides – or intends to provide – data not covered by any one external dataset. In this case, a local dataset should define a local IRI for the entity that dereferences to the relevant data in the local dataset. The local IRI should be linked to (potentially multiple) external IRIs by use of the owl:sameAs property.

Use direct links for edge entities: By "edge entity" we refer to entities for which the local dataset currently only provides – and plans to only provide – minimal information (such as a type and label) that is already covered by an external dataset, other than perhaps a single type of relation involving core entities. In this case, the local dataset need not define a local IRI for the entity and may instead choose to directly use the IRI from the external dataset containing more data about that entity.

The distinction between "core entities" and "edge entities" is rather informal, where judgement is required on the part of the publisher to select the best type of link to use. Conceptually the difference breaks down to the following pragmatic questions: Should clients be able to dereference the IRI for this entity to our local dataset? Will we offer data about this entity that clients will be interested in and is not easily dereferenced elsewhere? If affirmative – or even if in doubt – it is best to consider the entity as a core entity, define a local IRI, and define same-as links to external IRIs.

Example 8.12

Continuing from Example 8.10, let us focus on the following data about the author in the document for mbb:9781439501634:

```
@prefix mbb: <http://mybook.org/book/> .
@prefix mbp: <http://mybook.org/per/> .
@prefix mbv: <http://mybook.org/voc#> .

mbb:9781439501634 mbv:author mbp:SPrudhomme .
  # ...

mbp:SPrudhomme a mbv:Person ;
  mbv:name "Sully Prudhomme" .
```

Further let us assume that currently, when mdp:SPrudhomme is dereferenced, it returns (only) the following data about that entity:

```
@prefix mbp: <http://mybook.org/per/> .
@prefix mbv: <http://mybook.org/voc#> .

mbp:SPrudhomme a mbv:Person ;
  mbv:name "Sully Prudhomme" .
```

Minimal data are provided for mbp:SPrudhomme, and hence it *could* be considered an edge entity: in other words, the dataset is focussed more on books and less on authors. With reference to Figure 8.2, in the document for the book mbb:9781439501634, we could thus instead consider using the external IRI directly as the value for author:

```
@prefix mbb: <http://mybook.org/book/> .
@prefix mbv: <http://mybook.org/voc#> .
@prefix ne: <http://nobel.org/ent/> .

mbb:9781439501634 mbv:author ne:SPrudhomme .
  # ...

ne:SPrudhomme a mbv:Person ;
  mbv:name "Sully Prudhomme" .
```

This is a concise way to provide a link to an external dataset when it is assumed that the local dataset has nothing to add about an entity. Here we choose to still provide a label and a type for ne:SPrudhomme as some minimal data to keep the local document self-contained; of course, more data can be obtained by dereferencing the external IRI.

Now rather assume that in the local dataset we wish to describe the nationality of the authors of books; this is not covered by the data described for ne:SPrudhomme in the external dataset. Hence we might rather consider this entity to be a core entity, where in the document for mbb:9781439501634, we continue to use the local IRI mbp:SPrudhomme as originally presented, and in the local document dereferenced by mbp:SPrudhomme, we may represent the nationality as follows:

```
@prefix mbb: <http://mybook.org/book/> .
@prefix mbp: <http://mybook.org/per/> .
@prefix mbv: <http://mybook.org/voc#> .
@prefix wd: <http://www.wikidata.org/entity/> .

mbp:SPrudhomme a mbv:Person ;
  mbv:name "Sully Prudhomme" ;
  mbv:nationality wd:Q142 .

wd:Q142 a mbv:Country ;
  mbv:name "France"@en .
```

By using a local IRI, remote clients can dereference that IRI to find the additional data provided by the local dataset (in this case, the nationality). Here we choose to consider France to be an edge entity and use the Wikidata IRI to allow a client to dereference further useful data about the country, providing a type and label in the local document.

If we choose to use a local IRI for an entity such that remote clients can dereference our local data, we can still issue same-as links to remote sources. Indeed, where we know of multiple external IRIs referring to the same entity, we can add multiple same-as links; extending the previous document along these lines, in reference to Figure 8.2, we add:

```
@prefix mbb: <http://mybook.org/book/> .
@prefix mbp: <http://mybook.org/per/> .
@prefix mbv: <http://mybook.org/voc#> .
@prefix ne: <http://nobel.org/ent/> .
@prefix owl: <http://www.w3.org/2002/07/owl#> .
@prefix w: <http://wiki.org/entity/> .
@prefix wd: <http://www.wikidata.org/entity/> .

mbp:SPrudhomme a mbv:Person ;
  mbv:name "Sully Prudhomme" ;
  mbv:nationality wd:Q142 ;
  owl:sameAs ne:SPrudhomme , w:RSPrudhomme .

wd:Q142 a mbv:Country ;
  mbv:name "France"@en .
```

A client can now find additional data about the author from two remote sources by dereferencing the external IRIs in the same-as links and applying reasoning with respect to the semantics of owl:sameAs (see Section 5.4.1); the additional data include the following triples:

```
@prefix mbp: <http://mybook.org/per/> .
@prefix ne: <http://nobel.org/ent/> .
@prefix nv: <http://nobel.org/voc.ttl#> .
@prefix owl: <http://www.w3.org/2002/07/owl#> .
@prefix w: <http://wiki.org/entity/> .
@prefix wo: <http://wiki.org/ontology/> .
@prefix xsd: <http://www.w3.org/2001/XMLSchema#> .

mbp:SPrudhomme a nv:Person ;
  nv:vocation nv:Poetry ;
  rdfs:label "René 'Sully' Prudhomme" ;
  wo:yob "1839"^^xsd:gYear ;
  wo:war w:FrancoPrussianWar .

w:RSPrudhomme owl:sameAs ne:SPrudhomme .
ne:SPrudhomme owl:sameAs w:RSPrudhomme .
```

External links of this form are of fundamental importance for Linked Data, and more generally, for building a Web of Data. However, given the symmetric and transitive semantics of owl:sameAs – and the subtleties involved in the question of "are these two entities the same?" – care must be taken when defining owl:sameAs links [166, 204].

Example 8.13

Referring back to Figure 8.1, it may be tempting in a document
like `ex3:CoffeeParfaitRecipe` to define a same-as link of the form:

```
@prefix ...
ex3:Lemon owl:sameAs ex5:Lemon .
```

This would help us understand that the lemon in the recipe is related
to citrus, which may help draw conclusions about the recipe being unsuitable for people with citrus allergies. However, `ex5:Lemon` is defined
to be a species, and it would seem strange to claim that a recipe would
have a species as an ingredient. While there is certainly some relation
between both notions of lemon, specifying a same-as relation is highly
questionable, especially considering further data such as:

```
@prefix ...
ex5:Lemon ex5:evergreen true .
```

Instead of `owl:sameAs`, another relation may be more suitable:

```
@prefix ...
ex3:Lemon ex3:fruitOf ex5:Lemon .
```

We will return to the issue of *how* to generate links later in Section 8.5.

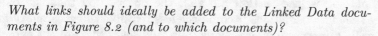

Exercise 8.2

*What links should ideally be added to the Linked Data docu-
ments in Figure 8.2 (and to which documents)?*

8.3.4 Vocabularies

In the context of Linked Data, a vocabulary is a set of terms that can be
used in an RDF document, typically focusing on a particular domain, and
typically defined with the goal to foster reuse across many sources in order
to increase interoperability. Most vocabularies focus on defining a set of class
and property terms. A vocabulary may, however, further define terms to refer
to a bounded set of prominent entities (i.e., individuals) of key importance
to a particular domain; for example, a geographic vocabulary may propose a
shared set of IRI terms for individual continents, countries, cities, etc.

Though not directly relating to a Linked Data principle, Linked Data best practices also offer guidelines relating to the use and definition of vocabularies that aim to reduce data diversity across sources and minimise the data integration challenges faced by clients. The guidelines are as follows:

Use existing vocabulary terms: Rather then reinventing new vocabulary terms over and over again to describe common information across different remote datasets, Linked Data best practices encourage the reuse – insofar as appropriate – of existing vocabulary terms across the Web; this may involve use of terms from multiple vocabularies in different namespaces. Where common vocabularies are reused across different websites, the interoperability of the corresponding data increases considerably.

Define new vocabulary with RDFS/OWL: Where appropriate vocabulary terms do not already exist for describing the intended data, new vocabulary should be defined. Following the Linked Data principles, these vocabulary terms should be dereferenceable IRIs. The dereferenced document should define the semantics of the corresponding terms using the RDFS and OWL standards. Where possible, these definitions should build upon – and thus link to – existing (external) vocabularies.

With respect to the first guideline, a wide variety of vocabularies have been published in the context of Linked Data that can – and should, whenever possible – be reused across the Web [389]. Regarding the second guideline, Bizer & Heath [181] (amongst others [8, 144]) encourage the use of RDFS with "a little OWL", meaning to avoid the more expressive features of OWL – such as class definitions (existentials, intersection, union, cardinalities, etc.) – when defining Linked Data vocabulary. Though again not a rule *per se*, avoiding class definitions can be justified in terms of the cost of reasoning over more expressive ontologies (see Section 5.6.3.1), the observation that the more specific the semantic definitions become the less reusable the vocabulary becomes, as well as anecdotal observations that publishers who are not experts on the semantics of OWL may make mistakes when using more expressive features. Along these lines, Linked Data publishers tend to use RDFS and the equality, class and property axioms of OWL when defining vocabularies, avoiding class definitions [144]. Non-standard profiles of OWL have also been proposed to capture the features most used in such settings [8, 144].

Of course, when vocabularies are published, it is important that they also follow the Linked Data principles, using dereferenceable HTTP IRIs to identify classes, properties and individuals [272], and providing links to other vocabularies [219]. A range of prominent domain-specific vocabularies have been published along these lines in the context of Linked Data. Furthermore, catalogues of vocabularies have been developed to encourage their reuse across the Web [389]. We will discuss such developments in more detail in Section 8.4.3.

Example 8.14

Based on Example 8.10, in an effort to reuse existing vocabulary, we may describe the data about our book as follows:

```
@base <http://mybook.org/data/9781439501634.ttl> .
@prefix bibo: <http://purl.org/ontology/bibo/> .
@prefix cc: <http://creativecommons.org/ns#> .
@prefix dcterms: <http://purl.org/dc/terms/> .
@prefix foaf: <http://xmlns.com/foaf/0.1/> .
@prefix mbb: <http://mybook.org/book/> .
@prefix mbp: <http://mybook.org/per/> .
@prefix mbr: <http://mybook.org/rev/> .
@prefix mbu: <http://mybook.org/user/> .
@prefix mbv: <http://mybook.org/voc#> .
@prefix schema: <http://schema.org/> .
@prefix sioc: <http://rdfs.org/sioc/ns#> .
@prefix xsd: <http://www.w3.org/2001/XMLSchema#> .

<> cc:license <http://creativecommons.org/licenses/by/3.0/> ;
   dcterms:modified "2018-08-08T20:20:20Z"^^xsd:dateTimeStamp .

mbb:9781439501634 a bibo:Book ;
   mbv:isbn13 "978-1439501634" ;
   dcterms:title "Les Vaines Tendresses"@fr ;
   bibo:authorList ( mbp:SPrudhomme ) ;
   schema:author mbp:SPrudhomme ;
   schema:contentRating mbr:frank9781439501634 .

mbp:SPrudhomme a foaf:Person ;
   foaf:name "Sully Prudhomme" .

mbr:frank9781439501634 a schema:Rating ;
   schema:author mbu:frank ;
   schema:bestRating 4 ;
   schema:worstRating 0 ;
   schema:ratingValue 3 .

mbu:frank a sioc:UserAccount ;
   sioc:id "frank" .
```

We now employ classes and properties from six (real-world) external vocabularies used by a variety of sites publishing Linked Data. In order to adopt these external vocabularies, the data model must be adapted accordingly; for example, whereas before the rating pointed to the book, now the book points to its rating with the schema:contentRating property; we also introduce the properties schema:bestRating and schema:worstRating as suggested by the Schema.org vocabulary to allow for normalising different rating schemes across different websites. Generally speaking, by reusing existing vocabularies in this manner,

the Linked Data published by the `mybook.org` domain of the running
example should be more interoperable – more easily integrated – with
other websites publishing Linked Data reusing the same vocabularies.

In using existing vocabularies, it is common for some minor incompatibilities to arise. For example, the documentation for the Schema.org
vocabulary defines that the author of a rating or creative work is expected to be a person or organisation; while this is not a problem for the
book, the review is denoted as being authored by a user, not a person.
When incompatibilities of this form occur, the Linked Data publisher
must exercise judgement as to whether the benefits of increased interoperability associated with vocabulary reuse outweigh the benefits of
defining new vocabulary that avoid such incompatibilities.

However, we still choose to define a new property `mbv:isbn13`: while
there exists a term `bibo:isbn13`, the property is not defined to be
inverse-functional since this would break OWL 2 DL compliance (which
does not allow inverse-functional datatype properties). On the other
hand, in our case, we are willing to trade OWL 2 DL compliance against
having a useful key for integrating data on books. Hence in the `mbv:`
namespace, we should define this new property that we have created.

```
@base <http://mybook.org/voc.ttl> .
@prefix bibo: <http://purl.org/ontology/bibo/> .
@prefix mbv:  <http://mybook.org/voc#> .
@prefix owl:  <http://www.w3.org/2002/07/owl#> .
@prefix rdfs: <http://www.w3.org/2000/01/rdf-schema#> .
@prefix xsd:  <http://www.w3.org/2001/XMLSchema#>.

# ...
mbv:isbn13 a owl:DatatypeProperty , owl:InverseFunctionalProperty ;
    rdfs:label "ISBN13"@en , "Autores"@es ;
    rdfs:comment "International Standard Book Number 13"@en ,
        "Número Estándar Internacional de Libros"@es ;
    rdfs:domain bibo:Book ;
    rdfs:range xsd:string ;
    rdfs:subPropertyOf bibo:isbn13 .
```

This provides some human-readable annotations for the term in English
and Spanish, as well as defining the types that should be inferred for
the subject and object. This definition further builds upon the Bibliographic Ontology (`bibo`) by defining the domain of the property to
be a class of that ontology. Furthermore, we define the property to be
a specialisation of the external (non-inverse-functional) `bibo:isbn13`
property. The stronger semantics of the `mbv:isbn13` property may now
enable the inference of new `owl:sameAs` relations between books, but
may also limit reuse of the property; for example, we could no longer
use the property directly on different physical copies of the same book.

Deciding when to reuse existing vocabulary versus defining new vocabulary, how to define new vocabulary, how best to extend existing vocabularies, how specific to make the semantic definitions of vocabulary – such questions are often the topic of debate, where finding a good solution requires experience, domain expertise, as well as compromise. Important vocabularies are thus often defined as part of a community or standardisation effort. In some cases, competing vocabularies may emerge that vie for position as the *de facto* standard. Mappings in RDFS/OWL can be used to bridge such vocabularies. We will discuss selected Linked Data vocabularies – and ways of finding existing vocabulary terms for reuse and extension – later in Section 8.4.3.

Discussion 8.2

FRANK: What is the difference between a vocabulary and an ontology? It seems like you use both almost interchangeably.

AIDAN: The precise meaning of both changes from author to author, but I prefer the idea of defining a vocabulary as a set of terms, and an ontology as potentially defining the semantics of the vocabulary in RDFS/OWL. Other authors may define a vocabulary as an ontology defining "lightweight semantics", meaning that more expressive features of OWL like class definitions are avoided.

JULIE: When extending existing vocabularies, what's to stop someone from breaking the existing vocabularies? What happens if someone states definitions that make an external class unsatisfiable or even leads to inconsistencies? Or what if someone defines some nonsense like that the class sioc:User is the sub-class of a class ex:InternetTroll that they invent? Wouldn't that cause all sorts of issues in legacy data using these existing vocabularies?

AIDAN: Naively, yes. But a software agent consuming Linked Data should not blindly trust all the data it finds – particularly when the agent plans to perform reasoning over RDFS/OWL axioms taken from the Web. Ideally such an agent will rather pay careful attention to the source of data on the Web, and proceed cautiously. There have been a number of proposals – such as "authoritative reasoning" or "quarantined reasoning" – for applying RDFS/OWL inferencing over Linked Data on the Web in a cautious manner; such methods only consider axioms from sources that are connected via links to a particular vocabulary during the reasoning process [322]. Taking your example, if you define a sub-class axiom to imply that all instances of sioc:User are instances of ex:InternetTroll, these reasoning methods will block that axiom unless it is published in or linked to by the document to which the IRI sioc:User dereferences. These reasoning methods have been demonstrated to work

over millions of Linked Data documents crawled from hundreds of
websites without the world imploding [322].

ANNA: What about the OWL 2 DL restrictions to maintain decidability? Are these followed by Linked Data vocabularies?

AIDAN: Some vocabularies follow OWL 2 DL restrictions, while others do not. For example, some vocabularies wish to define datatype
properties (e.g., `bibo:isbn`) as being inverse-functional (key) properties, which is not allowed in OWL 2 DL, but is supported by
rulesets like OWL 2 RL/RDF, and can be very useful for integrating Linked Data from multiple sites (e.g., automatically integrating
data about books from different websites based on them having
the same ISBN keys). In other cases, the definition of Linked Data
vocabularies may not satisfy OWL 2 DL restrictions for purely syntactic reasons, like not explicitly declaring datatype/object properties [263]. As for reasoning, typically some lightweight rule-based
style of reasoning is considered that can be applied over arbitrary
RDF graphs, but only captures a fragment of the full semantics of
OWL: incompleteness is more of an issue than undecidability [322].
In cases where OWL 2 DL-style reasoning (with respect to the Direct Semantics) is desired, non-compliant vocabulary definitions can
be approximated (e.g., dropping or replacing axioms that break restrictions) and/or patched (e.g., adding missing declarations) [263].

8.4 Linking Open Data

With the Linked Data principles in place and the best practices being defined, the Linked Data community began to think about how to realise their
vision of a Web of Data, and in particular, what concrete datasets could be
published following the Linked Data methodology. In parallel, the Open Data
community was growing in momentum – particularly in the context of science
and government – and was looking for methodologies on how to publish and
share data on the Web. The obvious synergy between both movements gave
rise to the creation, in March 2007, of a W3C Community Project called "Interlinking Open Data" – later shortened to the "Linking Open Data" project.
The motivating goals of this community project were twofold [63, 181]:

1. to bootstrap the Web of Data by creating and publishing open datasets
   following the Linked Data methodology; (and in so doing ...)
2. to introduce the benefits of publishing data under the Linked Data
   methodology to the broader Open Data community.

The Linking Open Data community would oversee a number of key developments leading to the first systematic realisation of a Web of Data. This

section provides an overview of these developments, where we first discuss the "Five-Star Open Data" scheme, which summarises the benefits of publishing Open Data as Linked Data. We then discuss some of the datasets that have been published as Linked Data, followed by a discussion of some of the key vocabularies that have been proposed in a Linked Data context.

8.4.1 Five-Star Open Data

The core message of the Linked Data community is, in essence, a bottom-up approach to bootstrapping the Web of Data that advocates starting with data and later (incrementally) adding semantics and links. This bottom-up philosophy is epitomised by the "Five-Star Open Data" scheme [46]:

⋆	PUBLISH DATA ON THE WEB UNDER AN OPEN LICENCE
⋆ ⋆	PUBLISH STRUCTURED DATA
⋆ ⋆ ⋆	USE NON-PROPRIETARY FORMATS
⋆ ⋆ ⋆ ⋆	USE IRIs TO IDENTIFY THINGS
⋆ ⋆ ⋆ ⋆ ⋆	LINK YOUR DATA TO OTHER DATA

—paraphrased from Berners-Lee [46]

Here, each additional star is promoted as increasing the potential reusability and interoperability of Open Data published on the Web.

The first star indicates that for data to be Open Data, it must be associated with an "open licence" that allows anyone to access, use and share the data – under at most an attribution and/or share-alike clause.[1]

Second, consider publishing Open Data as tables that are scanned and uploaded as PDFs; while such data satisfy the criterion of the first star, clearly the reusability of such data is harmed by the image format in which they are published. The second star of Open Data thus recommends that the data be published in a structured, machine-readable format that can be readily parsed and processed by clients interested in reusing the data.

Third, consider publishing Open Data as tables in Microsoft Excel spreadsheets; while such data satisfy the criteria of the first and second star, proprietary software may be required to (best) read the data, hindering reuse. The third star thus recommends that data be published in non-proprietary formats that are not tied to some specialised (commercial) software.

Fourth, consider publishing Open Data as CSV files in plain text; such data would satisfy the criteria for the first, second and third stars; however, assume that a table features a value "Santiago" in a cell. How can we know which Santiago is being referred to? Also, how can we link to the data specifically about Santiago from other locations on the Web? The fourth star thus

---

[1] See http://opendefinition.org/

recommends to use IRIs to identify entities described by Open Data, enabling the global identification and linking of entities across the Web.

Fifth, consider publishing Open Data as RDF files with dereferenceable IRIs that can be linked to over the Web; such data would satisfy the criteria for the first, second, third and fourth stars. However, even with a local IRI for an entity like Santiago, a client may still not know which Santiago is being referred to, making it difficult to integrate the data with other external datasets. If the data instead offered links to external datasets – such as offering a same-as link to wd:Q2887, the Wikidata IRI for Santiago de Chile, describing the country the city is in, its population, etc. – clients would have more context to determine which Santiago is being referred to, and could locate and integrate further data relating to the entities described.

Five Star Open Data then refers to data that are published on the Web in a manner that satisfies all five stars. The scheme aims to be inclusive: while even One Star Open Data is worth publishing, each star adds value to the data. While the fourth and fifth stars do not explicitly reference the use of RDF and Linked Data principles, their use is often assumed as they not only meet the necessary requirements, but are based on Web standards: notably, the fourth star is the first Linked Data principle, the fifth star is the fourth Linked Data principle, while the Linked Data best practices discussed previously offer guidance on how best to achieve these latter two stars.

8.4.2 Linked Open Datasets

The LOD project initially found traction through the efforts of academics and developers in research labs converting existing data – most prominently, the DBpedia project [247] extracting RDF data from Wikipedia – later spreading to companies like the BBC[2], Thompson Reuters[3], the New York Times[4], and various governmental agencies, resulting in the first systematic instantiation of a Web of Data, with data described using the Semantic Web standards and published according to the Linked Data principles and best practices.

As more and more Linked Open Datasets were announced, researchers sought a way to gain an overview of the developments. This led to the creation of the Linked Open Data Cloud; Figure 8.7 shows the most recent version available at the time of writing.[5] Each bubble refers to a different dataset, while each edge refers to links from one dataset to another. The diagram shown has 1,239 nodes referring to datasets with 16,147 edges denoting links

---

[2] https://www.bbc.co.uk/ontologies

[3] http://www.opencalais.com/

[4] https://developer.nytimes.com/

[5] Further detail on the cloud – including the most recent version – can be found at https://lod-cloud.net/.

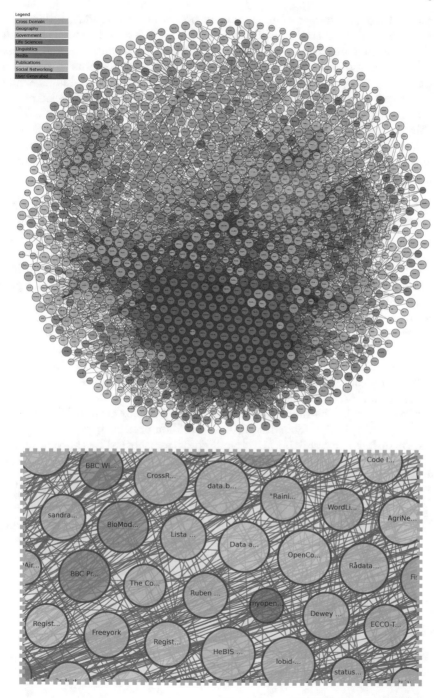

From https://lod-cloud.net/ ©①②

Fig. 8.7 Linking Open Data (LOD) cloud from March 2019 with zoomed-in sample

between them. Each dataset may contain potentially thousands, millions or even billions of RDF triples, while each edge may refer to thousands or even millions of links between datasets. Given the number of datasets and edges, we include a zoomed-in sample of the cloud. Different domains of data are captured by different colours: some datasets cover a number of domains, while others focus on a specific domain. We now discuss some prominent examples of both cross-domain and domain-specific Linked Open Datasets.

Many (but not all) of the cross-domain Linked Open Datasets are related in some way to Wikipedia, either having been extracted from Wikipedia, or having links to/from Wikipedia. The following are some of the key cross-domain Linked Open Datasets to be found in the LOD Cloud:

DBpedia [247] was one of the original Linked Open Datasets (and is thus traditionally depicted at the centre of the LOD cloud). The dataset is extracted from multiple language versions of Wikipedia using a variety of techniques. Data is mostly extracted from info-boxes,[6] but also from article categories, disambiguation links, etc. DBpedia v. 2016-10 describes 6.6 million entities, with a total of 13 billion triples (of which, for example, 1.7 billion are extracted from English Wikipedia).

Freebase [67] was a collaboratively edited dataset where users could directly contribute and curate structured data. The dataset contained both legacy data harvested from external sources, as well as user-contributed data. Linked Data exports were provided for accessing and linking the data. In 2010, Freebase was acquired by Google, and in 2014, Google announced it would shut down Freebase and support migration of data to the Wikidata project [377]. The final read-only version of Freebase from March 2015 contained 3 billion facts describing 50 million entities [377].

Wikidata [397] is a collaboratively-edited dataset hosted by the Wikimedia foundation (which hosts projects such as Wikipedia and Wikimedia). The dataset consists of imports from other datasets (such as Freebase), as well as direct user contributions. At the time of writing (May 2020), Wikidata contained over 1 billion statements describing 84 million entities; furthermore, more than 27 thousand users were active in the previous 30 days. Wikidata offers Linked Data exports and SPARQL query services for accessing, querying and linking to the data [121, 255].

YAGO [193] (or Yet Another Great Ontology) is a dataset extracted from Wikipedia, WordNet and GeoNames. In contrast to DBpedia, YAGO places more emphasis on quality over completeness, aiming for a smaller but cleaner dataset, with rich taxonomic relations; YAGO further features, for example, temporal and spatial annotations on triples that contextualise the validity of the claims they represent. As of 2016, YAGO was reported to have 1.2 billion triples describing 16.9 million entities [331].

---

[6] Info-boxes are the panes on the right-hand side of Wikipedia articles providing a summary of key factual data for an entity.

Aside from these cross-domain datasets, there are also a variety of Linked Open Datasets capturing data from specific domains; we describe a selection of some prominent datasets that happen to have an associated publication such that the reader can find more details in the literature:

Biblioteca Nacional de España (CULTURAL) [394] publishes information about the catalogue of the *Biblioteca Nacional de España* (Spanish National Library) as Linked Data, including works, authorities, etc.

Bio2RDF (LIFE SCIENCES) [43, 117] is a collection of over thirty different datasets from the Life Sciences domain (e.g., DrugBank, KEGG, MeSH, NCBI Gene, Pubmed) published as Linked Data.

IMGpedia (MULTIMEDIA) [127] extracts and publishes Linked Data describing the images hosted on the Wikimedia Commons; visual similarity relations between images are also computed and published.

Linked Open Numbers (MATHEMATICS) [398] describes the positive integers as Linked Data, including the predecessor and successor relation, primality, names in various languages, and so forth.

LinkedGeoData (GEOGRAPHICAL) [368] publishes geographical data about places, streets, etc., extracted primarily from the OpenStreetMaps website, but also including data from GADM and Natural Earth.

LinkedMDB (MOVIES) [177] is a dataset describing 38 thousand movies as Linked Data, drawing together a number of sources, including DBpedia, Freebase, OMDB, and the Stanford Movie Database.

LinkedSDMX (GEOPOLITICAL) [86] publishes statistical Linked Data about various geopolitical/economic indicators, integrating data from sources such as the UN, the IMF, the OECD, Eurostat, etc.

UniProtKB (LIFE SCIENCES) [78] publishes Linked Data about proteins and their functions derived from a variety of genome sequencing initiatives, annotated with information extracted from PubMed literature.

Again, as one may appreciate from Figure 8.7, here we have barely scratched the surface of the Linked Open Datasets that have been announced; furthermore, by limiting ourselves to only consider datasets for which we could find an associated publication in the literature (in English), we miss some other prominent datasets, such as from the *Bibliothèque nationale de France* (National Library of France; CULTURAL)[7], DBtune (MUSIC)[8], Geonames (GEOGRAPHICAL)[9], the Getty (CULTURAL)[10], the Library of Congress (CULTURAL)[11], PokéPédia (POKÉMON)[12], and many more besides.

---

[7] http://data.bnf.fr/en/about

[8] http://dbtune.org/

[9] http://www.geonames.org/ontology/documentation.html

[10] http://www.getty.edu/research/tools/vocabularies/lod/

[11] https://id.loc.gov/

[12] https://www.pokepedia.fr/

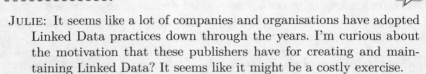

Discussion 8.3

JULIE: It seems like a lot of companies and organisations have adopted
Linked Data practices down through the years. I'm curious about
the motivation that these publishers have for creating and maintaining Linked Data? It seems like it might be a costly exercise.

AIDAN: The motivations are as varied as the datasets themselves. Libraries are interested in Linked Data since they wish, for example,
to build and share taxonomies (at which they are expert), interlink
their metadata with other libraries, allow users to find and query
their catalogue, etc. Governmental organisations are motivated to
publish Linked Data by the growing call for transparency, and by
the growing realisation that data are a public asset. In the sciences,
particularly those disciplines that are heavy on informatics (As-
troinformatics, Bioinformatics, etc.), huge amounts of dynamic data
are being collected by various research teams and institutes, where
Linked Data offers a way to share and interlink datasets, to coor-
dinate vocabularies, etc., without having to centralise everything.
Computer Science researchers are often motivated to publish Linked
Data as the datasets can (and have) become important resources
for their community, and related communities, used for evaluation
purposes, as background sources of knowledge, etc. Other datasets,
like Freebase, PokéPédia or Wikipedia, are community driven: users
are motivated by the goal of publishing cool data about their interests. As for costs, initially they can be high – especially in terms
of acquiring human know-how – but they have been reducing more
and more over time as tools and documentation improve.

JULIE: What about applications?

AIDAN: That's perhaps a more difficult question. As mentioned before,
Linked Datasets like DBpedia, Freebase and YAGO have been used
in a wide variety of research applications, including for Information
Extraction, Machine Learning, Question Answering, etc.; to name
one prominent example that combines these areas, the IBM Watson
system that beat top human contestants in the U.S. game-show
"Jeopardy" made use of such datasets [221]. On the other hand,
Wikidata is used for a variety of applications in Wikipedia, such as
improving how info-boxes are maintained across different languages,
performing quality checks, and so forth (see Section 2.3.1); Wikidata
is also used for Google's Knowledge Graph [377], and also Apple's
Siri service [255]. Though Linked Data success stories in their own
right, these aforementioned applications have involved hand-picked
Linked Open Datasets. More broadly, we have yet to see end-users
applications that *discover* Linked Open Datasets on-the-fly.

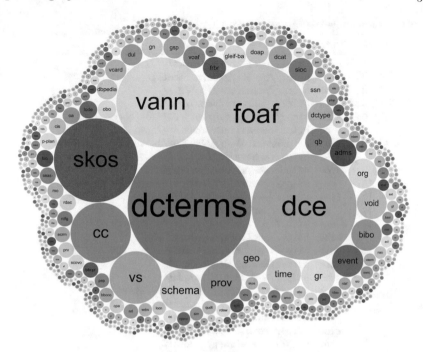

Fig. 8.8 Linked Open Vocabularies (LOV) overview from May 2020

8.4.3 Linked Open Vocabularies

Linked Data best practices emphasise the reuse of vocabularies by different publishers across the Web, where each vocabulary provides a set of classes and properties used to describe a given domain, and where the semantics of those classes and properties are defined using the RDFS and OWL standards. The goal of such reuse is to make data integration more straightforward by reducing diversity in how things are described. Along these lines, a number of lightweight vocabularies and ontologies have become de facto standards down through the years for publishing RDF in given domains [181, 389].

The Linked Open Vocabularies (LOV) service [389] collects vocabularies and provides a search and query service to help publishers find terms that they can reuse. Figure 8.8 shows an overview of 703 vocabularies indexed by the LOV system at the time of writing, where each bubble represents a vocabulary, and the size of the bubble is determined by the level of reuse of the vocabulary (the RDF, RDFS and OWL vocabularies are deliberately excluded). In Table 8.2, we provide the namespaces for the top 25 most reused vocabularies according to LOV; we now briefly describe these vocabularies.

Table 8.2 Namespaces of top 25 most reused vocabularies from LOV

№	Prefix	Namespace
1	dcterms:	http://purl.org/dc/terms/
2	dce:	http://purl.org/dc/elements/1.1/
3	foaf:	http://xmlns.com/foaf/0.1/
4	vann:	http://purl.org/vocab/vann/
5	skos:	http://www.w3.org/2004/02/skos/core#
6	cc:	http://creativecommons.org/ns#
7	vs:	http://www.w3.org/2003/06/sw-vocab-status/ns#
8	schema:	http://schema.org/
9	prov:	http://www.w3.org/ns/prov#
10	geo:	http://www.w3.org/2003/01/geo/wgs84_pos#
11	time:	http://www.w3.org/2006/time#
12	gr:	http://purl.org/goodrelations/v1#
13	event:	http://purl.org/NET/c4dm/event.owl#
14	bibo:	http://purl.org/ontology/bibo/
15	void:	http://rdfs.org/ns/void#
16	org:	http://www.w3.org/ns/org#
17	adms:	http://www.w3.org/ns/adms#
18	qb:	http://purl.org/linked-data/cube#
19	dctype:	http://purl.org/dc/dcmitype/
20	ssn:	http://www.w3.org/ns/ssn/
21	sioc:	http://rdfs.org/sioc/ns#
22	dcat:	http://www.w3.org/ns/dcat#
23	doap:	http://usefulinc.com/ns/doap#
24	gleif:	https://www.gleif.org/ontology/Base/
25	frbr:	http://purl.org/vocab/frbr/core#

dcterms (Dublin Core Terms): provides terms for describing metadata about information resources (documents), such as their creators, licences, dates, formats, subjects, references, versions, etc.

dce (Dublin Core Elements): the predecessor of the Dublin Core Terms vocabulary; provides basic properties for describing information resources, such as their creators, dates, formats, subjects, etc.

foaf (Friend Of A Friend): provides terms for describing people and organisations, documents associated with them, their online presence, as well as social connections between people.

vann (Vocabulary Annotation): provides properties for describing vocabularies and their terms, including changes between versions, example uses of terms, preferred prefixes for vocabularies, etc.

skos (Simple Knowledge Organization System): a W3C recommended vocabulary [273] for describing concept schemes – such as thesauri or taxonomies – including hierarchical relations, matching relations, etc.

cc (Creative Commons): a vocabulary for assigning licences to resources (such as documents), or for defining the conditions associated with licences, including their permissions, requirements and prohibitions.

vs (Vocab Status): offers properties for describing the status of a particular vocabulary term (e.g., `stable`, `unstable`), as well as for offering links to human-readable documentation about the term.

schema (Schema.org): a broad vocabulary proposed by Google, Microsoft, Yahoo and Yandex; most popularly used for embedding data in webpages describing entities (e.g., products, movies, recipes, etc.).

prov (PROV Ontology): a W3C recommended vocabulary [246] for describing the provenance of some resource, including the activities and agents involved, related resources from which it was derived, etc.

geo (WGS84 Geo Positioning): provides terms for specifying geographical points in terms of latitude, longitude, altitude, and for stating the geographical location of spatial entities using such points.

time (OWL Time): an OWL ontology defining various temporal notions, such as the days of the week, months, instants, durations, intervals, timezones, as well as a variety of properties for temporal relations.

gr (GoodRelations): a vocabulary focussed on e-commerce, with terms for describing products, offerings, stores, companies, locations, etc.; most often used to embed data in webpages about products.

event (Event Ontology): provides terms for describing events, which may be associated with a place, a time, an agent, a factor (a passive object involved), a product (what resulted), as well as sub-events.

bibo (Bibliographic Ontology): provides a set of classes for various types of works: books, code, emails, bills (of law), scientific papers, etc.; and a set of properties for describing them: identifiers, editions, issues, etc.

void (Vocabulary of Interlinked Datasets): can be used to describe datasets, including the graphs and partitions they consist of; the number of triples, properties and classes they contain; the links provided; etc.

org (Organisation Ontology): allows for describing organisational structures, including members, sub-organisations, units, sites, collaborations, purposes, roles, salaries, and more besides.

adms (Asset Description Metadata Schema): provides vocabulary for defining metadata assets (vocabularies, dictionaries, taxonomies, etc.), their repositories and distributions, representation, status, versions, etc.

qb (Data Cube Vocabulary): provides vocabulary for representing data cubes – multi-dimensional arrays of typically statistical data – including observations, dimensions, slices, attributes, measures, etc.

dctype (DCMI Type Vocabulary): defines a set of classes for entities that are commonly described by Dublin Core terms, including datasets, events, images, services, software, sounds, etc., as well as collections thereof.

ssn (Semantic Sensor Network Ontology): defines terms relating to sensor networks, including sensors, actuators, platforms, procedures, samples, deployments, inputs, outputs, results, stimuli, etc.

sioc (Semantically Interlinked Online Communities): offers terms for describing the presence and activities of users within various online communities, including user accounts, sites, threads, posts, replies, etc.

dcat (Data Catalog Vocabulary): a W3C recommended vocabulary [6] for describing data catalogues, the resources they contain, how they are distributed, how they are hosted, their relations and themes, etc.

doap (Description Of A Project): provides vocabulary for describing projects – primarily software projects – including repositories, homepages, mailing lists, forums, licences, programming languages, etc.

gleif (Global Legal Entity Identifier Foundation Base Ontology): publishes a base set of terms for describing legal entities, their legal relationships, their addresses, legal jurisdictions, etc.

frbr (Functional Requirements for Bibliographic Records): provides terms that are traditionally used for describing library catalogues, founded on works, expressions, manifestations and items (amongst other concepts).

As can again be seen from Figure 8.8, we have barely scratched the surface of the vocabularies that are available for reuse when publishing Linked Data. These vocabularies are defined using the RDFS/OWL standards, ranging from only RDFS definitions (e.g., dce), through RDFS with a "little OWL" (e.g., foaf), to RDFS plus more expressive features of OWL (e.g., time). As per the best practices defined in Section 8.3.4, many of the aforementioned vocabularies build on top of each other, defining relations in RDFS/OWL to terms in other vocabularies; furthermore, Linked Data publishers are encouraged to "cherry-pick" relevant terms from different vocabularies.

> **Project 8.1**
>
> *Using the LOV system (available at* http://lov.linkeddata.es*), find existing vocabulary terms that could be (re)used for representing the data in each of the Linked Data documents shown in Figure 8.1.*

8.5 Publishing Linked Data

Publishing Linked Data involves two core milestones: representing and serving data as RDF, and achieving links to/from external datasets.

The bulk of legacy data on the Web is not represented as RDF, where Linked Data is often generated from legacy data sources. Such data may use a variety of formats, from structured to unstructured, and anything in between. Though the techniques for publishing Linked Data from legacy sources are thus (necessarily) diverse, we can identify two conceptual scenarios: *conversion*, where legacy data have sufficient structure to be directly represented as the intended RDF with an appropriate mapping (often the case for relational data, XML, JSON, etc.); and *extraction*, where additional structure must be distilled from the legacy data in order to achieve the intended RDF (often the case for text, HTML, wikis, etc.). Furthermore, we identify two high-level options for conversion and/or extraction: *offline*, where the data are represented and stored in bulk as RDF in order to be served as Linked Data; and *online*, where legacy data are rather stored in their original format and where Linked Data documents are generated and served on demand over those data. From this perspective, both *conversion* vs. *extraction* and *offline* vs. *online* are viewed as dimensions rather than dichotomies: in practice, individual techniques may blur these conceptual distinctions, while pipelines for publishing Linked Data may involve both conversion and extraction of RDF data from legacy sources using both offline and online techniques.

Thereafter, legacy data – or even RDF data created from scratch – will rarely contain links to external datasets. Techniques are thus required to implement the fourth Linked Data principle: include links by using IRIs that dereference to remote documents. Generating links to remote sources per the guidelines outlined in Section 8.3.3 – particularly same-as links – can be challenging, but tools are available to aid publishers with this key task.

In this section, we discuss techniques for publishing Linked Data from legacy sources. We will follow a running example based on a movie portal.

Example 8.15

Anna gets a job at a major search engine, where each Thursday she's asked to work on a side project of her choosing. After some weeks of indecision, as a movie buff, she realises that in trying to choose the right movie at the right cinema, she has to visit the webpages of various local cinemas, where each offers different types of information, but none offer much background information about the movies themselves in terms of directors, actors, prizes, external ratings, etc. For this, she needs to visit various other websites and draw together information by hand.

Hence she starts to think about spending her Thursdays building a movie portal where users can search and filter movies in nearby cinemas based on times, directors, actors, ratings, etc., comparing times, distances and prices across cinemas. Furthermore, registered users can rate movies and receive recommendations and (opt-in) alerts for movies that will interest them, such as those by directors whose movies they have rated highly before, those that have been given a high rating by users to whom they are connected, and so forth. They may also, Anna is thinking, connect with nearby users who have similar tastes and maybe even organise to see a movie together if they so wish.

Looking to source some data about movies, Anna finds Linked Datasets like DBpedia, LinkedMDB and Wikidata with lots of rich, relevant info with which she can start to put together her movie portal. What she is missing now are data about movies showing in local cinemas. She starts by trying to scrape some data from the webpages of the cinemas, but each cinema uses a different format, she is limited in what data she can view, and data are changing all the time. Frustrated with this approach, she figures that since she's working for a major search engine, maybe they can organise something with a couple of large cinema chains in the area to have access to their database. Her boss tells her no, that the company should not give preferential treatment to certain cinemas, but maybe they could organise something so she could write a post on the company blog defining a data format in which *any* cinema could publish the data she needs on the Web in the format she wants; then to get the ball rolling, they could convince some of the major chains that if they publish data in the desired format, that the portal will be sure to draw more customers to (their) cinemas, with other independent cinemas likely to follow suit.

She thinks about what format of data she would like the cinemas to publish. Ideally the data would be published following some Web standards and be easy to integrate with the other sources she has. Also it should be extensible, in case she thinks other types of data might be useful in future. Ideally there would be a language and some tools available for querying the data. Also, she'd like to have a way to link back to the data sources so users can see from where the information is sourced, and she'd like a way to update dynamic parts of the data on the fly (rather than having to download a dump each time). And of course, all of this would be purely academic without techniques and tools to help the cinemas publish the data in the format she wants.

We begin this section by discussing the generation of RDF from legacy data in a variety of common formats. Later we discuss methods by which RDF content can be linked with other datasets and hosted on the Web.

8.5.1 Relational Data to RDF (RDB2RDF)

Many websites are currently backed by a relational database that manages the tabular data necessarily for dynamically generating webpages. The content of these databases is often only available to the public in an indirect and partial manner: through HTML pages that encode the results of a query expressible through the HTML-based forms of the website. At the level of the relational database, a user request is typically translated into an SQL query with a fixed structure that may fill in some criteria from the user's request. Direct querying of the underlying database itself is typically not permitted.

Example 8.16

Let us consider the following relational data from a cinema website, with information about the movies, times, screens, prices, etc.:

Movie

id	title	debut	until	mpaa	duration	director
M10001	Peterloo	2018-11-02	2018-11-27		PT2H34M	Mike Leigh
M10002	Overlord	2018-11-09	2018-12-04	R	PT1H48M	Julius Avery
M10003	Widows	2018-11-16		R	PT2H09M	Steve McQueen

Show

M_id	time	T_id	priceA	priceB
M10001	2018-11-22 14:00:00	A	7.00	5.00
M10002	2018-11-22 15:50:00	C	7.00	5.00
M10002	2018-11-22 20:50:00	C	8.00	5.50
M10003	2018-11-22 17:30:00	A	7.00	5.00
M10003	2018-11-22 20:50:00	B	8.00	5.50

Theatre

id	capacity
A	200
B	600
C	320
D	180

Here we see three tables (aka. relations): **Movie**, **Show** and **Theatre**. The primary keys are shown underlined; these are columns for which each row takes a unique (tuple) of values, thus uniquely identifying the row. Observe that in the case of **Show**, the primary key is composed of two columns indicating the movie and time. Foreign keys are shown with **X-col**, where **X** is the initial of a table and **col** is the column (primary key) of that table; values for a foreign key must exist in the target table. Incomplete data may be represented with a NULL (shown as a blank value); for example, since the movie entitled Widows was recently released, there is no fixed date yet for when it will stop showing.

The cinema website may offer a webpage listing today's shows. This webpage may be generated, for example, by taking the times and prices from the **Show** table filtered for today's date; and with a join on M.id, adding the movie title, advisory rating and duration from the **Movie** table. In SQL, such a query could be written as follows:

```
SELECT time, priceA, priceB, title, mpaa, duration
FROM Show
  JOIN Movie ON
    id = M_id
      AND time < NOW() + INTERVAL '1 day'
      AND time >= NOW();
```

(The conditions using NOW() are based on Postgres syntax.)

The website might offer functionality to find particular movies, such as, for example, movies showing within a certain time interval on a certain date with a particular advisory rating and duration limit. The query to generate results depends on the criteria specified by the user, which may involve a calendar interface for selecting the date and time interval, a dropdown box of options for advisory rating, and a slider bar for limiting duration. The corresponding query for generating the resulting webpage would be analogous to the following:

```
SELECT time, priceA, priceB, title, mpaa, duration
FROM Show
  JOIN Movie ON
    id = M_id
      AND time < ?
      AND time >= ?
      AND mpaa = ?
      AND duration < ?
```

Here each ? is a parameter that will be replaced by the corresponding user input; the overall query may even be precompiled by the database, allowing all queries of this type to be executed the same way, simply filling in the varying user criteria for each request.

In each case, the user is limited in terms of what sorts of queries the webpage allows them to express: they do not have access to the raw data in the underlying database and cannot write custom queries. Furthermore, these data cannot be readily combined with external sources on the Web, such as to generate and compare show times of all local cinemas with one request, filter movies by a list of preferred directors, search rating information from other websites, and so forth. For now, however, the cinema doesn't really care; their website offers the basics and is about as good as those of the competing cinemas in the area.

Discussion 8.4

FRANK: How does this previous example relate to the notion of the "Deep Web" discussed in the introduction of the book?

AIDAN: The page showing today's movies is probably part of the "Surface Web": per the first query, it does not require specific user criteria to generate, and probably it could be accessed by following a link such as Showing Today on the cinema website. However, the results page for the custom search – implemented with the second query – would generally form part of the "Deep Web"; it is not accessible by simply clicking links, where generating queries to scrape all possible results may not be feasible given the number of ways in which the various movie criteria may be combined.

In order to reduce the "barriers to entry" associated with publishing Linked Data, a natural direction is to explore techniques for converting relational data to RDF, which would assist publishers in generating Linked Data exports for the innumerable websites that store their content in relational databases, and thus potentially increase adoption of the Linked Data principles and best practices on the Web. Given that relational databases are inherently structured, a mapping is required from the legacy structure (relations/tabular data) to the target structure (RDF/graph data). Though a general purpose mapping can be defined and automatically applied for any relational database schema, better results can often be achieved through custom mappings that are designed for a particular schema and desired output.

Along these lines, the **Relational Databases to RDF (RDB2RDF)** suite of standards [14, 106] was recommended by the W3C for converting relational data to RDF. The two main standards are the **Direct Mapping** that allows fully automatic conversion of relational data to RDF [14], and the **RDB to RDF Mapping Language (R2RML)** language that allows for specifying custom mappings from relational data to RDF [106]. We now discuss these two standards in turn, starting with the Direct Mapping.

Historical Note 8.3

Works on mapping relational databases to RDF have a long history in the literature, most notably works relating to D2R(Q) [59]. Such works eventually led to the recommendation by the W3C, in 2012, of the two RDB2RDF standards discussed herein, namely the Direct Mapping standard [14] and the R2RML standard [106].

8.5.1.1 Direct Mapping

Given a relational database and a base IRI (used for naming) as input, the Direct Mapping provides a fully automatic way to extract RDF from the tables. The core idea is that a triple is generated for each cell of the table, where the subject is generated from the primary key of the row, the predicate from the name of the column of the row, and the object from the cell value itself. The type of object generated from a cell is decided from the type of the column in the relational schema, where for example numeric columns in a table will result in numeric literal values in the RDF graph. Additionally, each subject generated from a table is assigned a type generated from the table name. Finally, a mechanism is provided for generating links from the entities in one table to another based on foreign keys. Where a table cell is found to have a NULL (blank) value, the corresponding triple is omitted.

Example 8.17

Given the tables in Example 8.16 and the (fictional) IRI
`http://mov.ie/db/`, the following RDF data will be generated by the
Direct Mapping from the first rows of each table:

```
@base <http://mov.ie/db/> .
@prefix xsd: <http://www.w3.org/2001/XMLSchema#> .

<Movie/id=M10001> a <Movie> ;
  <Movie#id> "M10001" ;
  <Movie#title> "Peterloo" ;
  <Movie#debut> "2018-11-02"^^xsd:date ;
  <Movie#until> "2018-11-27"^^xsd:date ;
  <Movie#duration> "PT2H34M" ;
  <Movie#director> "Mike Leigh" .

<Show/M_id=M10001;time=2011-08-22T14%3A00%3A00> a <Show> ;
  <Show#M_id> "M10001" ;
  <Show#ref-M_id> <Movie/id=M10001> ;
  <Show#time> "2018-11-22T14:00:00"^^xsd:dateTime ;
  <Show#T_id> "A" ;
  <Show#ref-T_id> <Theatre/id=A> ;
  <Show#priceA> 7.0 ;
  <Show#priceB> 5.0 .

<Theatre/id=A> a <Theatre> ;
  <Theatre#id> "A" ;
  <Theatre#capacity> 200 .
```

First we recall that in Turtle syntax, an IRI of the form `<Theatre/id=A>`
is interpreted as a relative IRI that will be resolved against the base, generating the complete IRI `<http://mov.ie/db/Theatre/id=A>`. Thereafter, we highlight the following aspects of the Direct Mapping:

- Subjects encode the primary keys and the table name. Where the
  primary key involves two or more columns, all corresponding values
  are encoded into the primary key. Though not shown in the above
  example, in cases where a table does not define any primary key,
  each row is assigned a fresh blank node subject.
- Predicates encode the table name and column name; in the case of
  a link to an entity from another table, the string "ref-" is added.
- The cell values are generally expressed as literal objects. The types
  are based on the types of the columns, which we implicitly assume
  to be defined in the relational schema; for example, we assume that
  the column **debut** is defined with the type DATE in the relational
  schema, whose values would then be converted to xsd:date. The
  mapping of types from SQL to RDF is defined by the R2RML

standard [106] as shown in Table 8.3. Some XSD types supported by RDF have no analogue in SQL, as per the example where there is no corresponding type in SQL for xsd:duration; on the other hand other SQL types that are not listed will by default be mapped to a string value (though a system may choose to support further types).

- Where cell values are NULL, the corresponding triple is simply omitted from the output (per the mpaa of <Movie/id=M10001>).
- In the case of links based on foreign keys, the object of the triple is defined per the subject of a triple generated from the corresponding row of the target table. (This also holds when the target table has no primary key, in which case the object should be the same blank node as the subject of the corresponding row.)
- Types are generated from table names.
- IRIs are percent encoded to avoid problems in cases where the cell contains certain characters. Also, IRIs are based on the literal generated from the cell rather than the raw cell content. Hence we arrive at <Show/M_id=M10001;time=2011-08-22T14%3A00%3A00>, where the time value corresponds to an xsd:dateTime literal (rather than the raw cell value), and %3A encodes the colon symbols.

Remark 8.6

While Table 8.3 defines the high-level mapping of SQL types to RDF/XSD datatypes, there are some other minor details to consider:

- The reader may have noticed that INTERVAL is left undefined by the standard. This is because the mapping from SQL intervals to XSD is quite complicated (according to the R2RML standard [106]), and hence implementations are left to choose how they handle this type (the simplest option being to map it to a string value).
- The standard further allows any other SQL types not listed in the table and not relating to CHARACTER (strings) to be supported however the implementation chooses; this allows RDB2RDF tools to better support further SQL types while maintaining compatibility for the explicitly supported types of the standard.
- Since some SQL types do not have bounded precision, implementations are allowed to set practical bounds on precision.
- When creating lexical values, canonical forms should be used (e.g., preferring "2"^^xsd:decimal to "+02.0"^^xsd:decimal).

Table 8.3 Mapping of SQL types to RDF datatypes [106]

SQL type	Datatype	Lexical mapping
BINARY, BINARY VARYING, BINARY LARGE OBJECT	xsd:hexBinary	binary to hexadecimal
NUMERIC, DECIMAL	xsd:decimal	direct
SMALLINT, INTEGER, BIGINT	xsd:integer	direct
FLOAT, REAL, DOUBLE PRECISION	xsd:double	direct
BOOLEAN	xsd:boolean	ensure lowercase
DATE	xsd:date	direct
TIME	xsd:time	direct
TIMESTAMP	xsd:dateTime	replace space with 'T'
INTERVAL	*undefined*	*undefined*
other	*none* (plain)	string value

Exercise 8.3

Provide the triples produced from the Direct Mapping of the following tables. You may assume that **A_name** *indicates a foreign key referencing the table* **Award.name**, *that the columns* **year** *and* **since** *are defined with type* **integer** *in SQL, and that other columns are defined with type* **varchar** *(string). You may invent a base IRI to be used for the extraction. To keep the exercise more concise, you need only give the triples produced considering the first row of each table.*

Laureate

winner	year	A_name	genre
Sully Prudhomme	1901	Literature	
Theodor Mommsen	1902	Literature	history
Bjørnstjerne Bjørnson	1903	Literature	poetry
Frédéric Mistral	1904	Literature	poetry
José Echegaray	1904	Literature	drama
Ragnar Frisch	1969	Economics	
Jan Tinbergen	1969	Economics	

Award

name	since
Literature	1901
Physics	1901
Chemistry	1901
Medicine	1901
Peace	1901
Economics	1969

While the Direct Mapping offers a quick path for generating RDF from relational tables – the results of which will often be quite reasonable in terms of RDF modelling – better results can often be achieved with a manual mapping; for example, the Direct Mapping produces literals for columns not involved in a key (e.g., **director**), whereas it would be better in many cases to use IRIs to allow future extensibility of the data. Along these lines, for scenarios where one requires greater control over the mapping from relational databases to RDF data, the W3C recommends R2RML [106].

8.5.1.2 RDB to RDF Mapping Language (R2RML)

The R2RML standard [106] supports custom mappings from relational to RDF data. In comparison with the Direct Mapping, the R2RML standard permits flexible customisation of the RDF data generated from the database, but at the cost of requiring a mapping to be specified (typically done manually). Such mappings are themselves defined in RDF using vocabulary that are interpreted by R2RML tools. The core of an R2RML mapping is a set of one or more triples maps, where each triple map defines how a set of triples sharing the same subject are to be extracted from a row of a given table. We now outline the main structure of a triples map (including multiplicities):

`rr:TriplesMap`$^{[1-*]}$ Specifies the extraction of groups of triples, where each group is extracted from a row of a specified table and shares the same subject; within a given triples map we may/should define:

`rr:LogicalTable`$^{[1]}$ specifies the table from which the triples should be extracted; the logical table can be a physical table specified by name or a virtual table specified by an SQL query;

`rr:SubjectMap`$^{[1]}$ specifies the subject for each group; specifies zero or more classes of which each subject is an instance;

`rr:PredicateObjectMap`$^{[0-*]}$ specifies at least one predicate and at least one object for a triple:

`rr:PredicateMap`$^{[1-*]}$ specifies a predicate term;

`rr:ObjectMap`$^{[1-*]}$ specifies an object term.

Each parent is connected to a child by a predicate of the same name as the child type, but with a lower-case initial; for example, we can connect an instance of `rr:TriplesMap` to an instance of `rr:SubjectMap` with the predicate `rr:subjectMap`. We do not need to explicitly define types when they can be inferred from domain/range definitions on the R2RML vocabulary. Output triples are then built from subject, predicate and object terms, which may be specified as constants in the mapping – using the properties `rr:subject`, `rr:predicate`, `rr:object` – or mapped from the database using a map. The subject map is required; it specifies or maps the subject term and assigned zero-to-many classes. In the case that no predicate–object map is specified, the only triples produced will be to type the subjects according to the classes specified by the subject map (if any). Otherwise, each predicate–object map will specify and/or map the predicate and object terms used to produce complete triples for the current subject. If more than one predicate or object (map) is specified on an individual predicate–object map, all combinations of predicates with objects are used to create triples for the current row.

We now illustrate the main features of R2RML by way of an example mapping relational data to custom RDF.

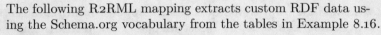

Example 8.18

The following R2RML mapping extracts custom RDF data using the Schema.org vocabulary from the tables in Example 8.16.

```
@base <http://mov.ie/db/> .
@prefix rr: <http://www.w3.org/ns/r2rml#> .
@prefix schema: <http://schema.org/> .
@prefix xsd: <http://www.w3.org/2001/XMLSchema#> .

<MovieMap> a rr:TriplesMap ;

  rr:logicalTable [ rr:tableName "Movie" ] ;

  rr:subjectMap [
    rr:template "http://mov.ie/db/m/{id}" ;
    rr:class schema:Movie
  ] ;

  rr:predicateObjectMap [
    rr:predicate schema:name ;
    rr:objectMap [
      rr:column "title" ;
      rr:language "en"
    ]
  ] ;

  rr:predicateObjectMap [
    rr:predicate schema:contentRating ;
    rr:objectMap [
      rr:template "MPAA {mpaa}" ;
      rr:termType rr:Literal
    ]
  ] ;

  rr:predicateObjectMap [
    rr:predicate schema:director , schema:creator ;
    rr:objectMap [
      rr:template "http://mov.ie/db/p/{director}"
    ]
  ] ;

  rr:predicateObjectMap [
    rr:predicate schema:duration ;
    rr:objectMap [
      rr:column "duration" ;
      rr:datatype xsd:duration
    ]
  ] .
```

Upon applying this R2RML mapping to the relational data in Example 8.16, the RDF data produced as a result will be as follows:

```
@base <http://mov.ie/db/> .
@prefix schema: <http://schema.org/> .
@prefix xsd: <http://www.w3.org/2001/XMLSchema#> ..

<m/M10001> a schema:Movie ;
  schema:name "Peterloo"@en ;
  schema:duration "PT2H34M"^^xsd:duration ;
  schema:director <p/Mike%20Leigh> ;
  schema:creator <p/Mike%20Leigh> .

<m/M10002> a schema:Movie ;
  schema:name "Overlord"@en ;
  schema:contentRating "MPAA R" ;
  schema:duration "PT1H48M"^^xsd:duration ;
  schema:director <p/Julius%20Avery> ;
  schema:creator <p/Julius%20Avery> .

<m/M10003> a schema:Movie ;
  schema:name "Widows"@en ;
  schema:contentRating "MPAA R" ;
  schema:duration "PT2H09M"^^xsd:duration ;
  schema:director <p/Steve%20McQueen> ;
  schema:creator <p/Steve%20McQueen> .
```

In this initial example we have described a single triples map, which leads to the extraction of three groups of triples from a single table. Each group is extracted from a single row and shares a common subject, with the subject of each group generated in the same way from each row. If we wished to extract groups of triples with subjects generated in different ways – using different tables, columns, templates, etc. – we would use (at least) one triple map for each such way in which the subjects of the desired output should be generated.

Aside from the aforementioned high-level features, RDB2RDF supports a range of lower-level features that enable fine-grained customisation of a mapping. Starting with rr:LogicalTable, while Example 8.18 demonstrated extraction from a physical table, another option is to specify an SQL query, where the triples will then be mapped from the table of results for the query.

Example 8.19

The Schema.org vocabulary defines schema:typicalAgeRange as a property to specify the age of the audience for which a creative work (e.g., movie) is generally targeted, where a string such as "2-4" indicates from the ages of 2–4, while "12-" indicates from the age of 12 onwards. Based on the MPAA ratings in the raw data, we could generate Schema.org-compatible triples indicating 18+ movies using the following mapping, where the logical table is specified as an SQL query that selects movies with an MPAA rating of 'R' or 'NC-17'.

```
@base <http://mov.ie/db/> .
@prefix rr: <http://www.w3.org/ns/r2rml#> .
@prefix schema: <http://schema.org/> .

<AdultMap> a rr:TriplesMap ;

  rr:logicalTable [
    rr:sqlQuery
      "SELECT * FROM Movie WHERE mpaa IN ('R','NC-17')" ;
    rr:sqlVersion rr:SQL2008
  ] ;

  rr:subjectMap [
    rr:template "http://mov.ie/db/m/{id}"
  ] ;

  rr:predicateObjectMap [
    rr:predicate schema:typicalAgeRange ;
    rr:objectMap [
      rr:constant "18+"
    ]
  ] .
```

This mapping will generate:

```
@base <http://mov.ie/db/> .
@prefix schema: <http://schema.org/> .

<m/M10002> schema:typicalAgeRange "18+" .
<m/M10003> schema:typicalAgeRange "18+" .
```

In this simple example, the SQL query selects only those movies with an MPAA rating of R or NC-17, generating a constant value ("18-") for each such movie on the property schema:typicalAgeRange. In the logical table we also specify the version of SQL used, in this case stating that the given query is compliant with the SQL 2008 standard; the version is optional. Note that any SQL query over the database can be executed, including one that joins multiple tables, aggregates data to compute counts or averages, etc. Furthermore, one could create a mapping with the above triples map (<AdultMap>) and the triples map of Example 8.18 (<MovieMap>) to extract both sets of data together.

Once we have specified the table from which we wish to extract triples – be it a physical table or a virtual table – we now need to begin to specify the subjects, predicates and objects of the triples we wish to extract. For each such position, we need a way to create RDF terms from zero-to-many values in a row of a relational table. R2RML thus offers three generic types of term maps that generate RDF terms from relational data, as follows:

rr:constant: Specifies a static RDF term directly.

rr:column: Creates an RDF term from the value in the row with the given column name; by default, the RDF term is generated based on the type of the column in SQL per the Direct Mapping, but the term type, datatype and language can be manually configured.

rr:template: Creates a custom RDF term that appends any number of values from different columns on the rows with static strings; the term type, datatype and language can be manually configured.

These term maps can be used to specify the generation of RDF terms within instances of rr:SubjectMap, rr:PredicateMap or rr:ObjectMap; in fact, we have already seen examples usage of each of the three options in Example 8.18 and Example 8.19. We now provide some more details.

In Example 8.19, we saw an example use of rr:constant to specify an object value that remains constant across all rows. R2RML also allows the use of an abbreviated syntax for specifying constant values.

Example 8.20

In Example 8.19, we specified a constant predicate and object:

```
 ⋯
rr:predicateObjectMap [
  rr:predicate schema:typicalAgeRange ;
  rr:objectMap [
    rr:constant "18+"
  ]
] .
```

We could alternatively have used a more verbose syntax:

```
 ⋯
rr:predicateObjectMap [
  rr:predicateMap [
    rr:constant schema:typicalAgeRange
  ] ;
  rr:objectMap [
    rr:constant "18-"
  ]
] .
```

Or indeed a more concise syntax:

```
[...]
rr:predicateObjectMap [
   rr:predicate schema:typicalAgeRange ;
   rr:object "18+"
] .
```

Here rr:object denotes a shortcut for rr:objectMap/rr:constant, and rr:predicate denotes a shortcut for rr:predicateMap/rr:constant. Indeed rr:subject denotes a shortcut for rr:subjectMap/rr:constant.

Moving to rr:column, the behaviour varies depending on whether it is used in a subject, predicate or object map. By default, IRIs will be generated for subject or predicate maps by appending the corresponding cell value to the base IRI; on the other hand, literals will be generated for object maps based on the type of the column in SQL (analogous to the Direct Mapping), where for example date in SQL is automatically converted to an xsd:date string in RDF while smallint, integer and bingint are mapped to xsd:integer, etc. (we refer to the standard for more details of these type mappings [106]). Any triple for which a NULL database value is encountered will be omitted.

Finally, in the case of rr:template, custom RDF terms can be generated by concatenating zero or more values from a row with static strings. Column names are enclosed in curly braces: '{', '}' (note that slash escaping can be used to escape braces in strings using '\{', '\}', and '\\' to escape slashes themselves). By default a template will generate IRIs in all maps (including an object map), with the values from the database being percent-encoded to ensure that valid IRIs are generated; in the case of relative IRIs, these will be appended to the base IRI. If any referenced column contains a NULL the returned value will be NULL and the corresponding triple will be omitted.

In cases where the default behaviour of rr:column or rr:template is not desirable, there are three ways to customise the term produced:

rr:termType: Specifies that an IRI (rr:IRI), literal (rr:Literal) or blank node (rr:BlankNode) should be generated.
rr:language: Specifies the language tag for literals.
rr:datatype: Specifies the datatype for literals.

These features must be used in a manner that complies with typical RDF restrictions, meaning that subject maps must generate IRIs or blank nodes, predicate maps must generate IRIs, whereas object maps can generate any term; furthermore, languages and datatypes can only be specified on literals and cannot be used together. We refer back to Example 8.18, which illustrates usage of various combinations of these features to customise RDF terms.

Remark 8.7

When generating blank nodes, a unique blank node will be generated for each unique string produced by the template.

Remark 8.8

There is no class-map. The term `rr:type` is the only way to specify the (constant) type of the subject in a subject map. Where type values should be dynamically generated from the data, a predicate–object map should be used (specifying the predicate `rdf:type`).

Remark 8.9

The R2RML standard further permits the definition of an *inverse expression* that allows to find the rows of the logical table that result in the creation of a given RDF term using (with the aid of the expression) the indexes of the database rather than regenerating each value from each row and comparing all such values with the current RDF term. We refer the reader to the standard for details [106].

Exercise 8.4

For the two tables in Exercise 8.3, create an R2RML mapping to produce the following triples (showing a sample for the first rows).

```
@base <http://nobel.org/db/> .
@prefix nv: <http://nobel.org/voc#> .
@prefix rdfs: <http://www.w3.org/2000/01/rdf-schema#> .
@prefix xsd: <http://www.w3.org/2001/XMLSchema#> .

nv:NobelPrizeLiterature rdfs:subClassOf nv:NobelPrize .
  …

<p/Literature#1901> a nv:NobelPrize , nv:NobelPrizeLiterature ;
  nv:winner <l/Sully%20Prudhomme> ;
  nv:year "1901"^^xsd:gYear .
  …
```

How might we change the mapping/output RDF to model the genres?

When extracting RDF from *multiple* tables, commonly the subjects extracted from one table may become the objects extracted from another table. While we could achieve this effect in R2RML by using an object map that corresponds to the subject map of another table, or using a logical table that joins both tables with an SQL query, R2RML provides a third option: a *reference object map*. Such a map – used instead of a (regular) object map – allows for specifying objects in one triples map that correspond to the subjects of another triples map. The idea is best illustrated with an example.

Example 8.21

In the following we again use the Schema.org vocabulary, this time to describe screenings of movies (shows) in a given movie theatre.

```
@base <http://mov.ie/db/> .
@prefix rr: <http://www.w3.org/ns/r2rml#> .
@prefix schema: <http://schema.org/> .
@prefix xsd: <http://www.w3.org/2001/XMLSchema#> .

<MovieMap> a rr:TriplesMap ;
  [ ... ] # as before ...

<ShowMap> a rr:TriplesMap ;
  rr:logicalTable [ rr:tableName "Show" ] ;

  rr:subjectMap [
    rr:template "http://mov.ie/db/s/{M_id}#{time}" ;
    rr:class schema:ScreeningEvent
  ] ;

  rr:predicateObjectMap [
    rr:predicate schema:doorTime ;
    rr:objectMap [
      rr:column "time"
    ]
  ] ;

  rr:predicateObjectMap [
    rr:predicate schema:workPresented ;
    rr:objectMap [
      rr:parentTriplesMap <MovieMap> ;
      rr:joinCondition [
        rr:child "M_id" ; rr:parent "id"
      ]
    ]
  ] .
```

In the latter predicate–object map, we define each object as being the subject of a specified "parent" triples map (<MovieMap>) according to the specified join condition, where rr:child indicates the name of the join column in the Show table and rr:parent indicates the name of the join column in the Movie table. The object(s) generated by this reference map will correspond to the subject(s) generated by the parent map for the rows in the parent table satisfying the join condition. Hence when combined with <MovieMap> as defined in Example 8.18, this map will generate further triples of the following form describing shows:

```
@base <http://mov.ie/db/> .
@prefix schema: <http://schema.org/> .
@prefix xsd: <http://www.w3.org/2001/XMLSchema#> .

<s/M10001#2018-11-22T14:00:00> a schema:ScreeningEvent ;
  schema:doorTime "2018-11-22T14:00:00"^^xsd:dateTime ;
  schema:workPresented <m/M10001> .

[...] # likewise for other shows and for data from <MovieMap>
```

Exercise 8.5

Provide an alternative R2RML mapping that produces the same result as seen in Example 8.21 but instead of using the latter reference map for schema:workPresented, uses a standard object map.

The join specified by the reference map is not restricted to be one-to-one: in case the join matches for multiple rows in the parent logical table, a triple will be added for each such row by the reference map (a triple for each unique object generated from each such row by the parent subject map). Furthermore, join conditions on multiple columns can be specified by adding multiple values for rr:joinCondition (each with a rr:child and rr:parent column specified); in fact, join conditions are optional where, without join conditions, a Cartesian product is applied, effectively mapping every subject of the child table to every object/subject of the parent table.

Remark 8.10

The standard is unclear for this author on what happens when the child and parent tables are the same and no join condition is specified; the informal description suggests that implicitly the reference object will only be generated from the same row as the subject, but the definitions do not seem to agree with the text, and the example provided is unfortunately ambiguous (using a table with one row) [106].

Exercise 8.6

Based on the two tables of Exercise 8.3, create an R2RML mapping using a reference object map to produce the following triples, where nv:inaugural *indicates the winner(s) in the first year of the prize.*

```
@base <http://nobel.org/db/> .
@prefix nv: <http://nobel.org/voc#> .

<p/Literature> a nv:NobelPrize ;
  nv:inaugural <l/Sully%20Prudhomme> .

<p/Economics> a nv:NobelPrize ;
  nv:inaugural <l/Ragnar%20Frisch> , <l/Jar%20Tinbergen> .

<l/Sully%20Prudhomme> a nv:Laureate .
<l/Theodor%20Mommsen> a nv:Laureate .
 [...]
<l/Ragnar%20Frisch> a nv:Laureate .
<l/Jar%20Tinbergen> a nv:Laureate .
```

(As a hint, please observe that the column **since** *in the table* **Award** *indicates the first year of each respective prize. In the absence of the* **since** *column, we could still use a logical table based on an SQL query to find the winners of the first year.)*

Finally, though the examples we have seen thus far relate to mapping relational databases to sets of triples (i.e., RDF graphs), R2RML can also be used to generate RDF datasets. Recall from Section 3.6 that an RDF dataset is composed of a default graph and a set of named graphs (where names can be IRIs or blank nodes). In order to generate RDF datasets, R2RML supports *graph maps.* Zero or more such graph maps can be attached to a subject map or a predicate–object map in order to specify that the triples extracted for the attached map should be assigned to those particular graphs. Named graphs can be specified using term maps as previously described; graphs must be specified as IRIs (i.e., they cannot be blank nodes, as allowed by RDF datasets). In case that no graph is specified, the extracted triples are written to the default graph, or, alternatively, the IRI rr:defaultGraph can be used to refer explicitly to the default graph. In cases where multiple graphs are specified, the triples will be written to multiple graphs. In the case that a set of graphs is specified on a subject map and another set on a child predicate–object map, the triples of that predicate–object map will be added to the union of both sets of graphs (if the union is empty, the corresponding triples will be extracted to the default graph).

Example 8.22

Consider the following R2RML mapping:

```
@base <http://mov.ie/db/> .
@prefix rr: <http://www.w3.org/ns/r2rml#> .
@prefix schema: <http://schema.org/> .
@prefix xsd: <http://www.w3.org/2001/XMLSchema#> .

<MovieMap> a rr:TriplesMap ;

  rr:logicalTable [ rr:tableName "Movie" ] ;

  rr:subjectMap [
    rr:template "http://mov.ie/db/m/{id}" ;
    rr:class schema:Movie ;
    rr:graphMap [
        rr:template "http://mov.ie/db/g/m/{id}"
    ]
  ] ;

  rr:predicateObjectMap [
    rr:predicate schema:name ;
    rr:objectMap [
      rr:column "title" ;
      rr:language "en"
    ] ;
    rr:graph rr:defaultGraph
  ] ;

  rr:predicateObjectMap [
    rr:predicate schema:director , schema:creator ;
    rr:objectMap [
        rr:template "http://mov.ie/db/p/{director}"
    ] ;
    rr:graphMap [
        rr:template "http://mov.ie/db/g/d/{director}"
    ]
  ] .
```

The result of applying this mapping to the tables of Example 8.16 will be an RDF dataset, where the default graph contains:

```
@base <http://mov.ie/db/> .
@prefix schema: <http://schema.org/> .
<m/M10001> schema:name "Peterloo" .
<m/M10002> schema:name "Overlord" .
<m/M10003> schema:name "Widows" .
```

The graph <http://mov.ie/db/g/m/M10001> will contain:

```
<m/M10001> a schema:Movie ;
  schema:name "Peterloo" ;
  schema:creator <d/Mike%20Leigh> ;
  schema:director <d/Mike%20Leigh>
```

and likewise for the two graphs <http://mov.ie/db/g/m/M10002> and
<http://mov.ie/db/g/m/M10003> describing movies.

The graph <http://mov.ie/db/g/d/Mike%20Leigh> will contain:

```
<m/M10001> schema:creator <d/Mike%20Leigh> .
<m/M10001> schema:director <d/Mike%20Leigh> .
```

and likewise for the graphs <http://mov.ie/db/g/d/Julius%20Avery>
and <http://mov.ie/db/g/d/Steve%20McQueen> describing directors.

Discussion 8.5

JULIE: But why do we need to convert the data to RDF? Why not just
    publish the data from the relational database directly on the Web?
AIDAN: We could dump the database to a set of CSV files and then
    publish these files on the Web directly, yes. But then we would
    only have Three Star Open Data (see Section 8.4.1). By mapping
    to RDF, we get that fourth star, using Web identifiers (IRIs) for our
    entities such that people can link to data about our entities from
    elsewhere on the Web. Furthermore, by publishing a CSV dump
    (or making our database openly query-able over the Web), our data
    would be less interoperable with other data on the Web. Per the
    running examples for movies, when we convert our data to RDF
    using the Schema.org vocabulary, once published, those data will
    be much more interoperable with the data published on other sites
    using the same vocabulary than if we had simply published the CSV
    files dumped from our particular relational schema. Aside from the
    Web, RDF has become popular for data integration scenarios within
    organisations, where the graph-based data model is used to abstract
    multiple sources of data, including relational datasets [357].

Further Reading 8.1

For further reading on the topic of extracting RDF data from
relational databases, we refer to the book chapter by Sequeda [357].

8.5.2 Other Legacy Formats to RDF

Relational databases are often used to dynamically generate content for web-pages and thus house a large swathe of legacy data on the Web. However, relevant data are also stored in other formats, possibly as static content. This is particularly true for many Open Data initiatives, be it relating to scientific, governmental or even commercial datasets. Such datasets are often published as static files in syntaxes such as CSV, XML, JSON, and so forth.

Needless to say, static data in such formats can be made more interoperable if rather published on the Web as Linked Data; per the Five-Star Open Data scheme (see Section 8.4.1), datasets published in such formats would be considered as Three Star Open Data, where a fourth star can be achieved by mapping the data to RDF with dereferenceable IRI identifiers. Unfortunately, each such legacy format requires a different set of techniques for mapping data to RDF, generally requiring manual intervention to achieve high-quality RDF in the output. Here we briefly describe some languages, techniques and tools to help map legacy data in some of the most popular formats to RDF.

8.5.2.1 CSV/TSV to RDF

CSV is a popular text-based format for tabular data, including relational data, spreadsheets, matrices, etc. Each line of the file represents a row of the table, while values in each row are separated using commas or tabs; in the latter case, the format is sometimes called Tab Separated Values (TSV). Otherwise, aside for some de facto conventions, most CSV/TSV files do not follow any formal standards; for example, the first row may or may not contain header information, the first column may or may not represent a key, etc.

Example 8.23

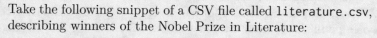

Take the following snippet of a CSV file called `literature.csv`, describing winners of the Nobel Prize in Literature:

```
Sully Prudhomme,1901,
Theodor Mommsen,1902,history
Bjørnstjerne Bjørnson,1903,poetry
Frédéric Mistral,1904,poetry
José Echegaray,1904,drama
[...]
```

No header is provided; this may rather be provided in an associated webpage or read-me. Furthermore, no context is provided within the file itself; e.g., it does not mention Literature (rather found in the filename or clear from the context in which the file is published). Such data is loosely relational (similar to the table found in Exercise 8.3).

Now rather consider the following TSV file, published on the Web with the name `genre.tsv`, describing weighted genres of movies.

	Action	Drama	Horror	Thriller
Overlord	0.3	0	0.5	0.2
Peterloo	0	1	0	0
Widows	0.1	0.7	0	0.2
...				

This time a header is provided, but the data are modelled in a completely different way to the previous CSV: rather than being modelled in a relational way, the genres are represented as a numeric matrix.

Discussion 8.6

FRANK: Perhaps a little off-topic, but why do you say that the TSV file in Example 8.23 is not "relational"?

AIDAN: Intuitively speaking, it is not how you would model such data in a relational database. Imagine creating a relational table structured analogously to the TSV file. Now how would you find the genres of the movie `Overlord` in SQL with non-zero weights?

FRANK: You would need to query for column names with non-zero values. Hmm, I'm actually not sure how you could do that in SQL. So a more relational modelling would be ...

AIDAN: ... would be a table with three columns: **movie**, **genre** and **weight** (with **movie** and **genre** being the key).

For brevity, we henceforth refer to both CSV and TSV formats as CSV.

While CSV is a simple and flexible format, making sense of such data often requires revising human-readable documentation. Likewise there is no single technique applicable to automatically map CSV data to RDF – at least while producing interoperable RDF that follows typical best practices.

In the case of relational-style CSV/TSV data with headers, one option is to load the data into a relational database and apply either a Direct Mapping-style conversion to RDF, or define an R2RML mapping that executes a custom mapping. Other tools – such as RDF plugins to Google's Open Refine[13] – allow for creating custom mappings from a CSV file to RDF via a user interface. The RDF Mapping Language (RML) – proposed by Dimou et al. [111] as a generalisation of R2RML in order to support logical sources beyond relational tables – also supports CSV files as a direct input format.

---

[13] http://openrefine.org/

An alternative approach is to use RDF to represent the metadata – rather than the content – of a CSV document. Along these lines, the W3C has recommended a vocabulary [324] for describing the schema of tabular data (including CSV/TSV data) in a JSON-LD/RDF format, which allows for assigning datatypes and annotations to columns, defining keys, etc.

On the other hand, CSVs may be used to represent statistical data as a matrix of numerical values. Though a variety of abstractions can be applied to statistical data, one that has become common is that of a **Data Cube** [155], which allows for modelling n-mode tensors of numerical values, and thereafter proposes a set of standard operations to query and process such data, key amongst which is the notion of a slice, which projects data with a given value on a certain dimension. In order to represent statistical data as RDF, the W3C has recommended the RDF Data Cube Vocabulary [102].

Example 8.24

Consider the content of genre.tsv from Example 8.23; this represents a 2-dimensional matrix of numeric data. Using the RDF Data Cube (qb:) vocabulary, we could represent these data as follows:

```
@base <http://mov.ie/db/> .
@prefix mv: <http://mov.ie/voc#> .
@prefix qb: <http://purl.org/linked-data/cube#> .
@prefix rdfs: <http://www.w3.org/2000/01/rdf-schema#> .
@prefix sdmx-m: <http://purl.org/linked-data/sdmx/2009/measure#> .
@prefix xsd: <http://www.w3.org/2001/XMLSchema#> .

mv:refGenre a qb:DimensionProperty ; rdfs:label "genre"@en .
mv:refMovie a qb:DimensionProperty ; rdfs:label "movie"@en .

<qb/MovieGenres> a qb:DataStructureDefinition ;
  qb:component [ qb:dimension mv:refGenre ; qb:order 1 ] ;
  qb:component [ qb:dimension mv:refMovie ; qb:order 2 ] ;
  qb:component [ qb:measure sdmx-m:obsValue ] .

<o/OverlordAction> a qb:Observation;
  qb:dataSet <qb/MovieGenres> ;
  mv:genre <g/Action> ;
  mv:movie <m/Overlord> ;
  sdmx-m:obsValue 0.3 .

<o/WidowsThriller> a qb:Observation;
  qb:dataSet <qb/MovieGenres> ;
  mv:genre <g/Thriller> ;
  mv:movie <m/Widows> ;
  sdmx-m:obsValue 0.2 .
```

...

In this description, we first define properties that denote dimensions (e.g., movie, genre, country, gender), measures (e.g., area, height, age, or simply value) and attributes (e.g., source, year, measure unit). Thereafter, we define the structure of a Data Cube: of which dimensions, measures and attributes is it composed. In this example, we further indicate an order, which offers hints on how users will typically interact with the cube, in this case browsing/querying by movie first, then genre. Finally, the cube is composed of observations, where each observation provides values for the dimensions, measures and attributes of the cube.

Here we have presented a rather simplified example to give the general idea of representing Data Cubes in RDF. The same pattern can be followed for n-dimensional data by simply adding more dimensions to the cube structure and correspondingly to the observations. Furthermore, multiple measures can be assigned per observation, representing, for example, a mean measure and a standard deviation measure. The Data Cube vocabulary also provides terms to categorise cubes, define slices of cubes by particular dimensions (e.g., horror weights), groups of observations (e.g., horror movies with non-zero horror weights), and more besides; we refer the reader to the standard for details [102].

8.5.2.2 XML to RDF

Another common data format used on the Web is that of the XML [77], which allows for defining documents following a tree-based structure. Both HTML and XML originate from the **Standard Generalized Markup Language (SGML)** [150], and thus share certain syntactic conventions. Unlike HTML, which is defined (primarily) for specifying the format of Web documents, XML can be used to represent and exchange data using custom (user-defined) tags. XML has been used in a variety of applications, including Rich Site Summary (RSS) for feeds, Scalable Vector Graphics (SVG) for images, Extensible Messaging and Presence Protocol (XMPP) for instant messaging, to name but a few examples. XML has also been broadly used as a format for ad hoc data exchange using informal, non-standard document structures.

XML has been standardised by the W3C [77], along with with XML Schema [313] for defining a document structure against which compliant XML documents can be validated, XPath [335] and XQuery [334] for querying and extracting elements from an XML document, XSLT [96] for transforming XML documents, and so forth. These XML standards have also had significant influence on the Semantic Web standards, where for example RDF/XML [42] allows for encoding RDF graphs as XML documents, SPARQL defines an output format based on XML [178], many of the datatypes supported in RDF are borrowed from XML Schema [313], and so forth.

Example 8.25

We provide an example snippet of an XML document describing biographical information about people involved in movies.

```xml
<?xml version="1.0" encoding="UTF-8"?>
<bios>
  <person name="Mike Leigh">
    <dob>1943-02-20</dob>
    <nationality xml:lang="en">Great Britain</nationality>
    <award>
      <category xml:lang="en">Best Director</category>
      <event>Cannes</event>
      <year>1993</year>
      <movie>Naked</movie>
    </award>
    <award>
      <category xml:lang="fr">Palme d'Or</category>
      <event>Cannes</event>
      <year>1996</year>
      <movie>Secrets &amp; Lies</movie>
    </award>
  </person>
  <person name="Julius Avery">
    ...
  </person>
  ...
</bios>
```

This document can be seen as conforming to the following tree structure, where we denote by <·> nodes, =·= attributes and * text elements.

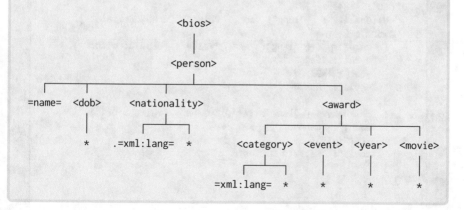

There are various methods by which legacy XML data can be surfaced as RDF. Perhaps one of the most common methods is to use XSLT [96] to declaratively define a transformation from an XML document to an RD-F/XML compliant document; supporting such transformations, the **Gleaning**

Resource Descriptions from Dialects of Languages (GRDDL) [99] standard
– recommended by the W3C – allows for linking from an XML document to
one or more XSLT documents on the Web that will transform (parts of) that
XML document to RDF/XML. An alternative is to use a language such as
XSPARQL [56, 323], which combines XQuery and SPARQL in one language,
allowing to map from RDF to XML, XML to RDF, or to query both in unison. It is further worth noting that the RDF Mapping Language (RML) [111]
described earlier also supports logical sources based on XML documents.

8.5.2.3 JSON to RDF

Another format that has grown in popularity on the Web is JSON [76]. Like
XML, JSON documents create a tree-like structure. However, while XML
supports a number of features that JSON does not (comments, a rich set of
standard datatypes, etc.), JSON offers a more lightweight syntax than XML,
and is more convenient to work with in certain programming languages (including, but not limited to, JavaScript). For these latter reasons, JSON has
become popular, in particular, as a format for returning data from **Application Programming Interfaces (APIs)** on the Web [175].

Example 8.26

We provide the same data as in Example 8.25, this time as a
JSON document (dropping the unnecessary root element <bios>):

```
[
  { "name": "Mike Leigh",
    "dob": "1943-02-20",
    "nationality": { "lang": "en", "value": "Great Britain" },
    "award": [
      { "category": { "lang": "en", "value": "Best Director" },
        "event": "Cannes",
        "year": 1993,
        "movie": "Naked"
      },
      { "category": { "lang": "fr", "value": "Palme d'Or" },
        "event": "Cannes",
        "year": 1996,
        "movie": "Secrets & Lies"
      }
    ]
  },
  {
    [ ... ]
  }
]
```

Again, a number of methods have been proposed to surface JSON as RDF. Key amongst these methods is the JSON-LD syntax [366]: as was discussed previously in Section 3.8.5, by adding a context to a JSON document containing information about namespaces, base IRIs, datatypes and languages, a JSON document can be directly viewed as an RDF graph (with some minor exceptions, where, for example, JSON-LD allows blank nodes in the predicate position of a triple). Another possibility is to use the extension of SPARQL proposed by Mosser et al. [278], which supports invoking JSON APIs from a SPARQL query as a SERVICE, extracting data from the response to be used as solutions for the SERVICE call. RML [111] further supports logical sources based on JSON documents, offering another option.

8.5.2.4 Text to RDF

While converting legacy data from relational databases, CSV, XML or JSON to RDF mostly involves mapping from one machine-readable structure to another, automatically extracting RDF from unstructured, human-readable text is a significantly greater challenge (as we saw in Section 1.2.2). Despite advances stemming from areas such as Deep Learning, contemporary techniques for automatically extracting structured data from text are limited either in the type of data they can extract, the precision with which they can extract data, or both. Were this problem "solved", it would obviate the need for a Web of Data: there would be little or no benefit to publishing structured content on the Web if automated techniques existed that could interpret and process the unstructured content of the current Web equally as well. In this case, the line between "human-readable content" and "machine readable content" would fade. Still – and perhaps thankfully, at least for the purposes of this book – we are far from such a scenario, where the problem of Natural Language Understanding (NLU) is informally considered an AI-complete problem, requiring an unprecedented form of Artificial Intelligence that not even advances in Deep Learning can yet begin to approach.

A variety of techniques have, however, been proposed in the research literature addressing this very challenge of distilling structured data from unstructured text – with varying degrees of success. Such works relate to the area of Information Extraction (IE) [256], which in turn builds upon techniques developed in the context of Natural Language Processing (NLP). While a comprehensive treatment of the works in this area are out-of-scope – and by themselves could fill (and indeed have filled [264]) a book as long as the present one – by way of example, we give a brief overview of some of the automated methods available for extracting RDF from text.

Example 8.27

Consider the following source text:

> Mike Leigh (born 20 February 1943) is an English writer and director. Leigh studied at the Royal Academy of Dramatic Art (RADA). He is known for his lengthy rehearsal and improvisation techniques with actors to build characters and narrative for his films. His aesthetic has been compared to the sensibility of the Japanese director Yasujirō Ozu. Leigh has won the Best Director award at Cannes for Naked in 1993 and the Palme d'Or in 1996 for Secrets & Lies.

Even for an expert human, modelling the information conveyed by this text as an RDF graph is exceptionally challenging, particularly considering the subtleties and uniqueness of the expression in the third sentence, for example. Still, the text does convey a considerable amount of factual information that could be readily modelled as an RDF graph.

In terms of Information Extraction, the methods that can be applied depend on what structured resources – ontologies, RDF data, etc. – are available. But assuming no such resources to be available, the first technique that can be applied is Named Entity Recognition (NER) [256], which will identify mentions of people (e.g., "Mike Leigh", "Yasujirō Ozu"), places (e.g., "Cannes"), organisations (e.g., "Royal Academy of Dramatic Art"), and perhaps other types of entities.

More ambitiously, one may try to extract structured data (relations) from the text; applying, for example, the FRED system [138] over the first sentence of this text, one receives RDF data as follows:

```
@prefix dbr: <http://dbpedia.org/resource/> .
@prefix dul:
  <http://www.ontologydesignpatterns.org/ont/dul/DUL.owl#> .
@prefix fred:
  <http://www.ontologydesignpatterns.org/ont/fred/domain.owl#> .
 ...

fred:generate_1 vn.role:Theme1 fred:Mike_leigh ;
  vn.role:Theme2 "0001-01-20" .

fred:situation_1 dul:associatedWith "0001-01-20" ;
  boxing:involves fred:writer_1 .

fred:writer_1 a fred:EnglishWriter , fred:Director ;
  dul:hasQuality fred:English ;
  fred:at "1943-02-01"^^xsd:date .

fred:EnglishWriter rdfs:subClassOf fred:Writer .
fred:Director owl:equivalentClass dbr:Film_director .
fred:Writer owl:equivalentClass dbr:Screenwriter .
fred:Mike_leigh owl:sameAs dbr:Mike_Leigh .
```

While this output succeeds in representing some of the (latent) structure of the original text – identifying for example the date, some of the classes involved, as well as providing useful links to DBpedia – some key data is missing, such as the fact that the date represents a date of birth. Furthermore, if we consider a similar input sentence:

Steven McQueen (born 9 October 1969 in England) is a film director and screenwriter.

The structure of the output changes significantly despite the fact that both sentences are expressing the same type of information:

```
@prefix dbr: <http://dbpedia.org/resource/> .
@prefix dul:
  <http://www.ontologydesignpatterns.org/ont/dul/DUL.owl#> .
@prefix fred:
  <http://www.ontologydesignpatterns.org/ont/fred/domain.owl#> .
  [...]


fred:generate_1 fred:locatedIn fred:England ;
  vn.role:Theme2 fred:Steve_mcqueen ;
  fred:temp_rel "1969-01-01"^^xsd:date .

fred:Steve_mcqueen a fred:Screenwriter , fred:FilmDirector .

fred:writer_1 a fred:EnglishWriter , fred:Director ;
  dul:hasQuality fred:English ;
  fred:at "1943-02-01"^^xsd:date .

fred:FilmDirector owl:equivalentClass dbr:Film_director .
fred:Screenwriter owl:equivalentClass dbr:Screenwriter .
fred:England owl:sameAs dbr:England .
fred:Steve_mcqueen owl:sameAs dbr:Steve_McQueen .
```

Thus we see that although there are techniques that can extract RDF from text, they are still limited in their ability to abstract the sentence structure from the data representation. Put more simply, the same information expressed in different styles of sentences may often lead to differently structured output data, affecting interoperability. We may also note that the Steve McQueen spoken about in this text is not the Steve McQueen identified by dbr:Steve_McQueen in DBpedia, but rather dbr:Steve_McQueen_(director). Again, such limitations are to be expected given the inherently challenging nature of the task.

Where an RDF dataset or ontology is provided as input to guide the Information Extraction process – a dataset or ontology that describes entities and/or concepts spoken about in a text – other techniques may be applied. For example, rather than applying NER to identify entities

such as "*Mike Leigh*", Entity Linking (EL) [256] tools can be applied
to also assign that entity in the text an existing identifier from an RDF
dataset (if available), such as `dbr:Mike_Leigh`. This then allows us to
know which entities in the structured data are spoken about in which
parts of a corpus of text. However, the EL task is in itself challenging
in the presence of ambiguous entities, such as `dbr:Steve_McQueen` (the
actor) and `dbr:Steve_McQueen_(director)` (the director) sharing the
same name within the same domain (movies).

Entity Linking itself does not produce RDF triples; however, given
an RDF dataset, a promising approach to extract RDF triples (encoding binary relations) from text is that of *distant supervision* [276].
The core idea of distant supervision is to first apply Entity Linking
to identify the entities from the RDF dataset spoken about in the
text. Where a sentence involves two entities found in the dataset –
e.g., "*Leigh*[dbr:Mike_Leigh] *studied at the Royal Academy of Dramatic Art
(RADA)*[dbr:Royal_Academy_of_Dramatic_Art]" – the RDF dataset is consulted
to check for existing relations between both entities; e.g.:

```
...
dbr:Mike_Leigh dbp:education dbr:Royal_Academy_of_Dramatic_Art .
```

That sentence can then be used as an example of how the corresponding relationship `dbp:education` may be expressed in text; from such
sentences are extracted a variety of features that are used to identify
the analogous relations between pairs of entities mentioned in similar
sentences but for which the relation has not yet been asserted in the
dataset. The distant supervision approach thus allows for extracting
triples that are interoperable with the input dataset (using the same
property to denote the same relation), but is mainly used to enrich
an existing dataset from text rather than to extract one from scratch.
Needless to say, not all triples extracted from such an approach can
be expected to be correct since, for example, multiple relations may
be present between two entities, a sentence may mention two entities
without indicating a relationship between them, the EL task may give
erroneous identifiers for entities mentioned in the text, and so forth.

Further Reading 8.2

For further reading on processing text in the context of the
Semantic Web, we refer to the book by Maynard et al. [264]. For further
reading on the topic of Information Extraction from text – as well as
semi-structured sources such as HTML – in the context of the Semantic
Web, we refer to the survey by Martinez-Rodriguez et al. [261].

8.5.2.5 HTML to RDF

HTML is the primary format for exchanging documents on the Web. Given the prevalence of legacy HTML content on the Web, methods for extracting factual information from such content would potentially be of major benefit for populating the Web of Data. But HTML is primarily used to create human-readable documents. As such, much of the information conveyed by HTML documents is conveyed in natural language, which we have seen to be challenging to process by automated means. In fact, were HTML content more machine-readable, this would obviate the need for a Web of Data in the first place! That said, HTML documents do sometimes provide some lightweight structure – such as titles, links, tables, lists, etc. – that, in some cases, can be exploited for the purposes of automatically extracting triples of higher quality than what would be possible over plain text alone.

Some methods for extracting triples from HTML are completely generic and do not presuppose a particular layout. The simplest can represent the document layout itself as RDF, using for example the XHTML Vocabulary [309]. Such an approach simply maps the existing structure of the HTML document to RDF rather than trying to extract information from its contents; as such, it is not useful for attaining the factual content that the HTML document may encode. Another generic approach to extracting information from HTML is to first extract segments of natural language text and then apply text-based information extraction approaches, as discussed previously; however, extracting high-quality RDF data from text is very challenging, where throwing away the structure of the HTML documents is wasteful given that this structure can often provide clues as to the factual content of webpages.

An alternative generic method that can be applied over collections of HTML pages is that of wrapper induction [131]: a *wrapper* can be thought of as a mapping from a HTML document to data in a desired (typically structured) format, whereas *induction* refers to the process of learning such a mapping. In terms of learning, supervised, semi-supervised and fully automatic approaches have been proposed [131]. In the context of Linked Data, for example, Gentile et al. [141] propose a distant supervision approach – similar to that discussed for relation extraction over text – whereby an RDF dataset and a collection of HTML documents are given as input; again, entities mentioned in the HTML documents are linked by their identifiers to the RDF dataset and existing relations between entities in the document are annotated; thereafter, paths in the HTML document that connect entities with known relations are extracted and applied to other documents to extract novel triples with those relations. Such wrapper-based approaches can work well assuming that groups of HTML documents in the input collection tend to follow a similar layout, perhaps being taken from the same website generated by the same script (but with different data on each page).

Example 8.28

Take, for example, the following HTML document describing
the movie Gattaca, with a header, a couple of sub-headers, a paragraph
of text, and finally a table with the cast and characters.

```html
<html>
 <head>
  <title>Gattaca (1997)</title>
 </head>
 <body>
  <h1>Gattaca</h1>
  <h2>Science Fiction</h2>
  <h2>1997</h2>
  <p>Gattaca is a science fiction movie directed by Andrew Niccol,
      centering on the topic of eugenics.</p>
  <table border="1">
   <tr>
    <th>Starring</th>
    <th>Character</th>
   </tr>
   <tr>
    <td>Ethan Hawke</td>
    <td>Vincent Freeman</td>
   </tr>
   ...
  </table>
 </body>
</html>
```

The first option for extracting RDF from such a document would be
simply to map its structure to RDF; for example:

```
@prefix dct: <http://purl.org/dc/terms/> .
@prefix xhv: <http://www.w3.org/1999/xhtml/vocab#> .
@prefix xsd: <http://www.w3.org/2001/XMLSchema#> .

<> dct:title "Gattaca (1997)" ;
   xhv:main <body> ;

<body> xhv:heading "Gattaca" , "Science Fiction" , "1997" ;
   dct:description "Gattaca is a ..." ;
   xhv:tab <tab1> .

<tab1> xhv:row <tab1-r1> , <tab1-r2> , ... .
 ...
```

However, this direct mapping-style approach does not capture the relations between the elements – that Science Fiction is the *genre* of Gattaca, that 1997 is the *release-year* of Gattaca, and so forth.

A second option would be to extract the text excerpts and apply text-based information extraction on these excerpts; however, information extraction from text is a challenging problem, and indeed per the above example, a lot of rich information may be trapped in the structural elements of the HTML documents (such as the year, the cast etc.).

A third option would be to generate a wrapper that maps structural elements of the HTML document to RDF triples. If we assumed, for example, a website publishing millions of webpages about movies using the above HTML layout, such a wrapper could be created manually, mapping the `<h1>` heading to the name of the movie, the first `<h2>` header to the genre, etc. – while a practical approach, it is not generic, since the wrapper would be specific to that HTML layout on that website and a new wrapper would need to be manually defined for another website. An alternative approach would be to try to learn wrappers based on the relations for an existing RDF dataset; for example, if provided as input an RDF dataset with the following triples:

```
@base <http://mov.ie/db/> .
@prefix schema: <http://schema.org/> .
@prefix xsd: <http://www.w3.org/2001/XMLSchema#> .

<m/M10001> a schema:Movie ;
  schema:name "Gattaca" ;
  schema:genre "Science Fiction" ;
  schema:director <p/AndewNiccol> ;
  schema:copyrightYear "1999"^^xsd:int ;
  schema:character <m/M10001#c1> ;
  schema:actor <p/EthanHawke> .

<m/M10001#c1> a schema:Person ;
  schema:name "Vincent Freeman" .

  ...
```

We can attempt to link the text elements of the HTML document (e.g., Gattaca) to terms in the RDF data (`<m/M10001>`), and then induce paths in the HTML document representing the relations between them; for example, we may find across multiple pages of the same website that the first `<h2>` element represents the genre of the `<h1>` element that precedes it. Applying this pattern to other webpages on that website (e.g., for newer movies) may allow to enrich the input RDF data with new triples. However, such an approach assumes that an appropriate RDF dataset already exists, and will struggle to capture new types of information; for instance, per the above example, we may lose information about which actor played which character, which is not given in the reference knowledge, and for which we thus lack examples.

Generic approaches for automatically extracting RDF triples from HTML thus have inherent limitations. A different strategy – already mentioned in passing – is to have a domain expert manually define a wrapper for a particular website. Although such an approach may often be practical, allowing for the RDF output to be carefully customised as required, it is also inflexible, requiring wrappers to be defined for each website of interest and potentially requiring wrappers to be updated as the websites change.

A final strategy, then, is to focus on automatically extracting triples from particular structural elements of HTML documents. Many such approaches target, for example, HTML tables, which offer (at least) some structure and are very common on the Web – and thus may present a tempting target for extracting information [261]. However, unlike relational or CSV tables, which are designed to be read primarily by machines, HTML tables are designed to be read by humans: rather than being designed to be easy to query and parse, one of the main design goals for HTML tables is to ensure that they look good to users. Various formatting changes can be employed to improve a table's aesthetics in a webpage, including splitting long tables, merging adjacent cells with the same value, nesting tables inside tables, and so on; these aesthetically-motivated changes often serve to obfuscate the data content from machines. HTML tables are also very diverse, with some used for forms, some for navigation bars, etc.; even those that carry "data" can be highly heterogeneous, and may be expressed as a relation (column headers only), transposed (row headers only), as matrices (column and row headers), and so forth. For these reasons, the automatic extraction of RDF triples from HTML tables is, again, a challenging problem; however, where an existing RDF dataset can be given as input, methods again based on distant supervision have had some relative success in this area [261].

A number of key Linked Datasets have been based on information extracted from Web documents in this manner, most prominently DBpedia [247] and YAGO [374], which are largely based on data extracted from the webpages of Wikipedia, and in particular the *info-boxes* of Wikipedia: the attribute–value tables presented in the top right corner of many articles, providing a factual overview of the entity described. In such cases, dedicated extraction frameworks have been proposed to target these specific sources of information while trying to maintain the highest quality output data possible [247, 374]. Given that Wikipedia had been operative for several years and hosted contributions from millions of editors before these datasets were proposed, being able to extract RDF data from this legacy source – even if not perfect – was a major development for the Linked Data community.

Further Reading 8.3

For further reading on works for extracting RDF from HTML documents, we refer to the survey by Martinez-Rodriguez et al. [261].

Finally, a growing number of HTML pages contain embedded structured data in formats such as RDFa (see Section 3.8.4), Microdata [290], or Microformats[14]. In a study of 2.2 billion webpages crawled in 2013 from almost 13 million websites, Meusel et al. [269] found, for example, that 26.3% of the pages and 13.9% of the websites featured embedded data in one of these formats. More recently, JSON-LD (see Section 3.8.5) has also become a popular format for embedding data in HTML documents, with data surrounded by the tags `<script type="application/ld+json">``</script>`. The most common vocabularies used in such embedded data are Schema.org and the Open Graph Protocol, corresponding to the applications discussed in Section 2.3.3. Such data can readily be parsed into RDF from HTML pages; although Microdata and Microformats are not native RDF formats, they can be – and have been [269] – directly converted to RDF [188].

Discussion 8.7

FRANK: But most websites are based on data, with a database in the background used to populate individual pages. How does it make sense to scrape the data from HTML pages?

AIDAN: Well in some cases – like Wikipedia – the database used to power the website just stores elements of the articles without really understanding what those elements refer to semantically. In other cases – like IMDb for example – indeed the database probably stores relations between entities like movies, people, and so on; in such cases, extracting RDF directly from the database – using RDB2RDF techniques – would be a lot cleaner than trying to extract it from the HTML pages. The majority of websites do not, however, offer access to their underlying data(base), but rather only to the surface HTML pages that can be generated from that data.

JULIE: But websites may not want people to have access to that data!

AIDAN: In some cases yes, in some cases no. It really depends on what website owners get in return for publishing their data. If their data are used to build applications that drive traffic to their website – per the applications in Section 2.3.3 – then more and more websites will chose to make more and more of their underlying data available. Ideally, public data would not need to be extracted or "backwards-engineered" from HTML but would rather be offered already in structured formats. Per the growing prevalence of embedding data in HTML, this is becoming more and more of a trend.

Finally we remark that beyond the Web, the sorts of techniques we have discussed in this section are gaining more and more attention in the context of constructing knowledge graphs internal to particular organisations [197].

---

[14] http://microformats.org/

8.5.3 Link Discovery

The previous section has mostly focused on how to convert from legacy formats to data in an RDF format using IRIs as identifiers. However, in the
5-star Linked Open Data scheme (see Section 8.4.1), we would still only have
achieved 4-star data: we are still left to link our data to other data. Though
we have discussed in Section 8.3.3 some of the conceptual ways in which a
local dataset can be linked to external datasets, we have not discussed practical methods by which such links can be actually derived: how we can find the
correct entities to link to elsewhere? In fact, even when only considering our
own local dataset, if it has been derived from multiple independent sources
in a way that may lead to different identifiers being assigned to the same
entity, we may face a similar linking problem within the local dataset.

Given as input a set of properties P and two RDF graphs G_1 and G_2
representing a source graph and a target graph, the goal of **link discovery**
is to generate novel triples of the form (x,p,y) where x is mentioned in one
graph, y in the other, and $p \in P$. Per the discussion in Section 8.3.3, same-as
links (where $p =$ owl:sameAs) are most commonly sought in the context of
publishing Linked Data; in this case, the problem is equivalent to that of
entity matching [122]. However, link discovery frameworks are often general
enough to support links involving other properties as well. On the other
hand, when only one graph is given as input – i.e., where $G_1 = G_2$ – then the
problem is sometimes rather known as **link prediction**.

In some cases, link discovery can be quite easily addressed. For example,
considering the case of linking two datasets about books where both use
standard ISBN codes, determining same-as links could be quite straightforward: first the books can be linked, and thereafter, these links can be used
to generate further links between authors, genres, etc. Assuming that both
datasets were described with the same vocabulary terms whose semantics
were defined in OWL – for example, to indicate that the ex:isbn property
is inverse-functional, that the ex:firstAuthor property is functional, etc. –
much of the linking could even be done automatically with reasoning [204].

Clearly however the former case is rather an ideal one. In practice, most
cases will present significant challenges to the linking process: the two graphs
being linked may use different vocabulary, they may not have any uniquely
identifying keys in common, the naming of entities may vary, multiple entities
may share the same name, the graphs may describe orthogonal data about
the entities leaving little in common between them, and so forth. Indeed in
some cases there may simply be insufficient "overlap" between two related
datasets for a high-quality set of links to be identified. Still, however, links
are of central importance to Linked Data for enabling clients to find data
sources of interest, and thus techniques have been proposed to maximise the
accuracy and efficiency of link discovery for as many datasets as possible.

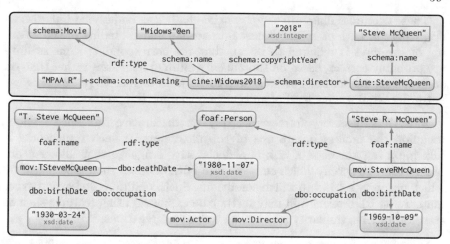

Fig. 8.9 Two example RDF graphs subject to linking

Example 8.29

Figure 8.9 presents a link discovery scenario where we would
like to identify which person in the bottom graph refers to the director
in the top graph (cine:SteveMcQueen). Based on name similarity, there
are two strong candidates in the bottom graph: mov:TSteveMcQueen and
mov:SteveRMcQueen. However, one of the candidates is an actor, and the
other a director, where the latter seems more fitting for a same-as link;
furthermore, we see that the actor died before the movie was released,
and hence, we could intuitively rule out that candidate. Based on the
presented data, we probably thus wish to create a same-as link between
cine:SteveMcQueen and mov:SteveRMcQueen – which would allow us to
integrate both datasets, combining cinema listings with biographical
details of the people involved in the movies showing – but the process
by which we can conclude that this link is (probably) correct is complex.

Example 8.30

As another challenging example, consider Figure 8.1 introduced
at the outset of the chapter. Focusing on ex1:Gaillimh and ex2:Galway,
we may intuit that both are cities based on the incident properties
ex1:city and ex2:city. We may further intuit that they are the same
city since the coordinates for ex1:Gaillimh are very similar to the coordinates on a supermarket in ex2:Galway. But again, deriving a same-as
link in this case presents us with significant challenges.

These examples illustrate the potential challenges underlying link discovery, where in both cases, an almost human-like understanding of the meaning of the data is required to assert that the corresponding same-as links are probably correct, based on (potentially fallible) heuristics rather than on crisp formal semantics. Furthermore, to be able to link large datasets, we naturally require some level of automation to scale the process.

Most link discovery frameworks rely on declarative link specifications to guide the process, where one of the most popular such frameworks is Silk [395]. At the core of Silk is a declarative language that allows a domain expert to specify which entities from both datasets should be linked by which property subject to which conditions. Such conditions go beyond exact matches on RDF terms and may further be expressed using features such as transformations, similarity metrics, as well as aggregations.

Example 8.31

We illustrate the main features of Silk by walking through an example – based on Figure 8.9 – of Silk's Link Specification Language, which allows a domain expert to specify rules and conditions by which entities are linked; the specification is then used to generate links.

We start by specifying some prefixes used in the rest of the document:

```
<Silk>
  <Prefixes>
    <Prefix id="dbo" namespace="http://dbpedia.org/ontology/" />
    <Prefix id="foaf" namespace="http://xmlns.com/foaf/0.1/" />
    <Prefix id="mov" namespace="http://mov.ie/v/" />
    <Prefix id="owl" namespace="http://www.w3.org/2002/07/owl#" />
    <Prefix id="schema" namespace="http://schema.org/" />
  </Prefixes>
  [...] <!-- continued later -->
```

We can then specify the locations of the graphs to be linked. In this case, we state that the source graph is a local file and the target graph is indexed by a remote SPARQL endpoint, providing locations for both.

```
  [...]
  <DataSource id="cin">
    <Param name="file" value="./cine.ttl"/>
    <Param name="format" value="TURTLE"/>
  </DataSource>
  <DataSource id="mov">
    <EndpointURI>http://mov.ie/sparql</EndpointURI>
  </DataSource>
  [...] <!-- continued later -->
```

Next we specify details of the linking rules; in this case we will specify one linking rule targeting directors in both graphs. We first assign an identifier for the rule and a property for the link:

```
[...]
  <Interlinks>
    <Interlink id="directors">
      <LinkType>owl:sameAs</LinkType>
[...] <!-- continued later -->
```

We can now specify a SPARQL-like query pattern that retrieves the candidates entities (the directors) in the source and target graphs:

```
[...]
        <SourceDataset dataSource="cin" var="d1">
          <RestrictTo>?m schema:director ?d1</RestrictTo>
        </SourceDataset>
        <TargetDataset dataSource="mov" var="d2">
          <RestrictTo>?d2 dbo:occupation mov:Director</RestrictTo>
        </TargetDataset>
[...] <!-- continued later -->
```

Next we specify the conditions under which pairs of entities from both sets should be linked. For this, we compute the maximum value of two string similarity measures – the Jaro–Winkler distance and the q-Gram measure – over the directors' names in both graphs:

```
[...]
        <LinkageRule>
          <Aggregate type="max">
            <Compare metric="jaroWinkler">
              <Input path="?d1/schema:name" />
              <Input path="?d2/foaf:name" />
            </Compare>
            <Compare metric="qGram">
              <Input path="?d1/schema:name" />
              <Input path="?d2/foaf:name" />
            </Compare>
          </Aggregate>
        </LinkageRule>
[...] <!-- continued later -->
```

We then state that only entity pairs with a score greater than 0.9 for this value should be linked with the previously specified property:

```
[...]
        <Filter threshold="0.9" />
      </Interlink>
[...] <!-- continued later -->
```

With this we end the link criteria. However, we may specify further links on different properties, on different entities, with different criteria, etc. In this case we will, however, simply end the link specification:

```
    ...
    </Interlink>
   </Interlinks>
  </Silk>
```

Per the above specification and the data in Figure 8.9, the following link will be generated (with a score of 0.905).

```
cine:SteveMcQueen owl:sameAs mov:SteveRMcQueen .
```

This previous example illustrates some of the main features of Silk; however, Silk provides a much wider range of features – of supported data sources, transformations (e.g., string operations), aggregation functions, and similarity metrics – than illustrated here [395]. Among these are Euclidean distance measures that would cover the scenario of Example 8.30. The framework further supports a range of optimisations, key amongst which is the notion of blocking, which in order to avoid the potentially quadratic ($O(n^2)$) number of pairwise checks between candidate entities, allows for first roughly grouping entities and thereafter only checking for eligible links within each group. For more details we refer the reader to the paper by Volz et al. [395].

In reference to Figure 8.9, it is perhaps worth mentioning, however, that to the best of our knowledge, there is no way to directly express the restriction that the director in the target graph cannot have died, say, two or more years before the year in which the movie in the source graph was released. While Silk offers a powerful rule-based linking framework, not all heuristics one might consider can be expressed; however, links could be further refined in a subsequent process (e.g., using SPARQL Update; see Section 6.5).

Aside from Silk, another popular link discovery framework is that of LIMES [291]. Much like Silk, LIMES supports user-generated link specifications that allow for first selecting source/target candidate entities, a property, link conditions, transformation operations, etc. However, unlike Silk, LIMES implements a variety of indexing techniques in metric spaces to narrow the search space for candidates, thus avoiding the need for pairwise checks. LIMES has also been extended with a variety of Machine Learning approaches to learn link specifications; amongst these we can find RAVEN [292], based on traditional Machine Learning classifiers; EAGLE [293] based on genetic programming, and many more besides [288].

In summary, link discovery is a fundamentally challenging problem, but one that lies at the very heart of Linked Data and – more broadly – our vision of the Web of Data. It is these links that would allow software agents to traverse the Web, automatically discovering and integrating the data needed to solve a given task from a variety of sources. A number of practical linking frameworks are currently available; however, the problem remains far from "solved" and novel techniques continue to be proposed and developed.

> **Further Reading 8.4**
>
> For further details of link discovery techniques proposed in the literature, we refer the reader to a survey by Nentwig et al. [288].

Discussion 8.8

ANNA: How does link discovery relate to the traditional data integration problem? In relational databases, for example, works on data deduplication, record linkage, etc., seem to have addressed similar problems to those mentioned here?

AIDAN: Fundamentally the problems are closely related, stemming from the need to identify elements of the data – records, tuples, identifiers, etc. – that refer to the same entity. The main difference in this context is the Web: while data integration has traditionally considered closed datasets in a local setting, here we are publishing the resulting links for others to reuse and build upon. The goal here is not to integrate data in the context of a given application, but rather to incrementally integrate data spanning the entire Web. So in summary, while the low-level techniques that can be applied may be similar, the high-level goal and the setting are quite different.

8.5.4 Hosting Linked Data

The final step for publishing Linked Data is hosting the RDF data on a Web server and ensuring that IRIs dereference to that content. However, in certain scenarios, accessing the data through dereferenceable IRIs alone may be inefficient, both for the client and the server; hence, other methods of data access may also be made available to clients. Finally, for clients to be able to know whether or not a Linked Dataset contains content relevant for them, what are the available options for accessing data, etc., it is also useful to provide structured metadata describing the dataset and its access methods.

8.5.4.1 Dereferenceable IRIs

Per the Linked Data principles, the requirements for publishing Linked Data are to uses HTTP IRIs to name things, to ensure that these IRIs dereference to content in standards such as RDF, and to offer links to external data by including dereferenceable IRIs from other datasets on the Web. In Section 8.2.2, we discussed the recipes for offering dereferenceable IRIs. In terms of implementing these recipes, there are three high-level options we can consider: (1) store content natively in RDF and serve it statically; (2) store content natively in RDF and serve it dynamically; (3) store content natively in another format and convert and serve it as RDF upon request.

1. The first option is to serve static RDF files through a Web server. This option delegates the burden of indexing the content of each file to the server's file system and the burden of retrieving the correct content for a requested IRI i to the Web server. Though simple, serving static files offers little in the way of flexibility, where the location and content of files must be managed manually or by custom scripts. This issue may become even more complex when one considers updates to the data, supporting content negotiation over different RDF syntaxes, and so forth. Problems with scalability may also arise: some file systems are not well-equipped to handle many small files. Hence serving static RDF files is more often adopted for quickly publishing a few small files (for example, a small ontology defining vocabulary terms) rather than large datasets.

2. The second option is to dynamically serve RDF from some form of RDF store, where a SPARQL engine is most typically used. This option delegates the burden of indexing and retrieving the content of each file to the RDF store. In the case of using a SPARQL endpoint, a common pattern is to redirect (or rewrite) a lookup on an IRI i to a query of the form DESCRIBE <i> on the endpoint, configuring the behaviour of DESCRIBE in the SPARQL engine to return the desired content; otherwise, custom CONSTRUCT queries on i can be used to fetch the desired RDF content. This option offers considerable flexibility, where the dereferenceable content of potentially manifold IRIs can be modified with a single SPARQL update command or by changing the query that fetches the dereferenced content, where the SPARQL (1.1) protocol already supports output in a variety of RDF syntaxes, and so forth. This option is also more scalable, where modern SPARQL engines are capable of storing billions of triples on a commodity machine. However, dynamically serving RDF in this manner does require installing an RDF store and configuring a Web server to rewrite or redirect IRI lookups to it; this initial cost may not be justified in cases where only a few files need to be served.

3. A third option is to store content in a non-RDF format, converting it and serving it as RDF on request. Content may be stored natively in a relational database, or served as XML, JSON, etc. At the time of the request for an IRI i, the content can be retrieved in its native format and a

method for converting the content to RDF can be applied, per an R2RML mapping, an XSLT document, by applying a JSON-LD context, or indeed any of the other methods previously discussed in Sections 8.5.1 & 8.5.2. The conversion may also be done by means of a custom script. The benefit of such an approach is that it obviates the need for duplicating storage in a non-RDF and an RDF format, which may complicate the management of data on the server; for example, if legacy applications on the server require a relational database, this approach obviates the need to maintain a relational and an RDF copy of the data. This option can thus be applied without major changes to the existing data management platform used to manage the data of a website, requiring an "RDF view" to be implemented on top of this platform rather than implementing a parallel RDF-based data management platform. The main downside of such an approach is the possibility of increased latency caused by retrieving the content required and converting it to RDF at runtime.

Of course, these options may be combined and blended to host dereferenceable RDF content on a Web server. Some RDF documents may be served statically, others generated dynamically from an RDF store, while others still are converted from non-RDF content. As another hybrid option, one could consider dynamically generating RDF documents from a non-RDF store the first time and then caching them in an RDF store in the expectation of repeated requests (of course this raises the issue of keeping cached RDF content up-to-date). Yet another possibility is to dynamically generate a single document from various sources, perhaps loading an RDF graph from a static file and merging it with the results of a SPARQL query and RDF data converted from a relational database. In summary, we see that there are many ways in which RDF content can be hosted and served through dereferenceable IRIs.

8.5.4.2 Linked Data Fragments

The standard way for a client to access the Linked Data they need is by using dereferenceable IRIs. However, in some cases, accessing relevant data through dereferenceable IRIs can be quite inefficient – or even infeasible.

Example 8.32

Consider a client wishing to find out the actors and actresses with which the director Steve McQueen has worked on the most movies from a particular Linked Dataset known to have this information. Assume we know the IRI for Steve McQueen and it dereferences to RDF data about him with a list of IRIs for his movies. We may subsequently dereference each movie IRI, where we may expect to find IRIs for all the cast members. Depending on precisely what information is dereferenced for an entity, we may further need to dereference the IRIs of some of the cast members to find their names. In summary, to find the data they need, the client must make several requests to the server, dereferencing a variety of IRIs, downloading each document returned, parsing it, and seeking the relevant data. Meanwhile the server may return a lot of information irrelevant to the client, such as biographical details of the director and cast members, ratings of the movies, etc.

In other cases, it may not be feasible for a client to find the data they need by dereferencing. Consider for example that the client does not know the IRI for the director, only that his name is Steve McQueen; or consider that the document dereferenced for the IRI of Steve Mc-Queen does not contain the movies he directed (rather the documents for the movies point to Steve McQueen as their director). In such cases, the client would not be able to directly access the data they need by dereferencing (at least, perhaps, without crawling the entire dataset).

Though not necessary to satisfy the Linked Data principles, it is thus common for Linked Data publishers to provide a variety of complementary ways for clients to access their data besides dereferenceable IRIs, including:

SPARQL Endpoints: Clients can issue a SPARQL query over the dataset, receiving direct results from the server.

Data Dumps: Clients can download an archived version of the entire dataset – or at least a large portion thereof – from a central location.

Triple Pattern Fragments: Clients can issue a query with a single triple pattern and receive an iterator of results from the server [393].

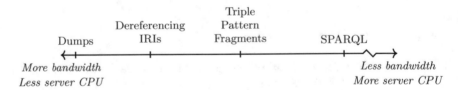

Fig. 8.10 Trade-off for access methods over Linked Data

In Figure 8.10 we summarise a core trade-off for different access methods [392], where responding to more specific/complex requests requires more CPU on the server-side but reduces bandwidth; on the other hand, less specific/simpler requests require less CPU on the server-side, but more bandwidth.

SPARQL endpoints allow clients to issue very specific requests to the server; for example, a client may in a single SPARQL query request the actors and actresses with which the director *named* Steve McQueen has worked on the most movies; the server can then directly respond with the requested results. Hence, when compared with dereferenceable IRIs, a SPARQL endpoint allows a wider range of requests to be answered efficiently and is much more parsimonious in terms of bandwidth: a client can express its specific criteria in a single request, and based on this, the server can return all and only the data of relevance to the client. Further given that dereferenceable IRIs are often themselves hosted using a SPARQL engine in the background to manage and serve RDF content, many Linked Data publishers opt to provide access to the underlying query engine through a public SPARQL endpoint [13].

However, hosting a public SPARQL endpoint can be costly for a server and – in turn – for a Linked Data publisher. Executing a SPARQL query may involve processing an arbitrary amount of data and may generate an exponential number of results; for example, a SPARQL query could ask for cliques of a particular size of actors/actresses where each pair has worked together in the same movie; over a large movie set, such a query would be very costly to compute no matter how optimised the engine. Hosting a public SPARQL endpoint may then see thousands of clients issuing arbitrarily-complex queries in parallel. For this reason, public SPARQL endpoints implement practical restrictions to prevent the server from being overloaded; these restrictions may include fixed thresholds on the number of results returned, the processing time for a query, and so forth [13]. Ultimately this limits the queries for which clients can expect (complete) results to be returned.

Despite these limitations, the public SPARQL endpoints of the most prominent Linked Datasets on the Web successfully manage to serve results for upwards of a million queries per day [342, 255]; however, not all queries issued to these endpoints can be successfully answered within the bounds of the practical thresholds they (are forced to) implement [342, 255].

For clients with a query in mind that is too expensive for the server to execute, what options are they left with? Such a client may consider instead trying to break the query down into multiple queries, but this may not always be easy to do (as in the case of cliques of actors/actresses, for example). A more general proposal to address this problem is to implement Web preemption [275], whereby a server can pause a query after it reaches a certain limit of processing, giving the option to the client to issue a further request to continue processing the query. This solution allows servers to bound the cost of individual requests, and in turn, to restrict the processing done for individual clients by limiting requests to a specific budget. However, Web preemption for SPARQL is still under development, where techniques have only been proposed thus far for a subset of the query language [275].

What about yet other clients who wish to run relatively simple queries but in volumes that would be infeasible to execute remotely? For such clients, a more practical alternative may be to download the entire dataset and process it locally. While this can often be achieved by crawling the dereferenceable IRIs on the server, such a crawl may – for a sufficiently large Linked Dataset – generate millions of (unnecessary) HTTP requests on the server.

A better option for clients who wish to work with the dataset locally is for the server to provide a dump of the dataset. A client can then download the dataset in an archived form. Dumps may be provided in a variety of syntaxes, with N-Triples or N-Quads being a popular choice for publishing dumps of an RDF graph or an RDF dataset respectively. Such syntaxes are easy to parse and processable line-by-line; although these formats contain no short-cuts and are thus less concise than other formats, their repetitiveness lends itself to excellent compression using standard methods (gzip, bzip2, etc.), saving storage and bandwidth. Custom formats have also been proposed for publishing dumps, including Header-Dictionary-Triples (HDT) [126], which achieves better compression than standard methods while also providing an index that allows for finding triples in the dump matching certain patterns.

Though relatively straightforward to provide a dump, there are a number of drawbacks. First and foremost, the client needs to install and maintain its own resources and software for being able to process data. Furthermore, providing dumps may be wasteful in terms of bandwidth, where a client may have to download all data just to access the portion they are interested in (e.g., casts of movies). More problematically, when the dataset changes, a client may need to re-download and re-process an updated dump.

The final Linked Data access method we consider – namely, **Triple Pattern Fragments (TPF)** [393] – tries to strike a balance between the strengths and weaknesses of the access methods previously discussed. A TPF service accepts from the client a query based on a single triple pattern. As a result, it provides an iterator over pages of results returned from the server, where the client can choose to request the next pages of results or issue another query.

When compared with SPARQL, TPF greatly limits the expressivity of a single request, which, as we have seen, requires that clients with more complex information needs decompose their complex requests into a sequence of simpler requests, potentially processing joins, aggregations, paths, etc., locally on the client's resources. The benefit of the TPF approach is that each individual request is now relatively easy for a server to respond to, with a more predictable cost than say an arbitrary SPARQL query request. In fact, the execution cost of a TPF request should be comparable to that for a dereferenceable IRI, requiring a single lookup on the server and streaming a predictable number of triples back to the client; in both cases, simpler requests improve the performance of caching. In contrast to dereferenceable IRIs, a wider variety of requests can be supported. The main drawback, versus SPARQL, is that more requests are required to serve more complex information needs, and indeed, intermediary data may need to be sent to the client for them to process joins, aggregations, etc., locally, which increases bandwidth usage. TPF thus offers an alternative access method that lies somewhere between dereferencing IRIs and hosting a SPARQL endpoint in terms of expressivity, server costs, and network usage. We briefly remark that a number of extensions to TPF – adding for example filters, limited forms of joins, etc. – have recently been proposed and studied [173].

Example 8.33

Consider again a client interested in the actors and actresses with which the director *named* Steve McQueen has worked on the most movies. This client may first issue a TPF request as follows:

```
?sm foaf:name "Steve McQueen" .
```

This request may return a number of possible IRIs of people named Steve McQueen, where the client may need to query the occupation for each one in turn until they find the director:

```
mov:TSteveMcQueen dbo:occupation ?oc .
```

...

```
mov:SteveRMcQueen dbo:occupation ?oc .
```

Assuming that the latter TPF request returns mov:Director, the next step is to find the movies that were directed by that person:

```
?mov schema:director mov:SteveRMcQueen .
```

Then for each movie, the client sends a new TPF request to retrieve the cast. Finally, the client can process these casts and count up the actors/actresses, issuing a final sequence of TPFs to find the names of the most frequent collaborators of Steve McQueen.

As per the trade-off shown previously in Figure 8.10, there is perhaps no single access method that is the best in all cases; rather it may be better for a server to offer multiple options to a client. Alternative access methods are abstracted by **Linked Data Fragments (TPF)** [392], where an individual Linked Data Fragment encapsulates an access method and is characterised by *data*: the results of a request; *metadata*: a description of the results of a request, for example, the number of results; and *controls*: how a client can interact with the server through that access method, for example, specifying a triple pattern in the case of TPF. An LDF server can then offer one or more LDF. Given a SPARQL query, a client can then communicate with the server to find the most appropriate LDF to use for a particular request, and execute the query following the controls provided. Unless the chosen LDF refers to a SPARQL endpoint, the client will need to generate an execution plan for the available LDF, which will typically involve executing joins and other query processing steps locally, as discussed previously.

The topic of efficiently consuming Linked Data using different access methods is an active area of research. A number of works have proposed algorithms and optimisations for running complex queries by issuing multiple requests to lower-level access methods. Hartig et al. [172] propose methods for executing SPARQL basic graph patterns on top of dereferenceable IRIs using a technique called link-traversal querying. Umbrich et al. [384] combine link traversal querying with SPARQL endpoints in order to find a query plan that retrieves fresh results efficiently in the presence of dynamic data. As afore-mentioned, a client with an appropriate query processing module can execute SPARQL queries on a TPF server [393], and extensions of TPF have been explored and compared theoretically [173]. Going further, a number of novel query languages – such as nSPARQL [311], NautiLOD [129], LDQL [174], and more besides – have also been proposed to allow clients to declaratively specify and execute more complex requests over such access methods.

In summary, a Linked Data publisher must minimally provide dereference-able IRIs through which their data can be accessed. However, to increase convenience for clients – and indeed to reduce the bandwidth and server CPU usage – a publisher may optionally make a number of alternative access methods available, including dumps, TPF endpoints, SPARQL endpoints, etc., where these access methods can be exposed to clients through LDF.

8.5.4.3 Dataset Descriptions

In the previous discussion we assumed that clients already know which Linked Dataset they would like to access data from, which access methods are avail-able to choose from, and where to find them. But how should clients know which datasets offer data about movies, for example? And given a partic-ular dataset of interest, how should clients know which access methods are available – and where? To aid clients to discover their datasets, publishers will thus often provide descriptions of their datasets in a structured format; upon finding this description, the client then has more information on which to judge whether or not the dataset is of relevance to them, and if so, what might be the best way to access its data given the task at hand.

While LDF offers a possible solution with respect to how clients can find and invoke different access methods over a Linked Dataset, it does not provide vocabulary for describing the content of a dataset, which may be needed for the client to discover the dataset of interest in the first place. One of the most popular ways to describe the content of a Linked Dataset is using the **Vocabulary of Interlinked Documents (VoID)** [7], which provides terms for describing high-level metadata about a dataset, technical details about how it is published and where it can be accessed, as well as a range of statistics that help to quantify and characterise its content. VoID descriptions are given in RDF and can optionally be integrated within the dataset itself, or published separately as Linked Data. We now provide an overview of the main features of the VoID vocabulary by way of an extended example.

Example 8.34

A VoID description begins by identifying the dataset and providing metadata about it, including, for example, an associated homepage, a title, the date it was last modified, a licence by which it can be used, the main subject of the dataset, and so forth.

```
@prefix void: <http://rdfs.org/ns/void#> .
@prefix xsd: <http://www.w3.org/2001/XMLSchema#> .
@prefix dct: <http://purl.org/dc/terms/> .
@prefix foaf: <http://xmlns.com/foaf/0.1/> .
@prefix sd: <http://www.w3.org/ns/sparql-service-description#> .

<#movies> a void:Dataset ;
  foaf:homepage <https://mov.ie> ;
  dct:title "Mov.ie Linked Data"@en ;
  dct:modified "2019-02-12"^^xsd:date ;
  dct:license <http://www.opendatacommons.org/licenses/odbl/> ;
  dct:subject <https://www.wikidata.org/wiki/Q11424> ; # film
  [...] # continued
```

Other general information about the dataset can be provided here, including its creators, the sources it uses, and so forth. VoID further provides a number of properties for defining technical aspects about how the dataset can be accessed, including features (such as RDF syntaxes) supported, the location of a SPARQL endpoint from which the dataset can be queried, the location of a dataset dump, examples of dereferenceable IRIs, as well as the main vocabularies used:

```
[...]
<#movies> a void:Dataset ;
[...]
  void:feature <http://www.w3.org/ns/formats/RDF_XML> ;
  void:feature <http://www.w3.org/ns/formats/Turtle> ;
  void:sparqlEndpoint <http://mov.ie/sparql> ;
  void:dataDump <http://mov.ie/dumps/all.nt.gz> ;
  void:exampleResource <http://mov.ie/db/m/M10001> ;
  void:exampleResource <http://mov.ie/db/d/Nike%20Leigh> ;
  void:vocabulary <http://xmlns.com/foaf/0.1/> ;
  void:vocabulary <http://schema.org/> ;
  [...] # continued
```

VoID further defines terms that allow for describing high-level statistics of the content of the dataset, including the total number of triples, entities described, classes used, properties used, distinct subjects, distinct objects, and dereferenceable RDF documents made available, which allows publishers to inform potential consumers as to the breadth and scale of the content of the given dataset in an agreed-upon way:

```
  ...
<#movies> a void:Dataset ;
  ...
  void:triples 104892342 ;
  void:entities 16124012 ;
  void:classes 14 ;
  void:properties 35 ;
  void:distinctSubjects 14819341 ;
  void:distinctObjects 38234912 ;
  void:documents 14819337 .
  ... # continued
```

Publishing such statistics once on the server-side obviates the need for potentially many clients to redundantly compute them from scratch. The statistics themselves can then be used in order to discover interesting datasets, to choose appropriate systems and techniques to manage a dataset locally, to optimise query evaluation, and so forth.

A dataset may be further partitioned into sub-datasets; in fact there are a number of ways in which this partitioning can be defined. First, custom partitions can be identified and linked to their parent dataset:

```
  ...
<#movies> a void:Dataset ;
  ...
  void:subset <#directors> ;
  void:subset <#cast> .
```

These partitions are themselves datasets and can be described as such:

```
  ...
<#cast> a void:Dataset ;
  dct:title "Mov.ie Cast Info"@en ;
  void:dataDump <http://mov.ie/dumps/casts.nt.gz> ;
  void:triples 48129126 .

<#directors> a void:Dataset ;
  dct:title "Mov.ie Director Info"@en ;
  void:dataDump <http://mov.ie/dumps/directors.nt.gz> ;
  void:triples 9347418 .
```

Here we describe two subsets of the data: one about casts and another about directors, providing links to separate dumps, as well as basic statistics about the number of triples in each dataset.

Another form of partitioning is based on properties and classes. Such partitions are again themselves datasets and are described as such.

A property-based partition is defined as all triples in the parent dataset that use a particular property; for example:

```
[...]
<#movies> a void:Dataset ;
[...]
  void:propertyPartition [
    void:property schema:director ;
    void:triples 2123742
  ] ;
  void:propertyPartition [
    void:property schema:director ;
    void:triples 2123742
  ] .
```

Here we state how many triples use these particular properties; we could also define other statistics as applicable to datasets.

A class-based partition, on the other hand, is defined in terms of all the triples whose subject is declared to be an instance of that class:

```
[...]
<#movies> a void:Dataset ;
[...]
  void:classPartition [
    void:class schema:Movie ;
    void:triples 71238123
  ] ;
  void:propertyPartition [
    void:property schema:Person ;
    void:triples 18239143
  ] .
```

The first class partition states that there are 71,238,123 triples whose subject is declared to be of type schema:Movie. Again class partitions can be described as if they were themselves datasets, which leads to, for example, the possibility of describing nested partitions:

```
[...]
<#movies> a void:Dataset ;
[...]
  void:classPartition [
    void:class schema:Person ;
    void:triples 18239143 ;
    void:propertyPartition [
        void:property schema:name ;
        void:triples 1023912
    ]
  ] .
```

This nested partition – referring to the set of triples in the parent dataset whose predicate is schema:name and whose subject is of type schema:Person – states that there are 1,023,912 names of people.

Here we have illustrated the main features of VoID; other features include the ability to define regular expressions on IRIs that describe the naming scheme used, the ability to define triples as link sets that connect two datasets, the ability to integrate VoID with the SPARQL Service Description vocabulary (see Section 6.7.3) describing how a dataset is indexed in a SPARQL endpoint, etc. For more on such features, we refer to the specification [7].

Remark 8.11

With respect to computing the VoID description of a dataset – and in particular the statistics of the dataset and its property and class partitions – a number of frameworks have been proposed. Amongst these, Makela [254] proposes to use a SPARQL 1.1 endpoint to generate VoID statistics, while Böhm et al. [65] rather propose to use the distributed MapReduce framework for large-scale datasets.

In summary, VoID allows publishers to describe a Linked Dataset in terms of its origins, topic, licencing, access method, content, and more besides. Such metadata can be used by clients to discover and interact with novel Linked Datasets on the fly. But how can clients discover the VoID description of a dataset in the first place? There are two main options. First, if a client knows the domain of a dataset (e.g., `http://mov.ie/`), then the VoID specification recommends that the VoID description be published, by convention, at the following well-known location on that domain [7]:

$$\text{http://mov.ie/.well-known/void}$$

A client knowing the dataset's domain can then simply retrieve the VoID description at the corresponding location for that domain. On the other hand, if a client does not know a dataset's domain – but rather simply knows that they are interested in Linked Datasets about movies, for example – they may rather consult a centralised catalogue of Linked Dataset descriptions, such as the DataHub[15], the VoID Store[16], SPORTAL [176], or a similar service.

8.6 Linked Data Platform (LDP)

Much of the content of the modern Web is user-generated. Many of the most popular websites – like Facebook, Twitter, Instagram, Reddit, Wikipedia, etc. – are platforms for users to interact with and exchange content. If we were, for a moment, to imagine a read-only version of such websites – where users serve purely as consumers of content, unable to produce and push new

---

[15] `https://datahub.io/`

[16] `http://void.rkbexplorer.com/`

content back to the platform – we can perhaps imagine that such websites would cease to offer users the very thing that made them so influential.

The previous section has dealt with a read-only vision of Linked Data, where clients can request RDF documents from a Linked Data server, but cannot push back content to that server. But if we were to conceive of the Web of Data as something that is *read-only* – where clients are not empowered to push content back to a server – we may, by this presumption, tend to overlook an important class of applications, namely *read–write* applications.

The **Linked Data Platform (LDP)** [365] lays the foundations for read–write Linked Data applications by specifying how a client can modify both RDF and non-RDF content on a server. These modifications are made through a HTTP interface, with the server providing information about what resources are currently available and what operations can be invoked upon them by a client, where the client can then invoke one of those operations and (where applicable) send the content with which those operations should be performed. In this section, we provide an overview of the LDP in terms of how clients and servers can communicate and what operations are supported.

Historical Note 8.4

LDP [365] – standardised in 2015 – was preceded by a number of works on read–write applications for the Web. The World Wide Web itself was originally conceived of as a collaborative platform that would allow clients to modify documents on a server [52], with HTTP supporting operations such as PATCH and DELETE for clients to request modifications to resources on the server. These read–write features were not well-supported by early browsers and became infrequently used, leading to a read-only inception of the Web. More collaborative platforms later became common on the Web – with the advent of weblogs, wikis, social networks, etc. – that allowed users to push content back to the server. Although such user-generated content changed the landscape of the Web – inspiring the name "Web 2.0" – the read–write aspect of these novel platforms was largely implemented in an ad hoc manner by different websites, often using asynchronous requests (AJAX/Javascript) on top of HTTP GET and POST to push content to and request modifications from the server. An extension to HTTP called Web Distributed Authoring and Versioning (WebDAV) – first standardised in 1999 and updated in 2007 [119] – allowed clients to request additional operations, such as copying, moving, locking and unlocking resources, as well as support for creating new collections of resources and atomic transactions. Around 2009, a variety of proposals began to emerge around the topic of read–write Linked Data [50, 47, 232]. All of these works, specifications and proposals served as antecedents to the working group that led to the eventual standardisation of the LDP [365].

8.6.1 Resources and Containers

LDP is built upon two main concepts: LDP *resources* and LDP *containers*. A loose but useful analogy is to think of LDP containers as (virtual) folders and LDP resources as documents, where containers then contain resources. Some documents are RDF documents while others are not. Each LDP container is represented with a special RDF document that represents its current state, in particular offering customisable links to the LDP resources it contains; with this document, the LDP specification considers LDP containers to also be LDP resources, which implies that LDP containers can contain other LDP containers (much like folders can contain other folders).

> **Remark 8.12**
>
> Strictly we should say *LDP Resources* to avoid confusion with the more general notion of a *resource* as anything with identity, but to avoid an acronym soup, we often say *resource*, which should be understood to mean an *LDP Resource* in this section; we will rather use the term *entity* to refer to the more general type of resource. We further will use the term *container* to refer to an *LDP Container*, noting that LDP and RDF containers have no relation.

More specifically, LDP is defined in terms of the following main concepts:

LDP Resource (LDPR): a document that can be retrieved via HTTP; there are two types of LDPR:

> **LDP RDF Source (LDP-RS)**: an RDF document that can be retrieved via HTTP;
> **LDP Non-RDF Source (LDP-NR)**: a non-RDF document that can be retrieved via HTTP.

LDP Container (LDPC): a collection of resources represented by an RDF document (an LDP-RS); there are three types of LDPC:

> **LDP Basic Container (LDP-BC)**: a container that links only to the resources it *contains*: the resources it has created and controls;
> > **LDP Direct Container (LDP-DC)**: a container that can additionally maintain a custom triple for each resource it contains;
> > > **LDP Indirect Container (LDP-IC)**: a container that can additionally maintain a custom triple for a particular entity mentioned in each RDF document it contains.

We make the following remarks with respect to these definitions:

- All definitions assume compliance with the LDP standard described in the following; for example, an RDF document that can be retrieved by

HTTP is not considered to be an LDP-RS unless the server hosting it supports the LDP operations that we shall soon cover.

- Per the nesting shown in the definitions, while a resource is either an RDF source or a non-RDF source (it cannot be both), a direct container is also considered to be a basic container, while an indirect container is considered to be a direct container (and transitively, a basic container).

- A container is represented by a resource (specifically an LDP-RS), where the specification thus considers containers to themselves *be* resources (of type LDP-RS); by this convention, when we say, for example, that a container is a collection of resources, we understand that resources can also be containers, and that containers can contain containers. Here we will thus use "(LDP) resource" to refer to (LDP) containers and documents.

- Another important distinction raised by these definitions is that between *containment* and *membership*: a container (LDPC) can be used to create resources (LDPR), where that container then *contains* (and controls) that resource. On the other hand, a direct or indirect container (LDP-DC or LDP-IC, respectively) can also maintain *membership* triples with custom properties that link to the resources that the container directly contains (LDP-DC) or to entities described by those resources (LDP-IC).

We provide a concrete example to help digest these concepts.

Example 8.35

We return to Example 8.15, and to Anna, who is still thinking about the design of her social cinema application based on Linked Data. She has collected RDF data about movies, directors, casts and so forth, and she has also linked these data with Linked Datasets like Wikidata, from which her application can periodically draw new and better information. She has also been successful in collecting embedded RDF data – described in Schema.org – from the webpages of some cinema chains about their screenings, including locations, times and even (in some cases) prices. With this, she can already build a search service that allows users to find upcoming screenings of movies by genre, or director, compare prices and ratings, and even subscribe for alerts.

But she is still missing the social aspect, whereby users could not only rate and discuss movies and cinemas, but also upload profiles and images, offer and receive recommendations, and perhaps even organise to go to the cinema together. She would also like to offer the cinemas control over data about them in the application, allowing them, for example, to update the available information about screenings, provide discounted rates, message users subscribed to them, and perhaps even introduce loyalty programmes for regular visitors using the application (or whatever else they might deem of interest, she thinks).

Realising that the application she envisages is read–write rather than read-only, she looks into using the LDP to allow her clients – movie-goers and cinema employees alike – to push content into the application and to have control over that content. Thinking about her problem in terms of containers and documents, she decides on the following initial structure to implement the LDP:

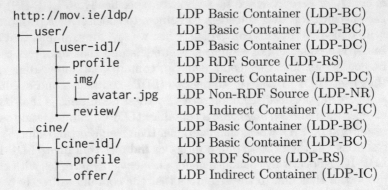

`http://mov.ie/ldp/`	LDP Basic Container (LDP-BC)
`user/`	LDP Basic Container (LDP-BC)
`[user-id]/`	LDP Basic Container (LDP-DC)
`profile`	LDP RDF Source (LDP-RS)
`img/`	LDP Direct Container (LDP-DC)
`avatar.jpg`	LDP Non-RDF Source (LDP-NR)
`review/`	LDP Indirect Container (LDP-IC)
`cine/`	LDP Basic Container (LDP-BC)
`[cine-id]/`	LDP Basic Container (LDP-BC)
`profile`	LDP RDF Source (LDP-RS)
`offer/`	LDP Indirect Container (LDP-IC)

In this folder-like structure, paths ending in slash are containers, while other paths are documents. A `[user-id]/` container will be instantiated for each movie-goer according to an ID they choose, and likewise a `[cine-id]/` container will be instantiated for each cinema. The `profile` document is an RDF document; its file extension is omitted to allow a client to select their preferred syntax via content negotiation, where LDP requires support for (at least) Turtle and JSON-LD.

Under this structure, once a new user (movie-goer) has authenticated themselves under a chosen ID, a container will be created for them with this ID within the parent `user/` container. As they add data through the application, these data will be stored in `profile` (for personal information, social connections, etc.). Any reviews that they submit will be stored as an RDF document within the `review` sub-container. Any images they upload will be stored in the `img/` sub-container, including an avatar they can upload for their profile. When a user uploads a new image to `img/` or a new review to `review/`, Anna would like to automatically add a triple indicating that the user created these new resources; using direct and indirect containers will allow her to create custom triples along these lines (the details of which are discussed later).

On the other hand, cinema employees – once authenticated with their ID – can connect to a container with their chosen ID within the parent `cine/` container to manage their cinema's data. Again, profile data for the cinema are made available in an RDF document called `profile`. Furthermore, data about the offers (screenings) from the cinema are maintained within the container shown, where a separate RDF document will be used to store data about each offer. The use of indirect containers will again allow the offer entities themselves (rather than the documents describing them) to be automatically linked to the cinema entity (rather than its container). We provide more details on this later.

A key point in this platform – and one of the motivating factors for the LDP standard – is that clients of the application now have two options to interact with their data: through the application's human-friendly HTML-based interface (as is now commonplace on the Web), or through the application's machine-friendly LDP-based interface. Anna further resolves to ensure that the application keeps both synchronised, meaning that updates through the LDP-based interface are reflected in the HTML-based application, and vice versa. This offers movie-goers the ability to use an LDP-aware client to review and modify the data that the application has about them, and likewise offers cinemas the option of using software to push content to the application rather than waiting for the application to pull content from them, or having to manually enter the content on the website.

Anna then begins to think to herself – if other websites followed the same principles, users could manage their data on several websites at once through such LDP interfaces, importing their data from one to the other, offering them control over their decentralised online presence. Maybe – with authorisation from the corresponding user – her application could even have containers in other future LDP-based applications, from which it could automatically push/pull content.

Daydreaming now over, she starts to think about what operations the clients of her LDP-based interface can effect within the various containers and documents she has defined in her structure.

8.6.2 HTTP RESTful Interface

We discussed resources and containers with which clients can interact through the LDP. But what precisely can clients do with these resources and containers? And how is this interaction specified?

The LDP is based on a HTTP **RESTful** interface, meaning that it is based on – and respects the RESTful semantics of – the HTTP methods DELETE, GET, HEAD, OPTIONS, PATCH, POST and PUT. Table 8.4 describes how these methods are used in the context of LDP and which must be implemented according to the standard; one may note that only read-only operations are required, though of course the expectation is that some of the other methods will also be supported on some resources for some users. Where these methods are implemented, the standard specifies a number of additional restrictions on how they are used, when they can be used, what effects they have, and what

Table 8.4 Optional and required HTTP methods for LDP servers

Method	Required?	Operation
GET	YES	Returns the resource's representation
HEAD	YES	Returns headers (same as GET but without content)
OPTIONS	YES	Returns the HTTP methods allowed on the resource
DELETE	NO	Delete the resources
PATCH	NO	Modify an existing resource
POST	NO	Create resources within a container
PUT	NO	Overwrite (or create) resources

responses are returned. A server that supports at least the required methods, with all supported methods implemented in a manner compliant with the LDP standard, is called an *LDP server*. We refer the reader to the specification for precise details on the requirements that an LDP server must meet [365], where here we rather give an extended example to illustrate how a client can interact with such a server.

Example 8.36

Following the LDP structure laid out in Example 8.35, assume that a new user registers with the username lev and an avatar image (uploaded to and saved by the server as avatar.jpg). Further assume that the application then initialises the following LDP resources:

/ldp/user/	LDP Basic Container (LDP-BC)
└─ lev/	LDP Basic Container (LDP-BC)
├─ profile	LDP RDF Source (LDP-RS)
├─ img/	LDP Direct Container (LDP-DC)
│ └─ avatar.jpg	LDP Non-RDF Source (LDP-NR)
└─ review/	LDP Indirect Container (LDP-IC)

Authenticated as lev, we assume that the user has read-only access to the /ldp/user/ container, but has read–write access on the /ldp/user/lev container and the resources it (transitively) contains.

Through the LDP interface, assume that the user now performs a GET on the basic container /ldp/user/lev, asking for the LDP-RS (RDF document) describing the container in Turtle format:

```
GET /ldp/user/lev/ HTTP/1.1
Host: mov.ie
Accept: text/turtle
```

Assuming all goes well, the server may then respond with a 200 OK response code and with a HTTP header as follows:

```
HTTP/1.1 200 OK
Content-Type: text/turtle; charset=UTF-8
Link: <http://www.w3.org/ns/ldp#BasicContainer>; rel="type",
    ↪                <http://www.w3.org/ns/ldp#Resource>; rel="type"
Allow: OPTIONS,HEAD,GET,PUT,DELETE,POST,PATCH
Accept-Post: text/turtle, application/ld+json, image/bmp, image/jpeg
Accept-Patch: text/ldpatch
Content-Length: 211
ETag: W/'ACC15E35A607DB49'
```

This header contains the following information:

Content-Type: indicates the syntax and encoding of the content in the body of the response.

Link: indicates the type of LDP resource at the requested location; this is required by the LDP specification in all responses.

Allow: indicates the supported HTTP methods that can be requested on that resource.

Accept-Post: indicates what content types POST accepts (this is a novel HTTP header proposed by the LDP specification [365]).

Accept-Patch: indicates what content types PATCH accepts (in Remark 8.14 we will provide further details on this option).

Content-Length: indicates the length of the content in bytes.

ETag: identifies the current version of the resource, which changes if and only if the resource's content changes; this is required by LDP in response to GET and HEAD calls. The ETag value may be computed in a number of ways: as a hash over the content, as an incremental counter of changes, or as a timestamp of the last change. The value is useful to check (with HEAD) if a locally cached version can be reused or if the resource needs to be refreshed from the server.

The content following this header would be along the following lines:

```
@prefix dct: <http://purl.org/dc/terms/> .
@prefix ldp: <http://www.w3.org/ns/ldp#> .

<> a ldp:BasicContainer ;
  dct:title "Mov.ie: lev's Data Portal"@en ;
  ldp:contains <profile> , <img/> , <review/> .
```

This is the RDF document (LDP-RS) that represents this basic container, describing the type of the container, the resources it contains, as well as providing other optional data, such as a name for the container.

Assume now that the user wishes to view their profile data through the LDP interface. They issue a GET on /ldp/user/lev/profile, receiving a similar HTTP header as before, and the following content, automatically generated for them when they registered:

```
@prefix dct: <http://purl.org/dc/terms/> .
@prefix foaf: <http://xmlns.com/foaf/0.1/> .
@prefix sioc: <http://rdfs.org/sioc/ns#> .

<> a foaf:PersonalProfileDocument;
  foaf:primaryTopic <#user> ;
  dct:title "Mov.ie: lev's Profile"@en .

<#user> a sioc:UserAccount ;
  sioc:name "lev" ;
  sioc:avatar <img/avatar.jpg> .
```

This is a regular RDF document without LDP-specific metadata.

Next they decide to remove their avatar; they do so using DELETE:

```
DELETE /ldp/user/lev/img/avatar.jpg HTTP/1.1
Host: mov.ie
```

If successful, the server will return a header-only response:

```
HTTP/1.1 204 No Content
Link: <http://www.w3.org/ns/ldp#Resource>; rel="type"
```

Upon performing a GET on the /ldp/user/lev/img/ container, assume that the LDP server responds with the following RDF document:

```
@prefix dct: <http://purl.org/dc/terms/> .
@prefix ldp: <http://www.w3.org/ns/ldp#> .
@prefix sioc: <http://rdfs.org/sioc/ns#> .

<> a ldp:DirectContainer ;
  dct:title "Mov.ie: lev's Image Collection"@en ;
  ldp:membershipResource <../profile#user> ;
  ldp:hasMemberRelation sioc:creator_of .
```

This time we see that the container is a direct container, currently not containing any resources. However, the last two triples of the document illustrate two novel aspects specific to direct containers: a membership resource and a membership relation. When a resource is added to the container, the LDP server will not only automatically add an ldp:contains relation, but also a membership triple linking the membership resource with the new resource per the membership relation.

To see these membership triples in action, assume that the user decides to upload a new avatar for their account. To do so, they will use PUT to upload a new image to /ldp/user/lev/img/avatar.jpg:

```
PUT /ldp/user/lev/img/avatar.jpg HTTP/1.1
Host: mov.ie
Content-Type: image/jpeg

[...]
```

where [...] begins the image data. Assuming the operation is successful, the server should provide the following header-only response:

```
HTTP/1.1 204 No Content
Link: <http://www.w3.org/ns/ldp#Resource>; rel="type"
```

Now if a fresh GET is performed on the /ldp/user/lev/img/ container, the LDP server will return the following RDF content:

```
@prefix dct: <http://purl.org/dc/terms/> .
@prefix ldp: <http://www.w3.org/ns/ldp#> .
@prefix sioc: <http://rdfs.org/sioc/ns#> .

<> a ldp:DirectContainer ;
  dct:title "Mov.ie: lev's Image Collection"@en ;
  ldp:membershipResource <../profile#user> ;
  ldp:hasMemberRelation sioc:creator_of ;
  ldp:contains <avatar.jpg> .

<../profile#user> sioc:creator_of <avatar.jpg> .
```

Aside from managing ldp:contains relations from the parent container to the resources it contains, by using a direct container we can also specify a membership resource to which relations will be automatically added (or removed) to/from any resource added (or removed) from the container. In this case, we have opted to automatically add/remove sioc:creator_of relations from the IRI of the corresponding user account to any images added to the image container. If we preferred, we could rather specify the membership relation in the other direction:

```
[...]
  ldp:membershipResource <../profile#user> ;
  ldp:isMemberOfRelation sioc:has_creator ;
[...]
```

which would result in membership triples of the following form:

```
[...]
<avatar.jpg> sioc:has_creator <../profile#user> .
```

One membership relation and resource may be specified per container.

The user now decides to subscribe to the cinema named hoyts. To do so, they may use the HTML-interface, or if they know the appropriate property recognised by the application, and the IRI for the cinema's account, they could issue a PUT to the LDP server with the header:

```
PUT /ldp/user/lev/profile HTTP/1.1
Host: mov.ie
Content-Type: text/turtle
If-Match: W/'F3F8B1603A72D582'
```

The If-Match: header specifies that the PUT should only be executed if the given value matches the current ETag value of the resource at that location. The following content is also sent with a new (final) triple:

```
@prefix dct: <http://purl.org/dc/terms/> .
@prefix foaf: <http://xmlns.com/foaf/0.1/> .
@prefix sioc: <http://rdfs.org/sioc/ns#> .

<> a foaf:PersonalProfileDocument;
  foaf:primaryTopic <#user> ;
  dct:title "lev's Profile" .

<#user> a sioc:UserAccount ;
  sioc:name "lev" ;
  sioc:avatar <img/avatar.jpg> ;
  sioc:follows <../../cine/hoyts/profile#user> .
```

The server will try to replace the profile resource with the content provided, and if successful, will return a 204 No Content response.

Finally, the user wants to add a review. First, they issue a GET on the /ldp/user/lev/review/ container, defined as an indirect container:

```
@prefix dct: <http://purl.org/dc/terms/> .
@prefix foaf: <http://xmlns.com/foaf/0.1/> .
@prefix ldp: <http://www.w3.org/ns/ldp#> .
@prefix schema: <http://schema.org/> .

<> a ldp:IndirectContainer ;
  dct:title "Mov.ie: lev's Review Collection"@en ;
  ldp:membershipResource <../profile#user> ;
  ldp:isMemberRelationOf schema:author ;
  ldp:insertedContentRelation foaf:primaryTopic .
```

The container is currently empty. As per a direct container, a membership resource and a(n inverse) membership property are defined. This time however, an additional property is defined, whose value in the added document will be linked to by the membership property.

To see indirect membership in action, assume that the user now wishes to add a review. They may again do this through the HTML-based interface of the website, but assuming they are aware of the expected data structure used and the IRIs required, they may also use the LDP-based interface. This time, rather than using PUT to create a resource at a specified location, they can rather use POST to submit the content to the parent container, with the following header:

```
POST /ldp/user/lev/review/ HTTP/1.1
Host: mov.ie
Content-Type: text/turtle
```

and the following content:

```
@prefix dct: <http://purl.org/dc/terms/> .
@prefix foaf: <http://xmlns.com/foaf/0.1/> .
@prefix schema: <http://schema.org/> .

<> a foaf:Document ;
  foaf:primaryTopic <#review> ;
  dct:title "lev's Review of Gattaca"@en .

<#review> a schema:Review ;
  schema:itemReviewed <http://mov.ie/m/M01013> ;
  schema:reviewBody "I liked the stairs"@en ;
  schema:reviewRating [
    a schema:Rating ;
    schema:bestRating 5 ;
    schema:worstRating 0 ;
    schema:ratingValue 4
  ] .
```

Given that the POST request has not specified a location for the resource, the LDP server may assign a name, assumed here to be r1 (note that if a review were previously posted at r1 and subsequently deleted, the LDP specification recommends to avoid reusing identifiers for deleted resources and prefer fresh identifiers each time [365, 344]). If the server succeeds in creating the resource, it may then return a header as follows:

```
HTTP/1.1 201 Created
Location: http://mov.ie/ldp/user/lev/review/r1
Link: <http://www.w3.org/ns/ldp#Resource>; rel="type"
Content-Length: 494
```

The Location: header indicates to the client where the resource has been created (as aforementioned, the location is automatically generated by the server rather than being part of the client's request). Issuing a GET on the /ldp/user/lev/review/ container again, we find new containment and (indirect) membership triples within the container:

```
@prefix dct: <http://purl.org/dc/terms/> .
@prefix foaf: <http://xmlns.com/foaf/0.1/> .
@prefix ldp: <http://www.w3.org/ns/ldp#> .
@prefix schema: <http://schema.org/> .

<> a ldp:IndirectContainer ;
  dct:title "Mov.ie: lev's Review Collection"@en ;
  ldp:membershipResource <../profile#user> ;
  ldp:isMemberRelationOf schema:author ;
  ldp:insertedContentRelation foaf:primaryTopic ;
  ldp:contains <r1> .

<r1#review> schema:author <../profile#user> .
```

Unlike the direct container seen previously, in this case the membership triple points to a resource inside the created RDF document – found using the inserted content relation – rather than the RDF document itself. Such triples are again added and removed automatically as new resources are added and removed from the container.

This extended example illustrates the main features of the LDP specification and how clients can interact with an LDP server via HTTP. The presented interactions were all successful; however, in reality an LDP server may choose to reject certain requests. To take one prominent example, the standard recommends that an LDP server reject any PUT request to a container that attempts to modify its containment relations. Furthermore, a more conservative LDP server may choose to reject the creation or modification of resources leading to a state that the application using the data may not be able to recognise. Where requests are not fulfilled for such reasons, a 4xx response code must be returned; furthermore an LDP server is required to specify to the client the constraints it imposes on the creation and modification of resources (we refer to the standard for details [365]).

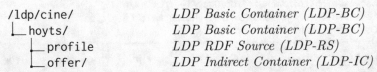

Exercise 8.7

Assume that we have an LDP client authenticated with the cinema user account hoyts, *with access to the following resources:*

/ldp/cine/	*LDP Basic Container (LDP-BC)*
└─ hoyts/	*LDP Basic Container (LDP-BC)*
└─ profile	*LDP RDF Source (LDP-RS)*
└─ offer/	*LDP Indirect Container (LDP-IC)*

The top-level basic container will contain basic containers for each cinema user account. The container for each account contains a profile described in RDF, as well as an indirect container that will be used to store offers made by the cinema associated with the account, with appropriate links maintained from the profile; here, the use of an indirect container will allow us to link the user account to the offers it makes.

More specifically, assume that `profile` *is a graph as follows:*

```
@prefix dct: <http://purl.org/dc/terms/> .
@prefix foaf: <http://xmlns.com/foaf/0.1/> .
@prefix schema: <http://schema.org/> .

<> a foaf:Document;
  foaf:primaryTopic <#cine> ;
  dct:title "hoyt's Profile" .

<#cine> a schema:MovieTheatre ;
  schema:name "Cine Hoyts" ;
  schema:screenCount 5 ;
  schema:geo [
    schema:latitute -33.4414991 ;
    schema:longitude -70.6505177 ;
    schema:address "San Antonio 144, Santiago, Chile"
  ] .
```

Also assume that offers from the cinema are described as follows:

```
@prefix dct: <http://purl.org/dc/terms/> .
@prefix foaf: <http://xmlns.com/foaf/0.1/> .
@prefix schema: <http://schema.org/> .

<> a foaf:Document;
  foaf:primaryTopic <#offer> ;
  dct:title "Widows, November 22nd, 2018, 20:30"@en .

<#offer> a schema:Offer ;
  schema:price 5000 ;
  schema:priceCurrency "CLP" ;
  schema:availabilityStarts "2018-11-22T17:50:00Z"^^xsd:dateTime ;
  schema:availabilityEnds "2018-11-22T19:59:00Z"^^xsd:dateTime .

<http://mov.ie/m/M10003> schema:offers <#offer> ;
  schema:name "Widows"@en .
```

Assume that we post such documents to the `/ldp/cine/hoyts/offer/` *container, which will generate a new resource named* `offn` *in the container, with n an incremental count of offers. Provide an RDF definition for the* `/ldp/cine/hoyts/offer/` *indirect container that will create membership links of the following form when offers are posted:*

```
...
<offn#offer> schema:availableAtOrFrom <../profile#cine> .
```

Remark 8.13

A separate specification was published by the W3C outlining Best Practices and Guidelines for implementing and using LDP servers [83]. Amongst these we can highlight:

- *Prefer relative IRIs (e.g., <>, <off3>) where possible*: they are more concise; furthermore, if an RDF document using relative IRIs is copied between containers, the identifiers will reflect their context.
- *Use fragment identifiers to represent entities (e.g., <#user>)*: this not only provides a way to ensure dereferenceable IRIs, it also helps distinguish information resources (documents and containers) from general entities (e.g., users, movies, etc.).
- *Represent container membership with hierarchical IRIs*: it is not required to have LDP containment follow a "folder-like" structure in terms of IRI paths, but it certainly aids readability to do so.
- *Include a trailing slash (only) in container URIs*: this again is not required, but per the previous best practice, it aids readability by following the intuition of containers being folders, especially when relative IRIs are used within those containers.
- *Minimise server-specific constraints:* this makes it easier for clients to work with an LDP server, per Postel's law in the context of making robust Web systems: "*be conservative in what you do, be liberal in what you accept from others*".

These best practices were exemplified throughout this section. Here we highlight five of the fifteen best practices and guidelines proposed. In fact, most of the other proposals are covered by the more general Linked Data principles and best practices that we discussed earlier, including, for example, making RDF terms used in resources dereferenceable, preferring the use of terms from established vocabularies where possible, using standard datatypes as broadly supported by RDF-based systems, etc. We refer the reader to the specification for further details [83].

Remark 8.14

Rather than using PUT to overwrite an existing resource, in the case of RDF documents, an LDP server may support PATCH, which can be used to request changes to the RDF document. The Linked Data Patch (LD Patch) format [55] was proposed for such cases, allowing to specify triples to add and triples to remove from an RDF graph.

We provide a relatively simple example to give a flavour of the LD patch proposal based on the RDF document /ldp/user/lev/profile from Example 8.36, where the user wishes to follow other cinemas after learning of the profit margins on popcorn at his regular cinema:

```
@prefix dct: <http://purl.org/dc/terms/> .
@prefix foaf: <http://xmlns.com/foaf/0.1/> .
@prefix sioc: <http://rdfs.org/sioc/ns#> .

<> a foaf:PersonalProfileDocument;
  foaf:primaryTopic <#user> ;
  dct:title "lev's Profile" .

<#user> a sioc:UserAccount ;
  sioc:name "lev" ;
  sioc:avatar <img/avatar.jpg> ;
  sioc:follows <../../cine/hoyts/profile#user> .
```

We could change the final triple to rather follow two other cinemas – cinemark and cineplanet – by requesting a PATCH with the header:

```
PATCH /ldp/user/lev/profile HTTP/1.1
Host: mov.ie
Content-Length: 478
Content-Type: text/ldpatch
If-Match: W/'CAC3BEF6F865647F'
```

and the following content using the LD Patch Format:

```
@prefix sioc: <http://rdfs.org/sioc/ns#> .

Delete {
  <#user> sioc:follows <../../cine/hoyts/profile#user> .
} .
Add {
  <#user> sioc:follows <../../cine/cinemark/profile#user> ;
    sioc:follows <../../cine/cineplanet/profile#user> .
} .
```

This requests that the previous sioc:follows triple should be removed for hoyts and two new ones added for cinemark and cineplanet.

Using PATCH is particularly useful to make small updates to large RDF documents rather than having to replace the entire document with PUT. Though the LD Patch format is based on Turtle syntax, it can be used to patch RDF documents represented in arbitrary syntaxes on a server (of course, a server supporting more than one syntax for the same resource should update all available representations of that resource). The LD Patch specification further includes features for manipulating RDF collections, as well as matching and updating elements based on query patterns; for more details, we refer to the specification [55].

Further Reading 8.5

Though we have covered the essential details of the LDP, many minor details are omitted, particularly in terms of implementing a compliant LDP server. For further technical details, we refer to the LDP specification [365]; for further examples, we refer to the LDP primer [270]; for further discussion on best practices to follow, we refer to the corresponding specification [83]; finally, for further discussion on LDP use-cases, we refer to the corresponding specification [34].

Discussion 8.9

FRANK: How does the LDP relate to the SPARQL Update language we saw in Section 6.5? Couldn't similar read–write functionality on Linked Data – and in fact even more functionality than offered by LDP – be supported using SPARQL Update?

AIDAN: Yes. It is perhaps similar to the relation between dereference-able IRIs and a SPARQL endpoint when talking about read-only Linked Data. Like in that case, one could implement LDP using SPARQL Update to help manage the RDF content in particular. However, there are some technical aspects that differ. First, authentication is perhaps more straightforward in the case of the LDP, where standard HTTP-based protocols can be used; on the other hand, implementing something similar on SPARQL Update – with fine-grained policies for users – would require a more advanced access-control framework specific to the SPARQL Update language [231]. Second, LDP can be used to manage storage of non-RDF content; an RDF graph in a SPARQL engine can link to such content elsewhere but storing raw image data, etc., in a SPARQL engine seems more questionable. Third, LDP offers some automatic triggers for updating triples in the hosted documents based on containment and membership; off-the-shelf SPARQL Update implementations do not offer such triggers (though they could be specified as updates). In summary, they offer two potentially complementary but different options for read–write applications.

JULIE: You spoke about users being able to access their data through the HTML-based application of the website or through the LDP-based back-end, and how that might increase the control users have over their own data on the Web. But what is to prevent a website from keeping application data managed in a private database and not making it available through the LDP interface?

AIDAN: Nothing; or at least nothing technical. The LDP specification does not enforce a website to make all of its data accessible and

modifiable through an LDP server: an individual website may make
all of its data, some of its data, or none of its data available through
an LDP interface. The LDP specification does, however, provide
the technical infrastructure for websites that *choose* the path you
mention – of offering its users and its content providers more control
over their data – to follow that path using Web standards.

JULIE: In that case, the standard has been around for some time already. Are there applications using it?

AIDAN: LDP is still a relatively new specification, but there are some interesting projects in development that use it. One of particular note
is the Social Linked Data project – better known by its acronym
Solid – led by Berners-Lee [259]. Like many good projects, it is
borne of frustration – of a frustration in particular with the increasing centralisation of data in the private databases of a handful
of a few very large and very powerful websites, who offer the users
generating the content very little control over that content, and
who have allowed that content to be misused on more than one occasion. Coupled with this frustration is the observation that social
networks, blogging platforms, etc., do not have to be centralised,
and that with technologies like LDP, these applications could, with
enough will, be decentralised, thus offering users complete control
over their data: what they store, what the data are used for, with
whom they are shared and for what purpose. Solid is based on the
idea of *pods*, which a user can host locally, and which store application data (profile information, movie reviews, personal videos and
images, etc.); users can store whatever data they like in their pod
and can then grant access as they deem fit to external clients. On
a technical level, pods are implemented using LDP, with optional
support for SPARQL; all of this is behind a user interface that hides
technical details. The Solid platform is still under development, but
it is one prominent initiative using the LDP specification.

8.7 Summary

While the previous chapters have dealt primarily with the data models
and languages defined under the Semantic Web standards, this chapter has
focused on Linked Data, which encompasses a now broad variety of complementary proposals on how these standards can (and should) be used to
publish, exchange and interact with data on the Web. We began by describing
the four Linked Data principles, which serve as the foundation for building a
Web of Data on the current Web architecture using the RDF standard. Thereafter we discussed a variety of best practices to improve – insofar as possible

– the interoperability of data published using the Linked Data principles with other data published likewise on the Web. We discussed the Linking Open Data initiative, which, in a nutshell, espouses the benefits of using Semantic Web standards to publish Open Data on the Web. We then discussed technical solutions for publishing Linked Data, including the conversion of legacy data to RDF, generating links to external datasets, and hosting Linked Data on a server. Finally, we discussed the LDP standard, whose goal is to foster read–write applications on top of Linked Data technologies, offering a possible route towards returning control of user-generated data back to users.

8.8 Discussion

> **Discussion 8.10**
>
> JULIE: It appears that a lot of data have been published using the techniques discussed in this chapter. But what about end-user applications? Who is using Linked Data and what for?
>
> AIDAN: The Linked Data principles have been around for well over a decade, as have many of the Linked Datasets. We have seen applications that use specific Linked Datasets, or a small collection of Linked Datasets, where for example Wikidata [397, 255] is becoming more and more integrated with Wikipedia, or where IBM Watson [128] – the system that beat human experts at the U.S. game-show Jeopardy! – has used datasets like DBpedia and YAGO. We have also seen use-cases explored in specific domains, where Bio2RDF [117] offers clinical researchers novel integrated views over datasets that they work with every day. Many industries now also maintain what they call "*knowledge graphs*", which are are large and often proprietary collections of diverse graph-structured data used in a variety of applications, including Google's Knowledge Panel, or Apple's Siri, etc.; such knowledge graphs draw on public datasets like Freebase or DBpedia, or more commonly Wikidata. However, none of these applications entirely fulfil the promise of Linked Data.
>
> JULIE: Why not?
>
> AIDAN: They have all worked with a specific collection of hand-picked datasets. In terms of end-user applications that are capable of automatically discovering new data sources on the fly, there are some prominent examples – as discussed previously – including Google's Rich Snippets or Facebook's Open Graph Protocol. These applications can potentially draw on data embedded within millions of

websites – be that RDFa, Microdata, JSON-LD, etc. – and they can incorporate data from new sources on the fly. But these applications do not entirely fulfil the promise of Linked Data either.

JULIE: Why not?

AIDAN: Although the data are not centralised, the vocabulary (largely) is. It is difficult to know precisely how companies like Google and Facebook use the embedded data they collect from the Web, but it would appear that their applications are hard-coded to assume the use of Schema.org vocabulary, or OGP vocabulary, or a small handful of other vocabularies. In other words, there is still a human in the loop who is interpreting the semantics of the terms used in the data and building end-user applications accordingly. The limitations of this approach are implicit in Exercise 8.7, which tried to use the Schema.org vocabulary to describe the times that movies would show in the cinema, but – though not mentioned at the time – ended up having to abuse the vocabulary a bit to get the data to fit. Were a user to define a better vocabulary for this – with semantics defined in RDFS or OWL, potentially extending the Schema.org vocabulary – they could perhaps support this vocabulary in their own application, but data in a custom vocabulary would not be recognised by applications hard-coded for Schema.org or OGP data.

JULIE: So which applications do leverage the promise of Linked Data?

AIDAN: The importance of the aforementioned applications should not be overlooked! But we are still missing end-user applications that can – or more emphatically, that *need* to be able to – discover novel sources of Web data on the fly and that *need* to be able to leverage data described in not just one or two or ten vocabularies, but any vocabulary published anywhere on the Web with machine-readable semantics. A *lot* of research has been dedicated to this topic – dedicated to consuming Linked Data in an automated, general way without any assumptions other than what the standards define – dedicated to searching, exploring, summarising, cleaning, integrating, validating, and more generally discovering and preparing sources of Linked Data for use in applications. But though a lot of groundwork has been laid, the types of applications that would be able to automatically and (pseudo-)serendipitously discover the right data and vocabularies on the Web needed for the task at hand – and thus fulfil the promise of Linked Data – remain illusive. It is now clear that such applications will not appear overnight. Rather they may evolve from the current applications we already mentioned – as they are extended to leverage more and more datasets and more and more vocabularies – or they may follow some new insights.

Chapter 9
Conclusions

In this book, we have extensively discussed the *Web of Data*, wherein the content of the Web is made increasingly machine readable, enabling the automation of more and more tasks. Towards increasing machine readability, we discussed the importance of having agreed-upon standards and best practices for modelling, querying, validating, linking and publishing data on the Web, as well as for capturing the meaning of data through formal semantics. In the past years, the Semantic Web community has proposed a wide range of standards and best practices along these lines, including the RDF data model, the RDFS and OWL ontology languages, the SPARQL query language, the SHACL constraints language, the Linked Data principles, the Linked Data Platform, amongst others. This book has presented these standards in detail, and discussed how they form the cornerstones of a Web of Data.

As discussed in Chapter 2, the Web of Data is not merely a vision for the future, but is also being realised in practice right now. The success of initiatives such as Wikidata show the value of publishing structured data on the Web not only for its many consumers, but also for publishers and editors who benefit from reduced redundancy in how data are represented and managed. In parallel, Schema.org, the Open Graph Protocol, and related initiatives have illustrated the types of concrete incentives that can encourage publishers on the broader Web to make machine readable content available on their websites. The hundreds of Linked Datasets that have been published on the Web in recent years – spanning a variety of domains – have also provided an important precedent for how not only data, but also vocabularies, can be represented, published, interlinked, extended, and exploited in a decentralised open manner on the Web. Finally, the increasing attention gained by knowledge graphs in recent years highlights that the standards and techniques discussed in this book have applications not only for the Web – which has been our focus – but also for managing, integrating, and consuming diverse data at large scale within enterprises and other organisations.

© Springer Nature Switzerland AG 2020
A. Hogan, *The Web of Data*, https://doi.org/10.1007/978-3-030-51580-5_9

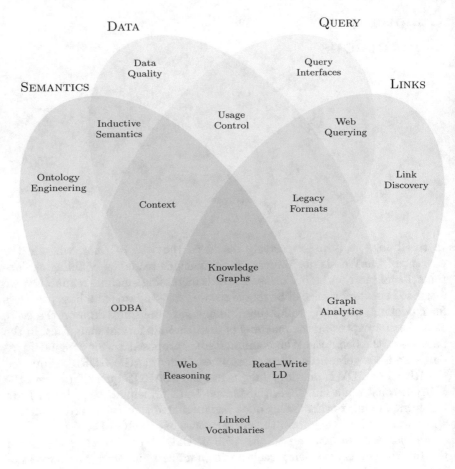

Fig. 9.1 Conceptual map of research trends for the Web of Data

In this last chapter, we look to the future of the Web of Data. We first enumerate and discuss some of the emerging research trends that may shape the next years, before concluding with some final remarks.

9.1 Research Trends

We now briefly summarise some of the key research trends for the Web of Data, some of which have been explored for a number of years already, and some of which are just now emerging. Our goal is not to give a comprehensive survey of all relevant trends; rather we discuss a subset of trends that illustrate diverse aspects of ongoing research relating to the Web of Data. Figure 9.1 provides a conceptual map of the trends that we discuss in terms of four high-level topics – DATA, SEMANTICS, QUERY and LINKS – where most trends touch upon multiple of these four topics.[1]

> **Further Reading 9.1**
>
> For further reading on research trends relating to the Semantic Web, we refer the reader to the survey by Gandon [136].

9.1.1 Data Quality

The Web is full of incomplete, out-of-date, inaccurate, misleading, biased, contradictory, and otherwise incorrect information, which may arise indeliberately (e.g., due to human error, poor-quality sources, etc.), or deliberately (e.g., spam, misinformation, vandalism, etc.). The Web of Data is no different, where data quality is an important issue. As one example, the Wikidata user &beer&love added a date of death for Stan Lee on Wikidata, even though he was still alive.[2] Soon thereafter, Apple's Siri and Google's Knowledge Panel began prematurely reporting Lee's death before it was flagged and removed.[3,4] While this was likely a case of deliberate vandalism, other issues relating to data quality may be more difficult to diagnose and resolve.

Data quality can be understood extrinsically in terms of how fit data are for an external purpose: a dataset that perfectly satisfies one use-case might be worthless to another use-case. However, data are often published on the Web without a principal purpose in mind, where it becomes necessary to look at the intrinsic quality of data in terms of dimensions that limit the potential purposes for which it can be used. For example, if the majority of statements that a dataset represents are false, this is a property of the dataset itself, and one that clearly limits the purposes it can satisfy. A number of works have then proposed and analysed intrinsic dimensions of data quality on the Web of Data, including the accuracy of coreference (owl:sameAs) links [166, 113], conformance of published data to Linked Data principles [199, 203],

---

[1] The conceptual map is intended to illustrate how different trends may shape the Web of Data, where certain categorisations are subjective. In particular, all trends involve DATA in some way, but for the purposes of the map, we only include those trends that focus on how data are represented, managed, assessed, etc., in that topic.

[2] Wikidata revision history for Stan Lee (Q181900), version id. 705733676: https://www.wikidata.org/w/index.php?title=Q181900&oldid=705733676

[3] "Siri Thinks Stan Lee is Dead—He Isn't" (Newsweek): https://www.newsweek.com/stan-lee-dead-apples-siri-mistakenly-tells-iphone-users-he-1009127

[4] "Siri Erroneously Told People Stan Lee Was Dead" (Gizmodo): https://io9.gizmodo.com/siri-erroneously-told-people-stan-lee-was-dead-1827322243

representativeness [364], completeness [217], etc. The goal of such research is not only to assess the quality of data available, but also to improve data published on the Web based on such assessments. We refer to the survey by Zaveri et al. [407] for a comprehensive list of quality criteria and measures that can be applied for RDF published as Linked Data.

9.1.2 Link Discovery

Key to the success of the current Web is the provision of links between relevant documents that help both humans and machines discover remote content of relevance to a given search or task. Likewise links are an essential ingredient of a Web of Data. Along these lines, the RDF model supports IRIs that can serve both as identifiers and links, while the Linked Data principles emphasise the importance of generating links to (and thus in turn receiving links from) remote datasets on the Web. Unlike on the current Web, links in the context of the Web of Data can be assigned specific (machine-readable) semantics, which can be very useful for integrating datasets. As an example, links using the owl:sameAs property can be used to denote coreferent resources in remote datasets; such links facilitate not only the discovery of related content elsewhere on the Web, but also the automatic integration of such content based on the semantics of the owl:sameAs property, which states that the data for both resources can subsequently be merged [166, 113].

Accurately identifying links with specific semantics – though key for building a mature Web of Data – raises unique challenges. First, the quadratic pairwise possibilities for linking between (even just) two datasets raises challenges with respect to efficiency. Second, the different ways in which analogous data can be represented in two different datasets presents challenges in terms of the precision of links produced with respect to the stated semantics. A variety of frameworks have been proposed to help address such challenges. The most prominent of these proposals are Silk [395], which relies on hand-crafted heuristics, and LIMES [291], which uses distance measures in metric spaces to identify candidates for linking. Work in this area is ongoing, where we refer to the survey by Nentwig et al. [288] for further discussion.

9.1.3 Context

There does not exist a notion of "universal truth" on the Web. Rather statements are often true in a particular context [161]. Some statements – such as "*Barack Obama is president of the United States*", or that "*the population of Boston is 646,000*", or that "*Pluto is a planet*" – depend on a temporal context, being true within a certain time period. Other statements may hold true only for a particular geographic region (e.g., "*Bitcoin is illegal*"), or according to a given source (e.g., "*the Earth is flat*"), etc. For this reason, it is better to view such statements as claims, rather than facts. Statements are associated with a particular context that may either be explicit (e.g., a claim that "*Barack Obama was president of the United States from 2008–2016*") or implicit (e.g., a claim that "*Barack Obama is the president of the United States*" found in a source last updated in 2011). More generally, ways to represent and reason about context are of importance to capture the subtleties of truth regarding claims on both the Web, and the Web of Data.

One way to represent context in RDF is to use reification (see Section 3.5.3), which allows for making statements about statements within the RDF model. However, the standard mechanism for reification proposed for RDF is arguably clumsy, where a number of alternatives have been proposed [294, 255]. Reification within the RDF model will always tend to be somewhat awkward, where other authors have rather proposed to extend the RDF model. A prominent proposal along these lines is RDF* [171], which allows using triples as the subject or object of other triples. RDF datasets (see Section 3.6) can also be used to represent context. Work has also been done looking at the performance of querying different representations of context for Wikidata [186]. An alternative approach is to use annotations, which not only allow to represent context, but also to define semantics specific to different contexts [409, 193, 143]. Open questions still remain, however, in terms of extracting context from sources, representing context in a standard way, querying and reasoning in a context-aware manner, etc.

9.1.4 Legacy Formats

While RDF is the standard data model proposed by the Semantic Web community, legacy data on the Web are often represented in other formats, such as Microdata, JSON, XML, CSV and so forth. Such data may be accessed on the Web as static documents, through API calls, etc. Furthermore, much of the data on the current Web are not explicitly structured, but often left implicit in the text and semi-structured elements (tables, lists, etc.) of HTML documents designed for human consumption. Rather than exclude such content from the Web of Data, there is ongoing research on how best to incorporate these formats and make them interoperable with RDF-based systems, which may involve representing the data as RDF, allowing them to be queried through SPARQL, and/or generating links from such content.

The challenge of incorporating legacy formats can be addressed on a number of fronts. First, syntaxes such as RDF/XML [41] and JSON-LD [366] serve as a bridge from their respective base formats (XML and JSON, respectively) to the RDF world. Second, high-level languages for mapping data in legacy formats to RDF have also been developed, where the RDB2RDF standards [14, 106] (see Section 8.5.1) can be used to import the relational data that underlie the Web into an RDF setting; RML [111] then provides a more general mapping language suitable for other formats. Third, languages have been proposed that allow RDF to be queried in unison with data in other formats, including XSPARQL [323] for querying RDF and XML, extensions to SPARQL that allow for querying data from APIs [268, 278], and more besides. Fourth, *information extraction* techniques can be used to link entities mentioned in text or other semi-structured elements (e.g., cells of HTML tables) to terms in an RDF graph, and to extract relations as RDF triples from such sources [261]. Further research along these lines would help to leverage existing data in legacy formats for populating the Web of Data.

9.1.5 *Graph Analytics*

Graph analytics have played a hidden but important role in shaping the Web as we know it. Measures of *centrality*, for example, can be used to identify the most important nodes in a graph, where the PageRank [302] centrality measure has played an important role in the success of Google, improving the ranking of search results shown to users by prioritising documents that have higher centrality in the directed graph formed by their links. Social network analysis [353] – which makes heavy use of graph analytics, such as centrality, clustering, density measures, etc. – has played a key role in understanding and shaping online social networks, such as Facebook, Twitter, etc. Graph analytics likewise have an important role to play on the Web of Data. However, while such analytics are typically applied to homogeneous graphs (e.g., with one or two types of relations, such as *links*, *follows*, etc.), RDF graphs are potentially much more complex, representing thousands of types of relations, necessitating the development of novel techniques.

Works on graph analytics for the Web of Data can be divided into three groups. The first group has proposed analytical techniques especially adapted for the Web of Data, including centrality measures that incorporate weighting schemes for different types of relations (i.e., different properties) within an RDF graph [224], works that incorporate the links between RDF documents on the Web into the ranking process [112, 198, 170, 109], and more besides [31, 4, 382, 133]. The second group uses graph analytics to draw conclusions about the Web of Data itself, relating to how robustly it is linked together [159], which ontological features are used in the most central documents of the Web of Data [144], and so forth. The third group proposes (typically distributed) frameworks for supporting the efficient execution of graph analytics over large-scale RDF graphs, including RAPID+ [330], Signal/Collect [372], Spartex [1], etc. Open questions still remain, however, with respect to how such graph analytics can be integrated with other aspects of the Web of Data, such as entailment or querying (for example).

9.1.6 Inductive Semantics

While ontologies allow for making the formal semantics of data explicit, a sufficiently large dataset has inherent semantics independent of such formal definitions. This semantics refers to patterns in how nodes of different types are connected, distributions with respect to the values they take on certain properties, and so forth. If we see data as representing observations of phenomena, then we can inductively extract semantics from these data in the form of patterns and hypotheses that help to characterise or model the phenomena that the data describe. This type of semantics, though fallible, is often quite useful; for example, from a film dataset, we might identify a pattern that movies tend to have directors born in the same country as the movie is filmed, which might help us to predict the nationalities of directors or the countries in which movies are set from incomplete data.

A variety of works have recently emerged in order to extract and exploit patterns in large graphs of data. Works on *graph summaries* aim to extract a high level structure from an RDF graph, which may take the form of quotient graphs [230, 164], lattices [151], relational-style schemata [314], and more besides [89]. Other works use machine learning techniques to learn models that generalise patterns from RDF graphs. *Graph embeddings* [399] learn numeric representations of a graph that (typically) allow for predicting the *plausibility* of a triple; for example, we may use a graph embedding to predict the most likely nationality of the director of a movie filmed in Japan. *Graph neural networks* (GNNs) [403], on the other hand, learn functions that aggregate input information from neighbours in a graph towards computing features for nodes; for example, we may train a GNN on examples of successful box-office movies – based on features for their location, production company, cast, etc. – that can predict which new movies will be successful. Finally, *rule-mining* [135] can be used to learn inference rules from an RDF graph associated with a given support; an example rule might infer that directors of a movie have the same nationality as the country the movie was filmed in, predicting that 90% of the rule's inferences will be correct. Exploiting inductive semantics for (RDF) graphs remains an active area of research: one that complements the formal definitions possible through ontologies.

9.1.7 Ontology Engineering

Ontologies form a central part of the Web of Data, allowing to formally define the semantics of terms that are used in the data exchanged by different parties on the Web, thus increasing interoperability. However, to enable such interoperability, it is important that the ontology – and the definitions it provides – are agreed-upon. Achieving broad consensus on the formal definitions particular to an ontology is far from trivial. Ontology engineering thus explores tools and methodologies that can help towards achieving consensus, which may consider either centralised settings (e.g., within a given organisation), or decentralised settings (e.g., over the Web).

We identify three main directions along which ontology engineering has evolved over the years. The first direction is in terms of *ontology engineering methodologies* [158, 319, 375, 373, 312], which describe resources and guidelines that help to structure the process of creating and refining an ontology. The second direction is towards developing *ontology engineering tools* [298, 222, 373] to help users (e.g., domain experts) define ontologies, visualise them, perform reasoning tasks, etc., thus lowering the barrier-to-entry for creating and maintaining ontologies. A third direction is towards the use of *ontology design patterns* [137, 64, 189], which capture abstract components that can be reused, specialised and composed with other patterns at the moment of creating an ontology. Traditionally speaking, much of the focus of ontology engineering has been on facilitating the ontology creation process within organisations, or other centralised settings. In the context of the Web of Data, more work is needed in order to explore the social processes [371, 320] as well as the methodologies [361] and tools needed [206] to create and maintain agreed-upon ontologies over the Web.

9.1.8 Ontology-Based Data Access

Although the SPARQL standard defines a variety of entailment regimes (see Section 6.6), implementing query answering with entailment is challenging, particularly for expressive ontological languages such as OWL 2 DL (for which boolean conjunctive query answering is not known to be decidable). In practice, current query services on the Web of Data – i.e., SPARQL endpoints – typically do not offer support for entailments. In order to lower the costs of supporting entailments within query engines, more lightweight ontological profiles have been proposed for which queries can be evaluated through query rewriting mechanisms that extend the query to capture additional answers that include entailments. This strategy – known as OBDA – has a number of advantages, key amongst which are (1) extended queries can be evaluated efficiently using off-the-shelf query engines, thus leveraging their existing optimisations; (2) under a query rewriting strategy, when base data are removed, it is not necessary to "revise" entailments as would be necessary under a materialisation approach that indexes entailments.

Within the area of OBDA, two main lines of research have emerged. The first is to identify profiles of ontology languages for which sound and complete (boolean) conjunctive query-answering can be conducted by means of the query rewriting strategy. A major milestone in this direction is the DL-Lite [84] profile, which in turn has guided the development and standardisation of the OWL 2 QL profile [280]. On the other hand, OWL 2 QL is relatively inexpressive, corresponding loosely to what can be expressed in the core of RDFS. Another line of research is to look at how additional features of modern query engines can be supported through an OBDA framework (for example, supporting bag semantics [295]) and indeed how these features can be used to support entailments with respect to more expressive ontology languages (for example, using recursion [405, 358]). Open questions still remain in terms of exploring both the theoretical limits and practical trade-offs between supporting more expressive ontologies and query languages, vs. the complexity and performance of the query answering task.

9.1.9 Linked Vocabularies

In order to build a diverse Web of Data, vocabularies are needed to provide agreed-upon terms for a variety of domains. Though closely related to research on ontology engineering, the priority shifts from finding consensus for a detailed set of semantic definitions towards achieving an initial and very broad consensus on a set of terms (i.e., vocabulary) to use for publishing data across the Web. These vocabularies are possibly associated with (often lightweight) semantic definitions using ontology languages such as OWL. This practice is already in place for Linked Data, where hundreds of new vocabularies have been defined – and existing vocabularies extended-upon – in a decentralised manner using ontologies (as discussed in Section 8.3.4).

We identify four main research directions along these lines. The first relates to defining vocabularies for broad use on the Web, as discussed in Section 8.3.4; of particular note is the Schema.org vocabulary [160], which has been adopted on 12 million websites. The second direction involves cataloguing and analysing the available vocabularies to facilitate their reuse across the Web, as supported by the Linked Open Vocabularies (LOV) system [389] (see also Section 8.3.4), as well as vocab.cc [369]. A third direction is towards building tools – such as Neologism [33], WebProtégé [206], etc. – that allow for collaboratively defining, documenting, visualising and maintaining vocabularies over the Web. A fourth line of research analyses trends in emerging Linked Vocabularies, where the results of Glimm et al. [144] show that the most prominent vocabularies on the Web tend to prefer lightweight semantics (mostly using RDFS features and avoiding OWL class restrictions) while the analyses by Matentzoglu et al. [262, 263] show that many OWL 2 Full ontologies available on the Web can be made OWL 2 DL compatible with relatively minor changes. Further progress can still be made on several fronts, particularly towards designing ontology engineering tools that facilitate reuse of vocabulary terms within expressive ontologies [345, 206].

9.1.10 Web Reasoning

With vocabularies gaining more and more traction on the Web, their (typically lightweight [144]) semantic definitions can be exploited through reasoning techniques, which can help, for example, to integrate data on entities with coreferent identifiers [204], to find additional answers to queries [383], to identify and repair inconsistencies in the data [69], and so forth. This decentralised ecosystem of vocabularies is, however, a novel phenomenon, and gives rise to novel challenges with respect to how to apply reasoning within this space. In particular, while reasoning has traditionally been applied in local settings over relatively small-scale, clean data, the Web reasoning setting involves very large-scale, messy data. Addressing these challenges is key to being able to leverage the semantics defined for terms across the Web.

A number of research works have investigated scalable and/or robust reasoning systems for Web data. In terms of scalability, various authors have investigated the use of distributed frameworks for applying incomplete forms of reasoning at large-scale [400, 386, 201]. In terms of robustness, the key challenge is to avoid (e.g., nonsensical) definitions from untrusted sources affecting the reasoning process over other sources; for example, if an isolated document on the Web defines that foaf:Person is a rdfs:subClassOf ex:Broccoli, we should not allow this definition to influence reasoning over the millions of documents on the Web using the popular FOAF vocabulary. There are two main proposals to address this issue: *quarantined reasoning* over a document only allows documents linked (recursively) from that document to be considered for reasoning [110, 383], while *authoritative reasoning* restricts the ontological definitions that will be used from a document based on which terms dereference to that document (e.g., the broccoli axiom would only be considered if published in a document that foaf:Person dereferences to) [69, 383]. We refer to the lecture notes by Polleres et al. [322] for further discussion of these themes. The aforementioned works tend to target more lightweight forms of reasoning for the Web, where there are many open questions relating to how to support expressive ontological features – e.g., existentials, disjunctions, etc. – when reasoning over Web data.

9.1.11 Web Querying

SPARQL is an expressive query language that can thus be costly to host services for [310, 13]. Optimisations for SPARQL in local settings – including indexing schemes [289], specialised data structures [21], optimal join algorithms [202], etc. – aim to reduce these costs. However, although state-of-the-art query engines can answer typical user queries rapidly, some queries are too costly to evaluate, particularly when services receive millions of queries per day [255]. Most SPARQL endpoints are thus configured with timeout and result-size limits to ensure that the overall service does not suffer due to expensive queries [13]. Clients needing complete results for expensive queries are left with little option other than to download and work with a dump locally. Research is thus ongoing to design languages and systems that provide more reliable query services to clients while reducing server-side costs.

A number of decentralised approaches have been proposed to support clients querying one or more sources on the Web of Data. SPARQL Federation (see Section 6.4) supports evaluating sub-queries on remote endpoints, where works on *federated query planning* aim to reduce the workload on participating endpoints while decreasing response times [352, 2, 12, 343]. *Link traversal querying* methods can evaluate queries directly over Linked Data by selectively dereferencing documents that are likely to yield triples relevant to a query [172]. While link traversal querying obviates the need for endpoints, it potentially requires a lot of irrelevant data to be transferred to the client. Other works try to strike a balance between SPARQL and link traversal, including *Triple Pattern Fragments* (TPF), which allows for answering queries on a server consisting of a single triple pattern, where joins – if required – are performed client-side [393]. Another proposal is to use *Web preemption* on SPARQL endpoints, where a server can pause a query after a fixed amount of time (or work) and the client must send a request to continue processing [275]; servers can then define quotas for individual clients by limiting the number of requests. More research is still needed to bring hosting costs and response times down – perhaps using *hybrid methods* that combine multiple strategies [2, 384, 173] – as well as for querying dynamic Web data [384, 114].

9.1.12 *Query Interfaces*

Although SPARQL provides an expressive language for posing queries against the Web of Data, relatively few users of the Web are likely to be familiar with its syntax. Hence research on query interfaces usable by non-experts is of key importance in order for the Web of Data to reach a broader audience. Ideally such user interfaces should not be locked to a particular functionality, but should rather allow users to generate queries in an intuitive but general manner. That said, there tends to be a trade-off between the expressiveness of a query interface, and its usability: more complex interfaces allow for generating more complex queries, but are often more difficult to use. Given the importance of the topic, a variety of works have explored this trade-off between expressivity and usability in query interfaces.

We can loosely categorise the query interfaces that have proposed thus far for the Web of Data into three main categories. The first category is that of *question answering systems* [249, 385], which accept a query in natural language and either convert it to a structured query (e.g., SPARQL) or try to answer it directly over the available data; while easy to use, these systems currently struggle to answer more complex questions. The second category is that of *facetted search* [300, 17, 277], where the user begins with a list of results (possibly given for a keyword search), and can then select facets upon which to iteratively refine the results shown; though intuitive, such systems typically only allow for expressing acyclic queries of a particular structure and for returning a list of entities as results (rather than, e.g., a table). The third category is that of *query builders* [265, 333, 255, 391], which assist users to construct graph patterns that can be evaluated over the data, typically employing visualisations, autocompletion, etc.; although such systems allow users to pose complex queries over a dataset, they typically are more difficult to use and require some knowledge of how the data are structured. Further advances are then needed towards improving the accuracy of question answering systems, the usability of query builders, as well as to support the inclusion of reasoning capabilities into such interfaces [17].

9.1.13 *Usage Control*

It would be naive to assume that any and all data can simply be published on – and made accessible to anyone through – the Web of Data. A large proportion of the data generated by users or organisations is of a sensitive nature, which raises both legal and ethical issues regarding their (re)use on the Web. While a simple strategy is to not publish sensitive data on the Web, rather making such data available in a limited way – e.g., to certain websites, organisations, users, etc. – would allow for novel applications and services to be provided for users while also offering protection from misuse of the data. As a general example, an application that has access to a users' location, past purchases, age, gender, etc., would potentially be able to personalise results generated from the Web of Data for that particular user, but clearly these are sensitive data whose use must be controlled in some manner.

A number of works have addressed issues relating to the *licensing* of data, where the Open Digital Rights Language (ODRL) [215] – recommended by the W3C in 2018 – provides a vocabulary for defining permissions, duties and prohibitions relating to how data may be used by individual parties; this standard can then be used for defining and reasoning over machine-readable representations of popular licenses [303]. An extension of ODRL, called the Data Privacy Vocabulary (DPV) [304], is currently being developed to further capture aspects relating to consent, legal norms, data processes, etc., in order to represent how personal data can be handled while upholding laws relating to *privacy*. *Access control* frameworks [231] then combine encryption and authentication mechanisms in order to enforce policies in terms of who can access what data under which terms. An alternative direction is to apply *anonymisation techniques* in order to avoid leaks of sensitive data, where work has been done on k-anonymisation for publishing data [329, 182], as

well as differential privacy for querying data [108]. Theoretical foundations
of anonymisation for RDF have also been explored [154]. As the Web of Data
matures – and as social awareness grows of the ways in which sensitive data
can be misused – such research will play an increasingly key role.

9.1.14 Read–Write Linked Data

The Web increasingly supports read–write capabilities whereby users can
not only read content on webpages but can also write or otherwise contribute
content on websites not under their control. Such principles underlie some
of the most prominent websites, including wikis, social networks, blogs, etc.
These read–write privileges enable the collaborative authoring and curation
of Web content. The same principles can be applied to the Web of Data, where
read–write privileges can enable users to collaborate on content [397]. Like on
the current Web, arbitrary users should not have complete write access over
data on remote websites, but rather the types of contributions they make
should be governed by policies, access control, etc. Likewise, on the current
Web, depending on the website, users may lose jurisdiction of their content:
they may not be able to control how it is used, by whom it is used, how long
it remains available, or indeed they may lose the ability to export or adapt
the content for their own purposes. Implementing read–write capabilities on
the Web of Data provides an opportunity to address such issues.

Along these lines, Berners-Lee proposed Read–Write Linked Data [47] as
a way for remote users to collaboratively edit and curate data on the Web in
a decentralised fashion. A major milestone towards this vision was the standardisation of the Linked Data Platform (LDP) [365] (see Section 8.6) which
lays the foundations upon which read–write Linked Data applications can be
built. A number of LDP implementations are now also available [35, 163, 251]
for such applications to avail of. However, while the LDP specification outlines key protocols, there are other practical details that still need to be
addressed in terms of decentralised authentication, access control, etc. Work
is ongoing, for example, on the Social Linked Data (Solid) platform [259],
which implements authentication, access control, update mechanisms, etc.,
on top of LDP in order to facilitate the creation of decentralised social applications that allow participating users to host and keep control of their
own data. Further developments along these lines are needed to fully realise
a read–write Web of Data, and in turn, a new generation of decentralised
applications where participating parties host and govern their own data.

9.1.15 Knowledge Graphs

As discussed in Section 2.3.2, knowledge graphs have been gaining more and more attention in industry and academia alike, where they serve as a graph-structured substrate of knowledge within a particular organisation [197, 297]. We distinguish two types of knowledge graphs: open knowledge graphs, which are published online for the public good (e.g., DBpedia [247], Wikidata [397], etc.), and enterprise knowledge graphs, which are typically internal to a company and used for the purposes of commercial use-cases (e.g., Google Knowledge Graph, etc. [297]). While knowledge graphs do not necessarily need to use the standards and techniques described in this book, they can be – and often are – used, particularly for the purposes of publishing open knowledge graphs online, which then form part of the Web of Data. On the other hand, enterprise knowledge graphs often benefit from sources on the Web of Data, pulling content from Wikidata [397], from Schema.org [160], etc.

In terms of research, knowledge graphs lie at the intersection of a number of areas, particularly in terms of graph databases, knowledge representation, logic, machine learning, information extraction, graph algorithms, and more besides [197]. This confluence of areas gives rise to novel research questions in terms of how to combine machine learning and knowledge representation, how to leverage graph algorithms for information extraction, and more besides. Currently, some of the main trends in this area are: *knowledge graph embeddings*, which aim to learn numeric representations of knowledge graphs [399]; *knowledge graph refinement*, which aims to assess and improve the quality of knowledge graphs along various dimensions [308]; as well as exploring *applications for knowledge graphs* in domain-specific settings such as to promote tourism [223], combat human-trafficking [376], and many others [197]. Though the Web does not always play a central role in knowledge graph research, the results developed for knowledge graphs – thus far involving researchers with diverse backgrounds and interests [197] – can be directly applied to the graph-structured datasets that form the Web of Data.

9.2 Final Remarks

There is one central tenet that underlies this book: tasks that are easy for humans are often difficult for machines, and tasks that are easy for machines are often difficult for humans. Finding how many times a digital copy of this book contains the string "Web" is something easily solved with machines, but difficult for humans to solve alone. On the other hand, the task of answering a quiz about this book – with questions such as *what is the twelfth research trend discussed in Section 9.1?* or *in which positions of an RDF triple can one place a blank node?* – would be much more difficult for machines to do accurately than for a human with good command of English. While machines are capable of much more efficient computation than humans – making it feasible for them to process large inputs in relatively little time – humans are better than machines at comprehension-based tasks that require a deeper understanding of natural language and the world around them.

Traditionally on the Web, machines have been delegated with the tasks of storing, finding, retrieving and displaying documents at an unprecedented scale, while humans are delegated with the tasks of generating content for those documents and comprehending them. This simple form of collaboration between humans and machines has led to the Web having had an extraordinary impact on society over the past decades. The traditional Web, however, does not provide solutions for tasks that require comprehension at large scale. Knowledge that cannot be gleaned from a single Web document, but rather remains implicit in the (human-like) comprehension of tens, hundreds, thousands or millions of Web documents, is left largely inaccessible to us users.

The Web of Data aims to make this implicit knowledge on the Web increasingly accessible by deepening the ongoing collaboration between human and machine. The goal is to automate comprehension of the Web's content at large scale by making that content – and requests over that content – more and more machine-readable. Key to building a machine-readable Web of Data is a consensus on core standards for how the data of the Web can be structured, how formal semantics can be made explicit, how queries can be expressed, how data can be validated, and how data and semantics can be linked together to form a Web of Data. Motivating and describing these standards has then been the principal undertaking of this book.

This Web of Data is no longer merely a goal, a vision, an idea: many of us now use the Web of Data on a regular basis (perhaps without realising it). If we use the Google search engine, for example, the Knowledge Panel and Rich Snippets provide us with additional metadata about our search, and its results, using techniques of the Web of Data. If we use Apple's virtual assistant Siri, we may receive answers sourced from open knowledge graphs on the Web of Data, such as Wikidata. Hidden beneath many of the applications we may use lie the principles, techniques and standards discussed in this book.

Still, this nascent Web of Data is far from reaching its full potential: the first stage of adoption has given rise to bespoke applications operating over lots of DATA, but with lesser emphasis on SEMANTICS, QUERIES and LINKS. The types of tasks that we discussed at the outset of the book – involving the needs of users like Julie, Frank and Anna – are not easily solved right now. Much like the current Web, however, the Web of Data should not be seen as something determinate, but rather as an ever-evolving technology that will start simple and mature over time. In the previous section we described a selection of research trends that form part of the technological road-map, and will continue to be subjects of investigation for the foreseeable future.

The Web of Data attempts to establish a bridge – or one might even say a tightrope – between machine precision and efficiency on one end, and human intuition and creativity on the other end. Given that the Web of Data focuses on machine readability, it is perhaps of no surprise that much of the work done thus far has likewise focussed on the *machine*. When thinking about the future evolution of the Web of Data, it is important that we do not lose sight of the *human*. The past years have yielded impressive and important developments in terms of techniques, languages, theoretical results, algorithms and optimisations relating to data validation, knowledge representation, query planning, etc. – all of which contribute towards empowering machines to help us make sense of the content of the Web. However, the human element – in terms of how users will interact with the Web of Data – is in some respects a much more complex subject to try and tame, and one that the research community has perhaps sometimes shied away from.

In a recent survey of the community [195], the two future challenges to which respondents assigned the highest priorities were *usability* and *incentives*, both of which pertain to the human element of the Web of Data. In terms of usability, a technology truly succeeds when it removes itself as the focus of one's attention, clearing the way for a user to be productive, and thereafter creative; many important aspects of the Web of Data are still far from this level of usability. On the other hand, while the potential incentives for a Web of Data can be argued on paper, and while concrete incentives for the Web of Data continue to emerge over time, what specific incentives will drive future adoption of the Web of Data – what will excite its users – are as difficult to anticipate now as they would have been for the Web in 1990.

While issues such as usability and incentives can be addressed systematically through further research in controlled settings, the most important experiment for us to continue with is that of putting the Web of Data into practice in order to address problems that people face, and to observe and learn from the result. Putting the technical developments of the past years into practice is a task that must be undertaken for the Web of Data to approach its true potential – and may also be the greatest challenge yet.

Glossary

A-Box [Assertional Box] A set of axioms about individuals in a DL ontology. 276, 278, 285, 286, 289, 302, 306, 308–311, 314

ABDUCTIVE REASONING The process of deriving a likely explanation for an observation based on known patterns or rules (alternative to deductive reasoning, inductive reasoning). 171, 645, 648, 653

ANTISYMMETRY A formal property of a relation whereby an element x being related to y and an element y being related to x implies that x equals y (related to asymmetry). 204

API [Application Programming Interface] An interface that can be invoked over HTTP, typically intending to offer software agents access to services or data over the Web. 580, 581, 631, 632

ASSERTION An axiom about individuals (often used for DLs). 243, 276–278, 282–285, 287, 294, 302–307, 314, 319, 645

ASYMMETRY A formal property of a relation whereby an element x being related to y implies that y is not related to x (opposite of symmetry). 204, 205, 208, 272, 277, 282, 303, 307, 308, 643, 656

AXIOM A claim with formal meaning. 200, 210–216, 218, 223, 224, 227, 238, 240, 241, 243, 246, 250, 251, 254–256, 276–290, 294–297, 302–307, 313, 314, 320, 322, 449, 540, 543, 544, 636, 643, 654

AXIOMATIC TRIPLE A triple that is entailed universally according to a specific semantics, even when no data are given. 158, 161, 165, 168, 169, 175–177, 179, 182, 313, 314, 424, 429

BAG SEMANTICS A semantics that preserves duplicates (alternative to set semantics). 330, 335, 350, 354, 355, 392–397, 405, 408, 635, 655

BASIC GRAPH PATTERN A set of triple patterns, sometimes considered to allow other expressions such as filters. 330–334, 336, 343, 350, 386, 388–393, 396–398, 404, 405, 408, 425–430, 433–439, 447, 602, 657

BINARY RELATION A relation between two entities. 79, 80, 129, 132, 133, 195, 584

BLANK NODE A type of RDF term used to represent the existence of something without identifying it with an IRI or literal. 61, 70–73, 76, 80, 81, 84, 85, 87–93, 98–100, 106, 108, 109, 123, 136, 139–142, 146, 148–152, 163, 174, 176, 177, 195, 222, 226, 244, 278, 314, 328, 330, 332, 340, 342, 344, 354, 364, 370, 374, 375, 379, 381, 382, 384, 387, 389, 391, 393, 394, 398, 403–405, 408, 416, 418, 419, 425–428, 458, 460, 465, 475, 485, 509, 532, 534, 560, 561, 568, 569, 572, 581, 640, 647, 652

BUILT-IN FUNCTION A function built into a language, often to deal with datatype values in a particular way. 33, 345

CACHE A temporary store of data used to avoid having to repeat the same processing various times. 408, 409, 600

CENTRALISATION Governance by a central organisation and/or from a central location (opposite of decentralisation). 45, 48, 53, 76, 448, 606, 623, 625, 634, 645

CLASS A collection of instances that share some commonalities; a term denoting such a collection. 31, 34, 37, 50, 51, 65, 77–79, 81, 83, 84, 89, 95, 101, 103, 108, 111, 113, 115–119, 121–126, 128, 130, 131, 157–161, 163–165, 167, 168, 172, 180, 181, 183, 185–187, 191, 194–196, 200–207, 210, 214–241, 243, 246, 248, 250, 252, 257–259, 261, 265, 266, 269, 270, 272, 273, 276, 277, 279, 281, 285, 292–298, 300–304, 312, 313, 316, 319–322, 353, 408, 409, 414, 424, 430, 436, 443, 444, 454–460, 462, 463, 466, 471, 474, 475, 492, 495, 519, 539–543, 551, 553, 563, 569, 583, 603–607, 635, 644, 648, 656, 657

COLLECTION An RDF representation of ordered, terminated lists of resources (alternative to containers; aka. a list). 83, 84, 87, 95, 99, 100, 157, 183, 195, 196, 221, 223, 250, 271, 273, 275, 316, 323, 370, 444, 445, 532–534, 549, 553, 585, 607–609, 621, 624, 644

COMPLETENESS A formal property of an algorithm for a decision problem whereby the algorithm returns true whenever the answer is expected to be true; a complete algorithm for an enumeration problem returns all true solutions (converse of soundness). 131, 137, 148, 167, 174, 180, 181, 193, 243, 256, 272, 276, 283, 292, 295, 298, 319, 386, 408, 449, 450, 529, 548, 560, 623, 630, 634, 637, 639, 646, 655

CONCEPT A class (often used for DLs). 144, 276–283, 288, 294, 303–307, 312, 314, 319, 409, 512, 552, 554, 583, 608, 609, 646, 648

CONJUNCTION A combination of formulae using AND. 22, 34, 253, 258, 259, 319, 334, 472, 502, 503, 505, 508, 509, 644

CONJUNCTIVE QUERY A structured query with a conjunction of conditions. 23, 25, 27, 257–259, 273, 299, 302, 305, 308, 310, 316, 333, 408, 634

CONTAINER A representation in RDF of ordered or unordered groups of resources (alternative to collections). 83, 84, 95, 126–128, 157, 161, 165, 169, 178, 181–183, 308, 429, 532, 533, 608, 644

CONTENT NEGOTIATION A HTTP feature allowing a client to request a resource in a preferred format. 527, 528, 596, 610

CoREFERENCE A condition whereby two or more terms refer to the same resource. 63, 68, 69, 196–199, 212, 629, 630, 636

CRAWL Traversing documents by following links on the Web in order to download said documents and create a centralised index. 522, 598, 599

CSV [Comma Separated Values] A plain text format for representing tables where columns in the table are delimited by commas, and where rows in the table are delimited by newlines. 17, 40, 54, 59, 109, 442, 545, 574–577, 581, 588, 631

CWA [Closed World Assumption] An assumption that any positive assertion (aka. fact) that is not entailed is false (alternative to OWA). 137, 452, 651

DATA CUBE A multidimensional array (aka. tensor) of values used to represent statistical data, often associated with operators for aggregating or slicing the data. 577, 578

DATATYPE A set of datatype values and a partial mapping from lexical strings (e.g., "2") to datatype values (e.g., 2). 34, 39, 51, 64–69, 78, 95, 98, 99, 101, 103, 121, 123, 128, 131, 134, 135, 153–156, 158, 159, 161–165, 172, 174, 177, 178, 196, 201, 213, 243–250, 276, 292–296, 303, 304, 306, 307, 312–314, 318, 320, 338, 341–344, 364, 428, 430–432, 435, 450, 455, 474–477, 482, 495–497, 504, 509, 542, 544, 561, 567, 568, 577, 578, 580, 581, 620

DATATYPE VALUE A value interpretable by machine – typically numeric, string, boolean, temporal, etc. – allowing operations such as comparison, ordering, multiplication, concatenation, negation, etc.. 20, 33, 34, 42, 123, 135, 155, 156, 158, 201, 215, 294, 296, 314, 341, 644, 645, 650

DECENTRALISATION Not being governed by a central organisation or from a central location (opposite of centralisation). 7, 47, 48, 55, 76, 611, 623, 627, 634–637, 639, 644

DECIDABLE A formal property of a decision problem whereby there exists an effective algorithm for the problem (opposite of undecidable). 193, 194, 215, 253, 263–265, 272, 274, 275, 281, 283, 284, 290–292, 296–299, 316, 319–321, 408, 439, 544, 634, 657

DECISION PROBLEM A problem that requires a true/false answer for any valid input. 257–259, 267, 299, 404, 406, 644, 645, 655, 657

DEDUCTIVE REASONING A process of applying rules or other logical formulae over premises to derive conclusions (alternative to abductive reasoning, inductive reasoning). 111–113, 171, 322, 643, 648, 653

DEFAULT GRAPH An RDF graph without a name in an RDF dataset. 85–87, 107, 108, 370–378, 414–416, 418, 420–423, 442–446, 572

DEREFERENCING Resolving a reference in order to return the referent; typically used in the context of HTTP where URLs, URLs, or IRIs are resolved to documents. 519–526, 528, 530–533, 535–538, 540, 543, 546, 555, 575, 595–600, 602, 603, 620, 622, 636, 637, 647, 649, 655, 657

EXTENSIONAL SEMANTICS A stronger if-and-only-if form of semantics; refers in particular to such a semantics defined informatively in the 2004 version of the RDF semantics for entailing triples in the RDFS vocabulary. 180

FEDERATION The evaluation of a query over multiple, independent query services. 410, 411, 413, 414, 443, 444, 447, 448, 637

FIRST-ORDER LOGIC A formal system used to express axioms with well-defined meaning permitting automatic deduction. 35, 128, 129

FUNCTIONALITY A formal property of a relation whereby it relates each resource to at most one other resource, as per a function (inverse of inverse-functionality). 206, 211, 274, 275, 277, 282–284, 294, 298, 303–306, 590, 648

GENERALISED TRIPLE An RDF triple that relaxes restrictions on which types of RDF terms can appear where, allowing blank nodes in the predicate position and literals in the subject and predicate position. 72, 106, 177, 314, 426

GRAPH HOMOMORPHISM A mapping from the nodes of one graph to the nodes of a second graph such that the image of the first graph under the mapping is a sub-graph of the second graph (weaker than graph isomorphism). 150, 404, 647

GRAPH ISOMORPHISM A one-to-one mapping from the nodes of one graph to a second graph such that the image of the first graph under the mapping equals the second graph (related to RDF isomorphism; stronger than graph homomorphism). 89, 408, 647, 652

GRAPH PATTERN A graph that allows variables that can be mapped to constants. 330–333, 346–349, 371, 388, 400, 420, 447, 638

GRDDL [Gleaning Resource Descriptions from Dialects of Languages] A standard for mapping from XML data to RDF using a provided stylesheet. 579

GROUND RDF GRAPH An RDF graph that contains only ground RDF triples. 136, 137, 139, 149, 151

GROUND RDF TRIPLE An RDF triple that does not contain a blank node. 137, 647

HASH RECIPE An implementation of dereferencing that involves affixing fragment identifiers to URLs in order to distinguish entity IRIs from the documents that describe them (alternative to the slash recipe, URL recipe). 522, 524–527, 655, 657

HERBRAND INTERPRETATION An interpretation that maps terms to themselves. 142, 143, 288

HL7 [Health Level 7] A set of international standards controlling the exchange of clinical data, including EHRs. 192, 646

HTML [Hypertext Markup Language] A lightweight markup language for formatting Web documents (inspired by SGML; related to XML and XHTML). 6–11, 15, 17, 18, 20, 37, 49–51, 64, 65, 96, 101–104, 106, 518,

IRREFLEXIVITY A formal property of a relation whereby it never relates any resource to itself (opposite of reflexivity).

JSON [JavaScript Object Notation] A lightweight syntax and tree-based data model for representing data that allows for describing objects with attribute–value pairs, where attributes are strings, and values can be strings, numbers, booleans, arrays, nulls, or nested objects.

JSON-LD [JavaScript Object Notation for Linked Data] A syntax based on JSON that can be used to serialise RDF graphs (alternative to N-Triples, RDFa, RDF/XML, Turtle) and RDF datasets (alternative to N-Quads and TriG).

KNOWLEDGE GRAPH A collection of data structured as a graph, often associated with machine-processable semantics.

LANGUAGE TAG A tag on a literal denoting the language of the literal.

LDF [Linked Data Fragments] A representation of various access interfaces for RDF, and how they can be invoked.

LDP [Linked Data Platform] A standard HTTP-based protocol for reading and writing data (typically RDF data) over the Web.

LEAN RDF GRAPH An RDF graph that does not simple-entail a proper subset of itself; in order words, an RDF graph without redundant triples containing blank nodes (opposite of non-lean RDF graph).

LINK DISCOVERY The problem of finding links between two datasets conforming to a particular property or set of properties.

LINK PREDICTION The problem of predicting missing links that are likely to be valid in a graph, which may consider a particular node and/or property as input.

LINKED DATA A minimal set of principles for publishing and interlinking data on the Web, involving the use of HTTP URIs or IRIs to identify entities that dereference to structured data describing those entities; alternatively, data published following these principles.

LITERAL A type of RDF term that is used for datatype values, plain strings, or language-tagged strings. 61, 64, 66–73, 76, 88, 95, 96, 98, 99, 103, 105, 121–123, 134–142, 145, 153–156, 161, 164, 165, 168, 172, 174, 176, 177, 194, 196, 200, 244, 247, 249, 277, 314, 318, 328, 338, 340–344, 364, 379, 384, 387, 426, 430, 432–434, 436, 437, 458, 460, 462, 475, 482, 483, 485, 495, 497, 502, 532, 559–562, 568, 644, 647, 649, 652

MATHEMATICAL SEMANTICS A semantics defined in terms of a mathematical structure. 131

METADATA Data about data. 7, 192, 463, 523, 534, 550, 552, 553, 577, 595, 601–603, 606, 614, 641, 658

MICRODATA A general and lightweight syntax for embedding data in webpages (alternative to RDFa). 50, 104, 109, 589, 625, 631, 653

MODEL An interpretation that satisfies a given set of axioms. 141–147, 151, 152, 154–156, 159–162, 166, 167, 169, 170, 182, 190, 192, 194, 251, 254, 257, 267, 269–272, 278, 284, 290, 291, 513, 515, 520, 533–535, 541, 569, 576, 623, 627, 630, 631, 633, 656

MODEL THEORY A formal mathematical framework for defining models. 129–131, 163, 166, 170, 180–182, 187, 188, 194, 197, 243, 266, 280, 296

n-ARY RELATION A relation between three or more entities. 79–82, 108, 533

N-QUADS A line-based syntax for serialising RDF datasets without abbreviations (serialises quadruples; based on N-Triples; alternative to JSON-LD, TriG). 107, 108, 600, 649, 656

N-TRIPLES A line-based syntax for RDF without abbreviations (a restricted form of Turtle; alternative to JSON-LD, RDF/XML, RDFa). 97–99, 106–108, 520, 527, 528, 600, 649, 650, 653, 657

N3 An extension of RDF with additional features for quantification and implication, as well as for defining graphs as nodes; a custom syntax for this extension (inspired Turtle, N-Triples). 99, 657

NAMED GRAPH A pair of an RDF graph and an IRI name (forms part of an RDF dataset). 82, 85, 86, 107, 108, 370–377, 415, 416, 418, 420–423, 442–447, 572

NON-LEAN RDF GRAPH An RDF graph that simple-entails a proper subset of itself; in order words, an RDF graph with redundant triples containing blank nodes (opposite of lean RDF graph). 93, 151, 152, 649

OBDA [Ontology-Based Data Access] The use of an ontology as a mediator to rewrite high-level queries to low-level queries over an underlying database or underlying databases. 309, 634, 635

ONTOLOGY An explicit machine-readable encoding of the semantics of a domain vocabulary using an ontology language. 35, 38, 40, 45, 56, 187–194, 214, 225, 242, 243, 250, 251, 253, 256–259, 263–269, 271–276, 278, 280, 281, 283–285, 288–293, 295–299, 302–306, 308, 309, 312, 314, 319, 321, 322, 425, 428, 435, 437, 452, 540, 542, 543, 548, 551, 553, 582, 583, 596, 633–635, 643, 650–653, 656

ONTOLOGY LANGUAGE A vocabulary with well-defined semantics that can be used to define ontologies. 35, 180, 186, 188, 273, 275, 276, 298, 627, 634, 635, 650, 651, 653, 657

OWA [Open World Assumption] An assumption that anything not known from the data is simply unknown, rather than false (alternative to CWA). 137, 151, 235, 253, 450, 476, 645

OWL [Web Ontology Language] An ontology language recommended by the W3C for specifying ontologies on the Web (extends RDFS). 35, 36, 55, 57, 68, 113, 114, 119, 128, 180, 182, 183, 185, 187, 188, 190, 192–196, 199–201, 203–205, 207, 210, 211, 213, 215, 216, 218, 220–222, 225, 226, 230, 231, 235, 240, 243–248, 250–259, 261, 263–269, 271–276, 278–281, 291–299, 303–309, 311–314, 316–322, 333, 424, 425, 428, 433–437, 439, 444, 447, 449, 450, 452, 453, 476, 515, 516, 530, 540, 542–544, 551, 553, 554, 590, 625, 627, 634, 635, 653, 656

PROPERTY A type of relationship, or a term denoting a type of relationship. 31, 33, 37, 40, 42, 43, 50–52, 77–80, 83, 92, 95, 101, 103, 105, 106, 108, 113, 115, 117–122, 125–127, 131, 133–136, 151, 157–161, 164, 165, 168, 169, 174, 178, 180–183, 185–189, 191, 194, 196–198, 200–215, 218, 225–244, 247, 250, 252, 253, 255, 257, 258, 261, 265, 266, 274–276, 281, 283, 290, 292–296, 298, 303, 308, 313, 316, 317, 320, 322, 352, 386, 414, 429, 435, 436, 439, 443, 445, 452, 454–459, 461–466, 468, 470–472, 474–478, 482, 484–499, 501, 502, 504–509, 519, 520, 532–534, 536, 539–542, 544, 551–553, 566, 578, 584, 590–594, 603–606, 609, 616, 629, 630, 632, 633, 652, 654, 657

PROPERTY PATH A path expression in SPARQL that can match arbitrary-length paths in an RDF graph. 351–355, 386, 439, 461, 478, 494, 508, 509, 511

PURL [Persistent Uniform Resource Locator] A URL (or URI) that resolves to a stable centralised redirection service, enabling persistence over time by allowing the redirection target to be changed over time. 531

QUADRUPLE An RDF triple extended with a fourth element; a way to serialise RDF datasets. 73, 74, 86, 87, 650

QUERY CONTAINMENT A relation between two queries whereby one is contained in another if and only if the results of the former query are a subset of the results of the latter query over any data (weaker than query equivalence). 406–408, 651

QUERY EQUIVALENCE A relation between two queries whereby one query is equivalent to another query if and only if the former query is contained in the latter, and the latter is contained in the former; in order words, two queries are equivalent if and only if they return the same results over any data (stronger than query containment). 406–409, 651

R-Box [Role Box] A set of axioms about roles (aka. properties) in a DL ontology. 276, 280, 283, 285, 286, 289, 297, 302, 304, 306, 308, 309, 311

R2RML A mapping language for converting data from relational databases to RDF (part of RDB2RDF; alternative to the Direct Mapping). 559–564, 567, 569–573, 576, 597, 646, 652

RDB2RDF [Relational Databases to RDF] A pair of recommendations for converting data from relational databases to RDF: the Direct Mapping and R2RML. 559, 561, 565, 589, 631, 646, 652

RDF [Resource Description Framework] A format recommended by the W3C for representing data as graphs. 21, 25, 36, 37, 40, 43, 50, 54, 55, 57, 60–64, 67–85, 87, 89–94, 96–101, 103–109, 111, 113–118, 120, 121, 123–135, 137, 139, 151, 153, 154, 157–163, 165, 166, 168–172, 174–178, 180–183, 186, 194–197, 221, 222, 226, 229, 238, 243–247, 249, 251, 253, 261, 265, 266, 268, 273, 276, 280, 281, 291, 295, 296, 311, 312, 319, 323, 325, 326, 331, 370, 384, 385, 404, 411, 414, 415, 421, 422, 424, 425, 428–430, 433, 434, 438–440, 442–450, 452, 453, 461, 500, 501, 507, 508, 512, 513, 515, 516, 518–520, 522, 523, 527, 529, 532–535, 539, 546, 551, 554–556, 559–564, 568–570, 574–583, 585–590, 595–597, 599, 602, 603, 607–610, 612–615, 618–624, 627, 630–632, 639, 644, 647, 649, 650, 653, 655, 656

RDF DATASET A default RDF graph and a set of named graphs. 61, 62, 85, 87, 93, 106–108, 198, 370, 371, 384, 406, 414, 415, 444, 454, 572, 573, 583–585, 587, 588, 600, 631, 645, 649–651

RDF GRAPH A set of RDF triples. 61, 74–76, 82–85, 87–94, 96, 98–101, 107, 108, 119, 120, 122, 129, 131–133, 135–145, 147–152, 154–156, 159–163, 167, 169, 170, 173, 176–179, 181, 185, 197, 198, 224, 254, 265, 266, 278, 281, 291, 295, 308, 312, 313, 316, 321, 325, 326, 328, 330, 333, 334, 336, 339, 346, 370, 374, 378–383, 393, 396, 403, 404, 406, 407, 425–431, 433, 437, 442, 444, 445, 448–450, 452–454, 463, 467, 476, 501, 511–513, 515, 519, 527, 533, 544, 559, 572, 578, 581, 582, 590, 597, 600, 620, 622, 632, 633, 645, 646, 649–653

RDF ISOMORPHISM A relation between two RDF graphs whereby they are isomorphic if and only if they are the same modulo (a one-to-one) relabelling of blank nodes (specialises graph isomorphism). 87–93, 96, 97, 99, 100, 141, 152, 382, 403, 408, 647

RDF MERGE A union of two RDF graphs preceded by a (one-to-one) relabelling of their blank nodes such that they do not share any. 90, 375

RDF TERM An IRI, literal or blank node. 61, 69–73, 76, 78, 87, 88, 105, 106, 130, 131, 133, 135, 142, 148, 150, 151, 157, 196, 197, 328, 329, 338, 340, 428, 431, 475, 486, 509, 511, 566–569, 592, 620, 647, 652

RDF TRIPLE A tuple of RDF terms of length 3, where the first element is called the subject (which may take an IRI or blank node), the second element is called the predicate (which may take an IRI), and the third element is called the object (which may take an IRI, blank node or literal).

61, 71–84, 86, 87, 90, 92, 94–98, 102–108, 113, 114, 116–120, 122–127, 129–131, 133, 136–138, 141, 142, 148, 150–152, 154–156, 159, 161, 162, 166, 167, 169, 170, 173–177, 179, 180, 182, 186, 195, 198, 200, 207, 209, 214, 217, 218, 242, 252, 256, 257, 277, 313, 314, 328–331, 370, 374, 375, 379, 380, 382–384, 388, 404, 415–423, 426, 427, 429–431, 433, 439, 444, 447, 448, 458–460, 462, 489, 494, 496, 502, 503, 505, 510, 516, 520, 533, 535, 538, 548, 553, 559, 561–563, 565, 566, 568–572, 581, 584, 585, 587, 588, 590, 596, 598, 600, 601, 603–606, 608–610, 614–618, 620–622, 631–633, 637, 640, 647, 651, 652

RDF/XML A syntax for serialising RDF graphs based on XML (alternative to JSON-LD, N-Triples, RDFa, Turtle). 94–98, 106, 520, 527, 528, 578–580, 631, 649, 650, 653, 657

RDFA [RDF in Attributes] A syntax for RDF recommended by the W3C that can be embedded within webpages (alternative RDF syntax to JSON-LD, N-Triples, RDF/XML, Turtle; alternative embeddable syntax to JSON-LD and Microdata). 50, 51, 101–103, 106, 446, 527, 589, 625, 649, 650, 653, 657

RDFS [RDF Schema] A concise ontology language recommended by the W3C for specifying lightweight ontologies on the Web (extended by OWL). 35, 55, 57, 113–115, 119–128, 131, 153, 158, 163–183, 185, 186, 188, 192–196, 200, 201, 203, 215, 216, 259, 263, 294, 308, 312, 314, 316, 319, 320, 424, 425, 428–430, 433, 449, 450, 452, 453, 460, 515, 516, 530, 540, 543, 551, 554, 625, 627, 635, 651

REASONING A process that draws implicit conclusions from explicit information (instantiated by abductive reasoning, deductive reasoning, inductive reasoning). 33, 56, 130, 163, 171, 182, 188, 193, 194, 199, 213, 240, 243, 256–259, 263–267, 273–275, 281, 284, 288, 291, 292, 294, 297–299, 303–305, 311, 313, 316, 319–322, 448, 538, 540, 543, 544, 590, 631, 634, 636, 638

REFLEXIVITY A formal property of a relation whereby it relates every resource to itself (opposite of irreflexivity). 130, 145–147, 165, 197, 201, 205, 228, 265, 277, 282, 283, 303–307, 649

REIFICATION A way of making statements about statements. 81–84, 95, 108, 157, 243, 532–534, 631

RELATIONAL DATABASE A database consisting of tabular data, often using the SQL query language. 16, 17, 19, 35, 59, 70, 76, 190, 191, 258, 298, 311, 324, 325, 337, 405, 409, 447, 448, 554, 556, 557, 559, 560, 562–564, 567, 574–576, 581, 588, 595–597, 632, 633, 656

RESOURCE Anything with identity (synonymous with entity). 38, 40, 60–63, 69–72, 76–83, 87, 95, 103, 104, 115, 117, 118, 120–122, 124, 130–136, 138–140, 142, 145, 146, 151, 153, 155, 164, 165, 167–169, 174, 181, 185, 187, 194, 196–198, 201, 205–208, 210, 213–217, 220, 221, 226–228, 231, 232, 235–237, 247, 250, 252, 257, 262, 263, 326, 450, 453, 552, 553, 582, 600, 607, 608, 630, 634, 644–646, 648, 649, 653, 656

REST [Representational State Transfer] A lightweight and scalable architecture for client–server interactions, where clients use a fixed protocol (typically HTTP) to request and potentially modify resources on the server, where resources contain links to other resources, and where the server does not maintain states (i.e., sessions) for clients. 611

RIF [Rule Interchange Format] A format recommended by the W3C for serialising and exchanging rules. 253, 316, 425, 437, 438

ROLE A property (often used for DLs). 248, 276–284, 290, 291, 294, 296, 303–308, 312, 314, 553, 632, 639, 640, 646, 648, 652

RULE A logical implication represented as an IF–THEN statement, where the IF condition is often called the body or antecedent of the rule, while the THEN conclusion is called the head or consequent. 26–35, 38, 45, 68, 114–116, 127–129, 143, 145, 171–177, 179–182, 199, 243, 253, 259, 261–263, 287, 304, 305, 311–316, 321, 322, 408, 409, 437, 438, 452, 498, 501, 502, 527, 540, 544, 592–594, 633

SATISFIABILITY A formal property of a set of axioms whereby there exists an interpretation that satisfies it, i.e., that assigns true to it. 119, 141–143, 148, 150, 153–155, 158, 160, 161, 165, 166, 168–170, 178, 181, 196, 227, 257, 258, 262, 266, 271–273, 280, 284–286, 288–290, 297, 298, 302–304, 306, 316, 319, 338, 373, 426, 459, 461, 472–475, 485, 502, 503, 505, 507, 523, 544–546, 571, 629, 650, 656, 657

SCHEMA A formal description of the high-level structure of a dataset that may be used for a variety of purposes, including managing, storing, indexing, querying, validating, and/or reasoning over a dataset. 17–19, 35, 45, 67, 103, 114, 120, 181, 190–192, 244, 246, 311, 313, 314, 386, 430, 432, 447, 448, 510–512, 541, 542, 553, 559, 560, 564, 570, 574, 577, 578, 589, 609, 625, 627, 633, 635, 640, 654

SEMANTIC SEARCH Advanced search functionality enabled by representations of semantics for the underlying content. 45, 48

SEMANTIC WEB A version/vision of the Web in which content is published in machine-readable formats and described with machine-readable semantics, offering greater automation for tasks; a collection of standards and techniques that have been developed towards realising this vision. 40, 56, 57, 182, 530, 546, 578, 584, 623, 624, 627, 629, 631

SEMI-STRUCTURED DATA Data that do not follow a strict structure (such as a relational schema) but can be parsed into tree-like or graph-like representations; sometimes used to mean data that mix unstructured (text) and structured (syntactic) elements, such as markup documents. 17–19, 584, 631, 632

SEO [Search Engine Optimisation] A methodology for increasing the traffic to a given website from a search engine or search engines, often by applying techniques to raise the ranking of specific webpages in search results. 51

References

1. I. Abdelaziz, R. Harbi, S. Salihoglu, and P. Kalnis. Combining Vertex-Centric Graph Processing with SPARQL for Large-Scale RDF Data Analytics. *IEEE Trans. Parallel Distrib. Syst.*, 28(12):3374–3388, 2017.
2. M. Acosta, M.-E. Vidal, T. Lampo, J. Castillo, and E. Ruckhaus. ANAPSID: An Adaptive Query Processing Engine for SPARQL Endpoints. In Aroyo et al. [19], pages 18–34.
3. B. Adida, M. Birbeck, S. McCarron, and S. Pemberton. RDFa in XHTML: Syntax and Processing. W3C Recommendation, Oct. 2008. https://www.w3.org/TR/rdfa-syntax/.
4. H. Alani and C. Brewster. Ontology ranking based on the analysis of concept structures. In P. Clark and G. Schreiber, editors, *Proceedings of the 3rd International Conference on Knowledge Capture (K-CAP 2005), October 2–5, 2005, Banff, Alberta, Canada*, pages 51–58. ACM, 2005.
5. H. Alani, L. Kagal, A. Fokoue, P. T. Groth, C. Biemann, J. X. Parreira, L. Aroyo, N. F. Noy, C. Welty, and K. Janowicz, editors. *The Semantic Web – ISWC 2013 – 12th International Semantic Web Conference, Sydney, NSW, Australia, October 21–25, 2013, Proceedings*, volume 8219 of *LNCS*. Springer, 2013.
6. R. Albertoni, D. Browning, S. Cox, A. G. Beltran, A. Perego, and P. Winstanley. Data Catalog Vocabulary (DCAT) – Version 2. W3C Recommendation, Feb. 2020. https://www.w3.org/TR/vocab-dcat-2/.
7. K. Alexander, R. Cyganiak, M. Hausenblas, and J. Zhao. Describing Linked Datasets with the VoID Vocabulary. W3C Interest Group Note, Mar. 2011. https://www.w3.org/TR/void/.
8. D. Allemang and J. A. Hendler. *Semantic Web for the Working Ontologist: Effective Modeling in RDFS and OWL*. Morgan Kaufmann/Elsevier, 2008.
9. J. Allen. *Natural Language Understanding (2nd Ed.)*. Pearson, 1995.
10. R. Angles, M. Arenas, P. Barceló, A. Hogan, J. Reutter, and D. Vrgoč. Foundations of Modern Query Languages for Graph Databases. *ACM Computing Surveys*, 50(5), 2017.
11. R. Angles and C. Gutiérrez. The Multiset Semantics of SPARQL Patterns. In P. T. Groth, E. Simperl, A. J. G. Gray, M. Sabou, M. Krötzsch, F. Lécué, F. Flöck, and Y. Gil, editors, *The Semantic Web – ISWC 2016 – 15th International Semantic Web Conference, Kobe, Japan, October 17–21, 2016, Proceedings, Part I*, volume 9981 of *LNCS*, pages 20–36, 2016.
12. C. B. Aranda, M. Arenas, Ó. Corcho, and A. Polleres. Federating queries in SPARQL 1.1: Syntax, semantics and evaluation. *J. Web Sem.*, 18(1):1–17, 2013.
13. C. B. Aranda, A. Hogan, J. Umbrich, and P. Vandenbussche. SPARQL web-querying infrastructure: Ready for action? In Alani et al. [5], pages 277–293.
14. M. Arenas, A. Bertails, E. Prud'hommeaux, and J. Sequeda. A Direct Mapping of Relational Data to RDF. W3C Recommendation, Sept. 2012. https://www.w3.org/TR/rdb-direct-mapping/.
15. M. Arenas, S. Conca, and J. Pérez. Counting beyond a Yottabyte, or how SPARQL 1.1 property paths will prevent adoption of the standard. In A. Mille, F. L. Gandon, J. Misselis, M. Rabinovich, and S. Staab, editors, *Proceedings of the 21st World Wide Web Conference 2012, WWW 2012, Lyon, France, April 16–20, 2012*, pages 629–638. ACM, 2012.
16. M. Arenas, Ó. Corcho, E. Simperl, M. Strohmaier, M. d'Aquin, K. Srinivas, P. T. Groth, M. Dumontier, J. Heflin, K. Thirunarayan, and S. Staab, editors. *The Semantic Web – ISWC 2015 – 14th International Semantic Web Conference, Bethlehem, PA, USA, October 11–15, 2015, Proceedings, Part II*, volume 9367 of *LNCS*. Springer, 2015.

17. M. Arenas, B. C. Grau, E. Kharlamov, S. Marciuska, and D. Zheleznyakov. Faceted search over RDF-based knowledge graphs. *J. Web Semant.*, 37-38:55–74, 2016.

18. L. Aroyo, G. Antoniou, E. Hyvönen, A. ten Teije, H. Stuckenschmidt, L. Cabral, and T. Tudorache, editors. *The Semantic Web: Research and Applications, 7th Extended Semantic Web Conference, ESWC 2010, Heraklion, Crete, Greece, May 30 – June 3, 2010, Proceedings, Part II*, volume 6089 of *LNCS*. Springer, 2010.

19. L. Aroyo, C. Welty, H. Alani, J. Taylor, A. Bernstein, L. Kagal, N. F. Noy, and E. Blomqvist, editors. *The Semantic Web – ISWC 2011 – 10th International Semantic Web Conference, Bonn, Germany, October 23–27, 2011, Proceedings, Part I*, volume 7031 of *LNCS*. Springer, 2011.

20. A. Artale, D. Calvanese, R. Kontchakov, and M. Zakharyaschev. The DL-Lite Family and Relations. *J. Artif. Intell. Res.*, 36:1–69, 2009.

21. M. Atre, V. Chaoji, M. J. Zaki, and J. A. Hendler. Matrix "Bit"loaded: a scalable lightweight join query processor for RDF data. In M. Rappa, P. Jones, J. Freire, and S. Chakrabarti, editors, *WWW*, pages 41–50. ACM, 2010.

22. F. Baader, D. Calvanese, D. L. McGuinness, D. Nardi, and P. F. Patel-Schneider. *The Description Logic Handbook: Theory, Implementation and Application.* Cambridge University Press, 2002.

23. F. Baader, J. Hladik, C. Lutz, and F. Wolter. From Tableaux to Automata for Description Logics. *Fundam. Inform.*, 57(2–4):247–279, 2003.

24. F. Baader, I. Horrocks, C. Lutz, and U. Sattler. *An Introduction to Description Logic.* Cambridge University Press, 2017.

25. F. Baader, C. Lutz, and S. Brandt. Pushing the EL Envelope Further. In K. Clark and P. F. Patel-Schneider, editors, *Proceedings of the Fourth OWLED Workshop on OWL: Experiences and Directions, Washington, DC, USA, 1–2 April 2008.*, volume 496 of *CEUR Workshop Proceedings*. CEUR-WS.org, 2008.

26. F. Baader, C. Lutz, and B. Motik, editors. *Proceedings of the 21st International Workshop on Description Logics (DL2008), Dresden, Germany, May 13–16, 2008*, volume 353 of *CEUR Workshop Proceedings*. CEUR-WS.org, 2008.

27. F. Baader, C. Lutz, and B. Suntisrivaraporn. CEL – A Polynomial-Time Reasoner for Life Science Ontologies. In Furbach and Shankar [134], pages 287–291.

28. F. Baader and U. Sattler. An Overview of Tableau Algorithms for Description Logics. *Studia Logica*, 69(1):5–40, 2001.

29. R. A. Baeza-Yates and B. A. Ribeiro-Neto. *Modern Information Retrieval – The concepts and technology behind search, Second edition.* Pearson Education Ltd., Harlow, England, 2011.

30. J. Bailey, F. Bry, T. Furche, and S. Schaffert. Web and Semantic Web Query Languages: A Survey. In N. Eisinger and J. Maluszynski, editors, *Reasoning Web, First International Summer School 2005, Msida, Malta, July 25–29, 2005, Tutorial Lectures*, volume 3564 of *LNCS*, pages 35–133. Springer, 2005.

31. B. Bamba and S. Mukherjea. Utilizing Resource Importance for Ranking Semantic Web Query Results. In C. Bussler, V. Tannen, and I. Fundulaki, editors, *SWDB*, volume 3372, pages 185–198, 2004.

32. P. Barceló, M. Kröll, R. Pichler, and S. Skritek. Efficient Evaluation and Static Analysis for Well-Designed Pattern Trees with Projection. *ACM Trans. Database Syst.*, 43(2):8:1–8:44, 2018.

33. C. Basca, S. Corlosquet, R. Cyganiak, S. Fernández, and T. Schandl. Neologism: Easy Vocabulary Publishing. In *Proceedings of the Fourth International Workshop on Scripting for the Semantic Web Workshop, SFSW 2008, Tenerife, Spain*, 2008.

34. S. Battle and S. Speicher. Linked Data Platform Use Cases and Requirements. W3C Working Group Note, Mar. 2014. https://www.w3.org/TR/ldp-ucr/.

35. S. Battle, D. Wood, J. Leigh, and L. Ruth. The Callimachus Project: RDFa as a Web Template Language. In J. F. Sequeda, A. Harth, and O. Hartig, editors, *Proceedings of the Third International Workshop on Consuming Linked Data, COLD*

2012, Boston, MA, USA, November 12, 2012, volume 905 of *CEUR Workshop Proceedings*. CEUR-WS.org, 2012.

36. S. Bechhofer, M. Hauswirth, J. Hoffmann, and M. Koubarakis, editors. *The Semantic Web: Research and Applications, 5th European Semantic Web Conference, ESWC 2008, Tenerife, Canary Islands, Spain, June 1–5, 2008, Proceedings*, volume 5021 of *LNCS*. Springer, 2008.

37. D. Beckett. RDF Syntaxes 2.0. In D. Wood, S. Decker, and I. Herman, editors, *W3C Workshop on RDF Next Steps*, Stanford, Palo Alto, CA, USA, June 2010. W3C.

38. D. Beckett and T. Berners-Lee. Turtle – Terse RDF Triple Language. W3C Team Submission, Jan. 2008. https://www.w3.org/TeamSubmission/turtle/.

39. D. Beckett, T. Berners-Lee, E. Prud'hommeaux, and G. Carothers. RDF 1.1 Turtle – Terse RDF Triple Language. W3C Recommendation, Feb. 2014. https://www.w3.org/TR/turtle/.

40. D. Beckett, G. Carothers, and A. Seaborne. RDF 1.1 N-Triples – A line-based syntax for an RDF graph. W3C Recommendation, Feb. 2014. https://www.w3.org/TR/n-triples/.

41. D. Beckett, F. Gandon, and G. Schreiber. RDF 1.1 XML Syntax. W3C Recommendation, Feb. 2014. https://www.w3.org/TR/rdf-syntax-grammar/.

42. D. Beckett and B. McBride. RDF/XML Syntax Specification (Revised). W3C Recommendation, Feb. 2004. https://www.w3.org/TR/rdf-syntax-grammar/.

43. F. Belleau, M. Nolin, N. Tourigny, P. Rigault, and J. Morissette. Bio2RDF: Towards a mashup to build bioinformatics knowledge systems. *Journal of Biomedical Informatics*, 41(5):706–716, 2008.

44. R. Berger. The undecidability of the domino problem. *Memoirs of the American Mathematical Society*, 66:72, 1966.

45. T. Berners-Lee. Semantic Web Road map. W3C Design Issues, Oct. 1998. https://www.w3.org/DesignIssues/Diff.

46. T. Berners-Lee. Linked Data. W3C Design Issues, July 2006. From https://www.w3.org/DesignIssues/LinkedData.html; retr. 2010/10/27.

47. T. Berners-Lee. Read-Write Linked Data. W3C Design Issues, Aug. 2009. https://www.w3.org/DesignIssues/ReadWriteLinkedData.html.

48. T. Berners-Lee. The Future of RDF. W3C Design Issues, 2010. https://www.w3.org/DesignIssues/ReadWriteLinkedData.html.

49. T. Berners-Lee and D. Connolly. Notation3 (N3): A readable RDF syntax. W3C Team Submission, Mar. 2011. https://www.w3.org/TeamSubmission/n3/.

50. T. Berners-Lee, R. Cyganiak, M. Hausenblas, J. Presbrey, O. Seneviratne, and O.-E. Ureche. Realising A Read-Write Web of Data, June 2009. Published Online: http://web.mit.edu/presbrey/Public/rw-wod.pdf.

51. T. Berners-Lee, R. T. Fielding, and L. Masinter. Uniform Resource Identifier (URI): Generic Syntax. RFC 3986, Jan. 2005. http://www.ietf.org/rfc/rfc3986.txt.

52. T. Berners-Lee and M. Fischetti. *Weaving the Web: The original design and ultimate destiny of the World Wide Web by its Inventor*. Harper, 1999.

53. T. Berners-Lee, J. Hendler, and O. Lassila. The Semantic Web. *Scientific American*, 284(5):34–43, 2001.

54. A. Bernstein, D. R. Karger, T. Heath, L. Feigenbaum, D. Maynard, E. Motta, and K. Thirunarayan, editors. *The Semantic Web – ISWC 2009, 8th International Semantic Web Conference, ISWC 2009, Chantilly, VA, USA, October 25–29, 2009. Proceedings*, volume 5823 of *LNCS*. Springer, 2009.

55. A. Bertails, P.-A. Champin, and A. Sambra. Linked Data Patch Format. W3C Working Group Note, July 2015. https://www.w3.org/TR/ldpatch/.

56. S. Bischof, S. Decker, T. Krennwallner, N. Lopes, and A. Polleres. Mapping between RDF and XML with XSPARQL. *J. Data Semantics*, 1(3):147–185, 2012.

57. B. Bishop, A. Kiryakov, D. Ognyanoff, I. Peikov, Z. Tashev, and R. Velkov. OWLIM: A family of scalable semantic repositories. *Semantic Web*, 2(1):33–42, 2011.

58. C. M. Bishop. *Pattern Recognition and Machine Learning*. Springer, 2006.

59. C. Bizer. D2R MAP – A database to RDF mapping language. In I. King and T. Máray, editors, *Proceedings of the Twelfth International World Wide Web Conference – Posters, WWW 2003, Budapest, Hungary, May 20–24, 2003*, 2003.

60. C. Bizer, R. Cyganiak, and T. Heath. How to Publish Linked Data on the Web. Technical Report – University of Mannheim, July 2007. http://wifo5-03.informatik.uni-mannheim.de/bizer/pub/LinkedDataTutorial/.

61. C. Bizer, K. Eckert, R. Meusel, H. Mühleisen, M. Schuhmacher, and J. Völker. Deployment of RDFa, Microdata, and Microformats on the Web – A Quantitative Analysis. In Alani et al. [5], pages 17–32.

62. C. Bizer, T. Heath, S. Auer, and T. Berners-Lee, editors. *Proceedings of the Workshop on Linked Data on the Web co-located with the 23rd International World Wide Web Conference (WWW 2014), Seoul, Korea, April 8, 2014*, volume 1184 of *CEUR Workshop Proceedings*. CEUR-WS.org, 2014.

63. C. Bizer, T. Heath, and T. Berners-Lee. Linked Data – The Story So Far. *Int. J. Semantic Web Inf. Syst.*, 5(3):1–22, 2009.

64. E. Blomqvist, K. Hammar, and V. Presutti. Engineering Ontologies with Patterns – The eXtreme Design Methodology. In P. Hitzler, A. Gangemi, K. Janowicz, A. Krisnadhi, and V. Presutti, editors, *Ontology Engineering with Ontology Design Patterns*, volume 25 of *Studies on the Semantic Web*. IOS Press, 2016.

65. C. Böhm, J. Lorey, and F. Naumann. Creating voiD descriptions for Web-scale data. *J. Web Semant.*, 9(3):339–345, 2011.

66. H. Boley, G. Hallmark, M. Kifer, A. Paschke, A. Polleres, and D. Reynolds. RIF Core Dialect (Second Edition). W3C Recommendation, Feb. 2013. http://www.w3.org/TR/rif-core/.

67. K. D. Bollacker, C. Evans, P. Paritosh, T. Sturge, and J. Taylor. Freebase: a collaboratively created graph database for structuring human knowledge. In J. T.-L. Wang, editor, *Proceedings of the ACM SIGMOD International Conference on Management of Data, SIGMOD 2008, Vancouver, BC, Canada, June 10–12, 2008*, pages 1247–1250. ACM, 2008.

68. P. A. Bonatti, M. Faella, I. Petrova, and L. Sauro. A new semantics for overriding in description logics. *Artif. Intell.*, 222:1–48, 2015.

69. P. A. Bonatti, A. Hogan, A. Polleres, and L. Sauro. Robust and scalable Linked Data reasoning incorporating provenance and trust annotations. *J. Web Sem.*, 9(2):165–201, 2011.

70. P. A. Bonatti, C. Lutz, and F. Wolter. The Complexity of Circumscription in DLs. *J. Artif. Intell. Res. (JAIR)*, 35:717–773, 2009.

71. I. Boneva, J. Dusart, D. Fernández-Álvarez, and J. E. Labra Gayo. Semi automatic construction of ShEx and SHACL schemas. *CoRR*, abs/1907.10603, 2019.

72. A. Bonifati, W. Martens, and T. Timm. An Analytical Study of Large SPARQL Query Logs. *PVLDB*, 11(2):149–161, 2017.

73. P. Bouquet, H. Stoermer, and B. Bazzanella. An Entity Name System (ENS) for the Semantic Web. In Bechhofer et al. [36], pages 258–272.

74. R. J. Brachman and J. G. Schmolze. An Overview of the KL-ONE Knowledge Representation System. *Cognitive Science*, 9(2):171–216, 1985.

75. J. Brank, M. Grobelnik, and D. Mladenić. A survey of ontology evaluation techniques. In *Proceedings of the Conference on Data Mining and Data Warehouses (SiKDD)*, pages 166–170, 2005.

76. T. Bray. The JavaScript Object Notation (JSON) Data Interchange Format. RFC 8259, Dec. 2017. https://tools.ietf.org/html/rfc8259.

77. T. Bray, J. Paoli, C. M. Sperberg-McQueen, E. Maler, and F. Yergeau. Extensible Markup Language (XML) 1.0 (Fifth Edition). W3C Recommendation, Nov. 2008. https://www.w3.org/TR/xml/.

78. L. Breuza, S. Poux, A. Estreicher, M. L. Famiglietti, M. Magrane, M. Tognolli, A. Bridge, D. Baratin, and N. Redaschi. The UniProtKB guide to the human proteome. *Database*, 2016, 2016.

79. D. Brickley and R. Guha. RDF Vocabulary Description Language 1.0: RDF Schema. W3C Recommendation, Feb. 2004. https://www.w3.org/TR/rdf-schema/.

80. D. Brickley, R. Guha, and A. Layman. Resource Description Framework (RDF) Schemas. W3C Working Draft, Apr. 1998. https://www.w3.org/TR/1998/WD-rdf-schema-19980409/.

81. D. Brickley, R. Guha, and B. McBride. RDF Schema 1.1. W3C Recommendation, Feb. 2014. https://www.w3.org/TR/rdf-schema/.

82. J. Broekstra, A. Kampman, and F. van Harmelen. Sesame: A Generic Architecture for Storing and Querying RDF and RDF Schema. In Horrocks and Hendler [207], pages 54–68.

83. C. Burleson, M. E. Gutiérrez, and A. Malhotra. Linked Data Platform Best Practices and Guidelines. W3C Working Group Note, Aug. 2014. https://www.w3.org/TR/ldp-bp/.

84. D. Calvanese, G. De Giacomo, D. Lembo, M. Lenzerini, and R. Rosati. Tractable Reasoning and Efficient Query Answering in Description Logics: The *DL-Lite* Family. *J. Autom. Reasoning*, 39(3):385–429, 2007.

85. D. Calvanese, G. De Giacomo, and M. Lenzerini. Conjunctive query containment and answering under description logic constraints. *ACM Trans. Comput. Log.*, 9(3):22:1–22:31, 2008.

86. S. Capadisli, S. Auer, and A. N. Ngomo. Linked SDMX data: Path to high fidelity Statistical Linked Data. *Semantic Web*, 6(2):105–112, 2015.

87. G. Carothers. RDF 1.1 NQuads – A line-based syntax for RDF datasets. W3C Recommendation, Feb. 2014. https://www.w3.org/TR/n-quads/.

88. G. Carothers, A. Seaborne, C. Bizer, and R. Cyganiak. RDF 1.1 Trig – RDF Dataset Language. W3C Recommendation, Feb. 2014. https://www.w3.org/TR/trig/.

89. Š. Čebirić, F. Goasdoué, H. Kondylakis, D. Kotzinos, I. Manolescu, G. Troullinou, and M. Zneika. Summarizing semantic graphs: a survey. *VLDB J.*, 28(3):295–327, 2019.

90. P. Champin, F. L. Gandon, M. Lalmas, and P. G. Ipeirotis, editors. *Proceedings of the 2018 World Wide Web Conference on World Wide Web, WWW 2018, Lyon, France, April 23–27, 2018.* ACM, 2018.

91. A. K. Chandra and P. M. Merlin. Optimal Implementation of Conjunctive Queries in Relational Data Bases. In J. E. Hopcroft, E. P. Friedman, and M. A. Harrison, editors, *Proceedings of the 9th Annual ACM Symposium on Theory of Computing, May 4–6, 1977, Boulder, Colorado, USA*, pages 77–90. ACM, 1977.

92. C. Chang, M. Kayed, M. R. Girgis, and K. F. Shaalan. A Survey of Web Information Extraction Systems. *IEEE Trans. Knowl. Data Eng.*, 18(10):1411–1428, 2006.

93. S. Chaudhuri and M. Y. Vardi. Optimization of *Real* Conjunctive Queries. In C. Beeri, editor, *Proceedings of the Twelfth ACM SIGACT-SIGMOD-SIGART Symposium on Principles of Database Systems, May 25–28, 1993, Washington, DC, USA*, pages 59–70. ACM Press, 1993.

94. G. Cheng and Y. Qu. Searching Linked Objects with Falcons: Approach, Implementation and Evaluation. *Int. J. Semantic Web Inf. Syst.*, 5(3):49–70, 2009.

95. C. Chung, A. Z. Broder, K. Shim, and T. Suel, editors. *23rd International World Wide Web Conference, WWW '14, Seoul, Republic of Korea, April 7–11, 2014.* ACM, 2014.

96. J. Clark. XSL Transformations (XSLT) Version 1.0. W3C Recommendation, Nov. 1999. https://www.w3.org/TR/xslt.

97. K. G. Clark, L. Feigenbaum, and E. Torres. SPARQL Query Results JSON Format. W3C Recommendation, Mar. 2013. https://www.w3.org/TR/rdf-sparql-XMLres/.

98. E. F. Codd. A Relational Model of Data for Large Shared Data Banks. *Commun. ACM*, 13(6):377–387, 1970.

99. D. Connolly. Gleaning Resource Descriptions from Dialects of Languages (GRDDL). W3C Recommendation, Sept. 2007. https://www.w3.org/TR/grddl/.

100. J. Corman, F. Florenzano, J. L. Reutter, and O. Savkovic. Validating SHACL constraints over a SPARQL endpoint. In Ghidini et al. [142], pages 145–163.

101. J. Corman, J. L. Reutter, and O. Savkovic. Semantics and Validation of Recursive SHACL. In *The Semantic Web – ISWC 2018 – 17th International Semantic Web Conference, Monterey, CA, USA, October 8–12, 2018, Proceedings, Part I*, pages 318–336, 2018.

102. R. Cyganiak, D. Reynolds, and J. Tennison. The RDF Data Cube Vocabulary. W3C Recommendation, Jan. 2014. https://www.w3.org/TR/vocab-data-cube/.

103. R. Cyganiak, D. Wood, and M. Lanthaler. RDF 1.1 Concepts and Abstract Syntax. W3C Recommendation, Feb. 2014. https://www.w3.org/TR/rdf11-concepts/.

104. C. d'Amato, M. Fernández, V. A. M. Tamma, F. Lécué, P. Cudré-Mauroux, J. F. Sequeda, C. Lange, and J. Heflin, editors. *The Semantic Web – ISWC 2017 – 16th International Semantic Web Conference, Vienna, Austria, October 21–25, 2017, Proceedings, Part II*, volume 10588 of *LNCS*. Springer, 2017.

105. M. d'Aquin and E. Motta. Watson, more than a Semantic Web search engine. *Semantic Web*, 2(1):55–63, 2011.

106. S. Das, S. Sundara, and R. Cyganiak. R2RML: RDB to RDF Mapping Language. W3C Recommendation, Sept. 2012. https://www.w3.org/TR/r2rml/.

107. J. de Bruijn and C. Welty. RIF RDF and OWL Compatibility (Second Edition). W3C Recommendation, Feb. 2013. http://www.w3.org/TR/rif-rdf-owl/.

108. R. R. de C. e Silva, B. de C. Leal, F. T. Brito, V. M. P. Vidal, and J. C. Machado. A Differentially Private Approach for Querying RDF Data of Social Networks. In B. C. Desai, J. Hong, and R. McClatchey, editors, *Proceedings of the 21st International Database Engineering & Applications Symposium, IDEAS 2017, Bristol, United Kingdom, July 12–14, 2017*, pages 74–81. ACM, 2017.

109. R. Delbru, N. Toupikov, M. Catasta, G. Tummarello, and S. Decker. Hierarchical Link Analysis for Ranking Web Data. In Aroyo et al. [18], pages 225–239.

110. R. Delbru, G. Tummarello, and A. Polleres. Context-Dependent OWL Reasoning in Sindice – Experiences and Lessons Learnt. In S. Rudolph and C. Gutierrez, editors, *RR*, volume 6902 of *LNCS*, pages 46–60. Springer, 2011.

111. A. Dimou, M. V. Sande, P. Colpaert, R. Verborgh, E. Mannens, and R. V. de Walle. RML: A Generic Language for Integrated RDF Mappings of Heterogeneous Data. In Bizer et al. [62].

112. L. Ding, R. Pan, T. W. Finin, A. Joshi, Y. Peng, and P. Kolari. Finding and Ranking Knowledge on the Semantic Web. In Y. Gil, E. Motta, V. R. Benjamins, and M. A. Musen, editors, *International Semantic Web Conference*, volume 3729 of *LNCS*, pages 156–170. Springer, 2005.

113. L. Ding, J. Shinavier, Z. Shangguan, and D. L. McGuinness. SameAs Networks and Beyond: Analyzing Deployment Status and Implications of owl:sameAs in Linked Data. In Patel-Schneider et al. [307], pages 145–160.

114. R. Q. Dividino, T. Gottron, and A. Scherp. Strategies for Efficiently Keeping Local Linked Open Data Caches Up-To-Date. In Arenas et al. [16], pages 356–373.

115. K. Donnelly. SNOMED-CT: The advanced terminology and coding system for eHealth. *Studies in Health Technology and Informatics*, 121:279–290, 2006.

116. P. Doran, V. A. M. Tamma, and L. Iannone. Ontology module extraction for ontology reuse: an ontology engineering perspective. In M. J. Silva, A. H. F. Laender, R. A. Baeza-Yates, D. L. McGuinness, B. Olstad, Ø. H. Olsen, and A. O. Falcão, editors, *CIKM*, pages 61–70. ACM, 2007.

117. M. Dumontier, A. Callahan, J. Cruz-Toledo, P. Ansell, V. Emonet, F. Belleau, and A. Droit. Bio2RDF Release 3: A larger, more connected network of Linked Data for the Life Sciences. In M. Horridge, M. Rospocher, and J. van Ossenbruggen, editors, *Proceedings of the ISWC 2014 Posters & Demonstrations Track a track within the 13th International Semantic Web Conference, ISWC 2014, Riva del Garda, Italy, October 21, 2014.*, volume 1272 of *CEUR Workshop Proceedings*, pages 401–404. CEUR-WS.org, 2014.

118. M. Dürst and M. Suignard. Internationalized Resource Identifiers (IRIs). RFC 3987, Jan. 2005. http://www.ietf.org/rfc/rfc3987.txt.

119. L. Dusseault. Web Distributed Authoring and Versioning. RFC 4918, June 2007. https://tools.ietf.org/html/rfc4918.

120. O. Erling. Virtuoso, a Hybrid RDBMS/Graph Column Store. *IEEE Data Eng. Bull.*, 35(1):3–8, 2012.

121. F. Erxleben, M. Günther, M. Krötzsch, J. Mendez, and D. Vrandečić. Introducing Wikidata to the Linked Data Web. In Mika et al. [271], pages 50–65.

122. J. Euzenat and P. Shvaiko. *Ontology matching*. Springer, 2007.

123. R. Fagin. Monadic generalized spectra. *Math. Log. Q.*, 21(1):89–96, 1975.

124. L. Feigenbaum, G. T. Williams, K. G. Clark, and E. Torres. SPARQL 1.1 Protocol. W3C Recommendation, Mar. 2013. https://www.w3.org/TR/sparql11-protocol/.

125. D. Fensel, F. van Harmelen, I. Horrocks, D. L. McGuinness, and P. F. Patel-Schneider. OIL: An Ontology Infrastructure for the Semantic Web. *IEEE Intelligent Systems*, 16(2):38–45, 2001.

126. J. D. Fernández, M. A. Martínez-Prieto, C. Gutiérrez, A. Polleres, and M. Arias. Binary RDF representation for publication and exchange (HDT). *J. Web Sem.*, 19:22–41, 2013.

127. S. Ferrada, B. Bustos, and A. Hogan. Imgpedia: A Linked Dataset with content-based analysis of Wikimedia images. In d'Amato et al. [104], pages 84–93.

128. D. A. Ferrucci, E. W. Brown, J. Chu-Carroll, J. Fan, D. Gondek, A. Kalyanpur, A. Lally, J. W. Murdock, E. Nyberg, J. M. Prager, N. Schlaefer, and C. A. Welty. Building Watson: An Overview of the DeepQA Project. *AI Magazine*, 31(3):59–79, 2010.

129. V. Fionda, G. Pirrò, and C. Gutiérrez. NautiLOD: A Formal Language for the Web of Data Graph. *TWEB*, 9(1):5:1–5:43, 2015.

130. P. M. Fischer, G. Lausen, A. Schätzle, and M. Schmidt. RDF constraint checking. In P. M. Fischer, G. Alonso, M. Arenas, and F. Geerts, editors, *Proceedings of the Workshops of the EDBT/ICDT 2015 Joint Conference (EDBT/ICDT), Brussels, Belgium, March 27th, 2015.*, volume 1330 of *CEUR Workshop Proceedings*, pages 205–212. CEUR-WS.org, 2015.

131. S. Flesca, G. Manco, E. Masciari, E. Rende, and A. Tagarelli. Web wrapper induction: a brief survey. *AI Commun.*, 17(2):57–61, 2004.

132. E. Franconi, C. Gutiérrez, A. Mosca, G. Pirrò, and R. Rosati. The logic of Extensional RDFS. In Alani et al. [5], pages 101–116.

133. T. Franz, A. Schultz, S. Sizov, and S. Staab. TripleRank: Ranking Semantic Web Data by Tensor Decomposition. In Bernstein et al. [54], pages 213–228.

134. U. Furbach and N. Shankar, editors. *Automated Reasoning, Third International Joint Conference, IJCAR 2006, Seattle, WA, USA, August 17–20, 2006, Proceedings*, volume 4130 of *LNCS*. Springer, 2006.

135. L. Galárraga, C. Teflioudi, K. Hose, and F. M. Suchanek. Fast rule mining in ontological knowledge bases with AMIE+. *VLDB J.*, 24(6):707–730, 2015.

136. F. Gandon. A survey of the first 20 years of research on Semantic Web and Linked Data. *Ingénierie des Systèmes d'Information*, 23(3-4):11–38, 2018.

137. A. Gangemi and V. Presutti. Ontology design patterns. In Staab and Studer [367], pages 221–243.

138. A. Gangemi, V. Presutti, D. R. Recupero, A. G. Nuzzolese, F. Draicchio, and M. Mongiovì. Semantic Web Machine Reading with FRED. *Semantic Web*, 8(6):873–893, 2017.

139. P. Gearon, A. Passant, and A. Polleres. SPARQL 1.1 Update. W3C Recommendation, Mar. 2013. https://www.w3.org/TR/sparql11-update/.

140. J. H. Gennari, M. A. Musen, R. W. Fergerson, W. E. Grosso, M. Crubézy, H. Eriksson, N. F. Noy, and S. W. Tu. The evolution of Protégé: an environment for knowledge-based systems development. *Int. J. Hum.-Comput. Stud.*, 58(1):89–123, 2003.

141. A. L. Gentile, Z. Zhang, and F. Ciravegna. Self Training Wrapper Induction with Linked Data. In P. Sojka, A. Horák, I. Kopecek, and K. Pala, editors, *Text, Speech and Dialogue – 17th International Conference, TSD 2014, Brno, Czech Republic, September 8–12, 2014. Proceedings*, volume 8655 of *LNCS*, pages 285–292. Springer, 2014.

142. C. Ghidini, O. Hartig, M. Maleshkova, V. Svátek, I. F. Cruz, A. Hogan, J. Song, M. Lefrançois, and F. Gandon, editors. *The Semantic Web – ISWC 2019 – 18th International Semantic Web Conference, Auckland, New Zealand, October 26–30, 2019, Proceedings, Part I*, volume 11778 of *LNCS*. Springer, 2019.

143. J. M. Giménez-García, A. Zimmermann, and P. Maret. NdFluents: An Ontology for Annotated Statements with Inference Preservation. In E. Blomqvist, D. Maynard, A. Gangemi, R. Hoekstra, P. Hitzler, and O. Hartig, editors, *The Semantic Web – 14th International Conference, ESWC 2017, Portorož, Slovenia, May 28 – June 1, 2017, Proceedings, Part I*, volume 10249 of *LNCS*, pages 638–654, 2017.

144. B. Glimm, A. Hogan, M. Krötzsch, and A. Polleres. OWL: Yet to arrive on the Web of Data? In C. Bizer, T. Heath, T. Berners-Lee, and M. Hausenblas, editors, *LDOW*, volume 937 of *CEUR Workshop Proceedings*. CEUR-WS.org, 2012.

145. B. Glimm, I. Horrocks, B. Motik, G. Stoilos, and Z. Wang. HermiT: An OWL 2 Reasoner. *J. Autom. Reasoning*, 53(3):245–269, 2014.

146. B. Glimm, I. Horrocks, and U. Sattler. Deciding $\mathcal{SHOQ}^\cap$ Knowledge Base Consistency using Alternating Automata. In Baader et al. [26].

147. B. Glimm, C. Lutz, I. Horrocks, and U. Sattler. Conjunctive Query Answering for the Description Logic SHIQ. *J. Artif. Intell. Res.*, 31:157–204, 2008.

148. B. Glimm and C. Ogbuji. SPARQL 1.1 Entailment Regimes. W3C Recommendation, Mar. 2013. https://www.w3.org/TR/sparql11-entailment/.

149. C. Golbreich and E. K. Wallace. OWL 2 Web Ontology Language: New Features and Rationale. W3C Recommendation, Dec. 2012. https://www.w3.org/TR/owl2-new-features/.

150. C. F. Goldfarb. Standard Generalized Markup Language (SGML). RFC 8879, Oct. 1986. https://www.iso.org/standard/16387.html.

151. L. González and A. Hogan. Modelling Dynamics in Semantic Web Knowledge Graphs with Formal Concept Analysis. In Champin et al. [90], pages 1175–1184.

152. J. Grant and D. Beckett. RDF Test Cases. W3C Recommendation, Feb. 2004. https://www.w3.org/TR/rdf-testcases/.

153. B. C. Grau, I. Horrocks, B. Parsia, A. Ruttenberg, and M. Schneider. OWL 2 Web Ontology Language: Mapping to RDF Graphs (Second Edition). W3C Recommendation, Dec. 2012. https://www.w3.org/TR/owl2-mapping-to-rdf/.

154. B. C. Grau and E. V. Kostylev. Logical Foundations of Linked Data Anonymisation. *J. Artif. Intell. Res.*, 64:253–314, 2019.

155. J. Gray, S. Chaudhuri, A. Bosworth, A. Layman, D. Reichart, M. Venkatrao, F. Pellow, and H. Pirahesh. Data cube: A relational aggregation operator generalizing group-by, cross-tab, and sub totals. *Data Min. Knowl. Discov.*, 1(1):29–53, 1997.

156. B. N. Grosof, I. Horrocks, R. Volz, and S. Decker. Description logic programs: combining logic programs with description logic. In G. Hencsey, B. White, Y. R. Chen, L. Kovács, and S. Lawrence, editors, *Proceedings of the Twelfth International*

World Wide Web Conference, WWW 2003, Budapest, Hungary, May 20–24, 2003, pages 48–57. ACM, 2003.

157. P. T. Groth, E. Simperl, A. J. G. Gray, M. Sabou, M. Krötzsch, F. Lécué, F. Flöck, and Y. Gil, editors. *The Semantic Web – ISWC 2016 – 15th International Semantic Web Conference, Kobe, Japan, October 17–21, 2016, Proceedings, Part II*, volume 9982 of *LNCS*, 2016.

158. M. Grüninger and M. S. Fox. Methodology for the Design and Evaluation of Ontologies. In *Workshop on Basic Ontological Issues in Knowledge Sharing, IJCAI-95, Montreal*, 1995.

159. C. Guéret, P. T. Groth, F. van Harmelen, and S. Schlobach. Finding the Achilles Heel of the Web of Data: Using Network Analysis for Link-Recommendation. In Patel-Schneider et al. [307], pages 289–304.

160. R. V. Guha, D. Brickley, and S. Macbeth. Schema.org: evolution of structured data on the web. *Commun. ACM*, 59(2):44–51, 2016.

161. R. V. Guha, R. McCool, and R. Fikes. Contexts for the Semantic Web. In S. A. McIlraith, D. Plexousakis, and F. van Harmelen, editors, *International Semantic Web Conference*, volume 3298 of *LNCS*, pages 32–46. Springer, 2004.

162. C. Gutierrez, C. A. Hurtado, A. O. Mendelzon, and J. Pérez. Foundations of Semantic Web databases. *J. Comput. Syst. Sci.*, 77(3):520–541, 2011.

163. M. E. Gutiérrez, N. Mihindukulasooriya, and R. García-Castro. LDP4j: A framework for the development of interoperable read-write Linked Data applications. In R. Verborgh and E. Mannens, editors, *Proceedings of the ISWC Developers Workshop 2014, co-located with the 13th International Semantic Web Conference (ISWC 2014), Riva del Garda, Italy, October 19, 2014*, volume 1268 of *CEUR Workshop Proceedings*, pages 61–66. CEUR-WS.org, 2014.

164. P. Guzewicz and I. Manolescu. Quotient RDF Summaries Based on Type Hierarchies. In *34th IEEE International Conference on Data Engineering Workshops, ICDE Workshops 2018, Paris, France, April 16–20, 2018*, pages 66–71. IEEE Computer Society, 2018.

165. V. Haarslev, K. Hidde, R. Möller, and M. Wessel. The RacerPro knowledge representation and reasoning system. *Semantic Web*, 3(3):267–277, 2012.

166. H. Halpin, P. J. Hayes, J. P. McCusker, D. L. McGuinness, and H. S. Thompson. When owl:sameAs Isn't the Same: An Analysis of Identity in Linked Data. In Patel-Schneider et al. [307], pages 305–320.

167. P. Hansen, C. Lutz, I. Seylan, and F. Wolter. Efficient Query Rewriting in the Description Logic EL and Beyond. In Yang and Wooldridge [406], pages 3034–3040.

168. S. Harris, N. Lamb, and N. Shadbolt. 4store: The Design and Implementation of a Clustered RDF Store. In *Workshop on Scalable Semantic Web Systems*, volume 517 of *CEUR Workshop Proceedings*, pages 94–109. CEUR-WS, 2009.

169. S. Harris, A. Seaborne, and E. Prud'hommeaux. SPARQL 1.1 Query Language. W3C Recommendation, Mar. 2013. https://www.w3.org/TR/sparql11-query/.

170. A. Harth, S. Kinsella, and S. Decker. Using Naming Authority to Rank Data and Ontologies for Web Search. In Bernstein et al. [54], pages 277–292.

171. O. Hartig. RDF* and SPARQL*: An Alternative Approach to Annotate Statements in RDF. In N. Nikitina, D. Song, A. Fokoue, and P. Haase, editors, *Proceedings of the ISWC 2017 Posters & Demonstrations and Industry Tracks co-located with 16th International Semantic Web Conference (ISWC 2017), Vienna, Austria, October 23–25, 2017*, volume 1963 of *CEUR Workshop Proceedings*. CEUR-WS.org, 2017.

172. O. Hartig, C. Bizer, and J. C. Freytag. Executing SPARQL queries over the Web of Linked Data. In Bernstein et al. [54], pages 293–309.

173. O. Hartig, I. Letter, and J. Pérez. A Formal Framework for Comparing Linked Data Fragments. In C. d'Amato, M. Fernández, V. A. M. Tamma, F. Lécué,

P. Cudré-Mauroux, J. F. Sequeda, C. Lange, and J. Heflin, editors, *The Semantic Web – ISWC 2017 – 16th International Semantic Web Conference, Vienna, Austria, October 21–25, 2017, Proceedings, Part I*, volume 10587 of *LNCS*, pages 364–382. Springer, 2017.

174. O. Hartig and J. Pérez. LDQL: A query language for the Web of Linked Data. *J. Web Semant.*, 41:9–29, 2016.

175. O. Hartig and J. Pérez. Semantics and Complexity of GraphQL. In Champin et al. [90], pages 1155–1164.

176. A. Hasnain, Q. Mehmood, S. S. e Zainab, and A. Hogan. SPORTAL: profiling the content of public SPARQL endpoints. *Int. J. Semantic Web Inf. Syst.*, 12(3):134–163, 2016.

177. O. Hassanzadeh and M. P. Consens. Linked Movie Data Base. In C. Bizer, T. Heath, T. Berners-Lee, and K. Idehen, editors, *Proceedings of the WWW2009 Workshop on Linked Data on the Web, LDOW 2009, Madrid, Spain, April 20, 2009.*, volume 538 of *CEUR Workshop Proceedings*. CEUR-WS.org, 2009.

178. S. Hawke, D. Beckett, and J. Broekstra. SPARQL Query Results XML Format (Second Edition). W3C Recommendation, Mar. 2013. https://www.w3.org/TR/rdf-sparql-XMLres/.

179. P. Hayes. RDF Semantics. W3C Recommendation, Feb. 2004. https://www.w3.org/TR/2004/REC-rdf-mt-20040210/.

180. P. Hayes and P. F. Patel-Schneider. RDF 1.1 Semantics. W3C Recommendation, Feb. 2014. https://www.w3.org/TR/2014/REC-rdf11-mt-20140225/.

181. T. Heath and C. Bizer. *Linked Data: Evolving the Web into a Global Data Space (1st Edition)*, volume 1 of *Synthesis Lectures on the Semantic Web: Theory and Technology*. Morgan & Claypool, 2011. Available from http://linkeddatabook.com/editions/1.0/.

182. B. Heitmann, F. Hermsen, and S. Decker. *k*-RDF-Neighbourhood Anonymity: Combining Structural and Attribute-based Anonymisation for Linked Data. In C. Brewster, M. Cheatham, M. d'Aquin, S. Decker, and S. Kirrane, editors, *Proceedings of the 5th Workshop on Society, Privacy and the Semantic Web – Policy and Technology (PrivOn2017) co-located with 16th International Semantic Web Conference (ISWC 2017), Vienna, Austria, October 22, 2017*, volume 1951 of *CEUR Workshop Proceedings*. CEUR-WS.org, 2017.

183. J. Hendler and D. L. McGuinness. The DARPA Agent Markup Language. *IEEE Intelligent Systems*, 15(6):67–73, 2000.

184. I. Herman, B. Adida, M. Birbeck, and S. McCarron. RDFa 1.1 Primer – Second Edition. W3C Working Group Note, Aug. 2013. https://www.w3.org/TR/rdfa-primer/.

185. I. Herman, B. Adida, M. Sporny, and M. Birbeck. RDFa 1.1 Primer – Second Edition – Rich Structured Data Markup for Web Documents. W3C Working Group Note, Aug. 2013. https://www.w3.org/TR/rdfa-primer/.

186. D. Hernández, A. Hogan, and M. Krötzsch. Reifying RDF: What Works Well With Wikidata? In T. Liebig and A. Fokoue, editors, *Proceedings of the 11th International Workshop on Scalable Semantic Web Knowledge Base Systems co-located with 14th International Semantic Web Conference (ISWC 2015), Bethlehem, PA, USA, October 11, 2015.*, volume 1457 of *CEUR Workshop Proceedings*, pages 32–47. CEUR-WS.org, 2015.

187. D. Hernández, A. Hogan, C. Riveros, C. Rojas, and E. Zerega. Querying Wikidata: Comparing SPARQL, Relational and Graph Databases. In Groth et al. [157], pages 88–103.

188. I. Hickson, G. Kellogg, J. Tennison, and I. Herman. Microdata to RDF – Second Edition. W3C Interest Group Note, Dec. 2014. https://www.w3.org/TR/microdata-rdf/.

189. P. Hitzler, A. Gangemi, K. Janowicz, A. Krisnadhi, and V. Presutti, editors. *Ontology Engineering with Ontology Design Patterns – Foundations and Applications*, volume 25 of *Studies on the Semantic Web*. IOS Press, 2016.

190. P. Hitzler, M. Krötzsch, B. Parsia, P. F. Patel-Schneider, and S. Rudolph. OWL 2 Web Ontology Language Primer (Second Edition). W3C Recommendation, Dec. 2012. https://www.w3.org/TR/owl2-primer/.

191. P. Hitzler, M. Krötzsch, and S. Rudolph. *Foundations of Semantic Web Technologies*. Chapman and Hall/CRC Press, 2010.

192. R. Hoekstra. *Ontology Representation – Design Patterns and Ontologies that Make Sense*, volume 197 of *Frontiers in Artificial Intelligence and Applications*. IOS Press, 2009.

193. J. Hoffart, F. M. Suchanek, K. Berberich, and G. Weikum. YAGO2: A spatially and temporally enhanced knowledge base from Wikipedia. *Artif. Intell.*, 194:28–61, 2013.

194. A. Hogan. Canonical Forms for Isomorphic and Equivalent RDF Graphs: Algorithms for Leaning and Labelling Blank Nodes. *TWEB*, 11(4):22:1–22:62, 2017.

195. A. Hogan. The Semantic Web: Two decades on. *Semantic Web*, 11(1):169–185, 2020.

196. A. Hogan, M. Arenas, A. Mallea, and A. Polleres. Everything you always wanted to know about blank nodes. *J. Web Sem.*, 27:42–69, 2014.

197. A. Hogan, E. Blomqvist, M. Cochez, C. d'Amato, G. de Melo, C. Gutierrez, J. E. Labra Gayo, S. Kirrane, S. Neumaier, A. Polleres, R. Navigli, A. N. Ngomo, S. M. Rashid, A. Rula, L. Schmelzeisen, J. F. Sequeda, S. Staab, and A. Zimmermann. Knowledge Graphs. *CoRR*, abs/2003.02320, 2020.

198. A. Hogan, A. Harth, and S. Decker. ReConRank: A Scalable Ranking Method for Semantic Web Data with Context. In *2nd Scalable Semantic Web Systems Workshop*, 2006.

199. A. Hogan, A. Harth, A. Passant, S. Decker, and A. Polleres. Weaving the Pedantic Web. In C. Bizer, T. Heath, T. Berners-Lee, and M. Hausenblas, editors, *Proceedings of the WWW2010 Workshop on Linked Data on the Web, LDOW 2010, Raleigh, USA, April 27, 2010*, volume 628 of *CEUR Workshop Proceedings*. CEUR-WS.org, 2010.

200. A. Hogan, A. Harth, J. Umbrich, S. Kinsella, A. Polleres, and S. Decker. Searching and browsing Linked Data with SWSE: The Semantic Web Search Engine. *J. Web Sem.*, 9(4):365–401, 2011.

201. A. Hogan, J. Z. Pan, A. Polleres, and S. Decker. SAOR: Template Rule Optimisations for Distributed Reasoning over 1 Billion Linked Data Triples. In Patel-Schneider et al. [307], pages 337–353.

202. A. Hogan, C. Riveros, C. Rojas, and A. Soto. A Worst-Case Optimal Join Algorithm for SPARQL. In Ghidini et al. [142], pages 258–275.

203. A. Hogan, J. Umbrich, A. Harth, R. Cyganiak, A. Polleres, and S. Decker. An empirical survey of Linked Data conformance. *J. Web Sem.*, 14:14–44, 2012.

204. A. Hogan, A. Zimmermann, J. Umbrich, A. Polleres, and S. Decker. Scalable and distributed methods for entity matching, consolidation and disambiguation over Linked Data corpora. *J. Web Semant.*, 10:76–110, 2012.

205. M. Horridge and S. Bechhofer. The OWL API: A Java API for OWL ontologies. *Semantic Web*, 2(1):11–21, 2011.

206. M. Horridge, T. Tudorache, C. Nyulas, J. Vendetti, N. F. Noy, and M. A. Musen. WebProtégé: a collaborative Web-based platform for editing biomedical ontologies. *Bioinform.*, 30(16):2384–2385, 2014.

207. I. Horrocks and J. A. Hendler, editors. *The Semantic Web – ISWC 2002, First International Semantic Web Conference, Sardinia, Italy, June 9–12, 2002, Proceedings*, volume 2342 of *LNCS*. Springer, 2002.

208. I. Horrocks, O. Kutz, and U. Sattler. The Even More Irresistible $\mathcal{SROIQ}$. In P. Doherty, J. Mylopoulos, and C. A. Welty, editors, *Proceedings, Tenth International Conference on Principles of Knowledge Representation and Reasoning, Lake District of the United Kingdom, June 2–5, 2006*, pages 57–67. AAAI Press, 2006.

209. I. Horrocks and P. F. Patel-Schneider. Reducing OWL entailment to description logic satisfiability. *J. Web Sem.*, 1(4):345–357, 2004.

210. I. Horrocks, P. F. Patel-Schneider, H. Boley, S. Tabet, B. Grosof, and M. Dean. SWRL: A Semantic Web Rule Language Combining OWL and RuleML. W3C Member Submission, May 2004. https://www.w3.org/Submission/SWRL/.

211. I. Horrocks, P. F. Patel-Schneider, and F. van Harmelen. Reviewing the Design of DAML+OIL: An Ontology Language for the Semantic Web. In R. Dechter, M. J. Kearns, and R. S. Sutton, editors, *Proceedings of the Eighteenth National Conference on Artificial Intelligence and Fourteenth Conference on Innovative Applications of Artificial Intelligence, July 28 – August 1, 2002, Edmonton, Alberta, Canada*, pages 792–797. AAAI Press / The MIT Press, 2002.

212. I. Horrocks, U. Sattler, and S. Tobies. Practical Reasoning for Very Expressive Description Logics. *Logic Journal of the IGPL*, 8(3):239–263, 2000.

213. U. Hustadt, B. Motik, and U. Sattler. Reasoning in Description Logics by a Reduction to Disjunctive Datalog. *J. Autom. Reasoning*, 39(3):351–384, 2007.

214. B. Hyland, G. Atemezing, and B. Villazón-Terrazas. Best Practices for Publishing Linked Data. W3C Working Group Note, Jan. 2014. https://www.w3.org/TR/ld-bp/.

215. R. Iannella and S. Villata. ODRL Information Model 2.2. W3C Recommendation, Feb. 2018. https://www.w3.org/TR/odrl-model/.

216. Y. E. Ioannidis and R. Ramakrishnan. Containment of Conjunctive Queries: Beyond Relations as Sets. *ACM Trans. Database Syst.*, 20(3):288–324, 1995.

217. S. Issa, P. Paris, and F. Hamdi. Assessing the Completeness Evolution of DBpedia: A Case Study. In S. de Cesare and U. Frank, editors, *Advances in Conceptual Modeling – ER 2017 Workshops AHA, MoBiD, MREBA, OntoCom, and QMMQ, Valencia, Spain, November 6–9, 2017, Proceedings*, volume 10651 of *LNCS*, pages 238–247. Springer, 2017.

218. I. Jacobs and N. Walsh. Architecture of the World Wide Web, Volume One, December 2004. https://www.w3.org/TR/webarch/.

219. K. Janowicz, P. Hitzler, B. Adams, D. Kolas, and C. Vardeman. Five stars of Linked Data vocabulary use. *Semantic Web*, 5(3):173–176, 2014.

220. T. S. Jayram, P. G. Kolaitis, and E. Vee. The containment problem for REAL conjunctive queries with inequalities. In S. Vansummeren, editor, *Proceedings of the Twenty-Fifth ACM SIGACT-SIGMOD-SIGART Symposium on Principles of Database Systems, June 26–28, 2006, Chicago, Illinois, USA*, pages 80–89. ACM, 2006.

221. A. Kalyanpur, B. Boguraev, S. Patwardhan, J. W. Murdock, A. Lally, C. Welty, J. M. Prager, B. Coppola, A. Fokoue-Nkoutche, L. Zhang, Y. Pan, and Z. Qiu. Structured data and inference in DeepQA. *IBM Journal of Research and Development*, 56(3):10, 2012.

222. A. Kalyanpur, B. Parsia, E. Sirin, B. C. Grau, and J. A. Hendler. Swoop: A Web Ontology Editing Browser. *J. Web Semant.*, 4(2):144–153, 2006.

223. E. Kärle, U. Simsek, O. Panasiuk, and D. Fensel. Building an Ecosystem for the Tyrolean Tourism Knowledge Graph. In C. Pautasso, F. Sánchez-Figueroa, K. Systä, and J. M. M. Rodriguez, editors, *Current Trends in Web Engineering – ICWE 2018 International Workshops, MATWEP, EnWot, KD-WEB, WEOD, TourismKG, Cáceres, Spain, June 5, 2018, Revised Selected Papers*, volume 11153 of *LNCS*, pages 260–267. Springer, 2018.

224. G. Kasneci, F. M. Suchanek, G. Ifrim, M. Ramanath, and G. Weikum. NAGA: Searching and Ranking Knowledge. In *ICDE*, pages 953–962. IEEE, 2008.

225. A. Katifori, C. Halatsis, G. Lepouras, C. Vassilakis, and E. G. Giannopoulou. Ontology visualization methods – a survey. *ACM Comput. Surv.*, 39(4), 2007.
226. M. Kay. XPath and XQuery Functions and Operators 3.1. W3C Recommendation, Mar. 2017. https://www.w3.org/TR/xpath-functions/.
227. Y. Kazakov, M. Krötzsch, and F. Simancik. The Incredible ELK – From Polynomial Procedures to Efficient Reasoning with $\mathcal{EL}$ Ontologies. *J. Autom. Reasoning*, 53(1):1–61, 2014.
228. Y. Kazakov and B. Motik. A Resolution-Based Decision Procedure for *SHOIQ*. *J. Autom. Reasoning*, 40(2–3):89–116, 2008.
229. G. Kellogg, P.-A. Champin, D. Longley, M. Sporny, M. Lanthaler, and N. Lindström. JSON-LD 1.1 – A JSON-based Serialization for Linked Data. W3C Candidate Recommendation, Mar. 2020. https://www.w3.org/TR/json-ld11/.
230. S. Khatchadourian and M. P. Consens. ExpLOD: Summary-Based Exploration of Interlinking and RDF Usage in the Linked Open Data Cloud. In Aroyo et al. [18], pages 272–287.
231. S. Kirrane, A. Mileo, and S. Decker. Access control and the Resource Description Framework: A survey. *Semantic Web*, 8(2):311–352, 2017.
232. M. V. Kleek, D. A. Smith, N. R. Shadbolt, and mc schraefel. A decentralized architecture for consolidating personal information ecosystems: The WebBox. In *Workshop on Personal Information Management (PIM)*, 2012.
233. H. Knublauch. SHACL Compact Syntax. W3C Draft Community Group Report, Jan. 2018. https://w3c.github.io/shacl/shacl-compact-syntax/.
234. H. Knublauch, D. Allemang, and S. Steyskal. SHACL Advanced Features. W3C Working Group Note, June 2017. https://www.w3.org/TR/shacl-af/.
235. H. Knublauch, J. A. Hendler, and K. Idehen. SPIN – Overview and Motivation. W3C Member Submission, Feb. 2011. https://www.w3.org/Submission/spin-overview/.
236. H. Knublauch and D. Kontokostas. Shapes Constraint Language (SHACL). W3C Recommendation, July 2017. https://www.w3.org/TR/shacl/.
237. H. Knublauch and P. Maria. SHACL JavaScript Extensions. W3C Working Group Note, June 2017. https://www.w3.org/TR/shacl-js/.
238. V. Kolovski, Z. Wu, and G. Eadon. Optimizing Enterprise-Scale OWL 2 RL Reasoning in a Relational Database System. In Patel-Schneider et al. [307], pages 436–452.
239. D. Kontokostas, P. Westphal, S. Auer, S. Hellmann, J. Lehmann, R. Cornelissen, and A. Zaveri. Test-driven evaluation of linked data quality. In Chung et al. [95], pages 747–758.
240. E. V. Kostylev, J. L. Reutter, M. Romero, and D. Vrgoc. SPARQL with Property Paths. In M. Arenas, Ó. Corcho, E. Simperl, M. Strohmaier, M. d'Aquin, K. Srinivas, P. T. Groth, M. Dumontier, J. Heflin, K. Thirunarayan, and S. Staab, editors, *The Semantic Web – ISWC 2015 – 14th International Semantic Web Conference, Bethlehem, PA, USA, October 11–15, 2015, Proceedings, Part I*, volume 9366 of *LNCS*, pages 3–18. Springer, 2015.
241. A. Krisnadhi, F. Maier, and P. Hitzler. OWL and Rules. In Polleres et al. [321], pages 382–415.
242. M. Krötzsch, F. Maier, A. Krisnadhi, and P. Hitzler. A better uncle for OWL: nominal schemas for integrating rules and ontologies. In S. Srinivasan, K. Ramamritham, A. Kumar, M. P. Ravindra, E. Bertino, and R. Kumar, editors, *Proceedings of the 20th International Conference on World Wide Web, WWW 2011, Hyderabad, India, March 28 – April 1, 2011*, pages 645–654. ACM, 2011.
243. M. Krötzsch, F. Simancik, and I. Horrocks. Description Logics. *IEEE Intelligent Systems*, 29(1):12–19, 2014.
244. J. E. Labra Gayo, E. Prud'hommeaux, I. Boneva, and D. Kontokostas. *Validating RDF Data*. Synthesis Lectures on the Semantic Web: Theory and Technology. Morgan & Claypool Publishers, 2017.

245. O. Lassila and R. R. Swick. Resource Description Framework (RDF) Model and Syntax Specification. W3C Recommendation, Feb. 1999. https://www.w3.org/TR/1999/REC-rdf-syntax-19990222/.

246. T. Lebo, S. Sahoo, D. McGuinness, K. Belhajjame, J. Cheney, D. Corsar, D. Garijo, S. Soiland-Reyes, S. Zednik, and J. Zhao. PROV-O: The PROV Ontology. W3C Recommendation, Apr. 2013. https://www.w3.org/TR/prov-o/.

247. J. Lehmann, R. Isele, M. Jakob, A. Jentzsch, D. Kontokostas, P. N. Mendes, S. Hellmann, M. Morsey, P. van Kleef, S. Auer, and C. Bizer. DBpedia – A large-scale, multilingual knowledge base extracted from Wikipedia. *Semantic Web*, 6(2):167–195, 2015.

248. A. Letelier, J. Pérez, R. Pichler, and S. Skritek. Static analysis and optimization of Semantic Web queries. *ACM Trans. Database Syst.*, 38(4):25:1–25:45, 2013.

249. V. Lopez, V. S. Uren, M. Sabou, and E. Motta. Is Question Answering fit for the Semantic Web?: A survey. *Semantic Web*, 2(2):125–155, 2011.

250. K. Losemann and W. Martens. The complexity of regular expressions and property paths in SPARQL. *ACM Trans. Database Syst.*, 38(4):24:1–24:39, 2013.

251. G. Loseto, S. Ieva, F. Gramegna, M. Ruta, F. Scioscia, and E. D. Sciascio. Linked Data (in Low-Resource) Platforms: A Mapping for Constrained Application Protocol. In Groth et al. [157], pages 131–139.

252. S. Luke, L. Spector, D. Rager, and J. A. Hendler. Ontology-based Web Agents. In *Agents*, pages 59–66, 1997.

253. C. Lutz, I. Seylan, and F. Wolter. Ontology-Mediated Queries with Closed Predicates. In Yang and Wooldridge [406], pages 3120–3126.

254. E. Mäkelä. Aether – Generating and Viewing Extended VoID Statistical Descriptions of RDF Datasets. In V. Presutti, E. Blomqvist, R. Troncy, H. Sack, I. Papadakis, and A. Tordai, editors, *The Semantic Web: ESWC 2014 Satellite Events – ESWC 2014 Satellite Events, Anissaras, Crete, Greece, May 25–29, 2014, Revised Selected Papers*, volume 8798 of *LNCS*, pages 429–433. Springer, 2014.

255. S. Malyshev, M. Krötzsch, L. González, J. Gonsior, and A. Bielefeldt. Getting the Most Out of Wikidata: Semantic Technology Usage in Wikipedia's Knowledge Graph. In Vrandečić et al. [396], pages 376–394.

256. C. D. Manning, P. Raghavan, and H. Schuetze. *Introduction to Information Retrieval*. Cambridge University Press, 2008.

257. C. D. Manning and H. Schütze. *Foundations of statistical natural language processing*. MIT Press, 2001.

258. F. Manola, E. Miller, and B. McBride. RDF Primer. W3C Recommendation, Feb. 2004. https://www.w3.org/TR/2004/REC-rdf-primer-20040210/.

259. E. Mansour, A. V. Sambra, S. Hawke, M. Zereba, S. Capadisli, A. Ghanem, A. Aboulnaga, and T. Berners-Lee. A Demonstration of the Solid Platform for Social Web Applications. In J. Bourdeau, J. Hendler, R. Nkambou, I. Horrocks, and B. Y. Zhao, editors, *Proceedings of the 25th International Conference on World Wide Web, WWW 2016, Montreal, Canada, April 11–15, 2016, Companion Volume*, pages 223–226. ACM, 2016.

260. C. Martínez-Costa and S. Schulz. Validating EHR clinical models using ontology patterns. *J. Biomed. Informatics*, 76:124–137, 2017.

261. J. L. Martinez-Rodriguez, A. Hogan, and I. Lopez-Arevalo. Information Extraction meets the Semantic Web: A Survey. *Semantic Web*, 11(2):255–335, 2020.

262. N. Matentzoglu, S. Bail, and B. Parsia. A Snapshot of the OWL Web. In Alani et al. [5], pages 331–346.

263. N. Matentzoglu and B. Parsia. The OWL Full/DL Gap in the Field. In C. M. Keet and V. A. M. Tamma, editors, *Proceedings of the 11th International Workshop on OWL: Experiences and Directions (OWLED 2014) co-located with 13th International Semantic Web Conference on (ISWC 2014), Riva del Garda, Italy, October 17–18, 2014.*, volume 1265 of *CEUR Workshop Proceedings*, pages 49–60. CEUR-WS.org, 2014.

264. D. Maynard, K. Bontcheva, and I. Augenstein. *Natural Language Processing for the Semantic Web*. Synthesis Lectures on the Semantic Web: Theory and Technology. Morgan & Claypool Publishers, 2016.

265. E. L. McCarthy, B. P. Vandervalk, and M. Wilkinson. SPARQL Assist language-neutral query composer. *BMC Bioinform.*, 13(S-1):S2, 2012.

266. D. L. McGuinness and F. van Harmelen. OWL Web Ontology Language Overview. W3C Recommendation, Feb. 2004. https://www.w3.org/TR/owl-features/.

267. G. Meditskos and N. Bassiliades. DLEJena: A practical forward-chaining OWL 2 RL reasoner combining Jena and Pellet. *J. Web Sem.*, 8(1):89–94, 2010.

268. A. Meroño-Peñuela and R. Hoekstra. Automatic Query-Centric API for Routine Access to Linked Data. In d'Amato et al. [104], pages 334–349.

269. R. Meusel, P. Petrovski, and C. Bizer. The WebDataCommons Microdata, RDFa and Microformat Dataset Series. In Mika et al. [271], pages 277–292.

270. N. Mihindukulasooriya and R. Menday. Linked Data Platform 1.0 Primer. W3C Working Group Note, Apr. 2015. https://www.w3.org/TR/ldp-primer/.

271. P. Mika, T. Tudorache, A. Bernstein, C. Welty, C. A. Knoblock, D. Vrandečić, P. T. Groth, N. F. Noy, K. Janowicz, and C. A. Goble, editors. *The Semantic Web – ISWC 2014 – 13th International Semantic Web Conference, Riva del Garda, Italy, October 19–23, 2014. Proceedings, Part I*, volume 8796 of *LNCS*. Springer, 2014.

272. A. Miles, T. Baker, and R. Swick. Best Practice Recipes for Publishing RDF Vocabularies, March 2006. https://www.w3.org/TR/2006/WD-swbp-vocab-pub-20060314/1. Superceded by Berrueta and Phipps: https://www.w3.org/TR/swbp-vocab-pub/.

273. A. Miles and S. Bechhofer. SKOS Simple Knowledge Organization System Reference. W3C Recommendation, Aug. 2009. https://www.w3.org/TR/skos-reference/.

274. L. Miller, A. Seaborne, and A. Reggiori. Three Implementations of SquishQL, a Simple RDF Query Language. In Horrocks and Hendler [207], pages 423–435.

275. T. Minier, H. Skaf-Molli, and P. Molli. SaGe: Web Preemption for Public SPARQL Query Services. In L. Liu, R. W. White, A. Mantrach, F. Silvestri, J. J. McAuley, R. Baeza-Yates, and L. Zia, editors, *The World Wide Web Conference, WWW 2019, San Francisco, CA, USA, May 13–17, 2019*, pages 1268–1278. ACM, 2019.

276. M. Mintz, S. Bills, R. Snow, and D. Jurafsky. Distant supervision for relation extraction without labeled data. In K. Su, J. Su, and J. Wiebe, editors, *ACL 2009, Proceedings of the 47th Annual Meeting of the Association for Computational Linguistics and the 4th International Joint Conference on Natural Language Processing of the AFNLP, 2–7 August 2009, Singapore*, pages 1003–1011. The Association for Computer Linguistics, 2009.

277. J. Moreno-Vega and A. Hogan. GraFa: Scalable Faceted Browsing for RDF Graphs. In D. Vrandečić, K. Bontcheva, M. C. Suárez-Figueroa, V. Presutti, I. Celino, M. Sabou, L. Kaffee, and E. Simperl, editors, *The Semantic Web – ISWC 2018 – 17th International Semantic Web Conference, Monterey, CA, USA, October 8–12, 2018, Proceedings, Part I*, volume 11136 of *LNCS*, pages 301–317. Springer, 2018.

278. M. Mosser, F. Pieressa, J. L. Reutter, A. Soto, and D. Vrgoc. Querying APIs with SPARQL: Language and Worst-Case Optimal Algorithms. In A. Gangemi, R. Navigli, M. Vidal, P. Hitzler, R. Troncy, L. Hollink, A. Tordai, and M. Alam, editors, *The Semantic Web – 15th International Conference, ESWC 2018, Heraklion, Crete, Greece, June 3–7, 2018, Proceedings*, volume 10843 of *LNCS*, pages 639–654. Springer, 2018.

279. B. Motik. On the Properties of Metamodeling in OWL. *J. Log. Comput.*, 17(4):617–637, 2007.

280. B. Motik, B. C. Grau, I. Horrocks, Z. Wu, A. Fokoue, and C. Lutz. OWL 2 Web Ontology Language Profiles (Second Edition). W3C Recommendation, Dec. 2012. https://www.w3.org/TR/owl2-profiles/.

281. B. Motik, P. F. Patel-Schneider, and B. C. Grau. OWL 2 Web Ontology Language Direct Semantics (Second Edition). W3C Recommendation, Dec. 2012. https://www.w3.org/TR/owl2-direct-semantics/.

282. B. Motik, P. F. Patel-Schneider, and B. Parsia. OWL 2 Web Ontology Language Structural Specification and Functional-Style Syntax (Second Edition). W3C Recommendation, Dec. 2012. https://www.w3.org/TR/owl2-syntax/.

283. B. Motik and R. Rosati. Reconciling description logics and rules. *J. ACM*, 57(5), 2010.

284. B. Motik, U. Sattler, and R. Studer. Query Answering for OWL-DL with rules. *J. Web Sem.*, 3(1):41–60, 2005.

285. B. Motik, R. Shearer, and I. Horrocks. Hypertableau Reasoning for Description Logics. *J. Artif. Intell. Res. (JAIR)*, 36:165–228, 2009.

286. S. Muñoz, J. Pérez, and C. Gutierrez. Simple and Efficient Minimal RDFS. *J. Web Sem.*, 7(3):220–234, 2009.

287. Y. Nenov, R. Piro, B. Motik, I. Horrocks, Z. Wu, and J. Banerjee. RDFox: A highly-scalable RDF store. In Arenas et al. [16], pages 3–20.

288. M. Nentwig, M. Hartung, A. N. Ngomo, and E. Rahm. A survey of current Link Discovery frameworks. *Semantic Web*, 8(3):419–436, 2017.

289. T. Neumann and G. Weikum. The RDF-3X engine for scalable management of RDF data. *VLDB J.*, 19(1):91–113, 2010.

290. C. M. Nevile, D. Brickley, and I. Hickson. HTML Microdata. W3C Working Draft, Apr. 2018. https://www.w3.org/TR/microdata/.

291. A. N. Ngomo and S. Auer. LIMES – A Time-Efficient Approach for Large-Scale Link Discovery on the Web of Data. In T. Walsh, editor, *IJCAI 2011, Proceedings of the 22nd International Joint Conference on Artificial Intelligence, Barcelona, Catalonia, Spain, July 16–22, 2011*, pages 2312–2317. IJCAI/AAAI, 2011.

292. A. N. Ngomo, J. Lehmann, S. Auer, and K. Höffner. RAVEN – active learning of link specifications. In P. Shvaiko, J. Euzenat, T. Heath, C. Quix, M. Mao, and I. F. Cruz, editors, *Proceedings of the 6th International Workshop on Ontology Matching, Bonn, Germany, October 24, 2011*, volume 814 of *CEUR Workshop Proceedings*. CEUR-WS.org, 2011.

293. A. N. Ngomo and K. Lyko. EAGLE: Efficient Active Learning of Link Specifications Using Genetic Programming. In E. Simperl, P. Cimiano, A. Polleres, Ó. Corcho, and V. Presutti, editors, *The Semantic Web: Research and Applications – 9th Extended Semantic Web Conference, ESWC 2012, Heraklion, Crete, Greece, May 27–31, 2012. Proceedings*, volume 7295 of *LNCS*, pages 149–163. Springer, 2012.

294. V. Nguyen, O. Bodenreider, and A. P. Sheth. Don't like RDF reification?: making statements about statements using singleton property. In Chung et al. [95], pages 759–770.

295. C. Nikolaou, E. V. Kostylev, G. Konstantinidis, M. Kaminski, B. C. Grau, and I. Horrocks. Foundations of ontology-based data access under bag semantics. *Artif. Intell.*, 274:91–132, 2019.

296. N. Noy, A. Rector, P. Hayes, and C. Welty. Defining N-ary Relations on the Semantic Web. W3C Working Group Note, Apr. 2006. https://www.w3.org/TR/swbp-n-aryRelations/.

297. N. F. Noy, Y. Gao, A. Jain, A. Narayanan, A. Patterson, and J. Taylor. Industry-scale Knowledge Graphs: Lessons and Challenges. *ACM Queue*, 17(2):20, 2019.

298. N. F. Noy, M. Sintek, S. Decker, M. Crubézy, R. W. Fergerson, and M. A. Musen. Creating Semantic Web Contents with Protégé-2000. *IEEE Intell. Syst.*, 16(2):60–71, 2001.

299. E. Oren, R. Delbru, M. Catasta, R. Cyganiak, H. Stenzhorn, and G. Tummarello. Sindice.com: a document-oriented lookup index for open linked data. *IJMSO*, 3(1):37–52, 2008.

300. E. Oren, R. Delbru, and S. Decker. Extending Faceted Navigation for RDF Data. In I. F. Cruz, S. Decker, D. Allemang, C. Preist, D. Schwabe, P. Mika, M. Uschold, and L. Aroyo, editors, *The Semantic Web – ISWC 2006, 5th International Semantic Web Conference, ISWC 2006, Athens, GA, USA, November 5–9, 2006, Proceedings*, volume 4273 of *LNCS*, pages 559–572. Springer, 2006.

301. B. Orgun and J. Vu. HL7 ontology and mobile agents for interoperability in heterogeneous medical information systems. *Comp. in Bio. and Med.*, 36(7-8):817–836, 2006.

302. L. Page, S. Brin, R. Motwani, and T. Winograd. The PageRank Citation Ranking: Bringing Order to the Web. Technical Report 1999–66, Stanford InfoLab, November 1999.

303. O. Panasiuk, S. Steyskal, G. Havur, A. Fensel, and S. Kirrane. Modeling and Reasoning over Data Licenses. In A. Gangemi, A. L. Gentile, A. G. Nuzzolese, S. Rudolph, M. Maleshkova, H. Paulheim, J. Z. Pan, and M. Alam, editors, *The Semantic Web: ESWC 2018 Satellite Events – ESWC 2018 Satellite Events, Heraklion, Crete, Greece, June 3–7, 2018, Revised Selected Papers*, volume 11155 of *LNCS*, pages 218–222. Springer, 2018.

304. H. J. Pandit, A. Polleres, B. Bos, R. Brennan, B. Bruegger, F. J. Ekaputra, J. D. Fernández, R. G. Hamed, E. Kiesling, M. Lizar, E. Schlehahn, S. Steyskal, and R. Wenning. Data Privacy Vocabulary v0.1. Draft Community Group Report, Nov. 2019. https://www.w3.org/ns/dpv.

305. C. H. Papadimitriou. *Computational complexity*. Academic Internet Publ., 2007.

306. P. F. Patel-Schneider. Analyzing Schema.org. In Mika et al. [271], pages 261–276.

307. P. F. Patel-Schneider, Y. Pan, P. Hitzler, P. Mika, L. Z. 0007, J. Z. Pan, I. Horrocks, and B. Glimm, editors. *The Semantic Web – ISWC 2010 – 9th International Semantic Web Conference, ISWC 2010, Shanghai, China, November 7–11, 2010, Revised Selected Papers, Part I*, volume 6496 of *LNCS*. Springer, 2010.

308. H. Paulheim. Knowledge graph refinement: A survey of approaches and evaluation methods. *Semantic Web*, 8(3):489–508, 2017.

309. S. Pemberton. XHTML Vocabulary. W3C Vocabulary, Jan. 2010. https://www.w3.org/1999/xhtml/vocab.

310. J. Pérez, M. Arenas, and C. Gutiérrez. Semantics and complexity of SPARQL. *ACM Trans. Database Syst.*, 34(3):16:1–16:45, 2009.

311. J. Pérez, M. Arenas, and C. Gutiérrez. nSPARQL: A navigational language for RDF. *J. Web Semant.*, 8(4):255–270, 2010.

312. S. Peroni. A Simplified Agile Methodology for Ontology Development. In M. Dragoni, M. Poveda-Villalón, and E. Jiménez-Ruiz, editors, *OWL: – Experiences and Directions – Reasoner Evaluation – 13th International Workshop, OWLED 2016, and 5th International Workshop, ORE 2016, Bologna, Italy, November 20, 2016, Revised Selected Papers*, volume 10161 of *LNCS*, pages 55–69. Springer, 2016.

313. D. Peterson, S. Gao, A. Malhotra, C. M. Sperberg-McQueen, and H. S. Thompson. W3C XML Schema Definition Language (XSD) 1.1 Part 2: Datatypes. W3C Recommendation, Apr. 2012. https://www.w3.org/TR/xmlschema11-2/.

314. M. Pham, L. Passing, O. Erling, and P. A. Boncz. Deriving an Emergent Relational Schema from RDF Data. In A. Gangemi, S. Leonardi, and A. Panconesi, editors, *Proceedings of the 24th International Conference on World Wide Web, WWW 2015, Florence, Italy, May 18–22, 2015*, pages 864–874. ACM, 2015.

315. A. Phillips and M. Davis. Matching of Language Tags. RFC 4647, Sept. 2006. https://www.ietf.org/rfc/rfc4647.txt.

316. A. Phillips and M. Davis. Tags for Identifying Languages. IETF Best Current Practice, Feb. 2014. http://tools.ietf.org/html/bcp47.

317. R. Pichler, A. Polleres, F. Wei, and S. Woltran. dRDF: Entailment for Domain-Restricted RDF. In Bechhofer et al. [36], pages 200–214.

318. R. Pichler and S. Skritek. Containment and equivalence of well-designed SPARQL. In R. Hull and M. Grohe, editors, *Proceedings of the 33rd ACM SIGMOD-SIGACT-SIGART Symposium on Principles of Database Systems, PODS'14, Snowbird, UT, USA, June 22–27, 2014*, pages 39–50. ACM, 2014.

319. H. S. Pinto, C. Tempich, and S. Staab. Ontology Engineering and Evolution in a Distributed World Using DILIGENT. In Staab and Studer [367], pages 153–176.

320. A. Piscopo and E. Simperl. Who Models the World?: Collaborative Ontology Creation and User Roles in Wikidata. *PACMHCI*, 2(CSCW):141:1–141:18, 2018.

321. A. Polleres, C. d'Amato, M. Arenas, S. Handschuh, P. Kroner, S. Ossowski, and P. F. Patel-Schneider, editors. *Reasoning Web. Semantic Technologies for the Web of Data – 7th International Summer School 2011, Galway, Ireland, August 23–27, 2011, Tutorial Lectures*, volume 6848 of *LNCS*. Springer, 2011.

322. A. Polleres, A. Hogan, R. Delbru, and J. Umbrich. RDFS and OWL Reasoning for Linked Data. In S. Rudolph, G. Gottlob, I. Horrocks, and F. van Harmelen, editors, *Reasoning Web. Semantic Technologies for Intelligent Data Access - 9th International Summer School 2013, Mannheim, Germany, July 30 - August 2, 2013. Proceedings*, volume 8067 of *LNCS*, pages 91–149. Springer, 2013.

323. A. Polleres, T. Krennwallner, N. Lopes, J. Kopecký, and S. Decker. XSPARQL Language Specification. W3C Member Submission, Jan. 2009. https://www.w3.org/Submission/xsparql-language-specification/.

324. R. Pollock, J. Tennison, G. Kellogg, and I. Herman. Metadata Vocabulary for Tabular Data. W3C Recommendation, Dec. 2015. https://www.w3.org/TR/tabular-metadata/.

325. E. Prud'hommeaux, I. Boneva, J. E. Labra Gayo, and G. Kellogg. Shape Expressions Language 2.1. W3C Final Community Group Report, Oct. 2019. http://shex.io/shex-semantics/.

326. E. Prud'hommeaux and C. Buil-Aranda. SPARQL 1.1 Federated Query. W3C Recommendation, Mar. 2013. https://www.w3.org/TR/sparql11-federated-query/.

327. E. Prud'hommeaux, J. E. Labra Gayo, and H. R. Solbrig. Shape expressions: an RDF validation and transformation language. In H. Sack, A. Filipowska, J. Lehmann, and S. Hellmann, editors, *Proceedings of the 10th International Conference on Semantic Systems, SEMANTICS 2014, Leipzig, Germany, September 4–5, 2014*, pages 32–40. ACM, 2014.

328. E. Prud'hommeaux and A. Seaborne. SPARQL Query Language for RDF. W3C Recommendation, Jan. 2008. https://www.w3.org/TR/rdf-sparql-query/.

329. F. Radulovic, R. García-Castro, and A. Gómez-Pérez. Towards the Anonymisation of RDF Data. In H. Xu, editor, *The 27th International Conference on Software Engineering and Knowledge Engineering, SEKE 2015, Wyndham Pittsburgh University Center, Pittsburgh, PA, USA, July 6–8, 2015*, pages 646–651. KSI Research Inc. and Knowledge Systems Institute Graduate School, 2015.

330. P. Ravindra. Towards optimization of RDF analytical queries on MapReduce. In *Workshops Proceedings of the 30th International Conference on Data Engineering Workshops, ICDE 2014, Chicago, IL, USA, March 31 – April 4, 2014*, pages 335–339. IEEE Computer Society, 2014.

331. T. Rebele, F. M. Suchanek, J. Hoffart, J. Biega, E. Kuzey, and G. Weikum. YAGO: A Multilingual Knowledge Base from Wikipedia, Wordnet, and Geonames. In Groth et al. [157], pages 177–185.

332. D. Reynolds. OWL 2 RL in RIF (Second Edition). W3C Working Group Note, Feb. 2013. https://www.w3.org/TR/rif-owl-rl/.

333. L. Rietveld and R. Hoekstra. The YASGUI family of SPARQL clients. *Semantic Web*, 8(3):373–383, 2017.

334. J. Robie, D. Chamberlin, M. Dyck, and J. Snelson. XQuery 3.0: An XML Query Language. W3C Recommendation, Apr. 2014. https://www.w3.org/TR/xquery-30/.

335. J. Robie, M. Dyck, and J. Spiegel. XML Path Language (XPath) 3.1. W3C Recommendation, Mar. 2017. https://www.w3.org/TR/xpath-31/.

336. S. Rudolph. Foundations of Description Logics. In Polleres et al. [321], pages 76–136.

337. S. Rudolph, M. Krötzsch, and P. Hitzler. All Elephants are Bigger than All Mice. In Baader et al. [26].

338. S. Rudolph, M. Krötzsch, and P. Hitzler. Type-elimination-based reasoning for the description logic SHIQbs using decision diagrams and disjunctive datalog. *Logical Methods in Computer Science*, 8(1), 2012.

339. A. Ryman. Resource Shape 2.0. W3C Member Submission, Feb. 2014. https://www.w3.org/Submission/shapes/.

340. Y. Sagiv and M. Yannakakis. Equivalences Among Relational Expressions with the Union and Difference Operators. *J. ACM*, 27(4):633–655, 1980.

341. J. Salas and A. Hogan. Canonicalisation of Monotone SPARQL Queries. In Vrandečić et al. [396], pages 600–616.

342. M. Saleem, M. I. Ali, A. Hogan, Q. Mehmood, and A. N. Ngomo. LSQ: The Linked SPARQL Queries Dataset. In Arenas et al. [16], pages 261–269.

343. M. Saleem, Y. Khan, A. Hasnain, I. Ermilov, and A. N. Ngomo. A fine-grained evaluation of SPARQL endpoint federation systems. *Semantic Web*, 7(5):493–518, 2016.

344. L. Sauermann, R. Cyganiak, D. Ayers, and M. Völkel. Cool URIs for the Semantic Web. W3C Interest Group Note, Dec. 2008. https://www.w3.org/TR/cooluris/.

345. J. Schaible, T. Gottron, S. Scheglmann, and A. Scherp. LOVER: support for modeling data using linked open vocabularies. In G. Guerrini, editor, *Joint 2013 EDBT/ICDT Conferences, EDBT/ICDT '13, Genoa, Italy, March 22, 2013, Workshop Proceedings*, pages 89–92. ACM, 2013.

346. M. Schmachtenberg, C. Bizer, and H. Paulheim. Adoption of the Linked Data Best Practices in Different Topical Domains. In Mika et al. [271], pages 245–260.

347. M. Schmidt, M. Meier, and G. Lausen. Foundations of SPARQL query optimization. In L. Segoufin, editor, *Database Theory – ICDT 2010, 13th International Conference, Lausanne, Switzerland, March 23–25, 2010, Proceedings*, ACM International Conference Proceeding Series, pages 4–33. ACM, 2010.

348. M. Schmidt-Schauß and G. Smolka. Attributive Concept Descriptions with Complements. *Artif. Intell.*, 48(1):1–26, 1991.

349. M. Schneider. OWL 2 Web Ontology Language RDF-Based Semantics. W3C Recommendation, Dec. 2012. https://www.w3.org/TR/owl2-rdf-based-semantics/.

350. M. Schneider and G. Sutcliffe. Reasoning in the OWL 2 Full Ontology Language Using First-Order Automated Theorem Proving. In N. Bjørner and V. Sofronie-Stokkermans, editors, *Automated Deduction – CADE-23 – 23rd International Conference on Automated Deduction, Wroclaw, Poland, July 31 – August 5, 2011. Proceedings*, volume 6803 of *LNCS*, pages 461–475. Springer, 2011.

351. G. Schreiber and Y. Raimond. RDF 1.1 Primer. W3C Working Group Note, June 2014. https://www.w3.org/TR/rdf11-primer/.

352. A. Schwarte, P. Haase, K. Hose, R. Schenkel, and M. Schmidt. FedX: Optimization Techniques for Federated Query Processing on Linked Data. In Aroyo et al. [19], pages 601–616.

353. J. Scott. Social network analysis: developments, advances, and prospects. *Social Netw. Analys. Mining*, 1(1):21–26, 2011.

354. A. Seaborne. RDQL – A Query Language for RDF. W3C Member Submission, Jan. 2004. https://www.w3.org/Submission/RDQL/.

355. A. Seaborne. SPARQL 1.1 Query Results CSV and TSV Formats. W3C Recommendation, Mar. 2013. https://www.w3.org/TR/rdf-sparql-XMLres/.

356. J. R. Searle. Minds, Brains, and Programs. *The Behavioral and Brain Sciences*, 3:417–424, 1980.

357. J. F. Sequeda. Integrating Relational Databases with the Semantic Web: A Reflection. In G. Ianni, D. Lembo, L. E. Bertossi, W. Faber, B. Glimm, G. Gottlob, and S. Staab, editors, *Reasoning Web. Semantic Interoperability on the Web – 13th International Summer School 2017, London, UK, July 7–11, 2017, Tutorial Lectures*, volume 10370 of *LNCS*, pages 68–120. Springer, 2017.

358. J. F. Sequeda, M. Arenas, and D. P. Miranker. OBDA: Query Rewriting or Materialization? In Practice, Both! In Mika et al. [271], pages 535–551.

359. K. E. Shafer, S. L. Weibel, and E. Jul. The PURL Project. *Journal of Library Administration*, 34(1–2):123–125, 2001.

360. P. Shvaiko, J. Euzenat, F. Giunchiglia, H. Stuckenschmidt, M. Mao, and I. Cruz, editors. *Proceedings of the 5th International Workshop on Ontology Matching (OM-2010) collocated with the 9th International Semantic Web Conference (ISWC-2010) Shanghai, China, November 7, 2010*, volume 689 of *CEUR Workshop Proceedings*. CEUR-WS.org, 2010.

361. E. Simperl and M. Luczak-Rösch. Collaborative ontology engineering: a survey. *Knowledge Eng. Review*, 29(1):101–131, 2014.

362. E. Sirin, B. Parsia, B. C. Grau, A. Kalyanpur, and Y. Katz. Pellet: A practical OWL-DL reasoner. *J. Web Sem.*, 5(2):51–53, 2007.

363. M. K. Smith, C. Welty, and D. L. McGuinness. OWL Web Ontology Language Guide. W3C Recommendation, Feb. 2004. https://www.w3.org/TR/owl-guide/.

364. A. Soulet, A. Giacometti, B. Markhoff, and F. M. Suchanek. Representativeness of Knowledge Bases with the Generalized Benford's Law. In *The Semantic Web – ISWC 2018 – 17th International Semantic Web Conference, Monterey, CA, USA, October 8–12, 2018, Proceedings, Part I*, pages 374–390, 2018.

365. S. Speicher, J. Arwe, and A. Malhotra. Linked Data Platform 1.0. W3C Recommendation, Feb. 2015. https://www.w3.org/TR/ldp/.

366. M. Sporny, D. Longley, G. Kellogg, M. Lanthaler, and N. Lindström. JSON-LD 1.0 – A JSON-based Serialization for Linked Data. W3C Recommendation, Jan. 2014. https://www.w3.org/TR/json-ld/.

367. S. Staab and R. Studer, editors. *Handbook on Ontologies*, International Handbooks on Information Systems. Springer, 2009.

368. C. Stadler, J. Lehmann, K. Höffner, and S. Auer. LinkedGeoData: A core for a web of spatial open data. *Semantic Web*, 3(4):333–354, 2012.

369. S. Stadtmüller, A. Harth, and M. Grobelnik. Accessing Information About Linked Data Vocabularies with vocab.cc. In J. Li, G. Qi, D. Zhao, W. Nejdl, and H. Zheng, editors, *Semantic Web and Web Science – 6th Chinese Semantic Web Symposium and 1st Chinese Web Science Conference, CSWS 2012, Shenzhen, China, November 28–30, 2012*, pages 391–396. Springer, 2012.

370. P. Stickler. CBD – Concise Bounded Description. W3C Member Submission, June 2005. https://www.w3.org/Submission/CBD/.

371. M. Strohmaier, S. Walk, J. Pöschko, D. Lamprecht, T. Tudorache, C. Nyulas, M. A. Musen, and N. F. Noy. How ontologies are made: Studying the hidden social dynamics behind collaborative ontology engineering projects. *J. Web Semant.*, 20:18–34, 2013.

372. P. Stutz, D. Strebel, and A. Bernstein. Signal/Collect12. *Semantic Web*, 7(2):139–166, 2016.

373. M. C. Suárez-Figueroa, A. Gómez-Pérez, and M. Fernández-López. The NeOn Methodology framework: A scenario-based methodology for ontology development. *Applied Ontology*, 10(2):107–145, 2015.

374. F. M. Suchanek, G. Kasneci, and G. Weikum. YAGO: A Large Ontology from Wikipedia and WordNet. *J. Web Sem.*, 6(3):203–217, 2008.

375. Y. Sure, S. Staab, and R. Studer. Ontology Engineering Methodology. In Staab and Studer [367], pages 135–152.

376. P. A. Szekely, C. A. Knoblock, J. Slepicka, A. Philpot, A. Singh, C. Yin, D. Kapoor, P. Natarajan, D. Marcu, K. Knight, D. Stallard, S. S. Karunamoorthy, R. Bojana-palli, S. Minton, B. Amanatullah, T. Hughes, M. Tamayo, D. Flynt, R. Artiss, S. Chang, T. Chen, G. Hiebel, and L. Ferreira. Building and Using a Knowledge Graph to Combat Human Trafficking. In Arenas et al. [16], pages 205–221.

377. T. P. Tanon, D. Vrandečić, S. Schaffert, T. Steiner, and L. Pintscher. From Free-base to Wikidata: The Great Migration. In J. Bourdeau, J. Hendler, R. Nkambou, I. Horrocks, and B. Y. Zhao, editors, *Proceedings of the 25th International Conference on World Wide Web, WWW 2016, Montreal, Canada, April 11–15, 2016*, pages 1419–1428. ACM, 2016.

378. J. Tao, E. Sirin, J. Bao, and D. L. McGuinness. Integrity Constraints in OWL. In M. Fox and D. Poole, editors, *Proceedings of the Twenty-Fourth AAAI Conference on Artificial Intelligence, AAAI 2010, Atlanta, Georgia, USA, July 11–15, 2010*. AAAI Press, 2010.

379. H. J. ter Horst. Completeness, decidability and complexity of entailment for RDF Schema and a semantic extension involving the OWL vocabulary. *J. Web Sem.*, 3(2–3):79–115, 2005.

380. B. B. Thompson, M. Personick, and M. Cutcher. The Bigdata® RDF Graph Database. In A. Harth, K. Hose, and R. Schenkel, editors, *Linked Data Management.*, pages 193–237. Chapman and Hall/CRC, 2014.

381. D. Tsarkov and I. Horrocks. FaCT++ Description Logic Reasoner: System Description. In Furbach and Shankar [134], pages 292–297.

382. Y. Tzitzikas, D. Kotzinos, and Y. Theoharis. On Ranking RDF Schema Elements (and its Application in Visualization). *J. UCS*, 13(12):1854–1880, 2007.

383. J. Umbrich, A. Hogan, A. Polleres, and S. Decker. Link traversal querying for a diverse Web of Data. *Semantic Web*, 6(6):585–624, 2015.

384. J. Umbrich, M. Karnstedt, A. Hogan, and J. X. Parreira. Hybrid SPARQL Queries: Fresh vs. Fast Results. In P. Cudré-Mauroux, J. Heflin, E. Sirin, T. Tudorache, J. Euzenat, M. Hauswirth, J. X. Parreira, J. Hendler, G. Schreiber, A. Bernstein, and E. Blomqvist, editors, *The Semantic Web – ISWC 2012 – 11th International Semantic Web Conference, Boston, MA, USA, November 11–15, 2012, Proceedings, Part I*, volume 7649 of *LNCS*, pages 608–624. Springer, 2012.

385. C. Unger, A. Freitas, and P. Cimiano. An Introduction to Question Answering over Linked Data. In M. Koubarakis, G. B. Stamou, G. Stoilos, I. Horrocks, P. G. Kolaitis, G. Lausen, and G. Weikum, editors, *Reasoning Web. Reasoning on the Web in the Big Data Era – 10th International Summer School 2014, Athens, Greece, September 8–13, 2014. Proceedings*, volume 8714 of *LNCS*, pages 100–140. Springer, 2014.

386. J. Urbani, S. Kotoulas, J. Maassen, F. van Harmelen, and H. E. Bal. OWL Reasoning with WebPIE: Calculating the Closure of 100 Billion Triples. In L. Aroyo, G. Antoniou, E. Hyvönen, A. ten Teije, H. Stuckenschmidt, L. Cabral, and T. Tudorache, editors, *ESWC (1)*, volume 6088 of *LNCS*, pages 213–227. Springer, 2010.

387. J. Urbani, R. Piro, F. van Harmelen, and H. E. Bal. Hybrid reasoning on OWL RL. *Semantic Web*, 5(6):423–447, 2014.

388. J. C. J. van Dam, J. J. Koehorst, P. J. Schaap, V. M. dos Santos, and M. Suárez-Diez. RDF2Graph a tool to recover, understand and validate the ontology of an RDF resource. *J. Biomedical Semantics*, 6:39, 2015.

389. P. Vandenbussche, G. Atemezing, M. Poveda-Villalón, and B. Vatant. Linked Open Vocabularies (LOV): A gateway to reusable semantic vocabularies on the Web. *Semantic Web*, 8(3):437–452, 2017.

390. M. Y. Vardi. The Complexity of Relational Query Languages (Extended Abstract). In H. R. Lewis, B. B. Simons, W. A. Burkhard, and L. H. Landweber, editors, *Proceedings of the 14th Annual ACM Symposium on Theory of Computing, May 5–7, 1982, San Francisco, California, USA*, pages 137–146. ACM, 1982.

391. H. Vargas, C. B. Aranda, A. Hogan, and C. López. RDF Explorer: A Visual SPARQL Query Builder. In Ghidini et al. [142], pages 647–663.

392. R. Verborgh, M. V. Sande, P. Colpaert, S. Coppens, E. Mannens, and R. V. de Walle. Web-Scale Querying through Linked Data Fragments. In Bizer et al. [62].

393. R. Verborgh, M. V. Sande, O. Hartig, J. V. Herwegen, L. D. Vocht, B. D. Meester, G. Haesendonck, and P. Colpaert. Triple Pattern Fragments: A low-cost knowledge graph interface for the Web. *J. Web Semant.*, 37-38:184–206, 2016.

394. D. Vila-Suero, B. Villazón-Terrazas, and A. Gómez-Pérez. datos.bne.es: A library linked dataset. *Semantic Web*, 4(3):307–313, 2013.

395. J. Volz, C. Bizer, M. Gaedke, and G. Kobilarov. Discovering and Maintaining Links on the Web of Data. In Bernstein et al. [54], pages 650–665.

396. D. Vrandečić, K. Bontcheva, M. C. Suárez-Figueroa, V. Presutti, I. Celino, M. Sabou, L. Kaffee, and E. Simperl, editors. *The Semantic Web – ISWC 2018 – 17th International Semantic Web Conference, Monterey, CA, USA, October 8–12, 2018, Proceedings*, volume 11137 of *LNCS*. Springer, 2018.

397. D. Vrandečić and M. Krötzsch. Wikidata: a free collaborative knowledgebase. *Commun. ACM*, 57(10):78–85, 2014.

398. D. Vrandečić, M. Krötzsch, S. Rudolph, and U. Lösch. Leveraging Non-Lexical Knowledge for the Linked Open Data Web. *Review of April Fool's day Transactions (RAFT)*, 5:18–27, 2010.

399. Q. Wang, Z. Mao, B. Wang, and L. Guo. Knowledge graph embedding: A survey of approaches and applications. *IEEE Trans. Knowl. Data Eng.*, 29(12):2724–2743, 2017.

400. J. Weaver and J. A. Hendler. Parallel Materialization of the Finite RDFS Closure for Hundreds of Millions of Triples. In Bernstein et al. [54], pages 682–697.

401. K. Wilkinson, C. Sayers, H. A. Kuno, D. Reynolds, and L. Ding. Supporting scalable, persistent Semantic Web applications. *IEEE Data Eng. Bull.*, 26(4):33–39, 2003.

402. G. T. Williams. SPARQL 1.1 Service Description. W3C Recommendation, Mar. 2013. https://www.w3.org/TR/sparql11-service-description/.

403. Z. Wu, S. Pan, F. Chen, G. Long, C. Zhang, and P. S. Yu. A Comprehensive Survey on Graph Neural Networks. *CoRR*, abs/1901.00596, 2019.

404. G. Xiao, D. Calvanese, R. Kontchakov, D. Lembo, A. Poggi, R. Rosati, and M. Zakharyaschev. Ontology-Based Data Access: A Survey. In J. Lang, editor, *Proceedings of the Twenty-Seventh International Joint Conference on Artificial Intelligence, IJCAI 2018, July 13–19, 2018, Stockholm, Sweden*, pages 5511–5519. ijcai.org, 2018.

405. G. Xiao, M. Rezk, M. Rodriguez-Muro, and D. Calvanese. Rules and Ontology Based Data Access. In R. Kontchakov and M. Mugnier, editors, *Web Reasoning and Rule Systems – 8th International Conference, RR 2014, Athens, Greece, September 15–17, 2014. Proceedings*, volume 8741 of *LNCS*, pages 157–172. Springer, 2014.

406. Q. Yang and M. Wooldridge, editors. *Proceedings of the Twenty-Fourth International Joint Conference on Artificial Intelligence, IJCAI 2015, Buenos Aires, Argentina, July 25–31, 2015*. AAAI Press, 2015.

407. A. Zaveri, A. Rula, A. Maurino, R. Pietrobon, J. Lehmann, and S. Auer. Quality assessment for Linked Data: A Survey. *Semantic Web*, 7(1):63–93, 2016.

408. A. Zimmermann. RDF 1.1: On Semantics of RDF Datasets. W3C Working Group Note, Feb. 2014. https://www.w3.org/TR/rdf11-datasets/.

409. A. Zimmermann, N. Lopes, A. Polleres, and U. Straccia. A general framework for representing, reasoning and querying with annotated Semantic Web data. *J. Web Semant.*, 11:72–95, 2012.

Printed in the United States
by Baker & Taylor Publisher Services